VOLUME I

PLANNING AND ORGANIZING

Atlanta 1996®

THE ATLANTA COMMITTEE FOR THE OLYMPIC GAMES

THE OFFICIAL REPORT OF THE CENTENNIAL OLYMPIC GAMES

VOLUME I   PLANNING AND ORGANIZING

This volume is comprised of a prologue, which covers the history of the Bid process, and 28 chapters, organized by program and functional area, which address in detail the preparations for the 1996 Olympic Games. For the benefit of future organizing committees, each chapter contains conclusions and recommendations.

VOLUME II   THE CENTENNIAL OLYMPIC GAMES

This volume is comprised of a prologue, three major sections, and an epilogue.

The prologue, entitled *Atlanta—Gateway for Dreams*, describes the city and its history.

Section I, *Spreading the Olympic Spirit*, begins with the arrival of the Olympic Torch in Los Angeles, California, on 27 April 1996, and progresses as the Torch Relay moves across the US, reaching Atlanta on 19 July, the day of the Opening Ceremony. This journey is juxtaposed with Atlanta's preparations for the Centennial Olympic Games during spring and summer 1996 and highlights of Cultural Olympiad exhibitions and events occurring prior to the official start of the Games.

Section II, *Celebrating the Games*, is a day-by-day account, 19 July–4 August, with highlights of Opening and Closing Ceremonies, athletic achievements, and descriptions of cultural events, as well as details of Games-time operations.

Section III, *Living the Dream*, gives information on the competition of each sport in the programme of the 1996 Olympic Games.

The epilogue, entitled *Nurturing the Memories*, describes some of the positive results of the Games on the city of Atlanta, including the status of the organizing committee's efforts to conclude the business of the Games and the use of some of the facilities built or given as part of the legacy of the Games.

VOLUME III   THE COMPETITION RESULTS

This volume is comprised of the detailed results for all athletes in all events. Also included as a reference is a section on medal winners and record-setting performances arranged by sport and discipline, as well as a section of venue maps for the major locations used during the 1996 Olympic Games.

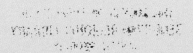

VOLUME I

PLANNING AND ORGANIZING

THE OFFICIAL REPORT OF THE CENTENNIAL OLYMPIC GAMES

PEACHTREE
ATLANTA

COLOPHON

The Official Report of the Centennial Olympic Games employs the typography and look developed for the 1996 Olympic Games by the Atlanta Committee for the Olympic Games (ACOG). The text type is Stone Serif. Univers is used for sidebar and tabular material. Display type is Copperplate Gothic. The Quilt of Leaves motif serves as a decorative element throughout the three volumes, in combination with the ACOG color palette in Volumes I and II.

Art direction by Loraine M. Balcsik. Design by Nicola Simmonds Carter and Loraine M. Balcsik. Typography by Loraine M. Balcsik and Robin Sherman. Four-color film was created by Bright Arts, Ltd., Hong Kong, with coordination by Imago, USA, Inc., New York.

Published by
PEACHTREE PUBLISHERS
494 Armour Circle NE
Atlanta, GA 30324

Manufactured in Singapore

First printing

Library of Congress Cataloguing-in-Publication Data

Atlanta Committee for the Olympic Games.
    The official report of the Centennial Olympic Games / the Atlanta
Committee for the Olympic Games.
       p. cm.
    Includes indexes.
    Contents: v. 1. Planning and organizing -- v. 2. The Centennial Olympic
games -- v. 3. the competition results.
    ISBN 1-56145-150-9 (set). -- ISBN 1-56145-168-1 (v. 1). -- ISBN 1-56145-151-7 (v. 2). -- ISBN
1-56145-169-X (v. 3)
    1. Olympic Games (26th : 1996 : Atlanta, Ga.) 2. Atlanta
Committee for the Olympic Games. I. Title.
GV722 1996.A86 1997
796.48--DC21   97-23578
                                             CIP

FOR SEVENTEEN DAYS in the summer of 1996 the world came together in peace and harmony in Atlanta for what became the largest gathering of athletes and nations in Olympic history. With arms linked and voices resounding, we celebrated the magnificence of our common humanity—the individual triumphs, the personal tragedies, the indomitable resilience of the human spirit.

With the conclusion of this XXVI Olympiad, we—the people of Atlanta—have realized our dream of hosting the Olympic Games, and our hearts are filled with gratitude to the Olympic Movement for the extraordinary opportunity. Our dream was achieved through the unwavering dedication and selfless participation of tens of thousands of individuals.

We thank each person; each smiling face and extended hand welcomed the world to our home and helped bridge the distances and differences that inevitably separate us, one person from another, one nation from another. These individual acts of goodwill exalted the Games and defined our place in Olympic history.

We understood Pierre de Coubertin's call to place sport at the service of humanity. The ideals of the Olympic Movement—joy in effort, the educational value of good example, and respect for universal ethical principles—deeply affected and inspired us. They united us in the initial Bid effort, and bound us together as our numbers swelled year after year.

We embraced the entire period of the Olympiad, just as we embraced Olympism as a way of life, and extended our programming across four years in the arts, education, and sport. We relied on our Olympic Spirit to accomplish our goals for the 1996 Games, and this served us well. We watched the Spirit ignite in our colleagues in schools, corporations, volunteer organizations, and government as together we worked cooperatively—always attempting to harmonize our efforts—to accomplish the tasks that lay before us.

This level of cooperation created Centennial Olympic Park, which symbolizes the grandeur of the Olympic Spirit and also its resilience. For it was here that the Olympic Spirit was tested and the people arose triumphantly to declare it would survive and flourish.

Just as the Olympic flame has guided us onward, each host city has contributed to the strength of the modern Olympic Games. Atlanta honored the traditions developed over the past century, and contributed new elements that reflect our place in the global community and our time at the close of the twentieth century. Our sophisticated competition venues were offered to the service of athletes. We endeavored in all ways to create playing conditions that were fair and that encouraged athletic excellence. Our broadcasting brought spectators around the world closer than ever to the competition.

We approached the Centennial Olympic Games with great idealism, with the belief that we could create a remarkable experience for all who participated. Our humanity will be the legacy of our conduct of these Games. We embraced the Olympic Movement, and it enriched and forever changed our lives.

This *Official Report of the Centennial Olympic Games* is our record of the staging of the event as well as a chronicle of its athletic achievements. We present these three volumes to our readers with pride, with faith in the future of the Olympic Movement, and with fulfillment for our place in its history.

William Porter Payne
President and CEO
The Atlanta Committee for the Olympic Games

TABLE OF
CONTENTS

ACRONYMS AND THEIR USAGE

The following terms are used in their acronym form throughout the *Official Report*, Volume I / Planning and Organizing, with the exception of the Bid and Management chapters, in which these terms are introduced.

ACOG–Atlanta Committee for the Olympic Games

ACOP–Atlanta Centennial Olympic Properties (will be spelled out on its first reference in the Marketing chapter)

AOC–Atlanta Organizing Committee

CEO–chief executive officer

COO–chief operating officer

IF–International Federation

IOC–International Olympic Committee

LOC–local organizing commitee

MAOGA–Metropolitan Atlanta Olympic Games Authority

NBC–National Broadcast Corporation

NOC–National Olympic Committee

OCOG–Organizing Committee for the Olympic Games

US–United States of America

USOC–United States Olympic Committee

The following acronyms appear frequently in the Official Report. The full term is given in the first reference in a chapter and whenever it appears in a chapter heading. If mentioned more than once in a chapter, the acronym follows the first reference.

ADA–Americans with Disabilities Act

ANOC–Association of National Olympic Committees

AOB–Atlanta Olympic Broadcasting

AONA–Atlanta Olympic News Agency

APOC–Atlanta Paralympic Organizing Committee

ASOIF–Association of Summer Olympic International Federations

AWC–Airport Welcome Center

CAD–computer-aided design

CD–compact disc

CODA–Corporation for Olympic Development in Atlanta

COP–Centennial Olympic Partner

DC–District of Columbia (when referring to the US capital, Washington, DC)

FAA–Federal Aviation Administration

FBI–Federal Bureau of Investigation

HOC–Hellenic Olympic Committee

IBC–International Broadcast Center

INS–Immigration and Naturalization Services

MAC–main accreditation center

MARTA–Metropolitan Atlanta Rapid Transit Authority

MOC–main operations center

MPC–Main Press Center

NGB–National Governing Body

OAF–Olympic Arts Festival

OGS–the Olympic Games Staff

OIC–Olympic identity card

OMS–operations management systems

OTS–Olympic Transportation System

OYC–Olympic Youth Camp

PC–personal computer

TOP–The Olympic Programme

UDC–uniform distribution center

VCR–videocassette recorder

VIK–value-in-kind

PREFACE

THE OFFICIAL REPORT *of the Centennial Olympic Games* was written by the professional staff of the Atlanta Committee for the Olympic Games. The content of the *Official Report* is strongly influenced by historical precedence and IOC requirements. The organizers and authors of this report have codified the experience and legacy of the Games for posterity and provided as much detail as possible to assist organizing committees in preparing for future Olympic Games.

This is the first of three volumes. As its title, *Planning and Organizing*, suggests this volume addresses the broad array of details, grouped by functional or program category, that were essential to creating the Centennial Olympic Games. Success depended on the combined actions of the thousands of people organized to mount the Games and their attention to detail. The plans, concepts, research and rationale for decision-making, problem-solving, and organizing that comprised our efforts are presented here as fully as possible, including recommendations for future organizers concerning what—with the lessons of experience—were identified as the critical ingredients to success. Where we encountered problems, we have tried to address them from a constructive perspective with the sincere hope of assisting future organizers.

These Centennial Olympic Games were for us, first and foremost, about people—the thousands who collaborated for years in developing the plans; the 53,540 volunteers who welcomed and assisted visitors to Atlanta and the Southern United States during Games-time, many of whom worked with the Organizing Committee and in their communities for years preceding the Games; the citizens of Georgia who provided such enthusiasm and goodwill in support of our mission; and the 197 nations and their dedicated athletes who gave to 5 million spectators and the worldwide audience of 3.5 billion television viewers spectacular performances.

The details of these experiences—from planning through staging through dismantling—are documented in these pages. The three-volume *Official Report* provides an avenue for understanding the magnitude of the effort and the challenges integral to presenting the Games.

The success of the 1996 Games lies in the hearts of the people who made them a reality. The memories of the collaboration and the goodwill and fellowship generated will shape our futures and be recalled as the most enduring legacy of the Games.

Ginger T. Watkins

Ginger T. Watkins
Editor
Atlanta, Georgia 1997

To the 53,540 volunteers
and employees who comprised
the Atlanta Committee for the
Olympic Games staff.
Their enthusiasm, dedication, and
loyalty made the 1996 Olympic
Games a personal, exciting, and
memorable experience for
millions of international visitors
and athletes.
As seems most fitting, the pages
of these three volumes are
anchored with their names.

MARTY W. AALTO • GAIL R. AARON • KAREN M.
AARON • ROGER AARON • WILLIAM H. AARON •
ANDRE P AARONS • KIM C AARONSON • MARIT
H AAS • PAUL T AASE • ARILD H AASTAD • RAN-
DOLPH ABARE • BELIYU ABATE • BILL ABBALLE
• MICHAEL ABBATE • CAROLINE T ABBEY •
BARBARA E ABBOTT • C PATRICK ABBOTT
• DARBY L ABBOTT • DEBRA W ABBOTT •
DOROTHY M ABBOTT • JACK W ABBOTT • JAMES
R ABBOTT • KAREN T ABBOTT • KIMBERLY M
ABBOTT • NANCY F ABBOTT • NICOLE G
ABBOTT • RAE E ABBOTT • SHERRILL C ABBOTT
• THOMAS K ABBOTT • VICKY S ABBOTT •
MUSTAFA ABDAL-AZIZ • LAWRENCE H ABDALLA
• SHARON D ABDEL-KHALIK • ZULFIOARALI
ABDUL • RAYYAH A ABDULLAH • SHARIF ABDUL-
LAH • YASMEEN ABDULLAH • YASMIN G ABDULLAH
• LURENA A ABDY • SATOSHI ABE • SERRA R
ABEL • DOUGLAS F ABELL • JODI L ABELOW •
RONNIE K ABERCROMBIE • CARL E ABERNATHY
• GARY Q ABERNATHY • GLENDA K ABERNATHY
• KEITH ABERNATHY • MAYA N ABERNATHY •
RICHIE M ABERNATHY • ROBERT ABERNATHY •
STEVEN H ABERNATHY • SUSAN M ABERNATHY
• TAMARA A ABERNATHY • TIMOTHY C ABER-
NATHY • WINIFRED S ABERNATHY • DORIS C
ABERNETHY • ALBERT D ABERSON JR • KIM R
ABNATHA • CORINNE H ABNEY • JAMES M
ABNEY JR • LINA C ABOGADIE • PATRICIA D
ABOINDE NJI • ANNE K ABOUCHAR • BASSEM B
ABOUKHATER • SOL H ABOULAFIA • ALBERT J.
ABOULAFIA MD • BETTY B ABRAHAM • BROOKE
E ABRAHAM • CAROL G ABRAHAM • MAY H
ABRAHAM • WARREN S ABRAHAMS • AVIS
ABRAM • MONROE J ABRAM ATC • WERONIKA N
ABRAMOWICZ • GLENDA A ABRAMS • JULIA H
ABRAMS • LINDA F ABRAMS • MARK K ABRAMS
• NICOLE ABRAMS • DEBORAH J ABRAMS RN •
CATHERINE B ABRAMSON • JEFFREY ABRAM-
SON • HERMES H ABRANTES • MELINDA T
ABREO • JENNIFER N ABSHIRE • NASSER R
ABU-AZZAM • FOUAD G ABUAKEL • GEMAL M
ABUBAKER • ZAINAB Y ABUELJEBAIN • OKAB M
ABUMADI • DAVID S ABUSAMRA • PABLO O
ACANDA • FRANCINE ACCARDI • PATRICK
ACCARDI • JIM A ACCORDINO • SUE C ACEE •
MARIA R. ACHECAR • LAWRENCE J ACHER
• NANCY H ACHESON • KENNETH J ACHILICH •
MARY I ACHILICH • KENNETH H ACHIRON
• LEONARD ACHIRON • ALAN H ACKERMAN •
GAYLE F ACKERMAN • KATHLEEN ACKERMAN
• MELISSA J ACKERMAN • WILLIAM J ACKER-
MAN • MICHAEL J ACKERMAN JR • JENNIFER L
ACKERSON • THERESA ACKERSON • KEVIN
ACOCELLA • PAUL F ACOCELLA • DENIECE B
ACOSTA • ERNESTO J ACOSTA • CHARLES L
ACREE • MICHAEL A ACREE • DIANE ACRENEAUX
• AMANDA S ACTON • JEROMY I ACTON • ALICIA E
ACUNA • AMY P ADAIR • TOM K ADAIR • CHRISTO-
PHER ADALA • SYLVIA B ADAM • LAWRENCE J
ADAMCIK • PAMELA S ADAMCIK • MARIA ADAM-
CZYK • MICHAL ADAMCZYK • LISA A ADAMI •
SACHI T ADAMI • JULIA B ADAMIAK • RICH
ADAMO • RICH ADAMO • MARK L ADAMS •
ANITA B ADAMS • ANNIE R ADAMS • BARBARA K
ADAMS • BENTLEY C ADAMS • BERT ADAMS
• BEVERLY W ADAMS • BRENDA C ADAMS •
CAROL S ADAMS • CATHY L ADAMS • CHALLIE E
ADAMS • CHARLES F ADAMS • CHARLES R
ADAMS • CHARLES R ADAMS • CHERYL L ADAMS
• CHRISTOPHER K ADAMS • CHRISTOPHER L
ADAMS • DANIEL S ADAMS • DARLEEN ADAMS •
DAVID W ADAMS • DEBORAH A ADAMS • DEBO-
RAH C ADAMS • DELORES L ADAMS • DIANE
ADAMS • DIANE B ADAMS • DOMINIC D ADAMS •
DONALD ADAMS • DUVAL C ADAMS • EDWARD L
ADAMS • ELIZABETH ADAMS • ELLA W ADAMS •
ELOISE S ADAMS • EMILY C ADAMS • EMILY S
ADAMS • FANNETTE C ADAMS • GARY T ADAMS
• GEORGE H ADAMS • GEORGEANNA M ADAMS •
GLENDA S ADAMS • HOLLY C ADAMS • IRA R
ADAMS • J ROBERT ADAMS • JACQUELYN F
ADAMS • JAMES K ADAMS • JANET S ADAMS •
JEFF W ADAMS • JENNIFER A ADAMS • JEN-
NIFER L ADAMS • JENNIFER M ADAMS • JERRY
A ADAMS • JOHN ADAMS • JOHN L ADAMS •
JOHN W ADAMS • JOSEPHINE C ADAMS • JULIE
K ADAMS • KELLY R ADAMS • LARRY E ADAMS •
LAURIE A ADAMS • LORRAINE ADAMS • MAR-
GARET G ADAMS • MARK C ADAMS • MARK R
ADAMS • MARTHA L ADAMS • MARY A ADAMS •
MARY E ADAMS • MARY H ADAMS • MARY K
ADAMS • MARY M ADAMS • MICHAEL R ADAMS •
NANCY S ADAMS • NATHANIEL ADAMS • NICOLE
ADAMS • PAMELA M ADAMS • PATRICIA E ADAMS
• PEG L ADAMS • PETER G ADAMS • PRISCILLA
B ADAMS • RANDALL W ADAMS • REBECCA J
ADAMS • ROBERT J ADAMS • ROBYN M ADAMS •
ROGER ADAMS • ROSCOE H ADAMS • ROSETTA
P ADAMS • RUSSELL J ADAMS • SAMUEL L
ADAMS • SHEILA ADAMS • STANLEY E ADAMS •
SUSAN H ADAMS • SUSAN H. ADAMS • TANYA J
ADAMS • TERESA ADAMS • TERRY P ADAMS •
THERESA L ADAMS • THOMAS E ADAMS • TY
ADAMS • VESTER L ADAMS • VICTORIA ADAMS •
WENDY L ADAMS • WILDA F ADAMS • WILLIAM T
ADAMS • WILLIAM W ADAMS • YOLANDA V
ADAMS • LATHANE ADAMS-CLARK • CAROL
ADAMS-MEANS • CLARISSA ADAMS FLETCHER •
HOWELL E ADAMS JR • WELLES ADAMS JR •
SHARON J ADAMS LEWIS • BOBBY J ADAMS MD
• MARYLYN A ADAMSKI • BRENDA C ADAMSON •
SONYA L ADAMSON • SUSAN A ADAMSON •
MICHAEL W ADCOCK • SUSAN W ADCOX • WILLIAM
ADCOX M.D. • KAREN B ADDAMS • WANDRA R
ADDERLY • FEDERICO ADDIECHI • TAMMIE L ADDIS
• ABBIGALE C ADDISON • CAROL C ADDISON •
CLARENCE L B ADDISON • DEANA M ADDISON •
MARK F ADDISON • SHANDY M ADDISON • JAMES
C ADDONIZIO • NIMOTA A ADEBOYE • JUDY C
ADEDUN • SANDRA R ADEN • BAMIDELE ADEO-
GUN • JACQUELINE V ADER • JEAN ADERO •
CHARLES F ADKINS • HARRIET M ADKINS
• JACQUELINE ADKINS • JESSICA B ADKINS •
JOHN L ADKINS • KRISTIE J ADKINS • MARY S
ADKINS • MATTIE M ADKINS • MELITTA A ADKINS
• TIMOTHY M ADKINS • TRICIA N ADKINS • JON
W ADKINSON • MICHAEL G ADKISON • BARBARA
F ADLER • CELIA G ADLER • EDNA ADLER •
GARY ADLER • MARVIN M ADNER • STEPHEN
VALENTINE ADOLPH • ZULEMA ADORNO • GABY
J ADRIAENSSENS • JOE L ADRIAN • STEPHANIE
A ADRIAN • ED AENCHBACHER • NATHAN V
AESCHLEMAN • ROBERT AESCHLIMAN • PATTI
W AESCHLIMANN • RAMATU M AFEGBUA-MAH-
MUD • DIONE D AFFLECK • TY P AFFLECK MD •
COOKIE AFTERGUT • CLIFFORD J AFTON • DEB-
ORAH A AFTUCK • RODNEY D AFTUCK • TIMMY J
AGAN ATC • NUPUR AGARWAL • FIFA AGBESSI •
SONYA AGBESSI • ESSEX AGEE • JEFFREY M
AGEE • KATHY L AGEE • ANGELA M AGEL •
JASON E AGIN • DAVID C AGLER • AARON D
AGNEW • KATHRYN H AGNEW • OLIVIER P
AGNEZ • ANNELORE K AGNIEL • NAVEEN AGNI-
HOTRI • AARON AGNOLI • RINALDO AGOSTINI •
ROSEMARY AGOSTINI MD • MAURIZIO M AGRES-
TA • DANIEL S AGRONOW • ABERRA A AGUEG-
NEHU • CESAR R AGUERO • SUE R AGUIAR •
IRAN R AGUILAR • LUTZ D AGUIRRE • MARIBEL
M AGUIRRE • MARTHA V AGUIRRE • ANDREW
AGUSTIN • AUGUSTINE AGYEMAN-BADU • E.
MARK AGYEPONG • NOOSHIN AHANGAR •
PATRICK AHERN • JIM W AHL • ANNA R AHLEN
• LARRY J AHLERS • SUE M AHLF • STEVE
CHARLES AHLGRIM • WILLIAM D AHLS • NEETU
AHLUWALIA • ANEESAH N AHMAD • SHABBIR
AHMAD • SUSAN AHMAD • JIM R AHMANN • JOHN
A AHMANN • MARIA E AHMANN • FARHANA
AHMED • JALAL U AHMED • MOHAMED A AHMED •
RAIHAN U AHMED • LINDA H AHN • SEUNGHYE
AHN • TAE-JIN AHN • KERRY L AHREND • BYRON
N AHRENS • CHANDLER B AHRENS • FATEMA A
AHSAN • PURNA AHUJA • MICHAEL K AIAU •
ADWOA O AIDOO • MUIBI A AIGORO • GAIL B
AIKEN • JANICE M AIKEN • MARGARET AIKEN •
SANDRA R AIKEN • LISA R AIKENS • DAWN M
AIKEY • SAMUEL D AIKIN • ETHEL L AINA JACK-
SON • JENNIFER L AINLEY • DAVID J AINSLEY •
FLEUR AINSLIE • STUART AINSLIE • EDDIE J
AINSWORTH II • FOHAT P AIRD • JULIUS A AITA
• SHANE T AITCHISON • TOPE Y AIYEJORUN •
MAMI AIZAWA • LYDIA P. AJHAR • MICHAEL
AJHAR • PAULA B AJISEFINNI • ABDUL Z AKBAR
• RINAT AKBAROV • SANDRA L AKBARPOUR •
KRISHNA V AKELLA • JUDITH L AKERMAN • KEN-
NETH AKERMAN • EMILY J AKERS • JANET T
AKERS • JOANN R AKERS • VIRGIL R AKERS •
MISAWA AKIHIKO • MISAE AKIMOTO • CECELIA S
AKIN • KENNETH G AKIN • MARSHA E AKIN •
NANCY E AKIN • WILLIAM A AKIN • OLU AKIN-
BOTE • DEBORAH L AKINDELE • FEMI M
AKINDELE • CLARA O AKINODE • TAI AKINOSHO
• DONALD W AKINS • JEFF K AKINS • MARY A
AKINS • ABIOLA O AKINWUNMI • JOSEPH A
AKOB • JACQUELINE AKOUKA • LINDA D
AKRIDGE • SEMEN AKSEL • GLENN D AKST •
SABRINA AKSTEIN • ABDULMONEM A AL-ALI
• SHARON L AL-HAYEK • YOUSIF A AL-MAIMAN •
SHAHID M AL-RAQIB • OSAMA K AL-SHAYKH-
YOUSEF • BUNMI O ALABI • DELE O ALABI •
SOLA O ALABI • ANTHONY N ALAKA • AKHBAR
ALI BAZ "ALAN COLUSSY, II" • DAVID R ALANIZ •
GAIL ALANIZ • AMY L ALANSKY • MARGARITA S
ALARCON • SAVAS ALATIS • KATHIE T ALBA •
KATHERINE ALBANY • MICHAEL ALBENBERG
• CAROL B ALBENESIUS • ALLAN EARL ALBER-
GA • ADELINA D ALBERGHINI • ALFRED C
ALBERGHINI • PATSY W ALBERS • WILLIAM F
ALBERS • JAMES R ALBERT • LILLIE B ALBERT
• MELIFAITE ALBERT • MICHAEL S ALBERT •
RENEE L ALBERT • MARK S ALBERT ATC • JEF-
FREY J ALBERT MD • CHRISTINE M ALBERTAZZI
• JASON D ALBERTIE • SHERRY L ALBERTINI •
TABOADA ALBERTO • MARGARET A ALBERTS
• CHRISTINA Y ALBERTSON • NORMAN ALBI •
MAXIMILIEN ALBI • ROBERT J ALBIN MD • MAR-
JORIE J ALBOHM CATC • ROBERT H ALBRECHT

• TINA M ALBRECHT • DARLENE S ALBREGTS •
VINCENT FA ALBREGTS • ANGELINE E ALBRIGHT
• CAREN L ALBRIGHT • JUDY H ALBRITTON •
KAMYLLA J ALBRITTON • KIMBERLY R ALBRITTON
• DUANE R ALBURY • ROBIN A ALBURY • SANDRA
E ALCALA • DANIEL R ALCH • CARL A ALCINDOR •
IZUMI Y ALCOBER • DICK ALCOCK • KRISTINA L
ALCORN • JACQUELINE M ALCOTT • DAVID M
ALDEN • JENNIFER L ALDERMAN • MARY E
ALDERMAN • WALTER ALDERMAN • SARA E
ALDERSON • LESLEY J ALDERTON • ABED A ALD-
ISI • ANDREW K ALDONS • THOMAS J ALDRED •
MARION D ALDRICH • JOANNE E ALDRICH
BUREL • JANEL P ALDRIDGE • JASON W
ALDRIDGE • RONALD J ALDY JR • RICHARD S
ALEMBIK • ERNEST E ALEMNJI • MONICA M ALEN-
CAR • ADAM H ALEXANDER • ALEXIS L ALEXAN-
DER • ANDREW L ALEXANDER • ASHLEY
E ALEXANDER • AUDREY T ALEXANDER • BAR-
BARA M ALEXANDER • BARBARA S ALEXANDER •
BERNARD H ALEXANDER • BERNICE E ALEXAN-
DER • BEVERLY A ALEXANDER • BILL ALEXANDER •
BOBBY R ALEXANDER • BRENDA ALEXANDER
• CHRIS ALEXANDER • EBONI L ALEXANDER •
EDWARD K ALEXANDER • ELIZABETH M ALEXAN-
DER • EVELYN R ALEXANDER • HUBERT T ALEXAN-
DER • JAMES A ALEXANDER • JAMES W ALEXAN-
DER • JOSEPH R ALEXANDER • JUDY A ALEXANDER
• JULIE M ALEXANDER • KAMLA ALEXANDER
• KAREN N ALEXANDER • KATHY R ALEXANDER •
KELLY D ALEXANDER • KEVIN M ALEXANDER
• LARRY B ALEXANDER • LAURA C ALEXANDER •
LAUREN G ALEXANDER • LIA D ALEXANDER • LINDA
D ALEXANDER • LINDA W ALEXANDER • MARCUS
ALEXANDER • MARGIE L ALEXANDER • MARGO
P ALEXANDER • MARIE F ALEXANDER • MARK S
ALEXANDER • MARSHA R ALEXANDER • MICHAEL N
ALEXANDER • MICHELE ALEXANDER • MIRIAM
ALEXANDER • RACHEL A ALEXANDER • RAHSAAN
K ALEXANDER • ROSETTA M ALEXANDER • SADIE
ALEXANDER • SADIE L ALEXANDER • SAM P
ALEXANDER • SHARON D ALEXANDER • SIHARATH
TA ALEXANDER • STEFANIE L ALEXANDER
• SURESH M ALEXANDER • TANYA F ALEXANDER •
THEODORE A ALEXANDER • THEODORE S ALEXANDER

• THOMAS A ALEXANDER • WILLIAM J ALEXANDER •
WILLIAM L ALEXANDER • ELMORE D ALEXAN-
DER DO • WILLIAM ALEXANDER III • COSTAS G
ALEXANDRIDES • PLAMEN D ALEXANDROV •
ERIC R ALEXIS • ELEAZAR O ALFARO • MIGUEL
ALFARO • DAWN E ALFONSO • TASLIN ALFONZO
• CHARLES R ALFORD • CHRISTINE B ALFORD •
DIANE ALFORD • DONNA C ALFORD • GWEN-
DOLYN C ALFORD • JAMES R ALFORD •
MICHELE W ALFORD • NANCY K ALFORD •
NANCY T ALFORD • ROBERT D ALFORD • SHEL-
LIE L ALFORD • UVANNEY J ALFORD • SHANTI
ALFORD BROWN • CYNTHIA L ALFORD RAESIDE
• BRITT N ALGER • KATHLEEN S ALGER •
SUZANNE-DESIREE D ALGIER • BETHANY L
ALGRIN • WALEED ALHAKAMI • KHALEFAH
ALHUMAIDA • AHMAD H ALI • KARIMAH ALI •
MAJID ALI • RAZIUDDIN ALI • KRISTINA A ALIA-
GA • MANUEL M ALIAGA • CHRISTINE E ALICEA
• THOMAS J ALIFFI • DANIEL J ALIG • JOHN S
ALINI • BUSTER ALITZER • EDWARD G ALIVERTI
• SHIRLEY A ALIVERTI • LAYLA I ALIZZI •
WARITH M ALLAH • EMAD Y ALLAHO • PATRICIA
C ALLAMAN • RENE O ALLAMBY • CRAIG H
ALLAN • JAMES ALLAN • JEFFREY L ALLARD •
BRIAN T ALLCOCK • THOMAS L ALLCOCK •
ANDREW J ALLDEN • DAVID J ALLDEN • GAYLE
E ALLDREDGE • JACQUELINE M ALLEE • REBEC-
CA M ALLEGRANZI • MICHAEL ALLEGRETTO •
ELIZABETH ALLEMENOS • ALISSA D ALLEN •
AMY ALLEN • ANGELA F ALLEN • ANN B ALLEN
• ANNE H ALLEN • ANNE S ALLEN • ARMAND A
ALLEN • BARBARA J ALLEN • BENNY R ALLEN •
BETTY C ALLEN • BEVERLY W ALLEN • BRADLEY
M ALLEN • BRENT B ALLEN • BRIAN J ALLEN •
BRITTANY V ALLEN • CARL B ALLEN • CAROLE
S ALLEN • CAROLYN L ALLEN • CELIA ALLEN •
CHARLES B ALLEN • CHRISTINE D ALLEN •
CYNTHIA B ALLEN • DALE L ALLEN • DANIEL M
ALLEN • DAVID ALLEN • DAVID L ALLEN • DEB-
ORAH J ALLEN • DESIA M ALLEN • DOMINIQUE
P ALLEN • DON W ALLEN • DONALD JR. F ALLEN
• DONNA S ALLEN • DORIS C ALLEN • DOUGLAS
ALLEN • ELIZABETH ALLEN • ELIZABETH S ALLEN
• EMORY E ALLEN • FRANK R ALLEN • GAILE M
ALLEN • GARY T ALLEN • GEORGE W ALLEN •

GERALDINE ALLEN • GIA S ALLEN • HELEN M
ALLEN • HIRAM C ALLEN • JACKIE L ALLEN •
JACQUELYN D ALLEN • JAMES E ALLEN • JAMES
K ALLEN • JAMES L ALLEN • JAN E ALLEN •
JANE E ALLEN • JAYAN S ALLEN • JEFFREY S
ALLEN • JENNIFER D ALLEN • JERRY ALLEN •
JOALVETTA A ALLEN • JOCELYN M ALLEN •
JOHN B ALLEN • JOSEPH R ALLEN • KATHRYN D
ALLEN • KENNETH L ALLEN • KENNETH M
ALLEN • KENT ALLEN • KIMBERLY A ALLEN •
KIMBERLY A ALLEN • KIRSTEN E ALLEN •
LAURA-ASHL ALLEN • LORI S ALLEN • LUCRE-
TIA G ALLEN • MARSHA M ALLEN • MARVIN K
ALLEN • MARY F ALLEN • MARY J ALLEN • MARY
L ALLEN • MARY M ALLEN • MELINDA M ALLEN
• MICHAEL V ALLEN • MICHELLE L ALLEN •
MITZI S ALLEN • NANCY C ALLEN • ODENE H
ALLEN • PATRICK C.N. ALLEN • RANDY ALLEN •
RICHARD ALLEN • RISHA N ALLEN • ROBERT B
ALLEN • ROBERT S ALLEN • RONNIE L ALLEN •
SALLY E ALLEN • SANDERS ALLEN • SARA B
ALLEN • SCOTT H ALLEN • SERESSA F ALLEN •
SHARON A ALLEN • SHERI D ALLEN • SHERRYL
J ALLEN • SHIRLEY C ALLEN • SHIRLEY E ALLEN
• STEVE W ALLEN • SUE ALLEN • SYLVIA ALLEN
• THADDEUS ALLEN • TODD ALLEN • TONIA B
ALLEN • TRACY Y ALLEN • VANESSA J ALLEN •
VERONICA F ALLEN • VICTORIA Y ALLEN • WEN-
DELL L ALLEN • WILBUR R ALLEN • WILLIAM L
ALLEN • WILLIAM O ALLEN • WILLIAM S ALLEN
• SCOTT W ALLEN PHD • RUTH A ALLEN ATC •
DORREL ALLEN C • GERALDINE ALLEN EMT
• PERCY ALLEN III • THOMAS G ALLEN III •
JOANNE B ALLEN MD • KRISTY V ALLEN SAT
• SHAWN P ALLENDER ATC • ASHLEY ALLERA •
LYNN E ALLEY • ALITHIA D ALLEYNE • LARRY
ALLGOOD • JOHN N ALLINSON II • JENNIFER G
ALLIS • AMY L ALLISON • CORNELL J ALLISON •
CORY ALLISON • DEBORAH L ALLISON • DIANE
S ALLISON • GERALD D ALLISON • MARY M
ALLISON • PATRICIA A ALLISON • REBEKAH J
ALLISON • STEVEN W ALLISON • TAMMY C ALLI-
SON • RUTH M ALLISON RN • AMY ALLMAN •
ROBYN R ALLMAN • STEPHANIE J ALLOMONG •
CYRIL R ALLOUCHE • BARBARA J ALLRED •

CLINTON D ALLRED • PAUL D ALLRED •
JEANETTE ALLRED-POWLESS • CHRISTOPHER
S ALLRED EMT • HOWARD D ALLRED JR • MARK
ALLWOOD • DANIEL ALM • ALBERT I ALMAND •
JAMES R ALMAND • LYNN B ALMAND • MAR-
GARET M ALMAND • PHILLIP J ALMAND • DIEGO
A ALMEIDA • ERLINDA M ALMEIDA • KEVIN C.
ALMEROTH • BRENT S ALMOND • PAULA M
ALMOND • STEVE W ALMOND • JON L ALMQUIST
• OMOKARO ALOHAN • SHELLEY M ALOI • SUSAN
L ALONGI • CARLOS R ALONSO • VICTOR M ALON-
SO • RACHEL L ALPERN • STEVE D ALPHABET •
ABDUL HADI A ALQATTAN • PAMELA J ALRED •
VICKIE C ALSABROOK • CHARMAINE A ALSAGER •
ANN L ALSTON • ANTHONY R ALSTON • AVA H
ALSTON • BARBARA ALSTON • ERIC R ALSTON •
ISAAC ALSTON • JULIETTE N ALSTON • MARCIA J
ALSTON • RACHEL L ALSTON • SABRINA J
ALSTON • MICHELLE D ALSTON WILLIAMS •
KRISTL ALT • UTE S ALT-CARBERRY • URSULA D
ALTEMUS • BRAD ALTENA • CRAIG J ALTERMAN •
JOEL J ALTERMAN • LEE A ALTERMAN • MARCIA L
ALTERMAN • TERRY L ALTERS • ARJEN M ALTHUIS
• CARRIE H ALTMAN • CECIL F ALTMAN • DAVID R
ALTMAN • EASTER L ALTMAN • ELIZABETH ALT-
MAN • HELEN R ALTMAN • JAMES S ALTMAN •
JENNIFER L ALTMAN • LAWRENCE C ALTMAN •
LINDA R ALTMAN • ARLENE S ALTMAN MT •
JAMES R ALTON • JUNE A ALTON • NANCY J
ALTON • RAE ANN ALTON • DEBORAH B
ALTSCHUL • RICHARD J ALTWARG • LORIN ALU-
SIC • VALDEANE A ALUSIC • CARLOS H ALVARA-
DO • DOLORES L ALVARADO • RUDY Z ALVARA-
DO • ANTHONY J ALVAREZ • FRANCISCO O
ALVAREZ • INAKI R ALVAREZ • JAVIER ALVAREZ
• JEFF B ALVAREZ • JORGE A ALVAREZ • NANCY
G ALVAREZ • RAMONA L ALVAREZ • REYES M
ALVAREZ • SUSAN L ALVAREZ • LUGAS G
ALVAREZ TABIO • DANIE ALVERO • CAROL Y
ALVES • CHARLES E ALVIS • JULIE L ALVOID •
ANNE T ALVORD • JUANA P ALZAGA • MARIANN
ALZATE • JOYCE M AMACHER • JUAN R AMADOR •
SONIA AMADOR • JAMAINE AMAKER • CYNTHIA L
AMANDOLIA • CHARLES SCOTT AMANN • HARUKA
AMANO • IKUHO AMANO • TSUKASA AMANO
• WALTER AMARAL • GEORGE P AMASON •

JOSEPH M AMATI • ANNA AMATO • ERICA L
AMATO • HERBERT K AMATO ATC • CHARLES P
AMATO JR • ROGER AMBAUEN • AMY N
AMBROSE • CHRISTOPHER W AMBROSE •
GEORGE R AMBROSE • MARGARET A AMBROSE
• MARVIN C AMBROSE • PAUL J AMBROSE •
VALERIE I AMBROSE • DURWARD F AMBROSE JR
• PETER J AMBROSE PHARM D • TRESSA R
AMBURGEY • WILLIAM T AMBURGEY • DAVE
AMEND • MARK T AMENDOLA • CAROLINA D.
AMERO • EARNEST M AMERSON • MARY A AMER-
SON • BARBARA A AMES • MARYANN AMES •
MICHAEL J AMESQUITA • JULIETTE T AMEY •
MARY E AMEY • NORSA J AMEY • ENRIQUE
AMEZQUITA • CHRISTOPHER D AMICK • MICHAEL
V AMICK • PETER L AMIDON • THARZIA R AMIE •
LORRETTA L AMIOT • BERNADETTE A AMIS •
ABDUL R AMLANI • NASIR P AMLANI • MAX E
AMMANN • MAX E AMMANN • RALPH S AMMANN •
POUL AMMENTORP-SCHMIDT • TIMOTHY C
AMMER • ALAN H AMMERMAN • SUSAN E AMMER-
MAN • CURTIS E AMMONS • JOHN L AMMONS •
LAURA T AMMONS • PAULA M AMMONS • ELIZA-
BETH C AMOS • GREGORY W AMOS • JEREMY S
AMOS • MARGENE K AMOS • REBECCA W AMOS •
ANTHONY L AMOS JR • MELINDA O AMOSU • ROS-
ALIND AMUNATEGUI • LAURA J AMUNDSEN •
HONG AN • SAHNG Y AN • RICHARD J ANASTASI •
DORAH B ANAYE-WHITE • TAIT A ANBERH • SON-
DRA L ANCELOT • BERTHA ANDALUZ • LEONARD
D ANDERS • MARK T ANDERS • PEGGY J ANDERS
• SONIA M ANDERS • DOUGLAS G ANDERSEN •
EILEEN P ANDERSEN • GRETCHEN L ANDERSEN
• JEFF P ANDERSEN • JODY C ANDERSEN •
KATHY ANDERSEN • LYNN L. ANDERSEN •
RICHARD H ANDERSEN • RUNE T ANDERSEN •
TREVOR T ANDERSEN • ALANA R ANDERSON •
ALLEN ANDERSON • AMALIA A ANDERSON •
ANNE M ANDERSON • ARNE J ANDERSON •
BARBARA S ANDERSON • BARBARA S ANDER-
SON • BETH L ANDERSON • BETTY ANDERSON •
BETTY A ANDERSON • BEVERLY D ANDERSON
• BROOKE L ANDERSON • BURMA D ANDERSON •
CAMERON K ANDERSON • CAROL B ANDERSON
• CAROLYN J ANDERSON • CHARLES ANDERSON

• CHARLES ANDERSON • CHERISH D ANDER-
SON • CHERYL S ANDERSON • CHRISTOPHER A
ANDERSON • CLARENCE E ANDERSON •
CLIFTON E ANDERSON • CURTIS M ANDERSON
• CURTIS M.F. ANDERSON • CYNTHIA Y ANDER-
SON • DAVE D ANDERSON • DAVID S ANDERSON
• DEBRA J ANDERSON • DONNEA N ANDERSON
• DORIS M ANDERSON • DOVETTE P ANDERSON •
DUANE ANDERSON • EDDIE D ANDERSON • ELIZA-
BETH A ANDERSON • ELIZABETH M ANDERSON •
ERICA L ANDERSON • ERIK K ANDERSON •
FRANCES L ANDERSON • GAIL V ANDERSON • GARY
L ANDERSON • GORDON M ANDERSON • GREGORY
ANDERSON • GRETCHEN ANDERSON • H.WALTER
ANDERSON • HARRIET B ANDERSON • JACQUELINE
D ANDERSON • JAMES E ANDERSON • JAMES M
ANDERSON • JANE A ANDERSON • JANET A ANDER-
SON • JANICE L ANDERSON • JASON C ANDERSON
• JEAN F ANDERSON • JENNIFER L ANDERSON •
JEROME D ANDERSON • JOHN S ANDERSON
• JUANITA A ANDERSON • JUNE ANDERSON •
KAREN ANDERSON • KAREN C ANDERSON • KATH-
LEEN M ANDERSON • KATHRYN W ANDERSON •
KEEGAN BROWN ANDERSON • KEITH A ANDERSON
• KELLY M ANDERSON • KRISTER K ANDERSON •
KYLE J ANDERSON • LISA C ANDERSON • LORI
ANDERSON • LORNA S ANDERSON • LUCAS
P ANDERSON • LUCILLE A ANDERSON • LYN-
NETTE ANDERSON • M. NAOMI ANDERSON •
MAKANYA D ANDERSON • MARGARET S ANDER-
SON • MARI L ANDERSON • MARKO D ANDERSON
• MARY A ANDERSON • MARY B ANDERSON •
MATTHEW R ANDERSON • MICHAEL D ANDER-
SON • MICHAEL K ANDERSON • MINDA K ANDER-
SON • MIWA S ANDERSON • NANCY L ANDERSON
• NANCY L ANDERSON • NATASHA ANDERSON •
NELSON R ANDERSON • NICHOLAS S ANDER-
SON • OCIE ANDERSON • PAMELA A ANDERSON
• PAMELA D ANDERSON • PATTY A ANDERSON •
PAUL W ANDERSON • RASHAHRA T ANDERSON •
RICHARD K ANDERSON • RICK D ANDERSON
• RICK E ANDERSON • RITA M ANDERSON •
ROBERT B ANDERSON • ROBERT G ANDERSON
• ROBERTA R ANDERSON • ROXROY ANDERSON
• ROY T ANDERSON • RUNO C ANDERSON •
RUTH A ANDERSON • SANDRA ANDERSON •

SARAH T ANDERSON • SCOTT C ANDERSON •
SCOTT W ANDERSON • SEAN ANDERSON • SELE-
NA D ANDERSON • SHEILA J ANDERSON • SHEILA
W ANDERSON • SHERRY E ANDERSÓN • SHIR-
LENE ANDERSON • SONJA G ANDERSON
• SOPHIA A ANDERSON • STACY L ANDERSON •
STEPHEN E ANDERSON • STEPHEN L ANDERSON
• STEVE R ANDERSON • STEVEN D ANDERSON
• STEVEN J ANDERSON • STEVEN R ANDERSON •
STEVEN S ANDERSON • TABITHA S ANDERSON •
TAMARA T ANDERSON • TERRY A ANDERSON •
TODD ANDERSON • VICKY H ANDERSON • WENDY
LYNETTE ANDERSON • WILFRED A. ANDERSON •
WILLIAM B ANDERSON • WILLIAM D ANDERSON •
WILLIAM D ANDERSON • WILLIAM G ANDERSON
• WILLIE J ANDERSON • WILLIE J ANDERSON •
WILLIE L ANDERSON • WILMA J ANDERSON •
NATALIE T ANDERSON-PLACE • BARBARA L
ANDERSON ATC • JOHN H ANDERSON ATC •
EARL E ANDERSON JR • GUSTAVE W ANDERSON
JR • HENRY F ANDERSON JR • CECIL ANDY M
ANDERSON PT • ANDREA M ANDERSSON • ELIZ-
ABETH P ANDERT • ERIC C ANDERTON • JEN-
NIFER L ANDERTON • LAZ EDUARDO ANDINO •
PAUL ANDJELKOVIC • KENJI ANDO • ROBERT P
ANDOH • ETELVINO V ANDRADE
• LIONEL ANDRADE • CRAIG S ANDRADE ATC •
VALERIE ANDREANI • DINAL S ANDREASEN •
JANIA ANDREOTTI • MARISA ANDRES • CATHER-
INE L ANDRESEN • NANCY A ANDRESEN •
AMELIA A ANDREWS • ARTHUR L ANDREWS
• BERNARD LOUIS ANDREWS • BOBBIE A
ANDREWS • BRENDA L ANDREWS • BRENT L
ANDREWS • CHRISTOPHER P ANDREWS • DEN-
NIS M ANDREWS • FELICIA N ANDREWS •
FRANK M ANDREWS • GEORGE H ANDREWS •
GERALDINE A ANDREWS • GLADYS L ANDREWS
• GUY P ANDREWS • J ALFRED ANDREWS •
JANET D ANDREWS • JANET L ANDREWS • JILL
G ANDREWS • JOHN ANDREWS • KATE E
ANDREWS • LAURA J ANDREWS • LYNN ANDREWS
• MADELON ANDREWS • MICKEY W ANDREWS •
MONTE ANDREWS • PATRICIA E ANDREWS • PAUL
G ANDREWS • ROBERT B ANDREWS • ROBERT D
ANDREWS • ROBIN C ANDREWS • SARAH S
ANDREWS • SHANNON G ANDREWS • THOMAS
B ANDREWS • TONYA L ANDREWS • WILLIAM L
ANDREWS • ROBERT ANDREWS EMT •
LAWRENCE M ANDREWS JR • MICHAEL D ANDRI-
ATCH • MICHAEL A ANDRIOLA • ETHAN L ANDRUS
• MARCO ANDUJAR • RUBEN ANDUJAR • DEBO-
RAH ANEKSTEIN • EMEKA B ANENE • BONNIE K
ANGEL • HENRY ANGEL • APRIL L ANGELES •
ROBERT C ANGELI • JOAN C ANGELINI • JESSE L
ANGELL • KEITH G ANGELL • MARGARET R
ANGELL • KARL ANGELO • WILLIAM M ANGELO •
MARIA M ANGELOVA • SARAH E ANGERMULLER
• NATALIE R ANGLE • RICHARD ANGLE • STACEY
D ANGLIN • MICHAEL J ANGRESANO • ANN M
ANGULO • SUZANA ANIC • LYNN ANIDI • KEISHA
ANITON • OLGA S ANKROM • MARY E ANNAVED-
DER • KERRY L ANNEL • JOSEPH L ANNEST
• WILLARD R ANNIS • BEVERLYN L ANSAH •
ELAYN Z ANSARI • KIM E ANSCHULTZ • HAROLD
B ANSLEY • KEVIN D ANSLEY • SAM B ANSON •
HADLI A ANSTINE • SELENA ANTALAN • FRANK
E ANTALEK • DANA ANTHONY • DEBORAH E
ANTHONY • FRED ANTHONY • JACQUELYN A
ANTHONY • JACQUELYN P ANTHONY • JANINE
D ANTHONY • JARRELL B ANTHONY • JUDY S
ANTHONY • LAVERNE V ANTHONY • MACK
ANTHONY • MAYNIE H ANTHONY • ROBERT
C ANTHONY • SHIRLEY ANTHONY • SMITH E
ANTHONY • STEPHEN C ANTHONY • XAVIER L
ANTHONY • VIRGINIA H ANTHONY MT • MARIA D
ANTOLINO • ANA I ANTON • ANNA T ANTON •
CAROLINE M ANTON • ANNE ANTONENKO • ADAM
ANTONIEWICZ • DAVID M ANTOPOLSKY •
MICHEAL ANTOSKOW • ZINA L ANTOSKOW
• ANDREW ANTWEILER • BRIAN ANWEILER •
YUSUKE AOI • SHUICHI AOKI • LUIS B APARICIO •
LOU A APLAND • DANIA G APONTE • JAMES P
APPEL • JEANNIE L APPEL • KATHY F APPELL
• PETER J APPELO • JANE W APPLE • MARY-
AUDREY APPLE • MEGAN S APPLE • BRUCE A
APPLE ATC • DAVID F APPLE JR MD • CHERYL L
"APPLEBERRY, CATC" • CONNIE J APPLEBY •
JOCILE S APPLEBY • AMIE L APPLETON •
PAMELA S APPLETON • ISAAC D APPLEWHITE
• ROBERT A APRAEZ • ROBERT A APRAEZ •
KAREN N APRIL • SADASHIV V APTE • LUIS
AQUINO • HIROKO ARAI • AOUS H ARAIM •
NAWAL ARAIM • OMAR A ARAIM • SINAN M
ARAIM • LOUIS R ARAIZA • CAROLYN N ARAKAKI •
MASAKO ARAKAWA • RUMIKO ARAKAWA • ARMIN
V ARANA • MERISA ARANAS • RICHARD ARANT •
JULIA S ARATA • PETER F ARATA • OSCAR A
ARAUZ • TINA P ARBES • GRADA ARBLE •
WILLIAM ARBOLEDA • DIANNE M ARBUCKLE •
ALLEN O ARCAND • SUSAN M ARCARO • ADDI-
SON A ARCE • FERNANDO ARCE • AFLACIA
ARCENEAUX • MARINA A ARCHBOLD • DAVID G
ARCHER • DAVID W ARCHER • DONNA M ARCHER
• GLENIS P ARCHER • JERMAINE ARCHER •
JOSEPH B ARCHER • PATRICIA A ARCHER ATC
• CYNTHIA V ARCHIE • MARY J ARCHILLE •
MICHAEL J ARCHILLE • JASON S ARCHINAL •
BIANCA N ARCHULETTA • ERNEST C ARCOS
• ROBERT R ARDALAN • JEFF ARDIS • GARY M
ARDITO • JEAN AREL • E M ARELLANO • KRISTIN
A ARELLANO • MARIANNE ARELLANO • JONAS B
AREM • MARCI A ARENA • JOHN R ARENBERG •
ELISABETH F ARENBURG • JENNIFER A
ARENDS • JOSHUA P ARENDS • MARK ARENDS
• IRAKLY G ARESHIDZE • COLLEEN I AREY •
STUART L AREY • VIRGINIA B AREY • PIO R
ARGENTA • BARBARA F ARGO • CAROL P ARGO
• GEORGE E ARGO • KIMBERLY J ARGO • LINDA
F ARGO • LURLINE G ARGO • NELSON E ARGO •
STEPHEN P ARGO • NECIP A ARI • GENE ARIAS
• MARI R ARICK • SAM J ARICO • CLAIRE ARIGA
• DICK ARILDSEN • VICTOR ARIYIBL • AFARIN
ARJMAND • HAMID ARJMAND • FREDERICK D
ARKIN • KAREN J ARKIN • MATTHEW D ARKIN
• MICHAELLE ARKIN • DAVID A ARLEN • SUSAN
J ARLEN • ALICE M ARLINE • CYNTHIA A ARMAN
• MICHELE ARMAO • JEFFREY T ARMBRUSTER •
LAUREL H ARMBRUSTER • CHARLES R ARMEN-
TO • JAMES M ARMES • PATRICIA ARMINANA •
ANGELA L ARMISTEAD • JARROD J ARMITAGE •
CARLY D ARMOUR • DAVID E ARMOUR • DORIS J
ARMOUR • HAZEL ARMOUR • LARRY ARMOUR
• MARSHA M ARMOUR • ROLENE R ARMOUR •
JAMES E ARMOUR JR • KAREN ARMS • ERNEST
C ARMSTEAD • ELAINE E ARMSTER • BETSY S
ARMSTRONG • CARY A ARMSTRONG •
CATHARINE B ARMSTRONG • CHRIS J ARM-
STRONG • DANIEL P ARMSTRONG • DAVID F
ARMSTRONG • EDWARD A ARMSTRONG •
FRANCES V ARMSTRONG • GARRET A ARM-
STRONG • GLEN B ARMSTRONG • JAMES C ARM-
STRONG • JEFFREY D ARMSTRONG • JESSE
ARMSTRONG • JO A ARMSTRONG • JUDITH
A ARMSTRONG • JUDY ARMSTRONG • KAREN F
ARMSTRONG • KATHY ARMSTRONG • KATHY R
ARMSTRONG • KETRA L ARMSTRONG • LEE
C ARMSTRONG • LISA J ARMSTRONG • MARK A
ARMSTRONG • MARY L ARMSTRONG • PEGGY
ARMSTRONG • PHYLLIS R ARMSTRONG •
RICARDO L ARMSTRONG • ROBERT M ARM-
STRONG • SHERRY A ARMSTRONG • TAMARA C
ARMSTRONG • WILLIAM S ARMSTRONG •
WILLIE D ARMSTRONG • LEWIS H ARMSTRONG
SR • KAROL S ARMWOOD • GUY C ARNALL JR •
NADENE G ARNAULT • CAMERON R ARNDT •
CARL H ARNDT • GAIL G ARNDT • KAREN D
ARNDT • ROGER L ARNDT • DEBORAH A ARNE-
SEN • JOSEPH C ARNETT • MARY E ARNETT •
STACEY A ARNETT • DOROTHY D ARNETTE
• VICKY E ARNETTE • GAY A ARNIERI • DAVID L
ARNOFF • ALEXIS S ARNOLD • ALISON K
ARNOLD • BETH L ARNOLD • CLAIRE L ARNOLD
• CYNTHIA D ARNOLD • DALE B ARNOLD •
DAWN E ARNOLD • EMILY THERESIA ARNOLD •
ERIC L ARNOLD • GAIL W ARNOLD • GERALD C
ARNOLD • HEATHER R ARNOLD • JAN M ARNOLD
• JENNIFER C ARNOLD • JERRY B ARNOLD •
JOANN J ARNOLD • JOSHUA N ARNOLD • LEWIS
GENE ARNOLD • OLIVIA L ARNOLD • PAMELA W
ARNOLD • PAT ARNOLD • RENEE B ARNOLD •
RICHARD H ARNOLD • ROBERT D ARNOLD
• ROBERT J ARNOLD • SUSAN A ARNOLD •
THERON H ARNOLD • THOMAS A ARNOLD •
THOMAS B ARNOLD • THOMAS C ARNOLD • TIM-
OTHY J ARNOLD • TRACY L ARNOLD • KYA
ARNOLIE • ROBERT A ARNOPOL MT • DOUG
ARNOT • BARBARA AROGETI • CHERRYMAE A
AROMAS • MELISSA H ARON ATC • AVIS Y
ARONOVITZ • BETSY J ARONOVITZ • BARBARA
G ARONSON • RICHARD M ARONSON • AMY I
ARONSON-FRIEDMAN • DOLORES M ARPI • GUY
LAURENT G ARPINO • DAISY V ARRECHEA •
HERNANDO ARRECHEA • CORRINE ARREDON-
DO • ALICIA A ARRICK • DEBORAH D ARRIETA •
BELINDA M ARRINGTON • CAROL L ARRINGTON
• CRAIG S ARRINGTON • DELL ARRINGTON •
GRANT H ARRINGTON • JOE B ARRINGTON
• JOSEPH ARRINGTON • KELLY ARRINGTON •
LAURIE L ARRINGTON • LAWRENCE F ARRING-
TON • LESHAUN E ARRINGTON • MALCOLM J
ARRINGTON • MARY H ARRINGTON • MICHELLE
L ARRINGTON • STEPHANIE C ARRINGTON-
HALEY • MARVIN S ARRINGTON JR • CECILIA A
ARRITOLA • ELBERT ARROWOOD • RHONDA A
ARROWOOD • MICHAEL F ARROYO • PETER
ARROYO JR • NEFISE Y ARSAN • RAMONA A
ARSCOTT • A RAYMOND ARSENAULT • JANE E
ARTEAGA • BARBARA J ARTERBURN • MARIO L
ARTESIANO • PAMELA M ARTHER • HELEN H
ARTHUR • JEFF D ARTHUR • JOSEPH M. ARTHUR
• LEN H ARTHUR • PATRICK S ARTHUR • PHYLLIS
J ARTHUR • ROSALIND E ARTHUR • ANDREW D
ARTIGUE • TERESA C ARTINGER • APRIL Y ARTIS
• FELICIA J ARTIS • JOHN D ARTLEY • REGINA
ARTS • DUANE T ARTZ • KRISTI B ARTZ • LYNN M
ARTZ • MICHAEL J ARUNDEL • CHUCK ARVIN •
MICHAEL G ARZABAL • LANDRIA K ASAMOTO •

CHRONOLOGY

1987

8 February—Atlanta attorney Billy Payne founds the Georgia Amateur Athletic Foundation (GAAF) and recruits Mayor Andrew Young to assist in bidding for the 1996 Olympic Games in Atlanta.

September—Atlanta submits its bid as the US candidate city to the United States Olympic Committee (USOC), becoming one of 14 American cities seeking to host the Games.

1988

February—A site-selection committee from the USOC visits Atlanta to meet with city leaders and tour proposed venues for the 1996 Olympic Games.

29 April—Atlanta is selected by the USOC as the US candidate city and will be bidding with five other cities—Athens, Belgrade, Manchester, Melbourne, and Toronto.

September—An Altanta delegation led by Mayor Young and Billy Payne travels to Seoul, Korea, for the 1988 Olympic Games to meet members of the International Olympic Committee (IOC) and learn more about hosting the Games.

November—The GAAF forms the Atlanta Organizing Committee (AOC) board of directors, which includes an advisory council and eight standing committees. The five "A's" bid logo is created, representing the resources that Atlanta offers: Access, Accommodations, Ability, Athletics, and Attitude.

1989

February—IOC President Juan Antonio Samaranch visits Atlanta to help celebrate the opening of the AOC's new offices. The AOC's Olympic theme is unveiled, "Atlanta and the Olympics: Yes! Partners with the World."

4 July—The AOC sponsors an Olympic Mile in the Peachtree Road Race, a 10 km competition attracting over 40,000 runners. Members of the IOC and the international press are present to see this start of a citywide billboard campaign to increase local awareness and interest in the bid effort. The volunteer campaign begins, with plans to attract 100,000 volunteers.

August—IOC members visit Atlanta prior to the IOC's 95th General Session in San Juan, Puerto Rico. Atlanta hosts the USSR vs. USA dual swim meet at Emory University.

September—Atlanta delegates attend the 95th General Session of the IOC and unveil an interactive video program that allows IOC members to tour Atlanta electronically. After the session, IOC members are flown to Atlanta for Labor Day celebrations, during which more than 7,500 runners participate in the "Run for the Bid" as a demonstration of public support for the Games.

1990

1 February—Atlanta's official five-volume bid document is submitted to the IOC offices in Lausanne, Switzerland.

April—The AOC hosts "Springtime in Atlanta," an event for visiting members of the IOC. Approximately 8,000 runners participate in the AOC's "Salute to Georgia Olympians" and the 5 km "Run for the Rings."

May—The IOC Study and Evaluation Commission, the Association of Summer Olympic International Federations (ASOIF), and the Association of the National Olympic Committees (ANOC) conduct official site inspections in Atlanta.

June—An Atlanta delegation attends the IOC Executive Board and ANOC General Assembly meetings in Barcelona, Spain, where the order of final presentations in Tokyo is determined. Atlanta will be first.

13–17 June—The AOC and Emory University host U.S. Olympic Academy XIV. The program concludes with Georgia Olympic Day, an opportunity for students throughout the state to have an Olympic-style experience. Work begins on developing an annual Olympic Day in the Schools program that will continue through 1996.

August—In an event sponsored by the AOC, the International Baseball Association hosts the World All-Star Amateur Baseball Game at Atlanta-Fulton County Stadium.

September—The AOC hosts the 68th voting member (of 88) of the IOC since Atlanta began its quest to stage the Games, an unprecedented number of IOC member visits for a bid city.

18 September—A delegation of more than 300 Atlantans and Georgians travels to Tokyo, Japan, to support Atlanta's bid for the 1996 Olympic Games at the IOC's 96th General Session. By a vote of 51–35, the IOC selects Atlanta to be the host city of the Games of the XXVI Olympiad. The decision is reached on the fifth ballot in voting by 86 members of the IOC. In Atlanta, celebrations abound.

1991

28 January—The Atlanta Committee for the Olympic Games (ACOG) is established as a private, not-for-profit corporation, and the ACOG Board of Directors is established.

14 June—ACOG and the United States Olympic Committee (USOC) form a joint venture—Atlanta Centennial Olympic Properties (ACOP)—to handle marketing efforts.

18 July—ACOG establishes the Children's Olympic Ticket Fund to raise money for economically disadvantaged children to attend the Games.

23 July—The ACOG Board of Directors adopts an unprecedented Equal Economic Opportunity Plan to ensure minority and female participation in Games employment and business opportunities.

18 September—The Olympic Experience, a high-tech public information center and retail store, opens in Underground Atlanta.

30 September—The Olympic Stadium Neighborhood Advisory Group holds its initial meeting. It is the first of 24 community-based groups formed to advise ACOG on Games planning.

1992

8 January—Groundbreaking is held on the campus of the Georgia Institute of Technology (Georgia Tech) for the first of 17 new housing facilities that ACOG will help fund for use as part of the Olympic Village.

21 January—ACOG releases a financial forecast outlining anticipated revenues and expenses for the 1996 Olympic Games.

23 January—The European Broadcasting Union extends a letter of intent to purchase the television rights to the Centennial Olympic Games.

2 February—The Coca-Cola Company becomes the first worldwide sponsor of the 1996 Games.

13 February—ACOG unveils the "Atlanta Centennial Torch," as the official logo of the 1996 Games.

5 March—NationsBank signs an agreement to become the first Centennial Olympic Games Partner.

7 April—To promote volunteerism before the Games, ACOG launches The Olympic Force, which will become a statewide network of more than 1,700 community groups representing 500,000 people.

8 May—The first annual auditions are held for the Atlanta Olympic Band, which will be comprised of 300 of Georgia's best high school and college musicians and color guard performers.

10 July—ACOG begins an expanded Dream Team program, annually selecting 100 Georgia teenagers as community youth ambassadors for the Games.

9 August—The Olympic Flag is passed to Atlanta Mayor Maynard Jackson at the end of the Closing Ceremony for the 1992 Olympic Games in Barcelona. Earlier in the event, an ACOG dance troupe performed and IZZY, the mascot of the 1996 Games, was introduced.

10 September—An 11-day statewide celebration begins, marking the arrival of the Olympic Flag in Georgia.

18 September—After an exciting concert at the Georgia Dome the previous evening that included a salute from US President George Bush, the Olympic Flag festival concluded exactly two years after the awarding of the 1996 Games to Atlanta, and the Olympic Flag is displayed at Atlanta's City Hall.

23 September—The US Congress authorizes the minting of a series of 16 commemorative Olympic coins.

November—The first of four annual service projects for Olympic Force members is held. The efforts include a food and toy drive to underprivileged families; collection of children's books for Georgia public libraries; refurbishing of arts and cultural institutions; and cleaning of state parks and historical sites.

1993

February—"Winterland," the first program of the Cultural Olympiad, opens. The month-long festival is a joint effort with 1994 Winter Olympic Games host Lillehammer.

9 March—Plans are approved to build Olympic Stadium on a site next to Atlanta–Fulton County Stadium (AFCS). After the Games, Olympic Stadium will be adapted to become the home of the Atlanta Braves baseball team, and AFCS will be removed.

17–18 March—The Association of Summer Olympic International Federations holds its annual meeting in Atlanta. ACOG is host to this gathering of more than 400 international sports officials and Olympic Family members.

23 March—ACOG joins with the Private Industry Council in initiating the Neighborhood Job Training and Employment Program for residents of areas around new Olympic venues.

21 June—ACOG announces its sponsorship of the 1996 Paralympic Games.

10 July—Groundbreaking is held for Olympic Stadium. Olympian Wilma Rudolph, in one of her last public appearances, is one of the speakers.

27 July—NBC-Sports is awarded exclusive rights to televise the 1996 Olympic Games in the US.

3 August—With input from local cultural leaders, ACOG unveils a four-year cultural program that will culminate in the Olympic Arts Festival.

6 August—Golden Park in Columbus, Georgia, is selected as the venue for softball, a sport added to the 1996 Games Programme by the IOC in 1991.

12 September—The Cultural Olympiad starts an eight-week festival "¡Mexico! A Cultural Tapestry" to commemorate the 25th anniversary of the 1968 Olympic Games in Mexico City.

18 September—At its 101st session in Monaco, the IOC approves the addition of beach volleyball, mountain bike cycling, and women's football to the 1996 Olympic Games Programme.

20 September—Four of six bidding cities—Birmingham, Alabama; Miami and Orlando, Florida; and Washington, DC—are selected to host preliminary rounds of football.

23 October—Opening Ceremony of the 1996 Games is 1,000 days away. In downtown Atlanta, ACOG unveils a countdown clock that spans one of the city's major highways.

1 November—The White House Task Force for the 1996 Olympic Games, chaired by Vice President Al Gore, holds its first meeting.

5 November—Don Mischer Productions is selected to produce the Opening and Closing Ceremonies.

19 November—Georgia Governor Zell Miller commits to the construction of Centennial Olympic Park in downtown Atlanta—a facility originally conceived by ACOG Chief Executive Officer Billy Payne as a central gathering place for Olympic visitors.

30 December—Sales of Olympic license plates to vehicle owners in Georgia begin, and will continue over the next two years exceeding 1 million—the largest commemorative license plate program in the state's history.

1994

27 January—The Cultural Olympiad Scroll logo is introduced.

30 January—"Atlanta 1996" debuts as one of the most highly rated programs on television the day it airs. In all, ACOG will produce eight programs for nationwide broadcast on NBC to highlight preparations for the Games.

10 February—The Georgia legislature passes a bill allowing accredited National Olympic Committee (NOC) physicians to provide medical services to their delegations during the Games.

24 March—ACOG unveils the design of the Olympic cauldron by artist and sculptor Siah Armajani.

15 April—The Cultural Olympiad and the National Black Arts Festival collaborate to present "Celebrate Africa!"

3 June—The Morehouse School of Medicine, SmithKline Beecham Clinical Laboratories, and ACOG announce plans to construct a new medical center for the school that will also provide doping control services during the 1996 Games.

15 June—ACOG breaks ground for the Georgia International Horse Park, which will be the site of equestrian competition.

25 June—Construction begins on the hockey venues as groundbreaking ceremonies are held on the campuses of Clark Atlanta University and Morris Brown College.

6 July—The Georgia Tech campus is the site of groundbreaking ceremonies for the Aquatic Center, which will host Olympic swimming, diving, synchronized swimming, and water polo competitions.

12 July—ACOG introduces the Look of the Games design, "A Quilt of Leaves."

4 August—Initial plans for the Olympic Transportation System for spectators are made public.

23–24 September—ACOG hosts the 1994 Pan American Race Walk Cup, marking the first test of an Olympic competition site.

4 November—Commemorative bricks to be used to pave the Plaza of Centennial Olympic Park are offered for sale.

22 November—Work on venues planned for Stone Mountain Park, a permanent facility for tennis and temporary sites for archery and track cycling, begins with a combined groundbreaking ceremony.

12 December—The Association of NOCs holds its annual meeting in Atlanta, with over 800 participants.

1995

17 January—Applications for Games-time volunteer positions are made available, starting an 18-month recruitment effort.

1 February—ACOG groundbreaking ceremony held at Lake Lanier for the canoe/kayak-sprint and rowing venue.

8 March—The 500-day countdown to the Games begins with the start of the Hanes Olympic T-shirt auction. Proceeds from the daily sale will go to the Children's Olympic Ticket Fund, the USOC, and Olympic Aid–Atlanta.

13 March—Construction of Centennial Olympic Park begins.

28 March—President Bill Clinton and Vice President Al Gore address ACOG employees and volunteers.

6 April—The specially designed torch for the 1996 Olympic Torch Relay is unveiled in Greece as ACOG joins with the Hellenic Olympic Committee in a ceremony commemorating the 99th anniversary of the first day of competition in the 1896 Olympic Games.

10 April—ACOG launches the first official Olympic Games site on the World Wide Web at http://www.atlanta.olympic.org.

13 April—ACOG celebrates the groundbreaking for the new basketball arena on the campus of Morehouse College.

24 April—The Cultural Olympiad hosts the Nobel Laureates of Literature in the largest such gathering ever.

1 May—Olympic tickets go on sale across the US as more than 35 million ticket catalogues are distributed.

7 May—ACOG hosts a meeting of 291 NOC delegates and chefs de mission to plan each delegation's participation in the 1996 Games.

23 May—Transportation officials and representatives of ACOG present a proposed traffic circulation plan for the Olympic Ring and downtown areas.

22 June—ACOG begins a series of 24 international and national competitions to test Games-time facilities, of which 13 are clustered in June–August as part of Atlanta Sports '95, involving more than 4,000 athletes.

19 July—ACOG celebrates one year to Opening Ceremony with a special employee event in an area adjacent to Olympic Stadium, while the IOC sends official invitations from Lausanne to 197 national delegations, inviting them to attend the Centennial Olympic Games.

23 July—The 15,000-mile, cross-country route of the Olympic Torch Relay is announced, along with plans for how 10,000 torchbearers will be selected.

16 September—ACOG hosts the Third IOC World Congress on Sports Sciences in Atlanta.

10 October—The design of the victory medal for the 1996 Olympic Games is unveiled. The Greek goddess Victory is emblazoned on the medal as well as the pictogram of the sport in which it is won.

29 October—Auditions begin for Opening and Closing Ceremonies performers.

1996

20 January—A four-month exhibition of 394 Olympic Games quilts begins at the Atlanta History Center. The quilts are handmade gifts that will be presented to the NOCs during team welcoming ceremonies at Olympic Village.

5 March—Olympic tickets are offered for sale over the Internet using IBM's electronic commerce software.

30 March—The Olympic flame is lit during a traditional ceremony in Olympia, Greece, and the first leg of the journey to Atlanta begins.

27 April—The US portion of the Torch Relay begins as the Olympic flame arrives in Los Angeles.

May—Work is completed on the temporary marina and other facilities needed in Savannah to support yachting. In an Olympic first, spectators can board boats that will sail out to the ocean racing lanes to provide a close look at the competition.

18 May—ACOG officially opens Olympic Stadium with music and ceremony during the International Amateur Athletics Federation Grand Prix, an athletics competition that has attracted a top international field and is the first sports event to be held in the new facility.

June—Self-study training materials are sent to 35,000 staff and volunteers, who also are scheduled throughout the month to attend venue orientations at the sites they will be assigned to during the Games.

1 June—The Olympic Arts Festival officially begins with the opening of several visual art exhibitions, which will expand to 25 over the next two months, and more than 200 theater, dance, classical music, and jazz performances will be held, involving some 4,000 performers.

1 July—The International Broadcast Center opens at the Georgia World Congress Center.

6 July—Both the Olympic Village and the Main Press Center begin operations.

13 July—Centennial Olympic Park opens to the public and immediately becomes the enormously popular, central gathering place for the Games.

17 July—The two-week Olympic Youth Camp at Berry College in Rome, Georgia, begins with a record 184 national delegations sending more than 500 young people to participate.

18 July—Thousands of ACOG staff and volunteers attend the dress rehearsal of Opening Ceremony at Olympic Stadium in response to the invitation that was included with their training materials.

19 July—With a packed house of 85,000 and more than 3.5 billion people watching worldwide via television, Opening Ceremony unfolds as a joyous, spectacular celebration of the Olympic Games.

4 August—The Olympic flame is extinguished during Closing Ceremony, and the Olympic flag is passed to Sydney, Australia, host of the 2000 Games.

5 August—The IOC holds a breakfast to honor ACOG staff members and managers for the energy, enthusiasm, and hard work they have dedicated to staging the 1996 Olympic Games.

10 August—ACOG hosts a final party to show appreciation for staff and volunteers, closing Centennial Olympic Park to the public for most of the day to accommodate the crowd of well over 25,000.

PROLOGUE
THE BID

detail of opening photo spread: **An exuberant crowd in Underground Atlanta celebrates the announcement that Atlanta will host the 1996 Olympic Games.**

OVERVIEW—The story has passed into legend. One man's vision to bring the Olympic Games to his city inspired thousands to participate in something beyond themselves, to demonstrate their human grace and offer their innate kindness to the world. Buoyed by their tenacity and their faith, this man's dream grew and the power of his dream united a community, a city, a state, a nation, and ultimately a world in sharing an experience so uplifting to the human spirit that for a span of time all peoples were united.

William Porter "Billy" Payne had witnessed a celebration of the collective effort of people joining together to accomplish a worthwhile goal. He believed he could create a comparable experience involving even more people by hosting the Olympic Games in his city of Atlanta.

Before he took his vision to Atlanta's business and political leaders, Payne formed the Georgia Amateur Athletic Foundation (GAAF), a not-for-profit corporation created with the mission of bringing the Olympic Games to Atlanta. He enlisted the support of his longtime friend, Peter Candler, and took a leave of absence from his law practice to serve as a full-time volunteer directing Atlanta's Olympic campaign.

Next Payne recruited a nucleus of diversely talented community volunteers with strong leadership skills, influence, and contacts who

could help him steer the Bid program. The "Atlanta Nine," as the group became known, included Candler, Ginger Watkins, Horace Sibley, Tim Christian, Cindy Fowler, Charles H. Battle Jr., Linda Stephenson, and Charles Shaffer. The Atlanta Nine combined their talents and financial resources to pursue the first goal in the Bid process: to be selected as the US candidate city by the United States Olympic Committee (USOC).

Payne then secured a meeting with Andrew Young, who was completing his term as Atlanta's mayor, and described the vision of the Olympic Games. Young saw the vision and how it could be accomplished. Although the city government did not become involved in the Bid process at this stage, Young gave Payne the city's official endorsement of the plan.

Payne knew the support of Andrew Young was critical. Young had served as the US ambassador to the United Nations and as a US congressman. During the civil rights movement of the 1960s, he was a top aide to the Reverend Martin Luther King Jr. and later served as the executive director of the Southern Christian Leadership Conference. Not only was Young critical to winning broad local and state support, his highly regarded worldwide reputation would be instrumental to the group's international relations, should the effort lead to the international level of bidding.

Atlanta had the infrastructure and many of the facilities necessary to host the Games, and the USOC ultimately cited these factors as the official reasons it selected Atlanta as the US candidate city. But it was the warmth, enthusiasm, and personal involvement of the GAAF members—their southern hospitality—that endeared the USOC to Atlanta.

This personal approach was initiated in September 1987 with the submission of the formal Bid to the USOC. Rather than mail their Bid documents as did all other contending cities, GAAF members delivered the materials in person to the USOC headquarters in Colorado Springs, Colorado. There they gave their formal presentation and met and discussed Atlanta's attributes with sports federation leaders. This effort differentiated Atlanta from its competition—13 other US cities.

The GAAF-produced video, entitled "Live the Dream," exuded Atlanta's enthusiasm and demonstrated strong local support, with appearances by Governor Joe Frank Harris, Mayor Young, and Martin Luther King III, the son of the American South's great civil rights leader. The written document delineated Atlanta's strengths as follows:

■ a world-class airport;
■ existing sports venues;
■ new construction plans for athletics and swimming venues as well as renovation plans for cycling and shooting facilities;
■ existing facilities for athlete Villages;
■ ample existing hotel rooms (more than 60,000);
■ an extensive rapid rail and bus transportation system;
■ experience in handling large masses of people because of the city's large convention industry; and
■ private funding through corporate sponsors, television rights, and ticket sales.

NATIONAL COMPETITION

Shortly after receiving Atlanta's Bid, the USOC Executive Board scheduled its annual meeting in Atlanta for January 1988. This meant 100 voting members were going to visit the city

personally just before the USOC Site Selection Committee's official visit.

In a show of warmth and friendliness characteristic of southern entertaining, the GAAF and dozens of other volunteers hosted the board for a memorable visit. An Atlanta home offered an elegant and intimate dining setting for the group. Afterward, volunteer drivers transported the officials to the High Museum of Art for a festive evening of entertainment by high school students from Atlanta's acclaimed Northside School for the Performing Arts, who appealed to members to select their city.

Also in January, a small group made its first trip to the Winter Games in Calgary to gather impressions and conduct preliminary research on hosting the Games.

When the Site Selection Committee came to Atlanta in February 1988, the seven members visited all existing facilities, including proposed competition sites and Village accommodations. A helicopter tour enabled the committee to view Stone Mountain Park, the proposed venue for archery, equestrian, road cycling, and shooting, as well as Callaway Gardens southwest of Atlanta and the city of Athens northwest of Atlanta.

The itinerary also included meetings with all top local political leaders, including the governor of Georgia, the mayor of Atlanta, the president of the Atlanta City Council, and the Speaker of the Georgia House of Representatives. Lunch was hosted by the Atlanta Chamber of Commerce and attended by prominent business leaders. By the time of the USOC Site Committee's departure, its members were extremely impressed with the GAAF's attention to detail, solid business and community support, and the overall enthusiasm for the effort. The only shortcoming they cited was Atlanta's limited amateur athletic experience.

However, there was a concern that the USOC would not recommend any city. Because the Olympic Games had been held in Los Angeles just four years earlier, some doubted whether the candidacy of any US city had a significant chance in the international competition. Yet in March 1988, the USOC signaled its interest. It narrowed the field of 14 competing cities to 2 and invited the remaining contenders —Atlanta and Minneapolis–St. Paul—to submit final presentations to its 102 Executive Board members at a meeting in Washington, DC, in April.

This announcement rallied the GAAF to a new level of activity. Payne was already working 14-hour days, still as a volunteer; other volunteers worked equally long hours. They increased their contact with USOC Executive Board members by mailing the formal Bid proposal to each member, hosting members in Atlanta to view the proposed competition sites, and meeting with national and international sports federation officials. If meetings were not possible, notes and personal phone calls, or both, substituted.

In keeping with their tradition of southern hospitality, members of the GAAF held a unique reception for the USOC Board on the eve of the GAAF's final presentation. Rather than hosting a party at a hotel, the GAAF selected a historic Washington home. Greeting guests was a 10-piece string ensemble lining the home's three-level staircase, with Young, Payne, and other committee members welcoming all. The next day, Payne, Young, and Governor Harris once again enthusiastically outlined Atlanta's and Georgia's strengths.

Judged by the USOC to have excellent organizing ability, venues, hotels, an airport, and rapid transit, as well as the ability to handle masses of people, Atlanta won selection as the candidate city.

MEETING THE WORLD

In May 1988, Atlanta entered international competition with five other cities vying to host the Centennial Olympic Games: Athens, Greece; Belgrade, Yugoslavia; Manchester, England; Melbourne, Australia; and Toronto, Canada.

Atlanta had come far, but was still facing a new beginning in the world competition. There were two major obstacles: many officials in the Olympic Movement felt 1996 was too soon to return to American soil following the 1984 Los Angeles Games. Also, with these Games celebrating the 100th birthday of the modern Olympic Movement, many in the IOC felt that the Games should return to their birthplace—Athens, Greece.

Quickly, Atlanta supporters formulated plans to strengthen their Bid and offer different perspectives on bringing the Games to the US. For example, they described the diversity of America's people, its regions, and its overall size and contrasted the number of times the US had hosted the Games of the Olympiad— only in 1904, 1932, and 1984—with the number of times Europe had hosted the Games—a total of 14. Furthermore, Los Angeles was the only city in the world to bid for the 1984 Games; therefore, in actuality, the IOC had not selected an American city for the Games of the Olympiad in almost 60 years.

As soon as their strategy was in place and their message was developed, the Atlanta team, led internationally by Charles Battle and joined by Robert Rearden Jr., began traveling the globe to tell it, and to make personal contact with all IOC members and a great many international sports officials. The strategy was the same one that had worked so well for the USOC Bid: personal contact. A first stop was Lausanne, Switzerland, the location of IOC headquarters, to meet with IOC President Juan

Antonio Samaranch. Other important early visits were made to Ecuador, Canada, Malta, and Mexico.

Andrew Young's international prominence enhanced the GAAF's visibility around the world and with IOC members, enabling the Atlanta team to tell its story.

With USOC support firmly solidified and the international Bid process officially under way, other resources were granted to the GAAF. All levels of government endorsed the Bid, and the business community began to provide financial support. The Atlanta Chamber of Commerce pledged the full support of its Atlanta Sports Council division and staff to help host amateur athletic events, a strategy crucial to proving Atlanta's worthiness. By the time Atlanta was given the honor of hosting the Centennial Olympic Games, the GAAF and other local groups had produced more than 30 national and international amateur sporting competitions.

Lessons from Seoul

A 20-member Atlanta delegation attended the 1988 Olympic Games in Seoul, Korea, to meet additional IOC members and gather information about hosting the Games. Following the tradition established in the US, the GAAF converted a traditional Korean home into an Atlanta House complete with staff and cuisine from the South. Intimate dinners and lunches were hosted daily to entertain IOC members and to facilitate the development of friendships and an ease of communication.

Payne and Young gave their first official presentation to the IOC Executive Board. Payne explained that the Atlanta team felt a responsibility to bring the Olympic Movement to the east coast of North America and near the Caribbean, an area that had never experienced the Olympic Games. Young, whom Payne had introduced as someone sensitive to the needs and priorities of other countries, briefly discussed Atlanta's capabilities, but emphasized

that the most important reason for bringing the Games to Atlanta was to inspire youth. Both men were encouraged when three officials, including President Samaranch, spoke further with them after the program officially concluded. The highlight came when President Samaranch offered to visit Atlanta in February 1989, much earlier than anticipated.

Atlantans had made tremendous progress in Seoul. They had spoken or met with 88 of 90 IOC members and had secured the information needed to begin planning for the IOC Bid documentation.

Before President Samaranch's visit, the GAAF held a workshop to consider its organizational structure and its goals and strategies. The meeting led to the creation of a 14-member Executive Board and adoption of the name, the Atlanta Organizing Committee (AOC), for business purposes. Andrew Young was named its chair, and Billy Payne, its president and CEO. Gerald Bartels, who was president of the Atlanta Chamber of Commerce, was named secretary, and Bob McCullough, a managing partner of Arthur Andersen and Company, became the treasurer. An Advisory Council was created representing a broad base of Georgians to support the AOC's efforts.

Soon after, the group unveiled its Olympic Games theme, "Atlanta and the Olympics: Yes! Partners with the World!" A logo also was released entitled, "Atlanta: A Star on the Rise." Five As in a star formation stood for access, accommodations, athletic facilities, attitude, and ability.

Building Momentum

IOC President Samaranch was given a true taste of southern hospitality when he visited Atlanta in 1989. Included were a ride on MARTA, Atlanta's rapid transit system; meetings with business and political leaders; lunch

"Atlanta: A Star on the Rise" was the name given to the AOC's Bid logo.

with Georgia Olympians; and a tour of sports facilities led by Young. A reception was held in the home of Rankin Smith, owner of the Atlanta Falcons, the city's professional American football team.

President Samaranch, in turn, praised Atlanta when speaking to the Georgia general assembly during his visit saying, "I think with public and private support, the beautiful Atlanta can be very, very strong. I think you have the right people working and fighting to get the Games to Atlanta." President Samaranch's main piece of advice before leaving? "Follow this way: work very hard and try to get the IOC members to visit the city. Good luck." Encouraged by President Samaranch's comments, Atlanta escalated its already intensive efforts.

The AOC opened its first office in midtown Atlanta. Although most of the staff members were still volunteers, work began in earnest to create the Bid documents. These documents were to be delivered to the IOC one year later.

A research team traveled to the IOC library in Lausanne to study previous documents for design and content standards. One local firm was contracted to design the proposal, and a second to write it. The writers moved into the AOC office for ease of sharing information. Through local sports authorities, volunteer committees were formed to document the city's ability to meet the international requirements of every sport.

Throughout the rest of 1989, and with increasing frequency during the next two years, Atlanta continued to host national and international amateur athletic events to increase its experience in this area. In March, the AOC hosted the International Amateur Swimming Federation (FINA) Executive Board meeting. Before summer, more than a dozen amateur sporting events, many of them international, were held in the city.

After each successful event and with each favorable response from the IOC, enthusiasm and momentum for the Games built in Atlanta. Not only was the business community providing a multitude of free services for the AOC's

preparations, but also more than 100,000 citizens had expressed their interest in volunteering for the Games—seven years before they were to take place! During the Bid effort alone, approximately 1,200 volunteers took part.

At the recommendation of the USOC, the AOC revised its Olympic Village and venue plans to consolidate these facilities. Revised Bid plans, which called for a $1 billion approach to hosting the Olympics Games, were released later in the year.

The enthusiasm of the people involved with the Bid effort was infectious. Volunteers, many of whom were professionals in their own right, came together to work for a shared vision— that of bringing the Games to their home. Their efforts ranged from stuffing envelopes to developing programs and traveling the world to promote the city's Bid.

To enhance excitement, the AOC launched a public awareness campaign in July 1989. Billboards and banners were displayed all around the city. A highlight of the effort was introducing the "Olympic Mile" in the city's annual 10 km Peachtree Road Race. Some 40,000 people ran the Olympic Mile in the race, which is held on the Fourth of July holiday and attracts participants from around the world. This event was also the first time the AOC hosted the international press.

The city's youth continued to be a primary focus, and later that summer the AOC initiated the Olympic Day in the Schools (ODIS) Program. Chaired and organized by volunteers, the program provided curriculum guides to help teachers incorporate Olympic values into all subject areas. The program culminated the next spring in Georgia Olympic Day, when students from around the state competed in academic and athletic contests in the style of the Olympic Games. Throughout ODIS Program's seven-year duration, more than 1 million young people participated in the program. Enthusiasm extended to schoolchildren who wrote to IOC members stating what the Games in Atlanta would mean to them. So touched were recipients that several sent personal responses.

An unprecedented showing of city support was planned for 24 August through 8 September 1989 in conjunction with the annual session of the IOC in San Juan, Puerto Rico. Before the session, three IOC members arrived in Atlanta for a four-day tour. Among the group's stops was the Martin Luther King Jr. Center for Nonviolent Social Change, where members

met with Coretta Scott King, widow of civil rights leader the Reverend Dr. King. Prince Albert commented that Dr. King's teachings were the same ideas upheld by the Olympic Movement, and the members in attendance complimented Atlanta and its plans for the Games.

Payne led an Atlanta delegation to San Juan and unveiled the AOC's now legendary presentation tool, a technically sophisticated interactive video that allowed viewers to fly through three-dimensional scenes of Atlanta and computer-generated models of existing and yet-to-be-built facilities. IOC members and 160 international media representatives experienced the video, which was produced in as-

sociation with the Georgia Institute of Technology. The AOC once again created an Atlanta House, which had become even more popular with international guests, who had heard of its reputation for southern hospitality.

As a precursor to the Bid documents, the AOC created the first major explanatory book denoting Atlanta's strengths, including a description of each venue, called the XXVI Book. It set high standards for the quality of design and information, a standard adopted throughout the Games process. The book was distrib-

uted in San Juan at the IOC Session.

Following the meeting, 24 IOC members—the largest number ever jointly to visit a bid city—came to Atlanta to experience its attributes. The showcase of support and enthusiasm from volunteers was unprecedented. There were facility tours, dinners in private homes, a sports competition for water polo and synchronized swimming, a cultural festival, and a 4 September 1989 road race called the "5K Run for the Bid," which was the highlight of the festivities.

Payne conceived the race, organized by the Atlanta Track Club, with the goal of attracting 5,000 participants who would display Atlantans' support. On the morning of the competition,

left: International Olympic Committee members toured the Martin Luther King Jr. Center for Nonviolent Social Change with King's widow.

right: 7,500 cheering runners supported the Atlanta Bid effort by participating in a road race on 4 September 1989.

top: This five-volume, leather-bound Bid document was submitted to the IOC in February 1990.

bottom: Youth of Savannah welcomed IOC visitors.

IOC members rode an express MARTA train to the race starting point. As they exited from the underground train tunnel, they heard the chanting of 7,500 runners: "We want the Games! We want the Games!" They walked into the vast crowd, visibly touched by the passion and support of Atlantans.

When the weekend concluded, 38 IOC members had visited Atlanta and given the city high marks, noting especially their confidence in Atlanta's preparedness and the enthusiasm of its residents.

Even after such an intensive weekend, efforts did not diminish. Throughout the rest of the year, the AOC sent delegations to key Olympic meetings around the world, while the state of Georgia began construction of the Georgia Dome, an important sporting facility that was the proposed venue for Olympic basketball and gymnastics.

The Official Bid

In January 1990, the AOC continued its community involvement campaign by debuting the Honor Marching Band in a nationally televised Martin Luther King Jr. Day Parade and March of Celebration in Atlanta. The band performed for more than 2 million people in 17 special events, concluding with a performance at Underground Atlanta on 18 September 1990.

February brought a historic moment and the completion of a major milestone: the submission of the official written Bid document to the IOC offices in Lausanne. The five-volume, leather-bound document, written and designed by the Atlanta team of George Hirthler and Brad Copeland, respectively, described Atlanta as a modern city with great expectations. Beautiful photography and colorful words also conveyed the distinct history and culture of the American South. Volume I contained greetings from famous Georgians and Americans. Volume II explained the history of Atlanta and the South, detailed the AOC's Cultural Olympiad plans, and proposed a torch relay that included all host cities of the modern Games. Volume III answered the 19 questions posed by the IOC to all bid cities, addressing issues of facilities, financing, and security, among others. Volume IV described the sports venues in detail, while Volume V explained how Atlanta would accommodate the media.

In sum, the plan called for $1 billion in spending, including $418 million for construction. Construction would include an 85,000 seat stadium for athletics, an aquatics center for swimming and diving, a water polo stadium, a track cycling venue, a shooting range, and an Olympic marina in Savannah, Georgia. In addition, twin dormitories for the athlete Village were included at a cost of $60 million.

Proposed sources of revenue were broadcast television rights fees, corporate sponsorships, ticket sales, Olympic coins, and other merchandise. No taxpayer involvement was proposed or required.

During the next three months, the AOC successfully hosted official site inspection visits by the IOC Study and Evaluation Commission, the Association of International Olympic Federations (ASOIF), and the Association of National Olympic Committees (ANOC). Based on the success of earlier visits, the AOC invited IOC members to gather in Atlanta for an event called "Springtime in Atlanta," to visit the city at its most beautiful with its dogwood trees and azalea bushes blooming. During this occasion, the AOC also held a festive community run called "Run for the Rings"—a salute to Georgia Olympians in which nearly 8,000 people participated.

IOC members also visited Savannah, the proposed site for Olympic yachting. In Savannah, more than 1,000 schoolchildren gathered in the city's historic squares, singing and greeting the procession as it drove through the city.

In June, at the IOC Executive Board and ANOC General Assembly in Barcelona, Spain, Atlanta learned two important facts. The IOC Study and Evaluation Commission had ranked Atlanta among the top cities competing for the Games and the IOC's draw for order determined Atlanta would be the first city to give its final presentation to the IOC Session in Tokyo, Japan, on 18 September.

The AOC's goal had been to learn from the IOC and to spread among its members the knowledge that Atlanta was ready and eager to

assume the role of hosting the Centennial Olympic Games. As it continued its mission of spreading the ideals of the Olympic Movement, the AOC sponsored the US Olympic Academy during the summer, held the first Georgia Olympic Day for youth, and hosted five amateur sports competitions.

The AOC had boosted its experience in amateur athletics by hosting dozens of international-level competitions. It had rallied the support of local, state, and national governments and

Atlanta's Dream Team, comprised of 58 youth ambassadors, went to Tokyo to lend support for the AOC's final presentation to the IOC.

business leaders. Atlanta had the infrastructure to accommodate the Games, and the AOC could build needed venues. Organizers had inspired hope across an entire state, among adults and children alike. They had hosted intimate parties and written notes recognized for their thoughtfulness and personal appeal. All these efforts were funded with $7 million raised almost entirely from merchandising and contributions from the local business community.

Now in September, the month the IOC would announce its decision, the AOC waited.

top: **Billy Payne surrounded by jubilant supporters after the announcement that the 1996 Olympic Games were awarded to the city of Atlanta.**

bottom: **When the final votes were tallied, Payne's dream was realized.**

Had Atlanta won the votes of enough IOC members? Sixty-eight had visited the city, an unprecedented number. In turn, AOC representatives had traveled to the homes or homelands of 85 IOC delegates in 70 countries. To lend support for the final presentation, a delegation of more than 300 Atlantans and Georgians—including a group of 58 enthusiastic students, aged 11–18, called the Atlanta Dream Team—traveled to Tokyo.

On 18 September 1990, Atlanta presented first. The hour-long program included a film and original song entitled "The World Has One Dream" and presentations by Young, Payne, Atlanta Mayor Maynard Jackson, and Governor Harris, communicating the message of the people of Atlanta who wanted the Games.

Six such presentations, one from each bid city, were heard that day, and then the vote was taken. At just after 0730 Atlanta time, and more than three joyous years after Billy Payne had shared his legendary vision with other Atlanta leaders, President Juan Antonio Samaranch spoke the magic words: "The International Olympic Committee has awarded the 1996 Olympic Games to the city of...Atlanta."

Spontaneous celebrations erupted throughout the city and across the state of Georgia. People rejoiced in their schools, offices, homes, and in public places. When the delegation to Tokyo returned to Atlanta on 24 September, a victory parade was held with more than half a million jubilant spectators and tons of confetti and ticker tape.

The dream of Payne, his fellow volunteers, and the community of Atlanta had come true—and a legend was born.

Atlanta 1996

CHAPTER ONE
MANAGEMENT
AND ORGANIZATION

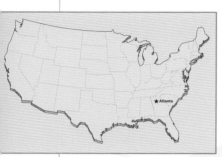

Map of United States of America

OVERVIEW—In what will undoubtedly be recorded as one of the most memorable and exciting moments in the history of Atlanta, the city was awarded the right to host the 1996 Centennial Olympic Games on 18 September 1990 at the 96th Session of the International Olympic Committee (IOC) in Tokyo, Japan.

As celebrations began in Atlanta and Georgia at the news of this honor, officials of the Atlanta Organizing Committee (AOC), the city of Atlanta, and the United States Olympic Committee (USOC) started the process of finalizing the agreement to form an organizing committee to stage the 1996 Games.

Under the terms of the *Olympic Charter*, the IOC entrusts the Games to a National Olympic Committee (NOC)—in this case, the USOC—which in turn delegates its duties to a duly established organizing committee. After the announcement, the plan was to have the Atlanta Committee for the Olympic Games (ACOG) established within six months to accept the responsibility of staging the Games.

ACOG was legally incorporated on 28 January 1991 as a 501(c)(4) civic organization to foster national and international amateur sports competition and to organize and conduct the Games of the XXVI Olympiad. This entity would operate under both the Tri-Party Agreement signed that same day by the city of Atlanta, the Metropolitan Atlanta Olympic Games Authority (MAOGA), and ACOG, and the agreement authorized shortly thereafter by the USOC and ACOG.

Staging the 1996 Games was unique in that it commemorated the 100th anniversary of the modern Olympic Movement and that these Games were presented entirely by privately raised funds. Equally important, due to several factors, ACOG determined the 1996 Games would be the largest Games to date and potentially the largest Games ever. The accessibility of the southeastern US, the seating capacity within the venues, and the incredible enthusiasm with which the Games were embraced by Atlantans, Georgians, Southerners, and indeed all Americans would attract thousands.

ACOG management accepted the obligations presented by the 1996 Olympic Games with enormous pride and commitment and maintained those requirements at the forefront of Games planning and execution. Its objectives were to create the best possible facilities and environment for Olympic athletes and in so doing, provide a legacy of sports facilities as well as programs that ensured the availability of the Olympic Experience while sharing with the world the hospitality that distinguishes the American South.

INVOLVEMENT OF OTHER ENTITIES

In addition to meeting the requirements of local, state, and federal government institutions, ACOG management worked closely with other entities directly involved with the 1996 Games.

International Olympic Committee

Under the *Olympic Charter*, the IOC is entrusted with the control and development of the modern Olympic Games, selecting the host city, and outlining the parameters for competitions, venues, the Olympic Village, the Olympic Arts Festival (OAF), and all elements of Olympic ceremony and tradition to which organizing committees must adhere.

For the 1996 Games, the IOC established two commissions: the Coordination Commission, which was responsible for reviewing Games preparations and updating the IOC Executive Board regarding progress and any issues that needed to be resolved, and the Centennial Commission, which ensured appropriate commemoration of the 100th anniversary of the Olympic Movement.

Members of the Coordination Commission, named in early 1991 by IOC President Juan Antonio Samaranch, held their first meeting with ACOG executives in August 1991. Chaired by Richard Pound, a member of the IOC Executive Board from Canada, the commission included other IOC members along with representatives of the International Federations (IFs), NOCs, and past Olympic Games organizers. The IOC's director general, secretary general, and sports director also were part of the commission.

The Coordination Commission met twice yearly with ACOG management. The two-day sessions were held at ACOG headquarters to provide an opportunity for commission members to meet with representatives of ACOG. The sessions began with a meeting of all commission members and ACOG executive management, followed by a series of committee meetings that focused on specific operational areas or issues, and finally a general meeting for review of all findings.

After each Coordination Commission meeting, ACOG managers were responsible for responding to questions and issues raised by the review group. Commission members also provided suggestions for solving problems and improving plans for Games operations. Results of each session were reported to the Executive Board.

The Centennial Commission focused on the commemoration of the 100th anniversary of the first IOC Session, which occurred in 1894 and was celebrated in June 1994 in Paris during the IOC's 103rd Session, as well as in certain aspects of the 1996 Games. The members reviewed ceremony plans and OAF programs of ACOG to ensure that the centennial of the modern Games would be celebrated appropriately.

In addition to these specially created commissions, standing commissions of the IOC provided considerable guidance and direction for their ACOG counterparts. For example, the Athletes Commission met regularly with ACOG management responsible for Sports and Ceremonies; the Radio and Television Commission closely reviewed plans being developed by Atlanta Olympic Broadcasting (AOB); and the Medical Commission maintained significant involvement with Medical Services, particularly in relation to drug testing and services and facilities for the care of athletes and other Olympic Family members.

Another critical aspect of IOC support for the Games concerned Olympic Solidarity, the commission responsible for ensuring the greatest possible representation of athletes and press from all countries. Through this program, many national delegations as well as 35 members of the press from developing countries were able to participate in the Games through funding for transportation, meals, and housing provided by Olympic Solidarity.

36 USC 380

The interlocking five-ring symbol of the International Olympic Committee is recognized throughout the world.

Throughout the preparations for the Games, ACOG management also reported regularly to the IOC Executive Board and each IOC Session.

International Federations

As stipulated in the *Olympic Charter*, ACOG consulted with the IFs for all technical arrangements related to the competitions. Personnel from each of the 26 IFs representing the sports programme of the Centennial Olympic Games were involved in determining the location of each venue, the physical layout of the field of play, and all other aspects of the venue devoted to the presentation of the sport. The IFs also reviewed the format for competitions, uniforms, utilization of equipment, and numerous other details.

The Sports Department was the primary link for this exchange of information and was responsible for ensuring that ACOG fully met the requirements of the IFs in preparing for the Games. During the Games, the IFs ensured that the grounds, tracks, courses, and equipment conformed to rules and provided technical delegates to verify all results before they were released to the media.

National Olympic Committees

The NOCs worked with ACOG in all areas related to their teams, particularly in regard to housing and services provided at the Olympic Village. In cooperation with the IOC and IFs, which are responsible for setting eligibility standards for each sport, the NOCs determined the number of qualifying athletes they would bring to the Games. In addition, the NOCs were encouraged to make pre-Games visits to coordinate their needs for housing, training sites, and transportation.

United States Olympic Committee

ACOG's involvement with the USOC included all areas typically addressed by NOCs, but as the host country NOC, the USOC management participated more extensively in the 1996 Games. While delegating the responsibil-

ity for staging the Games to ACOG, the USOC retained a management role for the 1996 Games through representation on the ACOG Board of Directors.

In addition, the USOC joined ACOG in establishing Atlanta Centennial Olympic Properties (ACOP), a joint venture responsible for marketing sponsorships and granting licenses for official products. This joint venture, whose chief officer reported to both the ACOG CEO and USOC co-chair, was created to raise a substantial portion of the funds needed to stage the Games.

Metropolitan Atlanta Olympic Games Authority

The state of Georgia's constitution prohibited the city of Atlanta from accepting certain IOC obligations; therefore, the Georgia general assembly created MAOGA in 1989 to enable Atlanta to bid for the Olympic Games.

Initially, MAOGA was formed with five members: the mayor of Atlanta, the president of the Atlanta City Council, and three people appointed by the mayor. In January 1990, MAOGA's charter was amended to allow eight members or more, and the organization ultimately established a 12-member board which met quarterly.

Under the Tri-Party Agreement entered into by MAOGA, the city of Atlanta, and ACOG, obligations that the city could not accept from the IOC were transferred to MAOGA. The obligations were then transferred to ACOG, with ACOG indemnifying both MAOGA and the city and state from any Games-related financial liabilities.

Terms of the Tri-Party Agreement also gave MAOGA the responsibilities to review ACOG construction contracts in excess of $250,000, approve venue changes within the city limits, and enter into any intergovernmental contracts on ACOG's behalf. In addition, MAOGA was designated as the entity that would construct and own Olympic Stadium. However,

ACOG funded and its Construction Department managed the building of the stadium.

To ensure effective financial reporting, MAOGA retained a major independent public accounting firm to audit information prepared and submitted by ACOG. This audit process confirmed annually there was no governmental financial liability.

Additionally, MAOGA was responsible for the development and implementation of numerous projects to enhance the city and communities around venues, working in conjunction with the Corporation for Olympic Development in Atlanta (CODA), established by the city of Atlanta.

Office of Olympic Coordination

The Tri-Party Agreement provided for the the city of Atlanta to create the Office of Olympic Coordination, reporting directly to the mayor and funded by ACOG. This office coordinated the city's involvement in the 1996 Games, including facilitation of agreements ACOG and city departments would have to reach related to law enforcement support, sanitation, and traffic management. These agreements constituted the city services contract, which differentiated Games-time responsibilities between the city and ACOG and determined how costs would be met.

THE BOARD OF DIRECTORS

As a not-for-profit corporation, ACOG was governed by a board of directors that was chartered in January 1991 to approve programs, policies, and financial investments. The 31-member group included the IOC members from the US and the head of the USOC—as stipulated in the *Olympic Charter*—and representatives from the AOC, USOC, local governments, the Atlanta business community, and communities hosting venues.

Andrew Young and Robert M. Holder Jr. were named as co-chairs of the board. Young, the city's former mayor and former US ambassador to the United Nations, had been instrumental in securing international support for

Atlanta's Bid effort. Holder, a recognized business and civic leader in Atlanta, had provided assistance and expertise to the Bid team.

For the first time in Olympic history, the president and CEO of the organization also led the campaign to win the right to host the Games. Throughout the planning and staging of the Games, William Porter "Billy" Payne had the full support of the ACOG Board of Directors. *(For a list of the members of the ACOG Board of Directors, see Figure 1.)*

The board created a nine-member executive committee to act, if necessary, on their behalf. Other committees of the board were Audit, Compensation and Executive Resources, Equal Economic Opportunity, and Finance. The committees worked closely with ACOG management to review programs and policies and recommended a course of action to the full board. The board was also supported by legal counsel, internal auditors, and a firm of independent public accountants that audited ACOG records.

Throughout its years of operation, the ACOG Board of Directors was responsible for authorizing the relocation of several Games venues and approving ACOG projections for a budget that ensured expenses would not exceed revenues. In addition, the board established and confirmed a number of key policies, including an aggressive Equal Employment and Opportunity Plan (EEOP), a code of ethics, and information disclosure.

Disclosure extended to the board itself. From its earliest days, a major portion of the board's quarterly meetings were open to the public and press. A news conference immediately followed each board meeting, allowing the media to receive additional information and ask questions.

As a corporate entity, the board was essential to the management of ACOG. Most members served on the board from the time of their appointment through the end of the Games,

ANDREW J. YOUNG, CO-CHAIR, BOARD OF DIRECTORS

Young, former US ambassador to the United Nations, three-term US congressman, and two-term mayor of Atlanta, played a key role in Atlanta's Bid effort.

Young was the pastor of small Congregational churches before becoming associate director of the National Council of Churches' department of youth work in New York City. He returned to Atlanta in 1961 to work as a top aide to Dr. Martin Luther King Jr. during the civil rights movement and to serve as executive director of the Southern Christian Leadership Conference.

Young has received many awards, including the Presidential Medal of Freedom, America's highest civilian award; the Legion d'Honneur (France); and more than 45 honorary degrees from universities such as Emory, Morehouse, Notre Dame, and Yale.

JAMES T BAILES • IRENE D BAILEY • ALEKSANDRA L BAILEY • ALEXANDER R BAILEY • ANGELA M BAILEY • ANN T BAILEY • ARSHON L BAILEY • BERNICE BAILEY • BEVERLY V BAILEY • BRADFORD J BAILEY • BRENDA H BAILEY • BRIGETTE A BAILEY • BROOKE D BAILEY • CHRIS BAILEY • COREY M BAILEY • DANIEL W BAILEY • DAVID C BAILEY • DEBORAH BAILEY • DEBORAH D BAILEY • DIANNE E BAILEY • DONALD H BAILEY • EILEEN H BAILEY • ELTON R BAILEY • EVELYN B BAILEY • GEORGE G BAILEY • GEORGE R BAILEY • HOWARD BAILEY • JACK D BAILEY • JACQUELINE S BAILEY • JAMES D BAILEY

19

ensuring a strong base of knowledge and experience. In addition, several individual members of the board shared their specialized expertise with ACOG management.

In June 1996, the board expanded to include five individuals who had been instrumental in preparing for the Games.

MANAGEMENT PHILOSOPHY FOR THE GAMES

In 1993, the ACOG Board of Directors adopted a mission statement to guide ACOG planning and decision making that pledged:

■ to conduct the Centennial Olympic Games with sensitivity, integrity, fiscal responsibility, and commitment to the needs of athletes;

■ to share with the world the spirit of America, the experience of the American South, and the vision of Atlanta; and

■ to leave a positive physical and spiritual legacy and an indelible mark on Olympic history by staging the most memorable Olympic Games ever.

Implicit in the mission statement was an understanding of the impact the Games would have on people, and therefore, a commitment to inclusiveness in Games planning, as well as an obligation to the athletes competing in each sport to provide the best Olympic experience possible.

Conduct of the Games

The mission statement provided the framework and standard of measurement by which ACOG managed the preparations and conduct of the Games.

Sensitivity. The hallmark of ACOG planning was an understanding of the importance of valuing the concerns of people who would be affected by the Games and bringing them together. This inclusiveness enhanced the quality of overall planning and the long-term relation

ships forged among people and organizations who were working together for the first time.

ACOG established more than 20 advisory groups composed of people with diverse backgrounds, interests, and concerns. Neighborhood task forces represented the residents of areas where new venues were being built. Other advisory groups concentrated on special interests, such as disability access and environmental responsibility.

Members of the advisory groups met regularly with ACOG management to express their views and make suggestions to plans as they were being developed. All the groups had an impact on the plans and the final version of numerous programs.

Changes recommended by neighborhood task forces helped ensure satisfaction with Olympic development in the communities surrounding the venues. The Committee on Disability Access helped ACOG present the most accessible Games ever. The Olympic Environmental Support Group (OESG) was instrumental in developing an environmental policy statement used to guide ACOG's construction of new venues and to promote energy efficiency and recycling throughout the Games. *(For more information, see the External Relations and Logistics chapters.)*

To address concerns of equality in the staffing and business opportunities the Games offered, ACOG adopted an EEOP to ensure meaningful participation from a diverse pool of employees and contractors in staging the Games. The plan provided for female and minority participation reflective of local work force and business capacity. The program also required that companies contracted to provide products and services to ACOG demonstrate the inclusiveness of their employment practices. The results that ACOG achieved through EEOP exceeded the accomplishments of most public sector businesses and government agencies by a substantial margin.

ROBERT M. HOLDER JR.,
CO-CHAIR, BOARD
OF DIRECTORS

The founder and chair of the board of Holder Corporation, one of Atlanta's leading construction companies, Holder is a director of Wachovia Corporation and National Service Industries, Inc.

He is honorary consul general of Thailand and past chair of the Atlanta Chamber of Commerce. Holder also serves as chair of the Carter Center Board of Councilors and co-chair of the Atlanta Action Forum.

Sensitivity and inclusiveness also meant making the Games available to a wide cross-section of people by minimizing the cost of participation. Tickets to many sports events of the 1996 Games were as little as $7 each, and the OAF presented numerous free events.

The creation of Centennial Olympic Park also helped ensure that the experience of friendship, diversity, and celebration integral in an Olympic Games as well as the excitement of witnessing human achievement was readily shared. The park was free to the public, allowing hundreds of thousands of people to join in the experience, whether or not they purchased a ticket to an event.

The establishment of the Children's Olympic Ticket Fund also demonstrated management's commitment to making the Games available to as many people as possible. Through this program, all honoraria received from ACOG Speakers Bureau presentations were used to purchase tickets for children in Georgia who might not otherwise have had an opportunity to attend the Games. *(For more information, see the Communications chapter.)*

These funds combined with contributions from the Centennial Olympic Games Hanes T-shirt Auction allowed nearly 17,000 young people in Georgia to attend sports competitions and OAF events.

Integrity. At the request of ACOG management, the ACOG Board of Directors approved stringent guidelines for a code of ethics that was applicable to board members, officers, and employees. The policy covered all aspects of ACOG's operation, with special emphasis on issues related to contract awards, hiring and employment practices, and the conduct of daily operations.

Specifically, ACOG's code of ethics prohibited all staff from accepting gifts and favors that might influence the discharge of their duties, disclosing confidential information, using their association with ACOG to secure unwarranted privileges or exemptions, and accepting employment from or rendering services to any organization that would be incompatible with their responsibilities to ACOG. The ethics policy also stipulated that individuals must disqualify themselves from participating in any action in which they had any financial interest and refuse to acquire an interest in any transaction that might be affected by ACOG.

A Board of Ethics, consisting of three persons selected by the Board of Directors, upheld and ensured enforcement of the code of ethics and addressed any situations reflective of the integrity of ACOG and its staff.

In keeping with ACOG's commitment to provide communications to the public and the media, the Board of Directors also adopted an information disclosure policy that made large amounts of information concerning the 1996 Games available to the public and the media.

Management and staff followed the advice and direction of ACOG's legal counsel, King & Spalding, an independent law firm, in adopting and implementing ACOG's ethics policies. In partnership with the law firm Arnall Golden & Gregory, they provided assistance to ACOG in developing contracts with third parties.

Fiscal Responsibility. ACOG had two financial objectives: satisfying obligations to the Olympic Family and the many constituencies of the Games, and ensuring planned expenditures did not exceed expected revenues. In striving to meet these goals, ACOG also was committed to leaving sports facilities as a physical legacy.

The long lead times essential to planning the Games, combined with the difficulty of anticipating changes in requirements from numerous entities and budgeting where there is

WILLIAM PORTER "BILLY" PAYNE, PRESIDENT AND CHIEF EXECUTIVE OFFICER

Inspired to bid for the Centennial Olympic Games in 1987 (see The Bid chapter), Payne took a leave of absence from his successful Atlanta real estate law practice to lead the effort. As president of the AOC, Payne served as a full-time volunteer in directing the Olympic Bid campaign, which was funded with $7 million raised almost entirely from merchandising and contributions from the local business community.

Born in Athens, Georgia, Payne has both an undergraduate degree and law degree from the University of Georgia (UGA), where he excelled academically as vice president of the student body and athletically as an All-American defensive end on UGA's 1968 SEC Championship football team.

ADOLPHUS DREWERY "A.D." FRAZIER JR., CHIEF OPERATING OFFICER

A former executive vice president of the North American Banking Group of First Chicago Corporation and First National Bank of Chicago, Frazier began his banking career with Citizens and Southern National Bank (now NationsBank) in Atlanta. He was the first president of Atlanta's Neighborhood Housing Services organization and managed the inauguration of US President Carter. He also led the team that reorganized both the US White House and Executive Office of the President.

little record of relevant experience, mandated flexibility and adaptability in financial strategies and creativity in determining ways to minimize costs. With ACOG's largest expenditures related to facilities for the Games, considerable focus was on the most efficient installation possible. Existing facilities were to be used to the maximum extent possible, recognizing the temporary nature of the Games, and no permanent structures were to be created unless a sound economic use for them after the Games could be demonstrated. In addition, venue sites were to be selected to minimize the need for additional construction and facilitate economic operation during the Games.

In managing all expenditures for the Games, ACOG followed detailed procedures for assessing the assumptions on which plans and their supporting budgets were made. Development of an annual master plan preceded the annual financial forecast, with frequent adjustments applied as total requirements and anticipated costs became more specific. Concurrently, all possible sources of revenue were explored so increases in costs could be offset by the availability of additional funds.

ACOG's estimates of both expenses and revenues were continuously monitored by two independent firms of auditors—one working on behalf of MAOGA and one retained by the ACOG Board of Directors. Concentrating not only on financial forecasts but also on all aspects of accounting and record keeping, the auditors consistently confirmed the overall validity of ACOG's plans.

Scrupulous attention to keeping expenses commensurate with revenues was essential because of ACOG's commitment to stage the 1996 Games without governmental financial support. That commitment was evidenced by the Tri-Party Agreement, in which ACOG indemnified the city and state from any financial liability.

The final financial reports for the 1996 Games confirmed that ACOG fully met its

promise of fiscal responsibility. Revenues of approximately $1.7 billion fully covered expenditures—which included a physical legacy of approximately $500 million in new sports facilities given to the local governments and educational institutions.

Commitment to Athletes. ACOG was dedicated to providing the best possible facilities and environment for athletes that would allow them to maintain their training before and during the Games, achieve spectacular performances when competing, and fully enjoy their Olympic experience. This commitment was fulfilled through programs including:

■ an Athletes Advisory Council, composed of Olympians, to provide consultation on the nature and scope of the Olympic events that affected athletes;

■ a Pre-Olympic Training Program, through which communities across the state and the South provided teams with training services, facilities, and hospitality prior to the Games;

■ an Envoy Program, in which volunteers were trained for two years to serve as the Games-time liaisons for the NOCs and facilitate the fulfillment of all requirements of the teams and their chefs de mission; and

■ Chefs de Mission Seminars, which provided unprecedented amounts of information prior to the Games, also helped to ensure effective coordination of team and NOC needs.

ACOG also devoted tremendous human and financial resources for the Olympic Village to deliver the largest array of services and programs ever available for athletes. The Olympic Village earned high praise from athletes throughout the Games.

ACOG realized its goal of presenting the 1996 Games so they were more available to athletes and countries than were previous Games. Programs were developed that removed barriers to participation, such as making funds available for qualified athletes who could not otherwise afford to attend the Games and providing more opportunities for athletes to qualify for

Olympic competitions. As a result of ACOG's efforts, more countries and athletes participated in the Games and medals were won by athletes from more countries than ever before.

Spirit and Vision

The Centennial Olympic Games provided a tremendous opportunity to share with the world the unique hospitality and the cultural riches that distinguish Atlanta and the South, and the dedication to volunteerism and enthusiasm for the Olympic Movement that exist throughout the US.

Beginning with the Bid, Atlantans expressed extraordinary enthusiasm for hosting the Games. They welcomed Olympic visitors and demonstrated through participation in numerous events their eagerness to experience the Olympic Games. Their efforts helped bring the 1996 Games to Atlanta, and they responded to the announcement of the IOC's choice by inundating the AOC office with calls and letters to volunteer for an event that would not occur for six years.

Soon thereafter, in April 1992, ACOG created the Olympic Force to direct the energy and interest of the people of Atlanta and Georgia into volunteer efforts that would benefit communities prior to the Games. Ultimately, some 1,700 organizations—representing more than 700,000 people statewide—expressed their commitment to volunteerism and the Games by joining the Olympic Force.

ACOG's Volunteer Services Department also established a corps of individuals who volunteered at ACOG headquarters, working in virtually every area of operations. Prior to the Games, volunteer drivers, tour guides, assistants on numerous projects, and members of the Olympic Force—in their efforts to improve the quality of life in their communities—repeatedly impressed visitors to Atlanta and Georgia with their commitment and dedication.

As summer 1996 approached, the volunteer team for the Games was assembled, numbering more than 55,000 people. They were capable, responsible, and tireless in assisting the members of the Olympic Family, spectators, and visitors to the greatest extent possible and in offering genuine welcome and hospitality. Volunteers were the heart of the 1996 Games and they measured up to every expectation.

This same enthusiasm and commitment to the Games was seen throughout the US when the Olympic torch arrived in Los Angeles 84 days before Opening Ceremony. As the Torch Relay progressed across the country, the crowds grew larger as people responded to the opportunity to share in the Olympic experience.

Along with the spirit of volunteerism displayed by Atlantans and others, exhibitions of southern culture were intended to further emphasize the warmth and hospitality of the region. The culture of the South was expressed through OAF programs and through the ceremonies of the Games. Dozens of southern artists and performers were showcased in OAF exhibits and special celebrations, such as the Southern Crossroads Festival held each day in Centennial Olympic Park, that displayed to visitors from around the world the dance, music, art, and crafts of the South.

In the Opening Ceremony, the story of the South was told through a music-filled performance called the Spirit of the South and in other elements of the program that highlighted the past and present of the region. Victory ceremonies combined the imagery of southern flowers and the traditions of Greece as medals were presented to winning athletes. The Closing Ceremony also gave spectators and a worldwide television audience a chance to experience the sights and sounds of the South from gospel to rock 'n' roll.

Positive Legacy

The full impact of the Centennial Olympic Games on the city of Atlanta, the South, and Olympic history has yet to be determined.

However, tangible evidence of the power and influence of the Games already can be seen.

Physical Legacy. World-class sports facilities are clearly among the enduring legacies of the 1996 Games. ACOG invested approximately $500 million in permanent projects—such as Olympic Stadium, the Stone Mountain Park Tennis Center, and the Wolf Creek Shooting Complex—that are already making Atlanta a national and international center for major sports events.

Centennial Olympic Park, which was inspired by the 1996 Games and partially funded by ACOG, continues to provide a festive gathering place for all Atlantans and visitors in the downtown area.

New housing on the Georgia Institute of Technology campus, which ACOG contributed as accommodations for the Olympic Village, will serve students well into the 21st century. Throughout Atlanta and other cities that hosted Olympic events, the Games also served as a catalyst for hundreds of new projects and facilities. These projects, both public and private, ranged from major renovation and expansion programs to refurbishment of small businesses.

Through CODA, more than $75 million in public and private funds was invested for the creation of city parks and spaces, pedestrian walkways, public art, and infrastructure improvements. CODA's accomplishments included development of long-range plans for revitalizing downtown neighborhoods as well as cooperative efforts with MAOGA, various governmental agencies, and not-for-profit entities that led to the construction or renovation of 700 housing units and additional new student housing in the Atlanta University Center.

Many other community-based projects were supported by a combination of local, state, and federal government funding and private investment. ACOG also contributed funds directly to some of these projects in an effort to stimulate additional action and improvements.

During the 1991–1997 period, the impact of the 1996 Olympic Games on the economy of Georgia is estimated at more than $5 billion—a sum that includes the funding and construction of new facilities, increased tourism revenue, and incremental tax benefits. Long-term effects on the economy are yet to be calculated, but the Games have ensured a solid base for future growth.

Spiritual Legacy. To help maximize the spiritual legacy the Games were sure to leave in Atlanta and the surrounding region, ACOG determined from the outset of its planning to extend the Olympic experience not just over 17 days in summer 1996, but throughout the entire XXVI Olympiad.

What management hoped would be the greatest of all Olympic legacies—the establishment of a deeper commitment to volunteerism—actually began even earlier, as evidenced by the volunteer spirit of the leaders of the Bid effort and the thousands who joined them. When ACOG created the Olympic Force, the response was overwhelming. Scores of people pledged to commit even more of their time to volunteer efforts, and those who had never volunteered before were encouraged to begin.

Following the plan to extend the Games experience over the Olympiad, Volunteer Services initiated a series of programs that continued until summer 1996. Olympic Force groups were asked to participate in a special volunteer campaign each year—from collecting food and toys for those in need to refurbishing state parks. The Olympic Force Medal of Honor was also instituted to recognize annually those groups and individuals who made outstanding contributions.

To involve as many people as possible in Olympic-related programs, volunteers were asked to support the numerous special events that ACOG presented during the years preceding the Games. The largest of these events—in

Exterior views of three of the permanent projects in which ACOG invested are shown above.
top: **Olympic Stadium**
center: **Stone Mountain Park Tennis Center**
bottom: **Wolf Creek Shooting Complex**

terms of number of volunteers who participated—was the 1992 Olympic flag arrival celebration.

Conceived as a means of bringing the Olympic Spirit and excitement to all Georgians, the celebration covered a 10-day period in September 1992—marking the arrival of the Olympic flag from Barcelona—and encompassed nine Georgia cities. Volunteer committees were established in each of the host cities, eventually placing some 2,000 people in volunteer positions. Many of the committees also were designated as Olympic Force groups, and hundreds of the 1992 flag arrival celebration volunteers later became Games volunteers.

The celebration events attracted approximately 300,000 Georgians, providing many their first look at the Olympic flag and the history of the Games as presented through a collection of Olympic memorabilia and a specially created video. In addition, workshops—free and open to the public—were conducted in each city to answer questions about the 1996 Games and explain how to become involved in preparations.

The 1992 flag arrival celebration also drew some 50,000 children from virtually every elementary and middle school in the state. Most of the students were participating in the Olympic Day in the Schools (ODIS) Program—a long-term initiative that ACOG created to touch the lives of future generations. Like the volunteer program, ODIS began during the Bid and then became part of ACOG's efforts to extend the impact of the Games. Centered on providing specially created curriculum materials about the Olympic Games to teachers, the program continued through the end of May 1996, reaching millions of young people.

ACOG also involved high school students in the Games each year with the selection of 100 youth ambassadors from around the state, who comprised the Dream Team. (For more information, see the Youth and Education chapter.)

Members of both high school and college bands were eligible for participation in the Atlanta Olympic Band; more than 350 top band and flag corps members each year were auditioned and assembled. The band began during the Bid and continued through the group's participation in the Closing Ceremony of the Games—providing a final, unforgettable Olympic experience for members of the 1996 group.

All pre-Games programs emphasized and promoted the Olympic ideals of excellence, teamwork, and respect for self and others. The programs brought organizations and people to work together as never before, resulting in cooperation, new friendships and alliances, and a shared pride in accomplishment. The Games offered an opportunity to establish international relationships that are likely to produce the cross-cultural exchange and understanding that embody Olympic ideals.

The Centennial Olympic Games made an indelible mark on Olympic history, as many important firsts were recorded: all NOCs which were invited to the Games attended; 40 percent of the competing athletes were women; magnitudes were achieved that potentially may never be surpassed, such as the largest available number of tickets and the most spectators and visitors ever to assemble. Memorable moments, such as the lighting of the Olympic flame by Muhammad Ali, were etched into the public consciousness.

Responsiveness to Public Interest. The 1996 Games generated overwhelming public interest from the selection of Atlanta as the host city through the final moments of the Closing Ceremony. ACOG responded in a variety of ways and sought to utilize this interest to foster the advancement of the Olympic Movement.

Information about the Games and the progress of preparations was made widely available through news releases and press conferences; brochures and Speakers Bureau presentations; the Olympic Experience, a public information gallery staffed by volunteers who provided information to visitors; newsletters for identified audiences, such as neighborhoods hosting

Views of three of the projects inspired by the 1996 Games and partially financed by ACOG are shown above.
top: **Georgia Institute of Technology student housing, which served as accommodations for the Olympic Village**
center: **Georgia Tech Aquatic Center**
bottom: **Centennial Olympic Park**

CARLA D BAKER CATC • ROBERT L BAKER III • ALFRED T BAKER JR • GORDON J BAKER JR • CHAMP L BAKER MD • MARIE BAKER WILSON • SANDOR BAKO • SHILPA P BAKRE • ZACH A BAKRIN • PATRICIA A BALABAN • GLORIA BALAGUE • DIANA S BALAS • JENNIFER S BALAS • LISA M BALAS • ALEXANDER T BALASCO • LUIS O. BALBOA • ASHLEY P BALCH • CHRISTINE L BALCH • EDWARD P BALCH • JEANA M BALCH • JEFFREY L BALCH • LINDA R BALCH • RANDALL M BALCH • ALAN S BALDEL • RYAN A BALDERSTON • CHELSEA L BALDING • TONY BALDING • ALBERTO BALDISSEROTTO •

Olympic venues; and the use of a World Wide Web site for the first time by an Olympic organizing committee.

The call center—operated entirely by volunteers—answered thousands of telephone inquiries per day, and Communications Department staff responded to letters from around the world.

Under the disclosure policy adopted by the ACOG Board of Directors, documents and records of the Games were available for public inspection. The involvement of those interested in the Games was sought through ACOG's advisory groups, which held sessions open to the public, allowing hundreds of people to obtain detailed information on areas of significant interest to them and to offer suggestions.

ACOG representatives were available to give progress reports on the Games to the communities by participating in neighborhood, business group, and town hall meetings, as well as other forums. Numerous organizations developing management case studies on the preparations for the Games were invited to send observers to ACOG's internal meetings and, as time allowed, to interview management and staff.

The objective of all these efforts was to share information about the Games and to encourage as many people as possible to become involved in the Olympic Movement.

MANAGEMENT STRUCTURE

After ACOG was established as a corporation, its organizational structure was designed with the help of worldwide management consultants McKinsey and Co. Departments were created primarily around the functional responsibilities that would have to be fulfilled during the Games, such as sports competition, ticket sales, transportation, and security. This structure allowed the organizers of various aspects of the Games to implement these plans.

ACOG's president and CEO, William Porter Payne, reporting to the ACOG Board of Directors, had responsibility for all aspects of the Games. The CEO directly managed all functional areas that had an external focus, from Ceremonies to Government Relations, and he worked with the USOC in overseeing the marketing efforts of the joint venture, ACOP.

In 1991, A.D. Frazier Jr. joined ACOG as COO, to report to the CEO on finance and accounting, construction of new facilities, and operation of the Games.

The departments created under the leadership of the CEO and COO were led by managing directors, who in turn established divisions responsible for various functional area projects and programs.

FIGURE 2: FUNCTIONAL AREA MANAGEMENT STRUCTURE

By the start of the Games, the ACOG management structure included managing directors with the following functional area responsibilities.

Reporting to the CEO

Sherm Day—Physical Legacy (Centennial Olympic Park)

Shirley Franklin—senior policy advisor (Community and Local Government Relations)

Bill McCahan—Marketing (ACOP)

Linda Stephenson—Olympic Programs (Cultural Olympiad, Volunteer Services, and Youth and Education)

Lindsay Thomas—Government Relations

Ginger Watkins—Corporate Services (Ceremonies, Creative Services, Look of the Games, Special Events / Guest Services, and Torch Relay)

Dick Yarbrough—Communications (Media Relations, Press Information and Operations, and State and Federal Government Relations)

Doug Bowles—assistant to the president

Reporting to the COO

Scott Anderson—Games Services (Accommodations, Food and Beverage, Merchandising, and Ticket Sales)

Doug Arnot—Venue Management

Charles Battle—International Relations (Olympic Family and Protocol and Olympic Village)

Morris Dillard—Operations (Logistics, Medical Services, Security, and Transportation)

Pat Glisson—Financial Services

Doris Isaacs-Stallworth—Administration and Human Resources

Rod Knowles—Technology

Dave Maggard—Sports

Bill Moss—Construction

Claire Potvin—Accreditation

Manolo Romero—Atlanta Olympic Broadcasting

Gary Slagle—Planning and Integration

Kay Wallace—deputy COO

The ACOG Board of Directors assembled at a meeting in May 1996.

As the Games approached, some divisions within departments became independent departments, especially when a multitude of operational details were managed. The Operations Department, for example, originally covered Accreditation, Accommodations, Logistics, Medical Services, Press Operations, Security, Technology, Ticket Sales, Transportation, and Venue Management. Several of these areas later became separate departments, with Logistics, Medical Services, Security, and Transportation remaining divisions of Operations.

The dynamic nature of this structure was essential, but sometimes problematic. The growth and redistribution of responsibilities occasionally resulted in gaps and overlaps in planning at the departmental level. However, as the organization moved toward a venue-based management process called venuization, in which all functional areas would be represented at the venues, an integrated approach to planning and operations was achieved.

The CEO and COO met daily to assess the planning for the Games, and then each held weekly and biweekly staff meetings with the senior managers. To bring together all the functional areas preparing for the Games and to ensure the most cohesive approach possible in shifting the organization to venue-based management, COO meetings regularly included all managing directors and their department heads. In addition, ACOG executives held open forums on numerous occasions to provide an opportunity for discussion with all program directors, managers, and supervisors. *(For functional area management structure, see Figure 2.)*

PLANNING PROCESS

The basis for ACOG's early planning was the extensive documentation prepared during the Bid process and the Bid books themselves. Prior to 1992, the focus was on broadly outlining program requirements. Programs—such as Accreditation, Sports, and Transportation—were defined as combinations of projects and activities directed toward achieving a specific purpose. Few financial commitments were made during this early period as staff compiled research materials on previous Games, performed quantitative analyses of functional area requirements, and gathered information and perspectives from various professionals and interest groups. This work resulted in preliminary plans that defined the scope of future planning efforts and ACOG's budget requirements.

Fundamental to this effort was the definition of key constituent groups—athletes and other members of the Olympic Family, including broadcasters, press, and sponsors—and the products and services they required. A database was created to document all the commitments made to the constituencies. Included in this review were Bid documents, the Host City Contract, marketing agreements, and the IF memoranda of understanding, as well as a listing of presumed expectations of constituents based on previous Games experience.

These documents were compared with the plans and programs of each functional area, providing ACOG an early opportunity to examine its plans from the standpoint of both provider and receiver.

Also important was the opportunity to prepare financial forecasts based on increasingly precise details. As budgets were developed on the basis of the plans, ACOG had to maintain its focus of staging a privately funded Games. This focus necessitated constant reassessment and careful decision making to maintain a critical balance between the celebration integral in the Olympic Movement and the achievement of balanced financial results at the conclusion of the Games.

Beginning in 1994, the emphasis turned to implementing and testing the various aspects of the plan to ensure delivery during the staging of the Games. A master scheduling system was combined with a budget reviewing system that allowed progress to be measured and budget data to be continuously updated. Concurrently, the planning process focused on integrating all functional areas through Venue Management.

STAFFING AND ADMINISTRATION

During the six years preceding the Games, ACOG's daily operations were similar to those of other corporations, although the rapid

increase in the size of the organization and its temporary status were unique, requiring a sophisticated approach to staffing and facilities planning.

Staffing

A Human Resources Department was established in April 1991, with the following goals.

■ Enable ACOG to attract, retain, and motivate the most experienced individuals.

■ Provide a framework for protecting the high standards of the Olympic Movement and code of ethics adopted by ACOG.

■ Contribute to the overall management decision-making process based on personnel management knowledge and skills.

■ Ensure equitable treatment of all applicants and employees in all aspects of human resources management.

ACOG-paid employees included full-time, part-time, and temporary staff. Full-time employees accounted for the majority of ACOG-paid staff until the start of 1996. At that time, almost all new ACOG positions were filled with temporary staff. Non–ACOG-paid staff comprised corporate-loaned employees paid by an outside corporation filling an approved ACOG position; value-in-kind (VIK) personnel assigned to ACOG under the terms of a sponsorship agreement; contract employees from companies under contract to ACOG to provide specialized professional and technical services; and employees assigned to ACOG under terms of the sponsorship agreement with Randstad Staffing Services.

At the end of 1991, ACOG-paid and non–ACOG-paid staff included the CEO, COO, 2 executive vice presidents, 7 senior vice presidents, 10 directors, and approximately 80 individuals in other staff positions. By 31 July 1996, this group had expanded to include a chief marketing officer (CMO), 15 managing directors, approximately 130 additional directors and program directors, 1,100 managers and assistant managers, and more than 3,000

MANAGEMENT AND ADMINISTRATION EMPLOYEES

Date	Staff Number
January 1993	58
January 1996	47
July 1996	43

Note: These staff numbers do not include contract, VIK, and volunteer personnel.

additional ACOG staff members—with Human Resources personnel handling the processing and administrative requirements associated with this growth in staff.

ACOG pursued an aggressive policy of inclusion as reflected in EEOP's plan, adopted by the ACOG Board of Directors in 1991, which provided equal opportunity for all qualified applicants and employees and prohibited discrimination on the basis of race, color, religion, national origin, sex, age, disability, or veteran status.

was notified about any concerns or questions. Human Resources, in conjunction with a consulting firm, was also responsible for the development of salary ranges. This approach required consideration of the dynamic environment and long hours associated with working for the Games, as well as the short-term nature of all positions.

In addition to compensation, ACOG-paid employees received benefits that provided insurance and other programs at rates comparable to those offered in private industry.

Billy Payne addresses Olympic Games staff members at a post-Games celebration held in Centennial Olympic Park.

Human Resources provided assistance to departments by helping to identify potential candidates through résumé database searches, advertising and search firms, corporations providing employees, and Randstad. The department also established relationships with local organizations and attended job fairs. By June 1996, Human Resources had amassed a résumé database containing over 38,000 records.

In January 1992, ACOG established a policy that required all ACOG-paid employees to successfully complete a drug test and background check prior to employment. The background investigations were conducted by the Georgia Bureau of Investigation. Only the applicant

In October 1995, ACOG announced a separation program effective at the conclusion of the Games. Designed to help ensure employees would remain motivated and enthusiastic, the program provided outplacement services such as assistance with résumé writing and interview skills, as well as retention incentives.

Internal Volunteer Program

Individuals who participated in the Internal Volunteer Program worked with ACOG staff prior to the Games and supported various projects in the ACOG offices and the special events and meetings ACOG hosted.

Many had been involved in the Bid effort and wanted to extend their commitment. Volunteers worked in all areas of operations, with assignments coordinated by the Volunteer Services Department based on the needs of the functional areas and the volunteers' availability, flexibility, willingness to fill an identified need, and skills.

The call center, which received several thousand calls each day to ACOG offices, was staffed entirely by volunteers, as were most reception desks. Volunteers also managed some ACOG programs, most notably the ODIS Program and the Speakers Bureau.

In 1992, after the internal volunteer program's first full year of operation, approximately 300 individuals were participating consistently. By April 1996, the number grew to more than 800, as the individuals assumed their Games volunteer positions. Over the five-year period, volunteers devoted 542,000 hours to preparations for the Games, with seven members of the program serving more than 5,000 hours each.

ACOG management praised the internal volunteers on a regular basis, hosting programs and commemorating their achievements with special pins representing various levels of service.

ACOG offered internship opportunities to college students through the Volunteer Services Department. Each intern was responsible for meeting his or her own expenses and college and university requirements. The internship program was available throughout all ACOG functional areas.

Internal Communications and Events

Human Resources, along with Corporate Services and Volunteer Services, coordinated communications and employee events to enhance morale and involve ACOG paid employees and internal volunteers in the excitement of participating in Games preparations.

Copies of the *Torch*—ACOG's published newsletter for Olympic Family members about the progress of the Games —were provided to employees with a biweekly internal newsletter featuring updates and employee recognition. Notices also were sent daily by E-mail and voice mail to all employees. Monthly luncheons were held to provide staff with information and entertainment. Major milestones were celebrated with special events and unique mementos, such as NBC T-shirts, 1,000-day countdown watches, and the 500 days to the Games certificates.

Other presentations were conducted periodically to preview various aspects of the Games, such as staff uniforms, or to express appreciation. At the end of 1994, bricks inscribed with staff names were placed together in a section of Centennial Olympic Park designated for staff. In March 1996, US President Clinton and Vice President Gore addressed staff and volunteers, delivering a message of thanks and inspiration. All employees and volunteers were invited to a private dress rehearsal of Opening Ceremony held on 17 July—one of the most popular activities.

Facilities

During the Bid phase, AOC occupied a single floor of an office building in midtown Atlanta. Immediately after the 1996 Games were awarded to the city, this space was increased to two floors to accommodate additional staff, marking the first of several office relocations and space reconfigurations. The Administrative Services Department was responsible for these relocations, which eventually required a full-time staff of coordinators and movers.

In May 1991, ACOG moved to the Inforum building in central Atlanta, which had 45,000 sq ft (4,185 sq m) of space to accommodate current staff and future hires anticipated in 1991.

By October 1991, however, considerably more space was required, and 15,000 sq ft (1,395 sq m) were added by year's end.

ACOG had planned to acquire and complete office space gradually, assuming additional space only when offices were at maximum capacity. Incremental staff growth rates made this approach impractical, and ACOG retained a contractor to review projected staff plans and associated office space through 1996 for each functional area and to develop standards for allocating space and furniture. The study determined that ACOG would require more space by 1993, forcing the acquisition of additional office areas.

By November 1992, ACOG began preparing an additional 83,000 sq ft (7,719 sq m) of space in the Inforum building. With such a large amount of space available, additions could be accommodated without relocating existing staff. During 1994, 10,000 sq ft (930 sq m) of space was acquired for the technology implementation center (TIC) and the Press Operations division in the Atlanta Apparel Mart, which is connected by an enclosed, elevated walkway to ACOG headquarters in the Inforum. While this space was being developed, existing facilities on the fifth and sixth floors of the Inforum were being redesigned, providing room for a second copy center and security command post as well as additional office space.

Nevertheless, it was clear that more space would be needed to accommodate the growing staff. In December 1994, ACOG acquired 180,000 sq ft (16,740 sq m) of space at a building two blocks from the Inforum. Renovation lasted from December 1994 to April 1995. In early 1996, an additional three floors with 41,000 sq ft (3,813 sq m) of space were acquired in this building to house staff joining ACOG in the final months of preparations. These offices were prepared only minimally, since the staff there would shortly move to Games-time locations. Other areas of the building were also adapted to serve as the main accreditation center (MAC) and the main ticket center during the Games.

As these facilities were being completed, work began on adapting ACOG offices at the Inforum to become an ACOG venue that would serve as Games-time headquarters. Construction began in March on specially equipped spaces for the Games main operations center (MOC), technology operations center (TOC), security operations center, sports coordination center, and an area for approximately 100 IBM technical staff to support the technology integration process during the Games.

While managing the succession of relocations and adaptations of new office space was a major responsibility of Administrative Services, the department also provided the support services essential to the daily functioning of ACOG offices. These services included operation of reception desks for all visitors, the call center or main switchboard, internal mail services, and copying centers. In addition, Administrative Services developed plans for handling emergencies, managed ACOG's office assets and inventories of equipment, established procedures for closing office spaces after the Games, and worked with the Finance Department regarding dissolution of the corporation.

Venuization

In 1994, ACOG management committed to the concept of venuization, which called for individuals from the functional areas that would be represented at a venue to work together as a team well before the start of the Games. Ideally, the teams—led by the venue manager and sports manager—would be located at their venues. However, with only a small number of venues available a few months prior to the Games, members of the venue teams had to be moved from their functional area to an area within ACOG designated for this purpose.

Given the lack of vacant areas in ACOG's offices, areas for venue teams generally had to be created within already occupied space, leading to multiple relocations of staff within offices

ACOG headquarters were located on two floors in the Inforum building in central Atlanta. As ACOG expanded, it eventually had to acquire more space in a building two blocks away on Peachtree Street.

to create a venue team location. Even more critical was the fact that many functional areas were not sufficiently staffed to devote full-time personnel to the venue teams. Additionally, many functional areas were reluctant to support venuization until the Games drew closer.

Atlanta Sports '95—a series of competition test events conducted by ACOG in summer and fall 1995—provided an opportunity to demonstrate venue-based management and the importance of building strong teams at each venue to coordinate all operations of the facility. Following these events, more venue teams were established at ACOG offices, but few were fully staffed. As an interim measure, the teams held meetings with all participants once a week or more frequently if necessary until their relocation to the venues.

Once the teams were established at the venues, they worked extraordinarily well together, forming the cohesiveness that results from being physically located together in a work environment and focusing on a common objective. In almost every instance, the longer the teams were together, the stronger their performance, indicating the effectiveness of the approach and the benefits of forming the teams early.

In the months prior to the Games, ACOG management almost universally supported venuization. However, it was challenging to determine the optimal time to transfer to venue-based management and to have the facilities and personnel in place to fully realize the shift.

GAMES-TIME MANAGEMENT

Management direction of the Games was the responsibility of the CEO, who led an executive management team directed by the COO. All competition and noncompetition venues and all functional area command centers—representing approximately 132,000 staff, volunteers, and contractors at more than 90 different locations—ultimately reported to members of this team.

The executive management team was officially in operation three weeks before Opening Ceremony, meeting each day. At that time, all the venue teams were in place and a chain of command had been established from venues and functional area command centers to ACOG headquarters.

On 19 July, the CEO and members of the executive management team began reporting daily each morning at 0830 to an IOC Commission chaired by President Juan Antonio Samaranch. The report focused on the previous day's operations, resolution of issues that had been raised in previous meetings, and the plans for the next day.

This information was gathered through daily reports submitted from all Games locations and from a series of COO-coordinated management meetings that were held at the end of the prior day and resumed each morning at 0630. Following the executive management team's meeting with the IOC, the COO would meet with managing directors to resolve the identified issues.

In addition to the meetings that brought together the management of ACOG and the IOC, members of the management team and certain IOC representatives were equipped with two-way radios that ensured instant communication with a critical group. The immediate accessibility provided by radio communication was an essential factor in clarification of issues and prompt problem resolution.

Information gathering and the ability to communicate promptly were fundamental to the management of the Games and were possible through the operation centers and reporting requirements that were in place by 1 July and, importantly, through a management philosophy that empowered people in the field to take the actions necessary to achieve ACOG's goals for the presentation of outstanding Games. Venue teams at competition and noncompetition sites took full responsibility for managing their venues within their scope of authority, as did the teams managing the functional area command centers.

Main Operations Center

With information as the key to effective management of large and complex undertakings, ACOG determined in fall 1995 that highly efficient command, communication, computer, and intelligence systems must be installed and functional before the start of the 1996 Olympic Games. A plan for an ACOG Games MOC was developed with information from the entire organization and approved by the CEO and COO.

The MOC was installed adjacent to ACOG's executive offices at the Inforum and equipped with technology that allowed MOC personnel to monitor every aspect of the Games on closed-circuit television and by computer and to communicate rapidly with any location. A desk for each functional area was staffed 24 hours a day by the senior leadership of the organization, with frequent guidance from managing directors.

The information that passed through the MOC included predefined and regularly scheduled reports covering key data pertaining to the operations of all venues, functional areas, and systems, as well as incident reports and other spontaneous information that identified matters needing critical response and resolution. With this data, the MOC was the conduit for resolving issues that could not be solved at the venues or functional command centers.

If required, and only upon direct authorization and leadership from the CEO and/or COO, the MOC could become the ACOG command, control, communication, computer, and intelligence unit to direct the Games and the activities of ACOG following preapproved emergency procedures. Although this action was never needed, ACOG was prepared for any eventuality.

Throughout the 1996 Olympic Games, the MOC served as the link in providing information to senior leadership as well as processing and communicating information across functional areas. Because representatives from all functional areas were stationed in the center, issues could be assessed rapidly and resolved or passed on to members of the executive management team. In essence, the MOC provided a communications hub and focal point that made it possible to quickly identify and resolve issues that crossed functional areas or extended beyond the bounds of a single venue or concerned matters beyond normal expectations.

Management of Venues and Command Centers

The MOC relied on information from the venues and the functional area command centers, each of which held meetings throughout the day to assess their performance and prepare for the next day.

At both competition and noncompetition venues, the venue managers were responsible for gathering information from their team members, resolving the problems within that venue, submitting daily reports, and referring any problems they could not resolve or that extended beyond the purview of their venue to senior management.

Functional area command centers operated in a similar fashion, especially the large centers, such as the TOC, which encompassed several hundred personnel and, like most of its counterparts, was responsible for centralized operations not specific to any one venue and for support of the technology personnel and resources assigned to all venues. Other large functional area command centers included Transportation, which was located outside of

ACOG offices at a site shared with local, state, and federal traffic management personnel, and Security, which operated with local, state, and federal law enforcement officials.

Many other functional area command centers were smaller, coordinating the flow of supplies, materials, and information to their personnel at the venues. Their reports sometimes duplicated information provided in the venue reports, which helped define problems and ensured all issues were addressed.

CONCLUSIONS AND RECOMMENDATIONS

In managing the 1996 Games, ACOG followed a strategic planning course that first established through a mission statement a context for the presentation of the Games and the desired accomplishments. A master plan was then developed to identify all the requirements set forth in the mission statement and the resources needed to fulfill those requirements. Challenges arose when requirements demanded more resources than were available, but the desired outcome—outstanding Games that created a memorable experience for athletes, officials, staff, spectators, and visitors—was achieved.

A number of recommendations can be made in the hope of serving future organizers. In this chapter, only those relating to the overall planning and execution of the Games are noted because other chapters in this volume provide recommendations regarding specific aspects and programs.

■ It is most essential to define the organization's objectives and priorities in planning and organizing the Games. Because of the size and scope of the Olympic Games and the many constituencies involved, it is not possible to meet the demands or earn the appreciation of all the constituencies. Senior management must focus immediately on establishing priorities in addressing the demands of various groups. This planning should involve a clear understanding of the contractual obligations of the organizing committee, the expectations dictated by tradition, and what the organizing committee determines it would like to achieve in enhancing the Games. Understanding the demands of each constituency is essential to the consistent and efficient preparation of the Games.

■ Also of extraordinary importance is recruiting event and business management staff and integrating them into the organization at the earliest possible point. Every Olympic Games is unique, but event operational experience is critical in developing cost-effective, realistic plans that can be implemented and in delivering results that meet expectations.

■ Finally, the approach to addressing the issue of functional area versus venue-based management must be determined from the beginning. The experience of the 1996 Olympic Games supports venue-based management, and dictates that it should be in place well in advance of the start of competition. At the same time, many of the requirements of the Games demand the creation of centralized functional areas. The course of action the organizing committee follows—which most likely will be a combination of the two management structures—and the definition of responsibilities must be clearly established and communicated throughout the organization.

CHAPTER TWO
ACCOMMODATIONS

OVERVIEW—ACOG's mission was to provide affordable, accessible, and plentiful housing in a hospitable environment for all who would attend the Centennial Olympic Games. The Accommodations Department was established to meet the housing needs of the constituent groups ACOG was committed to serve through the *Olympic Charter*: specifically, the Olympic Family, which included the IOC and its guests, NOCs, IFs, print and broadcast media, and sponsors. Additionally, the department was given the responsibility of coordinating accommodation options for the general public. Accommodations was not responsible for athlete housing, which was under the direction of the Olympic Villages Department.

Accommodations planning began with assessing the demand for housing from the contracted constituent groups and allocating the most appropriate type and location of accommodations. Demand assessment was a process that continued until Games-time.

Initial demand figures for the Olympic Family were derived from the Bid process, the Host City Contract, and guidelines provided by the IOC, as well as by comparing data from the Los Angeles, Seoul, and Barcelona Games. Accommodations staff met frequently with various departmental staff, NOCs, IFs, sponsors, media, and other integral groups to determine the actual housing requirements and encourage these groups to specify their requirements.

To estimate spectator demand for housing, ACOG developed a visitation model based on projected ticket sales. Initial studies indicated that spectators would require more than 52,000 rooms for the 1996 Games.

Assembling enough room inventory to meet estimated demand was the department's primary effort during the first two years of planning. ACOG needed to establish the inventory so allocations to the Olympic Family could be attained first. The first priority was to sign contracts with Atlanta's major hotels, followed by other Atlanta-area hotels, and with key institutions that had dormitories close to Olympic venues. Later efforts added private homes, condominiums, apartments, additional dormitories, and outlying hotels to this inventory.

The department allocated categories of accommodations and specific properties to certain constituent groups in accordance with IOC requirements as well as terms and conditions of sponsorship, licensing, and broadcasting agreements. Availability, cost factors, geographic requirements relative to venue assignments, and quality needs were other factors used in making allocations.

Most members of the Olympic Family were allocated to a network of centrally located hotels called the Olympic Family Hotel Network (OFHN). Designated for spectators' use was a network of other area hotels called the Olympic Games Travel Network (OGTN) and some private housing. Competition officials, press from developing countries, some contractors, and staff and volunteers were allocated other affordable accommodations in convenient locations, called the Host Campus Network (HCN). Private housing was offered to heads of state, sponsors, and other groups through Private Housing 1996, Inc. (PH'96).

ORGANIZATION

Ultimately, the Accommodations Department became three separately managed networks of inventory that corresponded to the initial allocations: the Host Hotel Network (HHN), comprised of the OFHN and the OGTN; the HCN; and PH'96.

The Accommodations Department was one of several functional areas reporting directly to the Games Services Department. The HHN and the HCN were coordinated by program managers and staffed with project coordinators as needed. Managing and coordinating the OGTN and the reservations vendor, PH'96, was the responsibility of the director of Accommodations. A financial consultant coordinated budget and revenue tracking for the department.

Once a group's accommodations were determined, a comprehensive process was required to convert these allocations into specific reservations.

Managing reservations was important. ACOG contracted with three reservation service vendors to allocate the customer to a specific property, invoice and collect payment, send confirmations, assign individuals to specific rooms, and process change requests. All payments were required well in advance of occupancy and were not refundable, but changes in arrival and departure dates, length of stay, and individual names were common for all networks.

HOST HOTEL NETWORK

The HHN was the inventory of all hotel, motel, lodge, and inn rooms that ACOG could, by contractual agreement, allocate. Established in 1991 with the help of the Georgia Hospitality and Travel Association, Inc., and several Atlanta-area hotels, its purpose was to ensure that hotel rooms would be available at fair prices.

The Host Hotel Contract

Early efforts were made to contract with as many hotels as possible. Prior to being awarded the Games, the Atlanta Organizing Committee negotiated with major Atlanta hotels to sign letters of intent to contract with ACOG should the Games come to Atlanta.

The basic contract was developed by incorporating the provisions in the letter of intent and the general format of hotel contracts used for similar events. Some provisions in earlier contracts were seen by the hotel community as unfavorable to their business and were therefore modified. Ultimately, one contract was developed for metropolitan-Atlanta properties and another for non-metro-area properties. The metro-Atlanta contract gave hotels access to purchase Games tickets to events of their choice without entering the ticket lottery and required the hotel to reserve some of its public space, such as ballrooms and meeting rooms, for allocation by ACOG.

Both contracts required a six-night minimum stay for all reservations, and both established dates in February, March, and April 1996 when ACOG could release unsold rooms without financial penalty. In both contracts, ACOG agreed to forward full payment to the hotels for all rooms reserved by 31 January 1996. Participating hotels promised to commit 80 percent of total room inventory from 17 July to 6 August 1996; to abide by ACOG's anti-ambush-marketing requirements; to sell all rooms at an Olympic rate, in compliance with Georgia's anti-price-gouging law; and to give ACOG minimal commission.

The price-gouging legislation, passed by the Georgia legislature at ACOG's urging, was established to prevent escalated pricing of hotel accommodations, which had occurred in previous Olympic host cities. Specifically, hotels

• ANGELA M BARNARD • JOHN CHARLES BARNARD • JOICE A BARNARD • NEVA-JANE BARNARD • RACHEL BARNARD • SEAN LIONEL BARNAVE • MARIA E BARNER • ANDREA B BARNES • ANGIE M BARNES • ANNA J BARNES • BARRETT L BARNES • BECKY A BARNES • BERNARD JR A BARNES • BOB BARNES • CAMMIE J BARNES • CHRISTOPHER V BARNES • DARRITA BARNES • DAWN M BARNES • DONALD F BARNES • DONALD H BARNES • ELDARADA BARNES • ERIC E BARNES • GLORIA A BARNES • HENRIETTA BARNES • JACQUELINE F BARNES • JEFF A BARNES • JOHN BARNES •

37

that had published rates over $100 per room-night could not increase their rates more than 5.7 percent, the sum of the consumer price index increase for 1993 and 1994. Lodging facilities with rates lower than $100 were not affected by the legislation, and thus many chose to raise their rates to $100 per room-night for the Olympic period.

While ACOG was supported by many area hotels, considerable marketing had to be done to bring more rooms into the network. Accommodations enlisted the help of the Governor's Office of Consumer Affairs, the Georgia Hospitality and Travel Association, Inc., and other hotel organizations in this marketing effort. In meetings with hoteliers, advantages of joining the HHN were emphasized, including rights to the HHN designation, the payment guarantee for all rooms reserved by 31 January 1996, and the absorption of credit card merchant fees by ACOG. By October 1995, these efforts had resulted in a total network inventory of 440 hotels and approximately 44,000 rooms.

Olympic Family Hotel Network

The OFHN was the group of hotels that provided ACOG's contractually obligated rooms for the Olympic Family. The Atlanta Marriott Marquis, an entire hotel designated as the Olympic Family Hotel during the Games period, was staffed as a venue by ACOG's Guest Services Department.

Since premium hotels, especially those near the Olympic Ring, were in greatest demand, the verification and validation of the demand for Olympic Family housing was extremely important. Accommodations required that each constituent group of the Olympic Family designate a contact person to determine demand.

All premium hotels in the HHN network in close proximity to the Olympic Ring, and cer-

tain outlying venues, were designated as OFHN hotels. Approximately 190 hotels with 29,500 rooms were allocated to the Olympic Family. Once a hotel joined the HHN, its inventory and other pertinent information were entered into a database used to track room allocations.

Room allocations were not made solely by the Accommodations Department, but were coordinated by a group's constituent contact. For example, ACOG's Sports Department assisted with IF allocations, ACOP representatives assisted with marketing allocations, and International Dignitary Relations with all NOC and international dignitary allocations. Press accommodations were coordinated with ACOG Press Operations. *(For more information, see the Communications chapter.)*

Once allocated, however, inventory was managed exclusively by Accommodations. Updating demand, clarifying allocations, invoicing groups, accounting for payments, maintaining inventory control, and communicating all of the above to the reservation services vendor were the responsibilities of the OFHN operations staff. In addition, operations staff was responsible for communicating with hotel owners and operators. All constituent groups were offered Accommodations' full reservations services, with athletes and the press being handled by other specific departments. While some declined—most notably, sponsor groups that chose to work directly with the hotels—most groups utilized the reservation services.

A significant strategy of the HHN was to reserve contingency rooms for any new sponsors or licensees. These rooms were paid for by ACOG prior to the required release date, therefore representing a potential financial liability if they remained unallocated and unsold. The majority of these rooms were released back to Accommodations in May 1996, but even so, some contingency rooms were not sold.

By 31 January 1996, all network hotel rooms—including rooms in the smaller, more remote hotels—that were unsold were released to the hotels. ACOG was committed to payments at least twice monthly after that date, and remittances were processed every two weeks beginning in mid-February. Every remittance transmittal gave detailed information regarding allocations, the status of room inventory, and payment information on every group or customer assigned to a specific hotel. A complete report was confirmed with ACOG and hotel management every two weeks.

The Accommodations team accurately projected that some room allocations—particularly to sponsors and licensees—were larger than needed. Because all rooms were prepaid with nonrefundable deposits and no provisions were made for cancellations, a resale program was developed. Constituents could return rooms to ACOG, and if Accommodations was able to resell them to a new customer, 65 percent of the original purchase price would be refunded. The majority of returned rooms were in top-quality hotels and good locations, and thus were resold.

Few major sponsors returned rooms to ACOG. While the terms and conditions prohibited the transfer of rooms, many sponsor groups that had experience with Olympic housing exchanged rooms among themselves, avoiding the 35 percent fee.

During Games-time, the OFHN staff continued to process changes in reservations and collect corresponding payments, identify and resolve issues, and sell contingency inventory when possible. *(For final room usage for the OFHN, see Figure 1.)*

Olympic Games Travel Network

The OGTN, established to provide travel services to the general public, consisted of hotel properties not allocated to the Olympic Family. Accommodations released approximately 14,000 rooms to a reservations service under an agreement to sell travel packages to the general public, including air travel; transfer, tour, and transportation services; rental cars;

and accommodations.

The OGTN sought to encourage demand by marketing to spectator groups. Housing was allocated to the OGTN from the HHN or provided in private homes by PH'96. The challenge for the OGTN was to assess demand and manage a reservations process in a fair and equitable manner, as well as promote attendance at the Centennial Olympic Games.

ACOG had promised domestic ticket holders that accommodations under its contract would be available immediately following the

FIGURE 1: FINAL ROOM USAGE FOR THE OLYMPIC FAMILY HOTEL NETWORK

Constituent	Rooms	Guests	Room-nights
IOC	874	2,366	12,651
Olympic Family (miscellaneous)	139	556	2,502
NOCs	2,963	5,926	35,556
IFs	1,119	1,679	20,142
Heads of state	200	300	1,600
Sponsors	8,963	102,178	178,812
Broadcast media	7,581	11,372	151,620
Press media	2,386	2,600	35,790
Contractors	2,263	4,211	44,204
Suppliers	415	2,030	8,485
Licensees	199	1,194	4,179
ACOG staff	864	5,767	13,928
Tour operators	360	4,320	6,480
General public spectators	41	492	738
Total	**28,367**	**144,991**	**516,687**

release of ticket lottery results. Thus, OGTN packages needed to be ready for distribution and sale at the end of September 1995.

Seven accommodations packages created by the reservations service offered different combinations of travel services. One offered only accommodations, which is significant because, under Georgia's anti-price-gouging laws, hotel rooms had to be available at the Olympic rate.

Once priced and approved by ACOG Games Services, the packages were offered in a 23-page catalog that introduced OGTN as ACOG's complete travel service. It was mailed on 28 September 1995 to 302,000 ticket-holding households in the US. Accommodations were offered to persons outside the US and non–ticket holders after 11 November 1995.

As the packages were being developed, it was determined that the original contractual provision with the hotels for six-night minimum stays was not appropriate for many general public spectators. A waiver from this obligation was sought from all hotels in the OGTN pool. A compromise offer to divide the 18-day Games period into six three-night blocks was proposed, and only one hotel refused to sign

A 22-page accommodations catalog was mailed to ticket-holding households in September 1995. The front cover and inside page are shown above.

the waiver. Packages were then created around three-day blocks of time with specified arrival and departure dates. Customers were advised that they could purchase as many as three blocks, or nine nights, per order.

Assuming that some people would attempt to reserve accommodations while searching for something better, the vendor wanted all sales to be final. However, because the catalog did not name specific hotels and consumers would not know the location of their assigned hotel until after their purchase, ACOG insisted consumers be given the right to cancel. A compromise was reached whereby customers

of the OGTN would have 15 days from the date of their confirmation letter to cancel with full refund.

A lottery process, named Fair Rooms, was created to ensure that all ticket-holding households that received the brochure had an equal chance to purchase the hotel rooms available in close proximity to the Games. All applications received during the first two weeks were entered into a computer program by package type and randomly selected, where demand exceeded the OGTN's supply. Letters were sent to the households with applications that had been selected to confirm that they would receive their requested packages. Additionally, the program assigned second- or third-choice packages when available. Early results indicated that most spectators were interested in the accommodations-only package.

Because of the 31 January release date, there was tremendous pressure to process sales quickly. In early January 1996, a second, smaller brochure offering the remaining inventory was created and mailed to ticket holders who had not responded to the first catalog, but results from this mailing were minimal.

Ultimately, domestic spectators' demand for accommodations did not meet expectations. When the 31 January payments were forwarded to the OGTN hotels, more than 7,000 rooms were released, unsold, back to the hotels. These were primarily in the outlying areas, and although some hotels allowed the OGTN to continue marketing their rooms, demand never materialized.

Having sold 16,244 packages serving 42,470 people, the OGTN planned for comprehensive customer service to cover nearly all phases of its operations. OGTN staff members were placed at all parking locations, motorcoach drop-off and pick-up sites, and an air-conditioned downtown hospitality center, the Retreat. Additionally, a 24-hour customer service center was established in the Accommodations office. In total, the OGTN sold 79,405 of the 296,000 room-nights allocated, or 27 percent.

The OGTN handled a significant amount of customer correspondence after Games-time. Some customers requested refunds for accommodations that did not meet their expectations. The reservations service vendor and ACOG developed a plan to respond to customers quickly by requesting that the hotel properties respond directly to the customers to resolve issues as they would with any other customer. When justified, customers were compensated through a fund established by the vendor and ACOG.

The HHN contracted for approximately 35,000 of the 44,000 rooms in its original inventory. The metro-area hotels enjoyed the longest, sustained stays with substantial group business; the properties peripheral to the metro area had less sustained occupancy. ACOG began releasing inventory back to member hotels as early as 31 January 1996. This trend of oversupply never reversed as Games-time approached, and thus the April, May, and June release dates resulted in even further reductions of inventory.

HOST CAMPUS NETWORK

The overall goal of the HCN was to provide clean, comfortable, safe, and accessible housing for all constituents with verified, budget-supported housing needs. HCN's responsibilities were to identify and verify constituent demand, allocate groups to specific campuses, oversee the budget, explore all potential HCN housing options within a reasonable distance from Olympic venues, and oversee the effective management of all HCN sites.

Seventeen sites, primarily colleges and universities, provided approximately 13,000 bed spaces. HCN also included grooms' housing, the complex of trailers constructed by ACOG at the equestrian venue.

This network offered a lower-cost housing option, used primarily by constituents for whom housing in groups would provide easier transportation accessibility, or groups who paid for their own housing and were looking for a low-cost option conveniently located to assigned venues. HCN offered housing near many Olympic venues where no other housing options were available. Also, campus sites provided opportunities for large groups to feel more comfortable by staying together at a single site, facilitating more efficient communication, transportation, dining, and other group logistics. The groups included competition officials, staff, and volunteers.

HCN provided housing for competition officials, extra team officials, press constituents from developing countries, NBC runners, subcontractors for various functional areas, athletes on stand-by for the rowing competition, members of ACOG's volunteer security team, grooms at the Georgia International Horse Park, Opening Ceremony cast members, some ACOG staff and volunteers, and certain spectator groups, such as youth groups seeking low-priced dormitory-style facilities.

Nonlocal staff and volunteers could request housing on an as-available basis. Some Atlanta-area staff members working more than 14 hours per day, with responsibilities requiring close proximity to the venue, could also request housing. These requests were submitted to Accommodations by each functional area. Despite careful planning and communication with ACOG, many staff and volunteer housing requests continued after established deadlines, with demand always exceeding supply.

Accommodations successfully attempted to contract for all available bed spaces at Atlanta-area college campuses. In addition, bed spaces were secured on campuses in close proximity to outlying venues.

MAOGA worked with Accommodations and

local developers to provide condemnation rights (transferred to MAOGA by the city) and establish Olympic purpose to enable three new housing projects to be built as part of the HCN. Olympic purpose was established since ACOG leased the facilities during Games-time. These facilities were Fuqua Hall at Atlanta Union Mission and new dormitories at Clark Atlanta University and Morehouse College. *(For HCN inventory by campus, see Figure 2.)*

ACOG developed a standard agreement for contracting HCN sites that included provisions

FIGURE 2: COLLEGES AND UNIVERSITIES IN THE HOST CAMPUS NETWORK

Site	Buildings	Bed-spaces	Rooms
Agnes Scott College	6	693	400
Atlanta Christian College	7	200	100
Atlanta Union Mission	1	97	97
Brenau University	12	278	175
Clark Atlanta University	9	1,659	1,170
Emory University	14	2,221	1,238
Georgia Baptist College of Nursing	1	262	147
Georgia International Horse Park	1	312	156
Interdenominational Theological Center	6	212	108
Lee College	2	125	75
Morehouse College	10	1,346	679
Morris Brown College	3	642	321
Oxford College	6	486	245
Savannah College of Art and Design	1	222	111
Spelman College	5	784	442
University of Georgia	5	3,044	1,522
Wesleyan College	4	400	200
Total Inventory	**93**	**12,983**	**7,186**

for rate; guaranteed rental period; specified number of beds, buildings, and facilities to be leased; security; exclusivity; insurance provisions; services to be provided; and ACOG and IOC requirements for sponsor protection and designation rights. ACOG paid 90 percent of rental fees in advance of occupancy, which was attractive to campuses. An HCN benefit program was developed to encourage participa-

tion. It included some opportunity to purchase tickets and Look of the Games banners, use of the designation right "member of the Host Campus Network," and employment and volunteer opportunities for staff and students.

The contracting process with most campuses took much longer than was expected, as each wished to negotiate specific issues. Since the contracts were negotiated before 1995, most agreements required amendments to allow for extensions of the lease period, addition of facilities, and operational details.

Allocation decisions were based on need for space, budget, and contractual obligations. The allocation process was difficult to manage, since demand fluctuated throughout the planning stages for the Games, and supply numbers were difficult to verify because of continued contract negotiations with some sites. Demand for downtown space always exceeded supply. Most contracting and allocations were completed by July 1995, but additions and changes continued until Games-time.

During the process, some groups required tours of campus facilities; therefore, the HCN tour program was established. Unlike hotels, campus dormitories were not always available for tours, since students lived in the facilities during the year, and conference groups occupied rooms during the summer. In the tour program, specific rooms at each campus were designated for tours, and students in these rooms agreed to have their rooms presentable as required by ACOG groups. ACOG required at least one week's notice to schedule a tour. The program ended in May 1996 to allow for final preparations.

Host Campus Network Operations

Games-time for the HCN began on 1 June 1996, when three housing sites opened for operation and occupancy. By 6 July, all HCN sites were operational. Flexibility was required by reservations and on-site management staff, as many guests arrived prior to their reservation dates, and every effort was made to accommodate them. Changes in departure dates caused by flight scheduling problems were also accommodated when possible. *(For final occupancy for the HCN, see Figure 3.)*

The vendor responsible for establishing overall operating and site-specific plans for most HCN facilities provided a team to oversee each project; developed complete operating plans for each site; procured necessary labor and supplies for operations, negotiating with third-party vendors as required; managed linen and laundry operations; and managed site restoration.

On-site operations consisted of three primary divisions: on-site management, front desk service, and housekeeping services. A housing manager and assistant manager who lived on campus were responsible for all aspects of site operations. They were available 24 hours daily. Larger campuses had additional assistants.

Front desk service managed check-in, checkout, and any changes, and provided information. Desk clerk positions were filled primarily by students recruited from each campus. While most desks operated 16 hours daily, the main front desk at each site operated 24 hours daily. The main desk was equipped with a computer linked to the central reservation system, which could provide printouts of daily occupancy, room availability, and housekeeping.

Housekeeping requirements were established by ACOG. Service was provided daily to competition officials, contractors, extra team officials, press personnel, reserve rowers, and spectator groups assigned to the HCN. Service for all staff and volunteers was provided weekly.

Some campuses provided room housekeeping service, but most provided cleaning only for public areas and community bathrooms. Others provided no housekeeping services at all. The service vendor provided supplementary services through subcontracted housekeeping companies to meet ACOG's service expectations. Linen and laundry services were coordinated with ACOG's Logistics Department.

Several HCN sites were located on campuses that were also competition venues or multipurpose sites for ACOG. At these campuses, Accommodations and vendor staff reported to

Venue Management and submitted their operational plans as part of the overall venue operating plan. For noncompetition sites, HCN coordinators assumed the venue management role for the sites and coordinated all elements of site planning, including operational plans, transportation, parking, food and beverage, and logistics.

In addition to paid desk clerks provided by the vendor, HCN enlisted more than 150 volunteers to assist in providing guest services. Volunteers were recruited from each campus,

FIGURE 3: FINAL OCCUPANCY FOR THE HOST CAMPUS NETWORK

Constituent	Bed-spaces	Guests	Bed-nights	Room-nights
Contractors	1,759	2,536	39,445	20,281
Competition officials	1,664	1,664	33,280	17,640
Extra team officials and grooms	1,029	1,100	20,580	10,290
General public	221	801	3,188	1,746
IFs	90	90	1,173	587
IOC	49	49	482	241
Organizing committees	150	150	1,350	720
Press	1,047	927	21,987	19,467
Security team	2,184	2,184	54,600	27,300
Staff and volunteers	4,353	5,043	98,539	49,405
Tour operators	100	100	1,600	800
Total	**12,646***	**14,644**	**276,244**	**148,477**

Note: 12,646 bed-spaces translates into approximately 6,619 rooms.

with a volunteer liaison to assist with recruiting, training, compiling of site information, and managing of the site's volunteers during Games-time. Volunteers worked at front desks, provided concierge and language services, assisted with check-in and check-out and site preparations, and performed other general tasks as needed.

ACOG Construction installed 39 trailers, or mobile homes, at the Georgia International Horse Park to house grooms, team veterinarians, and venue staff. Each trailer accommodated eight people in double rooms with connecting bathrooms. The trailers were furnished and serviced by Accommodations.

Host Campus Network Reservations

The vendor's reservation system for all HCN sites contained site profiles, including buildings and rooms; reservation data containing group and individual names, and arrival and departure dates; and room assignments. The vendor also prepared building site, group, and arrival and departure pattern reports; invoiced all paying groups; and collected deposits and final payments.

The system allowed for assigning individual reservations by group to a specified site, building, and room to simplify the check-in process. Because most campus space involved sharing rooms and bathrooms, assignments were based on gender. Rooming lists were provided by group contacts to facilitate this process. All communication with individuals was handled by a designated contact for each group.

The system operated 24 hours daily during the Games, while a second reservation center operated at the Airport Welcome Center at Hartsfield Atlanta International Airport. In addition, each site was connected to the central system by a remote computer.

Challenges

Operating the HCN presented several challenges. The first was contracting with campuses, determining reasonable rates and contract terms, and finalizing available bed-spaces, a process that continued well past initially established deadlines.

Secondly, some housing was not air-conditioned. ACOG provided temporary air-conditioning at two HCN sites for some 700 two-bed rooms. This project, managed by an external contractor, required upgrading power supplies, installing window units, and coordinating with campuses.

In addition, an insufficient supply of beds downtown continued to be an issue throughout the planning period. Waiting lists were developed to manage the excess demand, and by Games-time, all wait-list groups had either found housing on their own or were accommodated as a result of cancellations or nonappearances in the HCN.

One particularly controversial issue was the proposal to house competition officials in dormitory-style housing. ACOG was the first organizing committee in Olympic history responsible for funding this housing. The decision to use dormitory-style housing was based primarily on the intent to provide a village-type atmosphere similar to that provided for athletes, as well as to have access to many beds at limited locations, an obvious advantage from the standpoint of transportation and coordination. Unfortunately, many IFs and NOCs preferred hotels for these constituents. The compromise position was to provide dormitory accommodations with access to private or suite-style rooms for all officials. This decision affected other allocations, including moving press personnel from established locations. The competition officials' housing issue continued to be raised by IFs, with demands for unbudgeted amenities or relocation to hotel rooms. ACOG provided televisions, meeting space, and daily service for all these officials.

Another controversial issue involved the housing of extra team officials. At the request of the NOCs, ACOG agreed to provide village-type housing for these officials in one location for a daily fee that included transportation to and from the Olympic Village and dining privileges in the Village. Unfortunately, the renovations to some of the residence halls were not completed in a timely or satisfactory manner, which resulted in some NOCs moving their officials to hotels and demanding reimbursement for their room deposits. ACOG resolved these demands by analyzing the actual facts of each situation on a case-by-case basis.

In past Games, grooms did not pay for housing, but because ACOG incurred costs to furnish and service this housing, grooms were charged a daily rate, and a minimum stay was established. This was protested by several NOCs, as was the nonrefundable deposit required and the fact that NOCs had to pay for veterinarians to stay in the Olympic Village. ACOG eventually lowered the minimum stay requirement from 30 to 20 nights. Grooms' housing, despite the protests of some NOCs, was a very popular option and was fully occupied during Games-time.

Additionally, some guests were not pleased with sharing rooms and using community bathrooms, but most guests adjusted to the temporary inconvenience.

PRIVATE HOUSING '96

Recognizing that demand would probably exceed supply even with Atlanta's strong hotel base and the enthusiastic participation of the area's campuses, ACOG enlisted a group of real estate executives who had formed a private corporation for the purpose of leasing private homes, apartments, and condominiums during Games-time. Having won the formal sanction of ACOG, PH'96 of Atlanta conducted its business off-site and was controlled by its own board of directors and management. The ACOG sanction permitted ACOG access to the inventory of PH'96 while exercising some approval over its marketing, sales, and operational efforts in return for a commission. Though private homes and apartments were offered for lease during Games-time through

other agencies, PH'96 was the only provider supported and sanctioned by ACOG.

Olympic Family constituents and individual spectators seeking special accommodations found only in homes or estates were the focus of PH'96. It was projected that PH'96 would be in demand for a number of reasons: large homes and estates offered luxury amenities in private settings, apartments were available for long-term stays required by such groups as broadcasters and sponsors' technical crews and for guests seeking such conveniences, and condominiums typically offered the convenient facilities found in homes (kitchens, living rooms, garages, etc.) in locations close to many Olympic venues.

PH'96 also offered a number of hospitality services with their accommodations which could be purchased separately, including catering, housekeeping, private chefs, and transportation services.

As with the HHN, initial efforts of PH'96 were focused on acquiring inventory. Apartment owners were solicited to join the program, with many apartment complexes committing 5 percent of their inventory to the project.

During the development of the OGTN, Accommodations felt that the marketing abilities of its external vendor and the catalog being developed offered PH'96 an excellent opportunity to market its homes, condominiums, and apartments. Prior to this time, PH'96's marketing efforts had been minimal. Consequently, it was agreed that the vendor's rental inventory would also be offered in the OGTN catalog mailing.

Sales of PH'96 inventory were small—less than 3 percent of all orders. This trend did not change significantly during the course of the program. PH'96 options were also included in a second, smaller brochure, but home and apartment rental sales never increased significantly.

All PH'96 homes were required to pass inspections to meet certain standards for cleanliness, safety, quality, location, amenities, and insurance requirements. Qualifying homeowners signed rental pool agreements with PH'96, and their homes were entered into the supply database to be offered for a Games-time lease period. A local phone number was established for private homeowners to request rental information regarding the private home lease program.

Pricing for all PH'96 homes, condominiums, and apartments was based on the quality of the accommodations. For example, apartments were priced as standard or deluxe depending upon the amenities offered by the apartment complex. Homes were priced strictly on their assessed tax valuation; specific amenities such as swimming pools were not considered, and location such as proximity to a venue also was not a factor in determining a home's rental price. In addition, pricing was strategically aimed at a per-bedroom rate commensurate with hotel prices of similar quality. A minimum stay of six nights was established for PH'96 accommodations and, like the hotel offerings of the OGTN, specific dates for arrival and departure were established.

While continuing to accumulate an impressive supply of accommodations into inventory available for sale, PH'96 faced some significant challenges as the Games approached. First, all accommodations had to be inspected. This function was provided by various real estate and appraisal personnel who visited homes in person. While the criteria for inspection were specific, it was hard to coordinate with homeowners' schedules, and the whole process was expensive.

Marketing to some constituents was easy; those from some European countries with previous Olympic experience readily embraced the idea of staying in a private home. For domestic spectators, however, traditional hotel rooms were the preferred type of accommodation. Telemarketers were used in this effort, calling people who had contacted PH'96 through its hot line number to emphasize the attraction of homes. It was also challenging to match specific date and quality needs with available inventory. As the Games approached, it became apparent that the supply of private housing facilities would far exceed the demand.

Of the original 30,000 homes and condominiums in the PH'96 database, approximately 3,500 of these were inspected and approved, and only 634 private homes and 94 condominiums were leased for Games-time. The average lease period for homes and condominiums was 12 nights, typically consisting of two blocks of six-night stays. Approximately 40 percent of guests in private homes were domestic ticket holders who made their reservations through the OGTN. In total, 1,073 apartments were leased for an average of 24.5 nights each. In all, 200 apartment complexes representing 22 apartment companies leased apartments through PH'96. Approximately 18 percent of apartment guests were domestic ticket holders who made their reservations through the OGTN.

In addition, over 23,120 meals were served and 19 charter buses employed through PH'96 hospitality services.

ACCOUNT MAINTENANCE

Invoicing, collecting deposits and final payments, and adjusting accounts as changes to reservations were made were important functions of the Accommodations Department. In addition, managing expenses, processing budgetary transfers from other departments not included in the above schedule, and tracking the overall budget were important aspects

of the management of such an extensive housing program. A financial consultant was added to the department six months before Games-time.

Making timely, accurate payments to the 440 hotels and the many campuses was another important and time-consuming process involved in Accommodations management. Hotel payments were based on actual reservations for room types and lengths of stay, and different hotels had different payment deadlines and release dates. The campus payment schedule was established in advance. PH'96 managed the payment and collections process for its inventory.

Accommodations aimed to minimize expenses while maximizing the revenue potential of all housing networks. Revenues were generated through commissions charged on hotel rooms and private housing sales, as well as for all rental fees collected from paying constituents of the HCN.

GAMES-TIME OPERATIONS AND ACCOMMODATIONS USAGE

On 15 July 1996, four days prior to the Opening Ceremony, the Accommodations Department began its 24-hour daily operations, which lasted through the Closing Ceremony. The OGTN located its operations center in the Accommodations Department, where space was also provided for PH'96 to use as needed. Each entity—the OFHN, OGTN, HCN, and PH'96—had announced hot line phone numbers to their respective customers and sites for Games-time problem resolution through information and confirmation materials.

Games-time activities included last-minute accommodations assistance to the general public through the OGTN and the sale of excess rooms still available. Few calls were received in the late evening, so minimal staff was needed after 2300.

Activity subsided immediately after the Closing Ceremony. Duties for the post-Games period included closing campuses, gathering statistics, reconciling final accounts with hotels and other housing sites, and closing files in preparation for archiving. By 30 August 1996, all but one Accommodations employee had finished their assignments; the one remaining program manager was retained to finalize the department's activities.

Hotel inventory eventually peaked at over 45,000 rooms, and the HCN reached a total of

FIGURE 4: TOTAL ACCOMMODATIONS INVENTORY AND USAGE BY NETWORK

Network	Rooms	Guests	Room-nights
HHN: OFHN	28,367	144,991	516,687
HHN: OGTN	4,411	42,470	79,405
HCN	6,619	14,644	148,477
PH'96	7,186	36,694	64,800
Total	**46,583**	**238,799**	**809,369**

12,983 beds. PH'96 added approximately 2,500 apartments and 6,000 private homes and/or condominiums to the total inventory. *(For total accommodations usage by network, see Figure 4.)*

CONCLUSIONS AND RECOMMENDATIONS

In addition to providing housing for the Olympic Family, Accommodations was responsible for the challenging task of providing affordable and accessible accommodations for the general public who visited Atlanta. The hotels and residence halls were renovated and improved to create an Olympic environment and convey southern hospitality, and consistently honored the promised reservations and rates in accordance with the law. The operations of each network proceeded generally as expected. The following recommendations are offered to future organizing committees.

■ Establish contingency plans for circumstances such as bankrupt and closed hotels which already had prepayments, facilities incapacitated by disaster, and more routine situations, such as customer dissatisfaction, overbooking, and unanticipated arrivals.

■ Hotel contracts should call for a fixed standard rate for single- and double-occupancy sleeping rooms, although suites should continue to be individually priced.

■ Place the responsibility for making Olympic Family allocations under one department.

■ To avoid conflict between sponsors, NOCs, IFs, and other constituents, make Olympic Family allocation decisions at the highest levels of the organizing committee. The allocation of extra rooms to NOCs was particularly challenging due to difficulties in communication, continuous requests for changes, and the inability to collect payments in a timely manner.

■ Having an off-site external reservation and invoicing service impeded ACOG's ability to respond to changes in a timely manner. Use the latest computer technology to manage inventory and accounting on-site.

■ In creating inventory, consider that a large percentage of visitors may make alternate arrangements for their stay in the host city or delay making arrangements until immediately before the Games.

■ Housing for extra team officials and grooms should be managed by Olympic Villages, which has the best modes of communication with NOCs.

■ The technical competition officials and press should be allocated their own housing villages, as these groups expect to be housed together in proximity to their designated venues.

■ The organizing committee should have a standard policy regarding staff and volunteer housing, which is managed by the Accommodations function.

■ Extensive operational details should be included in the standard agreements for campus-style space, such as trash removal, after-use cleaning requirements, and damaged and lost key charges.

■ Contracting with an outside vendor for housing management services simplifies payroll and procurement for Games-time operations.

■ If private housing is used, recognize that not all units will meet clients' expectations, and housekeeping services need close monitoring.

CHAPTER THREE
ACCREDITATION

ACCREDITATION EMPLOYEES

Date	Staff Number
June 1993	2
January 1996	13
July 1996	58

Note: These staff numbers do not include contract, VIK, and volunteer personnel.

OVERVIEW—According to the IOC's *Entries for Sports Competitions* and *Accreditation Guide*, "The purpose of accreditation is to identify and register all persons involved in the staging of an Olympic Games, and to ensure that they may have access, in the quickest, safest, most practical and efficient way, to the sites and events which they must...attend within the framework of their function." Under IOC mandate and Rule 66 of the *Olympic Charter*, the Accreditation Department established, managed, and implemented appropriate accreditation policies and procedures and devised equitable and consistent ways to apply them.

An accreditation badge was issued to all individuals with a confirmed role or function at the Games to allow them access to perform their role or function. Accreditation, regarded primarily as a work permit, was granted to Olympic Family members whose presence at a venue or venues was permitted by *Olympic Charter* rules and to ACOG personnel and associated service providers deemed necessary to stage the Games. Using the accreditation database, responsible authorities approved applications before badges were issued.

The Olympic Family Department confirmed accreditation policies affecting members of the Olympic Family, including athletes, team officials, press, and broadcasters. Through ACOG Government Relations, the Olympic Family Department supplied information for discussions and negotiations with relevant US agencies—primarily the US Department of State and Immigration and Naturalization Service (INS)—leading to the development and implementation of the Olympic identity card (OIC).

In mid-1992, the IOC created its *Accreditation Guide* to introduce new definitions, particularly for accreditation categories. ACOG agreed to use the new guide as long as doing so did not result in increased financial responsibilities or operational difficulties.

The Accreditation Department was responsible for planning, organizing, and implementing the production and delivery of badges and the registration of all participants.

ORGANIZATION

During the first four years of accreditation planning, the Accreditation Department reported to the managing director of the Operations Department. The Accreditation Operations division was responsible for planning, organizing, and implementing the production and delivery of the accreditation badges, including registration of all participants. The Policy division was developed from and interacted primarily with Olympic Family and Protocol. A Steering Committee, comprised of representatives from ACOG functional areas, was formed to develop detailed accreditation policies. The result was an accreditation matrix that defined the type of accreditation, access rights, and other privileges granted to each constituency. The committee was also given the mandate to create operational sites for centers and technology development.

In response to problems observed with the preregistration and data management of all participants to be accredited at the 1995 test events, it was determined that more emphasis needed to be placed on the accreditation operations function. By late August 1995, all responsibilities for accreditation had been restructured into a separate Accreditation Department, within which two clearly defined divisions of Operations and Policy were established. A new director was hired, who reported directly to the COO.

OPERATIONS

The Operations division planned, developed, managed, and staffed all accreditation facilities. This division was separated into three subdivisions:

■ Facilities Planning, which organized all accreditation centers, rebadging centers, and venue accreditation offices;

■ Accreditation Personnel, which identified staffing requirements and recruited, hired, assigned, and trained all paid and volunteer personnel; and

■ Facilities Operations, which ensured operation of all accreditation facilities.

Accreditation Centers

Accreditation operated 10 full-service accreditation centers as well as facilities at most venues to process all constituents as efficiently as possible. Pre-Games goals were to complete the physical, technological, and logistical preparations for all of the centers well in advance of the Games. Plans specified principles and procedures, the scope and schedule of operations, technology necessary to support Accreditation at the headquarters and center levels, staffing requirements and schedules, signage needs, process-flow diagrams, daily checklists, relationships with other ACOG departments, and time lines.

Main Accreditation Center. The main accreditation center (MAC) opened 15 April 1995 and was used during test events and for training Accreditation staff. The center was also used for prebadging activities and bulk badg-

ing. The facility was located in ACOG's offices at 270 Peachtree Street in downtown Atlanta and was zoned with public access. The center was open 16 hours daily and operated by 298 staff members. It had 13 badging stations and 18 terminals to process accreditation for ACOG staff and contractors.

Airport Welcome Center. Planning for the 1996 Olympic Games was based on the idea that at least one million visitors would arrive by airplane. Hartsfield Atlanta International Airport expected as many as 150,000 passengers per day on the five days prior to the Opening Ceremony. The airport agreed to lease a hangar and adjoining parking facilities for use as an Olympic processing center which was named the Airport Welcome Center (AWC). Establishing this center near the city's main airport provided a convenient location for the initial processing of Olympic Family members away from the congestion inside the terminal. The objective was to move Olympic Family members quickly through the airport, transport them to the processing center for accreditation and baggage claim, and then provide transportation to accommodations.

The 110,000 sq ft (10,230 sq m) aircraft hangar used for the AWC provided space for logistical operations in the rear and offices on the second floor for ACOG functional area operations and management of the venue. In front of the hangar, a large paved area provided space for a terminal capable of accommodating 92 buses and a 40,000 sq ft (3,720 sq m) tent for baggage handling. Adjacent to the hangar, a separate, secure staging area was established for Olympic Village residents. All buses going to the Olympic Village were sanitized before entering the staging area, and a nearby maintenance building was used to x-ray baggage going to all Olympic Villages.

The Airport Welcome Center inside an aircraft hangar adjacent to Hartsfield Atlanta International Airport is shown before temporary construction *(top)* and just prior to Games-time *(bottom)*.

The AWC acted as the primary accreditation site for many Olympic Family members, NOC delegations, press and broadcasters, sponsors, accredited security personnel, and out-of-town volunteers.

Inside the hangar, a 71,000 sq ft (6,603 sq m) tent provided an air-conditioned, comfortable environment. The facility was operated by 667 staff members and accommodated 14 accreditation check-in computer stations, 28 accreditation badging stations, and 2 help offices, each with 6 help stations. A common entrance or atrium provided space for information, communication, and banking services; two accreditation badging areas for dignitaries and officials; and a sponsor hospitality area.

ACOG offered Olympic sponsors the opportunity to lease space at the AWC facilities to assist their executives and guests with arrival and departure arrangements, baggage handling, and ticketing. A total of 24 sponsors established operations at the site.

Delta Air Lines was the signature sponsor for the AWC. Delta provided three baggage carousels for arriving and departing bags, ample baggage storage racks, 18 full-service ticket counters, and a security checkpoint for departing guests. Delta also supplied staff and equipment to move bags from the main terminal to the AWC, identify athlete baggage for sanitization, and resolve issues related to lost baggage.

As a transportation terminal, the AWC provided bus service to more than 160 different locations throughout Atlanta and the Southeast. *(For more information on arrival and departure services, see the Transportation chapter.)*

Overall, the AWC processed accreditation for over 40,000 Olympic Family members and 45,000 sponsor guests. More than 75,000 individuals were accredited and 6,000 people uniformed. In addition, some 225,000 pieces of baggage were transferred through the baggage handling area.

Staff Processing Center. The staff processing center, which was housed in the uniform distribution center (UDC), was located in metropolitan Atlanta and began operating on 1 June 1996. The center employed 110 staff members, who used 10 terminals and 2 stations to accredit volunteers and rebadge some ACOG staff. This was a convenient accreditation center for volunteers, as they could receive badges and uniforms at the same time.

Olympic Family Hotel Center. The Olympic Family Hotel, located downtown in the Atlanta Marriott Marquis, had its own accreditation center that began operations on 5 July 1996. The Olympic Family Hotel center served the IOC, NOCs, IFs, and special guests. The facility was operated by staff equipped with two terminals at three stations.

Athlete Rebadge Center. The athlete rebadge center in the Olympic Village provided rebadging services for athletes only. It opened 5 July 1996 and was staffed by 20 people operating two terminals and three stations.

Venue Day Pass Offices. The Accreditation Department worked with Construction, Logistics, Technology, and Venue Management to design, place, and outfit at least one accreditation office for day passes at each competition venue, the Main Press Center, and the International Broadcast Center. The number of offices needed per venue was determined by the physical layout of the site and the number of people anticipated.

Operating plans were customized for each competition venue. Appendices to the plans included a key venue contact list, protocol for supplemental requests, lists of zones and other codes, an explanation of access control support, venue zones with anticipated challenges and solutions, pictogram and zone signage plans, and staffing responsibilities and requirements. Venue day pass offices opened on 1 July 1996.

Outlying Area Accreditation Centers.

Accreditation centers were operated in the cities hosting preliminary football matches—Birmingham, Alabama; Miami and Orlando, Florida; and Washington, DC. These centers were created to serve teams and officials who traveled directly to their competition city, rather than to Atlanta. Accreditation in the football cities operated within facilities that housed both accreditation centers and day pass offices.

Those involved in the yachting competition were accredited at the Savannah accreditation center, which opened 28 June 1996.

Each center began operating on 28 June 1996, and each had approximately 30 staff members, 2 terminals, and 2 stations.

Staffing and Games-Time Operations

Staff expansion was based on the opening dates of accreditation centers and venue offices. Virtually all staff were initially assigned to the MAC because it had the earliest start date—15 April 1995. This system provided excellent training for those who had never been exposed to accreditation center operations. Most importantly, staff members had the opportunity to adapt to the intense schedules required for successful accreditation operations.

Although individuals were assigned to either operations- or policy-oriented positions, everyone was expected to participate in resolving all issues and situations. The center manager was the final authority on all issues relating to new registration; record changes; constituent relationships; cooperation with Games Staffing, Volunteer Services, and Human Resources; management of help offices; database maintenance; and authorization of exceptions to policies. The center manager for operations managed facility design and layout, traffic flow, and queuing systems; logistics and delivery of equipment and supplies; equipment maintenance; Eastman Kodak Company and Technology liaison; center cleaning and maintenance;

building owner and security liaison; volunteer staffing; badge production, storage, and distribution; and special-group scheduling.

Accreditation and Security worked together to plan access control at the venues. Accreditation granted access privileges and provided the item that displayed those privileges. Security allowed the exercise of access privileges and enforced restrictions. Accreditation provided signage and ancillary access passes to be used by Security, as well as educational material and training on all access interpretation issues, including policy regarding supplemental access control items.

During the competitions, volunteer Accreditation officers provided access control support for Security staff regarding items, pictograms, and zones valid at a particular venue at a given time. Providing this support was a major challenge. Because many of the thousands of security personnel did not have sufficient training for enforcing a complex access and accreditation system, Accreditation officers often resolved conflicts and clarified issues.

Operating a multitude of venues with different constituencies and access needs stimulated the development of many ancillary and venue-specific accreditation items. Each venue was provided with badges that facilitated access between the time when security was in place and the time of full venue sanitization; day passes, which either enhanced existing privileges or gave a nonaccredited person access in exceptional circumstances; and passes worn by those nonaccredited individuals needing access only when venues were closed. Other ancillary items included broadcast compound passes, Olympic Family lounge passes, zone 7–only badges, cleaning staff passes, Logistics drivers badges, training site access passes, wristbands, and recovery badges and stickers for use after a venue concluded operations.

The number of ancillary items caused increased confusion, which Accreditation and Venue Management addressed through a brief seminar for all venue managers and venue security managers. The Practical Guide to Accreditation was also developed to serve as a reference guide to the myriad of items and policies.

Day passes were among the most misused accreditation items throughout the Games. Despite clearly defined rules, detailed lists of venue-specific exceptions, and management directives, many day passes were authorized for individuals who were not eligible to receive them. As in other Games, venue accreditation managers had to yield to venue and competition managers, who could authorize exceptions to policy on the issuance of passes.

POLICY

The *Olympic Charter* dictates that only those with an official role or function necessary to stage the Games are eligible for accreditation. Eligible persons are identified as Olympic Family and non–Olympic Family.

The IOC's *Accreditation Guide* defines Olympic eligibility. Based on this guide, individuals are identified under a large number of different accreditation categories.

The Policy division determined and implemented access rights for all constituent groups. It also identified, registered, and processed all individuals requiring accreditation following approved policies and procedures. The Policy division was primarily concerned with three areas:

■ Olympic Family Accreditation, which included coordinating the development, production, distribution, and management of OICs;

■ Non–Olympic Family Accreditation, which planned and implemented accreditation for staff, volunteers, service contractors, and law enforcement personnel, and identified other constituent groups that might require accreditation; and

■ Data Control, which ensured that the record of every person who might require accreditation was entered into the database and filed as a printed copy.

Additionally, the Policy division formulated regulations regarding zoning, the OIC, the Olympic accreditation badge, the radio-frequency (RF) badge, and the accreditation process.

Zoning

In order to regulate and control circulation within Olympic venues, each competition venue was divided into public areas accessible to all, including ticketed spectators, and areas reserved for accredited persons only. The latter areas were divided into zones that were restricted to persons with a functional need to be present.

Accreditation staff met with management and site designers for each venue to develop a logical zoning plan based on a generic set of zones of exclusion. The zones had the same generic definition at all competition venues.

■ 0, all zones
■ 1, field of play (competition areas)
■ 2, athlete preparation areas
■ 3, operations and administration areas
■ 4, media areas
■ 5, rights-holding broadcaster areas
■ 6, Olympic Family lounges
■ 7, accredited persons circulation areas

The Olympic Villages were divided into two zones: the international zone and the residential zone. Right to access the international zone was indicated by zone code V, and zone code R granted access to both the international and residential zones.

Zoning principles were applied consistently to venue perimeters and interiors. The concept of accredited circulation or flow (zone 7) between restricted islands (zones 1–6) was broadly applied. Sport- and venue-specific considerations played an important role in developing zoning plans. Pictogram and zone signage was developed in conjunction with each scheme.

The Olympic Identity Card

The OIC authorized Olympic Family members to enter the US to perform their Olympic duties during the Games. The OIC contained the holder's Olympic ID number, a personal identifier used to access the holder's record in the accreditation database promptly.

In 1993, ACOG began to develop OIC policies and procedures in conjunction with US government representatives. Most matters were addressed by either the State Department or INS, but a number of other governmental services were also involved, including the US Department of Justice, Department of Labor, Federal Bureau of Investigation (FBI), Department of the Treasury, and the White House.

While over a dozen different visa classifications for Olympic Family members would normally be issued, after lengthy discussions, it was agreed that the OIC would replace all necessary visa classifications except for the A visa issued to foreign diplomats. In spring 1995, operating procedures for the OIC were finalized, and it was agreed that the applicants' passports would not need to be submitted. However, in order to maintain their physical integrity, each OIC had to be submitted to the appropriate US consular post for approval and application of a tamper-resistant Centennial Seal.

When designing the OIC, ACOG used the IOC *Accreditation Guide,* which contains baseline requirements for information displayed on the cards. In addition, ACOG worked closely with the Forensic Document Laboratory of the INS to develop specifications for the OIC that would safeguard against counterfeiting, alteration, and photo substitution.

Prior to the Games, Accreditation focused on educating and establishing communication with NOCs and other organizations regarding the NOC process. ACOG personnel met with government officials in Washington, DC, and at the busiest ports of entry to explain the OIC process and answer questions. ACOG and the State Department also produced a video explaining the OIC process that was delivered to all US ports of entry and consular posts. A communication network encompassing ACOG personnel, senior State Department and INS officials, and the Olympic coordinators at US consular posts worldwide was also established. As a result, the majority of issues were resolved within 48 hours.

To address entry problems during Gamestime, an ACOG representative coordinated the international entry response team (IERT), comprised of field officers from government agencies and ACOG personnel. Operational 24 hours daily during June and July, the IERT resolved any issues that arose during the Games period, particularly at ports of entry.

Olympic Accreditation Badge

The final goal of the accreditation process was delivering to authorized individuals accreditation badges that identified them and visually displayed their specific access rights and privileges. A basic principle of Olympic accreditation is that each eligible participant may be issued only one badge. Dual or multiple applications must be individually analyzed and consolidated, where appropriate.

The accreditation category and the badge holder's name, photograph, function, and organization appeared on the accreditation badge.

Access rights were represented by pictograms indicating sports, competition venues, and noncompetition venues where access control was enforced, and symbols for zone codes and transportation privileges. For the Atlanta Games, 84 pictograms were used—31 sports and 53 service pictograms—as well as 7 zone code and 5 transportation code symbols. Inside venues, an accredited person's ability to circulate within and access restricted areas was determined by numerical codes for zones as noted earlier.

Numerous categories of accreditation badges were produced to identify people representing the various constituencies involved in staging the Games and allow them the access necessary to perform their role or function.

A transportation code was displayed next to the zone code on each badge. The codes were as follows.

■ T1 gave the bearer access to a private dedicated car and driver.

■ T2 gave the bearer access to a shared dedicated car and driver.

■ T3 provided access to the ACOG motor pool.

■ T4 provided access to an ACOG-organized bus system, such as the athlete or media networks.

■ T5 provided access to public transportation systems through a MARTA pass issued to all zone 7–accredited members during accreditation processing.

The Radio-Frequency Badge

Early in the planning process, the Security Department resolved that the accreditation badge would contain sophisticated technology that would allow it to be used for high-level security purposes. Hand geometry technology was chosen to accomplish this.

This technology incorporated a radio-frequency (RF) chip into the accreditation badge that was read when passed through specially designed and programmed portals. The badge for the 1996 Games allowed access only to points in the Olympic Village residential zone. Approximately 60,000 people required this access and were issued separate badges with RF chips, since the badge-producing equipment used for the Games was not compatible with hand geometry technology. The Accreditation Department's production of two badges for a very large population delayed the accreditation process at badging stations considerably.

The Accreditation Process

The accreditation process involved five steps:

■ preparation, production, and distribution of all required documents and instructions;

■ registration of all individuals potentially requiring accreditation into the accreditation database;

■ confirmation of eligible applicants;

■ validation of each applicant's access rights and other privileges; and

■ production and delivery of the accreditation badge.

Preparation and Distribution of Documents. Planning, producing, packaging, and distributing all necessary accreditation documents was an immense undertaking. A detailed instructional guide, the Olympic Identity Card Manual, was produced to complement OIC applications. A separate instruction manual was prepared for non–rights-holding media, since procedures and timing for distribution were different. Accreditation application forms were produced in 38 different categories.

The first documents for non–rights-holding media were sent in July 1995, while forms for rights holders were sent in December 1995. The forms were mailed to remaining Olympic Family organizations, most particularly the NOCs, in late January 1996.

Sport entry forms (inscriptions) and corresponding instruction manuals, arrival and departure forms and guides, and athlete biography forms also needed to be shipped to the responsible organizations. A warehouse was required to assemble, collate, and package more than 500,000 individual documents and ship them to some 250 organizations worldwide.

Non–Olympic Family documents—accreditation applications and background check waiver forms—were less complicated to prepare and distribute, as most organizations were local and therefore requested and obtained the necessary forms directly from the Accreditation Department.

Registration. All persons requiring accreditation were registered in the accreditation system. Data was either entered directly into the accreditation system or acquired from the Games staffing technology system (GSTS). Applications for staff, volunteers, and some contracted personnel were acquired from the GSTS. The entire database carried 265,811 individual records.

Olympic Family members were registered by the data obtained from their accreditation application forms, which were accumulated by their responsible organizations. The deadline for receiving most applications was 15 May 1996, but non–rights-holding media applications were due by 15 October 1995 and rights-holding broadcaster applications, by 15 March 1996.

Most contractors, AOB personnel, and service providers were required to complete an accreditation application form and sign a waiver to allow a background check. This process was coordinated through each responsible organization.

Confirmation of Eligibility. The submission of an accreditation application form did not guarantee an accreditation card. All persons registered in the accreditation system were confirmed in a Games-time role before they were eligible for accreditation. Eligibility for Olympic Family members was confirmed according to rules in the IOC's *Accreditation Guide.* In total, approximately 266,000 records were registered and 200,500 individuals badged.

Validation of Access Rights. All access rights were assigned in accordance with the requirements of each approved function. Thus, people needing accreditation were granted access to the venue(s) and the zone(s) within the venue(s) deemed necessary for the performance of their function.

The Accreditation Department coordinated with Venue Management, Sports, and other functional areas to develop a matrix that associated each position with the specific access rights (primarily the required zone codes) needed to fulfill the particular task on a permanent basis.

As names were assigned to approved functions and positions, Accreditation produced computer reports for review with the relevant venue and/or functional area manager and the responsible organization, as appropriate. On an exception basis, access rights were customized to meet the needs of persons fulfilling multiple functions or to address special zoning challenges at some venues.

Badge Production and Delivery. The procedure for delivering accreditation badges followed two approaches: bulk badging for distri-

bution at a later date, and individual badging for immediate delivery to an individual at an accreditation center.

Barring any complications or an unduly high volume of people, the badging process from check-in to check-out was no longer than five minutes. However, the badging capacity for the stations was overestimated; each station produced only 16–18 badges per hour rather than the 25–30 originally estimated.

Badge distribution to volunteers began on 1 June 1996, concurrent with the start of uniform distribution, while distribution to contractors began in early July. When the AWC opened on 25 June, individual badge distribution began. *(For the number of badges produced, including re-badges, per category per time period, during the peak badge production period of 7–19 July, see Figure 1.)*

OLYMPIC FAMILY ACCREDITATION

The accreditation categories used for members of the Olympic Family were in accordance with those prescribed by the IOC *Accreditation Guide.* ACOG expected that approximately 40,000 Olympic Family members would require accreditation, but the actual total was nearly 44,000. *(For a summary of accreditation statistical data, see Figure 2.)*

Athletes and Team Officials

The IOC determined strict criteria to regulate the number of athletes who entered and competed in each sport, discipline, and event. For the first time, well-defined qualifying standards were established for 24 of the 26 Olympic sports.

ACOG required several steps be completed to ensure that each delegation's operational needs were met, legal safeguards enacted, and the IOC's interests protected.

Contract employees received their accreditation badges at the main accreditation center.

FIGURE 1:
BADGES PRODUCED BY CATEGORY AND TIME PERIOD DURING THE PEAK PRODUCTION PERIOD

Category	To 30 June	1–6 July	7–14 July	15–19 July	After 19 July	Total
IOC		3	255	54	29	341
IF		2	39	88	11	140
NOC		17	177	521	94	809
G	10	7	49	514	244	824
GI	15	3	150	564	577	1,309
GT	7	9	153	559	650	1,378
Aa	94	617	3,763	5,593	1,327	11,394
Ac	8	72	259	162	18	519
Am		71	444	532	130	1,177
Ao	18	287	1,518	2,324	499	4,646
As	16	181	720	828	281	2,026
B	22	38	354	575	273	1,262
O	2	7	119	140	125	393
J	24	74	408	1,300	532	2,338
I *	10	11	334	816	1,989	3,160
Y			6	445	8	459
Subtotal	**226**	**1,399**	**8,748**	**15,015**	**6,787**	**32,175**
E	133	383	1,657	3,150	631	5,954
RT	887	1,179	3,844	3,241	729	9,880
AOB	837	655	1,585	1,048	461	4,586
Subtotal	**1,857**	**2,217**	**7,086**	**7,439**	**1,821**	**20,420**
ACOG	41,150	5,920	10,286	7,913	4,671	69,940
SC	17,619	13,603	22,440	17,200	16,181	87,043
Xs	4,914	3,112	4,541	2,153	1,904	16,624
Subtotal	**63,683**	**22,635**	**37,267**	**27,266**	**22,756**	**173,607**
Total	**65,766**	**26,251**	**53,101**	**49,720**	**31,364**	**226,202**

*Includes guest residents at the Olympic Family Hotel

Reception Procedures and Process. The NOC reception process was managed jointly by Accreditation, Olympic Villages, and Sports. The NOC chef de mission or other designee was required to complete the reception process before any delegation member received an accreditation badge or resided in an Olympic Village.

Sports was responsible for the receipt of sports entry forms, verification of qualification, and communicating with the IFs and the IOC on qualification and invitation matters. The Olympic Villages Department was responsible for reception meetings, financial matters, housing allotment, and general administration. Accreditation was responsible for *Olympic Charter* Rule 42 calculation, functions and access privileges for all delegation members, and the accreditation database.

Rule 42 guidelines determined how many team officials were allowed to reside in the Olympic Villages and how many extra team officials, not allowed to live in the Villages, could receive accreditation. The number of team officials allowed depended on the number of registered, qualified athletes; therefore, the final composition of the NOC delegation could not be determined until the reception process was completed.

Once these quotas were calculated, Accreditation reviewed the NOC delegation with the chef de mission, verifying each person's participation, function, and access privileges, while adhering to the quotas. After the final composition of the delegation was determined, Accreditation modified accreditation categories, functions, and access privileges before designating which persons on the original list could receive accreditation. Each NOC was required to pay all outstanding debts to ACOG prior to accreditation and occupancy of the Olympic Villages.

The reception process for the Centennial Games was more complex and challenging than at previous Games. The qualifying standards were new, complicated, and not easily understood by all NOCs. Some NOCs failed to grasp the intricacies of Rule 42 and discovered that their preferred operating structure was not permissible. Also, entry by name information, which influenced all aspects of the reception process, was not officially due until the day before the Olympic Villages opened because of

FIGURE 2: ACCREDITATION STATISTICAL DATA

Category	Description of constituents	Records registered	Individuals badged	Badges issued*
A	Test print	59	59	2,360
Aa	Athletes	16,466	10,705	11,394
Ac	Chefs de mission, deputy chefs de mission, and Olympic attachés	497	455	519
ACOG	ACOG	64,154	59,924	69,940
ACOG2	ACOG/MAOGA	1	1	1
Am	NOC medical personnel, physicians, physiotherapists, etc.	1,102	975	1,177
Ao	NOC team officials: coaches, team leaders, equipment managers, etc.	5,078	4,155	4,646
AOBa	AOBa	11	10	12
AOBb	AOBb	3,597	3,351	3,800
AOBc	AOBc	847	713	774
As	NOC extra team officials and grooms (not eligible for Olympic Village accommodation)	2,170	1,665	2,026
B	Miscellaneous: IOC commission members and personnel, IF technical delegates and board members, organizing committee senior executives, sponsors, Olympic project leaders	1,211	1,080	1,262
E	Journalists	3,653	3,021	3,145
EC	Press center support personnel	508	423	445
ENR	Non–rights-holding media	394	295	316
EP	Photographers	952	826	847
EPs	Sport-specific photographers	216	188	204
Es	Sport-specific journalists	396	310	333
ET	Press/photo technicians	371	308	317
EX	Local media	347	324	347
G	High-ranking official guests: sovereigns, heads of state or government, and sports ministers; presidents and directors-general of other Olympic organizing committees; and senior executives of TOP and COP sponsors and of rights-holding broadcasters	930	761	824
GI	Miscellaneous distinguished guests	1,394	1,165	1,309
GT	Transferable guest cards for the IOC, IFs, and NOCs, based on quotas	1,442	1,133	1,378
I	Miscellaneous guests: IF secretariat, horse owners, and Olympic Family Hotel residents	3,747	2,939	3,160
IF	IF presidents and secretaries-general (and one guest each)	134	129	140
IOC	IOC president, members, and senior management (and one guest each)	298	285	341
J	IF technical officials: jury members, technical commission members, referees, judges, etc.	2,255	2,171	2,338
NOC	NOC presidents and secretaries-general (and one guest each)	832	707	809
O	Observers from organizing committees and other major sport event organizers	376	332	393
RTa	High-ranking executives and team leaders of rights-holding broadcasters	220	195	211
RTb	Directors, producers, and commentators; technical, production, and administrative personnel of rights-holding broadcasters	7,253	6,642	6,969
RTc	Production, technical, and administrative personnel of rights-holding broadcasters, functioning exclusively at the IBC	2,891	2,576	2,700
SC	Service contractors	124,976	78,240	87,043
X	Law enforcement	5,825	4,511	5,873
Xo	Law enforcement (observers)	137	109	131
Xs	Law enforcement	847	666	771
Xu	Law enforcement (uniformed)	9,762	8,761	9,849
Y	Olympic Youth Camp participants	462	441	459
Total		**265,811**	**200,551**	**228,563**
Totals by group				
Olympic Family		55,595	44,206	48,009
ACOG staff and volunteers		64,155	59,925	69,941
AOB		4,455	4,074	4,586
Service contractors		124,976	78,240	87,043
Law enforcement		16,571	14,047	16,624
Others		59	59	2,360
Total		**265,811**	**200,551**	**228,563**

*All badges issued including rebadges.

HANS DIETER BECK • HELEN M BECK • JAMES E BECK • JAMES PAUL BECK • JENNIFER K BECK • JERRY W BECK • JIMMY B BECK • JOHN D BECK • JUDITH E BECK • KAY BECK • KENDRA L BECK • LYNNE H BECK • MARILYN Y BECK • PAULA S BECK • ROBERT E BECK • SACHIKO S BECK • THEODORA C BECK • TIMOTHY BECK • JAMES L BECK II • RICHARD D BECK JR • KRISTIN A BECK MT • JOY M BECKEN • BRODIE BECKER • CHARLES M BECKER • DARA BECKER • DIRK BECKER • JAMES M BECKER • JANET F BECKER • JOHN N BECKER • JONATHAN BECKER • KAREN A BECKER • KIMBERLEY M BECKER

59

qualifying event schedules, thus mandating completion of a large amount of work in a short time period.

Non–Rights-Holding Media

The initial accreditation quotas for the non–rights-holding press were delivered by the IOC in June 1995. Accreditation application forms and corresponding materials were sent to the NOCs as planned in mid-July with a return deadline of 15 October 1995. The deadline was met by most nations, but cancellations or substitution requests for approximately 15 percent of the E category followed.

In November 1995, the IOC Press Commission requested printed reports by nation of press accreditation forms already registered, in order to begin the quota reallocation process. By mid-November, the first reallocation of press quotas was confirmed by the IOC, and Accreditation forwarded the necessary application forms to the selected organizations.

A final reallocation was planned for March, but did not occur until May 1996. The delay of this allocation prevented approximately 600 journalists from obtaining an OIC. Instead, they had to comply with normal visa procedures.

All non–rights-holding media were transferred from the E category to the ENR category later in the accreditation process on advisement by the IOC. The obscurity of the rights of the ENR category media members was particularly apparent when at least four organizations lost their accreditation privileges during the Games because they infringed on broadcasters' rights.

Rights-Holding Broadcasters

Most groups and individuals in this category who handled accreditation for their organizations were familiar with the policies and procedures. After negotiations on numbers by category were completed, only minor adjustments were necessary.

Almost all application forms and OICs were completed correctly and on time. Most challenges came from the US broadcaster, NBC,

because of its immense size, and the South American Union, because of the number of its affiliates.

Other Olympic Family Members

The other Olympic Family members category covers a wide spectrum of groups and individuals ranging from IOC members, IF and NOC presidents and secretaries-general, IF technical officials, observers, Olympic Youth Camp participants, IOC and IF commission members and staff, and a variety of dignitaries and other guests. In general, most accreditation application forms were received on schedule.

Complications arose concerning the accreditation of dignitaries and other guests. ACOG policy, with the support of the IOC, required strict adherence to the definition of very high-ranking officials in the G category. Information on the eligibility criteria was well distributed, and favorable relationships were established with many organizations claiming G guests. However, immediately before and during the Games, many unannounced dignitaries and other guests presented themselves at the Olympic Family Hotel accreditation center. The Olympic Family Department was asked to verify or refute these requests based on agreed-upon and existing policies. Establishing the actual role of these persons and determining the appropriate accreditation categories and access rights in accordance with the policies proved challenging.

The management of transferable GT accreditation progressed well once eligible organizations understood the procedures and determined the breakdown between nominative and/or personal cards. In the GI category, more than 53 percent of those accredited were IOC guests, a higher percentage than anticipated. Additionally, there were numerous requests for more extensive access privileges than those designated.

The IOC determined strict criteria to regulate the number of accredited athletes.

NON–OLYMPIC FAMILY ACCREDITATION

Non–Olympic Family eligibility applies to persons not specifically covered in the *Olympic Charter* but who are directly or indirectly connected to the organization of the Games. This group includes staff and volunteers, host broadcasters, service providers, and security personnel. ACOG expected to accredit approximately 110,000 people in this category, but more than 156,000 were actually accredited.

Most non–Olympic Family persons were grouped under four main accreditation categories: ACOG, for staff and volunteers; AOB, for host broadcaster personnel; SC, for service contractor personnel; and X, for law enforcement personnel.

These constituents represented 78 percent—156,200 out of 200,500—of the total number accredited. They also accounted for 78 percent of the total number of badges produced, including rebadges—178,200 out of 228,600. The number of accredited people in the non–Olympic Family groups was approximately equal to the total number originally projected.

Despite extensive efforts to capture photos in advance and communicate the importance of early accreditation to non–Olympic Family members, thousands of non–Olympic Family constituents were badged during the peak period. The week before the Opening Ceremony, Accreditation produced 70,300 badges—more than double the badges Barcelona produced during the same period. More specifically, the peak day in Barcelona saw 7,200 badges produced, contrasted to the 13,273 badges produced in Atlanta on 15 July.

Staff and Volunteers

Much organizational focus was on the staffing process for volunteers and paid staff. Each department directly affected, such as Ac-creditation, Games Staffing, Human Resources, and Volunteer Services, appointed key personnel to interact with other ACOG functional areas.

Games Staffing and Computer Systems. The most challenging aspect of staff and volunteer accreditation was establishing procedures that worked well with computer systems (GSTS and the accreditation database) that were originally developed for different, and not necessarily compatible, purposes. Staff and volunteer records were transferred from GSTS into the accreditation database after completion of their required background checks.

The time line for assigning thousands of volunteers and properly constructing the accreditation system had to be tightly managed because it affected both computer systems. As the operational interdependencies became more complex, it was imperative to have accurate data. It was also critical that the managers from Accreditation, Human Resources, and Volunteer Services be familiar with computer systems and their operation. Overall, the interface between the GSTS and accreditation database worked well, and job assignments and access rights were effectively matched.

A key factor in the efficiency of this effort was the creation of the accreditation position-function table, which determined access rights for each job at each venue. The Accreditation Department produced a table of some 1,500 functions by regrouping many Games Staffing titles under more generic descriptions. However, some gains were offset when it was decided just two months before badge production began that a person could be assigned to only one position in GSTS. Any additional job assignments or responsibilities had to be translated into different zone codes or pictograms and managed directly by Accreditation. Of the 57,000 staff and volunteers, 16 percent or 9,400 had more than one assignment. All of these records had to be treated individually, therefore creating 1,020 new function codes in the accreditation database.

Pre-Badge Photo Capture. The equipment supplied by Kodak for badge production allowed photos of individuals who might need accreditation at a later date to be captured separately in stand-alone mode and stored in memory for future use.

To accommodate large corporate volunteer groups (Corporate Council companies) and volunteer organizations at remote sites, the photo capture process for volunteers started in March 1995, often before the volunteers were registered in the system. The process was accomplished by inviting groups to the MAC or by organizing a mobile unit that traveled to process specific groups.

Images captured with only a registration number were difficult to synchronize with the registration database. As a result, many exceptions had to be researched manually. On the positive side, advance photo capture enabled accreditation badges to be produced in bulk without the bearer's presence. About 22,000 volunteer badges were processed in bulk. These badges were printed as planned in mid-May and taken to the UDC for distribution with uniforms, which began 1 June.

Contractor Personnel

Contractors were defined as the non–Olympic Family workforce—other than ACOG staff, volunteers, AOB, and law enforcement personnel—needing access to Olympic venues to perform an approved function.

Registration. Accreditation processing for contractors followed the regular accreditation procedures for staff and volunteers, including a background check. The objective was to register as many contractor personnel as possible prior to the 15 May deadline for return of Olympic Family accreditation applications, and to process as many as feasible before most Olympic Family arrived during the two weeks prior to the Games.

The process started in early fall 1995, targeting known contractor organizations through

sponsors and venue operators. By 4 June 1996, 294 contractor organizations had been identified, but Accreditation registered more than twice as many in the next few weeks. In all, Accreditation registered 125,000 individuals representing 792 contractor organizations.

The late identification and registration of contractors complicated the Accreditation process during a critical period and, in some situations, delayed workers in getting to venues.

Two-Part Badges. The staff of many contractor organizations and the number of organizations greatly exceeded all expectations. In many cases, deadlines were not met; therefore, a two-part badge needed to be created for many companies.

The first part of the two-part badge system was a primary accreditation badge containing accreditation category, photograph, name, organization, and registration number, without any access rights or a bar code. Thirty-six percent of all contractors (27,800) and 8 percent of all law enforcement personnel (1,300) were issued these badges. The second part, also called the privilege pass, displayed the organization's name, access rights, and bar code. It was produced separately in more limited quantity and given to relevant organizations. Contractors were then responsible for issuing the privilege passes to their staff either as they arrived at the venue or as they were dispatched from an off-site location.

The two-part badge deflected many problems at the accreditation centers, since contractor personnel could be badged without assignment confirmation while the access rights required for their assignments were managed through the privilege pass. However, the two-part badge system confused access controllers at venues, and duplicate records management was ineffective. Further, if an individual's badge was canceled, it could not be detected at the venue, since the first part of the badge did not contain a bar code, while the bar code on the privilege part of the badge was still valid.

Law Enforcement

At previous Games, the term "security" often included law enforcement, military, private, and other security force personnel. For the Atlanta Games, the X accreditation category (and its derivatives Xo, Xs, and Xu), normally associated with all security personnel, encompassed only official law enforcement personnel (14,000 accredited). The total law enforcement personnel eventually accredited greatly exceeded the anticipated number. Law enforcement personnel were exempt from background checks, since they were verified through the OIC process or their agencies. Other types of security personnel were divided between the SC and ACOG categories. The SC category included contracted private security and most military personnel (18,000), while the Security Department's staff and volunteers (9,700) were accredited in the ACOG category.

DATA CONTROL AND TECHNOLOGY

Four full-time data entry clerks began work in March 1996, and 10 were added in May. It was anticipated that the data entry clerks would also manage the registration of contractors and law enforcement personnel during that period.

The workload increase was underestimated in both volume and timing, and data entry staff had to be increased to some 25 persons from May to early July. The greatest overload was caused by late applications from contractors and law enforcement personnel. Peak data entry for the SC and X categories was during the first weeks in July, when many data entry resources focused on Olympic Family matters. *(For the number of records entered in the accreditation database, see Figure 3.)*

One important prerequisite to a successful, efficient accreditation operation is data integrity. Strong directives requiring several steps of data verification and reconciliation were given to the data entry staff.

Although data entry staff was increased as application processing intensified, the number and urgency of applications was so great that they could not meet the demand. The insufficient number of staff required that many ACOG functional areas and contractor organizations assign personnel to assist with data entry for their

FIGURE 3:
RECORDS ENTERED IN ACCREDITATION DATABASE

Period	Olympic Family	E	RT and AOB	SC	X	Total
11 Dec 95–14 March	–	4,453	–	5,255	565	10,273
15 March–14 May	359	323	5,372	21,626	5,595	33,275
15 May–30 June	29,833	1,313	6,935	50,552	6,367	95,061
1–19 July	5,803	617	2,103	38,826	3,016	50,365
After 19 July	2,399	131	407	8,718	1,028	12,683
Total	**38,394**	**6,837**	**14,817**	**124,977**	**16,571**	**201,657**

Note: Excludes staff and volunteer records, which were acquired through the GSTS.

groups. Given the time limitation, there was no practical way to monitor the process and enforce consistent procedures for these personnel. Additionally, many forms were illegible, incomplete, or for personnel who had already submitted an application. In general, processing a large number of records in a short period of time causes errors and violates data integrity.

Technology, which was needed to support the data entry and data integrity functions, was also critical to the success of Accreditation. Among the essential elements was a central repository of information—a well-organized and accurate database to store information on persons to be accredited and listings of all responsible organizations, Olympic functions, accreditation categories, and access privileges. To support this system, management information systems must

SHARON BEHAN • MICHAEL J BEHR • SANDRA K BEHR • MICHAEL BEHUNIN • JUNE A BEIL • DANIEL D BEILMAN • MARY L BEILSMITH • KATHLEEN A BEINKE • BARBARA R BEIRNE • CHRISTOPHER J BEIRNE • CHRISTOPHER S BEIRNE • LEE B BEITCHMAN • LESLIE G BEITCHMAN • MERID BEKELE • JANET BEKENN • AILEEN M BEL • CARI LYNN BELANGER • JANE M BELANGER • JANICE A BELANGER • MARCEL BELANGER • MARIO BELANGER • ELENA J BELANSKY • MICHAEL S BELARMINO • ROSINA BELCASTRO • DEBORAH O BELCHER • RAYE J BELCHER • RONALD E BELCHER • TONYE D BELCHER •

63

provide reports and other analytical tools.

The accreditation system required information from and provided information to a number of other Games management systems, including Games Staffing, Sports, arrivals and departures, athlete biographies, background checks, Info'96, and results.

The most visible aspect of accreditation technology is the equipment used to produce the Olympic accreditation badge. New technology used at the Centennial Olympic Games produced an accreditation badge notably different from those at previous Games.

Accreditation was supported by the Technology Department for software and hardware applications. *(For more information about accreditation technology, see the Technology chapter.)*

CONCLUSIONS AND RECOMMENDATIONS

Olympic accreditation is an extremely complex and critical responsibility that requires extensive effort, resources, and internal cooperation. Accreditation guidelines for processes should be standardized and communicated to all functional areas, service contractors, and law enforcement agencies in order to facilitate having a fair, equitable, and consistent application for all concerned. The following recommendations are offered to future organizing committees.

■ In order to ensure consistency in the implementation of policies and procedures, all matters relating to accreditation should reside within one department.

■ The value of the accreditation process is determined by how well access control can enforce the system and policies at the venues. Since both operations are complementary and interdependent, accreditation and access control should reside in one department for training and implementation.

■ All management staff, particularly accreditation center and venue day office managers, should begin training programs at least six months prior to the operational phase.

■ Effective organization and management of the accreditation database is critically important. Work flow from reception meetings to data entry to file management to help offices in the processing area should be efficient and well-organized. A system function that searches for duplicate entries as data is entered is required to reduce the incidence of multiple entries.

■ The volume of accreditation data and the time required to enter it should not be underestimated.

■ Accreditation badge and uniform distribution to staff and volunteers should occur at the same location.

■ When determining the number of guests to be accredited, consider the added draw on associated resources the organizing committee must provide, such as free seating in the Olympic Family stands for events and Opening and Closing Ceremonies and transportation access privileges.

■ Stagger the processing of each constituent group to optimize the productivity of available resources and to avoid creating overloads on critical dates. All local applicants should be processed at least two weeks prior to the Games.

■ Schedule regular meetings with NOCs to resolve issues.

■ Standardize policies and procedures for access to venues prior to use of the accreditation badge.

■ Coordinating the OIC with government agencies should begin at least four years before the Games.

■ If bulk badging is implemented, the accreditation system should make a distinction between a badge that has only been printed and one that has been printed and delivered.

■ Future Games accreditation systems should have the ability to carry a table of all media quotas, by responsible organization and category.

ATLANTA OLYMPIC BROADCASTING

CHAPTER FOUR
ATLANTA OLYMPIC
BROADCASTING

OVERVIEW—Atlanta Olympic Broadcasting (AOB) 1996 was the ACOG department responsible for providing complete television coverage of the 271 Olympic sports competitions, ceremonies, and celebrations to an international viewing audience by coordinating with rights-holding broadcasters from around the world. As the host broadcaster of the Games, AOB's overall mission comprised four distinctive responsibilities:

- To design and operate the IBC, the center for the creation of all television and radio broadcasts of the Games. Located in the Georgia World Congress Center (GWCC), the IBC was the hub for both AOB's and rights holders' broadcast operations.
- To produce, develop, and deliver professional, unbiased international radio and television signals (often referred to as the international signal or world feed) from the venues to the International Broadcast Center (IBC).
- To provide facilities and services for rights-holding broadcasters such as broadcast equipment and telecommunication links.
- To maintain an Olympic Games archival service while producing features for international broadcasters.

By the conclusion of the Games, AOB had successfully supplied rights-holding broadcasters with more than 3,000 hours of coverage, transmitted to over 214 countries and territories worldwide. The 17-day cumulative global audience of more than 19.6 billion people made the Centennial Olympic Games the most watched sporting event in history.

International broadcasters attained rights-holding status after purchasing exclusive Olympic television rights from ACOG and the IOC. Television rights fees were ACOG's largest source of revenue, grossing a record $896 million, approximately 33 percent of total revenue generated. *(For information on television rights fees, see Figure 1 as well as the Financial Services chapter.)*

Early in its operations phase, AOB made the distinction between unilateral productions, which were produced by individual broadcasters, and multilateral productions, which were produced or created by AOB, and organized various services to support each type of production.

ORGANIZATION

Beginning in 1991 as ACOG's host broadcast planning group, AOB spent its initial development phase organizing and hiring personnel. In December 1991, ACOG selected an Olympic Games veteran with more than 25 years of experience in international broadcasting to lead the broadcasting operation.

AOB followed the model created by Radio Televisio Olimpica 1992 (RTO'92) in Barcelona when creating its broadcast operation. RTO'92 was the first host broadcaster in the history of the Games to be part of the local organizing committee. With the Centennial Games continuing to expand—attracting a record number of athletes, attending countries, and visitors—and the complexity of the broadcasting operation intensifying, ACOG also opted to internalize the broadcasting function.

AOB was separated into seven divisions: Planning and Information, Booking, Production, Engineering and Operations, Support Services, Broadcast Venue Management, and Business Affairs and Personnel.

Planning and Information

To ensure operational efficiency, the Planning and Information division coordinated and organized work schedules and information received from the other divisions of AOB. Planning and Information also tracked venue planning for AOB and other ACOG functional areas.

As the liaison between rights holders and AOB, Planning and Information also acquired and distributed information required by world broadcasters for proper coverage of the Centennial Games. Planning and Information wrote and edited all AOB publications and manuals, which were designed to fully articulate AOB's coverage philosophy. These publications included: the *Broadcasters Handbook,* Graphics Guide, Liaison Officer Training Manual, Preliminary Operations Plans, Production Guide, sport-specific Production Guidelines Manuals, Venue Operations Plans Manual, venue-specific Technical Managers Manuals, and three separate editions of the *World Broadcaster Meeting Manual.*

During the Games, Planning and Information staff assisted rights holders with acquiring information, using unilateral facilities, and administering the videotape library at all competition venues and the IBC.

Booking

The Booking division coordinated all rights-holding broadcasters' requests for facilities at the IBC, including space, furniture, equipment, electrical power, and bookable radio and television studios and edit suites. Booking also fulfilled broadcasters' unilateral requests at the

venues by reserving commentary positions, camera positions, and pre- and post-competition video feeds at all venues.

Production

The Production division produced the international video and audio signal from each sports venue. The signal was generated from a variety of full broadcast-quality cameras, which were selected and placed by Production. As a part of this signal, Production created the broadcast graphics for television coverage.

FIGURE 1:
REVENUE FOR TELEVISION RIGHTS

Broadcasting organization	Amount paid
NBC (US rights)	$456 million
European Broadcasting Union (EBU)	$247 million
Atlanta Japan Pool (AOJC) (a consortium of four Japanese broadcasting entities)	$99.5 million
Seven Network Australia	$30 million
Asia-Pacific Broadcasting Union	$5 million
Arab States Broadcasting Union	$3.75 million
Caribbean Broadcasting Union	$190,000
Canadian Broadcasting Corporation	$20.75 million
Korean Pool	$9.75 million
Organizacion de la Television Iberoamericana	$5.45 million
People's Television Network, Inc., of the Philippines	$1 million
Taiwan Pool of Taiwan and Chinese Taipei	$1.9 million
TVNZ/ASC of New Zealand	$8 million
South African Broadcasting Association	$6.75 million
Puerto Rico	$750,000

The graphics were based on ACOG's Look of the Games elements.

This division was also responsible for the production of ACOG's *Atlanta 1996* shows, which aired on NBC prior to the Games, and a

Atlanta 1996

The AOB logo incorporated elements of ACOG's torch mark logo as well as a symbol at the top representing the interconnectedness of worldwide broadcasting communications systems.

variety of other pre-Games projects, which will be discussed later in this chapter.

Engineering and Operations

The Engineering and Operations division provided the technical facilities, equipment, and staff required to implement the production plan at all venues and the IBC. Engineering and Operations coordinated data and timing systems, managed computer support and computer-aided design (CAD) systems, built commentary systems, and planned all broadcast telecommunications needs for AOB and rights holders. Engineering and Operations also set AOB's technical specifications and managed the development and procurement of special broadcast equipment.

Support Services

The Support Services division directed all logistical support, planning, and implementation of AOB operations. This division managed air and ground transportation, accommodations, shipping and receiving, accreditation, catering, uniforms, and the administration of all general services at the IBC. In addition, Support Services served as the liaison between ACOG and rights-holding broadcasters concerning their logistical needs and services.

Broadcast Venue Management

The Broadcast Venue Management division established a broadcast management team at each venue to oversee the broadcast operational plan. This team analyzed and defined AOB's on-site needs, managed the installation of broadcast equipment, and managed all AOB venue staff. As the liaison between AOB's venue operations and ACOG headquarters, Broadcast Venue Management coordinated all unilateral activity, ensuring that rights-holding broadcasters' requirements were met. This team also established procedural policies to ensure smooth

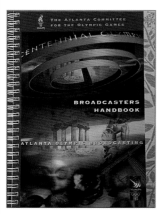

The **Broadcaster's Handbook** was given to all accredited broadcasters.

implementation of the operational plan and to resolve broadcast-related issues at the venues.

Business Affairs and Personnel

The Business Affairs and Personnel division provided financial, administrative, and personnel support to AOB. In addition, this division administered and coordinated all broadcast equipment, construction, and other vendor/staff contracts. The student Host Broadcast Training Program (HBTP) at Clark Atlanta University also evolved under the guidance of this division.

AOB Pre-Games Operations

By spring 1993, the leadership of all AOB divisions was in place. Pre-Games operations included broadcaster meetings and workshops, venue space allocation and planning, special training programs sponsored by AOB, additional staffing and contractor arrangements, and production.

International Meetings

In order to identify and meet the requirements of all international rights holders, the IOC, and its own staff, AOB held a series of international meetings prior to the Games. Much of AOB's production and technical plans evolved from information obtained during these meetings.

IOC Radio and Television Commission. The IOC Radio and Television Commission visited Atlanta on a regular basis beginning in May 1991. Its role was to review and comment on Games-time preparations. Following the initial meeting, the commission formed an ad hoc group of four people which held five additional meetings with various ACOG department managers to discuss any concerns. At that time, the commission set forth time lines for ACOG specifically related to the results system, media transportation, and venue CAD drawings. Either the commission or the ad hoc committee met frequently during the months prior to the Games to ensure that deadlines were being met.

Unilateral and World Broadcaster Meetings. While determining technical and logistical requirements at the venues and the IBC, AOB frequently held meetings to discuss its current broadcast plans with rights-holding broadcasters. Following these unilateral meetings, rights holders formulated plans for their own unilateral productions. These meetings also provided broadcasters with the opportunity to tour venue sites and receive updates on preparations being made for Games-time broadcast operations. During the three-year period prior to the Games, AOB hosted more than 200 broadcaster visits.

In May 1994, broadcasters worldwide attended the first of three world broadcaster meetings. Held prior to each Olympic Games, these meetings traditionally allow the host broadcaster to interact with rights-holding broadcasters regarding coverage plans and pre-Games preparations. In addition, they provide rights holders with the opportunity to discuss issues and concerns with the host organizing committee.

At AOB's first world broadcaster meeting, rights holders received the *1st World Broadcaster Meeting Manual*, which discussed AOB's plans for broadcasting the Games. The manual included preliminary CAD drawings of the venues, an overview of the IBC, and the telecommunications plan. Attendees also received the AOB rate card, which outlined AOB's pricing structure for a variety of items, including commentator positions, offices, radio and television studios, videotape machines, and related services and facilities.

Held in May 1995, the second world broadcaster meeting drew almost 300 broadcasters, who reviewed updated versions of the *World Broadcaster Meeting Manual* and received the AOB rate card. Attendees again toured venues and listened to ACOG progress reports on venue planning, press operations, technology, ticket sales, accommodations, and transportation.

The third world broadcaster meeting was held in April 1996. At that time, AOB distributed a revised edition of its manual and discussed its final plans for Games-time coverage. The meeting also provided broadcasters with a final opportunity to speak with ACOG staff members on a variety of Games-related issues.

Television Workshops. AOB conducted pre-Games television workshops for archery, equestrian, fencing, rowing, and shooting events. IF authorities and AOB staff believed that certain technological innovations could greatly enhance the coverage of these particular sports. Many ideas and suggestions generated during these workshops were included in the AOB production plan.

Management Workshops. Management workshops were held in May and June 1996. Management-level venue staff gathered to discuss issues relevant to their specific venue. Attendees included venue managers, information managers, support service managers, technical managers, producers, and directors. These workshops enabled attendees to share their expectations and operational plans for the Games. In addition, copies of the Venue Operations Plans Manual, Production Guidelines Manual, and Technical Managers Manual were distributed to appropriate staff. These venue- or sport-specific publications outlined information critical to successful venue operations.

Space Allocation and Planning

After AOB began its operational phase in 1993, the various divisions focused on meeting AOB's requirements at the competition venues and the IBC. Space allocation for broadcasters and identification of AOB equipment and production facilities at the venues were paramount. AOB conducted venue tours to determine camera and commentary positions, establish compound sites, and identify technical, logistical, and informational requirements.

Development of the IBC began after AOB established certain minimum broadcast parameters, which provided a framework for construction. In addition, these parameters confronted issues such as power and space allocations for both AOB and broadcasters.

The Host Broadcast Training Program

Launched in January 1994, the HBTP was a collaborative effort between Clark Atlanta University and AOB that provided more than 900 students from 20 colleges and universities in the southeastern US with the chance to work on a professional level in the worldwide broadcast of the Centennial Olympic Games.

The students worked with technicians and broadcasters from around the world in 10 select fields: archivist, audio assistant, camera operator, commentary systems operator, graphics assistant, liaison officer, logger, spotter, video operator assistant, and videotape operator. The first program of its kind, the HBTP provided a series of advanced communications courses and technology training designed to prepare students for actual international broadcasting experience.

In addition to these professional opportunities, the program offered a breadth of training not usually available in a communications curriculum. Key elements included direct, practical instruction and experience in state-of-the-art technology and intensive study of foreign languages.

In spring 1996, HBTP students who successfully completed the necessary courses were interviewed by teams of industry professionals, who evaluated each applicant's aptness for a position. The HBTP staff then scheduled interviews and AOB decided which students to hire based on the evaluators' recommendations for available positions. More than 600 HBTP graduates earned Games-time positions.

Staffing and Contractors

By early 1996, AOB's pre-Games staff had grown substantially, but the most rapid growth was still to come. More contractors from around the world began working with AOB

and the staff grew to 3,200, including volunteers and value-in-kind staff, just prior to the Opening Ceremony.

As staff resources were finalized, AOB reached agreements with MEI (Panasonic), the BellSouth Corporation, AT&T, Henry C. Beck, Inc. (HCB), and Georgia Power. *(For information on services provided through those agreements, see Figure 2.)*

AOB also concluded contractual agreements with several broadcast organizations with sport-specific broadcasting experience. These organizations agreed to provide the production teams and mobile units necessary to guarantee proper coverage of Olympic competition.

Production

While the vast majority of AOB images and graphics were broadcast during the Games, AOB produced a substantial amount of material beforehand. Prior to the start of the Games, AOB-produced material was seen both locally and nationally. It provided not only further information about the upcoming events, but also served as a training exercise for AOB's constantly growing staff.

NBC Specials. The 10-show series *Atlanta 1996* marked the first time in Olympic history that an organizing committee produced television specials for a rights-holding broadcaster. Each show was produced by AOB's production team and aired on NBC. The shows were designed to build awareness of and excitement for the Games; reveal news concerning Atlanta and the Olympic Movement; profile Olympic hopefuls; thank the Olympic sponsors; inform the public about buying tickets, coins, bricks, and other Olympic items; and generally educate the audience about the 1996 Olympic Games. The shows also provided a forum for ACOG to openly welcome visitors to the city and introduce key people involved in the Olympic effort. US President Bill Clinton, Georgia Governor Zell Miller, and Atlanta Mayor Bill Campbell all made guest appearances.

FIGURE 2:
ORGANIZATIONS AND SERVICES PROVIDED

MEI (Panasonic)
All broadcast-related equipment and responsibility for the design and installation at the Georgia Dome, IBC, and Olympic Stadium

BellSouth
Broadcaster video and audio circuits

AT&T
Additional supporting telecommunications services

Henry C. Beck, Inc.
The IBC's major construction contractor

Georgia Power
Primary and supplemental power supplies at venues and the IBC

The series began successfully on Super Bowl Sunday, 30 January 1994. Broadcast live from the Georgia Dome as part of the pregame activities for Super Bowl XXVIII, approximately five million viewers watched the first show, making it the highest-rated nonfootball program of any network on Super Bowl Sunday in 1994.

Other *Atlanta 1996* highlights included the fourth show in the series, which was a live-to-tape special revealing the Olympic Torch Relay route. It was hosted by US sportscaster Bob Costas and Billy Payne from the floor of Olympic Stadium, which was still under construction. Other specials announced the Olympic Coin Program, Olympic Aid–Atlanta in conjunction with UNICEF, and community heroes as torchbearers in the Torch Relay.

Torch Relay. AOB produced the opening Torch Relay video, which was shown on a massive projection monitor at the Los Angeles Coliseum on 27 April 1996, the first day of the Torch Relay in the US. AOB was responsible for choosing the music, creating graphics that displayed a detailed map of the route, and video editing.

AOB-Produced Videos. A variety of AOB-produced videotapes helped explain AOB's role and progress toward broadcasting the 1996 Games. "The Making of AOB" and venue update videos were given to broadcasters and organizing committees of future Games as sources of information, while staff used the footage for various lectures and presentations.

Test Events. With AOB staff providing guidance and instruction, HBTP students gained valuable experience in television production by working at the ACOG test events as well as other local sporting competitions. Certain competitions were taped and televised on the Clark Atlanta University local access channel.

While serving as a training tool for the HBTP, test events allowed AOB staff the opportunity to familiarize themselves with the demands specific to each venue. During the competitions, AOB staff conducted various camera placement studies to determine proper lighting requirements and also tested data and timing equipment. In addition, AOB collected footage for its various sports technical features, which were eventually made available to the international broadcasting community.

MULTILATERAL COVERAGE

AOB's planning efforts focused on the production of the multilateral feed. The multilateral feed was produced at the venues by AOB staff and consisted of both audio and video signals. From the venues, the feed was transmitted to the IBC, where it was distributed to more than 170 international broadcasting organizations. Rights-holding broadcasters were then allowed to edit the signals, supplementing them with additional camera feeds and their own graphics, to fit the viewing needs of their domestic audiences. After editing, the feeds were transmitted to various countries via satellite.

Often referred to as the international radio and television signal, the multilateral feed was produced in accordance with the broadcast guidelines established by the IOC Radio and Television Commission. These guidelines state that international radio and television signals must be produced objectively, avoiding undue concentration on a particular athlete and elements of national character in interviews and on-camera appearance of commentators.

The international television signal was provided in an analog composite format conforming to 525 National Television System Committee (NTSC) TV lines at 59.94 fields per second. NTSC is the current standard used in North America. International audio for television was a two-channel, stereo sound mix derived from a combination of acoustic microphones and contemporary digital processing technology. The stereo mix was customized for each sport and venue. Audio coverage consisted of ambient sound—the sounds from athletes, fans, and equipment in and around the field of play.

The international radio signal consisted of only general ambient sound at each venue and was delivered separately from the television signal. Components of the international signal included live sports coverage, graphics and computer animation, results and timing (various statistics along with the game clock), and event explanatory features.

Broadcast Coverage Cameras

Five hundred AOB cameras, most of which used CCCD technology, were used to broadcast the Olympic sports competitions. The type and size of the cameras varied, but all were positioned to provide views that would give the television audience a sense of athletes in motion as well as the human drama inherent in Olympic Games competition. Utilizing the latest technological advances, AOB's coverage set a number of precedents in Olympic history.

The GoCam, the Cablecam, and the Skycam were all used for the first time at the Centennial Olympic Games. A small self-steady tracking camera, the GoCam was capable of following an athlete along a rail, and was used in covering several different events, including track and field. The Cablecam provided an overhead angle by following an athlete along a cable. It was utilized at events such as canoe/kayak–slalom, where it was used to follow the athletes down the Ocoee River as they navigated the course. The Skycam, which moved both vertically and horizontally along a rectangular pulley, was operated manually and provided a unique overhead view of many events, including aquatics and gymnastics.

AOB crews utilized hard cameras and steadicams for more traditional shots. The hard camera, often the main camera, is a studio-type camera mounted on a tripod in a fixed position. The steadicam, a camera attached to a special body mount worn by a camera operator, has built-in stabilizers which hold the camera steady while the operator moves, providing fluid pictures. These cameras showcased action on the field of play; close-up views of competitors; and reactions of athletes and their coaches and families.

AOB utilized more than 100 point-of-view (POV) cameras, which provided viewers a unique perspective on Olympic competition, as well as a feeling of being involved in the action. These cameras were placed anywhere from inside the goal in handball to on a bicycle in track cycling.

AOB also positioned panoramic cameras around the city of Atlanta to capture and showcase the overall beauty and magnitude of the Games.

Summary Coverage

For events that did not receive live coverage, AOB offered summary coverage consisting of competition highlights and narratives that described the action. This type of coverage was often utilized for preliminary rounds of competition. Summary coverage was transmitted twice daily at specific times and was available to rights holders at the IBC. Broadcasters were alerted prior to the transmission of each summary and given an information sheet that served as a detailed script of the upcoming summary. *(For a list of sports for which summary coverage was provided, see Figure 3.)*

Transmission

Transmission procedures were similar for each sport. Approximately 15 minutes prior to the start of each event and following any pre-event feeds, a venue wideshot appeared with a location graphic, indicating the venue or competition location, and a timetable outlining that

---

FIGURE 3:
SPORTS UTILIZING
SUMMARY COVERAGE

Archery
Preliminaries

Badminton
Preliminaries

Beach volleyball
Court two

Equestrian
Three-day event
(dressage, endurance, and
jumping)

Fencing
Preliminaries

Modern pentathlon
First four disciplines

Shooting
Preliminaries

Table tennis
Preliminaries

Tennis
Outer courts

Yachting
All races other than
those covered live

particular session's upcoming events. Five to ten minutes prior to the start of an event, the international signal runup—a term which applies to the period just prior to telecast of the actual competition—began with 30 seconds of opening animation followed by an event graphic and other venue-specific graphics such as weather reports, descriptions of the events and competitors, and start lists.

At the conclusion of competition, a three-minute countdown to the international signal began. The countdown included final results graphics and event/session video replays. It concluded with another three-minute countdown with highlights and closing animation.

Graphic Look

The AOB graphic look complemented ACOG's Look of the Games by honoring the Centennial Olympic Games, celebrating southern elegance and grace, and utilizing the Look color scheme.

Many Games icons were incorporated into AOB's design, including the sport-identifying pictograms, 1996 Games logo, and the Olympic Rings. The pictograms appeared on various graphics and were tightly cropped for greater visual impact, while the Olympic Rings were displayed on all clock presentations for the first time in Olympic history. These graphics were developed on the DPMAX Paint System and were available to all rights holders and AOB four months prior to the Games, with minor modifications occurring until June.

Results and Timing

IBM, Swatch Timing, and ACOG Technology collaborated to provide all athlete-related data for the Games through a comprehensive results system. During the Games, the results system experienced problems, including late and often inaccurate information. The problems were especially acute in the first week, when rights

holders were often unable to obtain start lists at the IBC prior to contests or final results immediately following an event. *(For further information, see the Technology chapter.)*

Features

For the first time in Olympic television history, the host broadcaster provided a series of features for rights holders' unilateral use. These features, written and produced on videotape by the AOB features unit, were created to provide information and upgrade the broadcasters' telecasts. They covered Atlanta's past, present, and future and highlighted various city museums, parks, and neighborhoods. Each feature was ready to broadcast and ranged from 1.5 to 2.5 minutes in length. They contained a mixed audio track of music and sound effects and were accompanied by a suggested English script.

AOB also produced technical features on select sports that were broadcast during the runup by AOB production teams. Broadcasters were provided with a bullet-point script and the time in the runup when the feature would air.

UNILATERAL COVERAGE

While many broadcasters relied almost entirely on the multilateral feed provided by AOB, some rights holders wished to tailor their coverage to their unique audience. To meet the needs of these broadcast organizations, AOB offered a variety of unilateral and technical facilities at each competition venue, the Olympic Village, and, most extensively, the IBC.

Booking was responsible for supplying all unilateral material the rights-holding broadcasters needed to personalize their coverage.

Placement of graphics and colors was coordinated with AOB to ensure optimal coverage.

In addition, AOB assisted rights holders in procuring services from third-party companies, such as official equipment suppliers and telecommunications carriers.

Unilateral Facilities

In order to tailor and supplement the multilateral feed, AOB provided a variety of unilateral facilities for broadcasters' use. Many of the facilities could be reserved through Booking.

Commentary Positions. Some of the best seats at events were given to approximately 1,500 commentators responsible for broadcasting the Centennial Olympic Games to the world. In addition to the best sight lines to the field of play, the selection of these positions was partially based on the space available at specific venues. Each position included a table, three chairs, a commentary unit with two headsets and individual volume controls for incoming signals, and a color television connected to the venue cable access television (CATV) network. The CATV was a closed-circuit, multichannel television system used to distribute information, venue feeds, and return feeds. It was used by broadcasters and AOB production staff at the venues and IBC.

Positions at select venues were equipped with the commentator information system (CIS), a real-time competition results system developed jointly by AOB and IBM exclusively for Olympic Games commentators. CIS provided data such as start lists, timing, results and rankings, and medal standings. This touch-screen system was available at Opening and Closing Ceremonies and at the artistic gymnastics, athletics, canoe/kayak–slalom, diving, equestrian, rhythmic gymnastics, swimming, synchronized swimming, and track cycling events.

Commentators were assisted by approximately 300 liaison officers responsible for handling any commentary unit problems and results distribution.

Observer Seats. Located next to the commentator positions, more than 2,000 observer positions were available for reservation by accredited broadcast personnel for the Games. Unreserved seats for a session were distributed in the order in which they were requested.

Commentary Control Rooms. Commentary control rooms (CCRs) were located near the commentary positions at each venue, providing a site for initial mixing of background sound and the commentator's voice. The mixed program was fed first to the broadcast telecommunications center at the venue, then to the IBC. At the IBC, the final program was routed to the broadcaster's home country by the commentary switching center (CSC).

Commentary Positions with Cameras. Broadcasters had the option of purchasing POV cameras for use within their commentary positions. The cameras, containing 750 lines of horizontal resolution and full remote-control features, could be used for on-air commentary or viewing the field of play.

Additional Camera Positions. Two additional types of camera positions were available for use. Unilateral camera positions were available for broadcasters desiring to personalize their coverage throughout the Games. Electronic news-gathering (ENG) camera positions were available for those who did not need a permanent camera position. ENG cameras are hand-held cameras often associated with television news coverage. Rather than sending signals to a mobile unit in the compound, ENG cameras record images on tape for production at a later date.

Unilateral and ENG platforms were installed at the venues in sufficient numbers to satisfy the needs of the rights holders who wanted to complement the multilateral feed with unilateral coverage. AOB liaison officers at each venue assisted rights holders with access to the ENG positions. Unoccupied ENG positions could be used by broadcasters until the rightful owner claimed the position.

Injection Points. Broadcasters wanting to send prerecorded material back to their area in the IBC or to their home countries could book injection points. These injection points, located within the technical operations centers (TOCs) at selected venues, allowed broadcasters to book their playback and transmission material from the venues to their unilateral areas in the IBC.

Mixed Zone. As specified in the *Olympic Charter*, each competition venue included a mixed zone adjacent to the field of play, where broadcasters and other accredited media could conduct short interviews with athletes immediately following events. At Olympic Stadium, AOB offered bookable camera positions complete with a camera, operator, video and audio equipment, and a four-wire coordination circuit. Broadcasters were allowed to book their own permanent positions for live cameras in the mixed zone.

Media access to athletes in the mixed zone was first given to television broadcasters, then to ENG and radio broadcasters, and then to press and photographers. AOB liaison officers and personnel from ACOG Press Operations coordinated this activity.

Pre- and Post-Unilaterals. In order to personalize their coverage further, broadcasters could book pre- and post-unilaterals (live interviews or on-camera commentary) in predetermined areas at the competition venues. These positions were generally located just outside the field of play, near the mixed zone.

Bookable pre- and post-unilateral facilities included a camera, a microphone, an operator, and a four-wire coordination circuit to the IBC. Most pre-unilaterals began 45 minutes before the start of the international signal transmission, while post-unilaterals usually began eight minutes following the international signal

transmission. AOB held three 10-minute bookable pre- and post-unilaterals for each event.

Interview Room. ACOG Press Operations administered a formal room at each venue for interviews with medal winners following competition. Each interview room was equipped with necessary lighting and audio equipment in addition to ENG camera platforms.

Media Subcenters. Media subcenters, smaller versions of the Main Press Center (MPC), were located at each competition site and in the Olympic Village. Each subcenter contained a common work area equipped with tables, chairs, telephones, televisions, facsimile machines, printers, and Info'96—ACOG's computerized information system—terminals. The subcenters, staffed by ACOG Press Operations personnel, opened two hours prior to the start of competition and closed two hours following competition's completion.

Technical Facilities

While not bookable, various technical facilities were included in each venue plan.

Compounds. The broadcast compounds were large, open areas designed specifically to provide space for AOB and broadcaster mobile units, additional technical vehicles, and trailers. Located adjacent to or sometimes inside the venue, compound area access required AOB or rights-holding broadcaster accreditation. The size of each compound varied due to production demands and the space within each venue. Space for support facilities was also included.

Mobile Units. AOB placed mobile units inside the compounds to handle broadcast production. The mobile units transmitted the production feed from inside the venue to the IBC, where it was then distributed worldwide. Mobile units were stationed at all locations except at Olympic Stadium (athletics) and the Georgia Dome (gymnastics, handball), where semipermanent production control rooms and transmission facilities were constructed. All signals at these venues were routed through a master control room within the facility, which then distributed the signals to the compounds and the IBC.

At some venues, AOB had more than one mobile unit present. Venue coverage for certain sports required multiple live feeds and was available to broadcasters at the IBC. Athletics, gymnastics, judo, tennis, and wrestling had multiple feeds during the Games.

Technical Operations Center. AOB installed a TOC in the broadcast compound at each venue that served as the quality-control and transmission point for all multilateral and unilateral video and audio signals. In addition, these centers were the venue interface for camera and microphone splits, commentator cameras, CATV, data and timing, and public address. The TOCs also served as extensions of AOB's production unit by providing graphics, archiving, and super slow-motion equipment.

Audio. AOB audio coverage consisted of specific audio and background sound based on individual venues. The mix of these sounds provided the international television sound. Ambient sound differed from sport to sport. International radio sound consisted of only the ambient sound and was provided continuously 30 minutes prior to, during, and 30 minutes after an event.

Power. Two separate power distribution systems were utilized. The first supported only technical equipment, and the second supported nontechnical (domestic) requirements. Electrical power was available to broadcasters with facilities in the broadcast compounds, CCRs, and commentator positions.

Technical power was provided from power sources isolated from all other venue loads. Domestic power was provided to nontechnical areas located within the broadcast compounds. Power was available in phase 208 V, 60 Hz; single phase 208 V, 60 Hz; and single phase 120 V, 60 Hz formats. Power generators were located in each broadcast compound to provide backup technical power. Backup generator service was able to support all technical power requirements.

Venue Teams

In order to provide successful television coverage for rights-holding broadcasters, a broadcast venue management team was positioned at each venue. Each team was directed by a broadcast venue manager with the help of an assistant venue manager. Teams comprised a manager of production, a venue technical manager, a commentary systems manager, an information manager, a chief liaison officer, and a support services manager. A producer/director and production and technical teams covered the international television and radio signals produced at the various venues and sent the signals to the IBC.

INTERNATIONAL BROADCAST CENTER

The IBC was the headquarters for all AOB facilities and for rights-holding broadcasters. Located inside the GWCC, the IBC occupied 500,000 sq ft (46,500 sq m) of space distributed throughout three floors and three exhibition halls.

The IBC housed a variety of technical and production areas, including master control rooms, studios, transmission quality and control rooms, a central videotape area for archiving Games footage, bookable edit suites, and a host of general services.

Using a computerized booking system created by AOB, the IBC booking office processed all broadcaster requests for services and facilities and coordinated contracted services at the IBC and venues. Payments for pre- and post-unilateral requests, ENG camera platforms, and other bookable items were collected immediately before and during the Games.

The AOB information office at the IBC collected and distributed information to broadcasters, including statistics, results, start lists, and news releases when available. The main information desk was open 24 hours daily and offered information about results, historical data, Olympic competition rules, and historical facts about Atlanta.

Outside the information office, mail slots contained hard copies of the latest sports results and pertinent broadcasting information for each event. Common areas of the IBC offered CIS terminals and access to Info'96.

The information office was also responsible for the Broadcaster Information Channel (BIC), a part of the CATV system that helped supplement other information sources.

Inside the main entrance, visitors nonaccredited for the Games or for the IBC could receive a day pass from AOB's day pass office. During its three-month operating period, the day pass office issued 13,670 day passes, 8,000 of which were distributed during the Games.

The IBC also housed common services for broadcasters, including a bank, a newsstand, a post office, medical and dining facilities, and snack bars.

Technical Overview

Six technical areas were located within the IBC—the distribution center, transmission center, a CSC, bookable facilities, Archive Services, and a CATV system.

Distribution Center. All incoming video and audio signals from the venues were terminated, monitored, and equalized in the distribution center before being delivered to broadcaster areas and bookable facilities. Multilateral circuits were identified, synchronized, and phased, and then received additional technical monitoring before being distributed to rights-holding broadcasters. AOB and BellSouth management and technical personnel were present at all times to ensure the continuity and quality of each signal. Unilateral circuits were then committed to the appropriate broadcaster video and audio lines.

Transmission Center. Signals from rights holders were sent to the transmission center control for routing to their home countries. In the center, signals were monitored and tested for continuity, and identification signals inserted where appropriate. Signals were then sent to an international carrier for transmission.

Commentary Switching Center. The CSC distributed all incoming commentary and coordination circuits from Olympic venues and/or other locations to broadcasters' offices throughout the IBC. The CSC was also responsible for establishing circuits required by broadcasters between venues and/or other locations; cross-connecting two circuits between different locations and the IBC; testing, establishing, and monitoring broadcasters' international four-wire circuits; providing the coordination circuits and facilities needed for bookable venue unilateral transmissions, and switching these circuits to the broadcasters' home country or IBC unilateral areas; providing and operating circuits and facilities needed for AOB internal technical coordination of the international feeds; and establishing and supervising transmission from the off-tube booths. It was necessary to use 2,500 four-wire circuits to coordinate this vast network.

Bookable Facilities. A fully staffed radio studio and six edit rooms were available to rights-holding broadcasters through the booking office.

Archive Services. Recordings of all live venue feeds, IOC press conferences, and non-live ENG summaries were available to broadcasters through the AOB Archives Services function in the IBC library. Copies of all recordings made by AOB could be purchased by rights-holding broadcasters. Selected isolated camera-shot reels and playback reels from the various venues were also available in the library, as was all archival footage from the pre-Games period.

All video and audio signals were digitally recorded using Panasonic NTSC format. For

NBC, the US rights holder, operated within the IBC.

the video signal, only the host graphic presentations accompanied the pictures, while AOB utilized the television international sound for the audio signal. Detailed logs of each recording were provided.

An additional D-3 backup recording for each event was made at the various competition locations and contained the same video and audio information as the master recordings at the IBC. At the end of each competition day, these backup recordings were shipped to the IBC library for storage. Following the Games, the materials collected by AOB Archive Services were given to the ACOG and IOC archives in D-3 format.

Cable Access Television Network. The CATV network installed at the IBC was available to rights holders upon request. The CATV network had 60 channels and carried all international signals generated by AOB at the venues. Unilateral signals could be included by arrangement with the booking office.

TELECOMMUNICATIONS

AOB was responsible for providing rights-holding broadcasters with the international television and radio signals, producing the video and audio components at the venues, transporting those signals to the IBC for distribution, and facilitating the transmission of those signals around the world.

Television Contribution Network

The television contribution network was a communications system by which all unilateral and multilateral audio, video, commentary, telephone, and data systems were delivered from the Olympic venues to the IBC. Transmission methods included fiber optics, microwave, satellite, and wire line. The routing pathway for both unilateral and multilateral video and audio signals from Atlanta-area venues to the IBC was an optical fiber SONET ring configuration transmitted at the full bandwidth of 150 Mb per second. Signals from

outlying venues were transmitted to the IBC via optical fiber or satellite facilities under an agreement between AOB and AT&T.

Distribution Network

The distribution network was the delivery system for sending unilateral signals from the IBC to viewers worldwide. AOB, together with AT&T, assisted broadcasters in acquiring international transmission facilities. AOB reached an agreement with AT&T to provide video and audio transmission to international satellite uplinks and international commentary audio facilities.

CONCLUSIONS AND RECOMMENDATIONS

As the largest sporting event in the world, the Olympic Games provided AOB with one of the greatest challenges in the history of broadcast television. Over a 17-day period, the host broadcaster provided Games coverage for a cumulative television audience of approximately 19.6 billion people.

The success of AOB can be attributed to the production quality of the coverage; the addition of state-of-the-art POV cameras and other advanced technology; and increased coverage for the Games, with ample room and services for its own broadcast operations.

To ensure the success of the world broadcast feed:

■ Test the application of the results and information system one year prior to the Games to ensure reliability. This testing should be a stipulation of the contract with the technology sponsor company.

■ Complete CAD drawings of broadcast facilities at each venue must be distributed one year prior to the event. These drawings should incorporate all field-of-play issues, broadcast facilities, press areas, Olympic Family needs, and other venue-specific broadcast features in order of importance.

■ Establish a centrally located media village to expedite movement of media personnel to and from the IBC, MPC, and competition venues.

CENTENNIAL OLYMPIC PARK

CHAPTER FIVE
CENTENNIAL OLYMPIC PARK

OVERVIEW—Centennial Olympic Park was created to provide a celebratory gathering place for all persons in Atlanta during the Games and to leave a permanent legacy of green space within the Olympic Ring. Its creation was inspired by the experiences of ACOG management as they enjoyed other central gathering places in previous Olympic cities—especially the Plaza de España in Barcelona. They realized that the Centennial Olympic Games would be greatly enhanced by an area where local citizens and visitors, ticket holders as well as non–ticket holders, could gather to experience the friendship and celebration that are an integral part of any Olympic Games.

In November 1993, ACOG CEO William Porter "Billy" Payne proposed that an area close to the Olympic Village and within walking distance of the main hotel district and several competition venues be considered as this gathering place. This area consisted primarily of vacant land and buildings and a few small businesses. The area, described locally as "underutilized and undeveloped," had been one of unrealized redevelopment plans for years.

After discussions with both the private and public sectors, the state of Georgia, through support from the Georgia World Congress Center (GWCC), managed the development of the 21 acre (8.5 ha) site that became Centennial Olympic Park. The site was transformed into the gathering place envisioned by ACOG and exceeded all expectations as it quickly became a major attraction during the 1996 Games.

An estimated 5.5 million people visited the park during its operation. People gathered for rich cultural events, world-class entertainment, and sponsor exhibits, as well as to enjoy its refreshing fountain, trade pins, locate engraved bricks, and relax and socialize with others. An Atlanta newspaper headline described the park as "The Place to Be: The Epicenter of the Olympics."

ORGANIZATION

In 1993, as the vision of the park became a concrete plan, a small staff under the direction of the managing director of Olympic Legacy began the intensive coordinating process required for the development of a public park. The staff worked continuously through Games-time with all involved external organizations and ACOG functional areas.

Planning

When the US Housing and Urban Development Department announced it would provide a redevelopment grant to the Atlanta Housing Authority for Techwood and Clark-Howell Homes, one of the nation's oldest public housing projects, situated just south of the Georgia

Institute of Technology campus, ACOG saw the opportunity to link the site of the Olympic Village with the GWCC and Omni Coliseum through the creation of a park. The area would include a large gathering place for the Games. A smaller park would remain as a legacy of the 1996 Olympic Games.

After ACOG management privately discussed the park concept with a few key individuals, including Georgia Governor Zell Miller, the press became aware of ACOG's interest. In a public announcement on 19 November 1993, Billy Payne expressed his belief that the project could be funded without taxpayer money and stated that "if the park is to become a reality, the...business, political, and philanthropic community...must come together to [lead] this development."

The announcement of the park concept was received with virtually universal community support. Shortly thereafter, the Genuine Parts Company, the largest landowner in the proposed area, donated land valued at several million dollars to be the development cornerstone of the park. When the donation was announced during a press conference on 7 January 1994, the governor announced that support was sufficient to conduct a feasibility study and, most importantly, that the state of Georgia, through the GWCC, would take the lead position in assessing the project and, if the project was found feasible, would develop and permanently maintain the park.

Sprint Start Team

The GWCC Authority immediately selected a team to determine the feasibility of the plan for the park. This team was named the Sprint Start Team, denoting the urgency of the task. Members of the team, including representation from the Atlanta Chamber of Commerce, ACOG, the city of Atlanta, the Corporation for Olympic Development in Atlanta (CODA), and the GWCC Authority, as well as other Atlanta business community entities, responded by donating their expertise. Initially, the team solicited

input from focus groups comprised of more than 250 elected officials, community leaders, urban planners, and area residents. While participants voiced individual concerns such as total cost, size of the legacy park, and displacement of businesses, community support for the project remained high throughout its planning.

Preliminary estimates of resources available in addition to donated land and services were considered in the development of the working budget for acquisitions, site preparation, design, and construction.

The initial funds were provided entirely by the private sector. The Atlanta Chamber of Commerce directed a fundraising campaign, and the Woodruff Foundation contributed a large donation. The remaining funds were guaranteed by ACOG.

Individuals could contribute to the construction of Centennial Olympic Park by purchasing the engraved commemorative bricks used to pave pathways throughout the park.

To assess displacement issues, the team consulted local housing officials, social scientists, and other interested parties. One group that was consulted, the Atlanta Neighborhood Development Partnership, Inc. (ANDP), assisted with this evaluation and relocation.

A major success story was the relocation of the Sheltering Arms Day Care Center from within the park area to a site less than two blocks away. Sheltering Arms received a new, larger, more accessible center with training facilities and space for parking and landscaping.

top: **A master plan of Centennial Olympic Park incorporated the landscape quilt concept.**

bottom: **This aerial view shows the site where Centennial Olympic Park would be constructed.**

Sheltering Arms released a poster expressing appreciation for its new facility.

The Commemorative Brick Program

ACOG proposed to underwrite approximately 30 percent of the park's cost through selling commemorative engraved bricks. This program would also allow individuals to participate in the park's construction by purchasing personalized bricks.

The Home Depot assisted with the Commemorative Brick Program by marketing and selling the bricks nationwide in their stores and by telephone. Several of their associates also donated their services.

For a contribution of $35, a patron could have an inscription of up to two lines engraved on a brick to honor individuals and special dates, celebrate events, or recognize organizations. Approximately 500,000 bricks were sold, more than 100,000 during the Games, representing the most successful brick program in the US.

The bricks would provide the basis for the park design, forming the Centennial Plaza as well as many wide pathways. Specially designed kiosks in the park provided information on locating personalized bricks, which became a popular pastime as visitors admired, photographed, or traced their personal legacy in the park.

DESIGN AND DEVELOPMENT

Presented to the governor in late summer 1994, the feasibility study determined that adequate funding was available to develop the park in an appropriate manner within the necessary time constraints. The GWCC Authority held a design competition and chose EDAW, an international landscape design firm, to design the park, and Beers/Russell, a joint venture, to construct the park.

EDAW worked intensely from October 1994 through February 1995, and released the final design for Georgia's first urban park at a press conference hosted by the governor. EDAW described its park as a "landscape quilt in the city of trees." The quilt theme, selected by ACOG as part of its Look of the Games, was incorporated into EDAW's design to convey the cultural heritage of the American South. The landscape theme represents Atlanta's natural and topographic beauty.

EDAW first established an overall plan based on existing city streets, which would become pedestrian promenades through the park, leading to specific destinations and adjacent city blocks.

After this plan was adopted, EDAW incorporated the commemorative bricks into the pathways to symbolize stitching connecting landscape quilt pieces. Linking the different elements of the park and joining the park to the surrounding city with the bricks gave the pathways meaning to the thousands of individuals who supported the park through the brick program.

Bounded by the pathways, each piece of land—or "patch" of ground—was designed differently, depending on its location and use. For example, throughout the seasons, trees create variable patchwork appearances by their different shapes, leaves, flowers, bare branches, and degree of shade. The lawns, gardens, and plazas strengthened this patchwork effect and provided for different activities and various destinations.

Centennial Plaza was designed as a 100 x 100 m formal civic square. It commemorated the 100th anniversary of the modern Olympic Games and marked the formal gateway into the park. A court of 23 flags honored the host countries of the modern Games, and the Olympic Rings fountain displayed water jets, lights, and music.

ACOG staff worked with the GWCC Authority and EDAW to implement the design to accommodate crowds during the Games, with many of the permanent park features to be installed after the Games. During Games-time, the park contained 240,000 engraved bricks, the Fountain of Rings, pathways paved with an additional 100,000 engraved bricks, and an amphitheater designed to accommodate Games-time activities.

GAMES-TIME OPERATIONS

Concurrent with planning and design of the park, ACOG was planning and scheduling its Games-time entertainment and began solicit-

top: Plans for Centennial Olympic Park—envisioned as a place for people to gather, cool off, and celebrate the Olympic Spirit—incorporated water misters, shallow wading pools, and choreographed fountains.

bottom: A mature pecan tree was transplanted as a part of the park landscape plan.

ing assistance from potential sponsors. AT&T became the presenting sponsor for the park, assisting ACOG with overall planning, as well as planning its own Global Olympic Village. Other sponsors included Anheuser-Busch, General Motors, and Swatch.

Additionally, the Coca-Cola Company and the Georgia Department of Agriculture created exhibitions and activities for the enjoyment of park visitors. Events inside the park were free of charge. During the Games, the park was operated by ACOG under a lease from the GWCC.

The most popular attraction in the park was the Fountain of Rings in Centennial Plaza. People were constantly dancing in the water or gathering at the fountain to watch and photograph the activity. There were five daily 30-minute water shows when the water rings danced to music with an Olympic theme. The fountain was the single most photographed image of the 1996 Games.

Cultural Olympiad's Southern Crossroads Festival

The Southern Crossroads Festival was an event presented by AT&T that incorporated music, dance, food, slogans, and a bustling marketplace. Thousands of entertainers representing the American South performed on three stages throughout the park. *(For additional information, see the Cultural Olympiad chapter.)*

AT&T's Global Olympic Village

AT&T's Global Olympic Village, constructed primarily to host the families of competing athletes, also provided an exhibit for the public. It featured a large stage with state-of-the-art lighting and sound, and a large Astrovision screen. AT&T provided nightly entertainment from this stage, which could be seen from vantage points throughout the park. The stage was the site of nightly concerts, with performances by such popular entertainers as Ray Charles and Travis Tritt. Additionally, the Opening and Closing Ceremonies were broadcast on the screen for park visitors.

Sponsor Exhibitions and Activities

Anheuser-Busch's beer garden, known as Bud-World, was a 21,000 sq ft (1,953 sq m) air-conditioned facility. Inside, there was an impressive light show and video screens which showed everything from the latest videos to live feeds from NBC. Lines of visitors waited to enter from the morning's opening to the evening's closing, attesting to Bud-World's popularity.

Swatch built a half-acre pavilion designed to emulate the transparent glow-in-the-dark "jelly watch" in its collection. The pavilion housed a large exhibition featuring the history of timing, interactive activities, and a photo exhibit by Annie Liebovitz. The pavilion won awards for its architecture and lighting design.

General Motors constructed a 15,000 sq ft (1,395 sq m) pavilion in the southern tip of the park. A laser show occurred three or four times a night, garnering visitors' attention. The General Motors pavilion also housed an exhibition commemorating the centennial of both the modern Olympic Games and the automobile. The exhibition included a motion ride and a southern stock car in which visitors could be photographed.

The Coca-Cola Official Pin Trading Center located adjacent to Centennial Plaza was a favorite location for the popular Olympic pastime of pin trading.

The Georgia Agriculture exhibition, which highlighted the agricultural products grown in Georgia, was the park's state agency display. The robotics within the exhibit were a major attraction. The building has since become part of the University of Georgia Research Center campus.

The Superstore, one of the largest temporary buildings constructed for the Games, provided almost one acre (.4 ha) of air-conditioned shopping. It contained a broad selection of official Olympic Games merchandise.

The park also became the permanent home for four works of public art donated by individuals and organizations. The American Hellenic Educational Progressive Association (AHEPA) sponsored a sculpture honoring the centennial of the Games, named *Tribute to Olympia*. The impressive eight ton sculpture, created by the Greek-American artist Peter Calaboyias, is 17 ft high and 24 ft wide. A giant fan-like surface contrasts three 9 ft Olympic athletes representing different time periods: the first Games in ancient Olympia, the first modern Games in Athens, and the Centennial Games in Atlanta.

The Androgyne Planet, a sculpture commissioned by ACOG's Cultural Olympiad, was created by artist Enric Pladevall and fabricated in Vic, Spain (a city near Barcelona). It stands approximately 26 ft high and is made of matte-finish stainless steel, African teak wood, and bronze.

The *Gateway of Dreams*, a commemorative statue of Baron Pierre de Coubertin, the founder of the modern Olympic Movement, was donated by members of the US Pierre de Coubertin Committee (USPCC), which aided Atlanta during the Bid process. De Coubertin is depicted stepping into a gateway of ancient Greek columns, with seven doves descending out of the Olympic Rings to place a wreath of olive leaves on his head. De Coubertin approaches the moment of honor in the posture of an Olympic athlete about to receive a medal.

The *Allen Family Tribute* is an obelisk raised on a platform, dedicated to three generations of the Ivan Allen Family. In addition to Ivan Allen, Ivan Jr., and Ivan III bas reliefs, it also includes a narrative of their prominent contributions to the development of the city of Atlanta.

Adjacent Activities

With Centennial Park as the center of downtown activity, other activity centers around Centennial Park added to the festive atmosphere and entertained thousands of additional people. Those attractions included:

■ Coca-Cola Olympic City, a 14 acre (5.7 ha) site including interactive competition against Olympians plus live entertainment, merchandise, and an Olympic museum.

■ House of Blues, live musical performances, including performances from the nation's blues legends.

■ Anheuser-Busch's Budweiser Clydesdale Farm, a facility created to house the Clydesdale horse team that was driven through the park each day by a different celebrity. The facility was open daily to the public.

■ *The Sponsor Village*, constructed as the entertainment center for the TOP and COP sponsors of the 1996 Centennial Olympic Games, occupied 6 acres (2.4 ha) of the park. Each

sponsor, the IOC, and NBC built their own entertainment venues within the larger village.

Park Operations

Operations at Centennial Park were conducted much like Games-time operations at other noncompetition venues. It was expected that Centennial Park would be popular. Ultimately, it had more visitors than all other cluster venues combined.

Tribute to Olympia, **created by Greek-American artist Peter Calaboyias, contrasts Olympic athletes representing the first Games in ancient Olympia, the first modern Olympic Games, and the Centennial Olympic Games in Atlanta.**

Operating Centennial Olympic Park from 0530 until 0200 every day was challenging. The Centennial Park operations team succeeded with the help of experienced staff members and 74 enthusiastic volunteers.

Staff meetings for park management and exhibition management were held daily at 1000 and 1600. During other times, park management communicated through the venue communication center (VCC) located within the compound. The VCC monitored all radio traffic to ensure smooth communication between different functional areas, such as Security and Venue Management.

Park management's office compound was located west of the park in the GWCC parking lot. The lot served as both an office hospitality complex and a staging area for the buses serving the sponsor hospitality village.

The park was divided into two geographical sections for management purposes. The first section, south of International Boulevard, contained the Fountain of Rings and the Southern Music Amphitheater. The second section, north of International Boulevard, contained AT&T's Global Olympic Village and the Swatch and Anheuser-Busch exhibitions. Each area was managed by an assistant venue manager and a supervisor. For law enforcement purposes, the park was then subdivided into several more sectors, each with a sector chief and assistants. Each day, approximately 1,500 people were needed to operate the park, including its retail operations. Shifts began at 0530 each morning and ended after the park was cleared of guests at night. Overlapping security shifts assured coverage during busy times throughout the day and overnight.

Access Control. The public was invited to visit the park without cost, and ACOG established rules to ensure that activities within the park were consistent with the Olympic experience. During normal operating hours, park staff entered from the north at a staff check-in location. This same entrance was used by people entering the park after hours. Operating at capacity virtually every evening, the park required additional staff and security. Also, several crowd-control techniques were employed to direct people toward certain entrances and exits to facilitate movement.

Maintenance and Cleaning. Since the park operated 20 hours per day with large crowds of people, a huge effort was required daily to clean the facility. Contracted maintenance and cleaning staff were assigned to monitor specific sectors in the park. Some staff were responsible for collecting litter, others for emptying trash cans, and others for removing the trash bags from the park. The late-night crew cleaned the park completely with high-pressure water hoses.

Public Aid. Two first-aid centers were located in the park—one at the south end of the park and one at the north end. Visitors were directed to the nearest center unless help was required at the scene.

A lost-and-found station was located in the Randstad information station.

Program Entertainment. Entertainment in the park began each day at noon and continued until after midnight. Different entertainment options scheduled by the Cultural Olympiad Department could be found in most areas of the park. *(For more information, see the Cultural Olympiad chapter).*

Park Visitors

The park operated at virtually 100 percent capacity from sunrise until closing every night. An estimated 5.5 million people visited the park during its three-week operation. The crowds were large but manageable. Attendance peaked during high spectator traffic events at the Omni, Georgia Dome, and GWCC venues. As anticipated, there was also a large number of visitors during the nightly entertainment.

Peak attendance nights were Fridays and Saturdays, indicating the park's value as an entertainment center. Crowd estimates were more than 75,000 during the Ray Charles and Joan Osborne concerts.

Within the park, there was an overwhelming feeling of unity among the visitors. The Olympic Spirit was prevalent and acts of kindness and patience were frequent, adding to the manageability of the park during crowded times.

The Bombing at Centennial Park

On 27 July at 0125—the early morning of day 10 of the 1996 Centennial Olympic Games—a suspicious backpack was spotted next to a sound tower, and people were evacuated from the area. Unfortunately, the pipe bomb contained in the bag exploded before everyone could be moved away from the area. One person was killed directly from the blast, another died from a heart attack, and 110 others were injured. While the Olympic Games continued, Centennial Olympic Park closed for three days to enable law enforcement to investigate thoroughly. This act of terrorism incensed the citizens of Atlanta, Olympic Family members, and visitors from around the world, who refused to let their Olympic Spirit be diminished. This tragedy brought people together in a universal appeal to continue the Olympic Games in the spirit in which they were started.

Renewal and Remembrance. The park reopened on Monday, 30 July 1996 at 1000 with a memorial service and reopening ceremony. The 40,000 people who participated in the park's emotional reopening demonstrated their unwavering support of the celebration of the Olympic Games. Their presence testified to the power of the Olympic Spirit, evidencing that it could not be quenched by the tragedy of the bombing, but rather served to reinforce the Olympic ideal of bringing people together. The ceremony was attended by the family of the woman who lost her life, as well as by many injured by the bomb. Andrew Young spoke of the dream of the park and the emotions of the city, saying, "We're here to proclaim a victory, to celebrate a triumph of the human spirit."

The reopening of Centennial Park ultimately became one of the most inspiring events of the Games. Those who participated in it, saw it televised internationally, or read about it in any major publication sensed how profoundly the Olympic Spirit echoes in the hearts of the people.

The Legacy

Centennial Plaza and the Fountain of Rings remained open for visitors to enjoy after the Olympic Games. Approximately 15 (6.1 ha) of the park's 21 acres (8.5 ha) were closed to prepare the park for its permanent features, including grass, trees, new engraved brick walkways, a water feature resembling a free-flowing creek, and a visitors center. The park is scheduled to reopen in its final form in summer 1997. As a result of the Games experience, the design team, the GWCC, and EDAW modified the post-Games plan to include an area for concerts and a fence around the park for crowd control. Also, several plazas called quiltscapes will be added as a memorial to those killed and injured in the park and as a tribute to all the countries and athletes that participated in the Games.

Both the city of Atlanta and the state of Georgia will benefit from the permanent park and subsequent neighborhood improvements. It is anticipated that the area around Centennial Olympic Park will attract new entertainment facilities that will increase the popularity of the area. Private-sector developers are presently planning commercial and residential projects adjacent to the area. The many visitors to the park during the Games indicated that Centennial Olympic Park will remain an important legacy to residents and visitors in Atlanta.

CONCLUSIONS AND RECOMMENDATIONS

Centennial Olympic Park captured the true spirit of Olympism. It created a beautiful and symbolically rich place where people with different nationalities, languages, and backgrounds could together celebrate the overarching Olympic values of diversity and friendship. Both in terms of the crowds it drew and the sentiments it inspired, Centennial Olympic Park was the very heart of Olympic activity during the Atlanta Games. The presence of a safe gathering place which offers a variety of activities is invaluable at an Olympic Games.

Future organizing committees planning similar projects are especially encouraged to consider the following recommendations:

■ Open the park prior to the Games. Since crowds during this time will be smaller, the operations staff will have an opportunity to accustom itself to park management before the huge crowds arrive.

■ Conduct weekly meetings with all involved functional areas throughout planning stages and the Games.

■ Recognize that park operations are an enormous responsibility, as the park requires constant maintenance.

■ Notify the public of park operating hours and enforce them.

CHAPTER SIX
COMMUNICATIONS

COMMUNICATIONS
EMPLOYEES

Date	Staff Number
June 1992	13
January 1996	25
July 1996	39

Note: These staff numbers do not
include contract, VIK, and volunteer
personnel.

OVERVIEW—ACOG established the Communications Department to coordinate information sharing with the media and the public and to plan and operate all facilities and services accredited press would require to cover the 1996 Olympic Games. Interest in the 1996 Olympic Games was extraordinary, from the Bid through the Games' conclusion and for months afterward. Although local media, Atlanta residents, and outlying venue cities focused the most attention on the Games, national and international reporters and individuals worldwide also followed developments.

This enormous interest can be attributed to the historical significance of the centennial celebration of the Olympic Movement, as well as the globalization of the news industry. Most journalists routinely use computer databases that can easily review local press reports from any city; thus, coverage in Atlanta could be freely accessed throughout the US and other nations. In addition, many US and international news outlets have growing networks of offices with reporters assigned to numerous geographical areas. Prior to the start of the Games, more than two dozen national and international news organizations had staff based in Atlanta.

The importance of providing information to both the press and the public was recognized from the earliest days of the AOC and ACOG. After the IOC awarded the 1996 Olympic Games to Atlanta, a press chief was immediately appointed to work with the IOC Press Commission and the international press to determine their expectations. A Public Information Program was also instituted at this time.

During the years preceding the Games, working with the press was directed separately from the Public Information Program for an interim period. The two areas were consolidated approximately 18 months prior to the Games into the Communications Department, which reported directly to the ACOG CEO.

Communications' responsibilities on behalf of the media were to make information readily and easily available while preparing to meet the needs of the approximately 6,000 members of the press who would cover the Games and require a range of specialized facilities, equipment, and services. To address public interest in the Games, Communications also provided a large amount of free and easily accessible information and planned for the installation and operation of public information booths at Games venues to assist spectators and visitors.

ORGANIZATION

Communications staff were divided into four areas: Media Relations, Press Operations, Press Information, and Public Information.

Media Relations was responsible for pre-Games dissemination of Games information, including news releases, press conferences, and responses to inquiries, as well as coordination of all publicity efforts. During the Games, Media Relations worked with press and broadcasters on nonsports issues of the Games.

Press Operations planned and implemented all facilities and services for the press, including the Main Press Center (MPC) and press facilities at each competition venue and at certain noncompetition venues. This division also worked with Accreditation to distribute press credentials, Accommodations to secure press accommodations and coordinate reservations and payment, and Transportation to create a media transportation system that served press and broadcasters who were the constituency of the Atlanta Olympic Broadcasting (AOB) Department.

Press Information developed information for Info'96—the electronic communications system that served the Games—and assisted in creating the press data system that automatically transmitted results to press and broadcaster seating areas during competitions. In addition, Press Information prepared all sports-related materials for the media's use, took responsibility for announcements and other media relations activities related to all sports of the Games, and managed ACOG's Games-time news delivery system.

Public Information provided information to the general public, relying primarily on brochures, recorded messages on ACOG's general information phone lines, a Speakers Bureau, and a World Wide Web site. When the Games began, Public Information operated booths at every venue to disseminate information to spectators and visitors and to answer questions.

During the Games, Communications maintained a small headquarters group to manage operations in all areas. In addition, a small team of Media Relations personnel was located at ACOG headquarters to work with executive management as needed. All other Communications staff were based at the MPC or at the venues.

MEDIA RELATIONS

Media Relations staff worked with appropriate ACOG functional areas to determine the best communication strategies for issues that would affect the public. Media Relations also implemented publicity campaigns to promote ticket and merchandise sales, pre-Games Olympic Arts Festival (OAF) programs and test events, and recruitment of volunteers.

When releasing information, Media Relations adhered to disclosure guidelines designed to balance ACOG's status as a private entity with the interest of the media and general public in Games preparations.

Generally, the guidelines provided for inspection of hiring and purchasing policies; lists of employees, volunteers, board members, advisers, sponsors, licensees, and major vendors and contractors; quarterly financial status reports; provisions of significant contracts; reports to the IOC; and operating plans directly affecting the public such as ticketing and transportation. Although broad information was provided, controversies arose periodically as reporters sought greater detail while plans were still being formulated.

Press Guide

Media Relations created what became the most important tool for journalists, the *Press Guide*, which provided a comprehensive review of plans, policies, and programs for the Games—from finance and marketing to sports and venues—and also included facts about the Bid history, Atlanta area, and ACOG. The *Press Guide* was printed initially in 1991 and updated monthly through 1993. As plans for the Games were being implemented in 1994 and 1995, updates were less frequent. A major revision was issued in the beginning of 1996, and a final publication was developed for use during the Games. Copies were produced in English and French and occasionally in Spanish.

News Releases

News releases, supplemented with status reports, photos, slides, maps, diagrams, and video footage covering Games' preparations, were disseminated frequently. Initial releases covered finalization of venue locations, issuance of construction contracts, staff appointments, and new sponsors. As the Games ap-

In keeping with ACOG's commitment to communicate with the media and public, frequent news conferences were held.

proached, releases covered marketing and financial results, progress on new facilities, transportation plans, tickets, accommodations, OAF programs, volunteer activities, youth and education programs, and Games-related community events.

News Conferences

ACOG held hundreds of news conferences throughout the pre-Games period. Two standard sessions were held, one following each quarterly meeting of the ACOG Board of Directors and one after each review of the IOC Coordination Commission. Most news conferences, however, were conducted for specific

announcements, such as new sponsors and Games programs, the Olympic cauldron, the Look of the Games, and ticket designs.

In early 1995, news conferences were held on a biweekly basis to combine announcements, provide progress reports, and minimize the necessity for individual interviews with ACOG senior executives. These regular updates were well received by both the media and ACOG management, but special announcements continued the need for additional news conferences.

As 1996 began, at least three sessions per week were held, sometimes increasing to one or two per day as Games-time neared.

Venue Tours

Reporters, photographers, and broadcast camera crews were particularly interested in learning about the locations where Olympic competition would be held, especially the new venues being constructed. Staff from Media Relations and Construction or Sports conducted the tours requested by larger news outlet representatives. Individual requests and smaller groups were accommodated by the weekly venue tours offered by Guest Services. Over time, the number of requests more than tripled, and the demands on staff time and the need to limit distractions caused by constant visitors to the venues necessitated a change in the tour process. In mid-1995, Media Relations initiated a twice-weekly program of tours which encompassed the Olympic Ring, Stone Mountain Park, and Georgia International Horse Park.

Media were transported on 55-passenger buses, and Construction and Venue Management staff were available at the sites to answer specific questions. During the year prior to the Games, more than 4,300 members of the media participated in these tours.

Media Information Line

In early 1995, a media information line was established to handle the increasing number of calls from local, national, and international media. The staff was equipped with materials including the *Press Guide*, news releases, brochures, ACOG executive speeches, maps and directions to venues, and photographic and video images of venues, maps, logos, and other frequently requested visual elements of the Games. Early morning meetings were held each day to brief staff on new topics and provide updates essential to managing calls efficiently. At the beginning of 1996, inquiries increased dramatically, and responding promptly to calls became more challenging.

Issue Management

Media Relations also addressed numerous Games issues that generated significant public interest. For example, initial reaction to the official mascot of the Games, IZZY, prompted hundreds of inquiries, and the intense public debate and news coverage about the site and construction agreements for Olympic Stadium continued for several months.

Progress in raising sufficient funds to stage the Games had to be addressed regularly at the news conferences following the ACOG Board of Directors meetings. When progress seemed slow, reporters questioned whether taxpayers would have to pay for the Games; when reports were more promising, questions about the use of a surplus arose.

Changes in venue locations also were significant public issues, with the greatest attention focused on the site for preliminary volleyball rounds. Originally set in metropolitan Atlanta's Cobb County, the site became the center of a debate that reached national proportions when the county government passed an ordinance condemning homosexual and alternative lifestyles. Proponents on both sides of the issue sought to involve ACOG, which remained neutral. When ACOG relocated the

venue to nearby Athens on the University of Georgia campus, the change was based on the fact that the facility was better suited to the requirements of presenting the competition.

Throughout Games preparations and the Games themselves, issues continued to arise, and Media Relations helped ACOG management address these issues and minimize any impact they might have on the Games.

PRESS OPERATIONS

Press Operations—initially a joint responsibility of Communications and Operations—planned and installed facilities the press would need during the Games and managed services such as accreditation, accommodations, arrivals and departures, and transportation. Press Operations staff gathered information from the IOC Press Commission, international press members who have traditionally covered the Games, and NOC and IF press personnel to plan for the best facilities and services possible. They then worked directly with ACOG functional areas responsible for construction, ordering supplies, installing wiring and equipment, arranging food and beverage services, operating buses, and providing other support services for Games operations.

As preparations proceeded, members of the IOC Press Commission visited Atlanta for reviews and updates, and ACOG's press chief reported at various commission meetings. In addition, numerous press members came to Atlanta for informal briefings and tours and to cover ACOG's test events.

Both IOC Press Commission members and reporters suggested modifications to different aspects of the plans. Their recommendations—which ranged from reducing overall travel times for media bus service, to adjusting the height of photographers' stands—were adopted to the greatest degree possible.

JANET F BISHOP • JUDITH K BISHOP • KERMIT O BISHOP • KYLE R BISHOP • LAURA D BISHOP • LAURA S BISHOP • LEE BISHOP • MARTY M BISHOP • MARY ELIZABETH BISHOP • MICHAEL E BISHOP • MONICA R BISHOP • MURL R BISHOP • PATRICIA G BISHOP • ROBERT V BISHOP • SHERRY BISHOP • STEPHEN D BISHOP • T JANE BISHOP • WILLIAM C BISHOP • KAREN M BISHOP-BJORGEN • PAUL A BISHOP JR • JENNIFER I BISIGNARO • PATRICK BISSANTI • PATRICIA A BITJOKA • CATHY L BITNER • CINDY A BITNER • ELWANDA L BITNER • JAMES J BITSKO • CHERYL L BITTEL • COLLEEN L BITTINGER

93

Two significant issues were raised at a May 1995 IOC Press Commission meeting in Atlanta. The first related to the fact that installation of the MPC could not begin until 3 July because a trade show at the Atlanta Market Center would not conclude until that date. With this restriction, installation of the MPC would be extremely difficult to complete in time to meet the 6 July opening date. Press Operations was already negotiating for earlier availability of the space, and adjustments were achieved by paying the lessee to vacate one day earlier and by expanding ACOG's contract to allow occupancy of some areas by 15 June. Nevertheless, time remained very limited for installation of the MPC.

The second issue concerned the number and location of hotels for press accommodations. To address this issue, Communications management reopened discussions within ACOG regarding housing allocations for Olympic Family constituents. Additional hotel rooms downtown were designated for press, and more rooms were reserved at large hotels, which reduced the number of facilities being used.

Communications also worked with IOC Press Commission members to finalize certain key policies. As in previous Games, several events would be identified as high demand—meaning more journalists would want to attend than could be accommodated in the grandstand press seats. Reporters would be required to have tickets to attend these events, and the tickets, as in the past, would be allocated to NOCs for distribution to press from their countries. The policy for high-demand events during the 1996 Games was further defined to limit access to all press facilities, including the general work room and interview room, to only those with tickets. The exception was the super subcenter, which served the venues at the Georgia Dome and Georgia World Congress Center (GWCC). Nonticketed,

accredited media were allowed access to the super subcenter work room and interview rooms at all times.

An additional policy for the 1996 Games prohibited non–rights-holding broadcasters—holders of ENR accreditation—from bringing recording equipment into competition events or renting space in the MPC or competition venues.

Within the final year of preparations for the Games, Communications provided a series of mailings to the accredited media that included a Facilities and Services Manual, descriptions of arrival and departure services, and updates on transportation plans. A final mailing included information about the Press Gala—which would be held just prior to the start of the Games—and about the press bags that media received upon arrival for the Games.

Accreditation

The accreditation process began in April 1995 when IOC Press Commission members and the ACOG press chief met to allocate credentials to each NOC. They also established quotas for all categories of press credentials, i.e., E, EP, ET, Es, EPs, and ENR. Two other categories—EC for access only to the MPC, and EX for local press and representatives of national news organizations with Atlanta offices—were reserved for ACOG in response in part to the overwhelming demand for accreditation from US media.

The IOC Press Commission also determined the international news agencies that would receive credentials directly from the IOC or ACOG. This practice has been followed for the past several Games, with the agencies including Associated Press (AP), Agence-France Presse (AFP), Reuters, and the national agency of the host country. For the 1996 Games, United Press International (UPI) also was given a limited number of credentials, and the IOC included the Japanese news agency Kyodo, reflecting the fact that Nagano would host the upcoming Winter Games. In the absence of a national news agency in the US, ACOG credentialed *USA Today*.

The IOC notified NOCs in May 1995 of the number of credentials they would receive for the 1996 Games. The NOCs then determined which press institutions in their nations would receive applications.

Communications personnel mailed accreditation packages in July 1995—one year prior to the Games, as required—with a letter confirming the number of applications per category, the applications themselves, Press Accreditation Manuals, a Facilities and Services Manual for journalists, and other information.

In November, the IOC reallocated credentials based on the response to this first mailing and made a final reallocation in May 1996. By the end of the process, 5,954 credentials—the largest number ever—were issued. Journalists from 161 countries were represented—also the largest number ever. *(For the number of journalists accredited by category, see Figure 1.)*

The availability of EX and EC credentials led to extraordinarily broad coverage of the Games in Atlanta, each city that hosted a venue, and across the US. Coverage internationally was enhanced through the Olympic Solidarity program sponsored by the IOC and the Freedom Forum, whereby 35 journalists from developing nations were accredited to provide coverage of the Games for their citizens. The program provided transportation to and from the Games, housing, and meals for these journalists.

Accommodations

Meeting IOC requirements to house the accredited press presented significant challenges. Facilities sufficiently large to accommodate most journalists in a press village were either not available or unsuitable for various reasons.

While hotel rooms were an alternative that many journalists favored, large numbers of Olympic Family constituencies also sought this option. Demand far exceeded supply, especially for hotel space in the Olympic Ring area and rooms that were reasonably priced—priorities for the majority of the press.

Eventually, accommodations ranging from university-style housing to a variety of hotel rooms were made available. Many options were attractive to the press, and the university housing satisfied ACOG's pledge to provide low-cost facilities for a significant number of journalists. Approximately 800 rooms were rented at the university facilities. Food and laundry services as well as press centers were available at these sites. However, only some 700 of the more than 2,800 hotel rooms were located within the Olympic Ring. Many of the remaining rooms were clustered near the airport area not far from downtown, but others were as much as a 45-minute drive from the Olympic Ring. In all, 40 different sites in metropolitan Atlanta were used, placing considerable strain on the media transportation system.

Accommodations were allocated on a first-come, first-served basis. In addition, efforts were made to house representatives from the same news organizations in the same facilities.

Press members booked 2,450 hotel rooms, including accommodations in Athens, Columbus, Gainesville, Savannah, and the Ocoee River area. Hotel rooms for press covering preliminary football rounds were available through the local organizing committees.

Arrivals/Departures

Services for press included transportation from their point of arrival in Atlanta or Savannah to an accreditation facility, and then to the accommodations they had booked through ACOG in Atlanta or in Athens, Columbus,

FIGURE 1: NUMBER OF JOURNALISTS ACCREDITED BY CATEGORY

Category	Number
E	3,145
EC	445
ENR	316
EP	847
EPs	204
Es	333
ET	317
EX	347

• MICHAEL R BLACK • NATHANIEL C BLACK • NOLAN M BLACK • PATTY S BLACK • RASHAN J BLACK • RHONDA B BLACK • SONYA L BLACK • SUE K BLACK • SUSAN H BLACK • JOE BLACK PT/ATC • ALBERTA R BLACKBURN • ALICE F BLACKBURN • ARTHUR D BLACKBURN • DONNA L BLACKBURN • JACQUELINE L BLACKBURN • KARMELINE A BLACKBURN • KEITHA E BLACKBURN • LEON R BLACKBURN • LISA R BLACKBURN • LYNN H BLACKBURN • ROAMELIA W BLACKBURN • ROBIN D BLACKBURN • RODNEY W BLACKBURN • SARA D BLACKBURN • SHELTON H BLACKBURN • BENJAMIN A BLACKBURN II •

95

Gainesville, or Ocoee. Press going directly to the cities for preliminary rounds of football were accommodated and accredited in each individual city.

Arrival and departure forms and other materials were sent to all accredited press in late spring 1996. As expected, most press indicated Hartsfield Atlanta International Airport as their arrival destination and thus were accredited at the Airport Welcome Center.

Press accreditation proceeded smoothly in terms of records being readily available and accurate. Most delays resulted from the fact that press, broadcasters, and athletes were handled at one location without special lines designated for each group. For departures, press service included transportation from their accommodations to their departure locations.

Transportation

In addition to arrivals and departures, the media transportation plan included bus service that provided transportation between accommodations and the MPC, competition sites, and the Olympic Village. This bus service was available 20 hours per day prior to and after the Games and 24 hours per day throughout the Games. Press also were given passes that allowed free, unlimited travel on MARTA—Atlanta's rapid rail and bus system that operated 24 hours per day.

Service to and from the competition venues began three days before the start of an event with 4–6 or more trips daily. When competition began, service to Atlanta-area venues allowed media to arrive two hours before the start of an event, continued at 1–2 hour intervals, and was available until at least two hours after the conclusion of competition. At least 2–4 trips daily were available to venues in Athens, Columbus, and the Ocoee River area during competition periods.

As mandated by the IOC, the media system served both press and broadcasters—a constituency of more than 15,000. The hub and spoke concept that ACOG followed was the same approach used for media transportation systems in previous Games. Under this concept, media could board buses at their accommodations, go to a central point—or hub—and transfer to buses going to the competition venues and Olympic Village or to the MPC or International Broadcast Center (IBC). The system worked in reverse on return.

Initially, the hub was to be located within a short walk of the MPC and IBC. However, most prospective sites were in the area that subsequently became Centennial Olympic Park. After numerous reviews, the best option was identified as being about .75 mi (1.21 km) from the MPC and a short distance more from the IBC. This center, which became the hub, was known as the Media Transportation Mall.

This choice frequently prompted the media to spend more time traveling on buses, since shuttle service from the Main Transportation Mall to the IBC or MPC was added to the system. To help minimize the impact on the media, a press center was installed at the location with a small work room which provided access to results and other information.

The system added direct service from accommodations to a venue for media housed near venues outside the Olympic Ring that required transport to those venues only. Shuttle waystations also were established to allow media buses en route to venues outside the Olympic Ring to stop intermediately at a cluster of media hotels, permitting access to the system without going to the Media Transportation Mall.

Some complaints also were received about the proximity of loading areas near the press facilities at the venues, but security restrictions and the space shortage for these zones prevented this type of access.

Press parking was available at each venue for a fee, but the number of spaces was limited. Complaints were received about the locations offered, and several agencies requested and received refunds.

Overall, the media transportation services planned met IOC requirements and matched previously set standards. The delivery of these services, however, was not as effective as desired, primarily because of equipment problems with the buses and an initial lack of familiarity with routes on the part of some drivers. To address these problems, ACOG added more buses to the system and instituted direct shuttle service from the MPC to Olympic Stadium and from some press housing directly to the MPC. Considerable improvements were achieved.

The bombing in Centennial Olympic Park and the subsequent route restrictions and street closings adversely affected the media transportation system for several days. When more routine operations resumed, the system functioned with much greater efficiency.

Main Press Center

The center of press facilities and services for the Olympic Games is the MPC. The site originally selected for this facility for the 1996 Games was the GWCC, where the IBC was also located. However, as space requirements for both facilities were more fully defined, the MPC had to be relocated.

In 1993, plans were finalized to move the MPC to the Atlanta Market Center. This complex housed ACOG headquarters and was within walking distance of the IOC headquarters hotel, Centennial Olympic Park, the eight competition venues at the Olympic Center, and the IBC. It was spacious, but presented challenges in adaptation for Games-time because the 300,000 sq ft (27,900 sq m) of facilities encompassed three floors in two adjoining buildings.

Immediately following site selection, Press Operations began working with a consulting firm to develop detailed layouts of all areas for

the MPC. The staff also initiated discussions with sponsors, contractors, and vendors for equipping the space. In addition, meetings were held with representatives of large news agencies to gather their requirements for private offices, which would account for approximately one-third of all MPC space.

Also under development was the press rate card—a compilation of all equipment and services that would be offered to press agencies for purchase or rent during the Games. This project was incorporated with the planning for the MPC because most orders would be to equip the private offices news agencies would occupy at the facility.

Considerable debate occurred regarding rental rates for offices. The IOC Press Commission and large agencies urged a fee lower than that charged during the 1992 and 1994 Games. To provide recovery of ACOG's costs and respond to the requests, a compromise rate of $15 per sq ft was determined, lower than that for the 1994 Winter Games and slightly higher than the charge at the 1992 Summer Games.

Discussions were also held regarding prices for technology services and equipment offered on the press rate card. Compromises regarding price were satisfactory to most parties; however, the payment method implemented was not well received. The approach called for ACOG to collect money for space, furniture, and various other items while as many as nine different companies handled technology orders, resulting in press agencies managing numerous accounts for their orders.

In late 1994, when the MPC manager and assistant manager were hired, press rate card development was finalized and press agencies' orders were taken.

MPC full-time staff was supported by the MPC development team, which consisted of representatives from each functional area that would be involved in installing and operating the facility, including Accreditation, Financial Services, Food and Beverage Services, Language Services, Medical Services, Security, Technology, and Transportation. Press Information and Photo Operations also were represented since they would operate in the MPC during the Games.

The greatest challenge was the minimal time available for preparing the MPC. Some problems were overcome by initiating work on 1 March 1996 for the massive amounts of wire and cable needed to support MPC technology. Most of this work had to be performed in evenings and on weekends when the space was not occupied.

Also helpful was the 7 June 1996 availability of the 20,000 sq ft (1,860 sq m) space for the Kodak Imaging Center. This area was one of the most complex in the MPC in terms of technological requirements and layout. Two weeks later, the main entrance space and locations for numerous services were ready to be equipped.

Despite 24 hour daily efforts, the remaining space, which encompassed virtually all private press agency offices and the common work room, was not fully complete on 6 July when the MPC officially opened, although the facility was operational with staff, services, and equipment that met virtually all press requirements. As installation was completed during the next several days, problems resulting from the lack of time to test operations prior to opening also were resolved.

Scope of the Facility. The first floor of the MPC housed the primary entrances and security checkpoints; accreditation office; general and transportation help desks; check room and lockers; document distribution center; library; Kodak Imaging Center; news conference rooms; service areas; operational areas, such as

the switchboard, message center, and language services; offices for the IOC press chief, ACOG press chief, and Communications managers; and a small number of private offices rented by press agencies.

The second floor contained the main news conference room, a station where headsets were acquired, and the security command center.

The third floor held a large work area with seating for approximately 500 journalists, most private office space for news agencies, service center, AT&T calling center, sundries shop and international newsstand, full-service cafeteria, bar and lounge, and operational areas for the photo and information services.

Staff check-in areas and a break room were located on the fourth floor in space adjacent to that leased for the MPC.

Food and beverage stations were available on every floor. All space was fully air-conditioned, with smoking areas outside in easily accessible patio or balcony areas.

The MPC opened 6 July and operated 24 hours daily through 5 August, the day after Closing Ceremony.

Services. The MPC was designed to provide a variety of services to both individual reporters and photographers and to agencies occupying temporary offices.

Most services were on the first floor, where Games sponsors and several vendors operated kiosks that offered banking, shipping and delivery, copying and facsimile transmission, travel, laundry, and a variety of telephone, paging, and calling card services. In addition, MPC staff operated a message center and mail delivery center, a check room with rentable lockers, a medical center, and help desks.

Photographers had access to the full-service Kodak Imaging Center, which provided free film and processing. Canon and Nikon also offered on-site camera repair and loans.

In addition to equipment installed in private offices, telephones, facsimile machines, copiers, printers, and Info'96 terminals and printers were provided for use by the press and MPC staff. Large video walls in the first-floor entrance area and the third-floor common work area carried live feeds of competition at every venue as well as major news conferences held at the MPC.

Reporters representing news organizations without private office space could use the 500-seat common work room, with tabled workstations equipped with telephones and modem connections.

Research and reference materials were available in the library at no cost. Journalists also could review video footage from previous days of the Games on playback monitors. Headsets for simultaneous translation of major news conferences were also available free of charge.

For agencies that had placed rate card orders, a service center was available for problem solving and additional order placement. Photocopying and facsimile transmission services were provided near most private offices.

Both individuals and agencies had access to plentiful information about the Games. Start lists, results, and other competition data and Games information were continuously delivered to mail slots adjacent to the main work room and posted on notice boards. The document distribution center provided results books, IF books, team handbooks, and sponsor materials.

Food and beverage services were available in a cafeteria, bar and lounge, or at kiosks throughout the MPC. Several facilities remained open 24 hours daily. In addition, products of The Coca-Cola Company and Crystal Springs water were available continuously and free of charge. A sundries shop provided snack foods and other items, and newspapers from around the world were offered at two international newsstands.

Press Rate Card Orders. Press rate cards were mailed in mid-July 1995 as part of the media accreditation package. Agencies were asked to place their orders within three months, but virtually all agencies subsequently submitted changes to their orders despite a fee imposed for each change.

Office space in the MPC was offered on a first-come, first-served basis in anticipation of demand exceeding supply. Orders totaled about 30,000 sq ft (2,790 sq m) more than was available. Agencies that could not be accommodated were referred to other areas in the building and to a press center for nonaccredited media, provided by AT&T, located a few miles from downtown.

Office space and technology equipment and services were also available through the press rate card at the competition venues.

Agencies shipping freight for installation in their offices during the Games were required to use Circle International, ACOG's official customs broker and freight forwarder. Materials going to the MPC had to arrive no later than 23 June. In total, 143 tons of material were received and held at a warehouse for delivery to the MPC. The shipping and freight service also handled the removal and return shipping of agency freight.

Although time constraints lessened the availability of ACOG executives during the Games, they made efforts to accommodate requests for interviews.

Press Conferences. The MPC served as the site for news conferences and briefings other than those held at competition venues. During the 1996 Games, more than 500 representatives of ACOG, the IOC, NOCs (including athletes), and sponsors were involved in the 200 news conferences held at the MPC.

All ACOG and IOC briefings were conducted in the main news conference room, which seated approximately 400 people. Two smaller rooms were also available for news conferences and were equipped to handle any overflow from the main conference room. Through videoconferencing, reporters in the smaller rooms could watch the proceedings and ask questions.

Simultaneous interpretation in English, French, German, Russian, and Spanish was available for all official IOC and ACOG news conferences, including the Games status briefing held each morning. Use of all news conference rooms was free to IFs, NOCs, and other Olympic Family members.

AOB produced a direct feed of the IOC and ACOG news conferences that was broadcast on monitors throughout the MPC and at the IBC. In addition, summary transcriptions of these conferences and other major briefings were provided in printed copy and on Info'96.

Operational Issues. After initial installation problems were resolved, the MPC functioned extremely well. During the early days of operation, the ACOG press chief and other members of Communications management met with representatives from the major press agencies to hear their assessment of the facility and any suggestions for improvement.

Issues regarding day passes for access to the MPC continued throughout the Games with hundreds of press, either nonaccredited or not accredited for the MPC, trying to enter. Most wanted tours, which were available but restricted primarily to sponsor groups and observers who had made arrangements prior to the Games.

Following the bombing at Centennial Olympic Park, at the request of non–rights holders and in agreement with NBC, broadcast restrictions for news conferences at the MPC were temporarily suspended, allowing accredited non–rights holders to broadcast live from the conferences. This allowance was considered essential, given the enormous worldwide attention focused on the bombing. After the FBI and other agencies involved in the investigation ceased holding news conferences in the MPC, the restriction was reinstated.

Overall, the MPC received high marks from the press for the facilities provided, daily operations and services, and the convenience of the location. Disassembly of the MPC was completed by 8 August.

Press Subcenters

Press facilities were also required at every competition venue and certain noncompetition venues. IOC guidelines for serving the press, recommendations from IOC Press Commission members, and precedents from previous Games provided detailed direction for designing, equipping, and staffing these facilities.

Press Operations began the development process for the press subcenters in 1993, participating in cross-functional meetings and reviews to determine the layout and operating procedures for each venue.

Scope of Facilities. The scope and size of press facilities at venues closely matched those provided at previous Games. The number of grandstand seats reserved for press and the seats available in each work room were approximately the same as in Barcelona. In preparing for new sports and in refining capacity requirements for other sports, Communications utilized information from the IFs and from the most recent World Championships.

At each competition venue, press facilities included a press subcenter, press tribunes, photo positions, a mixed zone, and interview rooms.

The press subcenter was a smaller version of the MPC that served press as well as broadcasters. It featured a common work area, help desk, private offices for agencies, offices for staff, and food and beverage service.

Press tribunes were reserved grandstand press seating with unobstructed views of the field of play. Each tribune featured tabled and nontabled seating. Tabled seating offered electrical and telephone outlets and television monitors carrying the feed from that venue.

Photo positions were areas for photographers near and sometimes on the field of play and in press tribunes.

The mixed zone was a designated area where athletes and coaches met informally with media after competition.

Interview rooms, for press conferences and interviews with athletes and coaches following competition, offered sound systems and other audiovisual equipment needed by press and broadcasters. Simultaneous interpretation was available at selected venues, and consecutive interpretation was provided at all others.

Each competition venue also had an entrance dedicated for the press and broadcasters.

At noncompetition venues such as the Olympic Village, press housing, Media Transportation Mall, Centennial Olympic Park, and the OAF press center, facilities were more streamlined but offered quick access to Games-related information and staff trained to assist the press. The press centers at the OAF and Centennial Olympic Park were open to nonaccredited media as well as credentialed press.

Services. Most services centered on access to and delivery of information. The common work areas contained telephones, facsimile machines, copiers, television monitors, printers, and Info'96 terminals. Copies of start lists, recent results, news, and other materials were available in the press subcenter when press arrived and also posted on bulletin boards. Throughout each competition, reporters in the press tribunes were immediately delivered copies of results, news, and athlete quotes from the mixed zone.

Television monitors in the press subcenters and press tribunes carried the venue's live feed and the press data system for some sports. In addition, the monitors in the subcenters at the larger venues—including the Georgia Tech Aquatic Center, Olympic Stadium, and super subcenter—were programmed with live feeds from all venues.

Other services included facsimile transmission and photocopying, available through the help desk; language and technology assistance; purchase of AT&T prepaid calling cards for long-distance calls; rental of lockers; and rental of equipment offered through the press rate card. Products from The Coca-Cola Company, coffee, and water were available free of charge in the subcenters and frequently distributed by staff throughout the press tribunes and photo positions. Free snacks were provided at some venues, and all offered access to food and beverage stations. For photographers, a courier service ensured prompt delivery of film from the venues to the MPC for processing.

Operational Issues. Generally, operations at the competition venues proceeded smoothly; any problems were primarily related to technology and transportation. While Press Operations could not directly resolve most of these issues, the staff ensured that concerns such as the frequency of bus service and more rapid availability of results were promptly reported.

Complaints that mixed zones were too far from the press tribunes, which in turn were too far from the subcenters, were received at both Olympic Stadium and the Aquatic Center. In addition, reporters waiting in the mixed zones could not see the field of play. These problems had been partially addressed prior to the Games with the placement of additional television monitors in the mixed zones. In addition, quotes from athletes in the mixed zones were fed electronically to monitors in the press tribunes. At Olympic Stadium, a small work room was added adjacent to the press tribune, providing facilities for reporters to immediately develop and file stories during the sessions.

Problems were also encountered with press credentialed as ENR who violated the policy that restricted how much recording equipment could be brought into the venues. Most violations were handled with a warning; however, the IOC director of Public Information and the ACOG press chief did revoke some credentials due to repeated violations.

Throughout the Games, issues regarding the handling of high-demand tickets arose. Although Press Operations requested delivery of these tickets well in advance of the Games, they were not provided to IOC Press Commission members responsible for their allocation to the NOCs until 1–2 days before each event, giving NOCs little time to distribute them to reporters and photographers. Substantial confusion resulted on several occasions and unnecessarily complicated operations at the venues.

Photo Operations

Photo Operations, under the direction of a photo chief who reported to the deputy managing director of Communications, provided facilities and services both at the MPC and the competition venues, coordinated the International Olympic Photo Pool (IOPP), and managed the operation of the film courier system.

Kodak Imaging Center. The photo chief served as the liaison for equipping the Kodak Imaging Center in the MPC. The facility constituted the largest film processing center in the world during its operation. Services included complimentary Kodak film processing, printing, transmitting, and digital imaging. Kodak employees were responsible for the installation, management, and operation of the facility. During the Games, some 230,000 rolls of film were processed in the center.

Venue Photo Operations. At the venues, Photo Operations ensured the best possible positions for photographers near the field of play, finish lines, and victory stands. Positions closest to or on the field of play were reserved for the IOPP. At least 6 were designated at each venue, with 8 available for track cycling and 16 for athletics.

Other photo positions varied in location and number around the field of play and in the press tribunes; however, a variety of special accommodations was made to ensure full photographic coverage of each sport. For example, boats were provided for photographers at canoe/kayak-sprint, rowing, and yachting. Remote cameras were positioned at the Aquatic Center on girders, platforms, and underwater. A special bus for photographers followed pentathletes to the three different venues in which they competed.

At indoor venues, lighting on the field of play was a critical factor. IOC guidelines required a minimum of 1,400 lux, but this requirement had to be balanced with necessary television lighting, which is often lower. Broadcasters' demands resulted in less than optimal lighting for photographers for boxing, table tennis, and weightlifting.

International Olympic Photo Pool. An important responsibility of Photo Operations was the formation and support of the IOPP. Because more photographers were accredited for the Games than could be accommodated near the field of play, a pool was created that represented the IOC, the organizing committee, major news agencies, and the IFs.

The 1996 Games marked the first time that agencies in the IOPP could assign their accredited photographers on an as-needed basis, rather than designating specific individuals for the pool. In return for this flexibility, the three agencies in the pool—AFP, AP, and Reuters—provided their 150–200 best pictures from each day to the IOC, ACOG, and accredited news organizations for editorial use.

Film Courier System. The IOC requires that a courier service be provided to transport film from the venues to the MPC for processing at the imaging center. Photo Operations contracted with a professional transportation service that assembled an experienced team of drivers for the system. Motorcycles for the service were obtained from Games sponsor BMW. Driving times were matched to the competition schedule to ensure messengers arrived hourly at every venue during competition. Couriers delivered about 90 percent of the film processed at the Kodak Imaging Center.

Technology

The technology for the 1996 Games was expected to represent the best services available to the press. The amount and variety of equipment was remarkable, as were the capabilities of the systems that were developed.

The results system and Info'96 were the primary applications affecting the press. Through the results system, press at each venue received printed copies of start lists and results for the competition they were viewing. Info'96 provided this information for all sports as well as an enormous database of Games information and E-mail and bulletin board services for all accredited individuals.

Live television feeds of competition were also tremendously important to media, with all venue broadcasts available not only at the MPC but also at press facilities for the Aquatic Center, Emory housing, Olympic Stadium, the Olympic Village, and the super subcenter.

In addition, the press data system delivered start lists, results, and other information on an almost real-time basis to video monitors in press and broadcast seating for artistic gymnastics, athletics, basketball, diving, swimming, synchronized swimming, tennis, and track cycling.

Especially vital to large news agencies was the World News Press Agency (WNPA) feed. Offered on the press rate card, this system provided direct delivery of start lists, results, records, and statistics by modem to the agencies' computers.

When the Games began, sufficient time had not been available to fully test all hardware and software systems. Initial problems were encountered, and although they were resolved within a few days, the confidence the press placed in the technology was significantly damaged. Thus, all aspects of the service were subjected to critical review.

Overall, the WNPA feed did not meet performance expectations, and the shortcomings of the system were magnified by its importance to the major news services. Additionally, data migration, the speed at which information moves from where it is entered to other locations, did not occur as quickly as anticipated, causing delays in both Info'96 and the results system. For example, news items entered into Info'96 at a competition venue sometimes were not visible at terminals outside the venue for 30 minutes or longer, and the results system at the MPC sometimes was delayed in producing printed copies of start lists from venues until after competitions were started or concluded. *(For more information on the technology for the 1996 Games, see the Technology chapter.)*

MELINDA A BLOIS • KATHRYN J BLONDHEIM • MICHAEL F BLONDIN • ELIZABETH A BLOODGOOD CATC • BYRON BLOODWORTH • CHARLIE BLOODWORTH • JOHN D BLOODWORTH • JOHN T BLOODWORTH • KATHERINE W BLOODWORTH • KEMBA N BLOODWORTH • KENNETH W BLOODWORTH • SHIRLEY L BLOODWORTH • TERESA D BLOODWORTH • AMAN BLOOM • GREGORY D BLOOM • RUTH E BLOOM • STACY L BLOOM • SUSAN O BLOOM • SHEILA W BLOOMBERG • CAROL Z BLOOMQUIST • DAVID V BLOOMQUIST • RHETT BLOOMQUIST • MICHAEL J BLOUIN • BRET D BLOUNT • ELLEN L BLOUNT

103

Press Information

Communications was committed to significantly expanding the scope of information that would be provided to the media. Press Information was given this responsibility, with emphasis on Info'96 content, and establishing the press data system with Technology and AOB. Press Information was the liaison with Technology for developing start lists and results in formats most usable for press and broadcasters, and also created the preferred names process to ensure consistent use of athletes' names.

In addition, Press Information was responsible for the Atlanta Olympic News Agency (AONA), which served as ACOG's single news source during the Games and ensured delivery of news and information to accredited and nonaccredited media.

By the start of the 1996 Games, more data had been assembled for use by the media than ever before. Extensive descriptions of every aspect of the Olympic Movement and of ACOG as the host of the 1996 Games had been finalized. Venue profiles and information on each sport had been compiled as well as country profiles and their history in the Olympic Games. Historical results for every sport and facts and figures covering Olympic medals, athlete statistics, team statistics, and thousands of biographical records were also available.

During the Games, the major focus of Press Information was the production of sports-related information at the venues. Venue teams were organized at each competition venue, which included an information manager with extensive sports experience and supporting staff. These managers shared responsibility with Media Relations personnel operating from the MPC and ACOG headquarters in providing comprehensive news and information about the Games.

Concurrently, the Press Information research team continued to develop athlete biographies throughout the Games, operating from press facilities at the Olympic Village. An athlete biography form mailed to NOCs in January 1996 resulted in a 65 percent return rate, and this material was continuously updated. Additional forms were completed by athletes when they arrived at the Olympic Village. Approximately 20,000 biographies were available on Info'96.

With these services, the quality and scope of information was significantly improved over previous Games. Especially well received were such innovations as the extended start lists prepared for athletics and swimming, which provided records and rankings never before available on start lists. Also for the first time, area and national records for athletics and swimming and all comers records for athletics were continuously updated for printed copies of results and for scoreboards.

Atlanta Olympic News Agency

AONA incorporated the reports produced by Press Information staff at the competition venues with updates provided by Communications personnel at Centennial Olympic Park, the MPC, OAF, and the Olympic Village. AONA staff stationed at the MPC also provided schedules for news conferences and events of interest to the media, detailed notes of all ACOG and IOC briefings and other major news conferences, summaries of each day's activities, facts and figures about all aspects of the Games, and media advisories on issues ranging from ticketing for high-demand events to changes in transportation schedules.

Information produced by AONA was distributed through Info'96; the 1996 Olympic Games World Wide Web site; and WXIA-TV and WGST-Radio, the local news outlets for the Games. Printed copies were distributed to media at the competition venues, MPC, and IBC.

Along with Media Relations staff, AONA staff based at the MPC answered inquiries from reporters and arranged interviews and press conferences for ACOG executives. Hundreds of media inquiries were received daily from the 6 July opening of the MPC until the start of the Games. Once competition began, the number of inquiries at the MPC declined significantly as attention shifted to the competition. However, numerous requests to interview ACOG executives continued. Prior to and during the Games, very few individual interviews were conducted due to time constraints, although AONA staff did arrange briefings for groups of reporters or scheduled press conferences for the press to receive news directly from ACOG management.

When the bombing in Centennial Olympic Park occurred, AONA issued all ACOG statements and media advisories, provided notes from the numerous press conferences conducted in the MPC by law enforcement agencies, and coordinated with these agencies in responding to inquiries from accredited and nonaccredited media. One of the most important functions of AONA during this period was ensuring that only the most factual, current information was provided.

PUBLIC INFORMATION

The Public Information division managed several programs and prepared information for dissemination to the general public.

The Olympic Experience

A public information gallery called the Olympic Experience—featuring maps, models, and drawings of new venues, photographs of existing facilities, and displays of the Bid history, Olympic sports, and programs such as the OAF—was opened in 1991 in downtown Atlanta, and continued operations through 1996, hosting more than 750,000 visitors.

The Olympic Experience was also the site for one of several countdown clocks ACOG installed. Others were placed at ACOG headquarters, City Hall, and on an overpass of the major highway intersecting downtown Atlanta.

Another important Olympic Experience feature was a specially designed kiosk that instantly displayed answers to frequently asked questions with colorful visuals and video clips through an interactive touch screen. IBM provided the technology for the kiosk, and Public Information developed the content. Two additional kiosks were placed at the Welcome South Center, a downtown visitors' facility, and at Lenox Square, one of the busiest shopping centers in metropolitan Atlanta.

Speakers Bureau

A Speakers Bureau was established in 1991 to accommodate the hundreds of requests from area organizations that wanted to hear presentations about the 1996 Games. The speakers—all of whom were ACOG employees or volunteers—used speeches, notes, slides, videos, and other materials developed by Public Information to ensure consistent information was conveyed.

Speakers Bureau representatives spoke to more than 1,500 community, civic, corporate, and convention groups. ACOG accepted honoraria to the Children's Olympic Ticket Fund for Speakers Bureau presentations; contributions received comprised a significant portion of the funds used to buy tickets for children who otherwise could not have attended Games events.

Information Requests

Most information requests were for brochures and printed materials. A general information brochure, including a map of all venues and an array of facts, figures, and program descriptions, was produced immediately after Atlanta was awarded the Games. This brochure was updated and reprinted—in quantities of 50,000–100,000—on numerous occasions, but demand always exceeded supply.

Other documents addressed the process of volunteering for the Games, provided a self-guided driving tour of Olympic venues, and answered frequently asked questions. An Olympic sponsor, the BellSouth Corporation, developed a 32-page general information booklet in cooperation with Public Information that was inserted into phone books for the Atlanta area and distributed in early 1996.

Concerns regarding Games-time transportation issues in the Atlanta area prompted Public Information to work with Transportation and a major local newspaper to produce a comprehensive publication with maps, suggested routes, and travel times. The publication was distributed in a June edition of the newspaper, and ACOG distributed an additional 250,000 copies to city employers, MARTA commuters, and various community groups.

Concurrently, US ticket holders received the *Guide to the 1996 Olympic Games*. This publication, produced by Public Information, Games Services, and Creative Services, was intended for those who would be attending events and focused on directions to transportation services and parking, walking directions to venues, services available in and around the venues, and sports, OAF events, and other Games programs.

The document in greatest demand during the months prior to the Games was a detailed events schedule. Due to the number of sports sessions—more than 270—in addition to the extensive OAF events schedule, a summary schedule was assembled, as costs prohibited the production of such a large publication.

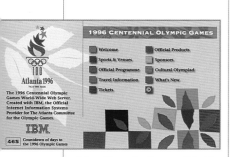

The Olympic Games World Wide Web site, the first designed for an Olympic Games, provided information about the Games to Internet users around the world.

Schedule information could be found, however, on the 1996 Olympic Games web site.

World Wide Web Site

Established in April 1995, the 1996 Olympic Games World Wide Web site marked the first use of the Internet by an Olympic organizing committee—and the first time that Olympic Games information was available to Internet users worldwide. The site was an instant success.

The site combined data from the *Press Guide* and general information brochures and from the latest competition and OAF schedules, with audiovisuals that ranged from slides and video programs to three-dimensional images and virtual tours of new venues. In addition, ACOG news releases were immediately added to the site as they were issued.

Popular features of the site included volunteer and merchandise order forms that could be submitted directly to ACOG. The greatest response was to the availability of tickets on the site. In March 1996, once tickets could be purchased on-line, an extraordinary 12–15 percent of all ticket purchases were conducted electronically.

The number of times the site was accessed began at 10,000 per day in April 1995 and grew to 400,000 per day just prior to Games-time. Once the Games began, usage of the 1996 Olympic Games site set Internet records—totaling approximately 200 million site visits for the 17 days of the Games. Approximately 60 percent of site visitors were from the US and 40 percent from other countries.

Call Center

Most calls requesting information came to ACOG's general switchboard or the call center, which responded five days a week, nine hours a day, for more than five years. The number of calls increased from several hundred per day in 1993 to an average of 2,500–3,000 per day in 1996.

Public Information staff members provided

the call center with constant information to equip operators with the data needed to respond to callers. When operators could not answer inquiries, they referred callers to a public information line to leave a voice mail message. Written responses generally were provided to these calls. Calls routed to Public Information increased steadily to approximately 125 per day by Games-time. Public Information staff members also responded to the thousands of letters and facsimiles sent to ACOG requesting general information about the Games.

Since many inquiries were related to information about Atlanta and the state of Georgia, Public Information established a collaborative arrangement with the Atlanta Convention and Visitors Bureau and with the Chambers of Commerce for Atlanta and Georgia. Each entity had supplies of the other organizations' brochures and materials, allowing each to serve as a complete source of information covering the Games, the city, and the state.

Games-Time Operations

During the Games, Public Information provided information directly to spectators and visitors through booths established in conjunction with Games sponsor Randstad at each competition venue and at Hartsfield International Airport, Centennial Olympic Park, the Olympic Experience, and a visitors center in downtown Atlanta. Public Information assumed an advisory role in determining the exact placement and design of the booths. Planning was concentrated on identifying and training the Public Information coordinators for each booth and preparing the materials to be distributed to spectators.

The booths were stocked with copies of the official map of the 1996 Olympic Games—produced by Public Information and Games sponsor UPS—and provided free to all spectators and visitors. Other materials available in limited supply included a guide to the OAF, a guide to accessible facilities, and listings of free events and activities.

The ACOG call center and World Wide Web site for the Games also provided avenues for communicating with the public, and AONA distributed information through the media. In the call center, approximately 100 volunteers managed the 25 phone stations installed for Games-time. Public Information staff provided training for these volunteers, developed answers for questions most likely to be asked, and met daily with the center coordinators to provide updates and other information needed to answer calls. During the Games, the center was fully staffed approximately 20 hours daily with a small number of operators available between 0200 and 0600 to handle emergency calls. Calls averaged 7,000–8,000 per day. Most inquiries concerned the schedule for sports and OAF events, possible delays caused by weather, and transportation information.

CONCLUSIONS AND RECOMMENDATIONS

The extraordinary worldwide interest generated by the Centennial Olympic Games, with the globalization of the news and broadcasting industry, mandated extensive, real-time communications in a variety of formats and applications. State-of-the-art technology with remarkable capabilities was available to the press, and extensive information was provided both to the press and the public.

The technology advances that make information more broadly accessible provide the Olympic Movement with even more opportunities to directly satisfy the public's immense interest in the Games. The following recommendations are directed toward achieving these objectives.

Media Relations

■ A World Wide Web site is essential for rapid, complete delivery of information to the media, with far less reliance on printed publications.

■ A media information line should be established at the earliest date possible.

■ Large press briefings should be scheduled well in advance to give international media the opportunity to attend and minimize the number of individual media visits to the organizing committee.

■ Notes from major news conferences should be distributed to the media and posted on the World Wide Web.

Press Operations

■ Senior experienced personnel for the MPC and venue facilities should be actively planning at least three years prior to the Games. Press chiefs for large venues should be full-time one year prior to the Games.

■ The MPC must be centrally located and available for occupancy and testing six weeks prior to the facility's opening date. The MPC should be staffed and operating with all management staff one week before opening. Operating 24 hours daily is not necessary until 2–3 days prior to the Games.

■ The ideal solution for press accommodations is a press village located within walking distance of the MPC.

■ Press transportation must have a hub within walking distance of the MPC and IBC.

■ A database should be built to consolidate all accommodation and rate card orders, mailing addresses, and other information related to the accredited press.

■ Restrictions related to ENR credentials should be clarified and communicated early and often to the press, NOCs, sponsors, and other constituencies.

■ In the competition venues, press tribunes should be located as close as possible to the mixed zone, especially for facilities hosting individual sports.

Press Information

■ The press data system should become part of standard planning, and the information provided by this system should be expanded.

■ The preferred names process needs to be continued but implemented beginning with the accreditation and inscription process.

■ Extended start lists should be provided for all individual sports.

■ The content of the technology systems critical to the press should be compiled by Press Information, with guidance and direction from Technology in how the material is accessed and presented. More testing of the technology systems is essential, as well as expanded training for personnel who will assist press in using the systems.

■ Consideration should be given to placing virtually all Games information for the media on a World Wide Web site that is established well in advance of the Games. Access to the site would be restricted to accredited media, who would have the opportunity to become familiar with the system prior to their arrival at the Games.

Public Information

■ A World Wide Web site is also essential to providing information to the public. Content should be presented in several languages.

■ Public information booths are necessary at Games-time, with more personnel assigned to the booths to answer general questions. A printed publication with general information and detailed maps should be provided free to all spectators during the Games.

■ A preliminary schedule of events should be made available in as many different formats as possible.

CHAPTER SEVEN
CONSTRUCTION

CONSTRUCTION EMPLOYEES

Date	Staff Number
June 1993	5
January 1996	4
July 1996	4

Note: These staff numbers do not include contract, VIK, and volunteer personnel.

OVERVIEW—From the earliest planning sessions in 1991, the mission of ACOG's Construction Department was to create a legacy of sports facilities through staging the Olympic Games that would further enhance the spiritual legacy of the Games—the emotions and memories inspired in the people who would attend. Newly designed and constructed as well as renovated spaces and facilities were needed that would meet the Games requirements of both ACOG and the IFs. It was important that all facilities achieve symmetry with community surroundings, provide a post-Games use, have no long-term impact on the environment, meet accessibility standards for people with disabilities, and be cost-effective. *(For information regarding how ACOG approached disability and environmental issues in its construction plans, see sidebar later in this chapter.)*

The Construction Department was chartered to supervise approximately $500 million in permanent and temporary facilities to support the 1996 Centennial Olympic Games. The crowning achievement was the $207 million Olympic Stadium—site of the Opening and Closing Ceremonies and the athletics competitions. From the Olympic Stadium to the new Aquatics Center at the Georgia Institute of

Technology and the Georgia International Horse Park in nearby Conyers, Construction accomplished its mission.

ORGANIZATION

In early 1991, the Construction Department began the task of developing the venues for the Games through planned phases. Due to the distinct nature of the phases and the diverse construction needs, ACOG chose to establish a small internal Construction Department and contract with external companies for the services needed in each phase.

The three main construction program phases were programming and planning, design, and construction, which included both permanent and temporary newly constructed venues as well as the adaptation of existing facilities. During the programming and planning phase, challenges were defined, while during the design phase, solutions were proposed. Concurrent with programming and planning, a site acquisition phase was occurring, during which contracts for the use of venues and sites selected for the Games were negotiated. Throughout the construction phase, the plans developed during the first two phases were implemented. Following the Games, venues were retrofitted and returned to each venue owner.

Comprehensive planning for an event of the magnitude of the Olympic Games involved incorporating three major components into each phase: developing the facility plan, identifying the nature of the event itself, and interacting with the community.

The facility plan addressed criteria such as the needs of multiple users (pre-, during, and post-Games), peak participant needs (usage at double and triple the average numbers), and the flow of participant groups through various routes, separating people into categories such as Olympic Family members, athletes, media, and spectators.

Identifying the nature of the Olympic Games as an event was another critical component. Event-specific requirements, especially temporary ones such as accommodating crowd sizes, needed to be identified clearly. Operation of the Games depended on developing very specific systems to accommodate food service, media needs, security, technology, and transportation, among others. Understanding these systems and what was required to accommodate their operations was paramount to the success of the construction planning for each venue.

Interacting with the communities which would host venues was an extremely important component of planning. ACOG carefully evaluated how construction of the venues would affect those neighborhoods and how those venue facilities could best provide long-term benefits and a positive legacy. It was also important to keep the residents of these communities informed about the schedules of certain construction activities, such as blasting, so they would be prepared for any disturbances.

PROGRAMMING AND PLANNING

Visual programming and planning, a proven architectural approach, was used by ACOG to define requirements for site and facility utilization. This methodology is a graphic communication process that addresses the qualitative aspects of activities and facilities, as well as the quantitative aspects of area and cost.

Sizemore Floyd Ingram (SFI) was contracted to provide the facilities programming and planning, which included documenting the requirements of all constituencies. Work began in June 1991.

Visual programming identifies overall challenges and divides them into smaller and smaller pieces of information that can be tested, understood, and modified quickly to meet changing requirements as they become known. This graphic and interactive process provided current information to Construction's programming team and ACOG every day.

The programming team assessed and displayed the information, allowing ACOG to make clear and well-informed decisions regarding each venue. Because of the breadth and complexities of the Olympic Games, an additional level of project planning was added, consisting of three major phases: data gathering, macro event modeling, and detailed venue programming.

After completion of the three phases, SFI held sessions to help ACOG determine the needs for the Games. The result was the production of the greenbooks, graphically oriented documents which compiled all needs for ACOG functional area venue support.

Data Gathering

Data relating to Olympic facilities was gathered, and a vision session was held with senior ACOG executives so the programming and planning team could understand the mission and legacy envisioned for the 1996 Centennial Olympic Games. Establishing clear and concise goals to be implemented through the facilities was important, as it would provide a comprehensive checklist for successfully completing each stage of the programming and planning, design, and construction processes. *(For a list of*

FIGURE 1: KEY TERMS

The terms listed below were significant in the planning and design of the venues. Spaces for these functional areas were further divided and became more detailed as the design of the venue evolved. Every effort was made to carry this numbering system from venue to venue throughout the process to create a continuity of terms. It was critical to the process that everyone had the same understanding of these areas.

1.0 Accreditation—an area designated for the validation of credentials for the athletes, Olympic Family members, and staff/volunteers working at the venues. This area was typically located adjacent to the entry points associated with the various user groups.

2.0 Ceremonies—spaces associated with the awarding of medals at each event. These spaces consisted of the awards platform (where medalists stand for presentation of medals), a staging area adjacent to the platform area, and a storage area for securing the flags and music of various national anthems.

3.0 Competition Area—the actual field of play of the venue.

4.0 Competition Related Services—the support area necessary for the athletes during the staging of the event, including locker/changing areas, lounge areas, and equipment storage.

5.0 Event Seating—the designation of seats of the various groups anticipated at the venue, including the public.

6.0 Venue Management—the spaces associated with the operations of the venue during the event, including office spaces, staff break areas, and work areas.

7.0 Sports Administration Federation Services—support spaces for the IF associated with the event, including offices, work rooms, and meeting rooms for IF staff and for juries and other competition officials.

8.0 Competition Management—office and office support space for the sport management of the venue.

9.0 Material Acquisition/Distribution—the necessary storage space and distribution points for consumable goods used during the event.

10.0 Media Operations—all space used by the various components of the news media and media support services during the event. This included spaces for a press subcenter (a working area for the press including support offices) and on-field positions for commentators, press, and cameras (both broadcast and photojournalist), as well as outdoor areas, such as a trailer compound.

11.0 Health Services and Medical Control—space for the medical requirements that had to be provided, including an area for sports medicine and doping control for the athletes and first aid for spectators and Olympic Family members.

12.0 Spectator Services—all spaces associated with providing spectator amenities, such as food concessions, information, and toilet facilities.

13.0 Olympic Family Services—all spaces associated with providing Olympic Family members with amenities such as lounge areas, reception areas, and escort waiting areas.

14.0 Security Services—spaces necessary to support Security staff during the event, including a command center, break areas, and outdoor areas such as SWAT staging areas.

15.0 Technology—support spaces needed to provide the technology associated with the event, including computer areas, telephone operations, and other electronic media requirements.

16.0 Food Service—spaces associated with the delivery and serving of food to the various user groups during the event.

17.0 Transportation—areas associated with transporting various user groups, including primarily exterior areas for parking, loading, and queuing to accommodate buses, cars, vans, and any other types of vehicles needed.

18.0 Ticketing—space required for the distribution of tickets at the venue.

---

key terms used in the planning and design of the venues, see Figure 1.)

Following the vision session, the programming team began a comprehensive global research effort, gathering any available information concerning past Olympic venues. This data was acquired from past Games reports, the IFs, published criteria, and interviews with experts. Each IF was also asked to validate or update its sport's requirements.

Macro Event Model

The second stage of programming and planning, building the macro event model, included a comprehensive series of interviews with ACOG's senior management concerning their preliminary systems concepts as they applied to operating the overall Olympic event. Systems concepts included areas such as ceremonies, construction, food service, spectators, sponsorships, security, and transportation. Building the model resulted in the development of a matrix which portrayed how each system would intersect within each venue.

During this time, SFI conducted evaluations of the Los Angeles, Seoul, and Barcelona Games to establish frames of reference for determining logical levels of services and functional requirements for each venue. Review of Barcelona's facilities allowed for a product test of each of the systems concepts discussed during the macro-level interviews. The planning team and ACOG senior management could see, from the abstract concept to the realized product, how these concepts could be developed.

The team then developed parameters for all core systems. A series of facility planning criteria related to individual venues was determined for each ACOG system. For instance, concessions systems developed a ratio of one point of sale for every 300 seats to build the model. Therefore, a ratio could be adapted from a relatively small venue to a large venue, such as Olympic Stadium. This approach allowed the team to develop a rational framework for criteria to use until more specific information was available at the time of an individual venue program request.

Detailed Venue Programming

Detailed venue programming began after planners reached an understanding of how the Games and their systems would work together as a total event. Space needs; quality service levels—temporary, portable, or permanent—as well as architectural and engineering systems; and budget options available for ACOG's consideration were determined during this phase.

Until this point, the programming and planning team had been organized according to its systems components, in a way that was similar to ACOG's organizational structure by operational system. The data gathering and assessment tasks for each component had been performed relatively independently. Facility criteria were identified by the programming specialists, site and existing facility analysis was prepared by the planning specialists, and cost and scheduling criteria were determined by the support specialists.

Following macro-level development, the SFI team was organized into five programming teams, each with responsibility for the architectural programming and planning for certain assigned venues. The 26-week venue programming process covered 29 venues and housing components. ACOG staff and SFI team members scheduled interactive sessions in order to accomplish this very intense and complex inquiry process.

First, questionnaires were developed for ACOG, IF officials, and post-Games venue owners to gather their initial requests for each venue. The information gathered was used to determine specific space requirements, priorities, and the flow of various participant groups through various routes. A workshop was then conducted to test each system within that venue.

The programming and planning team then proceeded to gather site, soil, access, utilities, and services data for each proposed sports competition site and to determine what issues remained and what the feasibility was for using each site for a particular sport. The majority of proposed sites were found to be suitable, although some needed adaptations were made, and several new sites were selected as more appropriate than others for the detailed venue program.

Construction's costing support team developed a comprehensive model to track cost as-

These two views show the Olympic Stadium site when construction had just begun (top) and when work was nearly complete (bottom).

DISABILITY AND ENVIRONMENTAL ISSUES

ACOG's design and construction activities took into consideration all issues of accessibility. Sites were also designed to have the least possible negative impact on the environment.

The Americans with Disabilities Act (ADA) provided the basis for constructing barrier-free facilities, and the design of the Olympic Stadium was the model for interpreting ADA guidelines for all venues. Designers studied the standards and principles set forth in ADA and applied them appropriately to each venue.

To help ensure accessibility in a new venue, Paradigm, a consulting firm, provided ACOG with detailed peer reviews based on progress drawings at five or more intermediate stages of design. These reviews, combined with meetings with the design teams, helped ACOG Construction officials monitor and control accessible elements of each facility design and develop consistent overall approaches to common ADA compliance requirements.

ACOG recognized that federal and state environmental regulations were in place that would control any improvements at all venues, especially the yachting and the rowing and canoe/kayak venues. Concerns about asbestos and underground storage tanks were anticipated and addressed appropriately. Concerns regarding animal and plant displacement and endangerment were addressed in the planning phases.

All ACOG facilities are models of design and construction successfully incorporating environmental and accessibility issues.

sumptions and test budgets from the programming and planning phase through the design and construction phases. The first task of the team was to review the Bid book assumptions and develop an understanding of the definitions used there. A primary market research survey was conducted to gather current cost information on the major construction systems anticipated for the Olympic facilities. Using the survey results, unit area costs were developed for each significant construction cost area. More than 250 specific unit-cost models were developed and applied to the individual space requirements of a venue in order to arrive at a working budget. Progressive budgets were developed, tested, and refined based on discussions with ACOG.

For each venue, a matrix of budget scenarios was developed, which included options for possible quality service levels that ACOG could consider, ranging from primarily temporary, to a mixture of permanent and temporary, to completely permanent venues. This flexible approach allowed ACOG to begin design and construction while maintaining the option of altering a venue budget based on Olympic needs.

The final venue program included a total project cost budget comprised of the hard costs of construction, such as building and site preparation, and the soft costs, such as design fees, furnishings, equipment, temporary and portable construction specialties (e.g., tents, trailers, and portable air-conditioning and generator units), and administrative items, including inflation factors, contingencies, and staff support.

A decision session was then scheduled so ACOG could review and make decisions on the options available. Following the session, a venue program was developed to provide the venue architects with facility criteria, space requirements, quality levels, and budgets the designer had to meet and the contractor had to deliver for ACOG. Accompanying the venue program was a schedule for architectural selection, design, and construction. Consistent

information in the venue program was provided to all potential architects and contractors before a final selection was made.

Individual venue budgets were considered provisional until all venue programs were complete, so that a total Games-wide venue budget could be determined and approved as feasible. At the completion of all the competition venue programs, a summary of each venue, its key provisions and scope, and alternative budgets were presented to the executive team for discussion, recommendations, and approval.

Following the completion of the programming and planning for competition venues, the SFI team began programming and planning the support venues, including the International Broadcast Center (IBC) and the Main Press Center (MPC). Several site options and locations were tested for adaptability, cost, location, services, and transportation.

The Greenbooks

During the Barcelona Games, the programming and planning team investigated and evaluated venues in terms of programmed needs of space, security, logistics, temporary and portable construction, and the flow of people, goods, and services. Additionally, Olympic operations systems outside the venues were evaluated. Upon return to Atlanta, the team conducted reviews with ACOG managers to determine if any adjustments or revisions were needed to the macro event model or the individual venue programs.

SFI helped ACOG determine the needs of the Olympic Games venues using a process new to most ACOG staff members: 2–5 SFI representatives met with staff members from each functional area included in the programming and planning process. The lead SFI staff member for a specific session asked questions of functional area staff members, while other members of the SFI team documented their responses on small cards. After information was collected from each group, all cards were hung on the walls, and the functional areas came together in one large session to review the collage of gathered information.

This session allowed the different groups to discuss openly the venue requirements for the Games as established by all the functional areas and to agree or disagree with the information as recorded.

The result of SFI's work was the production of graphically oriented, hardback documents called greenbooks. They contained the venue needs of all ACOG functional areas, requirements of the post-Games owner, anticipated schedules for completing construction work, and a budget estimate for each venue. Additional information was added to the greenbooks when venue locations changed or new site locations had to be considered.

Program Verification

Following visual programming and planning, a program verification process began. The Program Services Group (PSG) was contracted to perform this verification process, and used the completed greenbooks to verify that all the information provided within them was correct as written. Upon verification of a program by PSG, the ACOG Construction Department began the process of acquiring sites and selecting architects for venues.

Site Acquisition

Site acquisition was an important phase of the Construction Department as the competition, training, and logistical support sites were chosen for the Centennial Olympic Games. An attempt was always made to use existing facilities which would require as little adaptation as possible; however, due to the magnitude of the space requirements, sites for new facilities were also necessary.

Existing sites, 75 percent of which were on state-owned property, were acquired through a relatively standard lease agreement that provided for periods of use and compensation to the state or other owners. In some cases, the owners' lease form was used and adjusted to meet any special requirements. Provisions unique to Olympic competition and use were areas such as clean venues, proprietary rights, termination rights, mediation and arbitration procedures, operational considerations, construction obligations, and security considerations.

Generally, owners of existing sites were compensated by a rental payment and reimbursed for any support services provided. To help keep the rental and service reimbursement rates competitive, alternate sites were sometimes considered for the various competitions.

Undeveloped sites were acquired through a more complex lease agreement. In these cases, ACOG agreed to fund, build, and convey ownership of significant permanent construction on a site as an Olympic legacy and as compensation to the site owners, which were governments, government authorities, or private colleges and universities. Because of specific Olympic requirements, alternative locations were rarely available; therefore, competition was not a factor in the acquisition of most undeveloped sites.

When acquiring training sites, Construction attempted to use existing facilities as near as possible to the Olympic Village. Either a straightforward rental payment was made as owner compensation, or facility improvements (mostly for athletics) provided compensation in lieu of rent. Although many competition venues were used as training facilities, approximately 30 other training sites were acquired through standard lease agreements. Almost all these sites were located at local high schools, colleges, and swim clubs. Many of these facilities were available, allowing for strong competition.

More than 50 sites were acquired to meet the logistical support requirements of the 1996 Olympic Games. These sites included accreditation centers, dormitory housing accommodations, an equine quarantine facility, office and warehouse space, parking lots, ticket outlets, transportation centers, a uniform distribution center, welcome and information centers, and building rooftops (for general security and filming road races). Usually, security requirements for the logistical support sites were much less severe than those for competition and training sites.

Although ACOG Construction was not responsible for the development and construction of the Olympic Village, ACOG contributed significantly to the dormitories through a financial arrangement with the Board of Regents of the University System of Georgia. Construction of permanent dormitory housing was accomplished by the Board of Regents and became an Olympic legacy of student housing for the university system.

FIGURE 2:
ARCHITECTURAL DESIGN TEAMS FOR THE COMPETITION VENUES

Olympic Stadium
Heery International, Inc.
Rosser Fabrap International, Inc.
Williams-Russell & Johnson, Inc.
Ellerbe Becket, Inc.

Stone Mountain Park Tennis Center
R. L. Brown & Associates
Nichols Carter Grant Architects, Inc.
Rosser Fabrap International, Inc.
Tunnel-Spangler & Associates

Stone Mountain Park Archery Center and Cycling Velodrome
Bishop Planning Consultants, Inc.
M. Paul Friedberg & Partners
Harrington George & Dunn
Schurman Architects

Georgia Tech Aquatic Center
Stanley Love-Stanley, P.C.
Smallwood, Reynolds, Stewart, Stewart & Associates
B & E Jackson & Associates
Desmear Systems

Morehouse College Gymnasium
Moody / Nolan, Ltd

Georgia International Horse Park
Lord Aeck & Sargent
Delon Hampton & Associates
Tunnell-Spangler & Associates
Duckett & Associates
International Equestrian Design

Clark Atlanta University and Morris Brown College Stadia
Turner Associates
HNTB

Wolf Creek Shooting Complex
Harrington George & Dunn, P.C.
Lowe Engineers
CTA Architects / Engineers
Roy Ashley & Associates
Duckett & Associates

Lake Lanier
Armour, Cape & Pond
B & E Jackson & Associates

Wassaw Sound
Hussey, Gay, Bell and DeYoung

DESIGN

The entire design process, from the selection of architects and engineers through the completed design, lasted from July 1992 to the end of 1994. ACOG opted to choose architects on a venue-by-venue basis to ensure meeting completion timetables. A careful evaluation of designers was performed before their selection (including an evaluation of more than 1,000 unsolicited letters and brochures) to ensure that all the services needed to provide the best facilities were included. *(For a list of the design teams selected for the competition venues, see Figure 2.)*

In addition to ACOG-generated criteria, each IF had minimum requirements for the design of its specific field of play. IFs sometimes requested to approve documents to ensure that its standards were being met.

CONSTRUCTION

Central to the success of the Games was the goal of providing well-built and efficient facilities. A selection process similar to that used in the design phase was used to choose general contractors and construction managers for all venues. *(For a list of the contractors and construction managers of competition venues, see Figure 3.)*

One significant component of the construction plan was the use of temporary and portable equipment whenever possible to minimize construction of facilities not needed following the Games. A project management team, formed in December 1993, was responsible for the immense Temporary and Portable Facilities and Equipment (TPF&E) Program. The team also managed three primary venues in downtown Atlanta: the Georgia Dome, Georgia World Congress Center, and Omni Coliseum.

For the TPF&E Program, the team acquired more than 1 million sq ft (93,000 sq m) of tent space, 1,000 portable toilets, 150,000 temporary bleacher seats, 500 office and toilet trailers, and more than 25 MW of portable electric power. Priority was placed on quick installation and prompt removal of all such material to minimize rental costs and the impact on existing areas. (*Site plans for all competition venues are provided in Volume III of this report.*)

Newly Constructed Venues

In 1993, construction began on the first as well as the largest and most complex project—the Olympic Stadium. All newly constructed facilities were completed by the end of March 1996 so that any modifications could be made prior to the start of the Games. (*For the typical development schedule for new facilities, see Figure 4 on the following page.*)

Olympic Stadium. Opening and Closing Ceremonies, athletics competition, and the start and finish of the marathon were staged in Olympic Stadium, which was built on a 30 acre (12 ha) site, approximately 1.2 mi (1.9 km) from the center of the Olympic Ring. Plans unveiled in October 1992 required seating for 85,000 spectators during the Games, and 45,000 after the Games, as the facility would be converted into the home ballpark of the major league baseball team, the Atlanta Braves, beginning in 1997.

The master plan for the stadium included designs that would minimize the long-term impact on the surrounding community. The north end of the stadium seating bowl was built with precast concrete and some slab-on-grade construction. This construction method was used to simplify the stadium's post-Games conversion.

The precast construction method also allowed for easy changes to the stadium seating bowl for the Opening Ceremony. For that event, a large ramp replaced several hundred seats and was used by the athletes for entering the stadium, and by performers for other choreography during the evening. After opening festivities, the structure, which had been removed with its seats intact, was reinstalled prior to the start of the athletics events.

The team planning the Opening Ceremony requested a tunnel beneath the field of play for special effects during the show. This tunnel,

9 ft (2.7 m) in diameter, extended from the west side service level of the stadium to the center of the field. Adding this access, as well as all other utilities required, altered the original construction plans considerably.

Because of its future as a baseball park, the Olympic Stadium featured a track that was not surrounded with seating in its traditional shape, an idea that was new to some who had followed the history of the Games. The nonparallel seating section of the stands was farther from the Olympic Stadium's field of play than the seats on the east and west sides of the stadium. This future home plate area became a designated location for photographers. A moat was also created around the field for photographers so that spectator lines of sight from the stands were not interrupted by constant movement.

Following the Games, the stadium track was removed, modified, and given to Clark Atlanta University. The free-standing cauldron that housed the Olympic flame during the Games remained as a public work of art outside the north end of Olympic Stadium.

Stone Mountain Park Tennis Center, Archery Center, and Cycling Velodrome. Construction at Georgia's Stone Mountain Park, 16.5 mi (26.6 km) east of the Olympic Ring and Olympic Center, included a permanent tennis facility, along with a temporary archery range and cycling velodrome that were removed after the Games.

The tennis center was built in the northeast corner of the park because that location afforded the easiest access from public roads. It included a center court stadium with seating for 12,000, of which 8,000 would remain after the Games, as well as satellite and practice courts. The stadium and all other courts were given to Stone Mountain Park after the Games, with the temporary seating removed. The center is the largest tennis facility in the southeastern US

FIGURE 3: CONTRACTORS AND CONSTRUCTION MANAGERS OF THE COMPETITION VENUES

Olympic Stadium
Beers Construction
H. J. Russell Construction
C. D. Moody Construction

Stone Mountain Park Tennis Center
Winter Construction Company / Watson Building Constructors

Stone Mountain Park Archery Center and Cycling Velodrome
Foster & Company

Georgia Tech Aquatic Center
Gaston Thacker / Whiting Turner (GT / WT)

Georgia International Horse Park
Valley Crest Landscape, Inc. / Urban Organization, Inc. (Valley / Urban)

Clark Atlanta University and Morris Brown College Stadia
Turner / Mitchell

Morehouse College Gymnasium
Turner / Mitchell

Wolf Creek Shooting Complex
Metric Constructors, Inc. / A. L. Johnson Construction

Lake Lanier
M.G. Patton Construction Company / New South Construction Company

Wassaw Sound
Scott Bridge Company

and a great legacy to metropolitan-Atlanta citizens, including the largest amateur tennis organization in the world, the Atlanta Lawn Tennis Association.

A combination of cast-in-place and precast concrete with an exterior of buff-colored finished masonry, this facility coordinated well with the adjacent woods-lined golf course. All seats provided excellent views of the field of play, and the large plaza surrounding the stadium accommodated large crowds easily without creating spectator traffic-management

new sod was planted immediately prior to the Games. Adjoining the field of play was a large archery practice field. Temporary seats and field-of-play equipment were installed for this venue.

Following the Games, everything was removed except for some utilities which the park chose to keep for future use. Also, pine tree seedlings were planted on the lush green fields, and other larger trees that had been in temporary containers during the Games were planted permanently to create a new picnic area for park users.

FIGURE 4:
TYPICAL NEW FACILITY DEVELOPMENT SCHEDULE

Months

-3 -1 1 3 5 7 9 11 13 15 17 19 21 23 25 27 29 31 33 35 37 39 41 43 45 47 49 51 53 55 57 59 61 63 65 67

Venue contract negotiations

Design

Construction ←— Olympic Games

Field of play available for test event ◆

Installation of temporary/ portable facilities

Retrofit

The picturesque granite outcropping of Stone Mountain provided a scenic backdrop for the cycling velodrome. Because there was no identified operator for the cycling track following the Games, a temporary field of play was created. After extensive discussions with track designers from around the world, ACOG decided to construct the temporary facility using steel-supporting structures with a wooden track fabricated in sheets of laminated wood and finished with a special textured surface. All parts of this velodrome were fabricated in Michigan, then transported to the Georgia site for installation.

This was the first time that large sheets of wood had been used instead of the individual wooden sections typically used on cycling tracks around the world. The track was tested in events a year before the Games and received IF approval.

ACOG leased the track, seats, and most of the equipment used at this twin venue. After the Games, everything was removed, and the site was returned to Stone Mountain Park as a beautifully landscaped park for public use.

problems. The hard court surface, Plexipave, was approved for use at the Games.

In another area of the park, temporary archery and cycling venues were constructed adjacent to each other on undeveloped park land. A common mall area provided entry points for spectators going to either venue and provided separate entrances for the different participant groups.

Archery ranges were situated close to the center of the park. Located on a large, open green space, the field of play was constructed to accommodate the number of athletes approved by the archery IF. Because the range was used during the test events and an effort was made to maintain the beauty of the surrounding park,

above: **The archery range and cycling velodrome at Stone Mountain Park were temporary structures that were removed after the Games.**

right: **The tennis center was built as a permanent facility which was later left as a legacy to Stone Mountain Park.**

Georgia Tech Aquatic Center. The new $25 million Aquatic Center complex was constructed on a 14.6 acre (5.9 ha) site at the Georgia Tech campus near the main Olympic Village. The Atlanta Games marked the first time that one venue incorporated all aquatic sports: diving, swimming, synchronized swimming, and water polo.

The site provided spectators with a panoramic view of the city skyline. The open-air design was aesthetically pleasing and highly praised by athletes during both the 1995 test events and the Games. Georgia Tech, which received the roofed, outdoor facility after the Games for use as an intercollegiate aquatic center, has the option to enclose the structure, providing a championship caliber, year-round facility.

The main pool, which holds approximately 1.2 million gal (4.5 million l) of water, and the diving well, which holds 700,000 gal (2.6 million l), as well as the permanent seating stands were covered by a massive, permanent steel-framed roof measuring 85 ft (26 m) above the ground at its lowest point and rising to a height of 110 ft (33.5 m). An adjacent temporary roof covered 13,000 temporary seats.

Water polo athletes competed in a special, temporary above-ground pool with 4,000 temporary seats on two sides. This pool and seats were removed after the Games, and the grass surfaces beneath them replaced. The water polo finals were held in the main pool. The synchronized swimming competition occurred in the diving well. An existing pool adjacent to the diving well served as a warm-up facility.

Georgia International Horse Park. The Georgia International Horse Park in Conyers, 33 mi (53 km) east of Atlanta, contained permanent and temporary facilities which were constructed to accommodate all equestrian competitions: dressage, jumping, and the three-day event. The park was located on a 1,139 acre (461 ha) site.

Heavily wooded farmland provided a beautiful natural setting and was an enjoyable challenge to the team designated to design and construct this exciting venue. The facilities included a 32,000 seat arena (8,000 of which were permanent seats), 5 barns with 460 stalls, housing for grooms in specially built trailers, a steeplechase course, and a cross-country course.

The venue was designed with the health and safety of the horses in mind. The barns each had several ceiling fans and were designed to facilitate cross breezes. From design through

completion, scheduling for the park was critical to ensure that new grass plantings had enough time to grow, thus improving footing for the horses.

Following the Games, the venue was returned to the city of Conyers, which retains the facility as the Georgia International Equestrian Center. The organization has a plan for future use that includes the addition of a golf course and hotel.

Clark Atlanta University and Morris Brown Stadia. Hockey competition occurred at two sites located in the Atlanta University Center, a

The Georgia Tech Aquatic Center represented the first time in Olympic history that all the aquatic disciplines—diving, swimming, synchronized smimming, and water polo—were housed in one venue.

Both permanent and temporary facilities for equestrian competition, designed with the health and safety of the horses in mind, were constructed at the Georgia International Horse Park.

• JAMES H BOSTON • PATSY BOSTWICK • DAVID M BOSWELL • JUDITH F BOSWELL • TAMI W BOSWELL • MICHELE K BOTE • EMILY S BOTEIN • DIANE W BOTELER • MICHAEL W BOTELER • CYNTHIA BOTETT • JOHN J BOTH • MAXINE M BOTH • LIEZL BOTHA • DAVID S BOTHE • ELIZABETH E BOTHEROYD • JANET L BOTHWICK • VICTORIA L BOTSKO • GARY R BOTSTEIN • LAURIE K BOTSTEIN • SANDRA BOTTGER • CLIFFORD L BOTTIN • BARBARA BOTTINI • DAVID D BOTTJEN • BRENDA H BOTTONE • MARIA E BOTTONE • FRANCISCA G BOTTS • ROBIN M BOTTS • SARA B BOUCCHECHTER •

119

historically African-American educational collaborative. The center is located immediately west of downtown Atlanta and is bordered by residential developments, religious facilities, and public housing.

The main entry to both sites—one on the campus of Morris Brown College and the other across the street at Clark Atlanta University—is from Martin Luther King Jr. Drive, a major east-west street. A temporary pedestrian bridge was constructed over the street to connect the two sites. Because of grade variation, the bridge ends

The Morehouse College Gymnasium was constructed to accommodate the large number of teams competing in the preliminary rounds of basketball competition.

on one side with a staircase approximately three stories high.

The 5,000 seat stadium at Clark Atlanta was built on a bowl-shaped grassy field used for American football practice. Synthetic turf was used for the field of play. The city of Atlanta required that a new 108 in (274 cm) sewer be installed beneath the field of play to replace a deteriorating century-old brick sewer. The precast sewer sections were custom-built to extend the full length of the field and connect with sewers under the streets north and south of the stadium.

During the planning and design stages, Construction discovered that a portion of the land included in the programming phase belonged to another educational institution. An alternate layout was developed, providing post-Games use for football, collegiate American football, and athletics events. During construction, the base for a track was installed around the field of play, to accommodate the track from Olympic Stadium, which was moved there following the Games.

The 15,000 seat stadium built at Morris Brown College replaced Herndon Stadium, which was constructed in the 1940s. Neighborhood residents were concerned that the 13 acre (5.2 ha) site would lose some of its historical significance and that the actual demolition of the stadium would disturb and perhaps even damage nearby buildings. Morris Brown officials assured the community that the history of the stadium site would not be forgotten and preserved some of the historical sections of the site.

In terms of avoiding disturbance during construction, blasting was not an original part of the demolition plans; however, during the course of excavation, the general contractor encountered rock. ACOG Construction staff and the contractor communicated with neighborhood residents and kept them fully informed about the necessary blasting activities and their potential effects.

A major factor influencing the design of the stadium at Morris Brown College was the MARTA tunnel running east and west directly beneath the site. MARTA staff engineers reviewed and approved all preliminary and final construction plans to ensure compatibility between the two structures.

The stadium was built of precast concrete covered with a triple-brick pattern and included curved seating on both sides of the field. Although some individual bucket seating (featuring molded bottoms and backs) was provided on the "home" side of the stadium, most seats were aluminum bleachers. Temporary partitions installed to adapt the venue to the layout needed for hockey competition were removed after the Games to restore the layout to one suitable for American football.

A plaza area was built outside the main entrance to the stadium, and sidewalks were improved all around the new facility, creating a large arrival and gathering place for spectator activities associated with collegiate American football.

Early planning was required at both the Clark Atlanta and Morris Brown sites to enable quick retrofitting of the layout which was needed for the new school year in September.

Morehouse College Gymnasium. The site for preliminary rounds of Olympic basketball for both men and women was constructed on the campus of Morehouse College, also part of the Atlanta University Center. Although not included in the original Bid proposals, this venue was added to furnish the space needed for the large number of teams competing in the basketball event. The arena was constructed on an approximately 2 acre (.8 ha) site adjacent to the existing Archer Hall Gymnasium.

Construction activity also occurred in some existing buildings, used to accommodate other Games-related functions, such as cultural exhibits and housing.

The most recognizable challenge was adjusting the size of the site to accommodate a basketball court. Although the site measured nearly two acres, it was only slightly wider than the longest dimension of a regulation-sized basketball court. Once all the circulation space was added to both ends of the court, the building's width reached the minimum distance from the street as required by Atlanta zoning ordinances.

Wolf Creek Shooting Complex. The Wolf Creek Shooting Complex is located on 100

acres (40 ha) of rolling hills about 6 mi (10 km) southwest of Hartsfield Atlanta International Airport. All Olympic shooting competitions took place at the new site, which was built adjacent to an existing trap and skeet range. The Fulton County government owned the existing range and assumed ownership of the new facility after the Games.

In building the new complex, two major environmental concerns were addressed: protecting a wetlands area from encroachment or contamination and avoiding disturbance of the

waste landfill adjacent to the venue. Preliminary plans were to build five new ranges, but it was determined later that Olympic requirements could be met with three ranges. This change allowed the fall area for lead emitted during shooting to be moved away from the wetlands.

In addition to the existing range, the new facility contained three outdoor trap and skeet ranges with bunkers and three indoor ranges for shooting from 10, 25, and 50 m distances.

The Wolf Creek Shooting Complex, built adjacent to an existing trap and skeet range, housed all Olympic shooting competitions.

Enough space was available on the site to build additional ranges if necessary.

The 25 and 50 m buildings were semi-enclosed with a controlled ventilation system, allowing athletes to shoot from all positions inside the building at targets located outdoors. These two buildings had baffles overhead between shooters and targets to prevent bullets from leaving the ranges.

The ranges were equipped with state-of-the-art scoring equipment—the most advanced ever used in Olympic competition.

Lake Lanier. Facilities for rowing and canoe/kayak–sprint were built on Lake Lanier, 55 mi (88 km) northeast of Atlanta. The actual field of play was the point at which the Chattahoochee River feeds into Lake Lanier north of Gainesville, Georgia. A unique feature of venue construction was the installation of 17,300 temporary spectator seats on a 182,000 sq ft (16,926 sq m) platform supported by 202 steel piles that were driven into the lake. Fabrication of the platform required more than 860 tons (780 t) of steel and more than 52 mi (84 km) of aluminum planking.

This seating configuration was a first for the Olympic Games and provided the best lines of sight ever at these events, as it enabled spectators to see the racers from the starting line, rather than just the action at the finish line. Views were breathtaking from every angle.

The layout of this venue included different access points to each side of the lake, providing an easy, manageable way of separating the fans from the athletes and the Olympic Family.

The use of the lake was closely monitored by the US Corps of Engineers to minimize the damage to the site's environment. After the Games, all seats were removed, as well as all tents, trailers, and toilets. Shorelines were restored where any damage had occurred or where temporary roads had been installed for easier access.

The judges' tower, new boat houses, and permanent docks remained as a legacy for the city of Gainesville and Hall County, the post-Games owners.

Wassaw Sound. Constructing the venue for yachting competition in the Atlantic Ocean off the coast of Savannah, Georgia, was particularly challenging as no permanent facilities could be built because of environmental concerns about protecting populations of storks and turtles. The yachting IF often questioned ACOG's plans to provide temporary docks, and once the idea of using barges as docks was introduced, tests were performed to convince the IF that this approach would work. In fact, the barges worked extremely well, providing excellent ocean access, and were also less costly than other options.

The venue included an Olympic marina, a day marina, and a satellite Olympic Village. The Olympic marina was located on Wilmington Island on the property of a former resort hotel which had permanent docking facilities. The day marina, located on the north side of Wassaw Sound, was a 150,000 sq m temporary system consisting of floating barges with facilities and dock space. Both the Olympic and day marinas required extensive temporary facilities. Athletes prepared their boats at the day marina and either sailed or were towed to their events. Savannah, which is Georgia's oldest and second largest city, proved to be a very popular location with athletes and spectators.

ACOG installed lightning protection at several venues, including yachting, because of the tendency for storms to form quickly in the southeastern US in July and August. The yachting venue was struck by lightning on at least two occasions without any personal injuries or damage to property.

Inclement weather in the form of Hurricane Bertha struck the area eight days before the Games began. The entire ocean venue had to be demobilized, but the staff successfully reinstalled the site so it was operational in time for competition.

Existing Facilities

The existing facilities used for the Games were adapted with TPF&E to satisfy Olympic requirements. Designing and implementing this program was one of ACOG's greatest challenges. Because of the magnitude of the 17-day event, planning for these resources was critical. Ultimately, management of TPF&E was an overall success, confirming the strategies used during program verification and procurement.

TPF&E procurement strategies included the following key points.

■ Contracts were based on the scope of required work identified in late 1994, with the ability to adjust quantities based on unit prices.

■ The ability to obtain reserves of TPF&E such as tents, trailers, generators, seating, and toilets was part of the original contracts.

■ Commodity vendors and contractors were encouraged to form joint ventures with businesses owned by minorities and women.

■ Contractors were encouraged to complete fabrication 3–6 months prior to the Games. ACOG paid storage costs to ensure that supply problems would not arise.

Even though programming requirements continued to change until Games-time, this effective management process successfully filled the TPF&E needs at every venue. Equipment was delivered on time and in appropriate quantities, with no reports of excess amounts.

The two major challenges of the TPF&E Program were the integration of facilities requirements and scheduling and the consolidation of procurement responsibilities for TPF&E within ACOG.

Because facility requirements were not finalized prior to the contractor's having to fabricate and reserve ACOG's requirements, there were the risks of trying to place orders that could not be filled, paying an extreme premium for late orders, having to accept substandard items, and compounding already tight schedule constraints.

Fortunately, Atlanta has excellent labor and material resources; however, ACOG departments still had to compete with each other for the same resources.

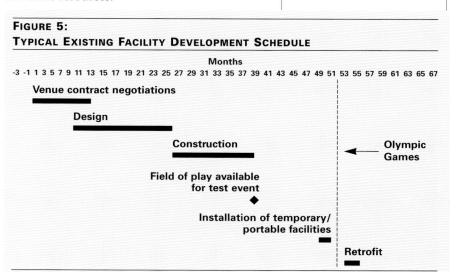

FIGURE 5:
TYPICAL EXISTING FACILITY DEVELOPMENT SCHEDULE

A number of existing facilities requiring minimal construction and TPF&E—usually to meet the *Olympic Charter* clean venue rule prohibiting advertising—were adapted for Olympic use. *(For the typical development schedule for adapting existing facilities, see Figure 5).*

Atlanta–Fulton County Stadium. This former home stadium of the Atlanta Braves was the venue for Olympic baseball competition. Adaptation was not needed, because the stadium as it existed already exceeded the requirements for Olympic competition. Located adjacent to the new Olympic Stadium, it was used also as a gathering place for athletes prior to Opening and

Closing Ceremonies. The area between the two stadia was used as a sponsor hospitality village.

Alexander Memorial Coliseum. The 10,000 seat arena, located near the Olympic Village on the Georgia Tech campus, and recently renovated as the new home for the Georgia Tech basketball team, was the venue for the Olympic boxing competition. Steps were taken to ensure that the site met clean venue requirements. Otherwise, only lighting improvements and a minimum amount of temporary equipment were necessary. An adjacent gymnasium was

The Georgia Dome was divided in the middle to accommodate more than one sports competition at a time.

used as a warm-up area for the athletes.

Georgia World Congress Center. Fencing, handball, judo, table tennis, weightlifting, and wrestling competitions were accommodated in this facility, which is one of the more heavily used exhibition spaces in the US. The layout of the facility and the vertical clearances contained more square feet and volume than was required for the Games. Temporary seats were installed in each venue area along with temporary equipment needed to serve each sport. One of ACOG's goals for this facility was to allow spectators to attend several events within one facility and provide spectators with convenient access to venues. The competitions held there drew full houses.

Georgia Dome. The Georgia Dome is part of a complex operated by Georgia state government that is both an exhibition space and the home of the National Football League's Atlanta Falcons. This facility had been used for many basketball games and athletics events, but at different times. Its use for Olympic basketball and artistic gymnastics marked the first time the arena was divided to accommodate more than one sport at a time. The venues were separated by a large, soundproof curtain.

The Dome has a permanent, transparent fabric roof that posed a problem for broadcasters because the quality of light could not be controlled. This problem was resolved by hanging a black fabric shroud inside the Dome to prevent any outside light from entering. This allowed lights to be added at desired locations within the facility, thus fulfilling broadcasters' lighting needs.

The Dome has a normal seating capacity of 72,000. When divided, there were approximately 34,500 seats for each competition, with warm-up space provided between the fields of play.

Georgia State University Gymnasium. Located within the Olympic Ring, Georgia State University was the site of Olympic badminton competition. The venue in the gymnasium had a capacity of 3,500 seats. Some changes were made to the ceilings to provide the minimum clearances specified by the badminton IF. Temporary air-conditioning and portable flooring were installed for the Games and removed at their conclusion.

University of Georgia Coliseum. The newly renovated coliseum at the University of Georgia in Athens, 50 mi (80 km) east of downtown Atlanta, was used for rhythmic gymnastics and preliminary rounds of volleyball. The facility accommodated 10,000 spectators and needed only minor adaptations, one of which was an enclosure built to provide practice space for athletes.

The Omni Coliseum. Located in the Olympic Center, this 16,500 seat arena was the primary venue for volleyball. A temporary portable floor was installed to create the field of play.

Road Courses. Streets throughout Atlanta served as venues for road cycling, racewalking, and the marathon. The cycling course stretched from downtown Atlanta northward through some of the most scenic neighborhoods in the city. The race walk course extended into the historic neighborhoods immediately south of the Olympic Stadium. The marathon course winding through the city was identified by a bright blue stripe painted on street surfaces. Temporary seats and viewing stands were installed at strategic vantage points. Look of the Games images, such as street banners, were installed along the courses.

Other Venue Locations

Local organizing committees outside Atlanta participated uniquely in the Olympic experience by completely developing some venues for their communities' use and providing them to ACOG for Games-time use. The following venues were leased to ACOG for the Games.

Atlanta Beach, located in Clayton County, Georgia, 20 mi (32 km) south of the Olympic Village, hosted beach volleyball competition. Seating for 12,600 was provided for the two courts.

Golden Park, the venue for women's fast pitch softball, was in Columbus, Georgia, located 105 mi (169 km) southwest of Atlanta. Athletes and officials stayed at a satellite Village in Columbus. The stadium had a seating capacity of 8,700 and featured adjacent practice fields.

Canoe/kayak–slalom events took place at the Ocoee Whitewater Center in the Cherokee National Forest in Cleveland, Tennessee, north of Atlanta, across the Georgia/Tennessee state line. This venue was developed by the US Department of Agriculture Forest Service and was the first natural whitewater slalom course in Olympic history.

Early rounds of football were played in existing facilities in Washington, DC; Birmingham, Alabama; and Miami and Orlando, Florida; Athens, Georgia, hosted the semifinal and final rounds. All these locations had been used for American football and were adapted for the Games by local developers.

RETROFITTING

Following the Games, venues were retrofitted and returned to each venue owner according to the stipulations in the individual contracts. All warranties and construction issues were resolved by May 1997, with the exception of the contract for Olympic Stadium. That contract required the full demolition of Atlanta–Fulton County Stadium and the configuring of the Olympic Stadium to accommodate baseball, with a completion date of 31 December 1997.

ELECTRICAL SYSTEMS

Electrical power systems provided for the 1996 Olympic Games consisted of the systems installed in permanent facilities as well as extensive temporary systems and/or system adaptations. Typically, the capacity and distribution level of electricity required at competition venues far exceeded the capability of the permanent facility configuration. Extensive temporary electrical power systems were required to support temporary facilities (i.e., tents and trailers) and all the technology needed for the Games. Games-time electrical loads consisted of temporary facilities, broadcast equipment, communications systems, and lighting systems. Additionally, in order to enhance the quality and reliability of critical broadcasting, lighting, scoring, and communications systems, more than 25 MW of on-site primary and secondary power systems were installed at every venue.

Georgia Power Company, the local utility for nearly all of the competition venues in Georgia and an Olympic Games sponsor, supplied most of the power. Because a significant portion of the venue loads were for temporary facilities

This temporary construction was adjacent to the course for canoe/kayak–slalom at the Ocoee Whitewater Center.

and equipment, consideration was given to generating power at the site for temporary facilities. However, an evaluation of the cost indicated that it was more economical to have Georgia Power install temporary utility transformers to distribute power from existing lines than to rent generators. At certain venues, however, in addition to utility power sources, twin generator sets operated in parallel and were used as primary power sources for broadcast equipment.

Extensive temporary electrical distribution systems were required to support temporary facilities. The configurations and components for such systems are significantly different from those of a permanent facility, causing challenges in developing venue designs. Inconsistencies in working with different building inspection officials who had varied experience with temporary distribution systems further complicated the issue.

The critical nature of venue loads for broadcasting, timing and scoring, communications, and field-of-play lighting necessitated having alternate and backup power systems. Early in the development of the venues, an evaluation was made of venue electrical loads and the quality and reliability of power required for each. Included in that evaluation was a review of the existing and proposed power systems supplying these loads. Based on that evaluation, a program to enhance the power systems supporting these loads was developed. This program included the application of on-site generators and alternate or redundant distribution system configurations. This program resulted in the application of approximately 85 generator packages, each with more than 25 MW of capacity supporting competition venues alone.

CONCLUSIONS AND RECOMMENDATIONS

The Construction Department and its contractors successfully planned, designed, and constructed all facilities and their components required for the Games. In the process, a lasting legacy for the state of Georgia was created.

The following recommendations are offered to future organizing committees.

■ Involve Venue Management before programming and planning are complete to avoid expensive design and construction changes late in the process.

■ Distinguish between the requirements and desires in the IFs' expectations for their fields of play.

■ Include regulatory agencies early in the process so they have a greater understanding of the magnitude and complexity of Games requirements.

■ Anticipate that electrical requirements will exceed projections, though some groups will overestimate their power needs.

■ Emphasize that planning as it relates to facilities must be completed at least nine months before use.

■ If temporary and portable facilities and equipment are to be used extensively, designate a single source responsible for procurement of leased items so that a consistent approach is maintained in terms of scope, contracting, risk avoidance, scheduling, and payment.

■ Consider as many alternate competition sites for each sport as early as possible in the acquisition process.

■ Ensure that indoor shooting ranges have walls, ceilings, and floors that are protected with baffling. The light intensity should meet IF and broadcasting requirements, with little variation in intensity level throughout the area.

■ For the outdoor trap and skeet ranges, include provisions for the environmental impact of lead emitted during shooting.

■ Focus early in the planning process on procuring labor and material resources to reduce competition among functional areas for the same resources.

Atlanta 1996.

CREATIVE SERVICES

CHAPTER EIGHT
CREATIVE SERVICES

OVERVIEW—From the beginning stages of Bid preparation through the conclusion of the *Official Report of the 1996 Olympic Games*, the AOC and ACOG placed great value on both creating a visual identity and ensuring the integrity of all collateral pieces. It was essential that ACOG have a strong and dedicated focus on the effective and proper use of its visual image and the publications that would tell the multifaceted story of the Centennial Olympic Games. The Creative Services Department was established to ensure excellence in the design and production of all visual manifestations of the Games. The influence of visual identity was far-reaching, including the entire spectrum of visual materials: publications, posters, photographs, videos, merchandise, exhibitions, and above all, the Look of the Games.

Each collateral piece that contained the logo was created to convey a certain message appropriate to a specific audience, in keeping with the high standards of the Olympic Movement.

ORGANIZATION

Throughout the first years (1987–1991), the core Creative Services staff focused on creating the visual message, confirming factual information, establishing guidelines, and contracting with design firms and designers for each collateral and video piece. During this period, it was believed that the involvement of several firms would contribute significantly to the enthusiasm of the community as well as the creative result of the end product. Although stringent guidelines were established for contractors, the response was extremely positive, and many firms and individual designers participated. For example, from 1988 to 1995, a holiday card was produced each year by a different designer, signed individually by ACOG, and mailed internationally to Olympic Family members.

From 1991 to 1993, a small staff continued to coordinate the work of design firms and produced reports to the IOC, programmatic collateral pieces, and communications to the community. Additionally, the department created logos and looks for each special event, including the 1991 reunion at Underground Atlanta commemorating the one-year anniversary of Atlanta being awarded the Games, the 1992 flag arrival celebration, and the 1993 Olympic Stadium groundbreaking.

Throughout Games planning, individuals and outside design firms were used on a contract basis. Once the Design Services division was established, it chose the firms and negotiated all these contracts.

Creative Services staffing grew steadily in 1994 as workload increased, and peaked in the final months before the Games. The department was organized into the following divisions, each with its own manager: Design Services, Editorial Services, Art Direction, Photography/Film and Video, and the Look of the Games. Each division is discussed in detail later in the chapter.

Each division's manager reported to the director of Creative Services, who reported to the managing director of Corporate Services. Also reporting to the director of Creative Services was a project coordinator who focused on three key programs: victory medals, staff uniforms, and the *Official Report*.

VISUAL IDENTITY

During Atlanta's early efforts to earn the right to host the Games, the AOC developed a colorful logo. This was a challenge, as IOC protocol precludes an Olympic committee from commercializing the Olympic Rings motif before winning the Bid. To suggest the Olympic Rings in the Bid logo design without actually using them, Atlanta designer Brad Copeland created an arrangement of five *A*s, each of which presented one color of the Olympic Rings. This Bid logo symbolized both Atlanta's initiative to host the Games and the international significance of the Rings. *(For more information, see The Bid chapter.)*

Atlanta
1 9 9 6

AOC Bid logo

Once Atlanta was awarded the 1996 Games, a new visual identity was developed. One of ACOG's first tasks in visual identification was to create a logo that would reflect the mission of the Centennial Olympic Games, be serviceable on products and materials, and be trademarkable both within the US and internationally. The focal point of this new identity was the ACOG torch mark, which became the official logo for the 1996 Olympic Games.

Games Logos

The first step in the Games logo development process was to confirm that its message would be appropriately conveyed and publicly accepted, so focus groups were conducted with the public throughout the region. Information from the focus groups was conveyed to a select group of design firms, and in fall 1991, Landor and Associates was chosen for its design interpretation of the centennial message.

The base of the torch mark logo, made of the five Rings and the number 100, resembles a classical Greek column and recognizes the centennial of the Games. The torch mark's flames gradually evolve into a perfect star symbolizing each athlete's pursuit of excellence. The gold color in this logo represents gold medals. The green represents laurel branches worn by winners in ancient times, as well as Atlanta's reputation as the City of Trees.

Before public announcement of the official Games logo, applications were filed to register the mark with the US patent and trademark offices, and in numerous civil law countries. *(For further detail, see the Marketing/ACOP chapter.)*

The torch mark logo—the Games' most important visual image—was approved by the IOC and unveiled to the public on 13 February 1992.

The torch mark logo, developed so that a system of derivative logos could be created from it, was utilized by both Atlanta Olympic Broadcasting (AOB) and the Cultural Olympiad. System logos were restricted in use to these two programs—the colors remained the same but were used with different degrees of prominence.

The AOB logo was created to establish the organization as the vital global broadcasting link for the 1996 Games. The sweeping swirl of the symbol encompasses all forms of communication, while the diagonal line at the focus of the spiral represents the single source from which all communications for the Centennial Olympic Games would originate. The kinetic spirals from the AOB logo rest on the five Olympic Rings and the number 100, giving the logo a look consistent with the ACOG torch mark logo. When used in color, the AOB logo appeared as a two-color, blue and white mark.

The Cultural Olympiad logo was created to evoke the spirit of innovation, energy, and dynamism celebrated in every culture. The symbol is a furled page, which could represent any image from a page of literature to a sheet of music. The base of the centennial torch beneath the upper segment provides a clear thematic link with ACOG. The five-color symbol, which included a specific match color, Cultural Purple, was its preferred version.

top: The torch mark logo, was the Games' most important visual image.

middle: The Atlanta Olympic Broadcasting (AOB) logo was created to establish AOB as the vital broadcasting link between the 1996 Olympic Games and the world.

bottom: The Cultural Olympiad logo was created to evoke the spirit of innovation, energy, and dynamism expressed by every culture.

MICHAEL L BOYTER • DUSICA BOZANIC • WILLIAM H BOZARTH • SCOTT H BOZE • ERIKA J BOZEMAN • JANET BOZEMAN • SUSAN Q BOZEMAN • KIRSTEN A BOZENHARD • CRAIG T BRAATEN • TODD M BRAATEN • REBECCA A BRAATHEN • STEVEN A BRABAW • CELESTINE A BRABBLE-BROWN • EDDY J BRACE • GILBERT B BRACEGIRDLE • MARY M BRACEGIRDLE • AMILCAR BRACERO • CAMILLA H BRACEWELL • DONALD F BRACEWELL • ELLEN H BRACEWELL • EMILY H BRACEWELL • JOHN B BRACEWELL • REBECCA BRACEWELL • WILLIAM BRACEWELL • BARBARA J BRACEY • RONALD BRACEY •

129

A family of typefaces for all ACOG print materials was selected as part of the overall corporate identity package developed in conjunction with the torch mark logo. The primary fonts used were Stone Serif, Copperplate, Univers, and Caslon Open Face.

Color Palette

Landor also developed the basic color palette of the Games. The deep, rich green—known as Georgia Green—came to be ACOG's signature color. Extensive work was required to standardize this color, as ACOG had to create a custom color formulated by Pantone, Inc., that would be applicable to all mediums. In the beginning years, the logo was only allowed to be reproduced in black/white, gold, green, or full color. Through the years, shades of colors were added to the original color palette to allow for certain product development (e.g., a blue stitched logo on a blue shirt). The torch mark logo and Georgia Green soon became universally recognized and synonymous with Atlanta.

Standards Manual

The Standards Manual was established to provide usage guidelines for programs, products, and collateral pieces. This was very important, as it became evident that written guidelines regarding use of the graphics and colors would be needed to provide and enforce consistency.

A complete version of the manual was created with the flexibility of adding chapters on other specific uses in future years, and was distributed in early 1993 to relevant ACOG and ACOP staff, sponsors, suppliers, and licensees. Each submission to ACOG was reviewed against this manual.

Standards were developed for the numerous auxiliary programs and constituents, such as the venue facilities, satellite venue support groups, local government entities, Cultural Olympiad programs, sports equipment suppliers, the hospital network, coin distributors, ticket agents, and the stamp program. Standards were created for the development of composite logos using ACOG, USOC, and corporate logos following

IOC guidelines. The primary guideline was that there had to be a clear division of two logos within one frame. Each was subject to approval by ACOP.

Mascot

What began as an effort to develop a futuristic Olympic Games mascot with universal appeal evolved into a successful program that focused on involving children in the Olympic Movement.

In late 1991, ACOG organized a design competition that included prospective mascot submissions from 20 designers and also reviewed suggestions gathered from the public as a result of a local newspaper promotion.

WHATIZIT—a computer-animated mascot created by a local design firm, DESIGNefx—was chosen as the most innovative concept because of its ability to change in appearance to represent different athletes and sports; hence its name, "What is it?" Selection of the mascot was announced in 1992. However, a major challenge was presented, as implementation of its computer image into printed images, costumes, and merchandise had not yet been fully developed at this time.

Initial reaction to WHATIZIT was not favorable among adults, but children were attracted to it. Their overwhelmingly positive reaction to the mascot confirmed ACOG's belief that its audience was youth.

ACOP Licensing began researching the mascot's appeal to children. As a result of studies from multiple focus groups, youth contests, and an animation studio, a number of adaptations were made to the mascot. For example, its name was changed to IZZY, and its appearance was altered to make it more adaptable to licensed products and animation.

ACOG Basic Color Palette

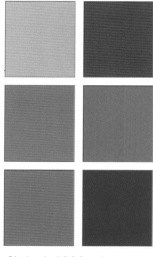

Six basic ACOG colors were developed by Landor and Associates.

TM. © 1992 ACOG

IZZY, the official mascot of the 1996 Games, appealed especially to children.

IZZY became part of a successful children's program through promotions such as the Macy's Thanksgiving Day parade and write-in story contests through *Parade* magazine. Additionally, stories were created for IZZY, promotions were launched—particularly in *SI for Kids*—and several sponsors used IZZY for promotions. ACOP Licensing produced a half-hour IZZY animated special that aired on cable television.

Thus, IZZY was an integral part of the Youth and Education Department and attended many schools and community events. *(For more information, see the Marketing/ACOP and Youth and Education chapters.)*

Exhibits

ACOG was the first summer organizing committee to offer a preview of its Games at the new IOC museum in Lausanne by installing an exhibition for the museum's opening. A semicircular display featured a model of the new Olympic Stadium in front of a backdrop of the Atlanta skyline. Video monitors highlighting Atlanta's plans for the Games operated continuously, while other displays featured Atlanta's torch mark logo, a stuffed toy of IZZY, and the five-volume set of ACOG's written Bid. The materials and video displayed were changed twice to reflect progress in Games planning.

In response to an invitation from the IOC, ACOG also created the centerpiece for the IOC pavilion at the Seville, Spain, World Exhibition in spring 1992. The 20 x 40 ft (6 x 12 m) exhibit invited guests to walk through the three-dimensional "One Hundred Year Time Line." Key moments in the history of the Olympic Games, the city of Atlanta, and related world events were intertwined to create a visual and auditory walkway from 1896 to 1996, culminating in a spectacular video montage of Atlanta's venue sites, sporting history, and community spirit. A brass and copper sculpture of Atlanta's torch mark logo was a featured element of the pavilion.

DEVELOPMENT OF THE LOOK OF THE GAMES

In addition to the Games marks, color palette, and mascot, the magnitude of the Olympic Games required a multitude of images that both enhanced the festive atmosphere of the events and provided the framework for all decorations and wayfinding signage. In mid-1993, Creative Services began to identify and evaluate design firms to perform the vital task of developing the central images of the Look. In order to bring people together to create a better whole, ACOG opted to assemble a consortium of talented designers to work collaboratively to develop the Look.

Inquiries from more than 500 prospective Olympic design firms were reviewed, other firms were contacted, and a preliminary field of 87 was identified. A detailed package on the Atlanta Games was sent to the firms, asking them to submit a comprehensive proposal. Thirteen firms responded to this offer, and each visited Atlanta in December 1993 to present materials to a review committee. After considerable review, ACOG selected six firms to commence the Look project. Five firms selected were design firms, and one was an architectural/project management firm. *(For details on each firm, see Figure 1.)*

The warmth, friendship, and hospitality of Atlanta and its people were central to the city's success in its endeavor to bring the Games to Atlanta. Therefore, the mission of the Look was to create a visual design that would express friendship, celebration, and the hospitality of the South. Imperative in the design was its capacity to be adapted readily and consistently to all mediums.

The development of a consistent Look for an Olympic Games is a relatively recent phenomenon. The Munich Games set a high precedent for the development of a consistent visual identity. The Los Angeles Games also did much to establish the concept of communicating the character of the Games through widespread and consistent use of distinctive colors, images, and temporary structures. The tradition was continued at Seoul in 1988 and Barcelona in 1992.

FIGURE 1: THE LOOK DESIGN TEAM

Copeland Hirthler Murrell Design and Communications
Atlanta, Georgia
The principals of this firm were veterans of the Atlanta Olympic effort who designed the Bid documents and early ACOG materials.

Favermann Design
Boston, Massachusetts
This firm has expertise in environmental graphics, sporting events, and urban design.

Jones Worley Design
Atlanta, Georgia
This firm contributed expertise in signage and wayfinding.

Malcolm Grear Designers
Providence, Rhode Island
This firm is known for fine, classical design.

Primo Angeli Design
San Francisco, California
This firm has extensive experience and success in branding, packaging, corporate identity, and uniform design.

Turner Associates
Atlanta, Georgia
This architectural and project management firm facilitated the process of developing the Look.

The Atlanta Look would need to appear prior to the Games in publications and other printed materials, but it was during the Games, at the venues and in the public areas, that it was most important for ACOG to create an attractive, inviting environment for spectators and television viewers worldwide.

The challenges inherent in developing a package of graphics and images that adequately conveyed hospitality, friendship, and the character of Atlanta were compounded by the fact that the Atlanta Games marked the 100th an-

top: **Rough sketches of the Quilt of Leaves were signed by its collaborative designers.**

bottom: **The Look of the Games Quilt of Leaves incorporated the two central images selected for the Centennial Olympic Games.**

niversary of the modern Olympic Games. The imagery of the Look would have to observe this historic event properly.

In January 1994, the six design firms assembled in Atlanta to develop the basic graphic images of the Look. Their mission was to create a Look that would impart a sense of the Olympic Spirit and the hospitality of the South. From this directive, three concepts were chosen:

■ harmony, in tribute to the countries of the world coming together at the Games;

■ radiance, in recognition of the glory of athletic achievement; and

■ grace, in celebration of the quality of an athlete in motion.

Using these concepts to guide their work, the firms spent January–February 1994 exploring possible Look images. After much exploration, two central images emerged—quilts and leaves.

Quilts were an especially appropriate symbol, as they embody the concept of unity within diversity. They also convey a strong sense of warmth, comfort, and welcome. Quiltmaking is a long-standing tradition in the South, as well as elsewhere in the US. Further research found that quilts were familiar to many cultures outside of the US. The appropriateness of the quilt image was illustrated most directly in the parade of participants in the Opening Ceremony. Each contingent of athletes in their respective national attire formed, in essence, a square of a quilt.

Atlanta is the most heavily forested city in the US, and its breathtaking springtime beauty of blooming dogwood trees and brilliant azaleas is well known. Adding to the aptness of the leaf image was its connection to the history and traditions of the Games. In the ancient Greek Games, victorious athletes were awarded laurels and olive branches for their achievements.

With the emergence of the quilt and leaf concepts and the collaborative efforts of the Look team and design staff, a basic black and white graphic was developed and given preliminary approval in early March. The Look team members were each assigned to develop specific applications of the Look. On 24 March 1994, the team assembled in Atlanta and presented the Look, now dubbed the Quilt of Leaves.

The individual firms took on specific assignments to further develop the Look until July 1994, when the Quilt of Leaves was unveiled to the public. Having successfully completed their mission, members of the Look design team remained involved in Games design work through specific projects.

The Look design program included very important, specific items, such as victory and commemorative medals and diplomas, uniforms, design elements of the Torch Relay, and pictograms, all coordinated by the Creative Services Department.

Victory and Commemorative Medals and Diplomas

Preparations for the design and production of victory and commemorative medals began in April 1994. The designer of the 1996 pictograms was awarded the contract to refine the design for the victory medals and design the commemorative medals.

The obverse of the medals adopted the design used since the 1928 Amsterdam Games. The design depicts the goddess of victory, Nike, holding a bundle of palm leaves in her left arm. Her right hand holds a wreath of olive leaves above her head. Behind her stands the ancient Coliseum with a horse-drawn chariot. An amphora is also included in the design.

The reverse of the medal displays the 1996 Games logo and the sport pictogram signifying the event won by the athlete. Each medal was also engraved with the name of the event in which it was won, signifying the first time medals contained sport-specific designs.

The obverse of the commemorative medal displays the torch mark logo with the words "Games of the XXVI Olympiad." On the reverse, the Quilt of Leaves appears with the words "Centennial Olympic Games."

In accordance with the *Olympic Charter*, both victory and commemorative medals were designed and produced by the same manufacturer. A total of 633 gold medals, 635 silver medals, and 661 bronze medals were produced, as well as 52,600 commemorative medals. Commemorative diplomas were designed in the ACOG design studio and then printed in French and English.

The commemorative medals and diplomas were distributed to all accredited members of the Olympic Family through their respective contact at ACOG, e.g., the Media Relations division of ACOG Communications, AOB, and

International Relations. ACOG staff and volunteers also received the diploma.

All moulds of the victory and commemorative medals and sets of the first-to-eighth placed athletes' certificates and commemorative diplomas were given to the IOC, in accordance with the *Olympic Charter*. Samples of the medals were also kept for ACOG's Olympic archives.

Uniforms

Design of uniforms for Games-time staff, volunteers, and officials began in July 1994. Two of

the Look design firms were engaged to begin creating the uniform design. The focus was to reflect southern warmth and hospitality; design clothing appropriate for a range of ages and sizes; make the uniform durable, cool, and easily washable; and incorporate the Quilt of Leaves pattern in the design.

Creative Services, Volunteer Services, and Hanes, the official uniform sponsor, held meetings to determine the colors and design of the various uniforms. There were five uniform types: casual, dress, business casual, official, and victory ceremonies. *(For more information about uniforms, see the Staffing of the Games chapter.)*

Torch Relay Design Elements

In early 1996, the Look of the Olympic Torch Relay was unveiled. The design combined vibrant colors and classical images to create a vivid representation of the Olympic Spirit. The

left: The obverse of the 1996 Centennial Olympic Games medals followed the design used since the 1928 Games.

right: Commemorative medals (obverse above and reverse below) were distributed to all accredited Olympic Family members.

dominant images of the Look of the Relay were a pictogram of torchbearers exchanging the Olympic flame, inspired by similar representations found on ancient Greek vases, and a stylized Quilt of Leaves motif. For the Torch Relay, this motif symbolized the different communities the Olympic flame passed through during its cross-country journey.

The Torch Relay Look was designed to uphold the sanctity of the Olympic flame and complement the Look of the Games. Colors and motifs were prominently displayed on torchbearer uni-

bands—one with the names of all Olympic Games host cities, and the other with the logo of the 1996 Centennial Olympic Games and the Quilt of Leaves motif. The torch was the tallest ever for a summer Olympic Games and the only one designed to be grasped in the middle.

Pictograms

To many spectators, pictograms are a familiar form of Olympic imagery. First introduced at the 1948 Games in London, they became an integral facet of Olympic Games design at the Tokyo

The 31 sports pictograms used extensively in the Look of the Games captured the grace of athletes in motion.

forms, vehicles, street banners, and many other aspects of the Torch Relay entourage.

Because the Torch Relay was sponsored separately from the Games, the logo used on all materials had to be different from the torch mark logo. A logo was created that combined the trademark of The Coca-Cola Company and the ACOG torch mark logo. Approved by the IOC at the Executive Board meeting in September 1995, the composite logo was one way a corporate sponsor was allowed recognition in conjunction with the Torch Relay. *(For information about sponsor recognition, see the Torch Relay chapter.)*

The design of the torch, one of the most vivid symbols of Games ideals, was very important. The torch was inspired by the simplest ancient torches—a cluster of reeds bound by twine—and also reflected the lines of classical Greek architecture. It featured 22 aluminum "reeds"—one for each Olympic Games; a center handle of Georgia pecan wood; and two gold

Games of 1964, serving an invaluable function as elegant and simple wayfinding devices. Abstract imagery had been most common in pictograms used at prior Olympic Games, but in the spirit of the 100th anniversary of the modern Olympic Games, ACOG selected pictograms of the human form that captured the commonality between the grace of a posed athlete and the graceful, personal quality of the South.

Prior to the Games, the sports pictograms were used extensively by licensees in Olympic Games merchandise and collectibles. Official use was restricted to documents and signage specific to individual sports and disciplines.

Sports pictograms were used extensively in the Look Program. To complement the sports pictograms and facilitate wayfinding, Creative Services also designed a series of service pictograms that were used extensively at Games-time.

OPERATIONS

Creative Services' operations focused on pre-Games and Games-time preparations within its five major divisions—Design Services, Editorial Services, Art Direction, Photography/Film and Video, and the Look of the Games—each outlined in the following sections.

DESIGN SERVICES

Great care was taken to protect the integrity and consistency of ACOG's design work. In 1993, a

whether four-color processing was required, estimated print run, specific paper requirements, when the job would need to be printed, and whether it should be printed by ACOG or by a contracted printer. A contract print-production specialist estimated the costs of jobs that required outside printing. These estimates, updated in early 1995 by a staff print-production specialist, helped management determine the number of staff members that would be needed.

After meeting with ACOG Financial Services and receiving assistance from their Public Infor-

larger ACOG design staff and studio were established under the supervision of an art director.

Approximately two and a half years prior to the Games, the division facilitated a project to identify the design and print requirements for all of ACOG. The intent was to estimate publications workload accurately in order to plan staffing and arrange potential printing sponsors and value-in-kind (VIK). This process involved a series of meetings with operating departments and functional areas. Some departments were able to estimate their needs, but others were not sufficiently advanced in their planning process to predict their requirements accurately. For some departments, the request for publications requirements actually served as a stimulus for their overall planning efforts.

As a result of this effort, a working document detailing more than 1,400 design and print jobs was completed. Details of each print job included estimated number of pages, page size,

mation division, all printing budgets from the various departments were centralized under the publications budget, a cost center managed by Design Services. A department's request to Design Services for a job requiring printing would be addressed immediately if it appeared on the approved publications list. If not, the approval of the director of Public Information and the managing director of Corporate Services was required, and the funding obtained from the operating budget of the requesting department.

This approach to printing and publications was effective in controlling costs and stimulating functional areas to focus on planning their needs. In addition, the data generated by this process led directly to a VIK arrangement with Xerox and a major paper supplier.

Following this thorough analysis of ACOG's publication requirements, workload projections were revised and additional graphic designers hired. By mid-1995, the Design Services studio was completely functional with an average weekly workload of more than 60 projects.

In fall 1994, the process for tracking the review and approval of all design work was revised and improved. This process provided for documented reviews of all design work by the art director, the director of Creative Services, the managing director of Corporate Services, the director of Marks Approval, and the corresponding functional area. Despite the large number of

A competition among ACOG designers resulted in both the ceremonies and souvenir ticket design, which reflected the Look of the Games.

documents that were submitted, the production manager was committed to the integrity of the production schedule and ensured that orders were processed quickly.

The technology used by the Design Services studio was a desktop publishing system installed by IBM and augmented by Xerox printing technology. The typical graphic designer's workstation included an IBM 486DX2 processor with up to 64MB of RAM, a CD-ROM drive for reading photo images, a wide variety of graphic design and text software, and an oversized monitor, which enabled designers to evaluate images and colors closely. The principal software packages used by the designers were Adobe Photoshop, Adobe Illustrator, and QuarkXpress.

The studio's work range included brochures, newsletters, advertisements for insertion in both local and national publications, service pictograms, accreditation and sports competition

forms, invitations to special events, certificates, conference agenda booklets, manuals, logos and symbols for pre-Olympic test events, posters, and other projects. The print-production specialist coordinated all jobs produced by contracted printing suppliers. Jobs requiring more than one color and complicated binding were always printed by contractors. Internal printing took place using an assortment of Xerox equipment, most often the Xerox DocuTech 135 Publishing System, which was capable of accommodating a wide range of one-color printing.

While most projects were designed in the Design Services studio, some were assigned to freelancers or contracted firms due to timing, scope, and workload. Design performed by contracted firms was sometimes problematic because some designers attempted to apply their own interpretations of ACOG's visual identity. In those cases, the design team worked closely with the contracted firm to ensure quality, consistency, and adherence to production schedules.

Among projects originally planned to be contracted was the design of the Games tickets, but an informal competition held among the Design Services designers resulted in an outstanding design, ultimately selected for both ceremonies and souvenir tickets.

Following the development of the Look in 1994, various ACOG functional areas requested the creation of a central drive or directory containing Look graphics and sports pictograms that could be used in internal documents and reports. A year and a half prior to the Games, these images were made available to internal users through ACOG computer networks along with a set of guidelines that imposed restrictions on their use. The images, though occasionally misused for external distribution, were greatly appreciated.

Two years before the Games, Design Services developed a standard set of preprinted materials (shells) for such commonly requested items as invitations, certificates, name tags, tent cards, and manual covers. These shells could then be processed through a laser printer with specific information. Using these shells helped ensure quality, consistency, and cost-effectiveness.

The staff remained active with design projects until shortly before Games-time, then were redeployed to either the sports daily programs project or the *Daily Olympian*.

EDITORIAL SERVICES

All official ACOG publications were either written or edited by the Editorial Services division. In 1993, the division developed a set of style guidelines to circulate throughout ACOG.

For projects assuming complete responsibility for writing, a staff writer was assigned to conduct research and interviews, prepare drafts, and circulate copy through an approval process designed to ensure accuracy.

When the division functioned only in an editing capacity, staff writers would review drafts prepared by other ACOG departments, edit them for proper ACOG style, return them to the originating department for changes, and then forward the revised copy for approvals. The production manager ensured that approvals were obtained from the Editorial Services manager, the director of Creative Services, the director of Public Information, the managing director of Corporate Services, and a manager or director from any ACOG department with relevant subject matter expertise.

All publications distributed in French were translated by the Language Services Department.

Periodic Publications

ACOG was required to produce periodic written reports for IOC Sessions and Executive Board meetings. Editorial Services prepared 24 such reports, which focused on planning and operational progress in all areas of Games preparations. These reports were prepared in English and then translated into French. They were typically shipped to the IOC in advance of the sessions.

The *Torch* was the official publication of the Centennial Olympic Games that began in the Bid organization as a single typewritten page. After ACOG was established, the *Torch* was enlarged and produced in full color. French translation was added in 1994. The *Torch* was written, edited, illustrated, and designed exclusively by Creative Services writers, designers, and photographers. The frequency of publication varied. Until 1993, it was published twice monthly, then monthly in 1994. In mid-1995, as the pre-Games workload increased, the *Torch* became a bimonthly publication. The final issue was published in July 1996.

Most issues were 8 pages; some were as long as 12 or 16 pages, depending on events at the

A tremendous variety of publications was written by Editorial Services.

time. The *Torch* was distributed to all ACOG staff, the ACOG Board of Directors, the IOC, NOCs, IFs, and sponsors, as well as community groups and state, local, and federal government officials.

The *Torch* served as ACOG's record publication, carrying news and feature items on all aspects of ACOG's work as well as photos of special projects, venue construction, pre-Olympic test events, Cultural Olympiad activities, and the announcement of new sponsors.

Other recurring publications written by Editorial Services included:

■ *Showcase*, a full-color newsletter produced several times a year for ACOP licensees;

IV • BRADLEY M BRANNICK • LISA BRANNOCK • BEN E BRANNON • BRADFORD M BRANNON • KARISA M BRANNON • KATIE G BRANNON • NANCY C BRANNON • PAT P BRANNON • RUSSELL L BRANNON • VICKI D BRANNON • JASON M BRANT • JOHN D BRANT • ERIC L BRANTINGHAM • DAVID L BRANTLEY • LINDA G BRANTLEY • MARGARET BRANTLEY • MICHAEL L BRANTLEY • MICHAEL S BRANTLEY • SUSAN P BRANTLEY • TERRY F BRANTLEY • JAMES BRANTLEY JR CATC • MARY M BRANYAN • YISU H BRASEL • KIMBERLY E BRASEL MT • ROBYN A BRASELL • DORIS H BRASFIELD • PATRICIA H BRASFIELD

■ *Resource,* a quarterly newsletter produced for the Volunteer Services Department and mailed to all volunteers and Olympic Force members;

■ *Outreach,* a quarterly newsletter produced for the Community Relations Department and distributed to residents of venue neighborhoods and community and special-interest support groups; and

■ *Inside ACOG,* a periodically published general interest newsletter for ACOG staff.

Editorial Services also wrote copy for the *Guide to the 1996 Olympic Games,* print ads, Cultural Olympiad print material, and brochures.

The *Daily Olympian*

The production of this Olympic Village newspaper was the exclusive focus of Editorial Services during Games-time. Volunteer reporters and editors were recruited in advance to aid this effort. Thirty-two issues were published in both English and French. Pre-Games issues consisted of four tabloid pages; Games-time issues expanded to eight pages. Some special issues were published in four-color printing. All others were two-color—black plus a second color that changed daily but was always drawn from the Look expanded color palette.

The emphasis of the *Daily Olympian* was on the athlete community in the Atlanta Olympic Village as well as the satellite Villages. Photos of athletes were used liberally. Feature stories focused on human interest themes. This approach ensured that more athletes received coverage and attention. A deliberate effort was made to include athletes from as many of the 197 competing countries as possible and feature athletes not already receiving significant media attention as a result of their performance on the field of play.

To ensure all athletes' names reached print, a special 28-page commemorative issue of the *Daily Olympian* was published on 3 August 1996. It contained a complete listing of the name, sport, and country of each athlete who com-

Production of the *Daily Olympian* was the exclusive focus of Editorial Services during Games-time.

peted in the Games. The list was obtained from the Sports database.

The *Daily Olympian* was well received by athletes. Daily circulation grew from 10,000 to 20,000 as Village occupancy increased. It was not uncommon for athletes to take as many as 10–20 copies of an issue as souvenirs. The newspaper received two awards for excellence from the International Association of Business Communicators.

Publications Required by the IOC

The first IOC-required publications produced were the sports explanatory books. Editorial Services and Design Services worked with Sports and Language Services to produce this boxed set of 26 books. Sports Logistics assembled the content and worked with competition managers and IFs on approvals. Editorial Services reviewed the copy for style and grammar. Design Services developed a colorful cover design and display box.

Content included the official program, equipment, rules, and diagrams of the field of play, as well as general information about Atlanta. Challenges were faced throughout the process of content and production schedule development. The initial set of books was presented to the IOC Coordination Commission in Atlanta in September 1995, and shipped to the NOCs and IFs later that month.

The Medical Services Department was required by the IOC to produce the *Medical Care Guide,* which provided an overview of the Games medical operations; the *Medical Controls Guide,* which explained athlete notification and sample collection procedures; and the *Drug Formulary,* which defined the permitted, restricted, and prohibited substances. The content was edited by Editorial Services, and the cover designs and printing handled by Design Services.

The final IOC-required document was the *Official Report,* a historical documentation of the Centennial Olympic Games. The first step was determining the content—a 1,500-page, three-volume set extensively detailing Games planning (volume I), a Games-time synopsis of the daily images and activities of the Games beginning with the Torch Relay (volume II), and a sport-by-sport listing of all athletes who competed and their final standings (volume III).

Peachtree Publishers, Ltd., was contracted to publish the *Official Report*, as well as to help develop its content and concept.

In preparation for the *Official Report*, ACOG staff began creating outlines of information required from each department in October 1995. Reports on pre-Games activities were due in March 1996. The success of this program was variable among departments as to content quality and timeliness of submission.

Photo assignments were made well in advance of the Games to ensure adequate coverage of all sports and key Games-time activities. ACOG retained full rights to all photography shot by volunteers, which included both hobbyists and professional photographers.

After the Games, five full-time staff members and numerous freelance writers were assigned to work with the publishing company's editorial and design staff to finalize format, text, and photos. Sales were offered to the general public before the final print date. An edition of 3,000 was printed; 2500 in English and 500 in French.

ACOG Resource Library

The ACOG resource library was established in 1991 by Public Information to provide a single resource and reference center and to maintain a historical record of ACOG's work. In 1994, a full-time professional librarian was hired to manage the growing collection of resources.

By the end of 1994, the full-service library housed an impressive collection of publications, newsletters, and media guides from various IFs and national governing bodies. Other books available were historical accounts of the modern Games and miscellaneous books and periodicals

from various countries, including many of the participating NOCs. Among the library's most utilized resources were *Official Report*s from previous Olympic Games.

The library also offered an assortment of videos, most of which featured inspirational moments and events ranging from competition clips from previous Games to Atlanta's winning the Bid. Assorted videos of venues, the upcoming Games in Sydney, and various ACOG programs such as the Dream Team Program, Centennial Olympic Park, and Olympic Preludes completed the collection.

The library subscribed to an on-line service to retrieve articles and updates on the Olympic Games, and had access to the Internet and the World Wide Web to obtain current information on a variety of subjects.

The ACOG library often worked in conjunction with the ACOP library by sharing resources to serve the information needs of ACOG staff and employees. Prior to the Games, the library was moved to the Main Press Center to allow access to all media. After the Games, the library was closed and converted into part of the Games archival project.

ACOG employed full-time personnel who provided guidance for archiving, itemizing, and inventorying approximately 6,000 boxes of records. In addition, 10 volunteers were assigned to inventory and catalogue memorabilia such as uniforms, ceremonies costumes and props, merchandise, canoes, torches, and victory medals, as well as the collection of photographs and videotapes.

ART DIRECTION

Originally part of Design Services, the Art Direction division was established in late 1994.

• ART BRAULT • FRANK M BRAULT • ACHIM BRAUN • CAROL J BRAUN • JEFFREY W BRAUN • JENNIFER S BRAUN • MARY C BRAUN • MICHELLE J BRAUN • SONYA L BRAUN • RACHEL E BRAUSCH • RICHARD O BRAUTIGAM • NANCY L BRAUTIGAN • SANDI BRAVERMAN • SUSAN B BRAVMAN • ANNA L BRAVO • DIANA BRAWDERS • EMMY L BRAWLEY • CHEVONNE D BRAWNER • DAVID A BRAWNER • DORIS Y BRAWNER • DREIDRA M BRAWNER • JULIE R BRAWNER • MATT T BRAWNER • WALLACE M BRAXLEY • BRIAN E BRAXTON • LEXTER V BRAXTON • WENDY K BRAXTON • ANNE M BRAY • CAROL C BRAY •

139

The division provided guidance and direction to other ACOG departments and ACOP Marks Approval on design issues. Its secondary focus was the ACOG Poster Program. In the final months before the Games, it provided extensive support to ACOG's noncompetition venue signage efforts.

Poster Program

In coordination with ACOP, it was determined that ACOG posters would be well suited to production and distribution by a licensee. At that point, the only poster in print was the Centennial Games logo on a green background.

In 1994, ACOG contracted with Fine Art Limited, already an ACOP licensee for limited edition prints and small sculptures, to add posters to its contract. The agreement established that ACOG and Fine Art Limited work together to decide which artists would create the posters in the series.

Art Direction developed the ACOG Poster Program to embrace a variety of images and artists. One principal aspect of the effort to ensure diversity among athletes was ACOG's requirement that images of competing athletes be free from any specific country markings or national flags. All artists who participated in the Poster Program were given the same set of guidelines, which included permission for them to sign their artwork personally.

The program included designer posters as well as fine art posters and limited edition prints. Limited edition prints were issued on a higher grade paper than posters, and their production involved a more elaborate color printing process. Each limited edition print was individually numbered and signed by the artist. Of the 63 posters in the program, 25 were available as limited edition prints. Each poster had a predetermined border that contained the Games logo and the phrase "Centennial Olympic Games" in English and French. The posters were divided into the following four categories.

Sports Series. A poster for each of the Olympic sports was produced by renowned artist Hiro Yamagata. Each poster in the series included the sport name, the artist's name, and the dates of the Games. Each poster was 18 x 24 in (46 x 61 cm). Fourteen were made into limited edition prints, each an edition of 60 handprinted lithographs.

Designer Series. These posters featured images created by graphic designers to capture some aspect of the Olympic Spirit. There were 13 posters of various sizes in this series. Among the subjects depicted in this series were IZZY, the torch mark logo, and the Atlanta skyline.

Look Team Series. Each of the six firms involved in the development of the Look was asked to design a poster. They were given broad freedom in selecting their content. The images they chose ranged from athletes to doves of peace to pictograms. All posters were 22 x 34 in (56 x 86 cm).

Artist Series. With the paintings created for these posters, artists used a more freestyle approach to portraying the Olympic Spirit. Eleven images comprised this series, with themes ranging from women in sports to the Olympic Village. Most were made available as limited edition prints. Among the artists whose work was represented in this series were Emma Amos, Patricia Cajiga, Michele Delacroix, Paul Goodnight, and James Rizzi.

As part of the agreement with the licensee, all fees to artists were paid by Fine Art Limited, which also assumed all production costs. Rights to the original paintings typically reverted to the artists, and ACOG received 100 copies of each poster and two of each limited edition.

Official Poster. As a Games tradition, one poster is selected by the IOC president as the official poster of the Games. Accordingly, IOC President Juan Antonio Samaranch selected a poster designed by Primo Angeli, one of the original Look designers, one week prior to the Games.

PHOTOGRAPHY/FILM AND VIDEO

Part of the Bid process required a small photography staff to photograph and catalogue pic-

IOC President Samaranch chose this image, designed by one of the original Look of the Games designers, as the official 1996 Games poster.

tures. In 1993, this staff became part of Editorial Services. Two staff photographers were responsible for cataloguing the negatives and photos so that images were available for use in all ACOG publications. The division was also responsible for determining rights issues associated with each photo. Volunteers and contractors were also important both for initial shots and for purchasing images from outside sources.

The Photography division's pre-Games responsibilities included archiving major events and programs and providing still photography support for ACOG publications, as well as the *Official Report*. In addition, staff photographers were regularly on duty to capture dignitary visits and respond to an assortment of daily requests from throughout the organization.

The Film and Video division was established in March 1993. Its primary mission was the video documentation of all ACOG events, such as groundbreakings, venue openings, and major Cultural Olympiad events.

This division centered on the production of radio and television commercials, video news releases, training videos, and a host of both production and postproduction projects. It also developed a broadcast color palette and video guidelines for Games sponsors. In 1995, the Photography division was merged with the Film and Video division, and together coordinated all ACOG still and video projects.

Video operations were diverse, ranging from the filming of archival footage of press conferences and board meetings to the preparation of ACOG video informational programs for IOC meetings and an elaborate program on the gathering of Nobel laureates hosted by ACOG in 1995. Footage from all sessions of the Nobel laureates gathering was made into a four-part broadcast special, later aired on public broadcast channels and distributed throughout the US to colleges and universities.

Time-lapse photography was used to record the construction of the Olympic Stadium from beginning to end. The footage was shot with 35 mm film from a fixed camera position and later converted into video.

In the weeks prior to the Games, the division worked with Sports Competition Production to produce a series of energetic, sport-specific features shown both prior to and at appropriate points during competition sessions. These video features provided spectators with a historical perspective of each sport. Features were produced for artistic gymnastics, athletics, baseball, basketball, diving, fencing, swimming, synchronized swimming, and water polo.

During Games-time, the Film and Video division also was responsible for feeding satellite video packages of the Olympic Arts Festival to the international media.

During Games-time, the full-time staff was supplemented by a pool of volunteer photographers whose primary mission was to photograph assignments in support of both the *Daily Olympian* and the *Official Report*.

The Photography/Film and Video division also assumed responsibility for obtaining copyright and broadcast releases for all images used in official ACOG programs and publications.

LOOK OF THE GAMES

The Look division was responsible for translating the Quilt of Leaves design elements into banners, fence coverings, flags, landscaping, signage, wall coverings, and other elements and applying them to the venues. The division began as a small unit, but grew as it assumed the responsibility of applying the Look at the venues and throughout Atlanta. A variety of external design firms played a major role in the application of the Look.

In 1993, the initial tasks of the Look staff were to determine all places where the Look could be applied to begin identifying possible fabricators, installers, and landscape firms. The first needed applications were the use of the Quilt of Leaves in ACOG's printed materials and

EMILY A BREEDEN • WESLEY L BREEDING • JAMES A BREEDLOVE • JOY H BREEDLOVE • KEI C BREEDLOVE • ANDREA H BREEN • ELEANOR BREEN • KATHRYN D BREEN • LESTER M BREEN • SKIP BREESER • KEVIN M BREHMER • WILLIAM H BREIDAHL • DANA L BREIG • JENNIFER M BREIMAN • ROBERT F BREIMAN • BOBBIE P BREITBEIL • ROBERT G BREITBEIL • VIRGINIA C BREITBEIL • MARY W BREITENBACH • AUGUST W BREMER • JOE E BREMER • MARTIN BREMER • NICOLA BREMER • WILLIAM BREMER III • SCOT BREMNER • CARLO A BRENA • BRYAN L BRENDLE • BARNEY BRENES •

141

the production of the complex Look kit of parts that would be used as the Look was applied to all venues and surrounding areas.

In early 1995, Look Program activities became more intensive, as procurement of the products required a long lead time. The Look kit was given to sports equipment companies that, with coordinated efforts, began to manufacture all sporting equipment.

Application to Venues

Prototypes of various structures and banners were created and tested in simulated indoor and outdoor competition environments to preserve the visual impact of the first applications until they could be seen by the public when the Games began in 1996. Coordination with AOB and NBC took place to ensure that Look elements would translate correctly, both in color and placement, in TV transmission.

In the second half of 1995, the Look Program divided the venues into two groups for specific applications of the Look. Twenty Look staff members and many outside contractors were required for the application. Each Look staff member was assigned to specific venues to coordinate installation, and was provided the tools to assist if necessary. The smaller venues were assigned to a group of Georgia-based architects and designers who worked with Look staff members from the kit of parts. One design firm, under ACOG's guidance, was contracted to apply the Look to the largest venues such as Olympic Stadium, Atlanta–Fulton County Stadium, the Omni Coliseum, the Georgia Dome, the Georgia World Congress Center, and the Georgia Tech Aquatic Center.

The fabrication of Look materials and the preparation of competition venues, the Airport Welcome Center, Main Press Center, International Broadcast Center, main accreditation center, and Olympic Village were coordinated with Construction and Venue Management. Special

emphasis was placed on the atrium decoration of the Olympic Family Hotel and the interior decorations of Olympic Family lounges.

By the end of 1995, all venue designs were complete and contracts for fabric, structures, and all Look materials were either awarded or under development. Using computer-assisted design (CAD) drawings, the Look was applied to the venues, especially at entrances, the field of play, television camera positions, and spectator areas. A specific description of the colors and graphics used on the field of play and the equipment needed to apply them were presented to each IF, AOB, and the IOC president for approval.

After design intent documents were prepared for each venue, ACOG received competitive bids on materials to be fabricated. Most contracts were awarded during January and February 1996. Typically, a 15 percent replacement factor was used when ordering materials. This factor proved to be accurate and compensated for any Games-time loss or damage.

Venue preparation began in late spring 1996, and all venues were fully prepared on schedule. The greatest challenge was preparing the plaza area between Atlanta–Fulton County Stadium and Olympic Stadium. Due to an Atlanta Braves baseball game at the Atlanta–Fulton County Stadium on the afternoon of 14 July, the plaza area could not be prepared until approximately 48 hours prior to the admission of ticketed spectators.

In addition to the venues, the Look was also applied to city streets, ACOG transit buses, and external fences through the special Sponsor Presence Program proposed to TOP/COP sponsors in late 1994. The program facilitated the production of more than 80,000 ft (24,384 m) of fence covering, 10,000 banners, and approximately 1,600 buses wrapped in vinyl Look graphics with logo identification for nine Games sponsors appearing in white at a ratio of 1:4 in order to preserve the graphic integrity of the Look Program and coordination among

Look of the Games elements were adapted to banners designed for each venue.

sponsors. In addition, the Look was applied to over 17 mi (27 km) of fence fabric, scaffolding for 116 temporary structures, and 5,000 highway banners—a total of 18.7 acres (7.6 ha) of vinyl with Look graphic images.

ACOG also aimed to create entryways that would enable spectators to recognize them from a distance. Structures made of steel and covered in fabric were used for this program. During the Games, the Look team reinstalled entrances as needed and moved elements from venue to venue. The program planned for the disassembly and recovery of items immediately following the Games.

Wayfinding. An important element of the Look Program was the creation of standard, easily readable signage and coordination with ACOG departments and local authorities, such as the state of Georgia Department of Transportation, for their application. The Look team created and distributed the visual standards and approved all proposed applications. ACOG Transportation helped determine the wayfinding signage required at major spectator entrances, while Venue Management advised concerning signage inside and on the fence outside the venues. A signage fabrication shop provided by Venue Management and the Look fabrication shop produced the majority of signage products, and local authorities used outside vendors to produce others. From the venues to the spectator terminals, wayfinding signs contained directions in English and French using sports and other pictograms. Signage shops allowed the immediate change and replacement of wayfinding signage.

Fabrication shop. The institution of an ACOG fabrication shop as part of the Look Program provided flexibility and speed. Established in partnership with a local Atlanta carpentry union, which used the shop to train apprentices,

the fabrication shop opened in late 1995. It offered extensive capabilities in woodwork, metalwork, and assorted utility projects. The facility performed routine work while providing the added convenience of local control and short-distance shipping.

Landscape

In 1994, ACOG began to evaluate and select landscape design firms to implement the Look through flowers and trees. Roy Ashley and Associates was chosen in spring 1995. Since Atlanta

is known as the City of Trees, the plan included placing trees and large containers of flowers in and around venues.

Trees and pots of flowers were placed inside venues and at entryways and the surrounding areas of venues. Special emphasis was placed on plantings and decorations within protocol areas and entrances. Permanent flower beds were planted at Hartsfield Atlanta International Airport, as well as Olympic Stadium and other venues. Wildflowers were planted on highway medians throughout metropolitan Atlanta. The Look division utilized 128 tractor loads of plant materials, including 632 shade trees, 1,077 crepe myrtle trees, 1,133 planter pots, and 157,000 lbs (71,000 kg) of wildflower seeds.

While many permanent installations were part of the construction program and coordi-

A rendering of the Olympic Stadium plaza showed how the Look of the Games elements would possibly be incorporated during the Games.

nated with the Look kit of parts and the Look landscape team, the majority of landscaping was temporary.

Subcontractors were used for the installation, maintenance, and procurement of these plants and flowers. During Games-time, watering trucks and hand-held containers of water were used each day after competition and when the venue was closed to maintain the landscaping. The plants were trimmed once weekly. Containers were specially designed and constructed of durable Styrofoam and painted gold so that weight was not a significant factor. The containers held large green plants and many smaller multicolored plants.

Quiltscape. To complement the Quilt of Leaves and afford Georgia citizens the opportunity to participate in the excitement of the Games, a community landscaping program known as Quiltscape was developed. As part of this program, an Olympic theme design and assorted plant materials were made available for purchase through the Games partner, Home Depot, in spring 1996. Community groups such as the Garden Club of Georgia joined in the Quiltscape project, along with state and county extension services.

CONCLUSIONS AND RECOMMENDATIONS

ACOG placed considerable value on establishing a visual identity through logos, symbols, colors, and the Look of the Games that represented a festive celebration of the Centennial Olympic Games. This visual identity, which became representative of and synonymous with the Games, had to be clearly translated and its high standards protected in all mediums. The following recommendations are offered to future organizing committees.

■ Create as much graphic material, photography, and video footage as possible internally to ensure the integrity and ownership of all materials.

■ Both horizontal and vertical images should be created. Graphics should be evaluated for their ability to be adapted, both vertically and horizontally, to applications such as large banners and small business cards.

■ All Look and signage graphic elements should be designed by a company with the expertise and resources to support architectural and engineering requirements for all three-dimensional elements. Secure the fabricators, supplier, and installer at least one year prior to the first installation date to ensure low cost and adequate production lead time.

■ Application of the Look to venues should be done in cooperation with the broadcasting and venue management departments.

■ The intensity of the installation and recovery schedules for Look elements should be considered when planning staff and contractor needs.

■ Arrange to have a full-time dedicated technical support person manage the installation and maintenance of the design studio's computer system.

■ Begin planning for and creating the *Official Report* early. To facilitate the success of this tremendous undertaking, assign staff writers and photographers from each department before the Games begin to assemble material.

CULTURAL OLYMPIAD

CHAPTER NINE
CULTURAL OLYMPIAD

OVERVIEW—Atlanta's Cultural Olympiad was among the most comprehensive and successful cultural programs presented during the modern Olympic era. From its origins during the Bid process to its magnificent finale, the 1996 Olympic Arts Festival (OAF), the Cultural Olympiad remained a high priority for ACOG.

The AOC designed a four-year Cultural Olympiad that would include a series of festivals presented each summer, culminating in the 1996 OAF. This series, entitled *The Dance of Life*, was based on Barcelona's ambitious multi-year Cultural Olympiad, but was treated as an integral part of the organizing committee's efforts rather than a separate activity.

After Atlanta was awarded the Games, Atlanta's Cultural Olympiad established as its mission to:

■ celebrate the rich and diverse arts and culture of Atlanta, the state of Georgia, and the South by presenting traditional and contemporary works by outstanding artists from the region;

■ present to the region distinguished international artists representing the five continental associations participating in the Games, symbolized by the Olympic Rings;

■ create programs with local arts organizations and foster new partnerships between local organizations and their international colleagues; and

■ create a legacy of new and broadened audiences and expand the vision through which Atlanta will be recognized as an international center for innovative arts, culture, and entertainment.

The result was a Cultural Olympiad that was large and inclusive, diverse in concept, and dedicated to presenting the rich cultural expressions of the American South.

A HISTORICAL CONTEXT

Establishing art and sport as complementary and mutually enhancing components of the Olympic experience has challenged nearly every Olympic host. The historic, even legendary, difficulties in defining, creating, organizing, and presenting a cultural program of international significance and quality within an organization focused on producing the world's largest, most prestigious athletic event have been met in different ways by the hosts of the modern Games.

Including art and culture as integral components of the Olympic Games dates from the early days of the modern Olympic Movement. Baron Pierre de Coubertin, the movement's founder, eloquently defined an Olympic Games that would celebrate humankind's highest achievements in both sport and art. In 1904, he wrote an article for *Le Figaro* in which he stated:

> In the golden age of Olympia, the harmonious combination of the arts, letters, and sport assured the greatness of the Olympic Games. And so it should be again.

This commitment to include the arts in every Olympic Games led de Coubertin to chair an IOC meeting in Paris in May 1906 to consider:

> to what degree and in what form the Arts and Letters could participate in the modern Olympiads, and in general be associated with the practice of sports in order to benefit from them and ennoble them.

The challenge of guiding the early Olympic athletic competitions prevented de Coubertin from implementing this concept until the Stockholm Games in 1912, when the first Olympic cultural events were introduced. Among various pageants and performances, the Olympic host committees from 1912 through 1948 presented a series of competitions in the fields of architecture, music, literature, painting, and sculpture called The Pentathlon of the Muses. The first noncompetitive approach to the cultural program was implemented at the 1952 Olympic Games in Helsinki, where only a single exhibition was presented.

The rapid growth in the quality and magnitude of Olympic athletic competitions compared to the relative obscurity of Olympic cultural programs led the IOC to reexamine the role of the arts and culture in a series of meetings that began in 1949. In 1952, the IOC Executive Committee reviewed the program of Olympic cultural competitions, and at the IOC Congress of 1954 in Athens, the *Olympic Charter* was formally amended as follows:

> The organizing committee will organize a demonstration or exhibition of Art (architecture, music, literature, painting, sculpture, sports, philately, and photography)... The program could also include ballets, theater performances, operas, or symphony concerts.

From that time, Olympic cultural programs have been as diverse in content and format as the host cities themselves. ACOG presented an ambitious program that spanned the full duration of its Olympiad.

ORGANIZATION

In 1991, under the guidance of the Cultural Olympiad director, the plan outlined in the AOC's Bid document was restructured to emphasize two central objectives: to develop the Cultural Olympiad into a series of partnerships with Atlanta's arts community and international cultural organizations, and to use the four-year Cultural Olympiad as an opportunity to encourage artists to develop new works and special programs for prospective presentation during the 1996 OAF. The format of four annual festivals gave way to a more fluid, evolutionary program with a variety of initiatives in each artistic genre. ACOG adopted these ideas, and began the process of defining Atlanta's Cultural Olympiad mission.

During its formative months, the Cultural Olympiad held meetings with representatives from many of Atlanta's cultural organizations to gain perspective on the status and interests of the local arts community. In July 1992, four producers were hired to develop programs in each of four major disciplines: music, visual arts, dance and theater, and humanities and special programs. The Cultural Olympiad then formed a committee of nearly 100 individuals representing Atlanta's cultural organizations, Olympic sponsors, and the chairman of the Fulton County Commission. This advisory committee was divided into four panels, one supporting each discipline, to assist the four producers.

The planning process, which was intended to unite the arts community, sometimes resulted in diverse objectives. The final selection of Cultural Olympiad programs and related distribution of ACOG's financial support were seriously debated before the committee published the Cultural Olympiad master plan in

The cultural logo incorporated elements of ACOG's torch mark logo as well as a symbol at the top reflecting the spirit of innovation and dynamism celebrated in each culture.

August 1993. This document defined the Olympiad's two major themes—southern connections and international connections—and a series of programs entitled *Arts Atlanta: Preludes to the Centennial Olympic Arts Festival*, later referred to as Olympic Preludes.

The conceptual development of all Cultural Olympiad programs took nearly a year to complete; however, several early, significant programs, including the formal launch and first Cultural Olympiad festival, were produced prior to the plan's publication.

The Atlanta Olympic Band, which performed at many functions before and during the Games, symbolized ACOG's commitment to youth and excellence.

The master plan was well received by the press. It presented the Cultural Olympiad's programs in "conceptual form, leaving specifics to future definition" and as "a living and dynamic work-in-progress." These concepts were the foundation on which arts organizations planned their programs during the

years preceding the Games. Organizations were invited to work with the Cultural Olympiad to create programs both representative of the themes expressed by the plan and serving their long-range institutional objectives. Organizations that worked with the Cultural Olympiad to produce arts events were known as collaborators.

OLYMPIC PRELUDES

The Cultural Olympiad staff and local arts organizations together developed the Olympic Preludes, a variety of cultural and arts events that occurred in the years preceding the OAF. Prelude events promoted the upcoming Centennial Olympic Games and the OAF, and also emphasized ACOG's commitment to encourage local organizations to develop new works by southern artists about southern themes.

The four international festivals held from 1993 through 1994 and the gathering in April 1995 of Nobel laureates of literature provided the Cultural Olympiad with early opportunities to develop logistical and production management skills in coordination with ACOG functional areas, which later proved invaluable to the operation of the OAF. The Cultural Olympiad's pre-Games events also helped ACOG departments develop policies and procedures regarding purchasing, contracting, risk management, technology, and other areas.

Multiyear Olympic Prelude Programs

Of the Olympic Prelude programs, those with the greatest impact on the OAF were the Atlanta Olympic Band, the Southern Play Project, *One Hundred Years of World Cinema*, and the Summer Dance Program.

Atlanta Olympic Band. The Atlanta Olympic Band, the first program initiated by the Cultural Olympiad, was formally inaugurated in Savannah on 18 September 1992, when the Olympic flag arrived in Georgia. The Olympic Band remained together throughout the Games, ranging in size from approximately 250 to more than 350 musicians during the Games. High school and college music teachers provided musical leadership.

The Atlanta Olympic Band annually auditioned Georgia's top high school and college musicians. Geographic distribution throughout the state and the diversity of the ensemble were important selection criteria. The band performed at many functions, including the Presidential Inaugural Parade in January 1993, the Macy's Thanksgiving Day Parade in November 1994, and the Opening and Closing Ceremonies of the Games.

The Atlanta Olympic Band symbolized ACOG's commitment to youth and excellence. This program's quality reputation and the pride it inspired greatly enhanced the Centennial Olympic Games.

Southern Play Project. The Southern Play Project supported participating theaters in their efforts to develop new works by southern playwrights writing on southern themes. The goal was to offer Olympic visitors plays that would help them understand the culture of the American South. Several theaters embraced this concept and staged new works.

Another component of the Southern Play Project was the National Black Arts Festival New Play Project, a multiyear collaborative partnership between the Atlanta-based National Black Arts Festival (NBAF), a biannual event, and the Cultural Olympiad. Its mission was to develop new works by African-American authors for prospective staging during the OAF. Four new works were selected by the NBAF and the Cultural Olympiad and received support during the workshop phase. One of those works, *Blues for an Alabama Sky* by Atlanta-based playwright Pearl Cleage, was presented by the Alliance Theatre Company during the OAF. Other works received public readings and workshop-level productions.

One Hundred Years of World Cinema. A two-year collaboration between the Cultural Olympiad and the High Museum of Art, this weekly series included films from more than 30 countries. Nine film series were screened at Rich Auditorium in the Woodruff Arts Center between June 1994 and July 1996. Each series included a selection of cinematic masterpieces and covered a broad range of cinematographic approaches. This series was one of the Olympic Preludes' most popular programs, attracting a full audience to almost every event.

Summer Dance Program. Like its theatrical counterpart, the Summer Dance Program was designed to encourage the development of new dance works by local organizations, bring local dance companies into contact with important choreographers from around the world, and create partnerships between both local and international dance companies.

The program included master classes for local dancers by a number of distinguished choreographers. It also led to the creation of a new work by Irene Tassembedo—an African choreographer and leader of the Parisian Compagnie Ebène—which was presented during the OAF. Other projects included two works developed and performed by the Dance Technology Project of the Atlanta Ballet, a collaboration between the Atlanta Ballet and the Georgia Institute of Technology's innovative new media center.

Regional Designation Awards. Additional Prelude programs deserve special mention. Regional Designation Awards, a concept developed in cooperation with the Southern Arts Federation, awarded the first Olympic imprimaturs in January 1993 to cultural institutions in the southeastern states for programmatic innovation and excellence. This program's success led to a similar program for humanities organizations that recognized excellence and encouraged participation in the humanities by cultural institutions throughout the state of Georgia

Four International Festivals

The inaugural event of the Cultural Olympiad was a first-ever collaboration between two Olympic hosts. The Cultural Olympiads of the Lillehammer Olympic Organizing Committee and ACOG met in late 1992 to discuss a plan to bring an exhibition of Norwegian art to At-

lights included a visit to Atlanta by Norway's Queen Sonya, and the world premiere of James Oliverio's *The Explorer*, a work commissioned by the Cultural Olympiad for the Atlanta Symphony Orchestra.

In spring 1993, the Cultural Olympiad presented *A Salute to Lausanne: Events Honoring the Opening of the IOC Museum*, an exhibition of the IOC's *Centennial Suite* featuring work by Swiss artists, with musical performances organized by the Georgia Museum of Art (Athens), Jubilee Cultural Alliance, the Embassy of

left: **A reception was held for Sonya, Queen of Norway, in conjunction with the exhibition of Norwegian landscapes entitled** *Winter Land: Norwegian Visions of Winter.*

right: **ACOG and the Lillehammer organizing committee collaborated to produce** *Olympic Winterland: Encounters with Norwegian Cultures,* **which included performances by Norwegian bands.**

lanta. These discussions led to a number of programs that united the two cultures under the aegis of the Olympic Movement. *Olympic Winterland: Encounters with Norwegian Cultures* (February/March 1993) was a multifaceted program that featured as its centerpiece *Winter Land: Norwegian Visions of Winter*, an exhibition of Norwegian landscape paintings at the Fernbank Museum of Natural History. Other high-

Switzerland, the Montreaux Jazz Festival, and the Swiss Council for the Arts, Pro Helvetia.

In fall 1993, the Cultural Olympiad, working with Teodoro Maus, Atlanta's consul general of Mexico, presented *Mexico! A Cultural Tapestry*, a large, multidisciplinary festival that brought more than 100 Mexican performers, musicians, visual artists, dancers, storytellers, films, and exhibitions to Atlanta in honor of the 25th anniversary of the Mexico City Games. For this event, the Cultural Olympiad commissioned its first public artwork, *Song for Atlanta* by muralist Gilberto Aceves Navarro, who worked with local artists and art students to create a mural that remains as a legacy of the festival.

In summer 1994, the Cultural Olympiad collaborated with the NBAF to present its largest festival prior to the OAF. *Celebrate Africa!* was a 10-day outdoor festival that featured an impressive artists' marketplace (Marche Africán) with performances, demonstrations, exhibitions, and more than 160 vendors. More than 350 artists and artisans participated in the festival. Theatrical, dance, and musical companies, many visiting the US for the first time, performed in events that attracted over 750,000 people. An educational program based on this festival was also developed for use by Georgia public schools.

Gathering of Nobel Laureates of Literature

An international gathering of writers and poets held in 1995, *The Nobel Laureates of Literature: An Olympic Gathering*, was among the Cultural Olympiad's most distinguished presentations. Eight laureates came to Atlanta for this historic presentation: Czeslaw Milosz (1980 Nobel prize), Claude Simon (1985), Wole Soyinka (1986), Joseph Brodsky (1987), Octavio Paz (1990), Derek Walcott (1992), Toni Morrison (1993), and Kenzaburo Oe (1994). Then–US Poet Laureate Rita Dove also participated in the event.

Ted Koppel, host of ABC-TV's *Nightline*, moderated the two panel sessions held at the Carter Presidential Center (400 seats), which were videotaped by Georgia Public Television for distribution through Georgia's educational broadcast system. The gathering also included a formal convocation dinner and public readings by each writer, which were held at Georgia Tech's Center for the Arts (1,000 seats). All of the gathering's events were fully attended and well received.

Prelude Operations

Each Prelude event presented distinct logistical and operational challenges. As ACOG functional areas were still in early planning stages, they were unable to provide full support in some areas, which made it difficult to obtain visas for international artists; resolve customs, logistics, and production issues; and obtain technology support for Prelude events.

Among the most important areas in which

The Nobel Laureates of Literature program of the Cultural Olympiad gathered eight poet laureates for panel discussions, public readings, and a convocation dinner with other Olympic guests.

the Cultural Olympiad needed support was contract administration. The Cultural Olympiad had difficulty negotiating and drafting contracts that met stringent Olympic requirements while honoring the conventional terms and conditions expected by artists and their representative institutions. Most of the early contracts were individually negotiated and drafted, and therefore had to be renegotiated when ACOG developed standard legal and language terms.

The Cultural Olympiad met most of its pre-Games accommodations, technology, transportation, and other logistical and production requirements with its own resources and support from ACOG's Special Events Department.

The majority of Olympic Prelude programs were offered free of charge. The free outdoor festival components of *Mexico! A Cultural Tapestry* and *Celebrate Africa!*, held in Atlanta's Piedmont Park, drew large, enthusiastic crowds. Exhibitions were also primarily free; when tickets were required, they were sold at or below market price.

Colorful brochures were produced for each festival and event and were distributed through direct mail and to the employees of

top: Mexican dancers performed as a part of the Olympic Prelude, *Mexico! A Cultural Tapestry.*

bottom: Celebrate Africa! was a 10-day outdoor festival in which more than 350 artists and artisans participated.

Olympic sponsors to encourage attendance, which was often less than originally anticipated. Sales for ticketed events were also generally less than planned.

1996 OLYMPIC ARTS FESTIVAL

The 1996 OAF was the largest, most comprehensive Olympic cultural event ever presented. It included nearly 200 dance, theatrical, and musical performances, more than 20 exhibitions, 17 public artworks, and an extensive festival, Southern Crossroads, all presented between 1 June and 3 August 1996. OAF events attracted the largest audience in history for Olympic cultural events—more than 2.6 million people.

Atlanta's OAF was also notable for employing promotional innovations that heightened its visibility by closely associating it with the Olympic Games. For example, OAF information was included in all event ticketing information distributed by ACOG.

OAF events adhered to the two major themes defined in the Cultural Olympiad mission. Designed to link the international artistic and cultural traditions of the Olympic Family with those of the South, the OAF was the most comprehensive multidisciplinary arts festival ever held in the southern US, involving nearly 100 Atlanta-based, national, and international performance and arts organizations.

Of the 41 OAF venues and public art sites, 37 were within the Olympic Ring. Activities were clustered in three major areas: the Woodruff Arts Center in midtown; downtown, including Centennial Olympic Park and historic Auburn Avenue; and the Atlanta University Center, just southwest of downtown. A limited number of venues were located near competition sites outside the Olympic Ring, including the Georgia Museum of Art in Athens and the Beach Institute in Savannah.

In addition to the core OAF programs, the Cultural Olympiad organized a statewide cultural celebration in collaboration with the Georgia Council for the Arts, which featured more than 90 events selected from several hundred proposals submitted from around the state. In addition, 24 Atlanta art galleries were included in the 1996 Olympic Arts Festival Official Guide.

Unlike cultural programs in previous Games, Atlanta's Cultural Olympiad was not a separate entity but rather part of the organizing committee and therefore could rely on ACOG functional areas for support with certain production services. In other areas, where the requirements were unique to the cultural program, the Cultural Olympiad provided its own support. These areas are described below.

Budget

The Cultural Olympiad produced the first detailed budget plan for the OAF in 1993, when little detailed information about individual productions was available. Producers estimated their requirements, but the process was incomplete because negotiations were just beginning; virtually no music, theater, or dance programs had been confirmed. In many cases, the estimates for these programs were fairly accurate; those that were not were balanced by transferring excess funds from other programs that required less support than anticipated.

Sponsorship

Because the Cultural Olympiad was part of the programming for the Centennial Olympic Games, sponsorships for individual events and exhibitions were offered to all Olympic sponsors. The Cultural Olympiad secured approximately $8 million in additional support for its programs through such sponsorships, mostly from a limited number of participants. *(For details on sponsored programs, see Figure 1.)*

Promotions

The Promotions division was responsible for producing Cultural Olympiad publications, including brochures, program books, and many other accompanying publications. It also coordinated and implemented a sales strategy with ACOG Ticket Sales for Cultural Olympiad events. In addition, this division implemented the OAF's Cultural Look of the Games pro-

gram, created and implemented a limited paid advertising program, managed the OAF merchandising program, and developed and coordinated Cultural Olympiad special events such as press conferences, awards ceremonies, and a variety of program openings.

Publications. OAF publications were produced by ACOG's Creative Services Department under the direction of the Cultural Olympiad manager of sales and promotions. Staff and contract writers and designers were hired to produce the following:

FIGURE 1: SPONSORED CULTURAL OLYMPIAD PROGRAMS

AT&T
Southern Crossroads, *AT&T Classical Music and Jazz Series*, and *AT&T Theater Series*

Equifax, Inc.
Rings: Five Passions in World Art

Avon
The *Olympic Woman*

American Security Group
Overall presenting sponsor of the OAF

AMC Theatres and Turner Classic Movies
One Hundred Years of World Cinema

General Motors
Southern Music Amphitheater of Southern Crossroads

Scott Hudgens Companies
World Events, a Cultural Olympiad–commissioned public artwork

The Imlay Foundation
An Olympic Celebration of Chamber Music

John S. and James L. Knight Foundation
Southern Play Project

Sara Lee Corporation
OAF Dance Program

National Endowment for the Arts
International Sculpture Exhibition

Swatch
An Olympic Portfolio: Photographs by Annie Leibovitz

David, Helen, and Marian Woodward Fund
Installation of *Androgyne Planet*, a Cultural Olympiad-commissioned public artwork, and the Southern Play Project

■ OAF ticket brochure (875,000)—mailed to more than 300,000 direct-mail ticket buyers and on request, and distributed to Olympic sponsors and throughout Atlanta at book, music, and record stores and at cultural venues;

■ *OAF Official Guide* (one million)—available free to visitors several weeks prior to and during the OAF at all OAF venues and at all ACOG visitor information kiosks;

■ OAF theater (58,000), dance (75,000), and music (45,000) playbills—incorporated all related OAF performances, highlighted OAF pro-

grams in other disciplines, and provided ticket purchasing instructions;

■ brochures for the *Olympic Woman* and *Centennial Collectibles* exhibitions;

■ brochures for the *Rings: Five Passions in World Art* and *Souls Grown Deep/Thornton Dial* exhibitions—produced by collaborators with Cultural Olympiad approval;

■ collaborator appreciation plaques (100);

■ collaborator and OAF participant certificates (5,000);

■ artists, staff, and vendor identification badges (15,000); and

top: Decorations for Cultural Olympiad venues matched the ACOG Look of the Games.

bottom: A total of 875,000 OAF ticket brochures were distributed by mail and throughout Atlanta at book, music, and record stores and at cultural venues.

■ *Map and Guide to Public Art*—produced in cooperation with the city of Atlanta Bureau of Cultural Affairs and the Arts Festival of Atlanta.

Sales and Marketing. Marketing Cultural Olympiad events has been historically challenging. Recognizing that previous Olympic cultural programs sometimes had been obscured by the Games, the Cultural Olympiad staff developed ways to gain greater visibility for the OAF. Among the most significant strategies was that OAF events were announced and tickets offered earlier than at any previous Olympic Games, in September 1995. This announcement was included in a package sent to more than 300,000 individuals who ordered Olympic tickets in the first direct-mail ticket sales phase. A two-page description of the OAF had also been included in the original Games ticket brochure, more than 35 million of which were distributed throughout the US.

The second marketing phase, telephone sales, began in February and continued through May, when over-the-counter ticketing locations opened throughout Atlanta. The results of the telephone phase could have been improved by more comprehensive training, a larger staff, and a sustained promotional campaign during the first few weeks.

Press coverage was coordinated with and supported by the Cultural Olympiad communications office. A limited advertising and promotions budget prevented large-scale marketing, although some OAF collaborators did promote events using their own budgets.

Sales were strong at the beginning of the mail-order phase, but then diminished until just prior to the Games. *(For details on the numbers of tickets sold and attendance at OAF events, see Figures 2 and 3, respectively.)*

Look of the Games. The manager of sales and promotions surveyed OAF venues with the ACOG Look of the Games coordinator in fall 1995. Pictures were taken at each venue so that elements could be scanned into a proposed design. Once plans were approved by each venue, Look staff confirmed hardware needs and banner measurements. To remain within OAF's Look budget, banner sizes and designs were standardized when possible. ACOG's Look division contracted the fabrication and managed the installation and removal processes.

Banners were usually hung during the week prior to exhibition openings, and at performance venues just prior to opening performances. OAF public art sites were identified by a wooden OAF Look kiosk. Within two weeks after the close of the OAF, all banners and other Look elements were removed.

Merchandising. An attractive, high-quality, full-color OAF souvenir book was a key component of OAF planning. In early 1996, the Cultural Olympiad decided that the book be written by Cultural Olympiad staff and designed and produced by an outside vendor. Concerns about design approaches resulted in a limited print run, and late delivery to ACOG Retail Operations resulted in few sales.

Other OAF merchandise, produced by approved licensees, included a series of pins, a T-shirt, and a poster. ACOG Retail Operations sold the products in several of its retail outlets during fall 1995. The Cultural Olympiad purchased additional quantities wholesale from the licensees and distributed them to staff, volunteers, special guests, and all OAF ticket sales brochure distribution outlets to help promote OAF ticket sales.

Some OAF collaborators chose to produce merchandise of their own. They were contractually obliged to design any event-specific merchandise in conjunction with ACOG and the Cultural Olympiad and have it produced by an ACOP licensee unless otherwise stipulated.

ACOG Retail Operations sold OAF and ACOG merchandise at only two OAF venues—the *Olympic Woman* and *Centennial Collectibles* exhibitions. Final net sales at both venues exceeded projections. The Woodruff Arts Center sold all OAF merchandise from a dedicated shop.

Special Events. The Cultural Olympiad staff selected a limited number of special events to be held during the OAF, and worked with ACOG's Special Events Department to budget, schedule, and plan these events, which included:

■ a reception held in honor of the *International Celebration of Southern Literature* at Agnes Scott College;

■ dedication of *World Events*, a public artwork commissioned by the Cultural Olympiad, followed by a reception for the Atlanta arts community on the opening day of the OAF;

■ morning press conference and evening reception to celebrate the opening of the *Olympic Woman* exhibition;

■ morning dedication of *Androgyne Planet*, a public artwork commissioned by the Cultural Olympiad in Centennial Olympic Park;

■ morning press conference followed by a celebration to open the Southern Crossroads Festival in Centennial Olympic Park;

■ evening reception to open the *Centennial Collectibles* exhibition at Atlanta Merchandise Mart; and

■ afternoon Palmares awards ceremony for *Centennial Collectibles* exhibitors and special guests.

For collaborators that held their own events, the Cultural Olympiad provided invitation lists, guidelines for maintaining ACOG's clean venue requirements, and Cultural Olympiad banners and personnel.

Communications

Cultural Olympiad press and media functions were managed by the ACOG Communications Department on a centralized client basis with a director of communications assigned to each functional area. This allowed ACOG to maintain a unified, corporatewide approach to communications, which resulted in a comprehensive strategy and position for

FIGURE 2: OAF TICKET SALES

Series	Number Sold
Classical Music and Jazz	32,305
Dance	39,471
Exhibitions	143,540
Puppetry	12,432
Theater	25,330
Total	**253,078**

FIGURE 3: OAF ATTENDANCE

Category	Attendees
Ticketed performances and exhibitions	253,058
Nonticketed exhibitions	90,000
Southern Marketplace	270,000
Southern Crossroads Festival	2,000,000
Total	**2,613,058**

• VICTORIA L BROOKS • YVONNE E BROOKS • ERNEST D BROOKS III • JAMES K BROOKS JR • MICHAEL W BROOKS MD • GREGORY S BROOKS PM • KATHLEEN H BROOM • WILLIAM L BROOM • KELLY A BROOMAN • ALLAN L BROOME • BOB C BROOME • CARTER E BROOME • CHRISTOPHER M BROOME • PATTI L BROOME • RONALD M BROOME • STAN W BROOME • JENNIFER J BROPHY • CAROL S BRORS-EN • DEREK L BROSCH • LEIGH V BROSCHAT MT • ANTHONY W BROSIO • GENE M BROSIUS • JOE BROSOFSKY • ROBERT BROTEMARKLE • JAMES M BROTEN • DONALD W BROTHERS • JAVON BROTHERS

155

its various departments. A specialist in arts communications was hired to direct press and media functions and later sponsorship, publications, and sales and promotion. This arrangement worked extremely well.

Media which covered only cultural events were assigned OAF press credentials. Close to 500 requests for OAF press credentials were processed prior to and during the festival. The OAF received significant coverage in print and electronic media, and nearly all of it was positive.

During the Games, the OAF press center was located in space provided by AT&T, adjacent to the Woodruff Arts Center and near a MARTA station. The Cultural Olympiad staff included the director of communications, the press representative and communications assistant, a venue manager, associate venue manager, and nearly 100 volunteer press representatives. The center offered the press a number of amenities, including calling card telephones, personal computers, facsimile machines, printers, copy machines, and Info'96 terminals. An interview room and complimentary beverage service were also provided. It was open daily from 0800 to 2400, from 8 July through the end of the Games.

Logistics

The Cultural Olympiad created its own Logistics division to develop comprehensive plans for and manage transportation, accommodations, volunteer recruitment and management, freight/customs, and warehouse operations, as well as coordinate requests with responsible ACOG departments. Each of these functional areas was managed by a dedicated coordinator hired 6–9 months prior to the Games.

Transportation. The first OAF transportation plan was produced in 1992, when an estimate of the number of vehicles, anticipated venues, performances, and other critical data was assembled and provided to ACOG Transportation. ACOG decided that a ticket to a cultural event would be valid for a ride to and

This attractive, high-quality, full-color souvenir book highlighted the events of the 1996 Olympic Arts Festival.

from that event on the Olympic Transportation System. Atlanta's cultural program was the first to provide transportation to ticket holders at no extra charge.

An OAF transportation coordinator was hired in March 1996. The final official vehicle configuration was seven cars, one cargo van, and seven passenger vans. Twenty volunteer drivers transported artists, equipment, and support staff to and from OAF venues and events. A total of 727 van trips, not including airport arrival and departure trips, were made in a 23-day period.

A detailed daily schedule for every OAF vehicle, completed several months prior to the Games, worked well as a blueprint, but inevitable changes required constant monitoring and expert management. Drivers were dispatched from a motor pool headquarters established at the Atlanta Civic Center, where the OAF controlled a number of parking spaces. Parking and street access permits, which were essential to the smooth operation of OAF transportation, were assigned in limited quantities.

Accommodations. Accommodations were a problem for many OAF participants. Although Cultural Olympiad staff began to define and communicate its needs more than three years before the OAF and had reserved a sufficient portion of its budget for housing, some of the housing assigned to OAF artists was inadequate or too far from the venues. Once the Games began, however, adjustments were difficult.

Venue Planning and Management

The OAF was presented in more than 40 venues and public art sites, each of which required varying degrees of support from OAF staff. Venues were designated as either A venues, which received the most significant level of support, or B venues, which were largely operated by the collaborating institutions and required little if any direct involvement from OAF staff.

All A venues received ACOG staff and volunteers, logistics support, Look of the Games banners and signage, OAF identification badges, OAF venue command center support, press and information tables, security, and technology. Some A venues received food and beverage service, ticketing, and transportation support. B venues received ACOG volunteers, a press and information table, and/or ticketing support, if needed.

Accessibility. The Cultural Olympiad made a concerted effort to ensure accessibility to all of its programs. An Atlanta-based company, Special Audiences, Inc., assisted the Cultural Olympiad in developing guidelines, analyzing proposed cultural venues for compliance with accessibility laws, and choosing events to receive support for hearing- and sight-impaired patrons. Many improvements were made to the venues, including braille lettering on elevators and entryways, and special signs and listening devices. One performance of each OAF play was accompanied by audio description; seven plays were interpreted in sign language.

Technology. Technology equipment supplied to the OAF communications center and venues included 23 telephones and phone lines, 8 facsimile machines, 7 copy machines, 3 Info'96 terminals, 2 Info'96 printers, and 55 pagers. The Cultural Olympiad had 26 computers, 8 of which were installed at OAF venues.

Venue Command Center Operations. The Cultural Olympiad created a base station through which the venues could communicate their needs and receive and deliver vital information. The OAF venue command center, which opened in mid-June 1996, was equipped with three telephones, facsimile and copy machines, and a base radio station that serviced both the OAF radio and security frequency daily from 0700 to 0100.

Stationed at the venue command center on a daily, rotating basis were representatives from OAF who coordinated services for the key functional areas and the Cultural Olympiad director or visual arts producer.

The venue command center staff held half-hour morning briefings throughout the OAF, which were attended by most OAF venue managers. These meetings raised key issues from the previous 24 hours, alerted all staff to issues and problems that might arise, and maintained communication between all involved parties.

OLYMPIC ARTS FESTIVAL PROGRAMS

OAF events were divided into distinct program areas: music, theater, dance, the visual arts, and humanities and special programs.

Music Program

The OAF presented a series of musical events from 15 July through 2 August that featured classical music and jazz, and included youth performances and regional contributions. This series was called the AT&T Classical Music and Jazz Series.

The series featured a variety of performances, such as *An Olympic Celebration of Chamber Music*, a gathering of some of the world's most distinguished musicians. It also included concerts by orchestras from former Olympic host cities, including the State Orchestra of Hellenic Music, which honored Athens as the first host city of the modern Olympic era.

The Atlanta Symphony Youth Orchestra and the Australian Youth Orchestra performed individually and then jointly, enabling Atlanta youth to symbolically pass the torch of the Olympic Spirit to the youth of Australia, host of the 2000 Olympic Games in Sydney. The Interlochen Arts Academy's World Youth Orchestra, featuring members from more than 30 countries, gave its first-ever Atlanta performance with the world premier of Alvin Singleton's *Umoja: Each One of Us Counts.*

Atlanta's own musical talents and institutions were well represented in this series. The

Atlanta Symphony Orchestra performed with Georgia native Jessye Norman and the Atlanta Symphony Chorus in a performance of Mahler's Second Symphony, with distinguished violinist Itzhak Perlman, and in the International Opera Gala in collaboration with the Atlanta Opera. The Atlanta Opera also gave two performances of George and Ira Gershwin's Pulitzer prize-winning musical, *Of Thee I Sing*.

Two major jazz programs were featured as part of the series: an Olympic Jazz Summit, created and organized by distinguished trumpeter Wynton Marsalis, that featured an all-star big band and an ensemble of dancers; and, to celebrate the 150th anniversary of the Smithsonian Institution, the Smithsonian Jazz Masterworks Orchestra performed the final concert in Symphony Hall.

Musical events were performed daily at the Atlanta Symphony Hall at the Woodruff Arts Center from 15 July through 2 August.

Theater Program

The range of subject matter explored in the OAF Theater Program fulfilled the Cultural Olympiad's mission to offer Olympic visitors a comprehensive understanding of the historic and contemporary forces that shaped the culture of the American South. Eight local and regional theaters participated in this theater series, presenting more than 80 performances between 11 July and 3 August. Some of these productions evolved out of the Southern Play Project. Two new works were commissioned by the Cultural Olympiad and Seven Stages, Inc., and premiered during the OAF. Other works in the series included plays that were collaborations between local and other theatrical companies, such as Theater Emory and the Saratoga International Theater Institute. Regional companies, such as the Alabama Shakespeare Festival, and international companies, such as the Royal National Theatre of Great Britain, also performed in this series.

Theater Emory collaborated with the Saratoga International Theater Institute to produce *Small Lives/Big Dreams*.

The Cultural Olympiad staff presented OAF theatrical productions in two facilities—the Alliance Theatre main stage and the studio theaters at the Woodruff Arts Center and at the main and second stages at the nearby 14th Street Playhouse, also owned and operated by the Alliance Theatre Company. This concentration of theater events contributed a festive atmosphere to these venues and allowed access to all performances from the Olympic Transportation System. The technical/production team designed a production plan that would integrate the individual requirements of participating theater companies. This lengthy process proved worth the effort.

Also part of the Theater Program was a four-year partnership between the Cultural Olympiad and the Center for Puppetry Arts, during which new works were created and premiered, a new museum was built to house a special exhibition, and the theater received a new lobby. This extraordinary organization presented more than 50 performances during the Games, including performances in collaboration with regional and international puppetry companies.

Dance Program

Five local and regional dance companies and seven national and international companies presented 29 dance performances between 10 July and 3 August. Local groups included the Soweto Street Beat Dance Company, which recently relocated to Atlanta from South Africa. Other participants were the Alvin Ailey American Dance Theater from the US, and companies from the Netherlands and Thailand.

The OAF Dance Program was presented in two large facilities—the Civic Center in downtown Atlanta and the Martin Luther King Jr. International Chapel at Morehouse College at the Atlanta University Center. The Civic Center seated more than 4,500, and the King Chapel, 2,500. Careful technical planning and production scheduling were crucial to the success of a program as large and complicated as the OAF's dance series. The production team successfully anticipated the technical challenges that could arise as a result of several different dance companies sharing a single performance venue.

Each company that performed at the King Chapel opened with an evening performance and followed the next day with a matinee, dismantling immediately after the performance so the next company could prepare to open the following evening. Productions staged at the Civic Center required more technical support and so were performed only two to four times each. Additional programming was also produced at the 14th Street Playhouse.

By presenting many diverse productions, the OAF Dance Program achieved its artistic goals while exceeding its most optimistic attendance expectations.

Visual Arts Program

Featuring over 20 exhibitions and 15 public artworks, the OAF Visual Arts Program was designed to explore both southern and international Olympic themes. Developing and managing the program, especially the public art component, was a monumental task that required numerous collaborative partnerships with local and international artists, museums, and cultural institutions that spanned more than three years.

Rings: Five Passions in World Art. The *Rings* exhibition, which focused on the international connections theme, was the centerpiece of the Visual Arts Program. *Rings* was the result of ACOG's and the High Museum's collaborative effort to produce an exhibition of visual art with international significance. The recently retired director of the National Gallery of Art, J. Carter Brown, secured to develop and coordinate the exhibition, had the experience, insight, and international prestige to realize this goal.

Establishing the contractual relationship with the High Museum took nearly 18 months. ACOG agreed to provide half the financial re-

sources and secure an additional signature sponsor to provide most of the balance; the High Museum needed to secure the remaining portion. In return, the Cultural Olympiad shared the revenues from ticket sales so its significant investment could be partially recovered. This concept of revenue sharing was unusual in the nonprofit museum world.

A large show such as *Rings* can take years to research and curate, design, secure loan agreements for, and present. The High Museum did an extraordinary job of managing this complex and challenging process.

The concept for *Rings* emerged in spring 1993 and is best expressed by the introduction to the exhibition catalog, written by J. Carter Brown:

> In conceiving this exhibition, I have taken, in a metaphorical sense, the concept of interconnectedness that those five [Olympic] rings so graphically embody as the guiding principle for an art exhibition of what we believe to be a wholly innovative kind. Its basis is in the emotional, affective (as distinct from purely cognitive) function of works of art, grouped under five rubrics: Love, Anguish, Awe, Triumph, and Joy.
>
> The present exhibition...brings together paintings and sculpture as diverse as possible, in scale and materials and originally intended function, objects that span more than seven thousand years of creativity, representing virtually all the major geographic areas and principle religious mainstreams of our world.

Brown warned exhibition organizers that the concept could be controversial, but it was agreed that it embodied the spirit of the Centennial Olympic celebration.

Souls Grown Deep: African-American Vernacular Art of the South. Souls Grown Deep was a landmark presentation of paintings, sculptures, and works on paper by self-taught artists from the southeastern US. More than 450 works by 30 contemporary artists were included in this extraordinary exhibition, a large percentage of which were loaned by local citizen William Arnet, a major collector of works by self-taught artists. The exhibition was a collaboration among the Cultural Olympiad, the Michael C. Carlos Museum at Emory University, and the city of Atlanta Bureau of Cultural Affairs. Since the Carlos Museum did not have sufficient space to accommodate the exhibition, the city of Atlanta provided a 30,000 sq ft (2,790 sq m) space in Atlanta's City Hall East, which the museum remodeled into an appropriate exhibition facility.

Because the space was not directly accessible by the Olympic Transportation System, the exhibition was not as well attended as it might have been, but it received universal critical acclaim from national and international press.

Clark Atlanta University Exhibit. Clark Atlanta University has collected paintings by African-American artists for more than 50 years. The collection had been displayed in substandard exhibition space for years, and had fallen into disrepair. A meeting in 1992 with the Clark Atlanta gallery director resulted in the Cultural Olympiad's commitment to fund the complete restoration of the collection for the 1996 OAF. The Cultural Olympiad's early commitment also gave the gallery director and officials the leverage to secure funding to convert the old Clark Atlanta library into a large new exhibition space, and thus facilitated a major legacy to Clark Atlanta faculty, students, and visitors. This exhibition, along with several others, was a key component of the Cultural Olympiad effort, *African-American Culture: An American Experience.*

Ulysses Davis Exhibit. While exploring the artistic community of Savannah, the site of Olympic yachting events, the Cultural Olympiad learned that the Beach Institute African-American Cultural Center was attempting to rescue the collected works of Ulysses Davis, a noted Savannah-based woodcarver. With a contribution from the Cultural Olympiad and additional funding, the Beach Institute was able to purchase the collection. The Beach Institute created a permanent display entitled *The Vision of Ulysses Davis, American Folk Artist.*

The Olympic Woman Exhibition and Program. The *Olympic Woman* chronicled the role of women in the modern Olympic Games from 1900 to 1996. The exhibition was composed of memorabilia, film, video, and photography from around the world. It was first proposed to ACOG by Bonnie Nelson Schwartz and Gloria Weissburg of Multimedia Partners, Ltd., in 1991. The exhibition opened in June 1996, and attendance grew when the Games began. ACOG and Spelman College developed a complementary *Olympic Woman* curriculum, which included a book, video, and other components, that was distributed to Georgia middle schools.

Centennial Collectibles. An exhibition of stamps and coins has been presented in conjunction with each Olympic Games, a tradition rooted in the fact that the production and sale of Olympic stamps and coins from each participating country has helped support the modern Olympic Movement. Collectors of Olympic memorabilia worldwide congregate at the Olympic Games to buy, sell, and trade Olympic memorabilia, including stamps and coins. In 1993, IOC President Juan Antonio Samaranch formed the Commission on Olympic Collectibles to unite what had always been autonomous areas of interest. The Cultural Olympiad was responsible for developing the Olympic Movement's first unified exhibition of stamps, coins, and memorabilia—*Centennial Collectibles: Olymphilex '96/Stamps, Coins, and Memorabilia.*

This exhibition was one of the most challenging to stage. The many constituencies, which included national postal administrations, philatelic and numismatic governing bodies and press, and hundreds of individual collectors and dealers, required constant attention from the Cultural Olympiad.

Organizers wanted to present the exhibition in downtown Atlanta, near the main Olympic hotels. The number of anticipated participants and the need for a trade show environment led organizers to reserve an entire floor (100,000 sq ft/9,300 sq m) of the Atlanta Merchandise Mart. Rental, utilities, maintenance, and security for this space absorbed the majority of the allocated budget.

More than 35 postal administrations and 45 dealers participated in the program and more than 60,000 people attended this event during its 18-day operation. It was one of the best-attended exhibitions of the Games.

Viewed by some as a central feature of the Olympic Games experience, the complexities of managing the multiple agendas of individual organizations and constituencies make this program very demanding.

Public Art. The Olympic Games provided an excellent opportunity to enhance the beauty of the city of Atlanta with public art during and after the Games. ACOG embarked on a program that eventually installed 12 new public artworks, several of which are permanent.

After conducting a study to identify opportunities for creating important new public artworks, ACOG decided to commission an artist to create a cauldron to hold the flame at Olympic Stadium. Several experts were engaged to serve on an advisory panel to select the artist. Chosen with the endorsement of all parties was Siah Armajani, an Iranian-born American sculptor whose work is world-renowned. Armajani's populist work has frequently involved sophisticated bridges and is deeply rooted in Jeffersonian democracy.

At an initial meeting, Armajani shared his concept for a spectacular 180 ft (55 m) bridge linking Olympic Stadium to a 120 ft (37 m) tower that would hold the cauldron. Numerous

contingencies were involved in developing the contract. Despite delays and complications, the artist continued to develop his concept, consulting regularly with ACOG officials and ultimately receiving the official sanction to proceed. When announced to the public, Armajani's concept for the Olympic bridge, tower, and cauldron was enthusiastically received.

Armajani's bold work was designed to symbolically and physically link Olympic Stadium to the community surrounding it. The bridge was designed so that the Olympic Rings, lo-

top: The majestic cauldron rose 116 ft (35 m) above the ground. The tower it rested on was linked to the north end of Olympic Stadium by a bridge.

bottom: The bridge that connected Olympic Stadium with the cauldron tower was designed to physically and symbolically link the stadium to the surrounding community.

cated at the center of either side of the bridge, served as structural components as well as symbols of international unity. At the tower end of the bridge, Armajani created a small house structure that joined the bridge with the tower, and through which a torchbearer would run and begin the climb to the cauldron, approximately 100 ft (30 m) above. The climb represented the extraordinary efforts of athletes

to achieve their goals; the cauldron at the top, a three-dimensional Cultural Olympiad logo, symbolized fraternity and the immense effort required to achieve greatness.

Art Partners on Location. The Cultural Olympiad collaborated with the city of Atlanta Bureau of Cultural Affairs in *Art Partners on Location*, a successful program through which public art was commissioned for Atlanta neighborhoods. The idea behind this collaboration was to create a new work of public art in each of the three neighborhoods surrounding Olympic Stadium. An array of artists was selected and presented to each neighborhood for final selection. Each artist chose the site and concept for the work together with the respective community. In two of the three neighborhoods, the artists asked residents to help create the works. This program provided a legacy to the neighborhoods that hosted the Games.

International Sculpture Exhibition. The *International Sculpture Exhibition* brought public artworks to Atlanta from around the world. Five important sculptures, each representing one of the Olympic Rings, were selected with the assistance of the Michael C. Carlos Museum and a distinguished international advisory panel. These sculptures were borrowed and installed around the city.

Humanities and Special Programs

In accordance with the Cultural Olympiad's theme of southern connections, the OAF included three programs that would expose Olympic Games visitors to the culture of the American South. These programs presented an exhibition of the African-American experience in the South, a discussion of southern literature, and a festival featuring southern music, dance, and artwork.

African-American Culture: An American Experience. This series of exhibitions, plays, dance and musical performances, and film presentations focused on the African-American

experience in the South. The curator and producer of the program developed a series of supplementary programs to support and reinforce the messages about African-American cultural contributions and expressions.

African-American Culture: An American Experience included *Folksay: A Living Exhibit*, a series of theatrical vignettes and oral histories developed from historical and archival sources and directed by Spelman College's distinguished professor of theater arts, Glenda Dickerson. Performances were held at the Atlanta University Center and along historic Auburn Avenue. Several churches in the area hosted daily afternoon gospel music concerts and performances of other African-American music, and the main quadrangle at Clark Atlanta was the site of a large outdoor performance stage that featured the university's and other Atlanta-based jazz ensembles. More than 550 artists and performers participated in these events, many of which were also presented at the Southern Crossroads Festival.

International Celebration of Southern Literature. Following the model of the 1995 gathering of Nobel laureates of literature, a three-day conference on literature from the American South was held in June 1996. Important southern writers such as Tina McElroy Ansa, Fred Chappell, Harry Cruise, Ellen Douglas, Ernest Gaines, George Garrett, Mary Hood, Terry Kay, Albert Murray, Reynolds Price, and Margaret Walker were assembled on the campus of Agnes Scott College with leading scholars of southern-US literature from Europe, Asia, and South America.

More than 500 people attended the conference, which included public readings, panel discussions, and informal gatherings that explored the contributions southern-US writers have made to American and world literature.

Tony Cragg's *World Events* was one of many pieces of public art displayed in the metro-Atlanta area for the Games.

Southern Crossroads Festival. From the earliest days of planning the OAF, the Cultural Olympiad was committed to presenting a large, multistage outdoor festival to showcase to Olympic visitors the extraordinary spirit and diversity of the culture of the American South. This festival, the OAF's largest program, was challenging to produce, and required more than two years of intensive effort, advice from many experts, and the collaboration of several institutional partners. During the 18-day festival, 1,114 artists and artisans participated in what became the Southern Crossroads Festival. Southern Crossroads was presented at Centennial Olympic Park, as it was both the literal and symbolic center of the Games.

Because of the Smithsonian Institution's successful and long-running annual Festival of American Folklife, Cultural Olympiad organizers wanted to involve the Smithsonian in their southern culture festival. The Smithsonian's Center for Folklife Programs and Cultural Studies became a coproducer of the festival. Coincidentally, the Smithsonian Institution was celebrating its 150th anniversary in summer 1996. Both parties decided to bring these two events together in the Southern Crossroads Festival.

Locally, the Atlanta-based Southern Arts Federation, an organization that traditionally coordinates, funds, programs, and presents performances for nine southeastern states, became the Cultural Olympiad's partner and collaborator in the development of Southern Crossroads. Their primary responsibility was to gather information about southern-US artists in every genre from which the Cultural Olympiad could select festival participants. The federation developed a comprehensive database that remains a significant legacy of the Cultural Olympiad.

The Atlanta History Center also became an early partner, assembling a panel of experts on southern culture and hosting the first meeting to begin defining the festival's major themes. It also agreed to curate and host an exhibition that would complement the festival by presenting a detailed and integrated view of the *American South: Past, Present, Future.*

During the festival, three performance stages in the park were used, one located in the south end and the other two in the north end, increasing the visibility of and access to festival events. Each stage had a distinctive character and purpose. The Southern Music Amphitheater had approximately 1,200 seats and standing room for 1,500–2,000 people. The stage operated daily from 1200 to 2400. It required two full crews per day, and was equipped with state-of-the-art sound and theatrical/concert lighting. Twelve or more ensembles were presented each day.

Designed for interactive participation between the audience and dance demonstrators and bands, the Dance Hall stage had seats for 400 and standing room for an additional 2,500–3,500 people. The stage initially operated from 1200 to 2100, but its hours were extended after the first four days to 2400. Again, two daily crew shifts were required. Twelve or more ensembles were presented daily.

The South on Record stage was designed to present broadcast-format programming and enabled audience members to interact with performers. There were 900 seats and standing room for 1,000 people. The stage operated from 1200 to 2100 and used a single daily crew. Eight or more ensembles were presented each day.

Performances at all stages lasted about 40–45 minutes with a 10–15-minute interval to prepare for the next production. Also, a demonstration area was created adjacent to the Southern Marketplace to accommodate two artisans. Approximately 20 people could view and interact with an artisan at work. Operating hours varied, but generally were from 1200 to 2000 daily.

Because of its size and location, Southern Crossroads presented enormous planning and production challenges. Nonetheless, it was enormously successful, attracting several million visitors to Centennial Olympic Park to participate in its exciting and diverse programs. It was by far the largest event of its kind ever presented in the South, and involved the most distinguished and gifted musicians and artists from the South than had ever before gathered at a single event.

CONCLUSIONS AND RECOMMENDATIONS

Perhaps the most important legacy of Atlanta's Cultural Olympiad is that its four-year program provided an unprecedented opportunity for organizations to improve and expand. Atlanta's OAF offered Olympic visitors an exceptionally wide range of cultural experiences and programs, significantly enhancing their Olympic experience. This linkage between art and sport is, as de Coubertin wrote in 1904, "as it should be...."

Atlanta's Cultural Olympiad consistently sought to integrate with ACOG's overall operations. The result was a successful operating model that significantly increased the visibility of the Olympic arts component, especially during the Games. The concept of a multiyear Cultural Olympiad has been embraced by the public, and future organizers are advised to consider the challenges inherent in the requirements of such an extensive program. These challenges include obtaining sufficient support from the organizing committee's functional areas before they are operational and dividing the Cultural Olympiad staff into two separate groups with pre-Games and Games-time planning responsibilities. The following guidelines will help future organizing committees plan Cultural Olympiad programs.

- Draft an early shell contractual agreement for consultants, artists, and exhibitions and required venues.
- Obtain early commitments from artists. This is essential to preserving negotiating flexibility and securing the most desirable participants.
- Thirty percent of the budget should be allotted for contingencies for production, since costs are always higher than anticipated.
- Establish clear guidelines for ticket distribution.
- Budget sufficient funds for a standard promotional campaign.
- Ensure that OAF's Look of the Games banners are large and plentiful enough to have an appropriate presence at the venues.
- Include matinee performances.
- Tightly control management of all projects from their venues.
- Be advised that it is difficult to attract public attention for events during the 10 days prior to the Games; however, during the Games, events were often oversubscribed.
- Select venues carefully; location is critical. OAF attendance levels greatly depended on an event's proximity to the Olympic Transportation System.
- Establish clear objectives and requirements for public artwork. Public art required tremendous resources and tended to attract controversy.
- Seek out programs that are distinctly Olympian, similar to Atlanta's *Rings, Olympic Winterland*, the joint concert between the Atlanta and Australian youth orchestras, and the *Olympic Woman*. The Olympic connection adds a sense of quality, drama, and pertinence to cultural events, a fact that can be used to increase their appeal to the general public.

EVENT AND GUEST SERVICES

CHAPTER TEN
EVENT AND GUEST SERVICES

OVERVIEW—One of ACOG's primary missions was to extend southern hospitality at its best, with friendliness, warmth, and efficiency. It was the responsibility of the departments of Special Events and Guest Services—components of the Corporate Services Department—to create and implement this image through providing events and hospitality services delivered in an atmosphere of graciousness and consideration.

Until spring 1995, Special Events and Guest Services operated as a single unit, as in the original AOC structure. However, the volume of events and visits by IOC and other officials soon required that each function be given its own director, reporting to the managing director of Corporate Services. Special Events and Guest Services not only worked together on many projects, but supported the other ACOG departments throughout the planning years.

Special Events created and implemented events for employees and external audiences, while Guest Services coordinated hotel reservations, travel arrangements, and gift procurement and distribution and planned Games-time Olympic Family programs.

SPECIAL EVENTS

This unit worked with every ACOG department in a client/agency relationship, creating and implementing events that supported the objectives of the department being served. Special Events had two divisions: one for internal and one for external events.

ORGANIZATION

The External Events group handled all meetings and events outside ACOG's offices. These included large-scale workshops, such as those held by ACOP for sponsors and licensees; major Olympic Family meetings, such as the Association of Summer Olympic International Federations (ASOIF) meeting with the IOC Executive Board, the Association of National

Olympic Committees (ANOC) General Assembly, Chef de Mission Seminars, and the 1995 Third IOC World Sports Sciences Congress; and press conferences, banquets, groundbreakings, grand openings, and other occasions. The 10-person department was responsible for every aspect of each event from catering, logistics, and making hotel arrangements (working through Guest Services) to staging, signage, and providing audiovisual support. Many events also required careful coordination with Risk Management and Community Relations.

The Internal Events group implemented all meetings with external constituencies and ACOG staff that occurred in ACOG offices, including board meetings, IOC Coordination Commission meetings, press conferences, and monthly brown bag lunches. This required a full-time staff of seven people, one of whom was dedicated to meetings and functions hosted by the CEO and/or the COO. This group also coordinated IZZY appearances through the Youth and Education Department, sponsor events, and community functions. The office maintenance contractor staff, which reported to this group, opened ACOG offices every morning by providing coffee in all break rooms, restocking soda machines, refilling water coolers, and preparing meeting rooms, complete with audiovisual equipment as needed.

Event Planning

Regardless of which division implemented an event, the event planning procedure was the same. The event was listed on the department's calendar, which was distributed throughout the organization to keep all staff apprised of current information. A specific event manager was appointed from within the department, and a support team was assigned. The event manager created an event plan, a template document that served as the basis for every event scheduled, to help ensure events were consistently well-planned. It also provided a mechanism for input from all staff associated with the event and enabled important information, such as contact names and phone numbers, to be shared with everyone involved.

Each event plan's overview described the event, noted its objectives, and indicated for which department/individual the event was being produced and who the event manager was. Each plan also provided:

■ the event venue's location and telephone number(s);

■ a time line noting when every preparatory step should occur and the team member responsible for each step;

■ a moment-to-moment schedule of the event day;

■ communication and audiovisual technology assignment;

■ any menu and bar service requirements;

■ placement of signage, decorations, equipment, and props;

■ transportation arrangements, including a map, parking assignments, and any specialized transportation needs;

■ a list of the name and telephone numbers of every person involved in the event;

■ the type and number of security members that would be present;

■ any issues associated with the event that might impede access for the disabled;

■ a list of the vendors and the corresponding purchase order numbers; and

■ all specific costs and the total budget.

After an initial meeting with the interested ACOG department, Special Events drafted the relevant event plan and made a formal presentation. Revisions were made as necessary, and the department funded the event via a budget transfer to Special Events. The proposed event site was surveyed to ensure proper sponsor representation, which included the removal of any visible brand signage that was visible. Depending on the complexity of the event, a rehearsal was usually scheduled. Following the event, an evaluation meeting with the client was held, including a final budget reconciliation.

In addition, there were a variety of functions held at ACOG offices and other locations which, while they did not require extensive planning, did require a well-produced setting. Special Events developed a kit of materials including table skirting, banners of various sizes, an assortment of flags, and other items that could be used for all departments.

Event Implementation

Special Events coordinated an event nearly every day, often producing several simultaneously. Following is a detailed listing of the special events the department produced.

Torch Relay staff member runs with a torch through a brown bag lunch gathering to the delight of all.

RECURRING EVENTS

■ **Brown Bag Lunches.** A tradition that began during the Bid process, brown bag lunches were designed to bring employees together on a regular basis in an informal setting. Until 1994, these monthly gatherings took place in the Centennial Room, ACOG headquarters' main conference room. Employees brought their own lunches and ACOG provided beverages. As ACOG's numbers increased, the lunches were moved to the large exhibition level of the Inforum building. Program content changed

IZZY stories displayed on the floor of the Georgia Dome.

monthly, with different functional areas delivering brief presentations about their activities. Brown bag lunches included remarks from ACOG CEO Billy Payne, new employee introductions, and employee birthday announcements. A major factor in the success of the brown bag lunches was that senior management attended regularly, setting an example that underscored the importance of communication within ACOG.

■ **Press Conferences.** These high-profile events were rarely the same and often impromptu. Special Events, together with Communications, created a template of services that would be provided at every press conference. Most often, press conferences at the Inform took place in the Centennial Room, which was equipped with proper lighting, appropriate signage, a registration table, mult box sound system, podium, backdrop, retractable screen, microphones, CD player, video equipment, and a camera platform. This

room accommodated approximately 70 reporters. When press conferences occurred outside the Centennial Room, most equipment and services were provided through a vendor.

■ **Regional Designation Awards in the Arts.** This annual awards program of the Cultural Olympiad also involved a reception for honorees.

■ **Volunteer Recognition Program.** With Volunteer Services, the department produced annual awards ceremonies to recognize volunteers' contribution to Games planning.

■ **Sponsor and Licensing Workshops.** Accommodations, transportation, and meeting services were coordinated for these ACOP events.

■ **IZZY Appearances.** The official Olympic mascot, IZZY, appeared regularly at ACOG and sponsor functions, schools, and public gatherings. Special Events staff managed IZZY appearances, which included hiring performers, scheduling performances, and arranging for travel and costume shipping. In total, IZZY made 498 ACOG-related, 571 school, and 223 sponsor-related appearances before the Games.

Games-time appearances added to the festive atmosphere. IZZY visited every venue at least once with daily appearances at Olympic Village, Centennial Olympic Park, and sponsor hospitality villages.

A conference room, designated the IZZY command center, was the place 50 volunteer performers received and returned costumes and teams received assignments. The program operated with 18 costumes—13 in use and 5 in reserve. During the Games, IZZY made 197 appearances.

MILESTONE EVENTS

■ **September 1991—Reunion at Underground Atlanta.** This public celebration commemorated the city's one-year anniversary as the host city of the Centennial Olympic Games. The event featured a replay of the IOC's announcement, the presentation of a commemorative T-shirt, and the opening of the *Olympic Experience*, ACOG's primary retail location and Olympic memorabilia exhibit.

■ **December 1991—First Centennial Olympic Partner Named.** A ceremony was held with NationsBank announcing the company's nation-

wide sponsorship of the XXVI Olympiad. Subsequently, announcements were produced for ACOP and ACOG for all sponsor and most other marketing agreements, many of which employed extensive audiovisual and decorative support.

■ **February 1992—Logo Unveiling.** A special press conference was held to unveil the torch mark logo, during which six huge banners featuring the torch mark logo and its colors were unfurled.

■ **April 1992—Olympic Force Launched.** This was the first of many events produced for ACOG's volunteer network. The annual awarding of the Medal of Honor involved a luncheon at the governor's mansion. Special Events also coordinated press conferences to announce the Olympic Force's 1992 food and toy drive, the grassroots and ITZAREADER programs, and annual meetings of Olympic Force coordinators. A Super Saturday celebration was held at five locations to mark the distribution of volunteer applications. Candidates attending could meet Volunteer Services staff, ask questions about the application process, and complete applications.

■ **September 1992—Flag Arrival Celebration.** Among ACOG's largest early endeavors, this event included a spectacular ceremony at the port of Savannah as the Olympic flag arrived on board the US Coast Guard barque *Eagle*. It was then transferred to a specially equipped train filled with an exhibit of Olympic memorabilia. The train toured the state, stopping in nine Georgia cities before arriving in Atlanta. More than 50,000 schoolchildren and 175,000 adults toured the exhibit. Ceremonies were held at each community where the train stopped. The event concluded with "Flag Jam," a star-studded concert at the Georgia Dome that featured Whitney Houston and was attended by US President George Bush.

■ **February 1993—*Olympic Winterland: Encounters with Norwegian Cultures*.** Special Events provided assistance for this month-long cultural presentation of the Cultural Olympiad, which included planning a reception for Sonja, Queen of Norway.

■ **July 1993—Olympic Stadium Groundbreaking.** Because of the prominence and legacy of the stadium with many active constituencies,

ACOG chose to make the groundbreaking a large celebration involving outreach to neighborhoods surrounding the site. Children from neighborhood schools painted a mural on a wooden fence at the site's entrance and participated in a relay to launch the ceremony. Members of the Atlanta Symphony Orchestra performed; and former Olympian Wilma Rudolph, in one of her last public appearances, addressed the crowd. The groundbreaking was performed simultaneously by eight dignitaries, including the governor of Georgia, the mayor of Atlanta, and the ACOG CEO, who drove small bulldozers to the site to break ground.

■ **September–November 1993—¡Mexico! A Cultural Tapestry.** Special Events produced the banquet celebrating the opening of this Cultural Olympiad festival's exhibit at the Michael C. Carlos Museum and the dedication of *Song for Atlanta*, a giant mural commissioned as part of the program. Guests were given photographs of the mural signed by artist Gilberto Aceves Navarro.

■ **October 1993—1000 Days to the Games.** To celebrate this milestone, a large countdown clock spanning a major highway was unveiled. An after-work gathering was held for all ACOG employees and a group photo was taken and distributed to all employees.

■ **January 1994—*Atlanta 1996.*** This series of television specials promoting the 1996 Olympic Games began on NBC just prior to the 1994 Super Bowl. To help Communications introduce the program to news media in Atlanta to cover the game, Special Events produced a preview party at the home of Evander Holyfield, Olympic boxer and world heavyweight champion. The event, which he hosted, included transporting 250 journalists by bus from downtown Atlanta.

■ **April 1994—*Celebrate Africa!*** The opening reception for this Cultural Olympiad festival, held at the Robert Woodruff Arts Center and High Museum of Art, featured different African foods and was attended by more than 800 people, including several IOC officials. Other events were planned in conjunction with the National Black Arts Festival held in Atlanta.

■ **June 1994—The Georgia International Horse Park Groundbreaking.** For this first of six venue groundbreakings, a template groundbreaking plan was created to make each ceremony consistent. The plan provided for banners, a ceremonial shovel, a portable podium, a program, refreshments, seating, and a sound system. Each venue owner signed the shovel after the event, and all participants signed a banner created specifically for each groundbreaking. The shovels will be displayed in ACOG's museum; venue owners kept the banners.

■ **August 1994—The Great Adventures of IZZY.** To help further promote IZZY's growing popularity, Special Events produced an unusual press event at the Georgia Dome. More than 60,000 stories written about IZZY's adventures by children from across the US and the world were displayed on the Dome's football field. Approximately 10,000 stories were hung from the ceiling of the Dome. US Secretary of Education Dick Riley, schoolchildren, and editors of *Parade* magazine, which promoted the story-writing activity, read many of the stories.

■ **March 1995—US President Clinton's first visit.** Approximately 500 days before the Games, US President Clinton and Vice President Gore visited ACOG's offices to inspire ACOG employees. The visit required extensive coordination with the US Secret Service.

■ **April 1995—*Nobel Laureates of Literature.*** Special Events coordinated the logistical planning of the two-day symposium of eight Nobel laureates of literature at the Carter Center. In addition to daytime sessions, this event included a dinner at the governor's mansion and several receptions, requiring considerable transportation coordination.

■ **January 1996—Olympic Games Quilt Exhibit.** A reception honoring the quilters who crafted more than 400 quilts as gifts for the NOCs and their flag bearers marked the opening of what became the Atlanta History Center's most popular exhibit. At an earlier event, a group photo of the quilters was taken at the state capitol.

■ **April 1996—100 Days to the Games.** With Volunteer Services, Special Events produced a fashion show to unveil Games uniforms to staff. Immediately following, a press conference was

held that included a live satellite feed from California with "Summon the Heroes" composer John Williams. This served as the premiere of this official musical theme and first public viewing of many Centennial Games features, including safety lanterns, sample medals, torches, victory bouquets, victory podiums, and renderings of venues dressed with the Look of the Games.

■ **May 1996—Olympic Stadium Grand Opening and IAAF Grand Prix.** The Grand Prix was the first competition held at Olympic Stadium. Although ACOG did not produce the competition, it produced and participated in an official

A groundbreaking ceremony using a designated shovel for all ceremonies.

opening ceremony. Youth from the Olympic Day in the Schools Program lined the field bearing flags that represented each country that would participate in the Olympic Games. One hundred individuals were selected from the stands to join dignitaries, including US Vice President Gore, in cutting a giant ribbon wrapped around the stadium that was carried by local neighborhood residents. A day-long media tour of the stadium preceded the opening.

■ **July 1996—Olympic Village Dedication.** Special Events produced two separate tours of the Village just prior to its opening. On the first day, selected officials participated in an official dedication, and members of the media were given guided tours of the Village for the remainder of the day. On the second day, nearly 100 local, state, and national officials were given tours and enjoyed a luncheon in the athletes' main dining hall.

WILLIAM ED BROWN • WILLIAM H BROWN • WILLIAM H BROWN • WILLIAM M BROWN • WILLIE A BROWN • ZARRON D BROWN • ZOLA J BROWN • RHONDA B BROWN-JOHNSON • DONALD F BROWN ATC • JOHN R BROWN ATC • BENJAMIN L BROWN III • GEORGE W BROWN IV • CECIL G BROWN JR • JAMES R BROWN JR • MERVIN T BROWN JR • MOSES BROWN JR • ALAN B BROWN MD • LAWRENCE S BROWN MD • CYNTHIA V BROWN NP • SHIRLEY BROWN PRESLEY • CECIL W BROWNE • AARON AW BROWNE • BARBARA A BROWNE • JOY V BROWNE • LESLIE BROWNE • MICHELE N BROWNE •

169

■ **July 1996—***Olympic Woman* **Exhibition Opening**. More than 250 guests attended a ribbon-cutting ceremony and reception to hail the opening of this historic exhibition.

■ **July 1996—Centennial Olympic Park Opening for Sponsors**. A day-long preview was held for employees of the four sponsors that had a significant presence in the park.

TORCH RELAY EVENTS

■ **Arrival of the Olympic Flame in Los Angeles**. Among the Torch Relay celebrations and festivities coordinated by Special Events was the

Information booths were provided at many meetings.

27 April 1996 arrival of the Olympic flame at Los Angeles International Airport on a charter flight carrying ACOG officials and senior members of the Hellenic Olympic Committee (HOC). In a private, brief reception at the airport, ACOG management and key members of the Bid team greeted the flame, still in its safety lantern. From there, the flame traveled by helicopter to the Los Angeles Coliseum where a large, public celebration took place, featuring the HOC's high priestess; the premiere of "Power of the Dream," the official song of the Centennial Games, and the first leg of the US Torch Relay.

■ **Riverboat Trip**. Various hospitality occasions coordinated by Special Events took place as the torch traveled from St. Louis to Hannibal, Missouri, by riverboat on the Mississippi River.

■ **Arrival in Washington, DC**. The event began on the US Capitol steps and continued with a celebration on the streets of the city. This was followed by a White House lawn party that concluded with a ceremony in the White House in which President Clinton participated.

■ **Ceremony in Selma, Alabama**. In this emotional Torch Relay event, ACOG co-chair Andrew Young carried the torch across the Edmund C. Pettis Bridge, scene of a historic civil rights confrontation, leading a group of children and civil rights leaders.

■ **Flame arrival in Georgia**. Governor Miller and the ACOG CEO welcomed the arrival of the torch in Savannah—the port which had welcomed the Olympic flag four years earlier—at the start of its nine-day tour of Georgia.

INTERNATIONAL EVENTS

■ **International Hospitality Events**. Special Events planned and facilitated all ACOG group travel and hospitality events at Olympic Family meetings throughout the world from the beginning Bid days in 1988 until the Games. On many of these occasions, hospitality houses, called Atlanta Houses, were established to demonstrate southern cordiality and to define and communicate ACOG messages to the IOC and the rest of the Olympic Family. Each hospitality program in conjunction with an Olympic Games required designated staff to coordinate the activities of ACOG management and sponsor guests for the duration of the Games, including creating guide books for various activities.

■ **March 1993—ASOIF and IOC Executive Board Meeting**. Produced for ACOG's Olympic Family and Sports Departments, this gathering of 407 sports officials was among the first occasions they had to review venue plans for the Games, meet the staff who would be coordinating the Olympic Village and sports competitions, and view preparations for the Games. Special Events provided all meeting services for this and all other major Olympic Family meetings. Services included arrangements for arrivals and departures, a concierge / information desk, entertainment, meal and banquet services, meeting room preparation, registration, signage in

French and English, and transportation. A special ASOIF logo was created to use on all gifts, signage, and publications.

■ **September 1994—The 1994 Pan-American Race Walk**. This was the first of 25 test events preceding the Olympic Games. Special Events was involved in the implementation of all test events. Operating as one department, Special Events and Guest Services handled all athlete meals and hospitality events for the competition, athlete and dignitary arrivals and departures, and housing, a major area of responsibility. The department applied the Look of the Games to banners, signage, and other items.

■ **December 1994—ANOC and IOC Executive Board Meeting**. Special Events produced this week-long gathering of more than 750 NOC, IF, and IOC officials, providing all necessary meeting services, such as registration, information desk/concierge, meal services, meeting room preparation, signage, arrivals and departures, room assignments, decoration, entertainment, sightseeing, and venue tours. A breakfast with envoys was among the events coordinated. In addition, Atlantans hosted delegates in their homes for more than 150 individual dinner parties. This event allowed Olympic officials to meet the people with whom they would be working during the Games, while sampling genuine southern hospitality. It also gave Atlanta families the opportunity to learn more about the countries participating in the Games and build personal relationships with the people involved.

■ **May 1995—Chef de Mission Seminar**. With Olympic Village staff, Special Events produced this four-day meeting during which NOCs began the detailed planning for bringing their delegations to Atlanta for the Games. Support activities included accommodations, meeting services, and transportation.

■ **July 1995—One Year to the Games Celebration**. ACOG marked this occasion with an outdoor breakfast and daylight fireworks display for staff at Atlanta–Fulton County Stadium, with a view of Olympic Stadium, which was nearing completion. To inspire the early morning crowds of press and ACOG staff, the event was hosted by ACOG co-chair Andrew Young at Olympic Stadium and CEO Billy Payne by audio link in Lausanne, where an official ceremony had just been held to invite the 197 NOCs to the Centennial Olympic Games.

■ **September 1995—Third IOC World Congress on Sports Sciences.** Working with Medical Services, Olympic Family and Protocol, and Sports, Special Events produced this week-long gathering of 500 international experts on sports sciences. Activities included coordinating attendees and producing extensive technical materials to distribute to medical attendees.

GAMES-TIME EVENTS

During the Games, Special Events arranged many meetings and banquets for the Olympic Family, including the following.

■ **10 July—IOC Juridical Commission Meeting.** Special Events coordinated this first official IOC meeting of the Centennial Olympic Games, providing all meeting services, such as registration and audiovisual support.

■ **11–18 July—IOC Executive Board Meeting and 105th Session.** Special Events, working with Olympic Family and Protocol, coordinated this meeting of the IOC Executive Board and full membership.

■ **13 July—Opening of Centennial Olympic Park to the Public.** A brief ceremony was produced to open the park officially. The ceremony included local and state government officials.

■ **14 July—Opening of the 105th IOC Session.** An evening of entertainment in the Woodruff Arts Center drew 2,000 attendees. Using a beautiful "Gardens of Georgia" setting, the event included a musical tribute to the South produced by the Cultural Olympiad and a menu featuring famous Georgia cuisine. A logo featuring the Georgia flower, the Cherokee Rose, was created for use on all session badges and publications.

■ **15 July—Governor's Dinner.** Georgia Governor Zell Miller hosted all IOC members and their spouses at a banquet at the governor's mansion. Special Events assisted the governor's staff in planning all aspects of the evening, including decor and menu.

■ **16 July—City Hall Dinner.** Atlanta Mayor Bill Campbell hosted all IOC members and their spouses at a banquet held at City Hall. Special Events served as a liaison for the mayor's staff in planning all aspects of the dinner.

■ **17 July—Olympic Youth Camp Opening Ceremony.** To mark the arrival of youth campers, there was an evening parade through downtown Rome, Georgia, near the Berry College campus where the camp was located. The parade concluded with fireworks.

■ **18 July—Southern Crossroads Festival Opening.** To launch this Olympic Arts Festival program, a ribbon-cutting ceremony included a local high school marching band, choir, dancers, and folk groups.

■ **18 July—Opening of *Centennial Collectibles.*** Special Events produced a ribbon-cutting ceremony for the Cultural Olympiad, in which IOC President Juan Antonio Samaranch and UN Secretary-General Bhoutros Bhoutros-Ghali participated.

■ **18 July—Olympic Patron Reception.** For Ticket Sales, Special Events coordinated an evening of entertainment for Patron ticket holders as part of their hospitality program. Held at a ballroom in the Georgia World Congress Center, the event offered buffets featuring food from each Olympic continent, an orchestra, and several US Olympians.

■ **18 July—Main Press Center (MPC) Reception.** A cocktail reception for the press was held in a hall adjacent to the MPC.

■ **18 July—IOC/NOC Team Physicians.** For Medical Services, Special Events coordinated the orientation meeting for team physicians held in the Olympic Village.

■ **19 July—IOC Executive Board and ASOIF Meeting—**Special Events assisted Olympic Family and Protocol in planning the logistics for this joint meeting.

■ **19 July—US Presidential Reception.** A reception with President Clinton was held for IOC members and government officials immediately preceding the Opening Ceremony. The event was held in the Olympic Stadium's Olympic Family lounge.

■ **20 July, 27 July, and 3 August—Licensing Receptions.** For ACOP, Special Events produced gatherings for licensees and their guests. Each event attracted about 150 people. The first was held at a local restaurant, the second at the NationsBank plaza, and the third at the "Top of the Ring" reception area in downtown Atlanta.

■ **21 July—IOC/ACOG Marketing Gala.** This major reception, produced by Special Events for ACOG, the USOC, and the IOC, was held at the Fernbank Museum of Natural History to thank all Games sponsors and their guests—more than 500 people. The Olympic Torch Relay was the theme and each sponsor's CEO was presented with an Olympic torch.

■ **30 July—Olympic Youth Camp Closing Ceremony.** To mark the camp's conclusion, an evening of entertainment was held which included a performance by a local musical theater group followed by a bonfire and dance.

■ **31 July—Centennial Olympic Park Reopening.** The park reopened in a ceremonial event which was created and coordinated in less than a day.

■ **3 August—Palmares Awards Ceremony.** For the IOC, Special Events coordinated the awards reception honoring exhibitors at *Centennial Collectibles.*

■ **10 August—Closing Party in Centennial Olympic Park.** This event, held to express appreciation for volunteers and staff, attracted more than 20,000 people. Special Events coordinated a barbecue and the sale of some Games items, including banners and pieces of Olympic Games uniforms. Every attendee was given a commemorative poster.

CONCLUSIONS AND RECOMMENDATIONS

From the simplest venue tour or international meeting to the largest venue opening celebration, ACOG's mission to provide an atmosphere of hospitality for the events it hosted was realized through the work of the Special Events Department. To accomplish the myriad of activities, great flexibility and readiness was required of the staff to plan and implement the activities of ACOG and all its functional areas, which had to give most of their energy and focus to Games-time planning activities. Future organizing committees are encouraged to consider the following recommendations.

- Keep in mind that great flexibility is required, as the number and size of events and visits to the organizing committee builds constantly toward Games-time.
- Standardize as much of the planning process and as many resources as possible to ensure continuity and efficiency.
- Creation of an inventory of owned items such as audiovisuals and decorations, with the proper technical staff for implementation, reduces expenses and risk of failures.

GUEST SERVICES

All ACOG departments used the Guest Services Department, a division of Corporate Services, to arrange for officials to visit Atlanta before and during the Games. "Guest" in the context of Guest Services refers specifically to three categories of visitors: the Olympic Family, distinguished guests, and ACOG business associates.

Before the Games, Guest Services booked hotel reservations, developed itineraries, made travel arrangements, planned tours, planned special programs for spouses, and provided dedicated hosts, hostesses, and drivers for these guests. The department was also responsible for all gifts presented to guests. During the Games, the department coordinated the operation of the Olympic Family Hotel—the Atlanta Marriott Marquis; developed and managed special activities, including the Children of the World and spouse programs; and managed ACOG's special gifts project.

ORGANIZATION

The Guest Services staff was divided into six areas of responsibility based upon the different categories of services provided to guests: accommodations, dedicated hosts and hostesses and drivers, gift programs, programs for IOC family members, tours, and transportation.

Guest Services' role in operating the Olympic Family Hotel involved coordinating most of these areas of responsibility with ACOG functional areas and hotel staff. Department staff was available to assist all ACOG departments with planning and coordinating visits for individuals and groups, including the development of itineraries.

By January 1996, the department's paid staff totaled 18 and remained at this number through Games-time.

Venue Tours

In May 1991, Guest Services established the Venue Tour Program. A training manual was written that included pertinent information regarding all competition venues and protocol. Forty volunteers with a working knowledge of Atlanta were trained extensively concerning ACOG's history and plans. The training sessions included site visits to the competition venues and discussions about media relations, protocol, and Games planning.

The volunteer guides led tours for individuals and groups, including representatives of the IOC, NOCs, IFs, government officials, media members, sponsors, and others.

Prior to ACOG securing automobiles from its vehicle sponsors, guides used their personal automobiles when taking 1–3 guests on tours. If the group was larger, Guest Services borrowed an ACOG van when possible or rented an appropriate vehicle.

Additional guides were trained and added to the program as needed. All guides participated in refresher courses when appropriate.

Tours were given to 105 guests in 1991; 304 in 1992; 665 in 1993; 1,415 in 1994; 3,987 in 1995; and 1,112 from January to July 1996.

Accommodations

Until 1994, each ACOG department was responsible for making the hotel reservations needed by its guests. As the volume of individual and group bookings increased, Guest Services employed an individual with experience in hotel convention services and reservations and assumed the task of securing accommodations for individual visitors in the special categories.

The department organized and maintained the booking process for guests by establishing contacts at area hotels, negotiating rates for Olympic business, creating official forms for the reservation process, establishing billing authorization procedures, and instituting approval processes for all invoices.

Guest Services was the liaison between the requesting ACOG department and the hotels. When accommodations were needed for individuals, ACOG departments informed Guest Services of their needs. Information was recorded in writing on a form that included the guest's name, arrival and departure times, desired room type, and billing information. With this information, Guest Services made the hotel reservations and secured the confirmation numbers. The department sent one copy of the reservation billing form to the hotel, another to ACOG's Accounting division, and one including confirmation numbers to the requesting department.

Guest Services was also responsible for arranging accommodations for groups visiting ACOG for meetings and workshops. The requesting department provided Guest Services with the hotel needs, which at times included meeting and banquet space. Using this information, Guest Services found an appropriate hotel to accommodate the group. Following a site visit, Guest Services negotiated the contract with the hotel and coordinated with ACOG's Procurement and Contract Administration (P&CA) division to have the contract signed and returned to the hotel. A copy of the contract was given to the requesting department and Accounting. *(For the number of room-nights booked, see Figure 1.)*

As the number of requests for accommodations increased, the department employed two additional staff members, one in February 1995 and one in November 1995, to assist with this program.

Dedicated Hosts and Hostesses

The Host and Hostess Program for special guests was launched during the Bid days and continued through the Games. To provide the finest possible hospitality, a volunteer host or hostess was assigned to IOC members and their families for the duration of their visits to the city. Many of these volunteers became the dedicated host or hostess for their assigned IOC member on all visits. These volunteers were responsible for ensuring the guest's arrival at meetings and hospitality functions and accompanying the visitors on other excursions in the area.

At Games-time, a dedicated host or hostess as well as a dedicated driver were assigned to every IOC member, IF president, and IF secretary-general, as well as to every president and secretary-general of NOCs with more than 50 athletes. Presidents and secretaries-general of NOCs with fewer than 50 athletes shared a host or hostess and driver. Dedicated hosts and hostesses and drivers were also assigned to visiting heads of state; the CEOs for the Sydney, Salt Lake City, and Nagano organizing

FIGURE 1: HOTEL ROOM-NIGHTS BOOKED BY GUEST SERVICES	
May–Dec 1994	3,467
Jan–Dec 1995	8,892
Jan–July 1996	9,603

tees; each member of Atlanta's IOC Coordination Commission; and the IOC marketing director. More than 500 guests were assigned dedicated hosts or hostesses and drivers during the Games.

Recruitment of hosts and hostesses for Games-time began in January 1995. Personal interviews were held with all candidates for the program. Successful candidates had to be at least 21 years of age and have strong interpersonal skills; excellent oral communication skills, including fluency in English, and in some instances, a second language; the ability to accommodate a flexible work schedule and variable hours; mature decision-making abilities; and had to be available for full-time work between 12 July and 6 August 1996. The selection process was completed by January 1996.

Once chosen, each dedicated host and hostess and driver completed the system assignment phase, submitting paperwork to the Volunteer Services Department. Their personnel data was entered into the ACOG system computer, and then each volunteer was accredited and supplied with the appropriate uniform.

Volunteer Services mailed a staff resource kit to each host and hostess. All other training materials and classes were developed and taught by Guest Services staff members.

Training began in January 1996 when the first of seven at-home study packets were sent to the volunteers. They included information about the Olympic Movement, ACOG, the sports of the Olympic Games, protocol, and sites in the metropolitan-Atlanta area. In addition, hosts and hostesses received an individually prepared packet containing biographical information on their assigned guests and information on the country they represented.

The first training class was held on 11 May 1996. After a general session, the volunteers were divided into groups of 20–25 for workshops on intercultural awareness and practical solutions to possible challenges that could arise during Games-time. In June, they visited competition venues within the metro-Atlanta area

and toured the Olympic Family Hotel. Hosts and hostesses also received training on use of the iDEN, the technological device they would use during the Games. The iDEN included a cellular phone, two-way radio, and alpha/digital pager in one small piece of equipment.

Games-time duties of the dedicated host and hostess included welcoming the assigned guest upon arrival in Atlanta; assisting in arranging meetings and appointments; facilitating arrival and departure at sports competitions, Cultural Olympiad events, and other official functions; and supporting special tours and visits in Atlanta and the region. The schedule of a dedicated host or hostess as well as the dedicated driver depended upon the schedule of the guest.

Transportation

During Bid days, a program to assign volunteer drivers to individual guests was established as part of a hospitality program. Dedicated drivers were recruited from the community and provided by the Georgia Power Company.

Guest Services developed a training manual for the drivers that included driving routes to competition venues and other sites in the metro-Atlanta area and information about the Olympic Games, protocol, and site parking.

The volunteer drivers participated in extensive training sessions that included classroom work and driving route practice. The training also included a visit to Hartsfield Atlanta International Airport, as a driver's assignment often began with meeting the guest there upon arrival in Atlanta. Additional drivers were recruited and trained as needed, and all drivers participated in refresher courses as appropriate.

The Guest Services transportation manager was responsible for securing volunteer drivers for individual guests and small groups and providing the drivers with written itineraries and cellular telephones.

During the Games, 562 volunteers served as dedicated drivers through Guest Services: 479 were loaned employees of the Georgia Power Company, and 83 were recruited by the Guest Services transportation manager. Guest Services was also responsible for recruiting, training, and coordinating volunteer drivers to serve artists performing at Opening and Closing Ceremonies.

In preparation for Games-time, the pre-Games training manual was modified to include Games-time driving routes and competition venue access information, provided to Guest Services by ACOG's Transportation Department.

Guest Services dedicated drivers participated in training sessions at the Olympic Family Hotel to prepare for Games-time duties. Volunteers were required to attend two half-day training workshops, in which drivers were divided into small groups to make the sessions more productive. The training included a detailed tour of the Olympic Family Hotel property to ensure drivers understood where all access points were located. Driving routes to the competition venues were discussed in detail using diagrams projected on large screens. Guest Services requested that each volunteer drive the routes numerous times in the months preceding the Games. The volunteers were also provided with addresses and directions to various NOC hospitality facilities. Dedicated drivers received at-home study assignments and an individualized packet containing biographical information about his or her special guest and country information.

Approximately one week prior to the arrival of the IOC members for the IOC Session and the beginning of the arrival of other Olympic Family guests, the dedicated drivers received their cars at ACOG's Fort Gillem warehouse. ACOG Transportation was responsible for assigning cars to the drivers, and a Guest Services staff member was present to assist.

Each dedicated driver also received a Games-time parking permit and two iDENs, one for the driver and the other for the dedicated host or hostess. Drivers were responsible for delivering iDENs to hosts or hostesses assigned to their guests and practicing using the equipment. This plan worked exceedingly well and gave the host or hostess and driver an opportunity to become acquainted prior to the Games.

Guest Services also supplied many of the drivers with a large umbrella, first-aid kit, and cooler, and issued them a charge card that could be used to purchase gasoline, oil, and car washes at selected sponsor stations.

During Games-time, the dedicated drivers and hosts/hostesses were divided into 15 teams, each managed by a volunteer team supervisor. Supervisors were responsible for coordinating individual issues, including collecting daily reports and receipts for gasoline and distributing meal tickets. Because many driving routes changed immediately prior to and during the Games, route maps had to be revised continuously. This was accomplished by having Guest Services staff drive the routes and design and copy updated maps for daily distribution to the drivers.

During the day, dedicated drivers were allowed to park in the Marriott Marquis parking garage. The drivers were allowed to take their cars home at the end of each work day.

Children's Program

Children of the World 1996, the first program of its kind in the history of the Games, was planned exclusively for the children and grandchildren of IOC members. In September 1995, Guest Services sent IOC members a letter and questionnaire requesting pertinent information, such as ages, interests, hobbies, and languages spoken, about any youth they would bring to Atlanta. Guest Services designed a program for these special visitors based on the

Children and grandchildren of IOC members enjoy activities with Atlanta pals.

information received. Fifty-two children and grandchildren of IOC members participated in the program.

The Pen Pal and Buddy Program paired children from the metro-Atlanta area with the children and grandchildren of the IOC members. Atlantans began to write their pen pals in spring 1996. On 20 July 1996, a party was held for these children and their Atlanta friends at a private Atlanta home.

A hospitality and activity center located in the Olympic Family Hotel was established for IOC family members aged 7–15. The center, managed by two ACOG Guest Services staff members assisted by a group of volunteers, was open 0800 to 2200 daily from 12 July through 4 August. The center was a place in which participating children could relax, make friends, and enjoy a host of activities, including art projects, magic shows, movies, video games, and visits by special surprise guests.

As part of the program, young IOC visitors became acquainted with Atlanta through trips to a bowling alley, television station, the Atlanta History Center, Centennial Olympic Park, Center for Puppetry Arts, Chattahoochee Nature Center, and Zoo Atlanta.

An agency was selected to provide private, in-room childcare to very young children for a charge. These child development professionals were fully trained in cardiopulmonary resuscitation and first aid, and were bonded and insured.

Spouse Program

The Guest Services Department was responsible for planning special activities for the spouses of IOC members and other special guests attending meetings in the years preceding the Games. These activities included luncheons and receptions in private homes, day trips to Callaway Gardens and the historic town of Madison, Georgia, fashion shows, and visits to the Atlanta Botanical Garden, Atlanta History Center, and the Martin Luther King Jr.

Center for Nonviolent Social Change. The department planned a program for the spouses of IOC members during the week the IOC was in session and during the Games through which the following events were organized and managed.

■ A "Day of Fashion" luncheon and fashion show featuring the fall collections of eight American designers and one Korean designer was held in a large ballroom. Saks Fifth Avenue assisted in coordinating the show, which was elegant, beautiful, and theatrical.

■ A luncheon was held at Avery Gallery, which specializes in antique prints, fine art, and handcrafted frames, followed by a shopping excursion to some of Atlanta's finest antique shops.

■ Corretta Scott King hosted a private tour of the Martin Luther King Jr. Center.

■ A special private tour was given of the Cultural Olympiad exhibition, the *Olympic Woman*, followed by a reception at the Commerce Club hosted by the president of Georgia State University.

■ A private tour of the exhibition *Rings: Five Passions in World Art* at the High Museum of Art was followed by luncheons at private Atlanta homes.

■ A day trip by chartered plane to Washington, DC, featured a luncheon hosted by First Lady Hillary Rodham Clinton and a private tour of the White House. This special day also included a driving tour of some of the capital's historic buildings and monuments.

Gift Program

Prior to the Games, Guest Services was responsible for procuring, inventorying, and distributing gifts for special guests. It maintained a large supply of gifts, including gifts for special ACOG programs, such as frames for the 1,000 days to the Games photographs and T-shirts commemorating other occasions. ACOG departments ordering gifts from Guest Services charged them to their own cost centers.

During the Games, Guest Services managed ACOG's Gift Program for distinguished visitors. Among various special guests, gifts were presented to:

- heads of state;
- IOC President and Mrs. Samaranch and other IOC members and their spouses, Mrs. Hillary Rodham Clinton, sponsor executives, and ACOG Executive Board members;
- presidents and secretaries-general of the NOCs and IFs;
- ministers of sport, executives of bid cities, and the executive committees of ANOC and ASOIF; and
- members of the IOC staff.

Gifts were wrapped and included personalized gift cards. They were distributed to guests' hotel rooms by volunteers and hotel staff.

Under the direction of its Gift Program manager, Guest Services was also responsible for coordinating the production of welcome bags that were placed in the Olympic Family Hotel rooms of all accredited guests. Volunteers filled the bags with a welcome letter from the ACOG CEO, the *Guide to the 1996 Games*, information on cultural programs, maps, and lapel pins.

OLYMPIC FAMILY HOTEL

At every Olympic Games, at least one hotel is selected to house the principle members, offices, and functions of the Olympic Family. It is generally referred to as the Olympic Family Hotel. During the Games, this venue is home to members, staff, and guests of the IOC, NOCs, IFs, other Olympic organizing committees, candidate cities for future Games, and heads of state. In addition, the venue hosts executive board meetings, the IOC Session, and numerous other meetings and functions before, during, and after the Games. Guest Services was primarily responsible for coordinating all Olympic Family Hotel operations.

Selection of the Hotel

ACOG coordinated with the IOC to contract with the Atlanta Marriott Marquis to serve as headquarters for the Olympic Family. The contract was negotiated by the Corporate Services Department, Accommodations Department, and P&CA division.

The Marriott Marquis, selected for its location, size, and ample meeting space, features a

Interior view of the Atlanta Marriott Marquis, which served as the Olympic Family Hotel.

spectacular open atrium at the center of a 50-floor hotel designed by Atlanta architect John Portman. With 1,671 guest rooms and more than 130,000 sq ft (12,100 sq m) of functional space, the hotel was large enough to accommodate all principle individuals, offices, and events of the Olympic Family. This was the first time in the history of the Games that all this activity took place within a single hotel. In addition, the hotel also had three entrances

BETTY-ANN M BRYCE • LISA M BRYCE SAT • SHARON L BRYDEN • ROBERT BRYDON • CAMMIE L BRYE • TIMOTHY S BRYNER ATC • DELORES L BRYSON • KATHY S BRYSON • KENNETH J BRYSON • ROBERT G BRYSON • DEWEY T BRYSON JR • EDWIN N BUAN • MARY KAY I BUAN • LUCY K BUBB • WENDY D BUBB • KEVIN E BUBECK • MICHAEL G BUBLITZ • PIERLUIGI G BUCCHI DE GIULI • ROBERTO E BUCCIERO • DOUGLAS M BUCE • STEPHEN J BUCE • ALYCE R BUCHANAN • CINDY F BUCHANAN • CLARK E BUCHANAN • DIANE C BUCHANAN • JAMES BUCK L BUCHANAN • MARIAH S BUCHANAN •

177

and exits, permitting many people to pass in and out at one time.

Contract Provisions

The contract between ACOG and the Marriott Marquis was developed and signed in 1994. The contract provided ACOG and the IOC the use and control of all meeting and reception areas in the hotel, with the exception of the Marquis Ballroom. The Imperial Ballroom, which seated 500 people, was the site designated for the daily Olympic Family breakfast. All other meeting rooms were used as IOC or ACOG offices.

The Marquis Ballroom was controlled by hotel administration, with the stipulation that functions would be held there subject to ACOG approval. ACOG was contractually obligated to promote the Marquis Ballroom to sponsors as the premier location for events. Nonsponsor events and sponsor-hosted events held in the Marquis Ballroom produced catering revenue for the hotel.

A clause in the contract ensured that the hotel charged its standard 1996 rates for all services, including audiovisual support, dry cleaning, facsimile transmission, food and beverage, and laundry.

ACOG was given exclusive control of the Marriott Marquis parking garage from 15 July through 5 August 1996. Of the 570 parking spaces used, 450 were designated for Olympic Family dedicated cars, and 20 for motor pool vehicles.

Payment for all rooms in the ACOG block was to be made to the Marriott Marquis in three installments beginning 31 January 1996 and ending 1 July 1996. Used by the hotel for financial protection, this strategy proved successful, as the burden for payment was on ACOG, which in turn lowered its financial exposure by requiring guests to prepay for their rooms. Sponsor product protection was guaranteed by the hotel.

Between the 1994 contract signing and the beginning of the Games, an issue arose that required further negotiation. The room charge per night initially included a continental breakfast to be served banquet-style for a maximum of 1,000 people per day. ACOG renegotiated for a more substantial breakfast by allowing the hotel to resell unoccupied rooms and charge its normal rate for rooms not used by the Olympic Family. Each day between 0630 and 0930 1,000–1,300 full breakfasts were served.

Offices

The Host City Contract stipulation that ACOG was to provide fully equipped offices for the IOC secretariat at the Olympic Family Hotel was an important concern to the IOC and ACOG. Most of the 59 IOC offices provided were located in meeting rooms that already existed in the hotel, but some had to be built by a general contractor.

Within the 29 offices, ACOG provided furniture, fixtures, equipment, and technology. Most of the furniture installation was supplied through a contract with the Marriott Marquis, but ACOG was directly responsible for providing all technology installations.

All temporary construction and equipment was removed from the hotel by 8 August 1996 by ACOG Logistics and Technology. *(For a list of IOC office inventory, see Figure 2).*

Hotel Venue Management

ACOG's venue management team for the Olympic Family Hotel resembled a typical hotel operating staff. The venue manager was responsible for integrating the needs of the IOC, NOCs, IFs, candidate cities, and heads of state into the existing operating plan of the Marriott Marquis. The venue manager worked directly with the general hotel manager and his steering committee members, which included directors of catering, convention services, food and beverage, group housing, loss

FIGURE 2:
IOC OFFICE INVENTORY

- 14 conference tables
- 23 Coca-Cola machines
- 4 IBM links
- 149 desks
- 3 pigeonhole boards
- 2 personal computers
- 510 chairs
- 22 message boards
- 8 Info '96 computers
- 3 sofas
- 59 French / English signs
- 21 typewriters
- 5 low tables
- 57 house phones
- 22 pagers
- 2 bookcases
- 93 network phones
- 25 radios
- 53 lockable cabinets
- 19 fax machines
- 106 20" televisions
- 152 trash cans
- 19 copiers
- 2 27" televisions
- 112 table lamps
- 5 shredders
- 4 video walls
- 2 safes
- 2 video multisystems

prevention, and services, as well as a front office manager, master account auditor, and room service operations manager. The venue manager was also responsible for integrating all ACOG functional area operations with the hotel: Accreditation, Airport Operations, Financial Services, Language Services, Logistics, Look of the Games, Medical Services, Merchandising, Protocol, Security, Technology, Ticket Sales, Transportation, and Volunteer Services, as well as coordinating with the US State Department, the direct link to heads of state.

The assistant venue manager assisted with all operations and was directly responsible for the appointment of hotel rooms, including reservations, confirmations, registration, arrival and departure processes, rooms billing review, room preparation, and luggage handling. The assistant venue manager also oversaw the operation of the message center, which supported all IOC and ACOG offices by taking messages and coordinating the delivery of all essential materials to the offices and guest rooms. Guest Services staff and volunteers supported the assistant venue manager in operating the message center and with responsibilities in the rooms division of the hotel.

During the Games, the entire venue management team met daily at 0730 to discuss issues and plan the day's activities. In these meetings, staff members reported on the current status of each functional area and presented any outstanding questions. The daily activity sheets, which included the hotel's occupancy levels and a schedule of activities, were distributed.

A credit review meeting also occurred daily. The venue manager, assistant venue manager, and food and beverage coordinator met with hotel staff to review the previous day's master account status. Any outstanding issues or problems were resolved daily. Any issues with the IOC or other organizations were also brought to the attention of the venue manager and addressed thereafter with the appropriate people.

IOC Relations

The relationship between the venue manager and the secretariat of the IOC is critical to the successful operation of an Olympic Family Hotel. The function of the venue manager was to act as a meeting planner for the IOC and coordinate the organization's needs with the capabilities of the hotel.

Meetings were held every six months with the secretary-general of the IOC and members of the staff to review issues relating to accommodations, accreditation, offices and technology, receptions and events, security, ticket sales, and transportation. Approximately six months before the Games, these meetings began to be held monthly. During the Games, they were held daily to review issues relating to guest arrival and departure, billing, ticket distribution, and transportation needs, as well as other IOC concerns.

Food and Beverage Operations

The food and beverage coordinator served as a direct link to the hotel's food and beverage, catering, and conference services directors. This individual was responsible for overseeing all hotel food outlets including catering at each event or function, daily breakfast service, event room preparation, food and beverage billing review, minibars, office refreshments, and room service.

The hotel's director of catering played a crucial role due to the number of proposals developed to meet the culturally diverse culinary needs of guests in the Olympic Family Hotel. For example, a strong blend of coffee was added to be served throughout the hotel. Also, menus were developed in English, French, and Spanish. This individual also controlled the computerized space reservations function and constantly updated the information upon the authorization and direction of ACOG's coordinator.

Look of the Games banners installed in the atrium of the Olympic Family Hotel.

Banquets served only sponsor-supplied beverages for all catered functions, primarily self-serve Coca-Cola and Crystal Springs water, under terms of a corkage-fee agreement negotiated with the Marriott Marquis.

The hotel provided room service featuring a menu that met most culinary needs and sufficient staff to respond to all requests within 30 minutes. Preordering was available by phone or electronically by television. Preorders were given top priority.

A surprising number of room service requests were made during the morning hours. An average 150 requests per day were made for breakfast. Lunch and dinner requests did not exceed estimates. Three telephone sales assistants provided by the hotel took orders. Staffing levels for room service waiters were estimated at 12 servers per shift.

Room service was also responsible for catering parties held on guest room floors. A hospitality catering coordinator from the hotel staff assisted with planning these functions.

Original plans were for all five restaurants in the hotel to operate seven days a week to meet Olympic Family needs. After the Games began, the plan was changed to operate three restaurants and a coffee stand kiosk for lunch and four restaurants for dinner. The most frequented place for lunch and dinner was the coffee stand kiosk, which served a full range of meals. Approximately 2,200 meals were served each day at restaurants restricted to Olympic Family use.

Two restaurants, Champion's and Pompano's, were open to the public at the request of hotel management. Security personnel prevented nonaccredited diners from entering restricted space through these restaurants and no problems were encountered.

Reserved seating for lunch was arranged for IOC members on the dates of the IOC Executive Board meeting and the IOC 105th Session. Apart from these times, no special requirements for seating were needed beyond the normal reservation system. Reservations were frequently placed for parties of 10 or more. There was no significant wait time for seating in the hotel restaurants.

In addition to existing restaurants, the hotel created a lounge area that served beer, wine, and light appetizers. High tea was offered in one of the hotel lounges from 1300 to 1500 daily. High tea was not as popular as had been anticipated because most guests were out of the hotel at this time attending sporting and other events.

Events and Functions

Various functions were held within the Olympic Family Hotel, including meetings, receptions, and dinners held by various IOC groups and sponsors. Nonaccredited guests attending events gained admittance through a specified entrance by showing their invitations and were admitted only to the hotel's exhibition and convention levels.

Opening and Closing Ceremonies Activities

Planning for the evenings of Opening and Closing Ceremonies demanded special attention because all guests in the hotel would be attending these two events. Coordination with Transportation regarding the transport all Olympic Family Hotel guests, including the IOC members and their guests to Olympic Stadium by motor coach, was of utmost importance. Bus depot locations and departure time schedules were posted for guests in the hotel elevators. Guest Services assisted IOC members and their guests during their departure.

Prior to Opening Ceremony, a reception hosted by the IOC was held in the Imperial Ballroom for 800 Olympic Family guests. A buffet from 1700 until 1930 on the evening of the Closing Ceremony served 500 guests.

Guest Accommodations

Guest Services worked closely with Olympic Family and Protocol to resolve all accommodation issues. Games-time arrivals began 1 July 1996, and departures continued until 9 August. A total block of 36,270 room-nights (1,600 rooms per night during peak nights 19 July through 4 August), including 1,531 suites

(60 suites per night during above-peak nights) was contracted by ACOG with the Marriott Marquis. *(See Figure 3.)*

Payment for the room block was due to the hotel in the following installments: 25 percent by 31 January 1996, 25 percent by 15 April 1996, and 50 percent, plus all taxes, by 1 July 1996. To meet this payment schedule, ACOG required payment from each Olympic Family constituent group one month before its due date. Olympic Solidarity, a unit of the IOC, offered financial support to the NOCs to cover their room payments.

A hotel registration form was developed with the assistance of the IOC and the Marriott Marquis to obtain information from Olympic Family guests. This form was distributed by the IOC on 1 March 1996 with a return deadline of 15 April 1996.

Members of the IOC were instructed to return their registrations to the IOC headquarters in Lausanne, Switzerland, where the forms were compiled and forwarded to ACOG. NOC and IF members and heads of state were instructed to return their registration forms to ACOG, where Guest Services staff compiled the information and entered it into an Olympic Family and Protocol database. The information could be sorted by affiliation category, arrival date, billing category, and room type, as well as alphabetically, and was sent to the Marriott Marquis for entry into its property management system.

Reports were frequently generated for comparison and analysis purposes. The venue management team was able to view the daily room reservation figures as well as arrival and departure patterns.

Arrivals and Departures

All IOC members and presidents and secretaries-general of NOCs and IFs were transported from the airport to the Marriott Marquis by their Games-time dedicated drivers. Using the iDEN device, each driver was in constant communication with the dedicated host or hostess, who was stationed curbside at the hotel upon arrival of the guest. Guests were then escorted to the accreditation center in the hotel for badging. Volunteers were stationed in the motor lobby to act as a liaison with the hotel's bell stand and ensure prompt assistance with luggage.

Upon receiving their accreditation badge, all guests, with the exception of the IOC members, were escorted to the hotel front desk to receive their keys and establish credit. The Marriott Marquis used its routine credit procedure of requiring a per-night cash or credit

FIGURE 3:

OLYMPIC FAMILY HOTEL GUESTROOM USAGE

Constituent groups	Projected room-nights	Actual room-nights	Projected peak	Actual peak
IOC	15,846	12,651	702	576
NOCs	11,359	11,746	596	597
IFs	1,813	1,740	115	96
Candidate cities	2,016	2,096	72	81
Heads of state	3,041	760	143	46

card prepayment for each room to cover incidental charges. ACOG and IOC staff worked closely with the hotel to ensure proper room assignments and adequate billing procedures. IOC members were pre-keyed so that check-in at the hotel was not necessary.

On a daily basis, IOC members and IF presidents and secretaries-general departed in their dedicated cars from the front of the hotel. NOC presidents and secretaries-general departed from the motor lobby. Each evening, the guest informed the host or hostess and driver of the expected time of departure the following morning. Upon arrival at the hotel, the driver parked the car in the hotel garage and waited for the host or hostess to radio that the car should depart the garage to meet the guest. Cars meeting guests in front of the hotel had one egress from the garage and those meeting guests at the motor lobby had another. Guests with dedicated cars were taken to the same point from which they departed upon their return to the hotel.

The third entrance of the hotel was designated for shuttle bus service to the venues and special events. A separate entrance was used for motor pool access.

Prior to each guest's departure, all accounts were reviewed and any issues resolved. Guests responsible for any individual charges were required to check out at the front desk and settle any remaining balances. Unused portions of deposits were refunded.

Upon departure, IOC members and IF presidents and secretaries-general were transported to the airport by their dedicated drivers. Other guests, includng NOC presidents and secretaries-general, traveled to the airport by motor coach. Both systems proved efficient and were well received by guests.

Hotel Security

All external points of contact had security personnel to provide access control and magnometers for inspection of packaging. Each vehicle entering the hotel garage required a special ACOG permit and had to pass through sanitization. Internal security also controlled access to guest room areas using the radio frequency accreditation badge. *(For more information, see the Accreditation and Security chapters.)*

Budget Results

The Olympic Family Hotel budget mainly covered costs of IOC and ACOG offices, IOC meetings and events, and the Look of the Games. Substantial funds were spent to alter the ribbon structure cascading the hotel's 50-story atrium to include the Look of the Games.

The original contingency for lost room revenue was removed from the budget. An aggressive selling and reselling process was developed to ensure that all guest rooms were occupied.

Conclusions and Recommendations

Guest Services ultimately assisted all ACOG functional areas in coordinating travel arrangements and programs for their guests. The pre-Games planning of events and services for the Olympic Family culminated in experienced operations of the Olympic Family Hotel.

The following recommendations are offered to future organizing committees.

■ Accurate driving routes must be developed early by the Transportation Department and shared with Guest Services in a timely manner.

■ Recognize that the assignment of dedicated vehicles to Olympic Family members is challenging due to the number of unscheduled individuals in each party.

■ It is essential to have an individual with extensive hotel experience as the venue manager of the Olympic Family Hotel so that the intricacies involved in operating a fully functional, preexisting hotel can be understood. Additionally, an assistant venue manager should be assigned 6–9 months prior to the Games to finalize the room block, registrations, the database, and other vital operations.

■ Functional areas should allot a portion of their budget to support their independent decisions concerning leasing of space and group placement within the Olympic Family Hotel.

■ It is important to coordinate with the IOC prior to signing the contract between the organizing committee and the hotel, as service levels must be scrutinized carefully before final selection. If a desired service does not already exist within the hotel, it is critical to include the demand and budget for it in the contract.

■ It is essential that the organizing committee require a minimum length of stay during Games-time. This precaution will dramatically reduce the financial exposure of vacant rooms and eliminate the necessity of relocating guests.

■ It is necessary that the IOC communicate its decisions regarding access issues prior to the Games to prevent Games-time confusion about accreditation access at all competition venues by volunteers.

CHAPTER ELEVEN
EXTERNAL RELATIONS

GOVERNMENT AND COMMUNITY RELATIONS EMPLOYEES

Date	Staff Number
January 1993	10
January 1996	19
July 1996	19

Note: These staff numbers do not include contract, VIK, and volunteer personnel.

OVERVIEW—Coordination and communication between the organizing committee and government and community entities is essential to the success of staging an Olympic Games. The number of involved jurisdictions and agendas compelled ACOG to emphasize these communication channels by establishing departments with responsibilities that were coordinated in purpose and direction, though distinct in constituency. The areas of responsibility were divided into: Federal and State Government Relations, reporting to the managing director of Communications, Local Government Relations, and Community Relations, which were both coordinated by the senior policy advisor.

FEDERAL AND STATE GOVERNMENT RELATIONS

Unlike previous Games, which were subsidized by government funding, the Centennial Olympic Games were funded through private sources. Despite this method of funding, establishing relationships with federal and state government agencies and officials remained important. Indeed, hosting an international event of the magnitude of the Centennial Olympic Games required identifying and implementing many legislative acts and permits.

The primary mission of ACOG's Government Relations Department was to facilitate communication and cooperation between ACOG departments and the US executive and congressional branches (federal) and the state of Georgia (state) government.

The department's secondary objective was to educate public officials on all aspects of the Olympic Games. In the early planning years, there was some confusion among officials as to the role of government entities in staging the

Games. In some cases, officials believed that ACOG should assume some public responsibilities, such as public safety, during the Games period, thus relieving the government from any involvement in the Games. In other cases, officials believed that the government should play a greater role in staging the Games than its traditional and constitutionally mandated public role. Government Relations maintained a dialogue with public officials over a period of several years that clarified each party's distinct role and secured strong government support for the Games.

The highly cooperative atmosphere established between ACOG's Government Relations Department and federal and state government entities contributed substantially to the success of the Centennial Olympic Games, ensuring that the public and private interests of all constituencies were represented and coordinated successfully, while providing long-term benefits to the host state and country.

ORGANIZATION

ACOG began an active government relations effort almost at its inception. In 1991–1992, Government Relations was a program under Sports and International Relations, with a former congressional staff member responsible for early planning. Federal liaison was facilitated by ACOG's appointed law firm from its Washington office. The Bush administration and the Georgia congressional delegation continued the strong support that had been developed during the Bid process. As early as 1991, federal legislation was passed to assist with specific Olympic requirements, and detailed discussions had begun with several agencies on various Olympic issues.

In January 1993, ACOG formally organized a separate Government Relations Department and appointed as its director a former member of Congress from Georgia to coordinate federal- and state-level efforts. Within a year, the department reached its ultimate size of five professional and three support staff members. ACOG's appointed law firm continued to operate as the ACOG office in Washington, DC, and the deputy director of Government Relations spent much time there to coordinate an increasing federal agenda.

In 1994, Government Relations was divided into two divisions, with the director assuming responsibility for activities at the state level and the deputy director for those at the federal level. Government Relations was placed under Communications to aid coordination between all ACOG departments with an external focus.

FEDERAL GOVERNMENT RELATIONS

ACOG worked with almost every existing congressional committee, executive department, and federal agency. The support of the federal government in staging the Olympic Games was quite extensive, ranging from charting currents for yachting maps and forecasting weather to managing the entry of people, goods, and animals into the country. Almost every federal agency became involved in the Games as the government acted to fulfill its traditional Olympic role.

From 1994 to 1996, the staff of Federal Government Relations was composed of a director; a manager responsible for transportation, grants, and entry; and a program coordinator responsible for National Weather Service support, agricultural issues, entry, and dignitary escort. This structure remained throughout the Games. Occasionally, consultants were engaged to facilitate specific tasks.

All Olympic-related requests for federal assistance to the state of Georgia and its cities were coordinated through the Federal Government Relations office, which allowed for the resolution of competing interests and prioritization of projects before submission to Congress or federal agencies. This effort helped Atlanta and other Georgia communities work effectively with each other and the federal government in preparing for the Olympic Games.

The Georgia delegates to the US House of Representatives and Senate took responsibility for all legislation for the 1996 Olympic Games. An Olympic legislative support group, comprised of the senior legislative staff of each congressional office, met several times a year to be briefed on Olympic legislative needs and discuss progress of the legislation. Once a year, the delegation met to receive an ACOG report on the progress of the Games.

Although there were several changes in delegation membership, each Georgia senator and representative took an interest in the Games and was active in securing support for Olympic legislation. Without the strong commitment of the delegation members, ACOG's Federal Government Relations effort would not have been successful.

JULIE C BUNVILLE • BONNIE A BUOL • FRANCISCO I BUONAFINA • SONIA BUONAFINA • DONNA BURBANK • JEFFREY BURBANK • WALTER S BURBANK • ANNA C BURCH • BILL A BURCH • BOBBY L BURCH • HAYLEY C BURCH • JIM BURCH • JOLA E BURCH • LUCILLE E BURCH • MARY C BURCH • MARY N BURCH • PAULA J BURCH • PIERRE D BURCH • JO-ANN BURCH NESBIT • DON M. BURCHELL • DONALD BURCHELL • CAROL A BURCHETT • LARRY L BURCHETT • JOE T BURCHETTE • BETTY S BURCHFIELD • RON A BURCHFIELD • MICHAEL J BURCIN • WILLIAM A BURCIN • MELANIE A BURDEN

185

In the executive branch, President George Bush's involvement and interest in the Bid effort led to the creation of the Interagency Task Force on the Olympic Games, designed to coordinate all federal activity related to the Games. This task force was in place in 1991–1992.

In 1993, when President Bill Clinton assumed office, a new task force was created, chaired by Vice President Al Gore. Senior White House staff were given responsibility for the task force's daily operations. Each cabinet

Billy Payne presents plans for Games venues to President Bill Clinton, Vice President Al Gore, Atlanta Mayor Bill Campbell, and White House official Mac McLarty.

secretary was appointed to the task force and asked to designate a senior official to assume responsibility for the Olympic effort. These senior officials formed the working task force.

The White House Task Force for the 1996 Olympic Games met once a year in 1993 and 1994, and twice a year in 1995 and 1996. The president and vice president of the US made several trips to Atlanta to meet with Olympic and government leaders about preparations, and each cabinet secretary made at least one Olympic-related trip to Atlanta during this four-year period to monitor the progress of federal efforts. In spring 1996, the vice president held several meetings focused specifically on security for the Games, and ensured a coordinated, responsive federal effort. This high level of involvement and attention allowed projects and issues to be completed in the proper time frame.

In a progress report published on 12 April 1996, the White House Task Force listed all federal support that had been provided for the 1996 Olympic Games and Paralympics. In addition to the assignment of Department of Defense (DOD) and law enforcement personnel from throughout the country detailed for security purposes, a unique program was developed to enable more than 1,000 local federal employees to fill critical positions as volunteers during the Games.

Locally, Olympic-related efforts were coordinated by the supervisor of each federal office in Atlanta through a group known as the Federal Executive Board, which focused on Olympic issues several years before the Games. Having federal representatives in Atlanta as active and involved partners ensured constant communication between ACOG and the federal government.

Federal Involvement

Due to the extent of the federal government's involvement in the Games, not all actions can be described. However, major department and agency activities are summarized below.

Department of State. This department was involved in three critical areas: establishing the entry procedures of Olympic Family members, assisting ACOG with protocol training for staff and volunteers, and providing security for visiting dignitaries. Unhindered entry for Olympic Family members that maintained appropriate security measures was accomplished through a unique Olympic identity card (OIC) process created by the department.

Department of Justice. Through its appropriate agencies, the Department of Justice (DOJ) provided legal enforcement activities in support of the Games. The DOJ helped establish the framework for the collaborative law enforcement effort of more than 50 federal, state, and local law enforcement agencies and provided grants to support state and local law enforcement efforts.

■ Immigration and Naturalization Service (INS), an enforcement agency of the DOJ at US borders, worked closely with the State Department in establishing OIC entry procedures. INS increased staff at major ports of entry and was able to process 40,000 Olympic Family members smoothly through ports around the country. An INS special response team at Hartsfield Atlanta International Airport operated 24 hours a day.

■ The Federal Bureau of Investigation (FBI), another agency of the DOJ, was responsible for the collection and dissemination of Olympic-related intelligence as well as for tactical response to incidents of terrorism. The Drug Enforcement Administration provided both air support to the FBI and personnel for local law enforcement support. The US Marshals Service provided personnel to escort high-risk athlete delegations and to supplement local law enforcement.

■ The US Attorney Executive Office, also a branch of the DOJ, assigned supplementary prosecutors to Atlanta to facilitate any increased judicial responsibilities.

Department of the Treasury. This department had two primary responsibilities: security and the Commemorative Coin Program. The US Secret Service provided security for heads of state visiting Atlanta and training to ACOG and law enforcement personnel on dignitary protection. The Bureau of Alcohol, Tobacco, and Firearms had primary responsibility for explosive ordnance management. The Office of Foreign Assets Control coordinated the issuance of licenses, allowing sanctioned countries to compete in the Games. In honor of the Olympic Games, the US Mint produced and marketed a set of 32 commemorative coins as part of the Commemorative Coin Program. Expanding on previous government mail-order operations, the mint distributed coins in the US through retail outlets and banks and overseas through multinational corporations. *(For more information, see the Marketing/ACOP chapter.)*

Department of Defense. The primary area of responsibility for this department was to provide security and logistical support for the Olympic Games. Through a US Army–directed

Olympic Joint Task Force, composed of civilians and military personnel from all of the services and branches, the DOD worked with ACOG, the Georgia National Guard, and law enforcement agencies at all levels of government to plan and provide support for the Games.

DOD security personnel began operations in Atlanta in June 1996, with the largest force in place from early July to mid-August. This group in particular inspected vehicles for explosives, drove athlete buses, and filled certain security posts at venues.

Department of Interior. This department completed a new visitor center complex at the Martin Luther King Jr. National Historic Site in Atlanta for Games-time visitors. The National Park Service formed a partnership with other government agencies and private organizations to establish the Welcome South Visitors Center in Atlanta to promote tourism in the Southeast.

Department of Agriculture. This government body was involved in a number of unique areas:

■ In the Cherokee National Forest, the USDA Forest Service designed and built the course used for the canoe/kayak-slalom competitions. Developed as a long-term economic project for the Ocoee area, the site was the first natural river used in this Olympic event.

■ The Urban and Community Forestry Assistance program provided annual grants for the nonprofit organization Trees Atlanta to plant trees in downtown Atlanta.

■ The Natural Resources Conservation Service procured native plant materials to be used at Olympic sites. Technical assistance was provided in the areas of soil stabilization, bioengineering, and wetlands.

■ The Animal-Plant Health Inspection Service provided quarantine and diagnostic services for horses entering the country. Plant protection and quarantine officers were stationed at all ports of entry to inspect passengers, baggage, and arriving aircraft.

Department of Commerce. The agencies of the Department of Commerce supported the Olympic Games as follows:

- The National Weather Service assembled one of the most advanced weather observation and warning networks ever created and provided weather support and information directly to the venues.

- The National Oceanic and Atmospheric Administration ship *Whiting* surveyed the yachting competition venue and provided data to the National Ocean Service, which produced accurate and current nautical charts.

- The National Telecommunications Information Administration provided a grant to the Georgia Division of Public Health to develop a health-related communications infrastructure in several Georgia counties hosting Olympic events.

- The Economic Development Administration provided grants for such community projects in Atlanta as Auburn Avenue Revitalization and the Ralph D. Abernathy Commercial Corridor.

- The Minority Business Development Agency assisted ACOG's Equal Economic Opportunity Plan by identifying minority businesses and assisting with seminars and workshops to improve minority participation.

Department of Labor. This department provided funding and technical assistance for a demonstration project for retraining and employment needs of approximately 225 residents of Olympic neighborhoods. This program, developed with ACOG, the Neighborhood Steering Committee, and the Georgia Department of Technical and Adult Education, allowed neighborhood residents to benefit from the employment opportunities created.

Department of Health and Human Services. Under this department, the Centers for Disease Control and Prevention located in Atlanta worked closely with ACOG to develop plans both to promote public health and to respond to heat-related illnesses and any public health emergencies. The Office of Emergency

Preparedness participated with the FBI in counterterrorism and emergency health and medical responses. The Food and Drug Administration conducted daily inspections of Olympic Village dining facilities.

The President's Council on Physical Fitness and Sports created many initiatives, including public service announcements with IZZY, the traveling exhibit *Flexing the Nation's Muscle: Presidents, Physical Fitness, and Sports in the American Century*, and council member participation in Olympic events.

Department of Housing and Urban Development. This department supported a range of programs to build affordable housing, create jobs, and stimulate economic development in distressed communities, most of which were coordinated through ACOG's Community Relations Department.

Department of Transportation. This entity was heavily involved with ACOG and state and local governments to assist with the complex and enormous transportation requirements for hosting the Olympic Games. The Department of Transportation worked with security agencies to prepare for any transportation-related terrorism or disasters. The department also installed state-of-the-art equipment to detect explosives at the airport.

- The US Coast Guard was responsible for all safety and security related to the Olympic water competitions in Savannah.

- The Federal Transit Administration (FTA) coordinated a fleet of more than 1,400 accessible buses loaned by more than 65 transit agencies from across the country and supported new rapid-rail stops and station improvements.

- The Federal Highway Administration (FHWA) supported highway, road, and street improvements as well as pedestrian walkway construction, bridge rehabilitation, and improvements to park-and-ride lots connecting to mass transit.

FTA and FHWA also helped install the most current information-providing technology at kiosks in MARTA stations, at facilities throughout the state, and on the Internet. They also funded Georgia's new statewide advanced transportation management system, providing real-time data on accidents and congestion.

■ The Federal Aviation Administration (FAA) supported improvements to Hartsfield International Airport, including security additions, an international runway apron expansion, installation of temporary control towers, and deployment of extra air-traffic controllers. The FAA also established critical Games-time security restrictions on airspace.

Department of Energy. This department, in conjunction with a number of public and private organizations, featured energy efficiency and renewable energy projects during the Games. Projects included:

■ photovoltaic panels for energy and a solar thermal water conditioning system installed on the roof of the natatorium to maintain pool temperature;

■ photovoltaic lights for the 10-acre (4 ha) parking lot at the new Martin Luther King Jr. National Historic Site;

■ a geothermal heat-pump system at the Georgia Institute of Technology;

■ strategies to reduce urban heat island effects; and

■ construction of a model house to demonstrate energy-efficient building systems and practices.

Environmental Protection Agency. This department assisted in the design and construction of a 16 mi (26 km) bicycle and pedestrian path from Georgia Tech to Stone Mountain Park. The Environmental Protection Agency (EPA) participated as part of the Olympic transportation support group in local efforts to increase commuter participation in public transportation. For two years, EPA provided full-time staff to ACOG to assist in the development of a solid-waste management and recycling strategy for the Games. Of particular note was a recycling project for recovery of construction and demolition debris.

Additional Agency Support. Other designated agencies within the federal government provided specialized support.

■ The Small Business Administration worked with ACOG to ensure that the Games provided economic opportunities for small businesses, by providing loans and surety bond guarantees.

■ The Office of National Drug Control Policy worked with the Atlanta Police Department to develop and test a geographical information-based system to counter illegal drug use. The technology package was a prototype, and the Games were a unique opportunity to test its full capabilities in an actual operational environment.

■ The Federal Emergency Management Agency (FEMA) collaborated with federal, state, and local officials and ACOG to ensure federal preparedness and coordination for disasters or emergencies that could have occurred. Interagency exercises, staffing of law enforcement and ACOG command centers, securing alternate operations sites, preparation for mobilization of equipment, and advance identification of a well-trained disaster team were among FEMA's preparations for the Games.

■ The United States Information Agency (USIA) provided assistance and materials to international journalists covering the Games. USIA foreign press centers worked with ACOG to provide support through the Southern International Press Center (SIPC) for nonaccredited journalists during the Games. Advance visits for approximately 80 journalists from around the world were held in conjunction with ACOG, SIPC, the Georgia Department of Travel and Tourism, and the Atlanta Chamber of Commerce.

In a unique exchange program, USIA and ACOG enabled teams from developing nations to come to the Atlanta area before the Games to acclimatize. USIA also produced an Olympic calendar and poster printed in English, French, and Spanish for distribution to its affiliates.

■ The Office of Personnel Management assisted in minimizing the number of federal employees in downtown Atlanta during the Games. Options included telecommuting, flexible work places, and alternative work schedules. This agency also approved ACOG's request to participate in a program allowing agencies to assign employees to ACOG for up to two years, resulting in 1,000 federal workers volunteering for critical positions during the Games.

■ The General Services Administration worked closely with federal agencies on procurement and general support needed for their Olympic efforts. Primary assistance was to DOD security operations, including design and construction consultation, transportation and travel services, property reutilization, supplies, information technology and communications support, and administrative and contracting services for security-related training.

■ The Corporation for National Service provided hundreds of Americorps members to assist with security and public safety needs at the venues, provided transportation services for people with disabilities, and assisted disabled senior citizens living in the Olympic Ring.

STATE GOVERNMENT RELATIONS

Positive relationships at the state level were also essential to the Games' success. ACOG's State Government Relations effort sought not only to develop good working relationships with necessary officials and agencies, but also to clarify the benefits the state of Georgia would receive from hosting the event.

Liaison efforts were founded on the exchange of information and the definition and clear understanding of the cooperative effort required to host an event of the size and scope of the Games.

Georgia Governor Zell Miller was an important partner in hosting the Olympic Games. As lieutenant governor, Miller had been very supportive of the Bid effort to secure the Games;

Georgia Governor Zell Miller, who offered ACOG his sustained support and guidance, spoke and appeared at many functions related to the Olympic Games.

as governor, his support and guidance to state agencies and departments ensured the necessary positive relationships.

To assist ACOG interactions with the state, the governor created the State Olympic Coordination Group and the State Olympic Law Enforcement Command (SOLEC), an organization comprised of representatives of law enforcement agencies. SOLEC established a command post with direct communications to the governor and coordinated state personnel providing security for the Games.

As the chief executive of the host state, the governor spoke and appeared at many functions related to the Olympic Games. He and his wife offered the use of the governor's mansion for ACOG-sponsored events. They hosted President Clinton and Vice President Gore in the residence, and even landscaped the grounds using the Look of the Games Quilt of Leaves pattern.

ACOG's State Government Relations represented ACOG in the coordination of efforts with state lawmakers and monitored activities with regard to legislation, informing all ACOG functional areas of new or existing legislation that would affect their respective departments. Two important state activities were a special Games license plate promotion and establishment of the legal entity to contract for state facilities. The majority of facilities used during Games-time were state owned, requiring negotiated rental fees for each. Many housing and competition venues were in state university campuses under the auspices of the Georgia Board of Regents. ACOG's contribution toward the lease and construction for each venue varied. An example was ACOG's contribution of $47 million, which enabled the Georgia Board of Regents to secure bond financing for much-needed dormitories on the Georgia Tech campus.

The following legislation was enacted in support of the Games:

■ expansion of Georgia state law, making ticket scalping for all entertainment events illegal;

■ limitations on hotel room rates during the Olympic period;

■ exemption of nonresident professionals, primarily in the medical field, from having to obtain a Georgia license in order to practice their professions on their constituencies in ACOG and Paralympic events;

■ extension of workers' compensation coverage to ACOG volunteers;

■ permission for some yachting competitors to wear personal flotation devices allowed by the International Yacht Racing Rules;

■ protection for certain trademarks and unregistered symbols against forgery and counterfeiting;

■ more stringent penalties related to possession, distribution, or use of explosives; and

■ approval of public safety–related funding.

ACOG's State Government Relations also liaised with agencies executing other Olympic-related programs and projects, such as the Revenue Department's Commemorative License Plate Program, the State Forestry Commission's donation of the Georgia pecan wood used for 15,000 Olympic torch handles, and the Soil and Water Conservation Commission's monitoring of soil erosion and sediment control. In addition, the Emergency Management Agency and the Red Cross of Georgia were consulted on emergency planning, and the Department of

Agriculture resolved the controversy over allowing horses with equine piroplasmosis to enter Georgia.

CONCLUSIONS AND RECOMMENDATIONS

Any undertaking as complex as the 1996 Olympic Games requires considerable cooperation from state departments and agencies. Coordination of information sharing and support with the federal and state governments is instrumental in ensuring the success of the Games. The following recommendations are offered to future organizing committees.

■ Establish centralized and frequently used communications channels to support the myriad requirements—from permits and licenses to emergency management assistance—which require clarity and understanding.

■ Opportunities to use governmental agency support are numerous and can provide invaluable assistance to the organizing committee.

■ Realize the time required to pass any federal or state legislation.

■ Monitor all legislation not directly related to the Games that may have an indirect impact on the staging of the Games.

LOCAL GOVERNMENT RELATIONS

Organizing and staging the 1996 Olympic Games directly affected numerous local government entities and required their involvement and support. ACOG's objective was not only to include these entities in planning, but also to keep them informed about the progress being made and about issues that related directly to their areas of authority.

Coordination with the city of Atlanta was a primary focus, given the Host City Contract and the fact that the majority of Olympic venues were within the city's boundaries. However, local governments also included Fulton County—of which the city of Atlanta is a

major part—and DeKalb County, which encompasses a portion of the metropolitan-Atlanta area and was also the jurisdiction for the Stone Mountain Park venues.

Venues in the Atlanta area also were located in Clayton County—for beach volleyball—and Rockdale County—for equestrian and mountain biking. Within each county, there were also municipal governments, such as the city of Jonesboro in Clayton County and the city of Conyers in Rockdale County. Municipal and county governments included entities such as boards and commissions that also needed to be addressed.

Initially, involvement with local government centered on the construction of new venues, with staff providing assistance in obtaining zoning permits, responding to environmental impact requirements, and arranging approvals for the extension of water, sewage services, and other utilities. However, transportation and security issues required increasing attention as planning efforts progressed.

ORGANIZATION

Under the direction of the senior policy advisor, Local Government Relations worked closely with Community Relations. A director led the department and was supported by a small team of staff and volunteers who coordinated efforts in various geographical areas and the government groups based in those areas.

Throughout the years preceding the Games, the Local Government Relations staff remained small. Its work concentrated on interacting directly with government entities through meetings and briefings and attendance at regularly scheduled public sessions, and then internally by contacting various functional areas that needed to provide information or prepare reports and required documentation.

PRE-GAMES RESPONSIBILITIES

In order to facilitate communication and interaction between ACOG and the various aspects of city government, Atlanta's mayor established the Office of Olympic Coordination soon after the 1996 Games were awarded to the city. ACOG was responsible for funding this effort.

Local Government Relations staff met regularly with Office of Olympic Coordination personnel to ensure a consistent exchange of information and plans between ACOG and city officials. The head of the Office of Olympic

Coordination regularly attended meetings of the ACOG Board of Directors and reported to members on city-related matters. The city was also represented at IOC Coordination Commission meetings to describe city programs and activities and to respond to questions from IOC members assigned to assess the overall readiness for the 1996 Games.

In addition to maintaining close contact with the mayor through the Office of Olympic Coordination, Local Government Relations worked with the members of the Atlanta City Council, the legislative branch of city government. ACOG staff members were present at regular meetings of the council, often providing reports and responding to issues related to the Games.

Still another aspect of Local Government Relations concerned MAOGA, created in 1989 by the Georgia general assembly. With most members of MAOGA's 12-person board active in the affairs of the city of Atlanta, the staff of Local Governmental Relations—along with other ACOG functional areas—was responsible for providing information and meeting the requests of this government entity. In addition, Local Government Relations provided support for MAOGA's initiatives to stimulate downtown development. Most initiatives related to new housing projects in areas affected by Olympic venues. Local Government Relations helped determine whether ACOG could be of assistance by committing, for example, to rent these facilities during the Games, thus providing a source of revenue that might enhance the projects. *(For more information on MAOGA, see the Management chapter.)*

In addition, Local Government Relations was closely involved with the Corporation for Olympic Development in Atlanta (CODA), an organization created by the city of Atlanta to revitalize public areas and improve city neighborhoods, using both public and private funds.

CODA's work and ACOG's efforts often intersected, with both Local Government Relations and Community Relations staff serving as liaisons.

Agencies with responsibilities ranging from issuing building permits and health and safety licenses to managing transportation and security were also important to the staging of the 1996 Olympic Games. Through participation in meetings and briefings, preparation of extensive reports and other documents, and numerous public forums, Local Government Relations helped ensure that ACOG staff understood and responded to the requirements and concerns of local government entities.

The most extensive efforts related to the negotiation of a contract for services with the city of Atlanta that covered provision of traffic management, police support, sanitation and trash removal, and other support traditionally managed by city municipalities. While ACOG needed some of this type of support from other cities hosting Games venues, the scope of services required in Atlanta—and the stipulations of the Tri-Party Agreement—prompted execution of a contract with the city of Atlanta. The impact of supporting the Games was far less extensive on other cities, and ACOG entered into informal agreements to provide recovery of overtime costs and some other expenses directly attributable to the Games.

The contract with the city of Atlanta was finalized a few months before the 1996 Games after a period of intense debate. Under the terms of the agreement, ACOG paid the city of Atlanta for overtime costs and expenses identified as in excess of the level of service typically provided by a city in the course of hosting large events.

Many functional areas at ACOG were involved in the city contract negotiations, with ACOG's COO assuming the lead role. Local Government Relations concentrated on maintaining communications between ACOG and various city departments and providing scheduling, circulation of document revisions, and other meeting services. These responsibilities were similar in all of the relationships Local Government Relations established with city and county organizations involved in the Games.

GAMES-TIME OPERATIONS

At Games-time, Local Government Relations staff worked primarily at a special facility established by ACOG to host local, state, and federal government officials for those associated with the Centennial Olympic Games as well as representatives of other jurisdictions.

The facility, called the Centennial Club, was located in an existing hospitality facility in the Olympic Ring. The club was in service 14 hours a day throughout the Games, providing a resting place for officials between venue visits and other activities. Throughout the Games, approximately 3,000 individuals used the club.

CONCLUSIONS AND RECOMMENDATIONS

Each organizing committee's local government relations department is unique to the political environment in which the committee must operate. ACOG's Local Government Relations met the primary objective established by ACOG management—to keep all relevant entities informed and create an environment for the successful negotiation and execution of the various agreements and contracts associated with staging the Games. A similar objective for other

CHARLIE BURRELL • D JEFFERY BURRELL • DIANE BURRELL • INDIA BURRELL • JAMIE L BURRELL • PHYLLIS J BURRELL • TYRONE L BURRELL • CHARLOTTE V BURRELL-HOWELL • SHERRI A BURRELL ATC • HARRY C BURRESS • JAMES H BURRESS • JEAN H BURRESS • JIMMIE L BURRESS • MILDRED A BURRESS • PAMELA H BURRESS • PETER D BURRIDGE • DEBORAH L BURRIS • MARGARET M BURRIS • MARK A BURRIS • DELVONNIE BURRIS-WILLIAMS • CELIA T BURROS • BILL R BURROUGH • LORI L BURROUGHS • SUSAN C BURROUGHS • JAMES E BURROUGHS JR • KELLY S BURROW •

193

organizing committees is essential. The follow-ing specific recommendations are also made.

■ Develop a database as early as possible to maintain information about the requirements, responsibilities, and enforcement authorization of every local government entity that might be affected by the Games, as well as how key con-tacts can be notified when important decisions are made by the organizing committee.

■ A review of all functional areas should be conducted to determine which local govern-ment organizations they might affect. Plans of action and guidelines of responsibilities for un-dertaking and communicating this work need to be defined and monitored for implementation.

■ Information and briefings need to be offered to large groups at the same time to minimize the impact on the organizing committee staff.

COMMUNITY RELATIONS

Community participation was important to At-lanta's selection as the host city of the 1996 Olympic Games. Recognizing this factor as a significant asset that should be incorporated into the preparations and staging of the Games, ACOG established a Community Rela-tions Department with a mission to:

■ Establish and maintain an open dialogue between ACOG officials and the many com-munities—representing both geographic areas and special needs—that would comprise the local constituencies of the Olympic Games;

■ Involve community leaders in Olympic Games planning, and integrate Games-related activities in a positive way into the neighbor-hoods hosting Olympic venues; and

■ Bring Atlantans together to improve the quality of life in these neighborhoods.

Implicit in this mission was a special focus on youth. Programs that could positively affect children and young people were a major em-phasis—from involving them in celebrations and special events to offering educational op-portunities and training programs that promised long-term benefits.

As plans for the Games evolved, the respon-sibilities of Community Relations were further defined to include facilitating ACOG's compre-hensive Equal Economic Opportunity Plan. The purpose of this plan, which was adopted volun-tarily, was to ensure that a diverse mix of em-ployees and contractors would be part of the efforts to stage the 1996 Olympic Games and to demonstrate that impressive participation lev-els could be achieved without the need for quo-tas or government mandates.

The fulfillment of the tenets of ACOG's overall mission statement "to leave a positive physical and spiritual legacy" can be largely at-tributed to the community involvement and special programs that ACOG fostered and the mutual understanding and appreciation that comes when a diverse group of people join to-gether in pursuit of a common goal.

ORGANIZATION

ACOG's Community Relations efforts officially began with the late 1991 naming of a senior policy advisor, who reported directly to the CEO. Throughout the pre-Games period, the number of staff remained small, reflecting the fact that much of the organization's work would be done through ACOG's representation and involvement in community committees.

Until 1993, most staff support was provided by volunteers. With Games-time approaching, six program managers were added. These man-agers plus a director of Community Relations and senior program manager worked closely with other ACOG functional areas, serving as resources for ideas and programs that would have an impact on the community and helping to communicate the various aspects of the programs ultimately adopted.

At Games-time, the Community Relations staff of 15 people became managers of teams of volunteers assigned to the venues. The teams included hundreds of individuals, many of whom had supported their communities throughout the preparations for the Games. Team managers reported to their respective venue managers and also kept the small headquarters organization of Community Relations informed concerning issues and how they could be addressed most effectively.

FRAMEWORK FOR COMMUNITY INVOLVEMENT

One of the most important aspects of Community Relations was involving citizens of the city of Atlanta and the other venue cities in ACOG's efforts.

Atlanta Area

Shortly after Atlanta was named as the host city for the 1996 Games, the city of Atlanta designated more than a dozen neighborhoods surrounding the Atlanta venues that would require special attention and development efforts. Community Relations began to meet informally with neighborhood leaders in these areas.

These informal meetings, conducted to discover community concerns about the Games and gather information for ACOG planning, formed the basis for establishing community advisory groups with representatives from each city neighborhood as well as additional groups near venues outside the downtown area.

These geographically based community groups were formed with the purpose of focus-ing on Olympic-related construction and how new facilities would affect their areas. They included the Olympic Center neighborhood advisory group, Olympic Stadium neighborhood advisory group, Olympic Village neighborhood advisory group, Stone Mountain Park neighborhood advisory group, and Wolf Creek neighborhood advisory group.

Because communities are not defined only by geographic borders, ACOG also established formal advisory groups to represent various special constituencies. These groups were:

■ Committee on Disability Access, a committee of approximately 300 people, most holding leadership positions in areas related to accessibility of facilities, assembled to help eliminate barriers in architecture, communications, and transportation.

■ Interfaith Advisory Group (IAG) panel representing a broad spectrum of religious beliefs, advised ACOG on ways to meet the spiritual and religious needs of members of the Olympic Family.

■ Olympic Environmental Support Group (OESG), comprised of 23 representatives from the fields of academia, business, environment, government, science, and the general public, helped ACOG establish and achieve environmental goals for the 1996 Olympic Games.

A community leader chaired each of these groups, which together represented more than 800 people. The strategy for each group was the same: to provide a forum for the exchange of information and views through regular meetings that involved representatives of the community, ACOG management, and others. Most groups met monthly or more frequently, and often formed subcommittees to address specific issues. Community Relations staff involved the appropriate functional areas to determine the feasibility of projects for these groups in terms of time and budget considerations.

The advisory groups began meeting in early 1993, and most discussions focused on the venue designs under development. Representatives of Construction and ACOG's contractors for design and architecture met frequently with group members. In the two years prior to the Games, discussions centered on transportation and security issues—in terms of their impact on the lives of the venue-area residents and the best methods for minimizing negative effects.

Less formally structured groups served in an advisory capacity to ACOG as representatives of the neighborhoods hosting the marathon and road cycling courses. These courses traversed major sections of the city, coming into contact with numerous residential and business areas. In addition, churches located along the courses were consulted respecting Sunday competition days. In the 18 months prior to the start of the Games, Community Relations—working with Security, Transportation, and Venue Management—met frequently with groups affected by the road courses to provide information on the preparations for the creation of the competition routes and associated support facilities and to discuss street closings, traffic rerouting, and other issues during the competitions. Churches along the courses were especially cooperative, often offering to host community meetings and then opening their facilities to spectators during the Games.

Community Relations also maintained a dialogue with numerous civic and cultural organizations, such as the Hispanic Chamber of Commerce and the Chinese-American Community Center. These relationships were essential to address the concerns of different ethnic groups

and facilitate the recruitment of bilingual volunteers and other cooperative arrangements.

In all, ACOG endorsed the formation of more than 20 advisory groups in the Atlanta area. The guidance that came from all advisory groups—and the communication they facilitated—was extremely important in shaping ACOG policies and programs and assisting in decision-making.

Venue Cities outside Atlanta

ACOG supported the efforts of local organizing committees of Olympic competitions outside the metro-Atlanta area through a division of Venue Management. This division employed the same mission and guidelines as Community Relations to address outlying site relations.

For the most part, the local organizing committees were concerned with gathering and disseminating information about the Games, pursuing opportunities for city beautification and economic enhancement, and recruiting volunteers for Games-time.

The first group to be established was the Savannah Olympic Support Council (SOSCO). Board and staff members were volunteers representing various segments of the city and surrounding county. ACOG staff in Savannah provided support to the committee, as did the competition manager and the venue manager.

The organizational structure for SOSCO included separate divisions for beautification, cultural affairs, youth and education, and small and minority business development. With SOSCO's assistance, programs in Savannah received state and federal funding and contributions from local private and public groups. By Games-time, the city's Riverwalk—where much commercial activity as well as many festivals and celebrations are centered—had been extended and a new municipal pier constructed. In addition, trees and flowering shrubs were planted at city entrances, and streets and bridge approaches to the city were beautified or repaired.

Arts Ashore '96 was created to stage a 100-day Olympic festival in Savannah that involved a broad cross-section of the community in the opening, closing, and medal ceremonies held for the yachting competition. With the help of SOSCO's youth and education division, Arts Ashore '96 brought more than 7,000 schoolchildren in the Savannah area together for a variety of programs.

SOSCO also helped fund other education projects, including a special curriculum for the schools and construction of a walled garden with tiles decorated by hundreds of young students to commemorate Savannah's role as the venue for Olympic yachting. The garden drew huge numbers of visitors during the Games and continues to be a popular attraction.

A major emphasis for SOSCO was volunteer recruitment for the series of test events held in Savannah beginning in summer 1994 as well as for the Games.

In Athens, the community effort began with the city's designation as host to the football competition finals and gained momentum in 1994 when the University of Georgia Coliseum was selected as the site for preliminary rounds of volleyball and then later for rhythmic gymnastics.

Like SOSCO, the local organizing committee in Athens concentrated on recruiting volunteers for the Games and supporting the creation of celebratory events around the various competitions to showcase the city to spectators.

In Columbus, Gainesville, and the Ocoee River area, local organizing committees followed similar planning efforts. Each channeled the enthusiasm created by the Games into economic development and the recruitment of volunteers, not only for the Games, but also for community projects aimed at beautification and revitalization.

Community Issues

In addition to concerns about how new venues and the staging of the Games would affect the people of Atlanta, issues arose that involved special interest groups' views and purposes. ACOG's position in addressing these matters was that the Olympic Games should not be used to promote one position over another in areas that are not directly related to the Games.

Much attention was focused on whether a volleyball venue should be located in northwest metropolitan Atlanta. *(This issue, which attracted significant attention, is discussed in the Communications chapter.)* A paramount consideration for ACOG in determining how to address this and other issues that were raised was maintaining the integrity of the Olympic Games. This was achieved by preventing the presentation of the Games from being diminished by disputes not directly related to the Olympic Movement and the needs of athletes.

SPECIFIC PROGRAMS

Community Relations was committed to improving all areas affected by the Games. ACOG, through its various programs, strove to accommodate the interests of various community groups.

Venue Modifications and Neighborhood Enhancements

From the beginning, Community Relations concentrated on the neighborhoods most affected by the construction of new venues and involving residents in the logistics of projects.

The participation of the advisory groups produced information for venue and surrounding area design. Examples include Olympic Stadium, where green spaces, trees, and plants were added to parking areas for beautification,

• VIVIANE M BUSHONG • CHRIS BUSS • AMANDA M BUSSER • JAMES A BUSSEY • YVONNE BUSSEY • SUSAN E BUSSIE • JOHN C BUSSLER • ERIN B BUTCHER • JAMES E BUTCHER • KATHLEEN A BUTCHER • ROBERT L BUTCHER • SANDRA K BUTCHER • STEVEN L BUTCHER • JANUS D BUTCHER MD • ANNE F BUTFILOSKI • BECKY F BUTLER • BRUCE C BUTLER • CHARLIE F BUTLER • CORINNE W BUTLER • DANIEL L BUTLER • DAVID A BUTLER • DEBORAH D BUTLER • DONNA C BUTLER • DONNA E BUTLER • DOZE Y BUTLER • DWAIN L BUTLER • EARL M BUTLER • ELIZABETH A BUTLER •

and the Atlanta University Center complex, where the height of light towers was adjusted to prevent light from shining into nearby homes.

Members of the Stone Mountain Park neighborhood advisory group wanted the least disturbance possible to Stone Mountain Park. The solution was to create temporary venues for archery and track cycling that would be removed after the Games so the site could be turned back into a natural meadow.

The Wolf Creek neighborhood advisory group provided suggestions related to the con-

ACOG hosted numerous meetings with advisory groups to discuss the progress of Games plans.

struction of baffles for the target range and plans for reducing the scatter of lead shot from the skeet competition. The environmental protection measures taken in the latter area led to an agreement to capture and recycle lead from the facility.

While Community Relations concentrated on support for newly constructed facilities, efforts were also directed toward supporting the advisory groups for neighborhood improvement plans that required funding from the public sector.

As programs were identified, priorities were set by a specially established federal funding group, which was chaired by the director of MAOGA and the president of CODA.

The largest single neighborhood enhancement grant went to the public housing area, Techwood Homes, near the site of the Olympic Village. The US Department of Housing and Urban Development provided $42 million to transform the area into a mixed-income community. Neighboring Clark-Howell Homes received another $19 million in funding. When construction of both communities is completed, some 900 housing units will have been added and the area will have been transformed.

Committee on Disability Access

The 1996 Olympic Games venues were a model of accessibility. More accessible seating was available for the 1996 Games than for any previous Olympic Games, and the Olympic Stadium—the centerpiece of the Games—was declared by US government officials as the most accessible facility in the world. In addition to the fact that a clear line of sight to the competition area was available to all disabled seating, concessions, rest rooms, and other amenities were constructed to be fully accessible.

The advisory committee members—all of whom served on a voluntary basis—worked closely with designers, architects, and construction crews to achieve these goals. Once structures were built, committee members ensured their usability by testing them for accessibility.

The committee's work was also directed toward making the Olympic experience accessible to the hearing and vision impaired. As a result, many ACOG publications were recorded on tape or transcribed into braille or large print. ACOG's general information phone lines and ticket lines were equipped to assist the hearing impaired. Interpreters were used for many Olympic Arts Festival (OAF) events, and various auxiliary aids and other services were available at the venues for those with disabilities. Public information booths at all venues also provided free copies of a brochure that outlined all the accessible features of the Games.

Another major emphasis of the committee's work was providing accessible transportation. *(For more information, see the Transportation chapter.)*

Olympic Environmental Support Group

Reflecting a mandate of the IOC to address environmental issues proactively, ACOG formed an advisory committee with the initial task of defining environmental goals for the 1996 Games. ACOG's guidelines for the committee emphasized the importance of minimizing any negative environmental impact of the Games on the host communities and creating a legacy for all future Olympic Games.

The objectives adopted as part of an environmental policy statement concentrated on five key areas and their accompanying directives.

- Venue construction: Build new facilities to have no long-term negative impact on the environment or surrounding community; require environmental audits before proceeding with construction; use existing sports and recreational facilities as efficiently as possible; and follow the latest environmental standards in local, state, and federal laws strictly.

- Energy efficiency and conservation: Achieve through the use of innovative technology.

- Natural resources protection: Preserve native vegetation, especially trees and endangered species, and restore sites to better environmental conditions than before the Games.

- Transportation: Rely heavily on mass transit and form partnerships with government, transit authorities, and private industry to use as many alternative energy vehicles as possible.

- Solid-waste management: Limit the creation of waste at all venues and recycle solid materials to minimize impact on landfills.

With the advice of the OESG, ACOG contracted with several environmental engineering and consulting firms to help finalize the site selection process and conduct environmental audits for all new construction and renovation projects. This work prompted several site changes for venues. Rowing and canoe/kayak-sprint were moved from Stone Mountain Park to Lake Lanier, and yachting was relocated from the Priest Landing site to Wassaw Sound in Savannah.

The temporary archery and track cycling venues planned for Stone Mountain Park provided the setting for the first hearings under the Georgia Environmental Protection Act. The resulting policies kept the land pristine and set the standard for future efforts.

The construction of Olympic Stadium was planned for the site of a parking lot adjacent to the city's existing stadium, minimizing the impact of this new facility. Plans also provided for the older stadium to be dismantled after its Games-time use and the site used for a parking lot. Olympic Stadium also provided significant opportunities for recycling. The 40,000 additional seats installed for Games-time use were removed and sold. The Olympic track was installed at a local university. Large amounts of concrete at the stadium were recycled and used in road surfacing when the stadium was modified after the Games.

While every effort was made to build new facilities on already developed land, several new venues were located in areas that had not yet been developed. As noted previously, the OESG helped identify methods of minimizing the environmental impact of these facilities, such as spectator seating on floating platforms at Lake Lanier to protect the surrounding wooded areas.

To enhance energy efficiency, ACOG used metal halide lights (which require much less energy than traditional lighting) where possible for indoor and outdoor competition areas. Other lighting fixtures were outfitted with fluorescent rather than incandescent tubing and energy-efficient electronic ballast.

At virtually every venue, natural resources were enhanced with the planting of numerous trees and plants. The most outstanding example was at Centennial Olympic Park, where 21 acres of green space, including 650 new trees and plants, were added to the city.

Prior to the Games, ACOG requested that all vendors and concessionaires reduce product packaging and use recycled and recyclable materials in goods provided for the Games. A comprehensive plan was enacted at each venue to separate solid waste so that as much as possible could be recycled or used for composting and waste-to-energy conversion. *(For more information on recycling, see the Logistics chapter.)*

Through the commitment of ACOG, the Games produced a minimal negative impact on the environment. The greatest long-term benefits may result from the example set for incorporating environmental responsibility into the hosting of major events.

Interfaith Advisory Group

The primary objective of the IAG was meeting the religious and spiritual needs of the athletes, their families, team officials, and other members of the Olympic Family during the Games. The group also provided advice on dietary laws, social customs, and religious practices of visitors from around the world.

The 40-member group outlined plans for religious centers at the Olympic Village, offering services in Buddhism, Christianity, Hinduism, Islam, and Judaism. In addition, prayer and meditation sites were identified at the Olympic Village. During the Games, committee members conducted a regular schedule of interfaith services. A team of volunteers also conducted services in an athlete's faith whenever requested. *(For more information on the IAG, see the Olympic Villages chapter.)*

Neighborhood Job Training and Employment Program

Very early in the planning process, members of the Olympic Stadium advisory group recommended a job training program that would help residents gain skills and experience for long-term employment in the construction industry. Expanded to a citywide effort, the Neighborhood Job Training and Employment Program (NJTEP) was created to provide at least 300 residents of Olympic venue host neighborhoods with classroom training and work experience at Olympic venues.

Community Relations began this effort using funding from ACOG and the Private Industry Council. An NJTEP steering committee, comprised of community leaders from the Olympic venue neighborhoods, was assembled to guide the program.

The steering committee sought additional funding from government agencies and private businesses to provide aptitude testing, drug screening, pre-employment training, monitoring of participants on the job site, and placement in other construction jobs after Olympic venues were completed. A total of $3 million was raised from public and private sources to support this program.

The Volunteers in Service to America (VISTA) program provided volunteers who served as mentors to NJTEP participants, recruited additional participants, and helped make child care and transportation arrangements.

Pre-employment training—including general education as well as specific construction trade classes—was offered by the Georgia Department of Technical and Adult Education. In addition, 60 women who participated in the program received customized training under a US Department of Labor program to prepare women for nontraditional employment.

More than 300 residents were employed, many of whom attained other construction jobs after the Olympic venues were completed.

Atlanta University Center Legacy

As the oldest consortium of historically black colleges and universities in the nation, the Atlanta University Center holds a special place in the Atlanta community.

Working with the presidents of the six member colleges, Community Relations was instrumental in ACOG's commitment of $51 million in physical and operational enhancements to the campuses. The projects included two stadiums, a gymnasium, a conference center, medical laboratory facilities, and tennis training facilities. The schools also benefited from hosting several OAF programs and the Host Broadcast Training Program, a joint project between Clark Atlanta University and Atlanta Olympic Broadcasting that provided more than 900 students with practical broadcasting experience. *(For more information, see the Atlanta Olympic Broadcasting chapter.)*

Youth Programs

Both ACOG management and community leaders shared a commitment to involving children and young people in the 1996 Olympic Games. Community Relations instituted numerous programs to help fulfill that commitment and provided support for efforts initiated by other functional areas and various organizations affiliated with ACOG. *(For more information, see the Youth and Education chapter.)*

Stadium Fence Painting. Community Relations focused on programs for young people primarily from the Atlanta area. Many activities related to the construction of new venues for the Games. One early activity was painting artwork on the fence surrounding the Olympic Stadium construction site.

Working with Atlanta public schools, Community Relations assembled 750 children from the Olympic Stadium neighborhoods for the project. In addition to providing an opportunity for artistic expression, painting the fence instilled the pride of ownership in neighborhood youngsters. The fence stood for two years, and as a particular tribute to the respect this artwork inspired, no incidents of vandalism ever occurred.

Inauguration of Sports Venues and Clinics. Olympic test events and official venue openings were other occasions to allow children in the surrounding neighborhoods to preview venues and learn certain sports. At the 1994 Pan American Race Walk, local students inaugurated the course the day before the official start of competition using skills learned during special classes at their schools with athletes from the US Olympic race walk team. At the hockey venue, neighborhood children who had just learned the basics of the sport were joined by Tipper Gore, wife of US Vice President Gore, who shared with them the importance of hockey and other sports in her life.

During the Games planning period, more than 8,000 Atlanta students—along with their parents, teachers, and coaches—participated in events at Olympic venues and in 30 youth clinics and demonstrations sponsored by Community Relations and Sports. More than a dozen Olympic sports were featured, including badminton, canoeing, canoe/kayak–slalom, cycling, fencing, handball, hockey, rowing, swimming, synchronized swimming, volleyball, and wrestling.

Internships. Internships with ACOG contractors and at ACOG offices involved young people in the Games and offered them valuable skills and work experience.

As part of their contractual commitment, many design and architectural firms selected for Olympic projects created internships for

Tipper Gore, wife of Vice President Al Gore, shares her hockey and other sport experiences with a venue neighborhood youth group.

for Olympic projects created internships for young people living in the neighborhoods surrounding the venues. Students from middle schools, high schools, and colleges had an opportunity to participate, depending on the type of program offered. Designers of the Olympic Stadium engaged high school students in a program that involved site design, facility layout, and building code review. The instruction and work experience for other programs involved similar activities as well as design competition. More than 200 students took part in these programs.

Several hundred additional young people worked as interns at ACOG headquarters in the four years leading up to the Games. High school students were placed in various functional areas each summer in cooperation with the Atlanta public schools systems and the Private Industry Council.

Children's Olympic Ticket Fund. This program was established in July 1991 to give economically disadvantaged children an opportunity to attend the 1996 Olympic Games. The Youth and Education Department was primarily responsible for coordinating the program.

During the Games, Community Relations volunteers assisted in welcoming and escorting the groups of children that participated in the program and distributing tickets, commemorative Olympic Games caps, and refreshments. Community spirit was developed among the many agencies that cooperated to assist the children by providing housing for participants from other areas of the state and assisting with transportation and services for the young people once they arrived. *(For more information, see the Youth and Education chapter.)*

Olympic Aid–Atlanta. Children in war-torn countries around the world were the target of Olympic Aid–Atlanta, an effort ACOG supported in conjunction with the sponsoring organization, UNICEF. Proceeds from the Centennial Olympic Games Hanes T-Shirt Auction also benefited this project, which provided medicine, school supplies, and trauma counseling for children in 14 countries. Additional funds

were raised during the Games by athletes and celebrities in various appearances at Centennial Olympic Park and other locations. Major donations also came from the European Union, the Robert W. Woodruff Foundation in Atlanta, and from US celebrities, surpassing the fund-raising goal of $7 million.

GAMES-TIME OPERATIONS

During the Games, Community Relations restructured its organization and assigned teams to clusters of venues and the neighborhoods surrounding them. The teams were managed by staff members, with several dozen volunteers assigned to each group.

In addition to supporting efforts at the venues and acting as a liaison between community leaders, government agencies, and Venue Management, the teams worked in the communities to keep residents and businesses informed about transportation and the effect on traffic flow. Team leaders reported to their respective venue managers and Community Relations headquarters staff.

CONCLUSIONS AND RECOMMENDATIONS

ACOG's Community Relations efforts helped create an enormously positive environment for staging the 1996 Olympic Games. In addition, involvement of the community in the planning process resulted in ideas that improved the construction, transportation, and operational plans of the 1996 Games.

The involvement of community constituents allowed those most affected by the Games to voice their concerns, contribute to decision making, and benefit from the presence of Games-related activities in their area. These efforts should start from the time the Games are awarded to a city and continue through the Closing Ceremony.

Proceeds from the Centennial Olympic Games Hanes T-Shirt Auction were contributed to the Children's Olympic Ticket Fund, the US Olympic team, and Olympic Aid–Atlanta.

Atlanta 1996.

Chapter Twelve

Financial Services

OVERVIEW—ACOG was created as a not-for-profit US corporation to stage the Olympic Games, and as part of the establishing agreements, committed to use private sources of funding and indemnify the city of Atlanta from financial obligations, share in the revenue sources with the IOC and USOC, and achieve a balanced budget.

In order to fulfill these commitments, ACOG established the Financial Services Department, with the mission of creating and implementing a financial structure through policies and procedures and functional area support to ensure the fiscal integrity of the corporation.

The systems and procedures developed by Financial Services provided a solid financial system for an organization that would grow in size from a small entrepreneurial entity to a Fortune 500 company within six years. All systems had to be sound enough to support a large, complex organization with a very short life cycle.

Inherent to ACOG's efforts were several challenges. First, the magnitude of the Centennial Olympic Games would be significantly larger than any previous Olympic Games. Moreover, the new revenue sharing formulas, that is, the established percentage of revenue received by the organizing committee, were less favorable than in previous quadrenniums. Also, contracts for the construction of competition venues had to be awarded before revenue from sponsorships or broadcast rights had been received, thus creating a significant cash flow issue.

Fortunately, ACOG began its efforts with a sound financial foundation, as revenue generated from merchandising after Atlanta was awarded the Games provided a support base.

The keys to the success of the Financial Services plan were allowing for the flexibility and adaptability to respond to changing and sometimes unanticipated events, enhanced by a willingness to take reasonable risks, without jeopardizing the fundamental mission; seeking creative ways to minimize costs, acknowledging that for a temporary event, there are many ways to create the necessary environment without permanent investment; and maintaining revenues and expenses in relative balance.

In addition to ensuring ACOG's fiscal integrity, Financial Services provided management information and problem resolution support for the CEO and COO, and was responsible for planning and implementing the dissolution and liquidation of ACOG following the Games.

ORGANIZATION

Financial Services began initially in 1991 with the confirmation of the chief financial officer (CFO) and a small staff. Initial plans included engaging firms to prepare audits; creating payroll, accounting, and internal audit/budget procedures; and establishing the function of controller in the organization. In 1992 and 1994, major staffing growth was necessary to meet the demands of the growing organization.

The department was divided into five divisions: Financial Planning and Analysis, Planning and Budget, Accounting, Procurement and Contract Administration (P&CA), and Risk Management. In addition, special support functions were coordinated by Financial Services—the Internal Audit function and the Paralympic Liaison function, responsible for dispersing certain allocated cash and value-in-kind (VIK) to the independently operated Atlanta Paralympic Organizing Committee (APOC).

FINANCIAL PLANNING AND ANALYSIS

The Financial Planning and Analysis division managed ACOG's revenue plan; it focused on strategic components of each revenue source and business relationships with key partners such as the IOC and the USOC.

This division completed special projects to help ACOG prioritize financial issues, guide decision making, and enhance the economic impact of the Games on the state of Georgia. It also evaluated and recommended programs with revenue opportunities that, once endorsed by ACOG, were transferred to the appropriate functional areas.

Financial Planning and Analysis emphasized detailed financial model building and forecasting. Financial pro formas were customized for each revenue source. Business arrangements were carefully analyzed to accurately project ACOG's net revenue and assist in finalizing business terms with outside entities.

To achieve a balanced budget while staging an event of this size and scope, all major revenue sources had to increase significantly relative to previous Olympic Games. Broadcast rights fees, sponsorships, licensing, and ticket sales represented 85 percent of revenue for Atlanta. The increased emphasis on these

elements balanced a lesser dependence on interest income not available to ACOG at the same magnitude as for the Los Angeles Games. Interest income provided only one percent of revenue for Atlanta. *(For percentage of revenue sources, see Figure 1.)*

A total $2.6 billion in revenue was generated, of which ACOG received $1.7 billion to finance the Games. Significant portions of the revenue generated supported Olympic organizations, including the IOC, the USOC, NOCs, and other Olympic-related entities. In addition, substantial portions of the revenue were reduced by accurate valuations of costs and allowances for VIK contributions—goods and services provided to ACOG by sponsors in exchange for rights and benefits.

Television Rights

Worldwide demand for the right to broadcast Olympic competition is crucial to the economic success of the modern Olympic Games. Broadcast rights fees were ACOG's largest revenue source, comprising approximately 33 percent of the total. Revenue was shared with the IOC, which was primarily responsible for negotiating broadcast rights arrangements. The USOC also participated in negotiations and received a revenue share from NBC, the US broadcaster. The Atlanta Games achieved record-breaking revenue levels, totaling approximately $900 million, which were received from 15 broadcast companies representing 169 countries. Atlanta received 60 percent of broadcasting fees, spending approximately $100 million to produce the host broadcast.

The royalties paid by NBC for US rights were higher than for previous Games, but less than anticipated due to timing and changes in the revenue sharing formula. NBC shared revenue from advertising sales in excess of $615 million to supplement the rights fees, providing an additional $18 million for ACOG. In addition, NBC supplied ACOG with air time for ten 30-minute television specials, including the associated advertising time.

Two major broadcast rights agreements (US and European) were critical to ACOG's financial plan, ensuring both the line of credit from NationsBank and approval from the governmental entity MAOGA to begin construction of Olympic Stadium.

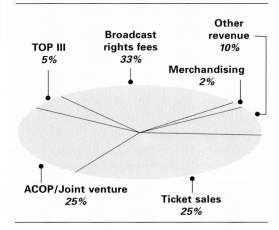

FIGURE 1:
PERCENTAGES OF REVENUE BY SOURCE

TOP III 5%
Broadcast rights fees 33%
Other revenue 10%
Merchandising 2%
ACOP/Joint venture 25%
Ticket sales 25%

Sponsorship Sales

The Olympic Programme (TOP) is the international level of sponsorship granted by the IOC for the international rights to use Olympic marks in corporate marketing programs. The program, named TOP III because it was the third such program in Olympic history, was critical to private Olympic financing and defined the terms of the major sponsor category. The program set sports marketing records, yet fell short of ACOG's expectations.

TOP III was challenging because sharing formulas had to be negotiated and agreed upon by the hosts of both the Winter and Centennial Games. Revenue from TOP sponsors represented 5 percent of ACOG revenue, or $81 million. Total TOP revenue was shared with the IOC, USOC, NOCs, and the Lillehammer Olympic Organizing Committee.

A major part of the revenue increase compared to prior Olympic Games was VIK rather than cash contributions. Revenue increased by 65 percent while VIK contributions more than tripled. Since the organizing committee is the TOP participant that can most effectively use VIK contributions, there was pressure to use more VIK in lieu of cash. ACOG's quantity of VIK from TOP was four times that of Barcelona's.

Another key revenue source was the marketing of national sponsorships—the Centennial Olympic Partners (COP)—subject to constraints defined by the IOC and parameters established by TOP III.

These sponsorships were controlled by the joint venture agreement between the USOC and ACOG that formed ACOP.

ACOP marketing was extremely successful, generating more than 25 percent of total ACOG revenue. ACOG's share amounted to $426 million.

Similar to TOP III, sponsor contributions were also more VIK intensive, representing half of the total sponsorship contributions. The added VIK necessitated stringent VIK management requirements to ensure goods and services were valued correctly, utilized optimally, and kept consistent with ACOG's budget and operational planning. *(For more information, see the Marketing/ACOP chapter.)*

Other Joint Venture Initiatives

The joint venture agreement specified how ACOG and the USOC collaborated to market the Games and how they shared revenue and expenses.

In addition to national sponsorships, the joint venture included licensing and coin programs and new market development. The licensing program far exceeded any previous program. Approximately 150 licensees with thousands of products had sales exceeding $500 million. These sales generated $91 million in royalties, netting $42 million for ACOG.

Data for all licensees was tracked on a Fox-Pro database and updated quarterly with the licensee sales and royalty reports. Both detailed and executive summary reports listed the data by mark, territory, product, and earned royalties versus minimum guarantee, among other data. Considerable effort was expended on collections from the licensees. Letters of credit were required to cover minimum guarantees.

The US Commemorative Coin Program was the largest Olympic commemorative coin program in US Mint history. Special emphasis was placed on sales efforts with NOCs as well as domestic sales through major US retail chains. ACOP shared the $26 million program proceeds with the USOC, the IOC, the APOC, and the NOCs. *(For more information, see the Marketing/ACOP chapter.)*

Ticket Sales

Ticket sales were critical to ACOG's financial plan. Atlanta had more tickets to sell than Los Angeles and Barcelona combined and capitalized on the quantity available and their high demand to significantly increase revenue.

Ticket sales, which represented 15 percent of the original forecast, ultimately accounted for 25 percent of the final revenue count. *(For more information, see the Ticket Sales chapter.)*

Other Revenue

Given the challenges presented by operating under a tight financial plan, ACOG devoted serious attention to smaller revenue sources, which were expected to generate less than

1 percent of total revenue. Over time, ACOG capitalized on a wide variety of small revenue opportunities, which ultimately generated 10 percent of total revenue. Significant among these were local sponsorships within the state of Georgia, donations from other organizations, commission on hotel rooms booked through ACOG, interest income, rate cards for the rental of equipment and facility space to constituent groups, and ticket service charges on ticket orders.

Parking and concessions also generated revenue, but not until Games-time. Other revenue sources, such as merchandise concessions, official souvenir program sales, and food and beverage concessions, were contracted to third parties in exchange for a minimum guarantee, with additional revenue based on sales activity.

Merchandising

Approximately 2 percent of total ACOG revenue was generated from retail operations. Although merchandising represented a small portion of total revenue, it played a key role in the early months of the organization, providing a significant portion of ACOG's cash flow.

Value-in-Kind Contributions

VIK contributions were a financial resource that required continuous management. During ACOG's early years, an estimate of VIK requirements by functional areas was needed to support sponsor negotiations. Once detailed, the contributions were assigned a value agreed upon by ACOG and the VIK sponsor.

VIK values in expense and revenue forecasts required careful monitoring, especially with budget modifications, to ensure the balance of VIK between revenue and expenses was not disturbed.

VIK contributions, generating 50 percent of total ACOG sponsorship revenue, reached unprecedented levels in Atlanta. Effective management of this resource was critical considering that ACOG was operating on a very tight budget consisting of both cash and VIK expenses. Additionally, as a result of joint venture revenue formulas, VIK usage and valuation affected the sharing ratios of cash between ACOG and the USOC. These factors forced such an intense focus on VIK that it often dominated the attention of the senior accounting and financial management staff, who often dictated operational approaches.

Several factors influenced the development of VIK policies and procedures issued in early 1994:

■ VIK required the same level of attention to authorization, budget, procurement, and reporting as any other expenditure transaction.

■ VIK required an expert to work with sponsors and their products, particularly regarding technology. A VIK coordinator was the department purchasing agent for ACOG in acquiring VIK. To facilitate the VIK coordinator's management of all VIK allocations from a sponsor, VIK budgets were often centralized.

■ Valuation of VIK, which affected ACOG, the USOC, and the IOC, needed to be fair to all.

■ To ACOG functional areas, VIK was considered the same as a cash expenditure. Education on this principle was very difficult.

■ The ACOG financial accounting system (AFAS) was used for managing VIK, but other systems were substituted when more practical.

Representatives from Financial Services divisions met weekly to monitor VIK management and provide a forum to resolve VIK issues expediently.

PLANNING AND BUDGET

Fundamental to both the development and management of the expense budget was the direct pairing and teamwork between Planning staff and Budget staff. While one group focused on coordinating ACOG-wide planning consistency, program integration, and project scheduling, the other worked to define and manage a financial plan that could be achieved in an extremely dynamic environment.

The Budget Office was responsible for the annual update of ACOG's full life cycle financial forecast and the daily management of the ACOG expenditure budget. It supported functional areas by dividing into three financial management support teams, each responsible for supporting a group of functional areas. The Budget Office was led by a director, and each support team was headed by a budget program manager. The teams were staffed by analysts who worked with budget program staff.

In late 1992, ACOG's Planning subdivision began detailed program planning using a technique called the work breakdown structure. This foundation involved the systematic breakdown and graphical portrayal of the major functions that comprised programs.

As programs were defined, major functions within them were itemized to determine the products and services ACOG would deliver and which constituents would receive them. Following this, program resource requirements (PRR)—the resources required to produce the products and services of each program—were identified. These PRRs, which included facilities, personnel, services, materials, and technical expertise, were entered into a financial forecast update model that contained all financial requirements for each functional program.

In 1993, the financial planning process shifted to the actual integration of financial plans, and a complete financial forecast and master plan were developed. This budget data was the foundation for building the expenditure portion of ACOG's financial forecast for 1994.

Development of time-phased schedules for projects and activities was the second major planning task. These schedules formed the basis of the Olympic master schedule system (OMSS), which consisted of three tiers of time-based information: detailed working schedules at the program and project levels; an integrated time line containing summaries of detailed program and project schedules called the master Olympic activity schedule (MOAS); and a major events summary, which contained milestones extracted from the MOAS.

The OMSS and AFAS were used to report on program-level projects and budgets to various constituency groups. Reports addressed the status of projects (including deliverables and milestones), near-term activities, budget status, and other related issues.

In 1994, the planning process shifted from a program orientation to a multifunctional venue orientation. First, the functional elements necessary for venue operations were defined. Venue management teams were developed during this period and began to draft operational plans for each competition venue in preparation for the 1995 test events.

The complexity of the project challenged ACOG to identify and respond to sensitive issues, such as program and constituent priorities, resource allocation, system design and implementation, and venue development. ACOG senior management, critical to advancing projects in the high-profile, high-pressure environment, confronted complex issues through open communication and were willing, if necessary, to compromise on matters that involved competing priorities.

Planning Integration and the Budget Office

During the development of the financial forecast update, the Budget Office coordinated extensively with Planning to ensure key opera-

tional assumptions were defined correctly in financial terms. Further, economic assumptions were reviewed and integrated with revenue and expenditure components of ACOG's economic profile.

To update the financial forecast, the Budget Office held financial planning work sessions with each functional program to evaluate financial priorities and view operational planning assumptions in financial terms. Planning staff also attended the work sessions, which focused on elements of a program's organiza-

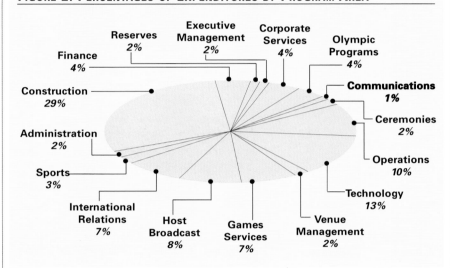

FIGURE 2: PERCENTAGES OF EXPENDITURES BY PROGRAM AREA

tional structure and its financial requirements, which included cost-center structure, staff plan and staffing costs, indirect staff-sensitive costs—per person cost allowances for space and equipment and statutory and nonstatutory compensation, direct program costs, and financial planning (revenue) integration.

A program's organizational structure, represented by its cost-center structure, was revised for consistency with its operational concept and plan. Typically, a program area would have one planning and management cost center,

EVAN A CALL • BONNIE L CALLAHAN • BRIAN T CALLAHAN • BRYANT K CALLAHAN • DANIEL L CALLAHAN • ELIZABETH A CALLAHAN • JACQUELINE D CALLAHAN • JOSEPH J CALLAHAN • JOYCE B CALLAHAN • KELI R CALLAHAN • KEVIN F CALLAHAN • MARGARET P CALLAHAN • MARGARITA T CALLAHAN • MEGAN B CALLAHAN • MICHAEL J CALLAHAN • PATRICK J CALLAHAN • RITA A CALLAHAN • TAMARA R CALLAHAN • TERI L CALLAHAN • THERESA M CALLAHAN • JUDY S CALLAND • JEFFREY G CALLARD • ANN M CALLAWAY • ANTONE TONY H CALLAWAY • BEN D CALLAWAY •

209

supported by individual operational cost centers. The concept of individual cost "buckets" was developed to group costs into specific centers for management accountability.

Staffing plans consisted of the number of positions required, including start and end dates, professional classification, and compensation levels and types. These were reviewed with Games Staffing, Human Resources, Volunteer Services, Venue Management, and Sports.

Indirect staff-sensitive costs—parametric estimates of general staff costs, such as space, supplies, and travel—were placed in the general operating budget. All other funding requirements for a program were categorized as direct program costs. Direct cost elements were correlated with individual planning parameters, such as functional delivery requirements, program resource requirements, and venue operating plans. Time-phasing of the expenditure budget requirements was correlated with the program and project development schedules.

The Planning and Budget division, led by the CFO, worked with program staffs to modify expenditure proposals and align them with achievable revenue forecasts. These budgets were then presented to the ACOG Board of Directors and executive management to establish financial priorities for the Games using a balanced budget scenario.

Once the ACOG Board adopted the financial forecast, its feasibility was reviewed by independent external auditors acting for MAOGA. The product of this quarterly review was a prospective financial review, modified to particular requirements of ACOG.

Excluding the Bid budget, ACOG officially updated its financial forecast four times from 1992 to 1995. Although ACOG chose not to officially update the forecast in 1995, an interim operating plan, termed a financial action plan, was sanctioned by the ACOG Board of Directors finance committee as a bridge between the 1994 and 1996 updates.

Daily Budget Management

The Budget Office reviewed proposed expenditure transactions daily for consistency with the approved operational plans and budgets. The goal of ACOG budget management was to ensure that funding commitments were made only for items allocated for in an authorized budget.

Hiring expenditures were presented to the Budget Office as employment requisitions—forms that were reviewed against the staffing plan and approved before a position was recruited or filled.

Procurement expenditures in the form of purchase requisitions were routed electronically through AFAS to the Budget Office. Upon system entry, purchase requisitions were coded to a specific cost center, object account, and project. If no budget, or an insufficient budget, was profiled to these coding parameters, it was routed to a "budget-hold" location for review by Budget Office staff. Once a requisition cleared, it proceeded electronically through the management hierarchy for approval.

Budget changes were regularly reviewed for requisitions inconsistent with plans and funding allocation changes were routed to executive management for consideration, where appropriate.

The Budget Office also managed contingency and reserve funds. There was a published contingency between revenue and expenses that was reevaluated with each annual financial forecast update. Each program request for incremental funding from reserves or contingencies required executive approval.

The Budget Office supplied budget status reports that were distributed monthly to departments. General monthly budget status assessments were presented to the CFO and COO and periodically discussed with the departments.

AFAS, a tailored version of the state-of-the-art financial software used on the internal computer network, was fundamental to Budget Office operations. Through the system's integration of budget management, financial reporting, general accounting, general ledger, and procurement modules, the office was able to monitor proposed expenditures, conduct budget status inquiries, adjust the budget for approved changes, and report budget versus actual results. The Budget Office maintained the cost-center structure and hierarchy and was instrumental in developing the expenditure portion of the chart of accounts.

To support the quarterly financial forecast review, the Budget Office maintained and updated an expenditure forecast summary. The financial impact of actual expenditures and budget reclassification transactions, financial exposures, and cost-saving opportunities were measured and recommendations developed for executive management decisions. *(For the percentage of expenditure by program area, see Figure 2.)*

ACCOUNTING

The Accounting division was divided into four subdivisions, each headed by a program manager who reported directly to the controller—Accounts Payable, ACOG Accounting (including Payroll), ACOP Accounting, and Cash Management/Treasury.

Accounting was centralized for all of ACOG, as well as ACOP, though some accounting tasks were performed by other departments or outside parties for efficiency. In these cases, Accounting was integrally involved in establishing procedures and monitoring compliance.

In late 1995, all Accounting personnel were assigned to venues. When ACOG venue management teams relocated to their respective venues in mid-1996, a financial services officer (FSO) and an accountant also moved to fulfill all financial duties at the venues. The FSO wrote and signed checks at venues, following ACOG policies and procedures manually rather than electronically. Daily reports were transmitted by facsimile machine from venues to headquarters and entered into the AFAS for consolidated reporting. Thus, recording of venue transactions was maintained on a real-time basis and not delayed until after the Games.

The accounting policies ACOG adopted were practical given ACOG's short life cycle. The policies were consistent with generally accepted accounting principles and were meaningful to an organization managing a limited pool of resources.

ACOG was structured as a 501(c)(4) organization until its 501(c)(3) tax status—which permits individuals and corporations to make charitable donations—was approved in 1992. The accounting cycle was a single six-year period. This allowed for annual operating results (net income or loss) to be deferred and treated as a balance-sheet item until the end of 1996. The accumulated retained earnings deficit was recorded as an asset, under the assumption that early losses would be recovered by the end of the six-year cycle.

Expenses were recognized on an accrual basis, and revenue was recognized on a cash basis. Expenditures for capital and intangible items were recognized immediately. All leases were treated as operating leases. Donations of VIK and personnel, for which the donor received no rights or benefits, were not recorded. Cost allocations from one department to another were approved as needed. Typically, this

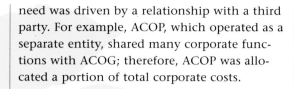

need was driven by a relationship with a third party. For example, ACOP, which operated as a separate entity, shared many corporate functions with ACOG; therefore, ACOP was allocated a portion of total corporate costs.

Accounts Payable

The Accounts Payable subdivision was responsible for creating the payment structure using AFAS. This accounting system, activated on 1 January 1993, integrated all financial functions on-line and in real-time. It included budget; requisitions, purchases, and encumbrances; accounts payable; general ledger and reporting; inventory control for asset management; rate card sales order processing; and accounts receivable.

In April 1993, the first detailed purchasing and accounts payable policies and procedures were issued. Initially, the general ledger chart of accounts, based on the Bid document budget, consisted of six cost centers and a few hundred accounts. In 1996, during the peak of operations, it consisted of more than 300 cost centers, with an additional 35 for ACOP, and 1,300 accounts. Additionally, a four-digit project code was used frequently for further segregation.

ACOG and ACOP Accounting

The complex financial operations of both ACOG and ACOP required two separate accounting teams.

The ACOG accounting team was concerned primarily with merchandising; asset management; construction—accrued on percentage completed; payroll and employee benefits; and monthly, quarterly, and annual tax reports with local, state, and federal agencies.

The ACOP accounting team collected cash revenue from agreements, evaluated and recorded VIK, distributed cash to partners and

recapitalized from them when necessary, compiled quarterly sales and royalty results of licensees, allocated net profits based on the joint venture agreement, and computed royalties owed to the IOC.

Financial results, including budget and revenue forecast highlights, were reviewed monthly.

Payroll Services. Automatic Data Processing (ADP) donated its payroll services to ACOG. Most staff were salaried, paid twice monthly, and used the direct deposit banking service offered.

Randstad Staffing Services, an international temporary agency, became a sponsor in mid-1994. Administrative and clerical staff were contracted through them; thus, Randstad coordinated all payroll services for those individuals.

Cash Management/Treasury

ACOG recognized from the beginning that the revenue flow would not be sufficient to support the organization as it expanded and particularly as construction accelerated. The ACOG financial plan was effective because of the cash flow infusion from an annually renewable line of credit from NationsBank. Executed in March 1992, it was initially set at $300 million; it tapered to $200 million in mid-1994, and was reduced to $50 million in December 1995. Borrowings peaked at $73 million in early January 1995. The line was repaid in May 1995.

The line of credit was unique in many respects. It was the first commercial line of credit provided to an Olympic organizing committee, as governmental cash flow generally met the needs of most organizing committees. In Los Angeles, broadcast rights fee deposits and the interest earnings on those deposits were sufficient to cover cash flow requirements.

This was also an extremely unique credit arrangement by normal US banking standards, because ACOG was a company with virtually no assets or revenue track record at the outset. Management of the line of credit was a high priority for NationsBank.

The cash management team was responsible for minimizing loan balances and maximizing investment earnings under the guidelines of a conservative investment policy.

Although considerable cash handling occurred at Games-time, most was performed by concessionaires. To comply with ACOG's security requirements, Accounting coordinated armored car schedules at the venues with all participating concessionaires. ACOG handled cash for ticket sales at venue box offices.

Control Management. The concept of control and oversight was crucial to the financial success of the Atlanta Games. ACOG was a private corporation, and although it guarded its financial information, it exercised more control management than most governments or publicly traded companies. ACOG placed as much importance on budgeting and control of expenses as it did on the acquisition of revenue. If excessive spending was not controlled, no amount of revenue could offset the depletion of available operating capital.

All budgets were provisional, that is, even though an item was budgeted, expenditures were not dispersed until approved by defined levels of ACOG management. This procedure was established to monitor expenditures and confirm their appropriateness to the priorities of the organization. Managers, managing directors, the CFO, COO, and CEO were each authorized to approve different expenditure amounts.

Other components of ACOG's financial control and management were AFAS; the central procurement of all goods and services; an active Internal Audit function and annual external audit; and active involvement by ACOG's Board of Directors, including periodic reviews by its finance and audit committees.

External review, unique to ACOG's political and economic circumstance, was imposed by NationsBank, its lending institution, and MAOGA. MAOGA had certain review rights granted by the Tri-Party Agreement, first on an informal and later on a formal basis.

MAOGA engaged an accounting firm to conduct these periodic reviews of ACOG's financial condition. These reviews were formalized as quarterly financial analyses to confirm ACOG's compliance with provisions of the Olympic Stadium contract; specifically, the maintenance of a contingency fund equal to 5 percent of uncommitted revenue with a $13 million minimum guarantee.

PROCUREMENT AND CONTRACT ADMINISTRATION

The P&CA division was divided into two subdivisions—Purchasing and Contract Administration, each headed by a program manager. Purchasing was comprised of buyers who specialized in high-volume transactions assigned by commodity codes. In the Contract Administration subdivision, administrators were assigned to specific ACOG departments to coordinate contracts requiring specialized terms and conditions. Contract administrators ensured the department was involved during contract negotiations of critical programs and requirements.

From the beginning, ACOG established procedures to conduct business fairly and equitably to positively reflect the community, and in January 1991, adopted an ethics policy. Through its Equal Economic Opportunity Plan (EEOP), ACOG strove to achieve unprecedented participation from both minorities and females in its business activities.

ACOG P&CA, like all financial management activities, began operations almost immediately, particularly for construction. The Construction Department directly administered activity using procedures established by P&CA; all other procurement activity was conducted directly by P&CA.

Purchasing

The P&CA division issued more than 30,000 purchase orders and over 6,000 contracts for the products and services required to stage the Olympic Games.

Tracking purchases with a limited staff was challenging, but P&CA operated with the mission to bring value to ACOG and ACOP by facilitating and executing the procurement of quality goods and services at the right time and at a reasonable cost while ensuring suppliers were treated in a fair, ethical, lawful, and professional manner.

In most cases, P&CA acted as an executor by researching all potential suppliers and pricing, processing, and issuing appropriate purchase orders or contracts. In other cases, P&CA was a primary facilitator of a team of representatives from P&CA, EEOP, and the functional user department. This team evaluated competitive proposals, reached a consensus, and recommended a bid award.

ACOG policy was to promote competition and quality performance, while maximizing the involvement of minority and female businesses, joint ventures, contractors, consultants, and suppliers.

Another important corporate objective was to conduct as much business as possible within the state of Georgia. P&CA expended 84 percent of procurement dollars in Georgia and 16 percent outside the state.

The Purchasing Policies and Procedures Manual was developed in 1993 and contained guidelines that ensured consistent practices were used for sourcing and pricing evaluations, requests for information (RFI), requests for quotations (RFQ), requests for proposals (RFP),

bidder's conferences, and blanket purchase orders. P&CA also worked under the guidelines that follow:

- purchase orders were to be given to vendors within three working days after receipt of an approved purchase requisition;
- senior buyers and contract administrators were to actively participate in locating and conducting business with minority- and female-owned businesses;
- invoice referrals were to be cleared within five calendar days of receipt;
- staff was to ensure vendors consistently provided on-time deliveries;
- staff was to establish and maintain positive vendor relationships utilizing lawful, professional, and ethical business practices;
- competitive bids, when applicable, were to be used to ensure fairness and cost-effectiveness.

Key Systems

P&CA utilized three modules within AFAS. The purchasing module provided the item master file and an address file for customers and suppliers to allow processing of purchase requisitions, consolidation of requisitions into purchase orders, and the issuance of electronic and printed purchase, loan, donated, and VIK order documents.

The contract administration module consolidated purchase requisitions into contracts for services or products and stored payment schedules and balance of dollars committed and paid against a specific contract.

The sales order processing module processed rate card item sales from ACOG constituents and was used to document liquidation sales.

Key Projects

In addition to daily purchase order and contract processing, P&CA led the development of standard or shell agreements to achieve consistency with contracts issued by ACOG. These shell agreements reflected standard terms and conditions, formats, and language that allowed contract administrators to seek legal advice on specific issues, including compensation and special technical provisions.

P&CA also developed an important VIK procurement process that applied the same operational and financial controls of the cash purchasing process to the VIK process.

By far, the largest P&CA project was sourcing and pricing potential needs and requirements for Games-time operations. As soon as products or services were identified and placed on a preliminary competition/noncompetition list, P&CA personnel gathered sources, price-break information, lead-time, and capacity information. This advance information allowed requisition consolidation in the system and purchase order issuance in minutes.

The final major project was P&CA's transition to the Material Sales division, which was responsible for liquidating ACOG's assets. Liquidation strategies were developed, followed by implementation policies. As procurement activity abated, P&CA personnel attended to liquidation/dissolution objectives, including the development of a master asset liquidation list, settlement and release agreements to limit corporate liability, a list of potential buyers and charitable organizations, and detailed procedures for the Material Sales division. *(Further discussed later in this chapter.)*

RISK MANAGEMENT

The Risk Management division was established in February 1992 to minimize and control the risk of human, material, or financial loss to ACOG and the Olympic Family. ACOG obtained commercial insurance for risks that could not be transferred, adequately reduced through risk control, or self-insured. Risk Management was divided into four subdivisions: Risk Assessment, Risk Control, Risk Financing, and Risk Administration.

The initial implementation of the Risk Management program was based on studies by a consulting firm and a group of local risk management experts from educational, business, and brokerage disciplines (the risk management professional support group), including interviews with ACOG executives and program directors to ascertain their management philosophy and approach to fulfilling Games-time obligations. The result was the establishment of a risk management plan that identified costs, including estimated staff, insurance premiums, and loss expenses.

The plan identified and classified operational exposures that potentially could cause human, material, or financial loss. A central concept was ACOG's role as a contractor of services, not a provider.

Risk Management services, which included insured and self-insured program administration, accurately assessed ACOG's operational exposures and facilitated insurance, loss control, and claims management program design.

Data obtained initially through Risk Assessment was used to market ACOG's insurance programs to insurance underwriters. Prior to marketing and implementing the insurance programs, an insurance brokerage firm analyzed ACOG's operations and assisted in refining and brokering the insurance and risk management needs. Risk assessments continued throughout the organizing committee's dynamic operations.

Risk Control developed, implemented, and monitored safety and loss control programs and was responsible for analysis of property conservation methods, facility inspections, safety training, and monitoring of regulatory compliance issues. Loss control and life safety policies were developed for defensive driving, golf cart operation, and emergency floor monitors; loss control surveys were conducted at all ACOG facilities during the course of the project. A safety manual was developed and distributed to ACOG functional areas.

Financial resources were reserved to pay uninsured expenses and losses within insurance program deductibles. Additional resources within the budget provided for the purchase of various commercial insurance, including property, casualty, workers' compensation, and Games cancellation.

Risk Financing handled insured and self-insured claims procedures, negotiation and payment, litigation tracking, and supervision.

Risk Administration was responsible for records and management information systems.

Insurance Programs

ACOG's core insurance program consisted of property, general liability, automobile liability and physical damage, workers' compensation, and excess liability. Its creation and implementation enabled ACOG to complete venue agreements and execute other agreements requiring such coverage. The core insurance program included a three-year rate guarantee and was auditable (based on actual exposures such as revenue, vehicular use, payroll, and property acquisition).

Insurance coverage often follows contractual obligations; therefore, a contract administration and management process was critical to the success of the core insurance program. Because of the large number of contracts projected for execution by ACOG, the Contract Administration Manual was developed that allowed a large percentage of contracts to bypass Risk Management review. An Internal Audit support function was established to monitor compliance with insurance and Risk Management guidelines.

Games Cancellation Insurance. Since the Games were privately financed, maintaining a comprehensive insurance and risk management program was critical to the financial underwriting of the Games. A significant revenue source was broadcast rights fees. Upon execution of the US broadcast rights agreement with NBC, ACOG procured the largest Games cancellation insurance in history. This worldwide placement, involving insurance markets in London, Europe, and the US, was effective December 1993. Similar to the core insurance program, Games cancellation insurance was written for a three-year period. Acquisition of this policy was required to comply with the agreements among ACOG, the IOC, and the city of Atlanta. Importantly, without this coverage, ACOG could not have maintained its line of credit with NationsBank.

Olympic Family Insurance. The *Olympic Charter* requires organizing committees to provide accidental injury and medical expense insurance for certain Olympic Family members, particularly athletes, judges, officials, the IOC, NOCs, and IFs. This requirement was particularly challenging in the US, as there is no national health care system. ACOG wanted to provide medical insurance that closely mirrored national health care. An analysis of Barcelona's medical insurance program provided the basis for ACOG's Olympic Family insurance program. This program included coverage for emergency sickness, an insurance term not included in previously underwritten US-based accidental injury/medical expense programs, was underwritten with a multiyear rate guarantee, and was auditable based on actual exposures. ACOG successfully negotiated nominal deductibles for its insurance programs and obtained, whenever possible, a fully insured program.

State of Georgia Risk Management Agreement. Many primary facilities used during the Games period were owned and operated by the state of Georgia. A comprehensive risk management agreement was negotiated between ACOG and the state of Georgia that allowed the use of state-owned properties. This risk management approach, completed in December 1994, simplified and expedited the contracting process for state-owned venues.

Volunteer Workers' Compensation Insurance. ACOG utilized the services of thousands of volunteers to stage the Games. This large number presented significant exposure to injury, medical treatment, and medical expenses. To address this issue, ACOG proposed, and the Georgia legislature passed, legislation designating ACOG volunteers as employees eligible to receive workers' compensation insurance. This milestone provided insurance to ACOG volunteers, while limiting ACOG's exposure.

INTERNAL AUDIT

Internal Audit examined and evaluated ACOG activities from a financial and operational risk perspective and aimed to identify and reduce ACOG's financial exposure by applying standard procedures such as audits and reviews.

Due to the rapid growth and short-term nature of ACOG, Internal Audit performed functions not traditional to the audit function. In some instances, Internal Audit implemented recommended changes identified through the audit process. Involvement in ACOG's operational development provided the opportunity to raise issues, make recommendations, and help implement solutions that considered operational risk as well as the ease of ACOG's dissolution.

From its inception, ACOG was subject to an unprecedented level of audit review. In addition to the designated outside auditor, ACOG was reviewed quarterly by its own independent audit firm to confirm the adequacy of its financial planning. In this context, ACOG expanded the traditional role of an Internal Audit function to one more proactive than reactive.

In August 1994, Internal Audit began with volunteers from the Atlanta chapter of the Institute of Internal Auditors (IIA) under the guidance of the department's director. IIA volunteer auditors provided expertise in addressing technical issues within functional areas.

Internal Audit provided continuous support to many functional areas. In June 1995, contract auditors from the external auditors were added to supplement the services provided by the volunteer auditors. This was an extremely effective approach.

The division focused on internal operations critical to staging the Games. Initial priorities were planning for audit activities and participating in negotiations of Games-time contracts. Later activities focused on evaluating purchasing cycle elements and reviewing operational plans prior to implementation. Numerous changes resulted from technical comments and observations provided in audit reports. Projects included:

- quality review of electronic data in AFAS;
- review of the materials management

system and monthly inventories of ware-housed materials;

■ statement of policy for safeguarding and asset control;

■ review of random award procedures for mail-order ticket sales and public housing;

■ audit of cash reconciliation for ticket sales activities;

■ audit of payments to Host Hotel Network participants; and

■ preparation of the activities plan for Games-time operations.

FIGURE 3: DISSOLUTION PLAN

Functional components	Preplanning phase		Operational phase			
	Pre–Games time		Short term August–October 1996	Long term November 1996–June 1997		
Staff	Finalize termination planning		Downsize to essential staff	Downsize to closeout staff		Downsize to zero
Venues	Finalize restoration plans		Restore to permanent configuration	Retrofit stadium	Reconcile complaints	Close out venue contracts
Assets	Identify assets		Capture and inventory assets	Sell or return assets		Close out assets
Obligations and agreements	Organize for closeout		Respond to claims	Settle claims		Close out agreements
Legacy and reports	Identify and collect items		Capture and store records and memorabilia	Prepare contractual reports		Transfer custody of legacy and memorabilia
Operations and finance	Refine post-Games plans/budgets		Prepare dissolution documents	Collect revenues / Pay bills	Reconcile and report on finances	Complete dissolution process

(vertical label: Centennial Olympic Games, 19 July–4 August 1996)

DISSOLUTION AND LIQUIDATION

ACOG utilized the services of a program and project management consulting firm to plan, coordinate, and integrate its dissolution and liquidation efforts. A small staff remained for the actual dissolution, performing activities that ranged from schedule integration and maintenance to status reporting and problem identification and resolution.

The CFO was responsible for dissolution efforts. Financial Service's main efforts were regarding accounts payable, accounts receivable, budget reconciliation, auditing, tax planning, and preparation for formal dissolution. As the functional areas dissolved, a task force assumed a proactive approach to collection duties.

Another successful endeavor was the collection, inventory, and marketing of intellectual property. Several bid committees and organizing committees purchased items from ACOG's intellectual property inventory. *(For a summary of the dissolution plan, see Figure 3.)*

Staff Dissolution

Planning for out-processing Games-time personnel began earnestly in September 1995. Personnel from Administration, Financial Services, Human Resources, Logistics, Planning and Integration (functionally responsible for noncompetition venue management), and Transportation comprised a task force and discussed the collection of ACOG property and determination of liability, reconciliation of all accounts, distribution of final paychecks, coordination with the Georgia Department of Labor, and administration of personnel records.

The task force created the Games-time out-processing center supported by Randstad and the Georgia Department of Labor, which provided pertinent benefits information. ACOG contracted with career consultants to provide outplacement counseling and assistance for employees, and sponsored a job fair at the Airport Welcome Center. More than 175 employers, including all sponsors, interviewed over 3,000 current and former ACOG employees.

A significant cost considered during dissolution was payroll. Clearly defined objectives of staff size and job descriptions ensured that dissolution proceeded in a timely manner.

Venue Restoration

The major preplanning effort for venue restoration was to identify, coordinate, and schedule the dissolution activities at all venues. This task was accomplished through coordination between Logistics, Planning and Integration, Transportation, and Venue Management. Much effort was expended to restore the venues to their original condition.

During the dissolution phase, repairs to damaged property at venues were negotiated by ACOG and Venue Management. The dissolution of construction contracts at all facilities built by ACOG's Construction Department required supervision from the designer and contractor as construction was finished and warranties relinquished to the owner.

Liquidation of Assets

In 1994, Financial Services issued a series of asset management policies. Among the policies issued was a liquidation policy that defined how the assets in ACOG's possession following the Games would be liquidated.

The primary objective of the liquidation program was to obtain the maximum amount of revenue from the sale of residual assets in less than six months after the Games. During the first quarter of 1996, P&CA personnel began to contact qualified material buyers to assess their interest in procuring ACOG assets at the completion of the Games. Parties that expressed an interest included salvage dealers, vendors, equipment brokers, liquidators, auctioneers, nonprofit and charitable organizations, and ACOG employees.

In May 1996, a formal RFP for a contractor was prepared and issued to approximately 46 parties identified during the initial search for potential material buyers. Responses to the RFP were received in early June and evaluated.

ACOG selected the proposal from a Georgia-based company that had been in the auction and liquidation business for 33 years.

After the selection, the challenge was to negotiate an acceptable contract. The contract was established on the principle of revenue sharing, therefore providing an incentive for the company to maximize the revenue from every auction.

The contract identified specific categories of items to be auctioned, including automobiles; boats; high-end furniture; miscellaneous equipment, furniture, and supplies; motorcycles and mopeds; racking; sports equipment; and stadium seats.

The agreement also allowed ACOG to add or delete items to the contract. A marketing budget, to be reimbursed by sales proceeds, was approved by both parties.

Public auctions and sales were held from August 1996 to January 1997 and were enormously successful because:

■ a fair and equitable contract was created and mutually agreed upon by ACOG and the vendor;

■ the vendor was responsible for removing any unsold or abandoned assets, and buyers were responsible for costs associated with removing purchased assets, thereby significantly reducing moving expenses; and

■ the general public supported all auctions and sales because the Olympic Games represented a positive experience in their lives.

Another significant aspect of the liquidation program was asset sales conducted by Material Sales (P&CA personnel). Material Sales, which generated most nonauction revenue, negotiated asset sales with the city of Atlanta, colleges and universities, liquidators and/or dealers, other sporting event organizations,

Public auctions and sales of Olympic assets generated nearly 175 percent more revenue than originally anticipated.

LINDA J CANTWELL • MICHAEL T CANTWELL • RAYMOND J CANTWELL • RYAN V CANTWELL • SHARON K CANTWELL • LILLIE M CANTY • PRECIOUS R CANTY • HOWARD A CANUP • JOANN M CANZONE • ZHIRUO CAO • KENNETH R CAOUETTE • ERWIN A CAPALONGAN • ANTONIO B CAPAROSO • PENNY L CAPAWANA • SHARON C CAPERS RN • BARBARA L CAPES • REBECCA E CAPES • LYNN CAPEZZERA • JUDITH G CAPIE • CHERYL A CAPITO HARRIS • LEE S CAPLAN • JAMIE J CAPONIGRO • KATHRYN A CAPORICCI • JACLYN CAPOUANO • ANGELO CAPOZZOLI • BRUCE A CAPPA • JANE M CAPPAERT

219

sponsors (when appropriate), vendors, and venue owners.

Retail sales for employees and the general public also generated substantial revenue. Employee sales were conducted for the sale of televisions and special furniture, and retail sales for the general public were conducted through an ACOG store in the Inforum, retail sales tables in the lobbies of most scheduled auctions, and a heavily advertised merchandise sale at the uniform distribution center held 12–14 December 1996. The results of the three-

FIGURE 4:
STATE TAX REVENUE IMPACT (IN MILLIONS)

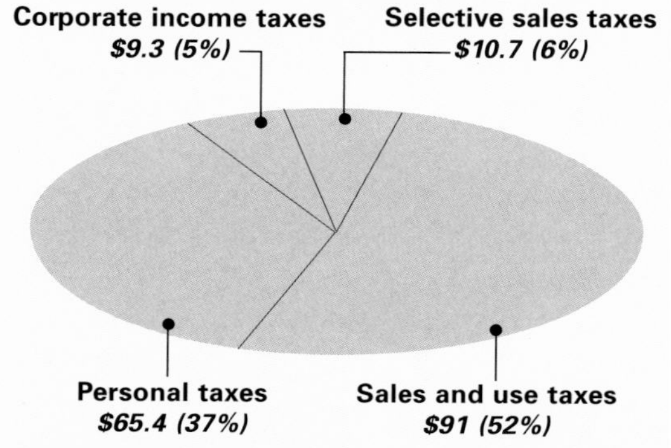

Corporate income taxes
$9.3 (5%)

Selective sales taxes
$10.7 (6%)

Personal taxes
$65.4 (37%)

Sales and use taxes
$91 (52%)

day sale exceeded expectations.

In summary, 58 percent of liquidation program revenue was generated from asset sales by Material Sales. The remaining 42 percent of revenue was provided by the public auctions that allowed ACOG to liquidate large volumes of goods in a professional and orderly manner. Overall, the liquidation revenue generated was 175 percent better than planned and ensured ACOG would dissolve financially successful.

Contract Resolution

Each contract between ACOG and vendors was reviewed when returning borrowed equipment and paying for lost or damaged items.

Settlement with sponsors for VIK usage and cash was more challenging because of the valuation determination, but was completed by the dissolution date, including the return of VIK equipment to the appropriate parties.

As immediate post-Games asset retrieval rapidly proceeded, it became evident that effort was required to identify and sort the ACOG-owned, sponsor-owned, and leased items. However, most items were properly returned with few managers requiring active accountability for property under their control during Games-time.

STATE OF GEORGIA ECONOMIC IMPACT

Studies were conducted in 1990, 1992, and 1995 to estimate quantitatively the economic impact that hosting the Games would have on the state of Georgia throughout the 1991–1997 period. The first study was completed at the time the Atlanta Bid was submitted. The 1992 study incorporated ACOG's first detailed budget and visitation estimates based on the preliminary event schedule. It also included pre- and post-Games visitation spending, which accounted for more than one-third of total projected visitation spending. The 1995 update incorporated the most current financial forecast and, for the first time, identified long-term impacts from hosting the Games.

Based on the 1995 study, the total economic benefit of hosting the Centennial Olympic Games on Georgia's economy was projected to be $5.1 billion from 1991 to 1997. Such an economic impact resulted from ACOG spending as well as visitor spending. ACOG spending generated approximately $2.6 billion of economic activity, while out-of-state visitor spending produced an additional $2.5 billion.

The initial injection of new dollars occurred primarily in and around Atlanta, Athens, and Savannah and to a lesser extent in the Columbus and Gainesville areas; however, the re-spending of these dollars or the induced economic impact affected even the smallest Georgia communities. This economic phenomenon, known as the multiplier effect, acknowledged that new dollars in the economy were subsequently spent within Georgia.

The greatest economic impact, measured by expenditures and new jobs, was experienced by those businesses involved in hospitality, business services, retail trade, construction, health services, transportation, wholesale trade, and personnel services. Approximately 77,000 full- and part-time jobs were created—close to 38 percent in the hospitality industry.

The 1996 Games generated an estimated $176 million in additional tax revenue for state government, primarily through general sales and use taxes, personal income taxes, selective sales taxes, and corporate income and license taxes. *(See Figure 4.)*

In measuring the economic impact the 1996 Games had on Georgia, the potential loss of visitor dollars from conventions and altered vacation plans was considered. Although this displacement was expected to be significant during the Games, it was measured throughout 1991–1997.

Many conventions scheduled during the Games, particularly small state and regional meetings, were simply rescheduled for another time. Likewise, dollars lost from residents choosing to vacation outside Georgia during the Games were anticipated to be within normal levels of out-of-state vacation spending. Usually, only the timing of the vacation was altered. In cases where Georgians chose to spend their vacations in the state to attend the Games,

the effect was essentially positive. Considering the combination of both positive and negative effects, displacement impact was expected to be neutral.

Conclusions and Recommendations

The challenge of the Financial Services Department was to manage the financial policies and procedures for a company with an extremely dynamic growth pattern which operated in a cash flow environment where expenses exceeded revenues until Games-time. Enforcement of these policies ensured that a positive balanced budget and positive financial legacy were met after the Games. *(For ACOG's financial statement as of April 1997, see Figure 5.)*

The following recommendations are offered to future Olympic organizing committees.

■ There should be an early acceptance of and commitment to a centralized approach to planning and integration.

■ A definitive strategic plan should be developed which prioritizes services to constituencies to guide allocation of limited resources.

■ Fair, uniform practices regarding the pricing, budgeting, utilization, and management of VIK among the IOC, NOCs, and OCOG should be established.

■ A thorough understanding of the financial implications of VIK valuation, utilization, and accounting should be ensured throughout the organization. The VIK process should adhere to firmly established priorities set by senior management.

■ One department should be designated to manage the rate card program to establish equity in prices and information, clear communications, and efficient management.

■ The objectives of the dissolution and liquidation process should be clearly defined, and the organization should ensure that appropriate staff remain available to fulfill these functions.

FIGURE 5: ACOG FINANCIAL STATEMENT AS OF APRIL 1997 (THOUSANDS OF DOLLARS)

Revenue

Revenue source	1993 Forecast	1994 Forecast	1996 Forecast	1996 Amended	Actual
Broadcast rights	$554,070	$555,500	$559,480	$559,480	$568,290
Joint venture	$537,390	$513,390	$462,460	$462,460	$426,448
TOP III	$119,090	$114,380	$77,600	$77,600	$81,180
Ticket sales	$225,790	$261,230	$422,090	$422,090	$425,140
Merchandising	$30,410	$28,700	$32,000	$32,000	$31,910
Other revenue	$122,260	$107,470	$151,670	$182,430	$188,050
Total	**$1,589,010**	**$1,580,670**	**$1,705,300**	**$1,736,060**	**$1,721,018**

Expense

Program	1993 Forecast	1994 Forecast	1996 Forecast	1996 Amended	Actual
Executive Management	$13,208	$16,087	$22,071	$24,765	$24,898
Associated Organizations	$9,011	$8,087	$7,818	$7,714	$7,655
Corporate Services	$42,003	$44,778	$68,102	$66,892	$65,879
Olympic Programs and Physical Legacy	$66,264	$52,481	$70,267	$67,851	$67,471
Communications and Government Relations	$22,829	$21,419	$26,365	$25,531	$25,553
Olympic Ceremonies	$21,663	$24,180	$31,215	$30,096	$26,647
Senior Policy Advisor	$5,910	$10,015	$9,391	$9,558	$9,487
Operations Management	$2,733	$3,550	$2,984	$2,982	$2,942
Logistics	$17,221	$24,374	$22,989	$41,753	$41,104
Transportation	$44,331	$40,482	$80,009	$88,320	$91,545
Medical Services	$3,768	$9,922	$7,018	$3,079	$3,365
Accreditation	$3,475	$2,660	$4,977	$2,975	$2,438
Security	$40,288	$51,359	$40,316	$34,089	$32,743
Technology	$187,843	$229,083	$223,483	$225,796	$218,983
Venue Management	$3,677	$6,036	$23,532	$38,419	$37,396
Games Services Management	$1,236	$1,144	$1,463	$1,890	$2,053
Games Services Marketing			$12,836	$13,500	$14,662
Accommodations	$1,925	$3,799	$15,429	$20,957	$22,136
Ticket Sales	$13,042	$15,412	$36,451	$34,210	$35,309
Spectator Services	$480	$1,131	$762	$780	$921
Food and Beverage Services	$4,666	$8,185	$14,375	$16,472	$21,686
Merchandising	$18,307	$16,647	$18,049	$17,825	$17,933
Host Broadcast	$95,120	$106,329	$115,503	$136,779	$141,343
International Relations	$3,684	$3,681	$3,749	$3,300	$3,355
Olympic Village	$121,290	$116,763	$111,174	$108,051	$109,784
Olympic Family Relations	$10,037	$10,979	$10,673	$9,639	$9,112
Sports	$73,255	$63,202	$59,024	$47,733	$48,460
Administration and Human Resources	$46,268	$38,118	$44,215	$43,767	$39,835
Construction	$491,119	$469,628	$465,227	$514,440	$494,239
Financial and Management Services	$76,694	$79,067	$69,938	$71,246	$69,958
Nondepartmental Reserves	$47,663	$42,072	$55,895	($4,349)	($6,543)
Reserves for Contingencies	$100,000	$60,000	$30,000	$30,000	$19,476
Reserves for Operations and Construction					$19,193
Total expenses	**$1,589,010**	**$1,580,670**	**$1,705,300**	**$1,736,060**	**$1,721,018**

Chapter Thirteen
Games Services

OVERVIEW—The Games Services Department was established to plan, procure, and contract the services necessary to promote a positive Olympic experience for all spectators and visitors of the Olympic Games. Those services included Accommodations and Ticket Sales, which are described in separate chapters of this report, and Food and Beverage and Merchandising, described in this chapter.

Although the services produced by Games Services were contracted to vendors, extensive efforts were made to coordinate their activities through a centralized operation to ensure efficiency and consistency among the departments that comprised Games Services.

Food and Beverage and Merchandising contracted with many different vendors and managed their level of service, ensuring successful delivery of products and services and maximizing revenues.

FOOD AND BEVERAGE

The goal of the Food and Beverage Department was to provide high-quality, affordable food and beverage service for all guests and staff of the Games to help encourage a positive Olympic experience. The department compiled the needs of both staff and spectators, contracted services at competition and noncompetition venues, and ensured consistent delivery.

The success of this mission depended on strict adherence to high standards of quality and fairness. At Games-time, food and beverage service was provided for over 2 million spectators and more than 100,000 athletes, dignitaries, media, and staff at 31 competition venues, 297 noncompetition sites, 3 sponsor villages, and all medical stations.

ORGANIZATION

In September 1993, Food and Beverage began operating as a separate division of Games Services. The first objective was to determine the food and beverage needs of the Olympic Family. Once determined, the division planned for budget development, catering, concessions, space requirements, sponsor product procurement, and support and delivery services in order to fulfill those needs.

Additional early planning focused on space requirements within the Construction Department's planning of new facilities and contract issues within all existing venue lease agreements to ensure that the rules for the service of potential product and IOC clean venue requirements would be honored. All negotiations with potential and confirmed Games sponsors in the food service category were handled by ACOP. (*For more information, see the Marketing/ACOP chapter.*)

In March 1995, as Venue Management began to confirm venue plans and other departments began to confirm schedules and staff numbers, it was determined that additional Food and Beverage staff and resources would be necessary. Requirements for contracting a master caterer to fulfill specialized non–point of sale food service and delivery and a master concessionaire for retail point of sale at all venues were identified, and negotiations began. Also, premium hospitality food and beverage service packages were planned and developed.

In March 1996, the department was organized according to the needs of constituents and assumed responsibility for coordinating and contracting with food service contractors, concessionaires, master caterers, and certain Olympic sponsors and suppliers. This responsibility included the development of and adherence to ACOG policies and procedures; staff training; coordination of final venue construction; operation of permanent and temporary facilities at venues; delivery of all products to facilities with adherence to logistics, quality control, and sanitation policies as established by public health officials; coordination with the Olympic Family and Protocol Department on the catering needs of the Olympic Family; finalization and delivery of meals and beverages to Games staff; and financial controls over Food and Beverage's budget and value-in-kind (VIK) distribution.

Communication with Games sponsors, suppliers, and contractors and coordination for successful food service delivery were of utmost importance throughout Food and Beverage's development, analysis of requirements, and delivery of services. Contracts were structured so that operators accepted operational and financial responsibility for their deliveries in return for retail spectator concession rights, which contributed greatly to the delivery program's success.

The challenges in existing contracts between food service vendors and venues, and contracts with Games sponsors and suppliers, mainly involved establishing achievable goals and the scope of service required. The most

problematic aspect of early planning was the exclusivity requirements of certain contracts with suppliers not capable of delivering the necessary volume of products and services. Using a number of vendors and suppliers was elemental to the program's success. (*For services and products provided by Olympic sponsors and suppliers, see Figure 1. For services and products provided by contractors, see Figure 2 on the next page.*)

FOOD SERVICE OPERATIONS

Efforts to provide food and beverage service to the Olympic Family, sponsor guests, and Games staff were planned separately.

These requirements were served at the venues by food and beverage compounds. The size and complexity of these compounds varied based on venue-specific production requirements. Trailer compounds were the minimum standard at each venue, including diesel or electric refrigeration and freezer trailers for water, ice, and perishables, as well as dry-storage trailers for nonperishable grocery items, paper and cleaning supplies, and equipment. Sponsors provided trailers for their VIK and donated products, which included soft drinks, bread, snacks, and beer, where permitted. Additionally, Food and Beverage and its contractors obtained additional refrigeration and dry-storage trailers under the provisions of a master distributor agreement.

A food and beverage manager at each venue managed ACOG staff and Olympic Family obligations at the venue and directed the concessionaire's retail activities. These managers developed time lines covering the first day of venue occupation through venue disassembly.

The Olympic Family

An appropriate level of service was provided at the venues for various constituents of the Olympic Family, including athletes, coaches,

**FIGURE 1:
SERVICES AND
PRODUCTS PROVIDED
BY OLYMPIC SPONSORS
AND SUPPLIERS**

The Coca-Cola Company
Soft drinks, juice,
sport drinks

Crystal Springs
Bottled water

Sara Lee Meat Group
Meat products

Anheuser-Busch
Beer

Fetzer / Korbel
Wine and champagne

Good Humor / Breyers
Ice cream products

McDonald's
Restaurant products

James River Corporation
Paper products

Campbell Taggart
Bread products,
confectionery, snacks

Brown Foreman
Distilled spirits

Douwe Egbert
Coffee

• JOANNE K CARLTON • JULIA E CARLTON • RICHARD K CARLTON • WILLIAM S CARLTON • THOMAS E CARLTON JR. • SUSAN M CARLUCCI • VICTOR F CARLUCCI • BRADFORD L CARMACK • CHRIS J CARMACK • DIANA CARMAN • DOUGLAS G CARMAN • JANE S CARMAN • PAGAN I CARMAN • DELENA Y CARMICHAEL • DONNA M CARMICHAEL • EVELYN L CARMICHAEL • JACENTA D CARMICHAEL • JAMES R CARMICHAEL • MELISSA CARMICHAEL • MELVIN E CARMICHAEL • MYRA M CARMICHAEL • VICKI S CARMICHAEL • WILLIAM P CARMICHAEL JR • DANIEL J CARMODY • PATRICK E CARMODY   **225**

FIGURE 2:
SERVICES AND PRODUCTS PROVIDED BY CONTRACTORS

	Location or Constituency
McDonald's Concessionaire	Olympic Stadium plaza, Stone Mountain Park, Atlanta Beach, Georgia Tech Aquatic Center, Georgia Tech Alexander Memorial Coliseum, Olympic Village
ARAMARK Concessionaire	Olympic Village, Olympic Stadium, Atlanta–Fulton County Stadium, Georgia Tech Aquatic Center, Georgia State University, Clark Atlanta University, Morris Brown College, Morehouse College
Sportservice Master caterer / concessionaire	Centennial Olympic Park, sponsor hospitality villages
The Lundergan Group Concessionaire / caterer	Lake Lanier, Georgia International Horse Park, Atlanta Beach, Stone Mountain Park, Wolf Creek Shooting Complex
Stone Mountain Catering Caterer	Stone Mountain Park Tennis Center
MGR Food Services Concessionaire	Georgia Dome, Georgia World Congress Center
Omni Food Services Concessionaire	Omni Coliseum
Spanky's Concessionaire	Savannah
Global Food Services Concessionaire	University of Georgia—Sanford Stadium and Stegeman Coliseum
University of Georgia Food Services University food service department	University of Georgia
Antioch Baptist Church Boxed meal production site	Staff and volunteer meals— noncompetition venues
Concessions / Paschal Concessionaire / boxed meal production site	Airport concessions, Airport Welcome Center, IOC/NOC concourse hospitality, staff and volunteer meals
Harry's Caterer / boxed meal production site	Staff and volunteer meals / Olympic Family meals
Cub Foods, Inc. Boxed meal production site	Staff and volunteer meals—warehouse sites
Valley Food Service Boxed meal production site	Staff and volunteer meals / Olympic Family meals
Marriott Management Services Caterer / boxed meal production site	Main Press Center, ACOG headquarters, noncompetition venues
Sysco Foods Food distribution	Master food distributor
Mid-South Ice Ice production	Ice distributor

and officials; the IOC and NOCs; press, media, and rights-holding broadcasters; and sponsors.

Athletes, Coaches, and Officials. Food and Beverage's objective was to offer athletes, coaches, and officials nutritious food and beverages that would be conducive to sports competition. The Olympic Villages Department was responsible for providing food service to those constituents housed in the main and satellite Villages, including athlete food service at the Village and boxed lunch service at remote sites. Food and Beverage and Olympic Village food service shared resources and worked with ACOP to make joint presentations to established and potential sponsors and suppliers to refine food service requirements.

To supplement the Olympic Village food service program, Food and Beverage assisted in serving hot meals to athletes, coaches, and officials at some remote venues. The Lake Lanier, Georgia International Horse Park, and Stone Mountain Park Tennis Center venues requested hot meal service due to their distance from the Village and the amount of time constituents would spend at the sites. Meals provided were comparable to those offered on Village menus, consisting of a high-starch, low-fat menu, with at least one vegetarian option at each meal. Local caterers or existing concessionaires were contracted to provide these services. When possible, requirements and menus were reviewed with Village food service staff to comply with specific IF's needs.

Food and Beverage provided a selection of fruit and snacks at the athlete lounges and fields of play. Athletes were also given unlimited, continuous beverage service in locker rooms, warm-up areas, and lounges, consisting of bottled water, soft drinks, and sport drinks. Continuous beverage service was also provided on the field of play during competition and, in some cases, fruit and coffee were provided as well. IFs determined the appropriate level of service for each venue.

Olympic Family Lounges. Food and Beverage was committed to offering exceptional southern-style food and a variety of beverages in the Olympic Family lounges at each competition venue.

Anticipating the number of guests at a given time at a venue was the responsibility of the Protocol Department, which managed the lounges. The amount of service required was forecast using the total number of Olympic Family seats available at each venue and adding a factor for the popularity of each session; this forecast was then used for menu planning and ordering.

Obtaining accurate estimates of the number of people, and therefore the quantity of food required, is central to the success of Olympic Family lounge food service in terms of availability and quality of food delivered. Menu decisions reflected constituencies' expectations as well as the capacity and capability of the service providers.

Food and Beverage utilized existing food service at a venue, the contracted concessionaire, or a subcontracted local caterer. The department provided all necessary food service equipment and decoration. Continuous service at buffet tables was provided through the contractor from one hour before competition began to one-half hour after competition ended. Three venues housed 40 percent of competition events and required 50 percent of the service provided. At Games-time, venue managers employed a flexible strategy with their service provider to modify the quantity of food and vary the menu.

Menus were planned according to the time of day and included hot and cold foods that emphasized the variety of southern cuisine.

Press, Media, and Rights-Holding Broadcasters. The department aimed to provide food and beverage service to press, media, and rights-holding broadcasters in a manner appropriate to their busy work environment both at the centrally located International Broadcast Center (IBC) and Main Press Center (MPC), and at the competition venues.

Press, media, and rights holders contracted for their own catering at the IBC and MPC in coordination with Food and Beverage. The internal agreements for these two facilities used existing contractors, which facilitated the sharing of resources, including purchased and VIK product distribution.

Media and rights-holding broadcasters were provided bulk food and beverage deliveries at the compound areas upon request, which were then distributed according to work areas. Delivery of food and beverages to the competition venues involved bulk delivery of provisions, as well as delivery of beverages in ice chests.

In the press lounges, snacks, soft drinks, sports drinks, coffee, tea, and bottled water were available. Soft drinks and sports drinks were available with unlimited-use Coca-Cola access cards (Coke cards), while bottled water in 5 gal water coolers, coffee, and tea were provided on tables. Beverage service was also provided to camera and commentator positions. Food and Beverage provided continuous service to the press lounges, ensuring that products were available and service areas were kept clean.

Press, media, and rights-holding broadcasters were also given priority lines at existing concession areas. The Georgia Tech Aquatic Center designed a concession area specifically for the press.

Sponsor Hospitality. The goal of the Sponsor Hospitality Program was to provide a relaxing place for sponsors to entertain guests with premium food and beverage service within walking distance to the three major venue clusters. Sponsor hospitality villages were established near Centennial Olympic Park, which served the park and center cluster venues;

BETTY LOU CARPENTER • CLARA E CARPENTER • DANIEL W CARPENTER • DAVID JOSHUA CARPENTER • DAVID L CARPENTER • EDWARD M CARPENTER • ELIZABETH E CARPENTER • ELLEN KAY CARPENTER • GAIL D CARPENTER • GARY L CARPENTER • GRACE A CARPENTER • JANICE M CARPENTER • JEAN Z CARPENTER • JERRI L CARPENTER • MAE-RONNIE CARPENTER • MARC CARPENTER • MARK A CARPENTER • MICHELLE L CARPENTER • PATRICIA N CARPENTER • ROBERT CARPENTER • ROBERT CARPENTER • SANDRA K CARPENTER • VICTOR W CARPENTER •

227

Stone Mountain Park, which served the outlying venues; and Olympic Stadium. The program was a collaborative effort between sponsors, ACOP, Food and Beverage, and the master caterer.

Construction of the sponsor hospitality villages was managed by ACOP. Food and Beverage coordinated with ACOP to provide all sponsor hospitality food and beverage service and contracted the master caterer to deliver the services. The master caterer divided services into operationally and logistically viable

Food and Beverage coordinated with ACOP to provide premium food and beverage service to all sponsor hospitality villages.

areas of responsibility, which it then subcontracted to other caterers for execution. Food and Beverage also served as the liaison and resource administrator between sponsors, the master caterer, selected subcontractors, and ACOP. Prior to the Games, customized menus were sold to each sponsor. Final menus at one sponsor hospitality village included more than 270 items.

Premium Hospitality. Early in 1994, Food and Beverage and Games Services management staff researched an additional hospitality program separate from sponsor hospitality. The program was designed to serve corporate groups that otherwise might not have access to the sponsor/supplier programs.

After reviewing sporting events with significant, successful corporate hospitality programs, plans were produced for premium hospitality programs at six venues. Due to space planning and potential performance issues, the initial plan was reduced to include only the program at the Georgia International Horse Park. The same concessionaire/caterer which provided most services for the equestrian venue also operated the international supporter's pavilion, where parties were produced for several equestrian federations (including the US equestrian team and British Equestrian Federation), as well as for athlete and NOC groups. In addition to providing for premium hospitality, this catering contract also included all Food and Beverage venue operations, including the Olympic Family lounges, grooms' meals, spectator concessions, and food service for staff, volunteers, and contractors.

Food Service for Games Staff

ACOG's goal was to support high morale of staff and volunteers by providing free, well-balanced, and nutritious meals utilizing sponsor products as much as possible. Contractors were also invited to purchase these services for their personnel. Food service for staff needed to be cost-effective, and the food had to be high quality and appetizing, plentiful enough to meet staff needs, and easy to serve and consume.

Initial Planning. The most important factor in staff meal planning was obtaining an accurate estimate of the number of meals needed. Venue staff counts were derived from the Games staffing technology system database and additional calculations were provided from each of the functional areas and venue management teams. To convert these figures into accurate estimates, the number of meals staff members would receive was based on the length of their shifts. One meal was provided to staff working 6–10 hours, two meals to staff working 10.5–15 hours, and three meals to those working 15.5 hours or more in a 24-hour period. Food and Beverage also determined that meal service needed to begin two and one-half weeks prior to the Opening Ceremony.

As providing staff meals was ACOG's expense, controlling the cost of meal production and distribution was another important concern.

Meal Service. Depending on the venue location and other factors, ACOG provided Games staff with boxed meals, daily food allowances and concession coupons redeemable at local concessionaires/retail units, hot buffets, or food ordered from local retailers. Sponsored beverages, including soft drinks and water, were available with all meals; coffee and tea were provided with breakfast at most venues equipped with electrical outlets.

Hot buffets were provided by contractors for some noncompetition venues including ACOG headquarters, the main accreditation center, the uniform distribution center, and the Airport Welcome Center, due to the length of their food service operations period. Some outlying and competition venues occasionally ordered pizza and sandwiches from local retailers.

The boxed meal was the most prevalent type of meal provided to Games staff, and the only type ACOG was fully responsible for assembling and distributing.

Breakfast, lunch, and dinner boxed meals were offered. A typical breakfast contained cereal, an egg, fruit, granola, milk, a pastry, and yogurt. Typical lunch and dinner meals contained a sandwich, chips, fruit, dessert, and a salad. A seven-day rotating menu was established for variety. Each boxed meal included a condiment and utensil kit. Additional snacks were also offered.

ACOG initially secured production of 1.2 million boxed meals for the period of 1 July–5 August, but functional area revisions to pop-

ulation counts caused this estimate to be revised frequently.

Several production facilities were contracted to assemble and transport boxed meals to the majority of venues, while existing food service concessionaires were contracted for remaining venues. Preliminary quantities were given to the sponsors and suppliers, master distributor, and production sites as early as 90 days prior to the Games in order to ensure production capabilities.

During Games-time, meal count revisions conducted at venues by food and beverage managers, who communicated to the Food and Beverage command center, which then contacted the appropriate producer. According to policy, 36 hours notice was required to change a meal order, but in most instances, less than 24 hours notice was given. This caused some difficulty, as production facilities attempted to control overproduction and minimize waste.

Meals were typically delivered to venues between 2400 and 0600 and stored in refrigerated trucks until meal service times.

Independent contractors could purchase boxed meals through the Catered Meal Program, which operated at both competition and noncompetition venues. Contractors submitted advance requests for the number of meals per venue, and were billed for that amount.

At most venues, the concessionaire transported meals from refrigerated storage to a staff lounge, where volunteers distributed meals at specified times. Meal delivery times were coordinated with Venue Management and Volunteer Services based on the competition schedules. At other venues, notably those at the Georgia World Congress Center, Food and Beverage volunteers were responsible for transporting meals from the two internal production facilities to one centralized distribution point.

Daily meal tickets redeemable at the point of consumption were issued to personnel when they registered at their facility. The points of consumption were staff and volunteer lounges that varied in size from tents seating 100 to converted gymnasiums seating 500.

Meal waste decreased as production facility and staff communications improved. Nonperishable prepackaged foods not consumed during a meal period were placed on buffet tables as snacks. Every day, perishable foods were given to a local food bank. Box containers were recycled in accordance with ACOG's recycling program.

Beverage Service

Unlimited, continuous beverage service was a priority, as many people would be working and competing outdoors or in a non–air-conditioned environment. Collaboration between some functional areas and The Coca-Cola Company, Crystal Springs Water Company, and Mid-South Ice was necessary to ensure adequate hydration and support staff. The operation plans at the venues included providing sufficient mobile refrigeration and freezer storage units.

Preliminary planning for beverage service was accomplished at the time staff meal requirements were calculated, as both efforts required similar information and criteria. The final plan for beverage allocation at the venues was to provide unlimited access to filtered tap water that staff could carry in 32 oz (950 ml) standard water bottles, ice, and soft drinks accessible through machines using a Coke card. Additionally, staff at noncompetition venues received bottled water in .5 l containers.

Athletes were offered unlimited beverages, ice, and fruit. It was estimated that competing athletes would consume four beverages, two pieces of fruit, and 2 lb (.9 kg) of ice per day of competition.

Food and Beverage managers defined initial estimates for ice and water and restocking quantities, and equipment requirements at

competition venues to develop the spectator water and ice plan.

The Coca-Cola Company provided vending machines for 12 oz (355 ml) cans and 20 oz (591 ml) sport bottles where space and electrical power allowed, and coolers and ice chests where appropriate. The Coca-Cola Company provided its own staff for product movement and distribution. Staff, volunteers, athletes, and coaches were given either unlimited- or single-use Coke cards for vending machines located at the venues.

Crystal Springs provided competition venues with refrigerated trailers stocked with .5 l bottles of water for athletes, media, press, rights-holding broadcasters, and security. Bottled water was maintained in ice coolers for distribution. Both electrical and gravity-fed dispensers, water bottles that fit into the belts of uniforms, and paper cups were provided for all other constituents, including staff, volunteers, and Olympic Family members. Remote sites, such as the equestrian venue, security outposts, and most noncompetition venues, used the .5 l bottles. Noncompetition sites with permanent facilities were also provided (primarily the Cultural Olympiad and some training sites) with dispensers where electrical power outlets were available. Either the concessionaire/ caterer or Food and Beverage volunteers provided labor to move water within a venue.

Deliveries were made to venues inside the Olympic Ring between 2400 and 0600. Delivery times at outlying venues were coordinated around competition times and peak traffic hours. Noncompetition venue deliveries were made according to preplanned restocking schedules.

Ice consumption estimates were based on the ice used at the test events in summer 1995. Since summer 1996 was not as hot or humid

top: Unlimited beverage service in locker rooms, warm-up sites, and lounges was available to athletes at all times.

bottom: Providing continuous, complimentary cold water and ice to staff and spectators was a top priority for ACOG.

as summer 1995, the amount of ice consumed at many venues was less than anticipated.

Since staff and volunteers at competition sites were accustomed to obtaining water in the .5 l bottles, when the 32 oz sport bottles became available, they had difficulty changing to refillable bottles and continued to request prebottled water. Consequently, consumption of water from .5 l bottles was higher than had been projected. *(For the total amount of water and ice consumed, see Figure 3.)*

SPECTATOR CONCESSIONS

Providing quality food to spectators was among Food and Beverage's primary concerns. Since the largest number of spectators in Olympic history were expected, the department wanted to ensure service that was fast, convenient, and unobtrusive to competition. By utilizing sponsor products and services and concessionaires at existing venues, and contracting outside concessionaires for temporary venues, Food and Beverage provided a pleasant, sanitary environment and an interesting variety of products at affordable prices.

Planning

The department's initial planning group developed preliminary plans and need forecasts by analyzing competition schedules, estimating per capita spending by guest per session, and considering actual per capita spending from the Los Angeles Games. A venue-specific food concession forecast also was developed from this information.

From the outset, it was planned that contractors would operate spectator food and beverage service. Food and Beverage focused on producing optimal concession contracts based on working sessions with candidate companies, site visits and interviews with non–Games sporting and special event venue owners/operators, and collaborative forecasting. The McDon-

ald's sponsor contract, signed in 1993, gave the company the right of first refusal for all food and beverage operational responsibilities.

In early 1994, Food and Beverage began to produce contractual requirements for competition venues. As venue planning progressed, criteria were established for developing venue-specific menus, including sports-specific demographics, length of session, proximity of venue to available spectator dining options and parking, and logistical, security, and access and exit considerations. The process of identifying, interviewing, and contingency planning also began during this period.

Following the research, ARAMARK was chosen as both a supplier and the contractor that would eventually become the second master concessionaire. ARAMARK also provided the majority of Olympic Village food service and management. Some additional planning allowed for the limited participation of other contractors prior to the conclusion of the planning process, creating a need to reconfigure venue operations as related to requirements of utilities and equipment.

Product and service levels were established based on typical stadia concession fast food menus, with the addition of some specialty items.

Concessionaires attempted to accommodate the more than 2 million spectators at the Games. The actual ratio of point of sale to spectators varied from 1:200 to 1:450, depending on the venue capabilities, the length of the session, and the sport. Concessionaires utilized cart sales in concourses and plazas, beverage-only points of sale, and sales to seated spectators where appropriate and permitted by the individual sports federation.

A special tent was designed at the Aquatic Center to ensure that concession lines would not interfere with spectator entrance and exit. ARAMARK designed the tent so customers

FIGURE 3:
TOTAL AMOUNT OF ICE AND WATER CONSUMED

Water
- cases of 24 0.5 l bottles 201,137
- 5 gal units 55,673

Ice
- 93,852 40 lb (18 kg) bags totaling 3,754,080 lb (1,702,850 kg)

KIMBERLY B CARSON • LINDA M CARSON • MARIE CARSON • NANCY CARSON • RALPH E CARSON • SARAH A CARSON • VANESSA CARSON • WENDY E CARSON • CHARLIE A CARSON JR • DAVID B CARSTENSON • REBECCA CARSTENSON • JOHN H CARSWELL • TIMOTHY G CARSWELL • WINNIE D CARSWELL • STEPHANIE CARTEE CROWE • ADRIAN G CARTER • ADRIENE M CARTER • ALLISON L CARTER • ALLISON R CARTER • ANGELIA L CARTER • ANN H CARTER • BELINDA C CARTER • BETTY M CARTER • BRANDIE C CARTER • BRYAN G CARTER • CANDACE M CARTER •

231

could enter, purchase prepackaged products, and pay as they exited.

Existing concessionaires utilized their own equipment and personnel, with the exception of one facility where Food and Beverage purchased new cooking and kitchen equipment and utensils and assumed responsibility for the assembly, installation, disassembly, transport, storage, and auction of this equipment. A portion of this equipment was provided by the Vulcan Hart/Hobart supplier agreement.

Coordination with Venue Management

Each venue's concessionaire developed a venue-specific organizational and staffing plan in cooperation with the venue Food and Beverage manager, which was configured around the competition schedule and coordinated with Venue Management. Deliveries to venues within the Olympic Ring occurred between 2400 and 0600. For outlying and noncompetition venues, deliveries were scheduled around competition schedules and peak traffic hours.

CONCLUSIONS AND RECOMMENDATIONS

The success of the food and beverage program is dependent on the consistency of service and variety of products provided by contracted suppliers and vendors for all constituencies. Every possible type of food service should be explored and considered in keeping with the policies of the organization for equitable and fair service and quality food and beverages. The following recommendations are provided to future organizing committees.

■ Prior to the finalization of contracts and commitments with sponsors/suppliers, all construction and delivery concerns must be addressed.

■ Involve the local health departments with ultimate jurisdiction over the venues early in the planning and training processes.

■ Contract or sponsor- and supplier-provided VIK labor needs to be contracted early and management resources clarified.

■ Structure the marketing/food service suppliers/distributors category so that a consortium of distributors is encouraged to participate, rather than any one company assuming responsibility, both financially and operationally.

■ Finalize contracts with master concessionaire(s), master caterer(s), and all primary subcontractors with venue assignments specified at least two years before the Games.

■ Contractor documents, including requests for proposals (RFPs) and contracts, should unmistakably define all financial expectations and terminology. RFP responses should be evaluated against established criteria.

■ Staff meals should incorporate boxed meals and alternatives, including hot and cold buffets, and concessions access. Budget realistically for alternatives, including a broad contingency.

■ Variety and creativity are the keys to a successful food service program. Dedicated concession stands, or dedicated lines for staff and volunteers, offer additional alternatives. Daily food allowances are useful if sufficiently budgeted and logistically available. Transport of hot or cold buffet meals is difficult from the standpoint of food safety assurance, and is not recommended.

Quality food and beverage was available to spectators with service that was fast, convenient, and unobtrusive to the sports competition.

MERCHANDISING

The Merchandising Department organized the sale of nonconsumable goods at all ACOG-owned and -operated or contracted locations before, during, and after the Games. The department's main concerns included profit and loss, concessionaire selection, contract negotiations, payment schedules, product selection, site selection, and store design.

Merchandising was part of the Games Services Department because of its service to the public and its revenue potential. ACOG's retail and wholesale operations began shortly after Atlanta was awarded the Games in 1990, and provided significant revenues throughout its existence. Revenue received before Games-time helped sustain ACOG planning operations. Venue sales also proved to be a substantial part of the merchandising program. Of the nearly $63 million in sales generated from 1991 to 1996, $9 million occurred between June and August 1996.

To sell apparel, memorabilia, souvenirs, and other collectibles effectively, the following four core merchandising methods were developed.

- retail sales (stores owned and operated by ACOG)
  - venue sales (concessions)
  - specialty store sales
  - liquidation sales (the Remains of the Games Program)

ORGANIZATION

As ACOG grew, a Merchandising Retail Operations division reported to various departments, first to an ACOG vice president of Special Projects until 1993, then to the ACOP vice president of Licensing until 1994, when it was placed under Games Services.

Merchandising was divided into two divisions: ACOG-owned and -operated retail and wholesale functions (Retail Operations), and merchandise concessions (Venue Sales). These functions were consolidated into the Merchandising Department reporting to the director of merchandising concessions.

All Retail Operations positions were held by full-time ACOG staff, with the exception of retail sales staff, which was 80 percent part-time. Volunteers were occasionally used to supplement the retail sales staff. Typically, an ACOG manager, assistant manager, and sales staff worked at each retail location. The stores reported to an operations manager and assistant operations manager. A merchandise manager (buyer) was responsible for procurement.

ACOG Retail Operations was contractually limited by Sara Lee's corporate sponsorship to operate no more than 20 retail locations to avoid adversely affecting the sponsor's distribution channels for permanent retail outlets. Due to operational and personnel considerations, ACOG limited retail activity to primary metropolitan-Atlanta malls. From 1992 to 1996, ACOG expanded its retail outlet locations from 3 to 16, and retail staff increased from 35 to approximately 225 associates at Games-time.

Staffing for wholesale and other sales consisted of one full-time person and a part-time assistant to solicit, order, and invoice all shipments.

Venue Sales had site-management responsibilities over its concessionaire. This was managed by three regional merchandise coordinators, each reporting to the ACOG merchandising director, who managed a group of

MERCHANDISING EMPLOYEES

Date	Staff Number
December 1992	85
December 1993	110
December 1994	123
December 1995	183
July 1996	227

Note: These staff numbers do not include contract, VIK, and volunteer personnel.

venues and acted as a liaison with other ACOG functional areas. The concessionaire hired the remainder of the staff.

ACOG-OWNED AND -OPERATED RETAIL OUTLETS

ACOG opened retail stores, carts, and kiosks prior to the Games to promote the upcoming athletic competitions and cultural performances, and to give shoppers an early chance to buy Olympic memorabilia, while providing

Merchandise carts from the AOC's first merchandising efforts promoted the Games and provided income for the organizing committee's operations.

the organizing committee with income for its operations.

Retail Operations focused on four functions: the procurement of merchandise to sell in retail outlets, at ACOG offices, to corporations for promotional purposes, and at special events; inventory management and sales analysis; the delivery, storage, and distribution of merchandise; and management of store operations and personnel.

Retail Products

From 1991 through first quarter 1993 (when licensees began to deliver their products), merchandise offered for both retail and wholesale

distribution was produced under a private label, developed by ACOG and supplied by local contracted vendors. This merchandise included items bearing the five *As* Olympic Bid logo, sold at ACOG retail outlets and wholesale by ACOG to selected metro-Atlanta retailers until April 1992.

Merchandise with the Atlanta Games torch mark logo was introduced at ACOG retail stores on 13 February 1992. In April 1992, all Bid logo merchandise was consolidated, moved to ACOG headquarters, and sold to employees. Some Atlanta retailers who had purchased merchandise through ACOG's wholesale program sold residual Bid merchandise throughout summer 1992.

Until official licensees began manufacturing and delivering products consistently from late 1993 to early 1994, there was a shortage of Olympic merchandise in the Atlanta retail marketplace. A 50 percent decrease in ACOG retail sales occurred during this period, which meant that retail space dedicated to Olympic goods was lost. ACOP and its licensees had to regain space in these stores for Olympic licensed products. Even as licensed merchandise was released on the market, Retail Operations continued to supplement licensed products with private-label merchandise in selected categories through second quarter 1995. After that time, Retail Operations used only licensed products.

ACOG worked with licensees to develop exclusive Olympic products. With Hanes, sublicensees and subcontractors were specifically designated to service ACOG retail only. Other major suppliers that produced exclusive products for ACOG retail were Aminco; The Game; Imprinted Products Corporation; Logo 7, Inc.; and Starter Corporation. Suppliers were selected based on pricing, delivery, advertising allowances, and design exclusivity. By late 1995, almost all ACOP licensees responded to the needs and requests from retailers for exclusive products.

Product selection was based on a system where inventory levels were determined by projected sales levels by merchandise category, current inventory, and existing orders. The goals were to maximize sales in response to customer trends, minimize price reductions, and maximize inventory turnovers.

From the outset, ACOG Retail Operations mainly focused on apparel sales (T-shirts, sweatshirts, hats, and outerwear), which increased steadily each year. Other significant product categories were pins and gifts. Pins represented 13 percent of sales by 1996.

Most sales locations included apparel, pins, toys, and Swatch watches. The scope of products offered was limited by the size of sales locations. For example, most cart locations could effectively display only 8–10 T-shirt designs, 4 collared shirts, and 2–3 sweatshirts. Larger stores carried wider assortments.

Contractual Arrangements

As a benefit of ACOG's not-for-profit status, ACOG retail outlets received favorable lease arrangements at shopping malls. The mall stores at Market Square, North Point, and Underground Atlanta provided shorter than normal lease periods to accommodate ACOG's post-Games closing schedule. The financial terms for stores called for 5–10 percent of net sales, payable to the landlord.

Some malls classified carts or kiosks as temporary businesses; therefore, lease periods were monthly, quarterly, or annually. From 1991 through 1994, lease terms for cart or kiosk locations were 5–10 percent of net sales, payable to the landlord. In some instances, common area fees shared by all tenants, such as payments to mall management for electricity, cleaning, and promotions, were waived.

In 1995, as mall management realized the revenue potential of ACOG's retail business, lease terms approached parity with prevailing market rates. Lease payments increased 8–20

percent, with primary malls increasing 15–25 percent in 1996.

Contractually, ACOG outlets operated under the same covenants that govern all malls. Carts and kiosks afforded ACOG the opportunity to test a specific market with nominal capital outlay or a long-term commitment; however, mall management reserved the right to exercise total control over cart placement and visual standards.

The initial capital investment in a cart averaged $5,000–$8,000, although most malls pro-

vided their own carts as part of their temporary leasing business agreements. Kiosk costs ranged from $14,000 to $50,000. The *Olympic Experience*, ACOG's primary retail location at Underground Atlanta, required an investment of more than $250,000. This investment included costs for original construction, two major visual upgrades, and video equipment replacements. Additionally, higher security, maintenance, and repair costs were required.

Site selection was based on mall sales per square foot, geographic location, and demographics. Because ACOG retail stores were not

The *Olympic Experience* was ACOG's primary retail location as well as an exhibit of Olympic memorabilia.

considered to be a destination for most shoppers, highly developed malls with established customer bases and proven marketing strategies were chosen to guarantee consistent traffic. Smaller shopping centers and freestanding stores were deliberately avoided.

Design

Cart and kiosk designs had to be integrated with each mall's overall design theme. Fixtures and visual standards, for example, were part of contractual lease agreements, and additional

The official Olympic mascot, IZZY, proved to be popular with children.

fixtures were solely at the mall's discretion. Given the large sales potential at Lenox Square mall, its management designated remodeling consultants to work closely with ACOG's contracted design team to approve development of 12 x 12 ft (3.7 x 3.7 m) kiosk configurations that accommodated ACOG's high sales volume and satisfied mall design standards. Store locations

had more latitude in both configuration and design flexibility, but they too required approval from mall management.

ACOG preferred to adhere to and promote its Look of the Games graphics; however, a formal design was not formulated early enough, and as a result, 12 different retail looks emerged. Where possible, the cohesive and recognizable ACOG Look supplemented original designs in later years.

Results

Favorable lease agreements, exclusive merchandise, focused assortments, quick inventory turnover, and advantageous pricing contributed to financial results considerably above retail industry norms. Gross retail profits ranged from 20 to 27.5 percent from 1992 to 1996, compared to specialty retail averages of less than 10 percent.

OTHER SALES

Revenue from sales at special events, bulk sales to corporations and other groups, and wholesale sales to non–ACOG retailers provided additional income needed for pre-Games operations.

Several events occurred during the four years prior to the Games which provided ACOG opportunities to promote its Olympic mission through merchandise sales. The most prominent was the Olympic flag arrival celebration and train tour in September 1992. For this event, ACOG purchased a Wells Cargo custom-designed 20 ft (6 m) concession trailer that appeared in nine Georgia cities during a 12-day period. Staffing costs for the five departmental staff members who toured with the operation and managed sales were absorbed in the merchandise overhead. The trailer was used at other special events and eventually sold to the Games' main concessionaire for merchandising at the venues.

Merchandising sold products wholesale to selected metro-Atlanta retailers from August 1991 through June 1994, with most 1994 shipments being plush toys.

ACOG also offered discounts on bulk sales to corporations and groups that used Olympic merchandise for corporate promotional (not for resale) purposes only. Initially, this program was aimed at local businesses and groups, but it expanded nationwide through sponsor affiliations. Licensees with contractual premium rights contributed to ACOG's corporate sales beginning in 1993.

The most notable special sales event was Atlanta's annual Peachtree Road Race, for which ACOG conducted a direct-mail campaign and pre-race sales in conjunction with the Atlanta Track Club.

VENUE SALES

The best opportunity for selling licensed merchandise and enhancing the spectators' Olympic experience was at the competition venues during Games-time. These locations included kiosks, program stands, table areas, tents, and trailers.

In early 1994, the critical issue was whether to contract venue business to a third party or operate the concessions as ACOG operated its retail outlets. ACOG decided to contract with a concessionaire after evaluating factors such as possible additional inventory and its eventual liquidation, experience, staffing issues, and other expenses.

Beginning in 1994 and throughout 1995, planning focused on site acquisition at the venues. Evaluation of crowd projections, traffic flow, and functional area requirements as well

as operating decisions by ACOG's Venue Management Department influenced the ultimate selections.

When additional merchandising sites were developed, the concessionaire had a contractual option to provide service. Among these sites were the lobbies of the hotels in the Olympic Host Hotel Network, the IBC, other noncompetition sites, and park-and-ride lots. All except the last were the responsibility of the concessionaire. Preferring that the public's first opportunity to purchase Olympic memorabilia be offered at one of the venues, ACOG restricted merchandising rights from park-and-ride lots under its control.

Concessionaire Selection

ACOG decided that public bidding by potential operators was a fair method of choosing a concessionaire. An RFP was sent to companies in the ACOG purchasing database that had expressed interest and to concession industry leaders. The RFP included the requirements and scope of the operation as well as the expected financial considerations, number of venues, anticipated attendance, and other information a potential concessionaire would need when deciding whether or not to submit a bid.

One month prior to the deadline for submitting proposals, ACOG hosted a public meeting where questions and comments could be addressed, allowing all potential bidders to receive the same information. After the meeting, the bidders had one month to submit written proposals.

Final vendor selection was based on an analysis of four components of each bid: financial considerations to ACOG, concession experience in Olympic or similar events, the ability to form a working partnership with ACOG management, and minority business participation.

Minority business participation was especially important to ACOG because of its work-

MELISSA A CASEY • MICHAEL L CASEY • MOLLY A CASEY • PAULA A CASEY • PRISCILLA S CASEY • ROBERT B CASEY • ROBERT J CASEY • ANGELA D CASH • BETTYE M CASH • BOB CASH • CINDY L CASH • JENNIFER N CASH • JIM P CASH • JUDY E CASH • LYN CASH • MARY M CASH • NANCY W. CASH • NEAL CASH • PETER J CASH • SALISSA J CASH • SAM CASH • STEPHEN E CASH • WILLIAM R CASH • DELOREAN CASHER • MARGARET E CASHWELL • CHRISPY CASIANO • CRISPINIANO CASIANO • REGIS R CASIER • ROBIN L CASILLO • LINDA L CASLAVKA • RICHARD J CASLER •

237

ing relationship with the local community. *(For more information, see the External Relations chapter.)*

As part of the evaluation, ACOG inspected the largest sites in which finalists currently operated. The director of Merchandising inspected operations at the World Cup, a Rose Bowl concert, and Atlanta Braves baseball games at Atlanta–Fulton County Stadium.

The contract was awarded to Eric Chandler Merchandising Partners (ECMP), a limited liability corporation formed exclusively for merchandising business. ECMP's senior management had extensive experience not only in Olympic concessions, but also Olympic management. ECMP's financial bid represented a substantial potential income and local minority interest in the project. The contract with ACOG required that ECMP pay the organizing committee a guarantee plus a percentage on a sliding scale.

Venue Merchandising Coordination

Merchandising staff coordinated with other ACOG departments in planning for venue sales, including:

■ Accreditation—contractor accreditation and venue day passes;

■ Construction—facility repairs and utility issues;

■ Creative Services—Look of the Games signage;

■ Financial Services—auditing of records;

■ Logistics—delivery schedules and waste removal and recycling;

■ Security—guards at sales locations and the warehouse, cash management, and resolution of counterfeit merchandise issues;

■ Sports—session times, program printing issues, and sales in the stands;

■ Technology—data, telephone, and other communication needs; and

■ Venue Management—attendance figures, communications protocol, parking, and scheduling.

Temporary stands, acquired by ACOG for ECMP's use as part of the contract, maintained the Look of the Games. Signage and visual elements were funded by ECMP, but required ACOG's approval and adherence to any applicable sponsor and operational guidelines.

Where furniture, fixtures, and equipment did not exist already, they were contractually the responsibility of ECMP, as were vehicles and most other equipment (e.g., golf carts). Certain sponsors and licensees, particularly Sara Lee (Champion and Hanes), Eastman Kodak Company, and Bausch & Lomb, had either contractual rights for dedicated stands at venues or exclusive signage. In all cases, the sales of such products were treated by ECMP as normal sales, and unless previously agreed to by ACOG, were incorporated into the normal payment calculations.

Venue Merchandise

The concessionaire was limited to selling only merchandise from ACOG licensees. ACOG provided sales information from its stores (e.g., best-selling designs, popular price points, terms, service, historical sales data on various products) to ECMP as a guide for developing the mix of goods.

The general concept regarding product mix was to focus primarily on T-shirts, hats, and pins, which would comprise 80–90 percent of venue concession sales. Exclusive designs, especially for apparel, represented specific venue events. This approach helped increase sales, minimize product choice risk, and distinguish the concessionaire from other vendors.

Logistics

The key logistical issue was the safe and efficient transport and storage of inventory. ACOG's Logistics Department maintained a central warehouse and provided trucks for transporting goods. Rented from ACOG and staffed by ECMP, the warehouse was centrally located near Olympic Stadium. ACOG retained oversight and access to all warehouse records.

ECMP's shipping procedures to the venues were self-policing within strict scheduling guidelines. ECMP had to sanitize and seal each truck prior to its departure from the warehouse. The seal number was then reported to the venue, and only a truck with an unbroken seal was permitted access to a venue.

Working closely with Logistics, ECMP developed a delivery schedule incorporating dock times as well as vehicle access points. The schedule, along with the geographic layout of the venues, dictated the number of delivery vehicles required.

Unauthorized Sales

Street vending not sponsored by ACOG had the potential to diminish sales at the venues. Under the contractual agreement, ACOG and ECMP collaborated on monitoring and seizing unauthorized merchandise. Judicially approved temporary restraining orders authorized law enforcement agents to seize items that infringed on trademarks. Additionally, ACOP worked closely with US Customs officials to seize any major shipments of unauthorized imported products. These efforts, coupled with the ability of vendors to purchase approved, licensed products, kept counterfeit merchandise to a minimum.

In an unforeseen development, vendors appeared on private property near venues but outside the jurisdiction of the services contract between ACOG and the city of Atlanta. Owners of commercial property, such as parking lots, could lease space to sellers with only a private property vending permit at a cost of less than $100. ACOG had no recourse over these locations unless unlicensed merchandise was sold.

This situation adversely affected not only ACOG's sales performance at the venues, but also the appearance of the city.

Venue Sales Results

Venue sales of approximately $9 million during the Games were less than ACOG had anticipated. Some contributing factors included the street vending discussed above and the success of the Superstore at Centennial Olympic Park. Also, some artwork developed by ECMP for apparel, despite focus group approvals, did not sell well. The apparel that sold best had event- or sport-specific designs and was sold only at the venue at which the event was held. The theory behind this is that spectators wanted to authenticate their visit to an event by buying a product only available at the venue.

SPECIALTY STORES

ACOG developed specialty stores to generate more revenue and create retail locations different from both the standard venue concession operations and the stores in shopping malls. ACOG envisioned the creation of a memorable shopping experience using state-of-the-art display capabilities and presenting a broader assortment of licensed merchandise. ACOG contracted with ECMP to operate the four stores described below.

As the concept developed for a central gathering place for all people wishing to experience the Games—the Centennial Olympic Park— ACOG recognized the need to create a central shopping location there for Olympic memorabilia, similar to the Storgatta in Lillehammer during the 1994 Winter Games. As the park evolved, Merchandising staff negotiated for prime real estate and significant square footage within the park's pedestrian corridor. The Superstore was constructed as the premier sales location in terms of selection, display, and entertainment for the spectators.

A second specialty store was the department store at the Atlanta Olympic Village. This store, located in the international zone, sold Village-specific souvenirs, electronics, and newsstand and sundry items in a location accessible only to accredited individuals.

A sponsor hospitality village specialty store, located adjacent to the Atlanta–Fulton County and Olympic Stadia, had a wider assortment of products than the standard venue locations.

The final specialty store was the Southern Marketplace, also located in Centennial Olympic Park. It offered non-Olympic items, particularly regional gifts and crafts.

Deliveries to the specialty stores, as well as their staffing, followed the same patterns and rules as the venue operations.

Specialty store revenues exceeded all expectations, amounting to more than $10.3 million.

Superstore

Miller/Zell, Inc., an ACOP licensee for point of sale store design and display, was retained to refine the design of the Superstore. Look of the Games design elements promoted the Centennial Olympic Games, and displays focused on past Games. The store itself was a freestanding, temporary structure designed and installed by DeBoer Structures. The air-conditioned, hard-sided tent was approximately 37,500 sq ft (3,488 sq m). Participating licensees designed their own concept shops, with fixtures and signage subject to ACOG approval. Each licensee paid a rental fee to cover the cost of the struc-

ACOG merchandise—such as Olympic T-shirts, sweatshirts, pins, and other gift items—was sold at many retail locations.

ture. The store had approximately 60 shops, ranging from 144 sq ft (13 sq m) to 3,500 sq ft (326 sq m).

Merchandise was typically sold on consignment and could be returned to the licensees after the Games. During the Games, licensees were required to staff their shops with the goal of improving sales by providing firsthand product knowledge and excellent customer service. This was a unique method of operation for the licensees and, after some initial hesitation to the staffing request, all the main spaces within the store were leased.

For the licensees, the advantages of participating were numerous. They could sell their products to the public in the main retail location, using their own techniques and fixtures; they had signage opportunities that were not available at the competition venues (typically reserved for sponsors); and they had recourse to liquidate goods following the Games.

The Superstore had a central staging area that could be used by licensees for promotional purposes, such as auctions and celebrity appearances. Also, a shipping service leased space to help customers send packages anywhere they desired.

The store had one set of entrance doors at the front and exit doors located outside the register area, designed to facilitate traffic flow and maximize the number of transactions. AT&T and National Cash Register donated 28 state-of-the-art point of sale systems in exchange for high visibility within the store.

Olympic Village Store

The Village store used an existing two-floor location within the international zone. The upstairs, approximately 5,000 sq ft (465 sq m), was used as a storage and resupply area for inventory and equipment. The downstairs, approximately 7,000 sq ft (651 sq m), was for sales. The floor plan was based on existing and augmented fixture capacities, as well as what items were needed to serve the athletes at the Village.

ECMP sublet a space to WH Smith to operate a newsstand, snack, and sundry shop. International as well as domestic publications were sold. Over-the-counter medications were approved by the Medical Services Department to ensure that no banned substances were mistakenly bought by athletes.

Another area was sublet to HiFi Buys, an Atlanta-based retail electronics store, with the understanding that no products competing with Panasonic sponsor products would be sold.

Other merchandise displayed an Olympic theme, and those licensees that participated in the Superstore were given a high profile in the Olympic Village store relative to space, product groupings, and assortments.

The Village store did very well, especially with athletes buying Olympic merchandise exclusive to the Village. Limited access to the Village meant that Olympic products sold there enjoyed a coveted status.

Sponsor Hospitality Village Store

The sponsor hospitality village store, an air-conditioned retail outlet of approximately 700 sq ft (65 sq m), sold basic Olympic merchandise, with a larger assortment than at the venue stands. The athletics and baseball competition schedules affected crowd size, and consequently the number of customers who visited the store, which had a subsequent impact on sales.

Southern Marketplace

With the Smithsonian Institution in Washington, DC, curating the Southern Crossroads Festival at Centennial Olympic Park, Merchandising contracted to have the Smithsonian Center for Folk Arts curate non-Olympic regional art, crafts, and gifts for the Southern

Marketplace, also in the park. The idea was to present authentic southern artisans' work for sale while having demonstrations by the artists to provide entertainment.

The marketplace was a standard canvas tent of approximately 3,000 sq ft (279 sq m) with a series of ceiling fans instead of air-conditioning. The facility conveyed the sense of a country store with a front porch.

At first, ECMP operated the store, with ACOG receiving 15 percent of sales. The Smithsonian purchased all merchandise and received a 10 percent fee on items sold. ECMP could return unsold items to the Smithsonian.

Because of all the parties receiving a percentage of retail sales, ECMP needed to raise prices significantly. This resulted in traditional gifts being sold at higher retail prices than in a standard country store. Despite the high volume of traffic, low sales prompted the Smithsonian to reimburse ECMP for its fixture costs and assume the store operations. The Smithsonian then lowered prices to traditional levels, and sales increased approximately 40 percent.

Special Marketing

Special Marketing was a program developed with a fashionable catalog firm and a cable shopping channel. Sales were not strong through either of these outlets. ACOG continued the Special Marketing Program through a sales agent who sold product categories, such as the entire Olympic basketball court sold to one collector. Some items, such as balls and flags, were offered as groups of related items to avoid a situation in which certain individual items would be in greater demand than others.

LIQUIDATION

The final responsibility of the Merchandising Department was the post-Games sale of remaining inventory (Remains of the Games). These items included not only merchandise

ANGELA A CATHEY • SHANNON S CATHEY • DAN T CATHY • RHONDA P CATHY • KERRI-ANN CATLAW ATC • JASON B CATLETT • REED L CATLETT • SHAUN P CATLIN • ANDREW R CATO • CATHARINE S CATO • LADONNA L CATO • LESLIE K CATO • MARTHA A CATO • VERNICE L CATO • MONICA CATON • JULIA AGDA CATRINOIU • LINDA M CATROPPA • DOUGLAS M CATTO • ROBERT J CATTO • LINDA J CAUDELL • NANCY CAUDELL-GLASSMAN • JOAN F CAUDILL • JUELLA M CAUDILL • TRAVIS M CAUDILL • JESSE A CAUDLE • JOEL P CAUDLE • LINDA S CAUDLE • GUDRUN E CAUFIELD •

241

previously offered for sale, but also items that had been used for the Games, such as balls, banners, uniforms, or other items that were deemed to be collectibles.

The ACOG Procurement and Contract Administration (P&CA) division had responsibility for the liquidation of the assets of the corporation. P&CA developed an RFP and ultimately selected an auction company to commence with liquidation. *(For more information, see the Financial Services chapter.)*

Before approving any items for auction, Merchandising identified selected items to sell at a premium both prior to and following the Games. Street banners, awards flags, and competition balls were the main sales efforts prior to the Games. After the Games, ACOG Retail Operations acquired the right to sell the remaining staff and volunteer uniforms. (During the Games, a competitive market developed among spectators who encouraged staff and volunteers to sell their uniforms because they were unavailable to the general public).

Immediately after the Games, ACOG began selling uniforms and street banners. At a party for staff and volunteers, a temporary concession tested the sale of these items. Subsequently, ACOG Retail Operations sold uniforms and banners from its warehouse through a mail-order program. Mail-order and store sales of uniforms totaled $352,000, an overwhelming response. Remaining inventory was sold in two employee stores, to the public at auctions, and at ACOG's Inforum offices.

There were not enough banners to satisfy demand. Many had been stolen, and these were by far the items staff, volunteers, and collectors most wanted. ACOG set a price allowing for fast liquidation of these items for the staff and volunteers, planning to sell remaining items to the general public. Orders far exceeded the available inventory, and to be fair, ACOG allocated only one banner per order. Additionally, there was a significant number of special requests, as well as commitments to college campuses where banners prepurchased by the schools had been stolen. To allow for some public sales of the banners, a limited number were pulled from inventory and included in the main auctions.

CONCLUSIONS AND RECOMMENDATIONS

The merchandising of apparel, memorabilia, souvenirs, and other collectibles generated significant income, as well as promoted the Centennial Olympic Games but, most importantly, provided individuals the ability to have a part of the Games experience for themselves and their friends. The following recommendations are offered to future organizing committees.

■ Encourage wholesale activity to sustain revenue flow and maintain space commitments within existing retail outlets.

■ The incremental value of special sales during special events is more promotional than revenue generating.

■ Demand for unique items not available in all retail outlets such as uniforms, balls, and banners enhances any central sales location.

Atlanta 1996®

Chapter Fourteen
Logistics

Logistics Employees

Date	Staff Number
June 1993	4
January 1996	35
July 1996	163

Note: These staff numbers do not include contract, VIK, and volunteer personnel.

OVERVIEW—ACOG organized the Logistics Department in summer 1993, under the direction of the Operations Department. The objectives of the department were to warehouse and transport the material goods needed to support the Games; quantify and coordinate the total furniture, fixture, and equipment (FF&E) needs; provide operational support in preparation, resupply, and recovery of Games equipment; and provide an efficient and globally conscious waste management program.

As Games-time approached, Logistics assumed additional responsibilities for other operations, including the import, quarantine, and export of equine animals; coordination of venue cleaning and housekeeping; transport of athletes' excess and oversized luggage between the airport and the Olympic Village; and provision of linen and laundry service to the Village and other specialized areas.

Organization

During the planning years, the Logistics Department's strategies for the support of the Games followed two distinct planning methods. The early methodology focused primarily on warehousing and transportation.

Considerable effort was directed to developing a comprehensive, computerized warehousing system. In 1994, a new module of the software used by ACOG Financial Services was selected to manage the warehousing, inventory, and venue distribution system. The full usage of this module was delayed by its complex technological installation and the extensive training that warehouse personnel required for its implementation. Due to the dependence on this module's inventory sorting capability, its late implementation posed a challenge to the logistical support required during the 1995 test events. Initially, Logistics staff members were unable to react quickly to the needs of ACOG's constituents and record all transactions on the new system. ACOG realized that in order to achieve the needed flexibility for delivery of materials, the system and planning efforts would have to be restructured.

The Logistics Department shifted away from its previous focus on warehousing to concentrate on creating a comprehensive customer service operation with the capacity to identify and procure the materials needed and distribute them in a timely manner. The new focus would provide the flexibility to support venue operations in a more cost-effective manner given the available resources.

Three key areas were addressed in the restructuring. In cooperation with Construction, Technology, Venue Management, and other ACOG functional areas, Logistics developed a process, called baselining, to define and optimize the space to be used at each venue and the FF&E needed for each functional area operating within that space.

Logistics changed its warehousing policies from bulk storage and single-order delivery to a simpler venue podding system (VPS), whereby each venue was allocated predetermined space for the storage of its FF&E.

Staffing strategy was the most significant area addressed. Logistics had originally planned to have a 3:1 ratio of warehouse employees to operational employees and hire venue logistics managers (VLMs) 90–120 days prior to the Games. The department's customer service strategy of providing assistance in planning and full delivery of materials required intimate knowledge of each venue; thus, Logistics began a concerted effort to hire all VLMs immediately, designating regional agents to be responsible for cluster venues as well as specially skilled staff to move equipment at venues.

In 1995, under its new structure, Logistics operated in four divisions—Logistical Support, Venue Logistics, Waste Management, and Administration.

LOGISTICAL SUPPORT

The Logistical Support division was responsible for logistical operations, which included shipping and receiving at all ACOG warehouses; providing transportation of needed items and services from the warehouses, vendors, and suppliers to ACOG and its constituents; coordinating international transportation and customs clearance; and developing policies and procedures for managing assets.

Logistical Support operated in four subdivisions—Warehouse Operations, Transportation, Customs Brokerage, and Asset Management.

Warehouse Operations

Four warehouses comprised the Logistics warehousing system, which received all ACOG, Atlanta Olympic Broadcasting (AOB), ACOP, and sponsor assets. The functions of receiving, storing, and shipping were performed at these ACOG warehouses, located in the

metropolitan-Atlanta area: the main distribution center (MDC); the Decatur distribution center (DDC), which also housed the uniform distribution center; the Fort Gillem warehouse; and the Savannah Port Authority warehouse. *(For the dimensions of facilities and items stored in the warehousing system, see Figure 1.)*

The warehouses separated and stored materials by venue for quality control and review by the VLM. The warehouses also supported venue operations through the provision of temporary labor and material resupply per VLM schedules and requests.

As materials arrived at the warehouses, the VLM verified receipt and proper packaging, then directed the warehouse staff in picking, packing, loading, and shipping those materials to their respective VPS within the warehouse or directly to the venue itself, when space was available.

Warehouse Operations implemented a seven-phase process for the ACOG warehouses to add structure and discipline to their warehousing efforts.

■ Phase 1: Arrival on dock—receiving crew accepted delivery, verified quantity, and entered receiving information into the computerized management system.

■ Phase 2: Put-away—warehouse crew moved items to their designated storage location and grouped like items for ease of locating. Designated venue items were moved to the VPS.

■ Phase 3: Confirm material requirements with venues—regional agents served as liaisons between the VLM representing customer needs and the computerized management system for reconciling inventory. The Logistics warehouse crew initiated the picking process.

■ Phase 4: Prepare to ship—regional agents initiated and monitored shipping preparations. The transportation crew was responsible for loading and staging.

■ Phase 5: Deliver order—Logistics Transportation coordinated the delivery schedule between the warehouse and the VLM. Regional agents monitored the process.

FIGURE 1:
THE LOGISTICS WAREHOUSING SYSTEM

Main distribution center
Storage capacity: 585,000 sq ft (54,405 sq m)
Stored: General commodities, technology items (Motorola and Panasonic), sports equipment and AOB items, and recovered ACOG assets for the liquidation process

Decatur distribution center
Storage capacity: 650,000 sq ft (60,450 sq m)
Stored: Technology items (Xerox), uniform distribution and Paralympic Games materials, and recovered ACOG assets for the liquidation process

Fort Gillem warehouse
Storage capacity: 60,000 sq ft (5,580 sq m)
Stored: Fixtures, equipment, Department of Defense items, and recovered ACOG assets for the liquidation process

Savannah Port Authority warehouse
Storage capacity: 112,000 sq ft (10,416 sq m)
Stored: Boats and general commodities to support the yachting venue

---

- Phase 6: Resupply—the VLM initiated this process through communication with the regional agent. Phases 1–5 were reactivated.

- Phase 7: Recovery—the VLM initiated this process and coordinated with the regional agent and the transportation and warehouse managers. Like items were grouped at venues and returned to the designated warehouse.

Generally, the goals established for warehousing were achieved. The biggest challenge was recovering assets in a short time period to reduce loss and theft, as venue owners began to restore venues for their own operations.

Transportation

The Logistics Transportation subdivision was responsible for material transportation from the ACOG warehouses, and directly from vendors and suppliers if necessary, to all Atlanta-area Olympic venues. The Savannah venue was supported by a local supplier and by the Logistics transportation fleet equipment in Savannah. Materials consisted of FF&E; sports, medical, and technology equipment and supplies; and all other miscellaneous items needed to support venues prior to and during the Olympic Games. Cargo vans, straight trucks, and semi-tractors and trailers were used. *(For an approximation of the size and scope of the transportation fleet, see Figure 2.)*

Partial support by Logistics was provided to the outlying venues in Birmingham, Alabama; Washington, DC; and Orlando and Miami, Florida, by common carrier.

Where warranted, specialized carriers were utilized to transport items or equipment with unique handling characteristics.

The Logistics Transportation subdivision maintained offices at the MDC and the DDC. The MDC coordinated distribution to all Cultural Olympiad sites, athlete meal transportation, transportation to and from the ACOG fabrication shop, distribution of results books

and other ACOG-requested publications, and management of canoe/kayak transportation.

The DDC office coordinated distribution of medical and technology equipment, linen, and maps and transportation to and from the computer equipment vendor.

Logistics Transportation began operating on a daily basis from 0730 until approximately 1800 as venues became available. Operating hours gradually increased until Games-time, when it operated 24 hours daily.

The department's transportation operation mirrored that of the warehouses and venues. As venue orders were fulfilled by warehouse personnel, Logistics Transportation communicated with the regional agent, the shipping manager or supervisor, and the VLM regarding order status and anticipated load and delivery times.

Three levels of priority were given to all shipments:

- Routine—assigned to all orders preloaded on trailers on a predesignated schedule. During resupply, this level was assigned to all orders not requiring expedited handling. Routine orders were delivered by the next resupply truck delivering to the venue. Each venue was guaranteed at least one resupply delivery per day.

- Rush—assigned to orders that had to be delivered to a venue within five hours. Rush orders were delivered by courier or by truck or another similar vehicle.

- Emergency—assigned to orders which had to be delivered within two hours, sometimes requiring the use of a staff member's personal vehicle. Emergency priority was used only for those items absolutely essential to the conduct of the Games or the safety or health of athletes, spectators, or ACOG staff.

The Logistics Transportation plan was well coordinated between the warehouses and the venues.

Customs Brokerage

After conducting a bid process among freight forwarding and customs brokerage firms, ACOG appointed Circle International,

Inc., as its official customs broker and freight forwarder in May 1994. Circle International was responsible for coordinating the international transportation, customs clearance, and distribution of materials and equipment used by ACOG, NOCs, IFs, athletes, media, sponsors, vendors, and suppliers in pre-Olympic training, test events, and the Games.

Circle International entered into a contractual agreement with ACOG which identified the required scope of work and a standing service tariff to be charged to the Olympic Family. The customs broker also provided full-time staff to the Logistics Department. This association marked the first time in Olympic history that the appointed broker was an operative part of the organizing committee with a fixed rate schedule for services confirmed in advance.

The US Congress passed Public Law 103-237 in May 1994 allowing for duty-free and governmental user-fee free entry of articles connected with staging the Games and associated events. The scope of this legislation far exceeded previous laws by requiring less entry documentation and removing quota requirements on imported Olympic-related goods. This legislation significantly reduced the cost to participants in Olympic events and facilitated a more efficient clearance process.

All material and equipment entering the US must be declared to US Customs before their release, and documentation must be filed for examination by the government agencies responsible for monitoring import. Items requiring additional government regulatory involvement such as food, radio frequency devices, or firearms and ammunition needed approval by their respective monitoring agency prior to release by US Customs and delivery to the importer.

ACOG and the customs broker held quarterly meetings with all government agencies affecting importation to determine where unique handling and/or procedures would be needed. The customs broker agreed to monitor those imports for ACOG and the NOCs to ensure items were properly identified.

In addition to these quarterly meetings, yearly port visits to US Customs offices in Los Angeles, Miami, New York, and Washington were made to personally update the individual port directors about ACOG's progress and discuss unique port requirements that might affect the import of Olympic items.

ACOG and the customs broker worked with NOC Services and NOC Relations and met with each NOC to discuss the entry and distribution program, as well as to address any individual concerns. In December 1994, in cooperation with the responsible government agencies, ACOG and the customs broker published the *Customs Manual for NOCs* to identify the various government agencies they would encounter; problem areas to avoid; routing information for smooth transport and import of their necessary equipment and materials; and export information needed after test events and the Olympic Games.

Logistics staff also assisted in creating the *Chef's Manual I* and *II* and the Chef's Calendar presented at the Chef de Mission Seminar in 1995. In addition, the Equestrian Manual, which addressed equine transport, and the Main Press Center (MPC) Manual, which aided the rights-holding press in their Games coverage, were produced.

In December 1994, ACOG hosted the Association of National Olympic Committees (ANOC) meeting to showcase the progress made by the city of Atlanta and ACOG in preparation for the Games. During this meeting, an information booth was established to answer questions and distribute literature. In spring 1995, a booth was available at the Chef de Mission Seminar, and informative seminars were held on import and export and the duty-free legislation.

The 1995 test events helped identify problematic areas where additional resources and coordination with government agencies was needed, primarily in the specialized customs knowledge of the completion and validation of ATA carnets, which are widely used for the international transport of team equipment. Yachting events held in 1994 and 1995 also identified the need for the placement of ocean containers for 112 teams in extremely limited quarters.

ACOG Imports. By March 1996, the many items necessary to stage the competitions were stored at the MDC for inspection and inventory. Initial imports were items for ACOG Sports and Construction. Under the *Olympic Charter*, ACOG purchased and imported over 250,000 items for sports such as athletics, table tennis, weightlifting, and yachting. All imports were coordinated through the customs broker, and in many instances, transported from supplier to site under its direction.

Additional ACOG-related imports included construction and track materials for completion of the Olympic Stadium, artificial grass for the hockey fields, and temporary seating, pools, and other structures for venues. Two sports-related imports requiring special attention were boats and horses.

Canoeing, kayaking, and rowing equipment posed specific challenges. Due to the size of equipment and the fragile nature of the boats, international transport was often costly and time consuming. Once in the US, teams often began their Olympic testing outside Atlanta, which required the customs broker to carry equipment from city to city prior to ACOG-sanctioned events. Logistics provided specially racked containers for boat transport.

The equestrian event required importing more than 250 world-class horses into Atlanta. ACOG established an import quarantine facility at Hartsfield Atlanta International Airport for US Department of Agriculture (USDA) testing.

■ *Yachting—Savannah, Georgia.* The Savannah venue held yachting team ocean containers in two locations, the Olympic Marina and the May Howard Elementary School. Space was allotted for 100 containers, but only 65 were used, most on marina property. Venue Logistics coordinated the delivery and installation of all containers, using a 25 ton (23 t) crane. Ten additional containers were placed for late-arriving teams.

Some larger teams with multiple containers used alternate storage sites in Savannah. Often, the customs broker leased space or requested donated space for these teams.

Individual shipments of masts, rudders, keel boards, and sails for pretraining and repair were delivered, as well as medical equipment for team doctors.

Following the Games, export arrangements were made to remove all containers from Savannah within one week.

■ *Rowing and Canoe/Kayak—Lake Lanier.* Site limitations at Lake Lanier prohibited mass placement of containers imported by the teams. Instead, containers were unloaded at the custom broker's Atlanta warehouse and their contents moved to Lake Lanier using contracted trailers. In some instances, the teams arrived with several boats on specially constructed trailers towed behind vehicles. In these cases, ACOG moved them to Lake Lanier by private vehicle or loaded them intact onto a trailer for transport.

Following competition, all individual boats were repackaged, either by the teams or with additional labor, and returned to Atlanta for export. Full containers were transported directly to the port according to instructions from the teams.

■ *Canoe/Kayak—Ocoee, Tennessee.* Services provided at this venue were similar to those at Lake Lanier. The limited space prevented the storage of transport equipment, and all teams had to unload their equipment upon arrival. Containers and trailers were returned to Atlanta for storage.

■ *Ceremonies*. The customs broker worked with the producers of the Opening and Closing Ceremonies to transport, clear, and deliver custom-made costumes from Port of Spain, Trinidad, to the Atlanta production facility adjacent to Olympic Stadium.

■ *DeBoer Tents BV/DeBoer Structures, Inc.* DeBoer was contracted with ACOP to provide structures and erect tents for the sponsor villages, the Superstore, and other venue sites. DeBoer engaged Circle International to provide the international transport of these tents and equipment from South Africa, England, and other European countries.

ACOP created certain deadlines which had to be met in order to avoid delay penalties. The customs broker and DeBoer created a transport matrix whereby the necessary materials could be loaded, shipped, and delivered to meet these deadlines. DeBoer's equipment required specialized containers called flattracks, which the customs broker leased. More than 75 containers of equipment were shipped and stored over a four-month period. The broker also assisted De Boer by providing forklifts, loading ramps, scissor lifts, pressure equipment, and cranes. In total, De Boer erected tent areas which covered approximately 50 acres.

Following the Games, DeBoer was required to remove all materials from the Olympic sites. The customs broker assisted DeBoer by providing the necessary equipment on a venue-by-venue basis and reserving the export containers.

■ *Torch Relay*. The customs broker initially shipped 1,000 torches from Atlanta to Athens for use in the 1996 Flame Relay in Greece. The customs broker worked with US Customs, Delta Air Lines, and ACOG management to ensure the Olympic flame's timely entry into Los Angeles by providing the district director of US Customs the documentation allowing for its immediate clearance.

National Olympic Committees. The customs broker began to receive freight for individual NOCs in May 1996. These materials were warehoused pending distribution instructions from each chef de mission. A distribution

plan for the Village was based on information received from the NOCs; however, the lack of complete information from the NOCs regarding the amount of freight they were shipping, the delivery parameters, or special handling requirements created challenges.

By mid-June 1996, several NOCs had accumulated large amounts of freight with complex delivery issues involving not only the Village, but hospitality houses, pre-Olympic training sites, and venues. In July 1996, the import operation grew so rapidly that within two weeks, the warehouse capacity of the customs broker had to be enlarged from 60,000 sq ft (5,580 sq m) to 260,000 sq ft (24,180 sq m), and it became apparent that the Village distribution plan had to be revised.

A complex delivery reservation system was designed so Village Logistics could schedule carriers into the Village or through the material transfer area (MTA). The scheduling process was devised so ACOG could confirm the responsible NOC was accredited and housed; Security was alerted as to the delivering carrier, its seal number(s), driver's name, and delivery time; and Village Logistics would provide personnel and equipment to assist with unloading the cargo.

Scheduling the increases in delivery with Village Logistics through the reservation process was difficult, resulting in delivery delays and the subsequent displeasure of the NOCs. Security difficulties also transpired, as prescreened vehicles were often delayed. Due to the unforeseen volume of freight, Village Logistics did not have sufficient staff or equipment available to assist with unloading heavy pallets.

As part of the custom broker's contract, an office was located adjacent to NOC Services to assist with problems, questions, and other matters. Because of the delivery problems and the ensuing complaints, one person was dedicated to assist Village Logistics with the reservation and acceptance process in order to clear the backlog of cargo consigned to the NOCs. A team of logistics material handlers and accompanying equipment was placed at the MTA to assist with delivery. This greatly improved the efficiency of operations at the Village and resulted in the successful delivery of all NOC freight prior to Opening Ceremony.

Broadcasters. All international rights-holding broadcasters contracted for the shipping and delivery services of Circle International. As the delivery process for the International Broadcast Center (IBC) began, problems with dock space allotment and insufficient personnel became apparent. Similar security problems to those encountered at the Village occurred at the IBC. Delivery vehicles were often denied entry or delayed, and sealed vehicles were opened for physical inspection, occasionally damaging the freight. As the schedule of deliveries decreased and more personnel were engaged, problems were overcome.

Following the Games, the IBC was required to remove all equipment and salvageable materials from the Georgia World Congress Center within four days. Two dock positions were allocated to deliver empty packing cases only and the rest to remove equipment. More than 30 people removed cargo 24 hours daily in order to meet the deadline.

Press Agencies. The customs broker received and prepared press agency freight for delivery, handled security screening, scheduled deliveries, and delivered cargo to the MPC dock. At the dock, all cargo was received and distributed by a facility-designated convention contractor.

Storing empty packing materials for use by press agencies following the Games was challenging. The customs broker leased space for storage and agreed to a tariff rate. The press agencies had free access to their materials to store excess equipment or parts.

The convention contractor also arranged for storage space, but indicated that agencies were not allowed access. Despite the MPC Manual instructions that the customs broker was the

officially appointed warehouse, some agencies encountered difficulties in engaging the convention contractor.

Sponsors. The customs broker assisted Panasonic with importing and distributing their value-in-kind (VIK) equipment. Equipment was imported and transported to the Panasonic facility in Suwannee, Georgia, where broadcast equipment was constructed for the IBC.

Reebok provided most of the footwear for ACOG staff, security personnel, and volunteers. The customs broker reserved warehouse space where shoes were selected for distribution. Through a process created by Reebok, shoes were tagged with the official ACOG merchandise hologram and distributed to retail stores, where ACOG staff acquired their uniform footwear.

The customs broker coordinated all domestic distribution of Swatch's timing equipment, which required specialized handling procedures, crating services, warehousing, and delivery, as well as precise delivery schedules to each venue. The customs broker also assisted Swatch's commercial division with the import and distribution of Swatch watches for ACOG staff and volunteers.

The customs brokerage process was successful primarily due to the early involvement of Circle International. In cases where functional areas, such as the IBC, MPC, and Olympic Village, did not coordinate their logistics activities with ACOG Logistics, problems did arise with deliveries and distribution. These problems were resolved once ACOG Logistics became involved.

Asset Management

The Asset Management subdivision defined the policies and procedures necessary to ensure the proper management of assets. Although each warehouse and venue managed its own inventory, all reported to this subdivision for inventory control. The department was also responsible for asset tagging procedures and conducted cycle-count inspections of selected areas to ensure quality control in inventory counts.

Asset Management's primary pre-Games focus was to develop a policy for removing items from ACOG headquarters and warehouses for delivery to the venues. Holographic tags were produced to identify asset ownership to aid ACOG Security in enforcing policy at venues.

A more difficult pre-Games task was the effort to coordinate the use of three separate materials management software systems for finance and purchasing, material planning and distribution, and warehouse receipt and inventory. A manual item-by-item validation between systems was necessary.

The Games-time function of Asset Management was establishing schedules for recovery of assets in a timely manner as venues finished operations. Implementation of the schedules was managed by VLMs.

VENUE LOGISTICS

Venue Logistics defined and prepared the material requirements for all venues, including training sites, the Airport Welcome Center, Centennial Olympic Park, Emory housing, equine quarantine, the MPC, the Olympic Family Hotel, the Olympic Village, and sponsor villages. It also provided dock management at venues, including maintaining ACOG, sponsor, and vendor delivery schedules.

This division played a major role in the scheduling and operations of venue preparation and disassembly. Venue Logistics worked with Warehouse Operations for all resupply and new material requirements and supported Asset Management in maintenance and inventory list updates.

The Venue Logistics plan was designed to provide the most efficient service for Games-time venue operations. To facilitate the flow

of communications and coordinate with the Venue Management structure, venues were divided into clusters—venues in close proximity—and regions—multiple venues grouped geographically. Each venue was planned for and operated by a VLM who reported to logistics program managers (LPMs) through a cluster manager and/or regional logistics manager.

During planning and implementation, the VLM was responsible for staffing, placement of FF&E, identification of warehousing needs, coordination with the customs broker, logistical operations scheduling, golf cart policy, and recovery and liquidation planning.

Adequate staffing was necessary to complete all Logistics functions. When planning staff levels, the VLM considered routine duties as well as contingency requirements, daily competition schedules, level of supervision required to perform tasks, and applicable time constraints. Often, Venue Logistics staff consisted of the VLM, two assistant VLMs, and a logistics crew.

The VLM worked with Venue Management to identify needed dock area space; design the dock area to ensure vehicle flow; identify shared space with other functional areas, bulk and lockable storage space, and equipment needed to facilitate all venue operations; and determine material flow patterns and challenges.

The VLM and Venue Management established venue baselines for all FF&E required. The VLM then met with each functional area manager to refine their requirements. The complete list of all materials was entered into the venue planning database (VPD). The VPD, combined with the detailed room identification matrix, was then used for distribution and recovery of all FF&E.

Each venue was given a standard central supply kit of FF&E to meet common operational needs.

The venue manager (VM) developed a construction schedule including dates, times, and

Moving athlete luggage to and from the Olympic Village required the support of the Logistics Department.

MAYA M CHANDIRAMANI • ANNE S CHANDLER • DANA D CHANDLER • DEAN A CHANDLER • FRANKLIN K CHANDLER • GERALD R CHANDLER • GWENDOLYN C CHANDLER • JAMES S CHANDLER • JANET K CHANDLER • JEAN B CHANDLER • JOAN D CHANDLER • JOSEPH B CHANDLER • JUDITH A CHANDLER • KELLY H CHANDLER • LAURA J CHANDLER • LENN H CHANDLER • LYNETTE W CHANDLER • LYNN S CHANDLER • MARCIA E CHANDLER • MARGARET M. CHANDLER • MARK CHANDLER • MARY C CHANDLER • MARY D CHANDLER • PAULA M CHANDLER • RUSSELL CHANDLER activities of prime importance to operational preparation. This information was included in a venue-integrated operations schedule, from which the VLM developed a matrix schedule including all responsible parties, contact names and numbers, and dates and times of deliveries. The logistics activity schedule was important to functional areas such as Sports and Technology, which played integral roles in the preparation and recovery schedule and thus relied on Logistics for the equipment to perform their tasks.

During the Games, Venue Logistics was responsible for managing all loading docks within venues and operating designated receiving docks and all material handling equipment. All deliveries were preplanned and included on the master delivery schedule and the daily delivery schedule, copies of which were provided to Security and Venue Management. Any vehicle not on the delivery schedule was denied access to the venue, usually held at the salle port, and reported to Logistics for immediate action.

Under the direction of Logistics and Venue Management, all venue staff disassembled the venue for which they had responsibility. All functional area managers coordinated disassembly efforts within their functional areas. A schedule of recovery activities was distributed prior to the final day of competition. The VLM then met individually with functional area managers to discuss venue disassembly. Logistics was responsible for accounting for all ACOG assets at the venue and ensuring proper packaging of equipment for shipment back to the warehouse or another ACOG facility. In some cases, ACOG materials were purchased by the venue owner and remained at the venue.

At venues where ACOG Construction did not have a presence, Logistics managed the planning and installation of temporary and portable items, including tents and restrooms. Logistics and Venue Management determined

The Venue Logistics crew was responsible for moving equipment from the warehouses to the appropriate venues.

space-efficient site plans at these locations.

The Logistics communication command center was established to serve as the central problem-solving network for situations that could not be resolved at the venues.

WASTE MANAGEMENT AND RECYCLING

The Waste Management and Recycling division determined the waste and recycling removal equipment and services needed at venues, procured the proper waste and recycling receptacles, and developed a management plan for all waste-hauling and recycling.

The division provided solid and biohazardous waste removal and recycling inside the competition venues and at Centennial Olympic Park and park-and-ride locations. Waste removal and recycling services at the IBC, Media Transportation Mall, MPC, and Olympic Village were also provided.

In fall 1991, the IOC, in partnership with the United Nations Environment Program, amended the *Olympic Charter* to emphasize environmental stewardship in staging the Olympic Games.

Atlanta was only the second host city to voluntarily address Olympic environmentalism in any pragmatic or operational way. Though not part of the Bid, ACOG enthusiastically supported the environmental policy, believing that there were better alternatives than disposing of the huge amount of solid waste the Games would generate in landfills.

ACOG's vision was to demonstrate the feasibility of alternatives on a large scale, as the Olympic Games provided many waste management challenges that commanded public attention. Therefore, a successful program could potentially inspire communities worldwide to implement sustainable programs. To realize this vision, ACOG developed an integrated plan by employing several leading waste management companies to test new ideas and technologies.

The challenge was not only to develop a sound environmental strategy, but also to ensure that waste was removed quickly and efficiently. There were many aspects to consider: security, space, narrow service windows, power, capacity, and budgets. The program also had to be user-friendly for spectators, staff, and contractors.

The first year was dedicated to several key planning tasks:

■ Waste generation model—developed based on waste generation rates from the 1984 Games in Los Angeles and from rates at sporting arenas across the country and in Atlanta. The average was about .28 lbs (127 g) per person per hour.

■ Budget model—developed based on preliminary estimates of spectators, number of venues, and the hauling equipment and service needed, including the waste haulers' hourly fee for truck rental, disposal, installation, and delivery.

■ Recycling goals—to be responsible and environmentally sensitive, setting a goal of diverting up to 85 percent of all generated solid waste from landfills.

■ Defining the scope of work—determining the proper waste and recycling equipment and services for waste disposal at Games-time.

The Environmental Protection Agency (EPA) provided an evaluation of the estimated waste to be generated by the Games and suggested source reduction language in supplier and vendor contracts to reduce the amount of potential waste. The EPA also loaned an executive to Logistics to work as an advisor to the Waste Management and Recycling division and provided for 100 of their full-time employees to volunteer at Games-time for the Waste Management and Recycling program. They supervised janitorial contractors, conducted public outreach, and helped maintain the integrity of the recycling plan.

In order to fulfill ACOG's environmental goals, several programs needed coordinated efforts, including venue cleaning, waste hauling, and recycling.

Venue Cleaning Program

In late December 1995, Logistics determined that professional cleaning assistance was required, and thus integrated a venue cleaning plan into the Waste Management and Recycling program. A cleaning management company was hired and worked closely with the VMs and Logistics staff to develop a program to fulfill this need.

The cleaning management company developed a cleaning master plan, established cleaning policies and procedures for venues, determined venue cleaning budgets, developed venue-specific cleaning specifications and standards, selected qualified contractors from the ACOG-approved vendor list, negotiated venue cleaning contracts, provided a cleaning manual for each venue, developed a resupply plan for all consumables, and prepared all equipment, personnel, and vendors.

During the Games, the cleaning management company coordinated the activities of all cleaning vendors, managed the cleaning contractors, and provided emergency cleaning as requested.

The tremendous amount of precleaning needed to prepare venues to Olympic standards was a challenge, as many cleaning personnel started on the day of the event.

Waste-Hauling Vendor

ACOG's original goal was to hire one waste hauler to service all venues. Five waste hauling companies were sent requests for proposals After reviewing specific criteria including management capability, available resources, minority participation, cost, and commitment to recycling, Browning Ferris Industries (BFI) was selected as the primary hauler; later, a combination of BFI, Waste Management, Inc., and

United Waste Services was needed to serve the program.

BFI operated a new 98,000 sq ft (9,100 sq m) materials recycling facility (MRF) that was used for separated and commingled (mixed) recyclable materials. A full-time executive was also loaned by the company to the Waste Management and Recycling division.

Recycling

In a supplier agreement with ACOG, CH2M Hill coordinated recycling services for the Games. This included selecting and determining the placement of bins, designing recycling graphics for bins and signage at venues, producing educational and promotional messages and materials, training staff and volunteers, and processing and marketing recovered materials to local customers. Local volunteers from the Georgia Recycling Coalition aided in Games-time management of the recycling program.

Pre-Games. It was determined that the warehouses would mainly generate cardboard, ferrous metal, office paper, plastic wrap, and wood. Cardboard was packaged in mechanical balers and shipped directly to the end market. Salvageable pallets were sent to a rebuilder. Mixed office paper and metal were collected by end market recyclers. Suppliers and vendors shipping supplies to warehouses were given guidelines to reduce the waste entering the warehouses. Where possible, packaging materials such as pallets, boxes, and packing foam were returned to the supplier for reuse. The materials of suppliers that shipped directly to venues became part of the venue recycling program.

Games-time. The Waste Management and Recycling division along with CH2M Hill determined that the largest percentage of waste would be generated by spectators and ACOG functional departments; therefore, a proactive purchasing program and meetings with packaging generators, including Food and Beverage

Department suppliers, were needed to manage waste flow. Waste Management and Recycling expected the waste to consist of recyclable items including food scraps, food service paper, mixed office paper, cardboard, plastic, and aluminum. The remainder was unknown miscellaneous waste.

Waste Management and Recycling also assumed that even though most spectators and staff expected a "hands-on" recycling program, an education and signage program would have to be implemented. Creative signage and public service announcements made throughout the venues helped educate and inform the spectators about the program.

A two-bin collection system, one for mixed waste and one for commingled recyclables, was established. Sixty-five gal (246 l) mixed waste receptacles, lined with green plastic bags, were used to collect food scraps, food service paper, and other unknown materials. Sixty-five gal (246 l) recycling containers, lined with clear plastic bags, were used to collect plastic and aluminum beverage containers. Recyclable materials were collected in one compactor and sorted at the MRF.

Mixed office paper receptacles, lined with blue plastic bags, were available in press offices, ACOG offices, and broadcasting areas to collect office paper, which was shipped to the MRF.

Trained cleaning staff collected mixed waste and recyclables and transported them to the central collection area. No sorting was needed; bags needed only to be placed in the right containers, according to color.

The central collection areas were used for the collection of both mixed waste and recyclables. A two-compactor system was used at the majority of venues. The mixed waste compactor collected green bags, which were then sent to Microlife USA's sorting/composting facility. Microlife USA was contracted to sort, recycle, and compost the mixed waste collected from the green bags.

Its resource recovery/composting facility was used to catch recyclables accidentally placed in the wrong receptacle. The sorted recyclables were sent to an end market. The facility then separated the waste flow further, recovering most waste, food scraps, and paper for composting. The residual waste was placed in a landfill.

The recyclables compactor was used to collect all clear and blue bags and loose cardboard. These were sent to the MRF for sorting, processing, and shipping mixed plastic and aluminum, bags of mixed office paper, and loose cardboard to end markets. Any rejected material was sent to Microlife's sorting/composting facility for processing.

The waste management system was designed to adequately manage 300 tons per day, and approximately 150 tons per day were handled. About 75 percent of waste removal services occurred between 1200–0600, which worked well due to the limited traffic flow of both vehicles and pedestrians.

The incidence of biohazardous waste, primarily from medical areas, was higher than expected, due to the improper sorting of non–biohazardous and biohazardous material. The waste material's limited storage required frequent collections.

Composting

The mixed waste material, containing between 60 and 70 percent food and food service items by weight, was first delivered to Microlife's sorting facility. A percentage of preseparated bagged material, paper, plastic, and aluminum came mixed with the unseparated waste. Wood pallets, paint cans, various ferrous metals, textiles, soiled cardboard, and waste paper were also present.

The material was hand-sorted over a 70 ft (21 m) conveyor system and the remaining organic waste (food waste, paper, and cardboard) was shredded and transported to a composting site in Conyers, Georgia.

Beginning in January 1997, the composted organic material was screened and matured for 3–6 months. Approximately 90 percent of the composted organic material was donated to municipal agencies for beautification projects. Ten percent went to landfills as rejected inert material.

Microlife ultimately processed 1,217 tons of waste. Its only serious problem was that it was not allowed to operate during the first seven days of the Games due to difficulties with the Fulton County Commission. Unfortunately, an

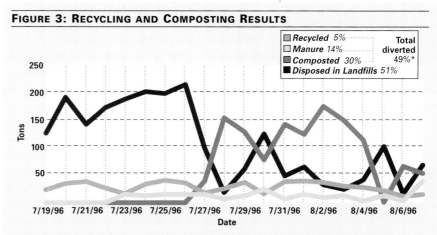

FIGURE 3: RECYCLING AND COMPOSTING RESULTS

Legend:
- Recycled 5%
- Manure 14%
- Composted 30%
- Disposed in Landfills 51%

Total diverted 49%*

Y-axis: Tons (250, 200, 150, 100, 50)
X-axis: Date 7/19/96 7/21/96 7/23/96 7/25/96 7/27/96 7/29/96 7/31/96 8/2/96 8/4/96 8/6/96

* An additional 273 loads of waste were attempted to be diverted, but were rejected for various reasons. These loads are included in the composted and disposed in landfills numbers.

estimated extra 1000 tons of mixed waste went into metro-Atlanta landfills during this period.

Recycling and Composting Results

ACOG's venue recycling program was responsible for successfully recycling 18 percent of the waste generated at the venues.

Of the 8.7 million lbs (3.9 million kg) of solid waste produced, two-thirds was used for composting and recycling. Furthermore, more than 10 million cans and plastic bottles were collected for recycling.

TRUDY L CHAPMAN • VERONICA CHAPMAN • WAYNE CHAPMAN • WENDY M CHAPMAN • WILLIAM E CHAPMAN • WILLIAM W CHAPMAN • GABRIEL CHAPMAN II • THOMAS G CHAPMAN JR • KELLEY W CHAPOTON • SUSAN C CHAPPELEAR • ANDERSON CHAPPELL • ERICA R CHAPPELL • JEANETTE E CHAPPELL • KATHERINE E CHAPPELL • KEVIN L CHAPPELL • NATASHA A CHAPPELL • SUZANNE E CHAPPELL • ROBERT E CHAPPELL JR • GREYSON S CHAPPELLE • ARTHUR M CHAPPLE • YASMIN CHARANIA • MARC M CHARBIT • PAUL H CHARBONNEAU • CHRISTIAN CHARBONNEL •

255

In addition, approximately 500,000 wooden pallets and 50 tons of scrap metal generated from warehouse operations were recycled. The Atlanta Food Bank organized a program to retrieve surplus food from Olympic venues to feed the homeless and hungry. This group collected 459,011 lbs (208,207 kg) of food.

(For an overall summary of recycling and composting during the Olympic Games, see Figure 3. The results include the seven-day period that was not operational.)

BUDGET AND ADMINISTRATION

Personnel in this area were responsible for the Logistics Department's internal administration. This included budgeting, staffing, and specialized contracted equipment and services.

Budget

The Logistics Budget subdivision managed the department's contracting and financial commitments. It also worked with various ACOG Financial Services divisions to ensure timely and cost-effective acquisition of needed items.

In late 1992, the proposed Logistics budget, completed with computer software used to plan warehousing, transportation loads, and routes, was submitted. As Logistics was restructured, a new budget was presented to the COO in 1995.

During Games-time, the Logistics budget was jointly managed from the Logistics command center and by the Financial Services officer at each venue.

Staffing

This subdivision was responsible for recruiting the thousands of candidates needed to staff the venues and warehouses. With ACOG Human Resources and Accreditation, Staffing attempted to streamline processing and thus reduce the time needed between identifying a suitable candidate and actual employment. Once individuals were employed, Staffing assisted with ensuring the employee was granted the accreditation privileges necessary to accomplish his or her task. A tracking report was developed by Logistics to monitor the progress of its employment applications.

Because Logistics staff, including contractors, needed access to all areas within all venues, obtaining these privileges was challenging to the accreditation system. Since unlimited access was highly sought after, any such request was intensely scrutinized. Logistics had to assist the Accreditation Department with granting the necessary privileges for Logistics crew members.

The Logistics accreditation effort became a 24-hour operation in early July in order to process the large number of staff needing badging. Large groups of Logistics contractors, vendors, or employees were processed at one time. To support access control, Venue Management issued temporary tags, which were adhesive-backed stickers to be placed on the ACOG-issued badge. However, some staff that had valid ACOG badges with proper zone access were denied access if the temporary tag was not attached. Staffing became more manageable shortly before the Games, although accreditation and security issues caused many unnecessary delays.

Materials Management and Planning

An integral part of Logistics was the Materials Management and Planning (MM&P) subdivision. This area compiled material requirements into a single data set used for modeling budgets and procuring services and marketing commitments. Data collection was done through the Logistics MM&P project team, in collaboration with the Procurement and Contract Administration (P&CA) and Internal Auditing divisions of Financial Services, Operations, Technology, and Venue Management.

This subdivision assessed overall ACOG material requirements for all venues and planned the most efficient utilization of assets and ACOG purchasing funds. It also developed standards for material requirements at all venues that adhered to ACOG's Look of the Games, AOB needs, and post-Games disposal strategies.

MM&P was the primary liaison between P&CA and ACOP. Total FF&E estimates were used by the Financial Services Department to forecast the funds necessary to procure assets. MM&P worked with P&CA to develop sourcing strategies and order-processing plans based on lead time, and a budget was allocated for purchasing items.

As part of the data collection process, MM&P met with each VM and VLM to determine baseline FF&E requirements using the venue baseline tool (VBT). This process provided the information Logistics required to co-ordinate and allocate VIK and purchased materials so as to allow the maximum utilization of ACOG assets and funds. Materials were tracked through identification, sourcing, requisitioning, purchasing, and receiving. A catalog of standard items was developed as a guide for venue personnel to determine functional area operational requirements.

To ensure an adequate supply of equipment such as portable lighting, forklifts, and trucks, the department reviewed prospective suppliers and negotiated its needs with the preferred vendor. Some items were supplied through Olympic sponsor agreements, including bicycles, boats, farm equipment, freight forwarding, generators, golf carts, lawn and garden equipment, linens, maintenance equipment, and waste receptacles.

The program checklist from Venue Management was imported on the VBT system and included a prearranged code for each functional area and location within the venue. The VBT was divided into four segments: ACOG information, construction information, furniture, and equipment.

Once completed, the information for all venues was given to the MM&P team to provide accurate numbers for acquisition of FF&E required at all venues. These numbers were then used in requisitioning materials for Games-time.

Information from the VBT was entered into the VPD, so locations could be assigned specific FF&E. Within this database, totals were completed for each item required for venue operations. With this information, additional requisitioning was performed for individual venues and supply/demand analyses were completed to compare existing inventory levels with anticipated demand.

The ACOG Financial Accounting System was used for requisitioning, purchase order development, receiving, distribution, and dissolution. Other software utilized by Logistics included inventory management and sales order processing. Inventory management was used as an inventory control tool. Sales order processing was used during test events to transfer materials from the warehouse to the venues and for the disposition of assets following the Olympic Games.

During Games-time, MM&P provided support to areas that required it. Staff reallocated assets, particularly golf carts, as usage patterns and operational needs at venues were clarified, and assisted with the linen and laundry distribution operation. Materials Management also supported athlete luggage handling during peak days and helped define roles and responsibilities related to initial venue recovery.

Exposition Group

The Exposition Group subdivision of the Logistics Department was the liaison between the Logistics Department and the Greyhound Exposition Services (GES) division of the Dial Corporation, which was the exposition services Olympic sponsor. It negotiated with GES to secure the most cost-efficient equipment and services, such as carpeting and draping, and supervised the ordering, delivery, installation, and dismantling of GES equipment in venues with the exception of the MPC and the Olympic Village, which were handled independently. Ad-

SUSAN B CHASE • SAMUEL CHASE II • CARL CHASE JR • HENRY H CHASE JR • AMY A CHASTAIN • ANN R CHASTAIN • BRADLEY J CHASTAIN • CASEY CHASTAIN • CATHERINE M CHASTAIN • CHARLES L CHASTAIN • EVERETT C CHASTAIN • JAY S CHASTAIN • JONI CHASTAIN • KEITH C CHASTAIN • LINDA A CHASTAIN • LORI L CHASTAIN • MARION S CHASTAIN • OLIVER J CHASTAIN • SAMUEL H CHASTAIN • SHIRLEY J CHASTAIN • VERONICA N CHASTAIN • ANA M CHASTEEN • CAMILLE J CHASTEEN • RAYMOND M CHATEAU • PATRICK H CHATELAIN • RICHARD C CHATHAM • STEVEN P CHATHAM •

257

ditionally, this group provided logistics management at Centennial Olympic Park and the sponsor villages at Olympic Stadium and Stone Mountain Park, because of the major role GES had at these venues.

When GES became a sponsor, Logistics and GES immediately began negotiations to establish services and pricing. After consulting with Venue Management, MM&P, and VLM, the orders for exposition services were placed by the Exposition Group.

To establish consistency within venues, the VLM became the single point of contact with the Exposition Group for subsequent venue needs.

Linen/Laundry

Five ACOG departments identified a requirement for clean linens such as towels, sheets, pillow cases, and blankets as an important part of their operations: Accommodations, Medical Services, the Olympic Village, Sports, and Venue Management.

The needs of Accommodations and the Village accounted for approximately 90 percent of all requirements. The budget was part of the Logistics Department and the primary planning and operating responsibilities were divided between the Village and Logistics.

The Olympic Village, which had the greatest linen needs, estimated its linen requirements based on the expected number of beds used, level of service provided, and sport-by-sport models of competition and training based on the number of athletes participating at a given venue on a given day.

A licensing agreement was reached with Fieldcrest Cannon whereby ACOG would receive linen products based on the forecasted needs. ACOG contracted the service of laundering the massive amount of linens to the Georgia Baptist Hospital Laundry Service (GBHL).

As the Village's expected occupancy levels rose, accommodation sites changed, and competition schedules and sites were revisited, the requirements were refined and reassessed for accuracy and savings opportunities.

In spring 1996, the Medical Services Department received a donation of disposable towels and sheets from a vendor, eliminating the need for any laundering or resupply of medical linens. Medical Services and Logistics determined initial linen quantities for each venue and only resupplied as needed.

Outlying venues also did not require resupply from the centralized laundry system, as it was not cost-effective. The VLMs at each of these venues arranged service with a local launderer.

Soiled linens were delivered to the laundry and returned to the venues after cleaning. Clean linen was delivered to the Village and the DDC, to handle the volume and address security concerns. A dedicated route established between the Village and the laundry operated between 1200–0600. To maintain proper inventories, an area in the Village was used as an internal linen distribution center.

For all other venues, the DDC served as the distribution center. This operation separated venues into accommodation sites or competition and training sites.

Control tickets were attached to the GBHL-supplied laundry carts, which recorded the type and amount of soiled linen being sent for cleaning by each respective site. These tickets were photocopied at the DDC and used as a cross-check for the next day's clean linen to be returned to the site. The carts were sent by semi-trailer to the laundry, where linens were sorted and cleaned. The carts were reloaded with clean linen per the control tickets. At the DDC, the clean linens were checked twice per the control tickets and loaded onto trucks for delivery that evening.

Five daily competition venue routes and two alternating day training-site routes were established, also based on geography and expected volumes. Trucks left the DDC between 1200–0600 with enough clean linen to evenly exchange items at all venues on its particular route.

1200–0600 with enough clean linen to evenly exchange items at all venues on its particular route.

After all venues closed, all linen was collected and returned to the DDC where it was consolidated, cleaned, packaged, and sold to a contractor.

Athlete Luggage Handling

Originally, handling athlete luggage was the responsibility of ACOG's Transportation Department with the assistance of Logistics for excess or oversized items.

When athletes began arriving in Atlanta, it became apparent that more logistical support was required for athlete luggage handling, including the delivery of lost luggage. The Logistics Department contributed that support.

This multivehicle operation, with staff members accredited for access to the Village, supported athlete luggage handling. Luggage was monitored as it was screened and vehicles were allocated if needed. Buses carrying athletes and trucks carrying their luggage attempted to depart for the Village at the same time. Problems with this new operation, such as the delay of luggage sorting, were corrected over several days, and the operation worked well.

Logistics established an office in the Village and successfully developed and implemented a plan for handling athlete departures from the Village.

Equine Quarantine

Logistics assumed responsibility for horse import, quarantine, and export in late 1995. An initial meeting was held with representatives from all entities involved, including the Animal-Plant Health Inspection Service division of the USDA, US Customs, US Immigration and Naturalization Service (INS), Georgia Department of Agriculture, the two major airlines that specialize in equine charters, Hartsfield International Airport, ACOG's customs broker, and the ACOG Sports Department. As a result of this meeting, a procedural manual was developed.

The customs broker chartered aircrafts to transport the animals, contracted for ground transport for the horses to acclimation farms and the Georgia International Horse Park, managed a reservation system in conjunction with two professional grooms' firms, and coordinated procedures for the federal agencies upon arrival of an aircraft. The existing equine facility at Hartsfield International Airport was only certified by the USDA for export, so Logistics employed an architectural firm and contractors to modify this facility for import and quarantine.

The Games-time operations of Equine Quarantine began in early June 1996 to comply with the 30-day acclimation period recommended for horses participating in competition. Most inbound charter flights were scheduled to arrive at 0300 to avoid hot temperatures. Flight arrivals were coordinated with Hartsfield International Airport officials, who arranged to close a runway during unloading. After INS officers boarded the aircraft to inspect the documentation of passengers, the horses were unloaded, removed from the shipping containers, and taken inside the quarantine facility to be examined by USDA veterinarians for parasites and blood testing for Piroplasmosis, an equine disease. ACOG staff then took the horses to their stalls, where they remained until blood tests were completed.

Meanwhile, in the customs facility, officers of the USDA Animal-Plant Health Inspection Service and a US Customs officer inspected grooms' articles for illegal plants, food, or other items. Once cleared, the grooms proceeded to nearby accommodations to await the results of the equine blood test.

Equestrian events required the importation of horses, which necessitated establishing facilities and procedures for equine quarantine and testing.

horse was not released from quarantine as a result of a positive blood test and was eventually returned to its country of origin.

Export procedures were less rigorous. US government regulations require only a five-hour rest period for horses prior to their export. The USDA certified the Horse Park as a temporary export facility, from which the horses were taken to their aircrafts.

CONCLUSIONS AND RECOMMENDATIONS

The accumulation of required material, careful inventory management, venue delivery and installation, and the development of a complete recovery plan are the main elements of a successful logistics department. Prior to the Games, the amount of materials expected and the warehouse space necessary to support it can only be estimated, as actual needs are not documented by departments until venue occupation. This necessitated supplying departments with standard kits of FF&E and called upon Logistics staff to be prepared to meet additional needs during Games-time.

The following recommendations are offered to future organizing committees.

Logistical Support

■ The MM&P function needs to occur before a thorough assessment of the warehousing requirement can be made. When evaluating potential warehouse facilities, the location and total cost of refurbishing the facility should be the primary considerations.

■ To make the warehousing task more efficient, a simple, user-friendly software system for tracking all materials must be implemented early.

■ Standardize materials and supplies, to the greatest extent possible, for efficiency, consistency, and cost containment.

■ The designated freight forwarder/customs broker should be chosen early in the organizing process and should be integrated into the logistics process across all departments to ensure legal compliance and consistency of information and services.

■ The airline charter process must be sufficiently communicated so that relevant government agencies can be notified and personnel and equipment available to clear and unload the planes.

■ The exit process from the Olympic Village needs to be planned in as much detail as the arrival process. Regulations on baggage handling and outbound charters need to be emphasized and the distinction between freight and luggage needs to be clearly defined.

■ The asset management plan needs to include a fully developed recovery component.

Venue Logistics

■ Centralization of a function should be organization-wide. Duplication of services by individual departments during Games-time can cause problems.

■ Storage of empty packing cartons and materials is important to large constituent groups such as the broadcasters and press media. Keeping these materials on-site would allow for prepacking and expedite the exit process.

Waste Management

■ The planning offices for important contracted services should be located in proximity to the function to facilitate communication. Distance and isolation can disrupt the flow of some venue operation–related information.

■ The degree of public relations support for the environmental program corresponds directly to its success.

■ The venue cleaning program should be directed by the venue management function.

Administration

■ Close coordination with Accreditation, Human Resources, and Security is required to provide all needed access for personnel and deliveries.

Chapter Fifteen
Marketing / ACOP

OVERVIEW—Atlanta Centennial Olympic Properties (ACOP) was created on 14 June 1991 as a joint marketing program between the USOC and ACOG. In the 1990 Host City Contract with the IOC, the USOC and the organizing committee were required to, "cooperate fully so that there is only one joint marketing program between them." The intent of this requirement was to establish and implement a program to market the right to use Olympic marks, license the sale of Olympic merchandise worldwide in a manner consistent with the spirit and image of the Olympic Games and Olympic Movement, engage in marketing activities to raise revenue to support the US Olympic team and the 1996 Games, and avoid the creation of competing ACOG and USOC programs that could lead to sponsor conflicts and marketplace clutter.

ACOP's mission was to raise a substantial portion of the funding for the Centennial Olympic Games and the 1994 and 1996 US Olympic teams through the sale of sponsorships, licensing, and other fund-raising programs. ACOP presented a single, unified marketing program for the 1996 Games and the US Olympic teams.

Sponsorship programs were developed and implemented by ACOP, including participation in the IOC's international marketing program, The Olympic Programme (TOP) III, and the national partners program, Centennial Olympic Partners (COP). Licensing programs were divided however, as ACOP managed ACOG marks licensing, while the USOC managed the licensing of its marks separately. However, both programs collaborated on the sale and distribution of products. Similarly, charitable fund-raising, lottery and license plate programs, and certain other local or specialized programs were developed separately by the two entities, but marketed together. The result of the joint venture was the most successful marketing program in Olympic history.

Early Activities

ACOP was required, per the 14 June agreement, to develop its marketing plan by 1 October 1991. The plan was designed to generate maximum revenues for the Games, USOC, and ACOG, and to reduce market confusion by collecting and packaging together as many Olympic-related marketing opportunities as possible for coordinated presentation to potential sponsors, licensees, and suppliers.

ACOP developed and implemented adequate procedures that ensured Olympic marks were used in conjunction with high-quality products and services and were consistent with the image of the Olympic Movement.

ACOP was managed jointly by the ACOG CEO and a USOC co-chair, who together established the policies and managed and supervised the operations of the program. ACOG's CEO was responsible for the daily implementation of the marketing plan, provided that he jointly manage the execution of sponsorship, supplier, licensee, contributor, and similar agreements with the USOC co-chair and USOC president.

The joint venture agreement did not allow the USOC to use, market, or sell ACOG marks without sharing the profits with ACOG, and ACOG could not use, market, or sell USOC marks without sharing the profits with the USOC. Staff and related expenses were to be shared in the same proportion as the revenue split.

ORGANIZATION

In order to facilitate and implement a successful marketing program, ACOP staff was divided into six divisions: Sponsor Sales, Sponsor Support, Licensing, New Market Development, Olympic Program, and Marketing Operations.

Staffing

After the consummation of the joint venture agreement in late 1991, ACOP began to establish its focus and assemble its staff. In spring 1992, a chief marketing officer, vice presidents, and administrative staff began the development of the detailed operations plan.

By January 1993, the ACOP staff expanded to include directors for New Market Development, Marketing Operations, Licensing, and Sponsor Support.

Volunteer, paid, and loaned personnel at the end of 1995 totaled 97. The Games-time organization was staffed by ACOP personnel and volunteers added to the Sponsor Support division.

After the Games, a small staff remained to conclude ACOP activities and to transfer remaining responsibilities to ACOG and the USOC; the legal conclusion of the venture was effective 31 December 1996.

SPONSOR SALES

The Sponsor Sales division was responsible for developing the base of companies that would invest to acquire the right to be associated with the Olympic Movement, and use that association to enhance their businesses. In 1991, McKinsey and Company produced a comprehensive market research report profiling companies that had made major advertising and promotional commitments in the past. The sales plan was to approach these companies and propose that they acquire Olympic Games/US team rights as a strategic investment that would allow them to participate in a comprehensive total marketing program.

Such a program required identifying which key constituents would be affected by Olympic-related marketing activities and the objectives that were to be achieved. For business constituents, marketing opportunities were typically consumers, distribution channels (distributors or retailers), suppliers to the company, and employees. The purchase of a sponsorship allowed companies to:

- launch and showcase new products;
- cultivate new market segments;
- alter or shape corporate image;
- motivate/incite employees; and
- develop unique Games-time hospitality programs for key customers, suppliers, and other constituents.

The size of investment required to acquire sponsorship rights and benefits necessitated that ACOP articulate to potential sponsors how the Olympic association could be integrated advantageously into their present marketing strategies and plans.

Market research data and testimonials of companies involved with prior Games demonstrated a virtually universal awareness of Olympic trademarks, and the positive way people view the Games regardless of their gender,

Atlanta 1996
®

36 USC 380

The ACOP logo incorporated the ACOG torch mark logo and the USOC logo.

RICK C CHIANG • CHRISTOPHER CHIAPETTA • ANTHONY J CHIARANTANO • ELIZABETH W CHICADO • STACY A CHICK • ANNA CHIEN • SAU-YAN CHIEN • CHARLES P CHIHASZ • SARA J CHIHASZ • MICHAEL CHIKIRIS • JAGADEESH C CHILAKAPATI • WADE H CHILCOAT • SARAH ANITA CHILCUTT • JON M CHILD • KATHRIN R CHILD • MARTHA LEE CHILD • DAVID B CHILDERS • ELIZABETH B CHILDERS • JAMES H CHILDERS • KAREN B CHILDERS • KENNETH C CHILDERS • MARY J CHILDERS • SHIRLEY T CHILDERS • TERESA A CHILDERS • WILLIAM S CHILDERS • BRENDA K CHILDRESS •

263

race, age, income, or education, thus convincing companies of the positive return-on-investment potential resulting from sponsorships. In support of sponsor investments, the most comprehensive sponsor services program ever developed was created.

Worldwide Sponsors, Centennial Games Partners, and Sponsors

The Host City Contract required that ACOP participate with the IOC in the process of marketing the international sponsorships of The

Corporate logos were displayed frequently to recognize the important support provided in the staging of the Games.

Olympic Programme III, hereafter referred to as TOP. TOP sponsors were given worldwide rights in all countries which had NOCs participating in the program.

ACOP was not authorized to grant the right to use Olympic marks in connection with any product category included in TOP, and any revenue received in connection with TOP was deemed revenue to ACOG and not ACOP. ACOP participated in all discussions and negotiations with the IOC concerning TOP sponsors and provided marketing services for them.

The following 10 companies were the TOP sponsors for the 1992–1996 quadrennium.
- The Coca-Cola Company
- Eastman Kodak Company
- VISA
- Bausch & Lomb
- Xerox
- Sports Illustrated/TIME International
- Panasonic
- IBM
- John Hancock
- UPS

The national partnership program—Centennial Olympic Partners, hereafter referred to as COP—involved the following companies, which had rights comparable to TOP sponsors but for marks used exclusively within the US.
- NationsBank
- Sara Lee Corporation
- The Home Depot
- Anheuser-Busch
- McDonald's
- Swatch
- AT&T
- Delta Air Lines
- Motorola, Inc.

In addition to the TOP/COP sponsor programs, a sponsor level program was developed that granted, solely in the US, a more limited set of rights and benefits to the following companies.
- Sensormatic
- York
- Randstad Staffing Services
- BellSouth Corporation
- Georgia Power Company
- Blue Cross/Blue Shield
- Scientific Atlanta
- Borg-Warner Security Corporation
- Columbia TriStar Television—*Wheel of Fortune* and *Jeopardy!*

- General Motors
- BMW
- Holiday Inn
- Avon
- Nissan
- World Travel Partners
- Texaco USA
- International Paper
- American Gas Association
- The Dial Corporation
- Textron
- General Mills
- Brunswick Corporation
- Merrill Lynch
- WXIA-TV

Sponsor Rights and Benefits. As a result of their investment, companies acquired a comprehensive set of rights and benefits as part of their association with the Olympic Movement. Defined sponsorship rights provided sponsors access to Olympic marks, designations, symbols, and imagery for use in conjunction with business activities. Depending on the type of sponsorship, the marks could include the IOC five rings, the USOC five rings, the Atlanta torch mark logo, and the Atlanta Games mascot, IZZY. In addition, certain phrases trademarked by ACOG, such as *Atlanta 1996*, were also available to sponsors.

Approved designations varied from generic designations (official worldwide sponsor of the 1996 Olympic Games, official Centennial Olympic Games partner, official sponsor of the US Olympic team) to more company- or product-specific designations (official timer of the 1996 Olympic Games, official outfitter of the US Olympic team). Symbols, such as the official pictogram of the 1996 Olympic Games, and imagery, such as the Look of the Games colors and patterns, were other rights granted uniquely to sponsors for commercial programs, such as advertising, promotions, and contests; recognition programs; and premium items.

A broad, comprehensive benefits package was also created for sponsors. The size of the sponsorship investment determined the quantity of benefits provided. Typically, a TOP or COP sponsor would have access to 400 hotel rooms, with two Opening and Closing Ceremonies tickets per room and four event tickets per day per room, with a 1:1 ratio of tickets for high-demand and low-demand events. Sponsors were allowed to select their accommodations in the order in which they signed as a sponsor.

Additionally, TOP and COP sponsors were allowed to acquire space in the three sponsor hospitality villages, built to provide high-quality fa-

cilities in which sponsors could entertain guests during the Games. Sponsors were also provided automobiles for executives and guests, preferred parking locations, and a certain number of accreditation badges that provided broad access privileges and were transferable.

Sponsors were also given the largest recognition program in Olympic Games history, the most far-reaching sponsor protection program ever implemented, and the most comprehensive and longest-available sponsor services program ever provided, which will be discussed later in the chapter.

Other first-time activities developed for sponsors were several unique support programs, such as the Centennial History Collection and the

A symbolic representation of the Games was presented to each corporation providing support.

History of the Olympic Games kiosk, for which ACOP used its experience, access to information and memorabilia, and creative resources to develop a versatile display that could then be used by all sponsors multiple times.

Supplierships

Companies with the capability and tradition of providing operational items, resources, and sports equipment for the Olympic Games became suppliers. The supplier-level financial commitment did not equal that required for

Workshops were held for sponsors that focused on Games-time operational issues and ways companies could use their marketing rights to enhance their businesses.

sponsorship rights and benefits, and therefore received restricted rights and benefits. For example, the official supplier of basketballs was allowed to use the Games mark on its equipment.

Business Suppliers: ABF/Worldway Corporation; Aggreko, Inc.; Alfred Karcher, Inc.; Allsport; American Meter Company; ARAMARK; Auto Desk, Inc.; Beaulieu of America, Inc.; Brother International Corporation (USA); Buckhead Beef Company, Inc.; Carolina Handling;

LLC/Raymond; CH2M Hill; Circle International; Competitive Media Reporting; CTI Resources, Inc.; DeBoer Structures; Digital Music Express; Dohring Company; Douwe Egbert; Drake Beam Morin, Inc.; Exide Electronics Corporation; Fetzer; Fluke Corporation; Gallery Furniture; Good Humor/Breyers; James River Corporation; Jet Set Sports; Korbel; Kubota Corporation; Leisure Club International, Inc.; Media One, Inc.; New Holland North America, Inc.; Norfolk Southern Railway Company; Qzar, Inc.; Reebok; Reed & Barton; Rentokil Environmental Services; Simmons Company; Stainless Image, Inc.; Vulcan Hart/Hobart; WGST; World Color Press; and ZEP.

Sports Equipment Supplierships: Adolph Keifer & Associates; American Athletic, Inc.; Federal Sports Technologies, Inc.; Hayashi/Top Ten; Hydra Rib; Infra-Red Sauna Systems, Inc.; JOOLA; Mavic, Inc.; Mettler-Toledo, Inc.; Mistral Sports Group; Mizuno, USA; MONDO S.p.A.; Penn Racquet Sports, Inc.; Perry Sports; Robbins Sport Surfaces; Senoh; Sport Supply Group, Inc.; Sunfish Laser; Taraflex; Tuf-Wear Manufacturing, Inc.; Uesaka Iron Works; Yakima; and Yonex.

SPONSOR SUPPORT

The most comprehensive sponsor support program ever developed was created as part of the overall sponsor marketing plan. Since sponsorships required the largest investments in history, a very comprehensive support program was necessary. The Account Director Program, through which sponsor liaisons were managed, was developed, as was a broad strategy that focused on three major support areas— Sponsor Services, Sponsor Protection, and Sponsor Recognition.

Account Director Program

The Account Director Program was implemented in 1992 in recognition of the scale and scope of activities sponsors would be pursuing to maximize their investments, and the multitude of Olympic organizations with which they would need to interact. Account directors were assigned to all sponsors to act as their primary contact with Olympic organizations and apprise them of various Olympic-related activities and programs in which they could participate. Account directors worked with two to five sponsor accounts, depending on the size and diversity of sponsor activities. One account director was assigned to provide support to the supplier companies. Through interactive communication, account directors were a valuable component of sponsors' Olympic programs, responding to sponsor requests, assimilating appropriate resources, and introducing sponsors to new programs or opportunities.

Sponsor Services

Sponsor Services was formed in 1993 to coordinate the fulfillment of sponsor contracts with all ACOG functional areas. The focus of Sponsor Services was to plan, manage, and communicate sponsors' operational support needs during the pre-Games and Games-time periods.

Sponsor Services developed two distinct exhibits for sponsor usage. The Centennial History Collection, a 10,000 sq ft (930 sq m) exhibit of historic memorabilia collected throughout the 100 years of the modern Olympic Games, contained over 1,000 items borrowed from collectors worldwide. The display was portable, so sponsors could schedule to use it for trade shows, conventions, corporate headquarters, plant sites, or civic facilities. The exhibit was utilized by virtually all TOP/COP sponsors and was brought on a tour for four months in Europe, sponsored by Swatch.

Also available to sponsors was the History of the Olympic Games, a 400 sq ft (37 sq m) interactive, traveling multimedia kiosk that featured: Great Moments in Olympic History; the Atlanta Centennial Games—Background, Plans, and Video Interviews with Games Executives; the

History of the Olympic Games; and a fourth component whereby a sponsor could create and insert unique product or company information. This single touch-screen kiosk was designed for sponsor use with smaller audiences.

From 1993 to 1995, Sponsor Services held numerous workshops for sponsors and licensees that focused on Games-time operational issues and methods sponsors could use to enhance their visibility through their sponsorships. In 1993 and 1994, Sponsor Services also conducted annual workshops for the Licensing division.

Sponsor Services was responsible for the marketing activities at the Lillehammer Winter Games. An ACOP office was established there to support sponsors and their activities in Norway. Daily marketing meetings were attended by the IOC, Lillehammer Olympic Organizing Committee, and the USOC to discuss sponsor issues.

In 1994, the Sponsor Presence Program, designed to blend the Look imagery with sponsor-specific identification in high-visibility areas, was created with ACOG Creative Services. A package providing more than 400 street banners, 4,500 ft (1,372 m) of venue wraps, and 155 bus wraps was offered to TOP/COP sponsors at the November workshop. Nine sponsors purchased the package.

In 1995, the Sponsor Advisory Council for TOP/COP was formed to allow a senior representative from each company to meet with ACOP executives for frank dialogue and issue resolution.

Sponsor Services also organized and conducted a five-day venue tour for all sponsors in

Artist rendering of the sponsor hospitality village at Olympic Stadium.

May 1996. Sponsors were given an extensive tour of every venue, including tours of sponsor parking and venue access locations.

Sponsor Hospitality Villages. Sponsor Services developed the three TOP/COP sponsor hospitality villages for which ACOP was contractually responsible—at Olympic Center, Olympic Stadium, and Stone Mountain Park. Site selection and preliminary designs were completed in late 1994. In the final designs, the center village, which was next to Centennial Olympic Park, and the stadium village were each nearly 5 acres (2 ha) in area and included multiple structures.

The Stone Mountain Park village was a single 30,000 sq ft (2,790 sq m) tent, with dining facilities, bars, and television viewing areas. A marketing club was located in both the center and stadium villages. Eighteen of the 19 sponsors participated, as did the IOC. The minimum purchase provided 2,000 sq ft (186 sq m) that was customized in both the center and stadium villages, general access to the Stone Mountain Park village, and an associated amenity package. Sponsors could expand their customized facilities at the center village by leasing additional area. The largest individual sponsor facility was a 10,000 sq ft (930 sq m) hospitality tent.

Preliminary research for potential suppliers of the products and services required to build and operate these villages began in January 1995. This process was assisted by procuring some of these services through marketing supplierships. Two primary supplierships were De-Boer, which provided structures, and Aggreko, which supplied air-conditioning and power distribution.

During 1995, Sponsor Services focused on three main areas: planning for the construction and dismantling of the villages, planning their operation, and managing a matrix of commitments of ACOG departments responsible for delivering services to sponsors during Games-time.

Bimonthly vendor integration meetings were held with all primary vendors that would be working in the villages along with the architect and Sponsor Services staff.

Site preparation and construction began on the center village in April 1996. Since no site preparation was required for the stadium village, its preparation began on 1 June 1996, and the Stone Mountain Park village began on 8 July. After the Games, all three villages were dismantled within three weeks.

The result of the multiyear planning process was a Games-time hospitality program larger than any conducted previously for any major event, and it achieved unparalleled success. Sponsor response to the quality of the hospitality program and the thoroughness and efficiency of the programs within it was a reflection of the commitment ACOP made to assist sponsors in maximizing their investments.

Sponsor Protection

Sponsor Protection was responsible for ensuring that sponsors' rights were not compromised by competitors which might try to create the impression that they were connected with the Olympic Movement, and for monitoring and correcting any attempts to use Olympic-related marks, designations, or imagery that violated the US Amateur Sports Act. With the anticipated size of the Centennial Olympic Games and the high regard the US holds for the Olympic Games, it became apparent that protecting the rights for which sponsors had made significant investments would be challenging. Celebrating the 100th anniversary of the Olympic Movement in the US created the extreme potential for ambush marketing.

In 1992, after evaluating historical ambush marketing problems at the Olympic Games and other major sports-related events in the US, a strategy was developed comprising a national strategy, an Atlanta Games-time strategy, and other enforcement activities.

National Pre-Games Strategy. A historical evaluation revealed that the general public was not aware that ambush marketing is inappropriate and illegal. Altering the incidence of and public attitude toward ambush programs required portraying the problem more visibly and clearly.

A document was created that described the legal problems incurred from unauthorized use of Olympic marks, designations, and imagery vis-a-vis the US Amateur Sports Act, and the illegality of intentionally confusing or misleading the public through advertising. The document also described how, through embarking on an ambush campaign, a company ultimately disempowers the entire Olympic Movement and the athletes it claims to support. The document focused on those illegal and undesirable actions within the context of the code of ethics by which businesses and advertising agencies guide their policies and activities, thus making them more apparent to the public and corporations.

With the plan developed, the next step in spreading broad awareness was mailing a letter to more than 1,000 advertising and public relations agencies that defined the problem and asked them to rethink pursuing such activities with clients which were not Olympic sponsors.

A multimonth media interview campaign including major trade magazines and local and national press followed. These efforts resulted in some excellent features by the media that started 18 months before the Games and increased in frequency and intensity as the Games approached. This was supplemented by many interviews on network and cable television that provided even more information.

In addition, the media was made aware of other preparations to protect sponsors during the Games. A media tracking firm was employed to identify any unauthorized television, radio, and print ads by nonsponsors. A market research firm was used to conduct public opinion research to evaluate whether ads were confusing or misleading, as preparatory work for developing plans for legal action, if necessary. An advertising agency prepared several ads to run in major media that would specifically identify companies engaging in ambush marketing if they persisted after notification. Additionally, outside legal counsel, which had been actively involved with the preparatory work during the 24 months preceding the Games, was commissioned to work quickly and directly on any such activities.

This Games-time action plan, which complemented the pre-Games awareness/prevention campaign, was provided to various media, which supported and broadly covered the efforts. This program resulted in cooperation from many agencies and corporations. Individuals were more aware of whether or not a company was legitimately associated with the Games or the US Olympic team. The result of the efforts was virtually no ambush activity occurring in the country.

Atlanta Games Strategy. Much attention was devoted to planning for problems that could arise in Atlanta during the Games. During the years preceding the Games, a comprehensive inventory of all billboard locations; large, highly visible buildings; and other high-profile advertisement locations was incorporated into a computer database.

This information, in conjunction with the ongoing ambush marketing communications with major outdoor advertising companies, placed ACOP in a position to monitor activities via these very visible means of public communication. As a result of this preparatory work, ACOP was able to respond rapidly to advertisements that encroached or confused the public and correct the situations.

The other major Games-time activity was the challenge of ensuring no ambush activity took place in and around the competition venues. A venue marketing team was at each of the 31 competition venues during every competitive session. Teams worked with Security to prevent items from entering the venues, and with Venue Management to ensure no orchestrated ambush activity occurred during the competitions. Such activity could potentially occur through numerous means, such as flags, placards, visors, seat cushions, and drink containers. To staff such an endeavor, 175 volunteers were recruited and provided with a comprehensive training program.

Enforcement Activities. Sponsor Protection continuously worked with the USOC to enforce its rights granted under the US Amateur Sports Act. Throughout four years, more than 16,000 telephone calls were received and over 3,900 cease-and-desist letters sent, most frequently to businesses across the country unaware they were violating federal law. Typically, a positive response followed notification. Rarely, when this did not occur, stronger legal action was taken.

Another activity conducted with the USOC was working with US Customs to prevent unauthorized merchandise from entering the country. A training program for US Customs was developed and presented 68 times to customs agents at the ports of entry, resulting in their full attention and cooperation.

Sponsor Recognition

The goal of the Sponsor Recognition division was to make the public aware that sponsors were primarily responsible for making the Games possible, and therefore should be recognized as being unique and special because of this. This centrally developed program resulted in the broadest recognition program in Olympic Games history.

Public Relations. During the pre-Games period, Public Relations staff provided services directed at raising sponsor visibility. They arranged major press briefings to announce sponsorships and coordinated Sponsor Recognition press releases to business and Olympic media. In addition, Public Relations provided assistance and Olympic Games/US Olympic team materials for sponsor-specific events as requested.

A special program designed by Public Relations was the Sponsor Demonstration and Seminar Program. The program, held in Atlanta, Chicago, and New York during 1996, included inviting the press to seminars which featured sponsors headquartered in their geographic areas. Sponsors designed space at seminar locations in order to demonstrate to the press the products and services defined by their sponsor category. During the session, a senior executive from each participating sponsor spoke for five minutes to outline why it had become a sponsor and how it was using that sponsorship to meet business objectives.

Additionally, four workshops were held for sponsors' public relations staffs. These sessions focused on maximizing the public relations value of the sponsorship and exposing them to available resources and assets.

Public Relations also provided news releases that focused on situations where a sponsor was involved directly in an operational aspect of staging the Games. This not only acknowledged sponsor contributions, but also helped validate the applied use of their products, services, and personnel.

Sponsors were recognized in every general distribution publication produced by ACOG and the USOC. In addition, special stories were published about sponsors as they were announced to provide individual as well as group recognition. These publications were distributed to hundreds of thousands of people.

During the Games, Public Relations orchestrated a number of half-hour media briefings for sponsors to describe the various activities they were participating in during the Games period.

Advertising. Through various advertising media, an image recognition strategy was devised in 1993 that necessitated a print campaign during the 1994 Olympic Winter Games with a focus on the TOP and COP sponsors. This first advertising campaign included 12 pages of advertisements that appeared in *Sports Illustrated (SI)* over a three-week period. The ads featured pictures of athletes with the underlying theme that sponsors were partners to the athletes and the Games.

The second advertisement campaign, that began in late 1994 and continued through 1995, showed an athlete as the centerpiece, framed by each TOP and COP sponsor logo and a short vignette about the sponsor. The vignettes were written by the TOP/COP sponsors and focused on their individual Olympic-related messages. The campaign included 22 pages of advertising that were printed for several months in *Fortune, People, Southern Living, Sports Illustrated*, and *Time*'s Man of the Year publication.

The third ad campaign was the 1996 pre-Games/Games-time emphasis program, which had two versions. One featured the logos of the TOP and COP sponsors, and the other, the logos of all sponsor family members. The program appeared 18 times within the publications mentioned above.

A series of television ads was also developed to create a new look at athletes in action. A special project was initiated whereby aspiring athletes in multiple sports disciplines were filmed as they prepared for the US Olympic team. Each athlete then did a voice overlay to describe how the support of sponsors made it possible for them to train and compete in the Games. These ads, with an overlay of the TOP and COP sponsor logos, were shown as 60-second commercials during each of the 10 NBC Olympic Games special programs that began in early 1994. This footage, available to sponsors for use in their own commercials or video projects, was also used in other video-based projects, such as public service ads created to run as pre-feature film ads in movie theaters.

Another significant type of advertising was placing TOP/COP sponsor print ads on billboards around Atlanta immediately before and during the Games. Through the generous billboard space contributed by an outdoor advertising company, sponsor messages were conveyed to spectators visiting Atlanta.

Games-Time. During the Games, the objective was to recognize sponsors with extensive, high-profile visibility to spectators attending competitions. Every competition venue was

ACOP demonstrated displays of Olympic licensed merchandise at major trade shows.

surveyed to determine which locations would provide the most exposure to the 180 specially designed recognition kiosks. Of these kiosks, 120 carried the logos of the TOP/COP sponsors, and the other 60 carried the identities of all 43 sponsors. The kiosks used the Look color and image schemes. In addition, a profile of each sponsor was developed for Info'96.

LICENSING

The objectives of ACOP's Licensing division were to create and maximize revenues, establish and sell the ACOG mark and designation (brand) through licensed products, protect the trademarks, and sell licensed products internationally. The concept was based on analysis of each potential merchandise category with plans to offer nonexclusive licenses to the best companies in each category. The marketing strategy was to promote interest in all sports and Olympic themes year-round, in addition to Games-time. This strategy was very successful, despite the challenge of maintaining multiyear interest in the US.

The selection criteria for licensees were quality licensed products, marketing ability and experience in their category and distribution channels, and financial stability.

The original plan called for four collections of specially licensed products: authentic, kids, historic, and general. The challenge in separating the collections was that most prospective licensees demanded licenses for all, which ultimately were granted to shorten the selling process and achieve higher guarantees. Licensees typically would then direct their efforts at the programs that would yield the greatest results. The total number of licensees in the program in the US was 124, including the largest licensing agreement in Olympic Games history with the Sara Lee Corporation. Internationally, 24 companies, distributors, and NOCs had licensing rights in more than 60 countries.

A holographic hang-tag program was researched and implemented to create an authentic, protective system and enhance the look of the products. In deference to the requirements of some licensees, a holographic sticker was produced that could be applied to existing hang-tags. *(For a complete list of US merchandise licensees, see Figure 1.)*

Licensee Support Program

The Licensee Support Program made the license more valuable and therefore, more salable.

Through this program, ACOP was able to acquire licensees at the highest rates and largest guarantees in Olympic Games licensing history.

ACOP occupied significant exhibit space at the Super Show and the National Sporting Goods Association Show. During the early years, this helped establish that ACOP would contribute serious efforts to support product sales.

The retail support team visited major retailers and arranged vendor days. The team also focused on creating promotions—point of sale materials including banners, concept shops, countertop displays, and videos designed to increase sales for licensees and retailers; a public relations and ad campaign; and multiple licensee workshops.

The public relations plan contributed to the program through support of the Olympic mascot, IZZY, contacts with collectors, gift ideas, and unique products.

The advertising plan was launched via a unique feature requiring licensees to pay fees into an ACOP cooperative budget which was used to fund advertising and promotion programs to promote Olympic Games brand awareness that would benefit all licensees. Funds were also spent on trade journal ads through ACOP's ad agency.

The following campaigns were part of the Licensee Support Program.

■ An *SI* subscription was given to approximately 1,000 national retailer buyers and executives. Quarterly, an ACOP "wrap" was designed and included with that week's issue. The wrap included information about the program, an advertisement, and the name and address of each licensee. During that period, the advertisement appearing in *SI* was also placed in appropriate trade journals.

■ During the 1995 holiday season, a gift guide was inserted in *People*, *SI*, and other magazines. The guide contained illustrations of licensed products, and licensees wishing to participate paid for specific placement in the guide.

■ Periodic updates to trade journals and consumer periodicals, announcements of new licensees, press kits for trade shows, and video

ACOP produced *Showcase*, a licensing newsletter distributed regularly to communicate innovative programs.

news releases during appropriate selling seasons further implemented the public relations plan. Major efforts also resulted in contests in *Sports Illustrated for Kids* (*SI for Kids*).

Special Programs. The Coca-Cola Company was licensed to create the ACOG Pin Society, a quality program with newsletters, a book, membership pins, and special sales. The successful program had approximately 75,000 members and generated significant pin sales.

Some licensees created products for the 1994 Lillehammer Games for sale in the US. More successful in northern US cities, it was a helpful test case for future work. Additionally, an ACOG store was opened in Lillehammer that had exceptional business.

The Swatch Program was among the most successful licensing agreements coordinated by ACOP. Historic marks (official posters and Games marks from the past 100 years) enhanced the early stages of the program. Subsequently, Swatch designed several other collections that outsold the first. Swatch eventually became ACOP's second highest royalty-producing licensee, managing successful sales programs in more than 60 countries.

A number of premium promotional programs were also launched. One of the most successful was McDonald's Canada, Germany, and Austria promotions, which included substantial savings on the purchase of caps and watches. ACOP ensured the items were produced by ACOP licensees, and more than 1 million ACOG watches were sold in Germany during a two-week period.

Another unique promotional event included the painting of a GM-sponsored race car with a special flag and ACOG motif. The sale of commemorative products from this race yielded successful promotional value and revenue.

In order to enhance exposure, ACOP licensed Mattel to produce an Olympic Barbie doll. The result was the sale of more than

---

FIGURE 1: US MERCHANDISE LICENSEES

- AA World Class Embroidery
- Aerial Photography Services, Inc.
- Aladdin Industries, Inc.
- American Toons
- Aminco
- Anheuser-Busch, Inc.
- Applause
- A.T. Cross
- AT&T
- Avon Products, Inc.
- Balfour
- Bausch & Lomb
- Beaulieu of America
- Big Dog Sportswear
- Bogarz
- Bridgestone Graphics Technology, Inc.
- Brother International Corporation
- Brown-Forman Beverages Worldwide
- C-2 Office Gear
- Carlson Marketing Group, Inc.
- Carlton Books
- Champion
- Champion Jogbra
- Cherians / Foamina USA, Inc.
- Coach
- Coca-Cola USA
- Collect-a-Card
- College Concepts
- Copywrite Products L. L. C.
- Crystal Springs Water Company
- Cutler Sports Apparel
- DiscUS Sports, Inc.
- Drew Pearson

- Easton Events Company
- EK Sports / Everything Kids
- Emerson USA
- Equity Marketing, Inc.
- Essex Manufacturing Co., Inc.
- Favorite Recipes Press
- Fieldcrest Cannon, Inc.
- Fine Art Ltd.
- First Colony Coffee and Tea Co., Inc.
- Flik Flak (division of SMH, Inc.)
- Fort, Inc.
- General Mills
- Golden Harvest Products
- Group II Communications, Inc.
- Haddad Apparel Group, Ltd.
- Hallmark Licensing, Inc.
- Hanes / Hanes Her Way
- High Five Sportswear
- H. M. Gousha
- Ho Ho Art & Craft International Co., Inc.
- The Home Depot
- The Hunter Manufacturing Group
- Identity, Inc.
- Imprinted Products Corporation
- IMS Studio 6
- Jonathan Grey
- Kendall-Futuro Company
- L'eggs

- Lion Brothers
- Lipert International, Inc.
- Lledo, Inc.
- Logo 7, Inc.
- Mack II, Inc.
- Macmillan USA / Frommer's Travel Guides
- Maggie Lyon, Inc.
- Mattel
- MBI, Inc.
- Michael Anthony Jewelers
- Milestone Publishing
- Miller / Zell, Inc.
- Mirage
- Molten
- Mondo, S.p.A.
- Motorola
- Moving Products
- Oak Hill Farms
- One-on-One Sports
- Pacific Rim Trading Caps
- Perry Ellis (a division of Salant Corporation)
- Pindar Press
- Pittsfield Weaving Company
- Play-By-Play Toys & Novelties
- The Postcard Factory
- RGA Accessories, Inc.
- Ralph Marlin & Company, Inc.
- Reebok
- Reed & Barton
- Responsive Marketing, Inc.
- Salamander
- Salem Sportswear
- The Seckinger-Lee Company

- Southern Living
- Spalding Sports
- Speedo / Authentic Fitness
- Sport Supply Group
- Sports Image
- Starline Creations, Inc.
- Starter Corporation
- Sunbelt Marketing Group
- Sunfish Laser
- Sure Shot
- Swatch (division of SMH, Inc.)
- Swingster Marketing
- Swiss Army Brand
- Tag Express
- Terry Manufacturing
- The Game
- Topline Products, Inc.
- United Innovations
- UPP Entertainment Marketing
- USA.OPOLY, Inc.
- US Gold
- US Label
- US Playing Card Company
- Waterford Crystal, Inc.
- West Georgia Golf Company
- WEK Enterprises
- Wincraft
- Winner International
- Yonex Company, Ltd.
- Zak Designs
- Zippo Manufacturing

100,000 Barbie doll sets, as well as exceptional coverage in many consumer periodicals.

ACOP licensed *Southern Living* to produce a direct-mail product catalog which superbly represented many products. Royalties from catalog sales covered catalog production expenses.

ACOP also licensed QVC, the interactive TV sales network, to create a number of programs on their shopping channel. In addition to generating more product sales, ACOG became more visible to consumers.

IZZY Marketing. Creating and marketing products of the Olympic mascot, WHATIZIT, presented challenges. Problems included reproducing certain features of the figure, such as its floating lightning eyebrows and the cloud of stars that surrounded its head.

In response, ACOP licensing in conjunction with KidFacts, a research firm specializing in assessing entertainment concepts with children, and Sagon-Phior, a creative firm that helped develop youth-oriented merchandise, began to research the mascot's appeal to children. Children in focus groups throughout the country expressed their desire to make WHATIZIT more youth-like. ACOG considered their advice and then implemented their suggestions. The revised character was unveiled in June 1993, and ACOG invited children to choose its name. Within two weeks, children in 16 countries had submitted more than 3,300 names. A panel of Atlanta-area children selected IZZY.

As part of the introduction of IZZY's new name and personality, *Parade* magazine invited children to write stories featuring the character. ACOG promised to award a certificate to each child who wrote a story and display the stories during the Games. More than 1,600 schools participated, submitting more than 170,000 stories by Games-time. ACOG invited the US Secretary of Education and local school chil-

dren to read some of the stories, which were displayed in the Georgia Dome prior to the Games. All stories were incorporated into the *Centennial Collectibles* exhibit in the Atlanta Merchandise Mart, and many children were able to locate their stories displayed on the walls and other areas during the Games.

ACOP, with the help of Film Roman, Inc., an award-winning animation studio, transformed IZZY into an animated figure. A half-hour animated IZZY special loaded with imagery and lessons for children from the Olympic Games was televised on TBS's Cartoon Network three times beginning in fall 1995.

Even before the special aired, the licensing of IZZY products had already helped him become the most widely employed mascot in Olympic history. Among other IZZY products, there were bedding sets, bookbags, coloring and activity books, party supplies, pins, plush toys, school supplies, stickers, and tableware, as well as a fan club. A giant IZZY balloon appeared in Macy's Thanksgiving Day parades from 1993 to 1995—each with television audiences of approximately 65 million people—and flew over Atlanta during the Games.

International Marketing. International markets offered an opportunity for ACOP Licensing to capitalize on the worldwide enthusiasm that would surround the Centennial Olympic Games. The challenge was to establish agreements with the NOCs and, where appropriate, obtain access for ACOP licensees, which would allow them to distribute products in the respective countries.

As indicated previously, the multicountry Swatch agreement was the largest and most successful international licensing program in Olympic history. Other significant milestones were arranged with agencies in several countries such as Germany, Mexico, and South Africa. The agreement with Japan Olympic Marketing, Inc., also proved successful, generating a record level of royalties for an event taking place in another country. Another first was a licensing agreement negotiated with the Chinese Olympic Committee that allowed for ACOP marks usage on licensed products in the People's Republic of China. *(For a complete list of international licensing agreements, see Figure 2.)*

Although the international marketing program was successful and record-setting, it did not achieve its full potential due to the slow process of negotiating contracts.

Games-Time Support. In addition to hosting three receptions during the Games for licensees, ACOP coordinated an effective anti-counterfeiting program. By contracting the legal and investigative work, ACOP developed a program that placed 15 teams of four (two investigators and two federal marshals) on the streets during the Games to address counterfeit merchandise. Due to the coverage plan and the effectiveness of these teams, virtually all counterfeit merchandise found was voluntarily surrendered to the investigators. In total, more than $5 million of counterfeit merchandise was removed, ensuring minimal unlicensed marks use during the Games.

MARKETING COMMUNICATIONS CENTER

The marketing communications center (MCC) was a resource center designed to preserve and protect the value of the Olympic Games sponsors' investments by providing Games-time support for the marketing functions of Licensing, Sponsor Protection, and Sponsor Services, as well as for the Clean Venue Program. It began 12-hour daily operations on 1 July 1996 to assist with pre-Games support, but operated 24 hours daily during the Games.

The mission of the MCC was to provide quality customer service to sponsors by resolving problems, making qualified referrals to other departments, and providing current systemwide and emergency information.

The MCC, staffed by ACOP personnel with assistance from other ACOG functional area staff, was in direct, constant contact with the ACOG command center and the venue communications center, which communicated Security, Sports, and Venue Management information, as well as other sponsor-related issues for dissemination to sponsors and licensees. The MCC also resolved contract infringement issues and sponsor hospitality logistics during the Games, and kept the ACOG command center apprised of issues from ACOP sites at the sponsor villages and the Airport Welcome Center, as well as systemic operational problems in various functional departments.

Clean Venue Program

Rule 51 of the *Olympic Charter* provided the foundation for guidelines governing clean venues for the Olympic Games. It was ACOP's responsibility to implement and coordinate the Clean Venue Program. Guidelines for signage control were drafted and refined over a two-year period with the IOC and ACOG. Cooperation and understanding from ACOG functional areas were essential to the success of this program. Venues were divided into four distinct areas with different levels of signage control: Level A, field of play; Level B, venue seating/stands; Level C, concourse; and Level D, within accredited area and outside the venue.

All signage and branding visible within the competition areas, or from the spectator seats, press areas, suites or skyboxes, and broadcasting perspective were eliminated from the field of play and venue seating/stands levels. ACOG was required to cover existing signage, equipment, participants' apparel, audio and video announcements, and other miscellaneous items.

The IOC rules were that sponsor corporate identification in Levels C and D must be connected with a service provided by the sponsor, and that sponsor identification not connected with a service would be considered advertising

---

FIGURE 2: INTERNATIONAL LICENSING AGREEMENTS

ALI—Korea

Able Pacific—Chinese Taipei

Australian Olympic Committee

Avon Products—Chinese Taipei, Malaysia, Saipan, Thailand

Billion Max—Indonesia, Hong Kong, Malaysia, Singapore, Thailand, India

British Olympic Association

Brazilian Olympic Committee

Canadian Olympic Association

Chinese Olympic Committee

Coach—Chinese Taipei, Guam, Hong Kong, Singapore, Japan, Indonesia

Deutsche Sport Marketing—Germany

Empire International—Philippines

Grinaker Sport Management—South Africa

Israel Olympic Committee

Japan Olympic Marketing

Lillehammer Olympic Organizing Committee—Norway

Motorola—France, Germany, United Kingdom, Malaysia, Philippines, Singapore

Nutrexpa—Spain

Swatch—62 countries

Sara Lee—Canada, France, Hong Kong, Italy, Malaysia, Puerto Rico, Philippines, Singapore, Spain

St. Jacks—El Salvador, Guatemala, Costa Rica

Starion International—United Kingdom

Tycoon Enterprises—Mexico

US Gold—24 countries

KRISTA L CLARK • KRISTIN R CLARK • LAURA E CLARK • LAWRENCE L CLARK • LEIGH G CLARK • LINDA D CLARK • LISA P CLARK • LONA L CLARK • MADELINE E CLARK • MARIE F CLARK • MARK V CLARK • MARSELIS K CLARK • MARY CLARK • MARY L CLARK • MATTHEW J CLARK • MICHAEL A CLARK • MICHELLE J CLARK • NANCY B CLARK • NICOLE M CLARK • NINA R CLARK • PATRICE G CLARK • PATRICIA A CLARK • PATRICIA D CLARK • PENNY J CLARK • PETER YUICHI CLARK • REBECCA A CLARK • REBECCA C CLARK • RICHARD D CLARK • ROBERT J CLARK • RONALD T CLARK • RONALD W CLARK •

275

and not be permitted. This included, but was not limited to, corporate or brand names on existing signage; staff uniforms; wayfinding, merchandising, and food and beverage signage; audio announcements; and air-space restrictions, which controlled the use of aircraft, including blimps and aircraft-trailing banners.

NEW MARKET DEVELOPMENT

The New Market Development division's mission was to pursue additional program opportunities that would generate new revenue. The Olympic Report Program and the Sound of the Games Program were chosen and developed based on the products and services the company(ies) offered, and because they could be implemented within ACOP parameters.

In addition, this division managed ACOP marketing responsibilities with the US Mint to develop and cultivate the Commemorative Coin Program.

Commemorative Coin Program

To commemorate the Centennial Olympic Games in Atlanta, the US Mint offered a series of 16 coin designs that captured the spirit of the Olympic Games, as well as highlighted a number of the sporting events. The program generated substantial gross sales, and was the largest Olympic commemorative coin program in US Mint history.

The series included more coin designs than any previous program—four five-dollar gold coin designs, eight silver-dollar coin designs and four clad (cupro-nickel) half-dollar coin designs. The gold coin designs depicted the overall themes of the Olympic Games—a torch runner, Olympic Stadium, the Olympic flag arrival celebration, and the lighting of the cauldron. The silver coins featured artistic gymnastics, cycling, high jump, rowing, tennis, and track and field designs, as well as two Para-

The US Mint's Olympic Commemorative Coin Program captured the spirit of the Games in 16 coin designs.

lympic designs—a blind runner and a wheelchair athlete. The clad coin designs included basketball, baseball, football, and swimming designs. Each design was also minted in two coin finishes—proof, a highly polished mirror-like finish, and uncirculated, a matte finish. With two finishes for each design, the entire set numbered 32 coins.

Congressional legislation allowing the mintage of these coins included in their sale price a built-in surcharge that varied by coin type. The surcharges were paid to ACOP, and then divided between the IOC, Atlanta Paralympic Organizing Committee (APOC), ACOG, and the USOC.

Eight coin designs were released in 1995 and the remainder were released in 1996. The complete set was only offered during a special subscription period in early 1995. Sets included in this offering were a 16-coin proof set, a 32-coin proof and uncirculated set, and an 8-coin silver-dollar proof set. Sales of these sets accounted for approximately 50 percent of total coin sales.

Coins were sold internationally through distributorships established in more than 40 countries, representing the largest international program ever created by the US Mint. International sales accounted for approximately 35 percent of all coin sales. A portion of each international coin sale was paid to the NOC of the country where the sale was made.

The US Mint also promoted the Olympic coins to its direct-mail customers. In addition, a new retail program was implemented to reach customers who did not traditionally buy coins. These Olympic souvenirs in new, consumer-oriented packaging with value-added premiums, were sold in a variety of major retail chains. These items were also offered through a direct-mail program. Total coin sales from these two programs accounted for approximately 10 percent of all coin sales.

"Olympic Report" Radio Program

A specially tailored daily radio program was created and aired for seven months in 1996.

The radio network consisted of more than 250 radio stations in over 160 cities, towns, and communities across the US, and also internationally over the armed forces radio network. A new 2.5-minute program was provided daily to each participating station to be aired three times during the day. Each tape contained an interview conducted by Olympic gold medalist Bruce Jenner with various people involved with the Centennial Olympic Games. Each interview presented different insights about the Games that ranged from historical recollection about memorable events to a more specific focus, such as preparations for the 1996 Games. Sales to companies that wanted to advertise in conjunction with these broadcasts created a unique new revenue flow to support the 1996 Games and the US Olympic team.

Sound of the Games Program

Five audio compact discs (CDs) tailored for a specific musical genre were created by leading music producers. The CDs were sold both individually and in a specially designed Olympic Games commemorative music set. The classical release *Summon the Heroes* spent seven weeks as the #1 album on the Billboard Classical Music Crossover Charts. The rhythm & blues release single "Reach" spent three weeks as the #1 single on the Billboard Adult Contemporary Chart. The Latin release *Voces Unidas*, the first Latin Olympic album ever, went triple platinum for Hispanic music sales. The jazz release *People Make the World Go Round* featured 1984 gold medalist, Wayman Tisdale. The country release *One Voice* featured Closing Ceremony star and Georgia-native Trisha Yearwood singing her song "The Flame."

Television Marketing

Another new revenue source resulted from Olympic interest expressed by KingWorld, a major television program syndicator. Two of the most widely watched television shows in the US—*Wheel of Fortune* and *Jeopardy!*—created opportunities for Olympic Games/US team visibility and marketing.

In addition to creating greater awareness of the Games and generating incremental revenue from merchandise sales, both shows also selectively featured Olympic-themed shows, including an Olympic champions week in which former gold medalists competed against each other.

OLYMPIC PROGRAM

The Olympic Program division was established to create and maintain marketing relationships between ACOP and the USOC departments, APOC, three US Olympic Festival organizations—San Antonio, Texas, in 1993; St. Louis, Missouri, in 1994; and Denver, Colorado, in 1995—and the US national governing bodies (NGBs) for the summer and winter sports.

All NGBs had existing autonomous marketing programs directed at selling sponsorships to assist the endorsement of developing athletes. Many NGB sponsors were major corporations, and although most sold sport-specific products, the potential for conflict existed given the anticipated scope of the Games' Sponsor Program.

In 1992, a new program was developed that involved acquiring sponsor marketing rights for most US summer and winter sports, whereby NGBs would relinquish their sponsor marketing rights to ACOP for 30–35 defined product categories in return for revenue to be paid through the quadrennium. The intent of offering this revenue commitment was to protect sponsors from potential ambush from competitors that

CLARK MT • RHONDA K CLARK SAT • BARBARA CLARKE • BARBARA P CLARKE • BETTY LOU D CLARKE • BOBBY CLARKE • CECILE M CLARKE • DANIEL CLARKE • DANIEL M CLARKE • DARNELL CLARKE • DARRELL L CLARKE • DENNIS A CLARKE • GLYNN CLARKE • GORDON A CLARKE • GREGORY M CLARKE • HALEY C CLARKE • IDA-ANNE H CLARKE • JAMES O CLARKE • JAMES P CLARKE • JENNIFER Y CLARKE • JOHN CLARKE • JOSEPH R CLARKE • KATHERINE CLARKE • LAURIE N CLARKE • LORI E CLARKE • MARC E CLARKE • NANCY J CLARKE • RAYMOND C CLARKE • ROBERT N CLARKE •

277

might choose to sponsor NGBs to develop high-visibility promotion programs.

A formula was developed that determined the value of sponsor rights and contracts were negotiated with each NGB. All seven winter NGBs participated in the agreement which lasted through the 1994 Lillehammer Games, and 24 of the 28 summer NGBs participated through 1996.

The investment made to acquire these marketing rights represents the largest benefit ever delivered to the sponsor family by an organizing committee. In addition, the Glory of Olympic Sport Program—a package of commercial marketing rights from participating NGBs—was created and seven sponsor companies acquired these rights.

Marketing Operations

In addition to managing the daily marketing operations, the Marketing Operations division was responsible for trademark registration protection, marks approval, and ACOP's dissolution.

Trademark Registration Protection

ACOG aggressively pursued trademark registration protection, both in the US and abroad. In the US, ACOG filed to register more than 30 marks, including the Atlanta torch design, the mascot design, the Cultural Olympiad logo, sports pictograms, the Atlanta Olympic Broadcasting logo, and the Look designs.

The Olympic logo and Olympic mascot designs were the subject of extensive foreign registration activity. Applications for registration of the Olympic logo were filed in 46 countries in multiple product classes covering all products proposed to be manufactured, licensed, and distributed under this mark by ACOG and its licensees. Marks were first filed in the US and civil-law countries in the order they were

received, and were then followed within the six-month priority period by filings in Paris Convention countries. Applications for registration of the Olympic mascot were filed in 36 countries. Registration for the mark was requested in classes generally encompassing clothing, exhibition services, jewelry, leather goods, pins, publications, and toys.

In connection with filing foreign trademark applications, ACOG consulted attorneys with expertise in each trademark jurisdiction.

Marks Approval Process

Marks Approval was an extremely critical operation within ACOP. This subdivision reviewed and responded to all requests from entities with contractual marketing rights to use the various Centennial Olympic Games marks. These marks included the ACOG torch mark logo, official mascot IZZY, Look quilt pattern and centennial seals, sports pictograms, supplier mark, Cultural Olympiad mark, licensed product collection mark, historic marks, and venue marks. In addition, marks approval for the USOC team mark and the IOC five rings mark was coordinated with those organizations and handled within the Marks Approval subdivision.

It was here that all programs with marketing rights, wherever they originated, became visible. Typically, the marketing rights described in the various contracts were written on a conceptual level. The actual rights on an executional level were determined by Marks Approval to ensure the rights could coexist in the marketing plan without contract overlaps and inconsistencies.

All submissions were reviewed for contractual compliance, third-party association, graphic compliance, appropriateness of image, and consistent use of the Games message.

Actual marks usage submissions totaled 45,000, averaging 2,000 per month during peak periods and requiring cooperation with 560 different entities with various rights. Therefore, it was critical to develop methods to organize the operation and accommodate the volume and 10–business-day processing time. In addition, the process had to involve ACOG senior management to address Games image and message concerns, the USOC to address consistency in the US market, and the IOC to address consistency within the Olympic Movement. Formal weekly meetings were held with ACOG and an IOC representative and daily discussions were held with the USOC.

A standards manual that detailed graphics and business applications standards for Olympic marks use and a manual that defined standards for the official mascot IZZY were developed by Creative Services. The manuals were issued to sponsors, licensees, broadcasters, and select ACOG and ACOP employees who needed the information to perform their work. *(For further detail about the standards manual, see the Creative Services chapter.)*

In order to control the volume and diversity of the anticipated submission activity, a computer-based document management system was created. This system was menu-driven and captured the type of marks use and property utilized as well as the requesting client and time line data.

Due to the critical nature of the response processing time, it was important to maintain an adequate written record of the steps taken to review a submission and issue a response. All submissions were to be accompanied by a completed marks approval form stamped with the date it was received, then assigned a number in the database, and finally sent to a reviewer for approval. Once the review process was complete, the form was transmitted via facsimile machine to the requesting entity and date-stamped with the information. In addition, the facsimile confirmation sheet was attached to the form.

Office Management

Financial Planning and Analysis. The marketing revenue planning mandated the simultaneous pursuit of diverse multiple revenue programs as well as extensive revenue forecasting. Revenue sharing agreements between ACOG, the USOC, and the IOC were primarily administrated by ACOG's Financial Services Department, while ACOP focused on creating revenue.

In order to develop an expense plan for an unparalleled marketing program, executional flexibility had to be incorporated by setting expense parameters as a percentage of projected revenue for three areas—sponsor benefits, direct operating expense, and licensing. Projects were allowed to be changed as long as they continued to address the commitments and objectives of the organization, and the overall set of projects under the expenses for the three program areas remained within the approved percentage of revenue parameters.

Contract Administration. To maintain secure contractual information, a program director was appointed to research contractual rights questions, act as a liaison with ACOP's external lawyers, verify legal billing, and serve as the central depository for all ACOP contracts. The program director was also responsible for screening new business proposals and NOC access rights requests, managing the expense budget, and coordinating with ACOG's Accounting division.

Market Research. A market research function and a reference library were established within ACOP to provide background information on prospective sponsor companies, licensees under consideration, retail organizations, new market opportunities, and potential ambush campaigns, as well as to perform fact checks on submissions received by Marks Approval.

A diverse set of publications, on-line databases, and access to a network of financial industry experts were intertwined to provide a

FAYE J CLAY • JOSEPH D CLAY • MYRTIS CLAY • RENIA CLAY • ROSA K CLAY • SHERYL T CLAY • YOLANDA Y CLAYBROOKS • CHERYL CLAYPOOLE PT • DIEDRE K CLAYTON • GALE CLAYTON • GLEN D CLAYTON • JEAN E CLAYTON • JEFFERY CLAYTON • JON R CLAYTON • KERRIE E CLAYTON • LAWRENCE L CLAYTON • LORRIE E CLAYTON • MAKUNDA D CLAYTON • MARGARET PEGGY S CLAYTON • MAUREEN A CLAYTON • MYRNA A CLAYTON • PHILLIP D CLAYTON • RAYDEAN S CLAYTON • RICHARD E CLAYTON • ROBERT F CLAYTON • SARAH CLAYTON • SARAH L CLAYTON • LORI E CLEARWATER

279

marketing research support function that rivaled that of many corporations in terms of data diversity and access. More than 500 information sources were used and over 1,900 research projects developed.

ACOP Dissolution Process. As provided in the 1991 joint venture agreement, ACOP's dissolution was mandated on 31 December 1996, and continued thereafter only to conclude its affairs, liquidate its assets, and satisfy claims.

A further written agreement in August 1995 provided that the USOC co-chair would assume all authority and that all remaining non-cash assets of ACOP, excluding memorabilia requested by ACOG, would be delivered to the USOC by 31 March 1997, after liquidation of ACOP's tangible assets into cash.

In January 1996, ACOG established an ACOP dissolution planning group. The topics addressed included the legal dissolution of the corporation, employee matters, asset recovery and liquidation, collection and preservation of information and archives, financial dissolution, and claims resolution.

An inventory of ACOP-owned assets was completed and provided to ACOG and the USOC by 30 June 1996. ACOP assets were included in the ACOG asset auctions, although the proceeds were accounted separately.

Second, procedures were established for handling files and other information to be shipped to the USOC. A categorization process was established for labeling and storing files for easy access and copying computer files to disks.

Appropriate samples of licensee and sponsor use of the marks were made available to ACOG for use in its proposed history, and for the USOC and IOC. Relocation and consolidation of office space was also determined to accommodate MCC needs, disposition of excess value-in-kind, employee termination, and equipment and storage needs.

The dissolution process progressed smoothly in accordance with the established procedures. The final file transfer to the USOC occurred in early spring 1997.

CONCLUSIONS AND RECOMMENDATIONS

The joint marketing program created by ACOG and the USOC represented the most extensive collaboration in Olympic history between an NOC and an organizing committee to maximize revenues for both entities.

By developing a broadly based marketing

FIGURE 3: GROSS REVENUES	
Sponsors / suppliers	$633 million
Licensing	$91 million
Commemorative coins	$26 million
Other marketing	$10 million
ACOP Total	**$760 million**

and support plan, ACOP was able to set records for raising revenues that provided funds to ACOG, the USOC, IOC, APOC, the NGBs, and a number of NOCs, as well as covering the expenses of the joint venture. *(For ACOP's gross revenues, see Figure 3.)*

CHAPTER SIXTEEN
MEDICAL SERVICES

OVERVIEW—The mission of the Medical Services Department was to provide the best available medical support to Olympic athletes, Olympic Family members, spectators, ACOG staff and volunteers, and all other visitors. Medical Services enhanced the knowledge of sports medicine by building and strengthening relationships among local, national, and international medical communities.

All medical care complied with the *Olympic Charter* under the guidance of the IOC Medical Commission, which was responsible for implementing the IOC Medical Code. The code provided for the prohibition of doping, determined the prohibited classes of substances and prohibited methods of use, established a list of accredited laboratories, obliged competitors to submit themselves to medical controls and examinations, stipulated provisions relating to the medical care of athletes, and provided for sanctions to be applied in the event the medical code was violated.

Within the Olympic Village, medical care for athletes was readily available at several locations, and NOCs were provided separate space within their residential areas for their own medical services if requested. Within all Olympic venues, a medical team operated to provide immediate medical care to athletes, Olympic Family members, spectators, staff, volunteers, and any others needing assistance.

An exceptionally high level of medical care was both planned for and provided at the 1996 Games. Hospitals selected for the Olympic Hospital Network enthusiastically responded to the challenge of supporting the Games, and thousands of people from the metropolitan-Atlanta area medical community volunteered their services and expertise. Scores of medical providers and suppliers, such as ambulance companies and medical supplies and equipment manufacturers, generously supported the Games. The US sports community also provided athletic trainers, doping control personnel, sports medicine physicians, and volunteers.

ORGANIZATION

Medical Services, a part of the Operations Department, was directed by a chief medical officer (CMO) and a program director. With a staff of approximately 15 individuals, they developed services for all competition and noncompetition venues.

Planning began in 1992 with a review of medical performances and reports of past Games. Many previously developed concepts guided ACOG's strategy in developing its Olympic medical support group (OMSG) and Olympic Hospital Network, and assembling the ACOG Medical Services staff.

The OMSG, a volunteer medical planning advisory board comprised of local, state, and nationally recognized medical professionals, was built on Atlanta's existing medical infrastructure, which has a long history of voluntarism. The OMSG deployed more than 300 medical volunteers who were divided into 23 subcommittees, each of which were based on a medical specialty and managed by a volunteer expert.

The Olympic Hospital Network was comprised of various facilities that provided planning support, personnel, equipment, and supplies. Atlanta hospitals were asked to support one or more Olympic venues or key groups of Olympic participants. In return, the hospitals received Olympic recognition and hospital staff gained access to purchase tickets.

The ACOG Medical Services staff was appointed, each taking functional responsibility for a designated area, such as athlete medical care, Olympic Family care, or equipment and supplies management. For the development of competition venue services, staff agreed to support certain pre-Olympic test events. The Medical Services Department ultimately grew to include 30 staff members and more than 4,000 experienced medical volunteers.

MEDICAL OPERATIONS SYSTEM

Throughout preparations for the Games, the IOC Medical Commission worked closely with Medical Services to ensure that correct arrangements were made for all medical services, including medical command system operations, staffing, equipment and supplies, public health, and disaster planning—all of which comprised the Medical Operations System.

Medical Command System

For Games-time operations, the department created a system of interacting communications—or command—centers to facilitate the management, communication, and coordination of competition and noncompetition venue medical services, including those venues in outlying cities. Major medical incidents at venues were recorded and reported to their command centers from where medical dispatchers were assigned. Each venue command center worked closely with the main medical command center at ACOG headquarters. Other command centers included the Olympic Family Hotel, doping control command center, and the data collection center.

Main Command Center. The main medical command center at ACOG headquarters operated 24 hours daily to coordinate all medical needs, including deployment of medical personnel and communication among all sites. The command center also resolved problems that could not be handled at the venue or Village level. Medical command center staff included the CMO, a triage nurse, a representative from the state public health department, a regional medical coordinator, and functional area resource support.

The staff utilized facsimile machines, computers, and telephones to communicate with medical personnel at all venues and deploy transportation such as emergency vehicles. This center, which received periodic venue updates, relayed security reports to appropriate venues, monitored all situations within local hospitals, and released approved medical information to the press. Weather information, especially heat index data, was always available at the command center.

Any information for the CMO and the program director was communicated through the main medical command center, where a physician who maintained direct communication with the CMO and the program director was present during operating hours each day. Members of Medical Services and Operations management reviewed data and confirmed policy for several hours each day in the main center.

Olympic Family Hotel. The headquarters of the IOC Medical Commission, located within the Olympic Family Hotel, was the site where daily meetings were conducted by the IOC Executive Board and Medical Commission. The headquarters of the CMO and program director were located within the hotel, as was an

FIGURE 1: FUNCTIONAL COMPOSITION OF MEDICAL VOLUNTEERS

Venue	Admin	Trainer	Doping control staff	EMT/ Paramedics	Physicians	Nurses	Total
Competition venues							
AFS	21	17	9	43	11	12	113
AMC	15	28	8	16	11	6	84
AQU	18	36	42	32	16	9	153
ATB	9	10	16	16	6	4	61
CAU	13	23	0	13	8	5	62
CGP	4	8	9	11	10	21	63
GDM	24	33	16	30	17	12	132
GHP	17	20	10	42	23	12	124
GSU	14	19	10	5	5	5	58
GWC	24	59	50	61	22	16	232
LAK	10	31	29	18	8	5	101
MAR	4	14	1	0	12	33	64
MBR	6	16	10	12	8	7	59
MRH	15	20	-	17	4	5	61
MRI	6	23	15	0	14	10	68
OCO	12	13	10	17	11	16	79
OMN	14	17	13	30	11	6	91
OST	39	28	47	84	30	19	247
RCC	3	7	8	0	2	0	20
SMA	10	51	16	19	10	4	110
SMC	10	48	14	34	13	6	125
UGA	19	5	17	56	12	11	120
UGC	11	12	3	12	4	4	46
WLF	12	9	9	10	4	5	49
Subtotal	**330**	**547**	**362**	**578**	**272**	**233**	**2,322**
Noncompetition venues							
AGS	0	9	0	0	0	0	9
ATL-HART	0	0	0	0	0	18	18
CPK	17	0	0	69	9	15	110
EMU	0	16	0	0	0	0	16
IBC	2	0	0	0	12	17	31
INF	87	0	0	14	10	7	118
IYC	1	0	0	0	2	0	3
MPC	15	0	0	0	2	17	34
OFH	20	3	0	0	20	16	59
TRS	0	248	2	0	5	0	255
WEL	2	0	0	0	6	14	22
Subtotal	**144**	**276**	**2**	**83**	**66**	**104**	**675**
Villages		**Accredited ACOG polyclinic staff**					
CLV	1	8	7	*	*	*	16
COV	0	11	26	*	*	*	37
OLV	64	116	112	29	142	35	498
SVV	3	25	35	*	*	*	63
Subtotal	**68**	**160**	**180**	**29**	**142**	**35**	**614**
Total	**542**	**983**	**544**	**690**	**480**	**372**	**3,611**

Provided locally

ACOG doping control liaison to the IOC Medical Commission. Additional administrative support offices were also located there.

Venue Command Center Communications. At each venue command center, a medical volunteer served as the medical dispatcher and was responsible for handling all medically related calls from within the venue. The dispatcher relayed information to appropriate members of the medical team and other venue volunteers, and then resolved medical incidents with the venue medical officer (VMO). Incidents were reported to the main medical command center.

Press Relations. Press activities relating to Medical Services were coordinated through the main medical command center and ACOG Press Operations. No Medical Services staff or volunteers communicated with the press. Hospitals did not release information regarding Olympic-related admissions unless approval was granted by ACOG's press chief officer and the CMO and a release form was signed by the admitted patient.

All press-related activities regarding doping control were handled by the ACOG press chief and the IOC.

Staff

ACOG Medical Services staff were responsible for recruiting and scheduling more than 4,000 medical volunteers that were deployed in Villages and in competition and noncompetition venues. In some cases, volunteers were from outside the metro-Atlanta area and required housing. (*For the functional composition of the medical volunteer group, see Figure 1.*)

Equipment and Supplies

ACOG staff worked with medical equipment and supplies vendors and members of the Olympic Hospital Network to acquire both the donated and purchased resources necessary for Medical Services operations. Information was distributed to medical staff on the use and replenishment of equipment and supplies. During Games-time, the main medical command center was responsible for redeployment of assets.

Public Health

Professionals from a number of federal, state, county, and city agencies helped ACOG ensure that Atlanta residents and all Olympic visitors would be safe from public health risks. Environmental issues and health promotion were the focus areas. A smoke-free policy was developed for all venues, consistent with the IOC goal of promoting physical health through sports. The policy also disassociated the Games from tobacco advertising and sponsorships. A public health task force addressed drinking water and air quality, food sanitation, waste disposal, and swimming pool water quality.

A brochure promoting good health practices was sponsored by Atlanta-based health insurer Blue Cross of Georgia and was distributed with spectator ticket information. Other promotions, notably for heat-related illness prevention, were emphasized at the Villages and venues.

Disaster Planning

ACOG worked closely with all appropriate federal, state, and local agencies to develop and augment disaster plans.

Three levels of emergency response were developed. Level A response included medical emergencies that could be resolved by the medical team and ambulance service assigned to the venue. Level B response indicated that the venue team required additional resources, which were deployed from nearby venues by the main medical command center. Level C response meant that required resources were not available at the venue, and through the main command center, appropriate public agencies were called for assistance.

THE OLYMPIC HOSPITAL NETWORK

The Olympic Hospital Network, consisting of hospitals in Atlanta and all other venue cities, provided outstanding medical services for athletes, Olympic Family members, spectators, staff, and volunteers. Each hospital was chosen for its excellence in providing medical care, as

well as for its proximity to the venues. Nine hospitals were selected to provide medical care for all metro-Atlanta venues. Crawford Long Hospital served athletes and Georgia Baptist Medical Center served the Olympic Family, and the seven additional hospitals adopted venues, where they served as the main providers of medical care for spectators, ACOG staff, and volunteers.

In outlying venue cities, fewer hospitals were needed. In most cases, the outlying venue city identified two hospitals: one to serve athletes and Olympic Family members, and one to serve all others. In some cases, the athletes, Olympic Family members, staff, and volunteers were treated in the same facility; however, special precautions were taken to isolate athletes and Olympic Family members from the other hospital patients.

Hospitals that adopted venues provided supplies and equipment for the volunteer medical staff to use in the venue during operating hours.

OLYMPIC VILLAGE OPERATIONS

As home to 16,500 athletes, trainers, and coaches, the main Olympic Village, located on the campus of the Georgia Institute of Technology, required carefully planned access to medical care. The polyclinic, sports medicine center, training sites, and the international zone first-aid station, all staffed by medical volunteers, were available to Village residents, but their medical services often extended beyond the Village. NOC medical teams were given separate space within their residential areas upon request.

Similar medical services were offered at satellite Villages in Columbus, Cleveland, and Savannah, Georgia, and at the preliminary football sites.

Located in the residential zone of the Olympic Village, the polyclinic was the location where athletes and Olympic Family members could receive medical care 24 hours daily. The facility provided a full range of primary care services and was the central location for storage of athlete medical records. Nearly 500 medical personnel, including 142 doctors and 35 registered nurses, staffed the polyclinic.

Located in the polyclinic and also open 24 hours daily, the main pharmacy dispensed drugs from the Olympic drug formulary list of IOC-approved medications. It ordered drugs requested by ACOG and NOC physicians. All usage of nonformulary drugs had to be approved by the IOC Medical Commission.

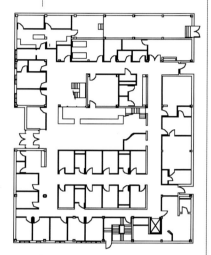

The polyclinic in the Olympic Village operated 24 hours daily to provide a full range of medical services for athletes and Olympic Family members.

left: floor plan of polyclinic

right: view of entrance and reception area

Smaller pharmacies and polyclinics were located at outlying sites. In these areas, full pharmacy services could be obtained at the network hospitals.

The sports medicine center in the Olympic Village offered services of athletic trainers and physical and massage therapy. The volume of staff and supplies acquired was based on data from the Barcelona Games and supplemented as required. Health professionals in the metro-Atlanta area volunteered on a 14-day rotation, receiving two days off. Supplies were donated by the official athlete care hospital.

Medical Services staff coordinated care between the sports medicine center and the venue sports medicine areas, managed all equipment and supply allocations, and coordinated volunteer staffing. At each location, the chief athletic trainer was responsible for supervising medical care methods and the use of related supplies.

The medical services provided for athletes at each training site were determined by the risk level of the sport and any special request from the Sports Department. All sites had access to emergency medical service. Training that required sports medicine staffing primarily involved a team's athletic trainers. Athletes were referred to the polyclinic if nonemergency physician care was needed.

The international zone of the Olympic Village maintained a first-aid station that served all visitors to the Village. A VMO managed the staff, which included physicians, nurses, mobile first-responder teams trained by the American Red Cross, and roving medical teams.

Individuals requiring additional care were referred to the polyclinic; individuals with more serious problems were evaluated at the athlete and Olympic Family hospitals, as appropriate.

VENUE OPERATIONS

The philosophy governing Medical Services at venues was to provide immediate and temporary care of athletes, Olympic Family members, spectators, staff, volunteers, and any others who suffered injury or sudden illness, and to provide services that helped prevent medical emergencies. All care was managed by physicians. Patients were referred to designated hospitals for advanced or longer-term care.

Medical care at competition venues was divided into three areas for athletes, Olympic Family members, and spectators, staff, and volunteers.

Medical care was organized in tiered levels, ranging from physicians and nurses in fixed venue stations to mobile first-responder teams roving within a venue. Each venue was equipped with advanced cardiac life support (ACLS) capability and one ACLS ambulance. One ambulance was available for every 20,000 spectators.

A VMO directed all medical services and personnel operating within each venue. An assistant VMO served as acting VMO in his or her absence. A venue medical administrator (VMA), reporting directly to the VMO, coordinated all medical logistics, personnel, and administrative needs in each venue. An assistant VMA served as acting VMA in his or her absence. Support was also provided by ACOG regional medical coordinators.

Individuals volunteering for venue medical services included physicians, nurses, paramedics and emergency medical technicians, American Red Cross first-responders, dispatchers, runners, administrative clerks, physical therapists, massage therapists, and athletic trainers. Volunteers from outside Georgia filling some medical positions required state certification or licensing. Volunteers with strong leadership skills were selected to assist in planning for competition venue operations. These volunteers assisted with planning during 1995 and served as key venue medical planners during test events. During the Games, they were appointed as VMOs, VMAs, and venue assistants.

Factors used to determine the number of first-aid stations included the number of venue attendees, access level into the venue, risk of heat-related illness, venue terrain, the nature of the venue sport, and whether the venue was indoor or outdoor.

Certain venues, such as the Georgia World Congress Center and the Georgia Dome, had centralized first-aid stations covering multiple events in the same facility. Each sport within the venue had at least one mobile first-responder team assigned to spectator areas.

The size of each station varied according to the venue and its existing capabilities; however, each had the minimum space necessary to care for and ensure the privacy of two patients at one time. Each unit met minimum space requirements of 400 sq ft (122 sq m) and

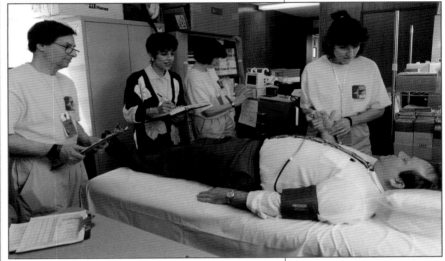

had air-conditioning, electricity, and water. A toilet was located in or near each station. This medical care model applied to all venues.

ACOG Medical Services staff members were trained to be prepared for any situation that might require medical attention at the Games.

Athlete Medical Care

The mission regarding athlete care during the Games was to provide efficient, equitable, high-quality medical care that focused on returning injured athletes to activity as quickly as possible. For this purpose, athlete medical care was provided in the Olympic Village, at each venue, and at training sites.

The primary location for athlete medical care was a venue sports medicine station located near the field of play. Other locations included warm-up areas and, where available,

YOLANDA C COBHAM GILBERT • EDWARD R COBIA • ALTONIA A COBLE • STEVEN A COBURN • DAVID V COCA • BEN F COCHRAN • BRENDA A COCHRAN • ELEANOR J COCHRAN • JEFFREY S COCHRAN • KATHRYN COCHRAN • LARONDA R COCHRAN • LELDON COCHRAN • NADRA L COCHRAN • TAMRA L COCHRAN • TANYA S COCHRAN • TRACY L COCHRAN • WILLIAM R COCHRAN • DREW J COCHRANE • KATHLEEN M COCHRANE • PATRICIA COCHRANE - CASE • EMANUEL T COCIAN • CAROL L COCK • TREGEL M COCKBURN • BURNETTE COCKFIELD • EMILY S COCKRELL • TIMOTHY P COCKRELL •

287

the recovery or holding areas in each venue. Athlete stations were secure from spectators and press.

Sport-specific requirements at each venue and the presence (or absence) of an athlete's official medical delegation determined whether the venue sports medicine staff functioned as the primary, secondary, or tertiary medical provider. When the ACOG medical team was the primary provider, they were the first to respond to on-field medical problems. When designated as a secondary care responder, ACOG physicians assisted if the respective NOC physician requested that they do so. In the tertiary care situation, a physician provided by a particular IF had primary duties, reinforced by the NOC and then the ACOG Medical Services staff.

Each venue sports medicine station was staffed with a physician, nurse, and at least one athletic trainer; additional staff were added if necessary. Each station provided treatment tables for use by official team athletic trainers and medical personnel. However, ACOG provided supplies only when ACOG Medical Services staff provided consultation or treatment.

Olympic Family Medical Care

At least one mobile first-aid team was assigned to the Olympic Family area in each venue. The team was in direct radio contact with the venue dispatcher and VMO and worked in conjunction with the Olympic Family nurse and/or physician, one of whom had defibrillation capability. The mobile team began evaluation and treatment and, if necessary, assisted the patient to a first-aid station.

If further medical care was needed, transportation was obtained through the VMO, who also notified the main medical command center about the patient's condition.

All these procedures fell within Olympic protocols for treatment of Olympic Family members and were under the supervision of the VMO.

Spectator, Staff, and Volunteer Medical Care

Spectators were treated at the first-aid stations in the venues. In minor cases, some spectators were treated by roving mobile teams. As a rule, there was one mobile aid team, comprised of one emergency medical technician and one paramedic, for every 20,000 spectators. These numbers were altered if deemed necessary by factors such as limited access or higher usage.

Higher usage rates were seen in crowds with less than 30,000 people or with older or ambulatory spectators, events with increased pedestrian traffic, multiple daily sessions, outdoor events, and warmer temperatures. Usage rates varied between 0.68 and 6.8 incidents per thousand spectators.

Mobile aid teams, responsible for certain areas within venues, were supervised by the VMO and dispatched by the medical dispatcher. The teams carried equipment that was adapted for each crowd and matched venue-specific requirements. First-responder teams were also provided.

After initial assessment, the mobile aid teams in consultation with the VMO chose to treat patients at their seats with no further intervention, transport patients to the first-aid station for physician evaluation and treatment, or transport patients directly to the hospital by ambulance.

If a spectator required nonemergency medical care beyond that available in the venue, the spectator was referred to an outpatient clinic or was sent to the venue's designated hospital. Patients provided their own transportation to the referred facility unless their condition was considered unstable or emergent; then the spectator was sent by ambulance to the closest hospital.

Staff and volunteers were treated in the same manner as spectators. Medical care focused on returning staff members to their venue positions as quickly and safely as possible.

Spectator Care Beyond Venues. An OMSG subcommittee developed a program for spectator medical care beyond Olympic venues. A network of primary care medical facilities, strategically located around Atlanta, supplemented the existing nonemergency medical care system during the Games. A physician was available in the triage area of these facilities from 0800 to 2000 to advise and make appointments. Booklets were placed in metro-Atlanta area hotels indicating the triage telephone number for nonemergency medical care and a map of area hospitals and participating outpatient facilities.

ACOG worked closely with public agencies, the Salvation Army, and local churches to ensure that free water was distributed. Hydration stations were established in areas with pedestrian concentration.

Noncompetition Venue Care

The philosophy governing medical care at noncompetition venues was the same as that of competition venues. For advanced or longer-term care, physicians referred patients to designated hospitals or, if appropriate, to the polyclinic. Noncompetition venues included the Main Press Center (MPC) and International Broadcast Center (IBC), Centennial Olympic Park, Olympic Family Hotel, Olympic Youth Camp (OYC), training sites, and the Airport Welcome Center, as well as the Olympic Village.

Medical care was provided at the IBC and the MPC. Medical aid stations were staffed during regular operating hours, but remained open 24 hours daily during peak times. Physicians and nurses provided routine first-aid and triage care. Emergency transportation was also available.

A medical aid station in Centennial Olympic Park was staffed by physicians, nurses, and mobile responders. Emergency transportation was available to the nearest Olympic support hospital.

Olympic Family medical care was provided at the Olympic Family Hotel and the venues. The hotel had a 24-hour first-aid station staffed with physicians and nurses. One mile from the hotel, the Georgia Baptist Medical Center served the Olympic Family.

The OYC had a resident registered nurse and a physician on-call. Emergency transportation was available to a nearby Olympic support hospital.

At training sites, the level of medical service provided for athletes was the same as for the training sites within the Olympic Village.

Roving emergency medical teams covered the airport. Staffing was determined by flight arrival schedules. Two ACLS ambulances remained at the site at all times. Transfer could be made to the support hospital in minutes for life-threatening conditions.

MEDICAL CONTROLS

A range of functions, termed medical controls, were determined by relevant state and federal laws, as well as IOC-mandated requirements. These included doping control, gender verification, temporary physician licensing, and controlled substances handling.

Doping Control

"The International Olympic Committee was, in fact, the first international organization to become truly concerned with doping in sports," said IOC President Juan Antonio Samaranch in ACOG's *Medical Controls Guide.* "It was also the first to attempt to deter this harmful practice, which can seriously damage the health of our athletes."

The IOC has since embarked on a project to educate the public and athletes worldwide about the importance of being drug-free. Moreover, it has established procedures to prevent the misuse of drugs during the Games.

The ACOG Doping Control Program met all IOC-required drug testing standards. Doping Control staff collected and tested urine samples during preliminary and medal rounds, and conducted random sampling as specified by the IOC Medical Commission. In addition, testing occurred whenever a world, area, or national record was broken. ACOG worked closely with the IFs to customize the doping control procedures for each sport.

An updated version of the Versapak sample kit system, which included collection vessels, bottles, containers, and transport bags, was utilized.

The Doping Control Program was coordinated and managed from three locations: the doping control command center located at ACOG headquarters, a doping control office located at Agnes Scott College, and the Nile Room at the Olympic Family Hotel.

The doping control command center, operational from 20 July to 4 August 1996, from 0800 until 2200 daily, served as the main communication center for all doping control services. This command center communicated with each doping control station, the testing laboratory, and the IOC Medical Commission.

The doping control office at Agnes Scott College was staffed daily from 0700 until 0100 to handle scheduling and transportation and to resupply needs, such as sample kits. Vans were provided to transport personnel and supplies.

The Nile Room was a secure room where the doping control sample kits were stored and distributed on a daily basis to IOC Medical Commission representatives for use at venue doping control stations. In addition, the Nile Room served as the transportation desk for the IOC Medical Commission carpool. Forty cars were required to transport IOC Medical Commission members and the ACOG doping control medical team to venues. The Nile Room was staffed with four volunteers daily from 0700 until 2230. A daily roster and schedule were posted in the Nile Room.

Doping control stations were located at all competition venues. All stations were air-conditioned and included a check-in area, waiting room, separate processing and consent areas, and restrooms. The stations were organized and supplied by the site coordinator under the direction of the IOC Medical Commission representative and the doping control medical officer.

The ACOG Doping Control Committee coordinated activities for station services, site coordination, escort coordination, and the doping control offices.

In accordance with the *Medical Controls Guide,* doping control personnel at each station included 1–4 medical officers, 2–6 technical officers, 1–2 site coordinators, 1–4 escort coordinators, 2–50 escorts, and security personnel outside and inside all stations. All personnel were extensively trained volunteers who worked entire days without shifts. Seven trained, qualified doping control medical officers were available from ACOG for use as deputy IOC Medical Commission representatives at the doping control stations if necessary.

The Atlanta branch of SmithKline Beecham Clinical Laboratory, Inc., was certified by the IOC to test samples during the Games. For the first time during an Olympic Games, the lab testing that was conducted involved the use of high-resolution mass spectrometry, which improves the ability to detect performance-enhancing drugs. The IOC required renovation of the SmithKline laboratory to include three of these devices. The laboratory director augmented laboratory staff with key personnel from other IOC accredited labs, notably the Institute of Biochemistry of the German Sports University in Cologne, Germany, and the University of California, Los Angeles, Olympic Testing Laboratory. *(For the number of doping control samples received per day, see Figure 2.)*

The Morehouse School of Medicine in Atlanta provided SmithKline with a center where it could conduct doping research and educational training. During the Games, Morehouse provided laboratory equipment and staff.

SmithKline assisted Morehouse with funding, equipment, and training personnel to develop several other research projects before, during, and after the Games. The primary research focused on new areas of performance-enhancing drug abuse and on methodologies to improve existing testing techniques. Studies included the misuse of beta agonists. The beta agonist study is a continuing one, performed in conjunction with the National Aeronautics and Space Administration (NASA). An important legacy of the Games resulted from the construction of a 330,500 sq ft (30,737 sq m) multidisciplinary research center, which housed five research and education outreach programs.

Versapak sample kits were stored in a secured warehouse until needed, and then were delivered to the Nile Room. IOC Medical Commission representatives delivered sample kits to each station daily. At the end of each day, the same IOC Medical Commission representative returned any unused kits to the Nile Room.

A designated security officer was stationed at each doping control station entrance, permitting only authorized personnel to enter. All individuals entering a station were issued one of three color-coded doping control security passes, which designated IOC Medical Commission members, doping control team members, and athletes and their representatives.

A lockable cabinet in each station secured

the sample kits, necessary forms, urine collection vessels, transportation bags, and seals to be used each day.

After stations closed each day, sealed sample kits were transported by a courier service from the venue doping control stations to the laboratory in a secure manner.

Under IOC Medical Commission guidance, the doping control medical groups provided three guides printed in both English and French to athletes, NOCs, and IFs. The *Medical Controls Guide* explained athlete notification and sample

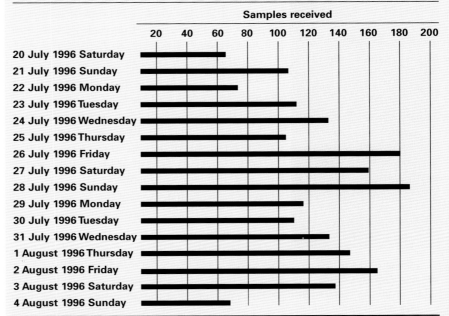

FIGURE 2: DOPING CONTROL SAMPLES RECEIVED PER DAY

collection procedures; the *Drug Formulary* defined and listed permitted, restricted, and prohibited substances; and the *Medical Care Guide* provided an overview of the Games medical operations including medical command system structure, protocol, and methods for the care of all constituents.

A doping control notification and official record form, transport form, and accompanying color-coded envelopes were also developed and approved by the IOC.

Gender Verification

Gender verification of female athletes has been required for Olympic competition since 1968. For female athletes without previously approved verification, a testing program was established which allowed rapid processing. All 3,626 participating female athletes at the 1996 Games required a valid gender verification card issued by the IOC prior to competition.

Gender verification, under the direction of the head of the Genetics Department at the Emory University School of Medicine, was performed at the polyclinic in the Olympic Village. A collection center on the second floor of the polyclinic had a separate entrance ensuring privacy for testing.

The presence of the sex-determining region of Y gene (SRY) was assessed by obtaining a buccal cytology brush sample, isolating crude DNA, and applying the polymerase chain reaction in an automated 96 well plate format. Testing results were available 1–4 hours after specimen collection, depending on the number of athletes tested. A maximum of 500 samples could be processed in a 24-hour period. If the initial screen was positive, the SRY test was repeated to rule out false positives. Cytogenetic blood chromosome analysis and endocrinologic evaluation could be performed for intersex medical problems.

All test results were reported to the chairman of the IOC Medical Commission or his designee. Athletes who screened positive were asked to allow further testing or examination.

Qualified medical geneticists and gynecologists were available to further evaluate athletes that tested positive, if requested by the IOC Medical Commission. Other qualified specialists, such as psychiatrists, urologists, and endocrinologists, were on-call to assist female athletes in a sensitive and professional manner. During the Games, none of the athletes screened were excluded from competition because of screening results.

Temporary Physician License

Physicians living outside the state were able to apply for a temporary license to practice medicine during the Games through an act passed by the Georgia state legislature. Applications for the temporary licenses were sent to NOCs in November 1995.

Physicians granted temporary licenses could treat their nationals at all ACOG medical sites including broadcast and press centers, competition venues, NOC designated areas, the Olympic Family Hotel, and Village polyclinics.

As a courtesy, temporary-licensed doctors also had access to their athletes, team members, and accredited nationals at the Olympic hospitals, allowing them to visit their patients, review medical records, and consult with attending hospital physicians.

Their privileges did not allow for admitting patients, ordering and performing procedures, or writing prescriptions in the hospitals, but did allow attendance at specialized procedures, such as those performed in the operating room, with permission from the attending hospital physician.

The temporary license did allow foreign physicians to write prescriptions in outpatient settings for their nationals. Written on special medical prescription forms, they were honored by the polyclinic pharmacy.

Controlled Substance Handling

Many drugs routinely used by physicians worldwide are regulated by the US Drug Enforcement Administration (DEA), which established procedures for teams participating in the 1996 Games. Any controlled substances required by non–US team physicians that were

Cover of the ACOG *Medical Controls Guide*, one of three guides required by and issued under the guidance of the IOC Medical Commission; it was distributed to athletes, NOCs, and IFs.

THE ATLANTA COMMITTEE FOR THE OLYMPIC GAMES

MEDICAL CONTROL GUIDE

Atlanta 1996

brought into or out of the country, had to accompany the physician and be part of his or her emergency kit. The DEA could review this inventory if necessary.

Individual team members with controlled substances obtained lawfully in their country for medical use could enter or leave the US with the substance if it was contained in the original packaging prescribed for that individual, and if the individual gave the US Customs Service the trade or chemical name of the substance or the name of the practitioner who dispensed the substance and prescription number.

Regarding new prescriptions, if narcotics or other substances controlled by the DEA or Georgia laws were ordered, only a physician with a DEA-issued identification number could write or dispense the prescription. The IOC Medical Commission had to be informed as well.

All medications were dispensed from handwritten prescriptions only. Team physicians could prescribe only to members of their delegations. Although more than one prescription could be written for an athlete, each prescription was written for a maximum of seven days, with no refills.

SPORTS SCIENCE RESEARCH

Prior to the Games, the IOC Medical Commission and ACOG sponsored the Third IOC World Congress of Sports Science meetings to discuss the biological, physiological, physical, and psychological sciences associated with elite athletes in sports.

The meeting was held for five days in September 1995 and attracted more than 1,000 attendants. Participants displayed approximately 250 different scientific papers, poster exhibits, and technical exhibits.

For every Olympic Games, the IOC asks the host organizing committee to support a variety of sports science projects coordinated by the

IOC Subcommission on Biomechanics and Physiology of Sport. In late 1990, an ACOG liaison to the IOC Subcommission was named, consequently becoming the coordinator of biomechanics research for the 1996 Games.

A request for research ideas was distributed, and by the end of 1994, the IOC subcommission selected projects in 11 sports. A senior researcher was appointed to conduct the research for the selected sports.

During the Games, a large pool of graduate students and staff from Georgia State University volunteered their assistance, which ranged from serving as venue research managers to helping collect data. More than 100 researchers were involved in the projects. About half came from outside Atlanta and required housing and transportation. Additional support was provided from Georgia State and Georgia Tech, as well as equipment suppliers.

Correctly coordinating the research required working with individual venue competition managers as well as Atlanta Olympic Broadcasting (AOB), as many projects involved the use and placement of more than 30 high-speed recording devices and cameras. Computer editing equipment was also used to help view the collected data, which was often available immediately to athletes and coaches, and was used later for publication in journals and for future study.

One project established an IOC coaching center to help athletes and coaches during the Games. The center provided facilities for athletes and coaches to view the computerized video, which was digitized and stored on a file server immediately after an event. This allowed for quick, in-depth qualitative analysis for alterations of technique or strategy before the next competition. The center focused primarily on artistic gymnastics, athletics, basketball, and diving, but other sports were recorded if requested by a coach. The center, operated with support from Georgia Tech volunteers, proved to be successful and is recommended for future Games.

Another project also provided same-day results for swimming performance. On the final night of swimming competition, the director of this project and his group produced two comprehensive volumes (male and female) of data and distributed them to all NOCs with swimmers competing in the 1996 Games.

Under direction of the coordinator of biomechanics research, more than 40 printed manuscripts from all 1996 Games projects are expected to be printed by the end of 1997.

Activity Data

The Centers for Disease Control and Prevention (CDC), a federal government agency in Atlanta, provided substantial assistance with data collection. The CDC provided 14 people to report and log all medical incidents. This group, performing as a subset of Medical Services, was located within ACOG headquarters and utilized the ACOG computer network system.

Medical encounters or incidents were defined as visits to an ACOG medical facility, requiring some type of medical care and a physician-completed form. More than 10,000 incidents were reported. Additionally, more than 20,000 visits to medical facilities were made for reasons other than medical treatment, including athlete massages, injury taping, and requests for information. *(For a summary of Games-time medical encounters, see Figure 3.)*

FIGURE 3: SUMMARY OF MEDICAL ENCOUNTERS (4 JULY–7 AUGUST 1996)

- 10,723 medical encounters were recorded
- 7,333 (68%) involved accredited individuals
- 1,804 (17%) were athletes
- 4,469 (42%) were injuries
- 9,829 (92%) were initial visits
- 1,053 (10%) were heat related

CONCLUSIONS AND RECOMMENDATIONS

An exceptionally high level of medical care was planned for and provided by ACOG. The Olympic Hospital Network proved to be extremely successful due to the extraordinary response from the metro-Atlanta area and other venue cities' hospitals to the challenge of providing medical services for the Games, and the generous services donated by medical providers and suppliers. Atlanta has an extensive medical infrastructure and members from the community volunteered by the thousands to offer their services and medical expertise.

The following recommendations are offered to future organizing committees.

■ Establishing a doping control testing laboratory is an enormous, time-consuming task. This process should begin very early and in close consultation with the IOC Medical Commission.

■ Because most Games medical staff are volunteering their professional expertise and time, the difficulties involved in recruiting them for test events prior to the Games need to be recognized.

■ Publications and communications of the standards of the IOC medical controls on an international level is paramount to the success of the athletes and competitions.

Chapter Seventeen
Olympic Family
and Protocol

Olympic Family and Protocol Employees

Date	Staff Number
June 1993	9
January 1996	30
July 1996	35

Note: These staff numbers do not include contractor, VIK, and volunteer personnel.

OVERVIEW—The Olympic Family and Protocol Department, created in 1992 under the International Relations Department, coordinated ACOG's presence at all IOC meetings, Olympic Family international meetings, and other gatherings. Olympic Family and Protocol also:

■ administered the needs of the IOC; the NOCs; the presidents, secretaries-general, and executives of the IFs; the organizing committees of future Games and bid cities; and all high-ranking dignitaries and government officials;

■ provided an expert Language Services Department to provide necessary assistance;

■ planned victory ceremonies that appropriately honored Olympic medalists; and

■ represented the Olympic Family's interests in all plans and preparations of ACOG functional areas.

ORGANIZATION

Olympic Family and Protocol was comprised of four departments: Olympic Family, Language Services, Protocol, and NOC Relations.

The Olympic Family Department facilitated all ACOG relationships with the IOC and other Olympic Family constituencies. The Language Services Department was responsible for providing translation and simultaneous interpretation services and recruiting, evaluating, and training language volunteers to staff all venues during the Games. The Protocol Department managed Olympic Family lounges and reserved seating areas, protocol services at the Olympic Family Hotel (the Atlanta Marriott Marquis), protocol services in venues and Olympic Villages, and victory ceremonies. The NOC Relations Department coordinated relations between ACOG and all NOC delegations, processed Games-time accommodations requests, recommended and coordinated with Olympic attachés, helped locate pre-Olympic training sites, and published a regular NOC newsletter.

The Airport Operations Department began as part of Olympic Family and Protocol. However, in November 1995, when the Airport Welcome Center (AWC) was being planned, Airport Operations became part of the Welcome Center venue team. Thereafter, Olympic Family and Protocol maintained close contact to ensure that the appropriate level of service was provided for arriving and departing Olympic Family members. *(For more information on the AWC, see the Accreditation chapter.)*

OLYMPIC FAMILY

The Olympic Family Department was responsible for IOC Relations, coordination with the consular and diplomatic corps, International Dignitary Relations, international entry issues, the Observer Program, and development of accreditation policy for the Olympic Family.

IOC RELATIONS

To enable the IOC and ACOG to coordinate in meeting their mutual goals, regular communication took place between the president of the IOC and the ACOG CEO. Senior management of the IOC administrative staff communicated directly with members of ACOG's management team. In addition, the IOC president nominated special representative commissions to study specific subjects pertaining to the 1996 Olympic Games and formulate recommendations to the IOC Executive Board. These included the Coordination Commission, the Medical Commission, the Press Commission, and the Radio and Television Commission.

Most logistical and operational aspects of coordination between ACOG and the IOC were facilitated by the IOC secretary-general, who made several visits to Atlanta during the pre-Games period. The secretary-general met with representatives of Accommodations, Accreditation, Corporate Services, Olympic Family and Protocol, Olympic Programs, Olympic Villages, Security, Ticket Sales, and Transportation to ensure planning was on schedule and that IOC requirements had been met. The secretary-general and her secretariat also made arrangements for the IOC's 105th Session, held from 14 to 18 July 1996.

Many specific matters were coordinated with the IOC through its specialized group of directors. This involved frequent contact with the directors of Sports, Olympic Solidarity, Marketing, Medical Services, the IOC's International Cooperation Department, Logistical Affairs, and Control and Coordination.

ACOG appointed an official IOC liaison in February 1993, who reported directly to the IOC secretary-general and ACOG's Olympic Family and Protocol director. She assisted both organizations in obtaining information for Games preparations, scheduling meetings and visits, and coordinating many other functions. In February 1996, the IOC loaned ACOG a French-speaking liaison with particular expertise in IOC protocol.

Reports to the IOC

From its inception, ACOG was required to forward semiannual reports in English and French to the IOC Executive Board providing detailed accounts of progress in preparation for the Games. Two years before the Games, these reports were submitted quarterly. Additionally, ACOG was required to provide oral and written reports about ACOG activities to the IOC Executive Board and the IOC Session upon request. In many cases, the same report was presented to the IOC Executive Board and the IOC Session. ACOG representatives reported to every IOC Executive Board meeting and IOC Session from December 1990 to July 1996.

IOC Coordination Commission

To monitor preparations for the Games, the IOC established a Coordination Commission. On 3 April 1991, ACOG representatives met with the chair of this commission and the IOC secretary-general to discuss the specific responsibilities and functions of the commission. The first commission meeting was held in August 1991; subsequent meetings were held biannually until the final year, when three meetings were held at four-month intervals. Each meeting was followed by a press conference.

The role of the IOC Coordination Commission was to monitor ACOG's progress in Games preparations; provide assistance and expertise

GLORIA T COLLEY • MARY E COLLEY • CAROL A COLLICA • JACK E COLLIE • ANGELA J COLLIER • ASHLEY A COLLIER • AUDREY L COLLIER • BARRY K COLLIER • BETTY J COLLIER • CARMELITA V COLLIER • CARYN E COLLIER • CHERRY A COLLIER • CHERYL A COLLIER • CURTIS COLLIER • EVA B COLLIER • FABIENNE B COLLIER • GARY P COLLIER • GLENDA H COLLIER • JACQUELYN E COLLIER • JANICE COLLIER • JUANITA E COLLIER • KATE COLLIER • LISA C COLLIER • MICHAEL J COLLIER • REID COLLIER • ROBERT B COLLIER • SONYA M COLLIER • TOMMY A COLLIER • WALLACE M COLLIER •

297

to ACOG; facilitate coordination with the IOC, NOCs, and IFs; and provide periodic reports on the organization of the Games to the IOC Executive Board.

The function of ACOG's IOC liaison differed during the Games period. The composition of the IOC Coordination Commission was revised and expanded and, under the leadership of President Samaranch, its members met daily with ACOG management to discuss and resolve various issues relating to the conduct of the Games. ACOG's IOC liaison, stationed in the

left: The IOC Coordination Commission held biannual meetings with ACOG staff.

right: The IOC Coordination Commission visited the Olympic Stadium during its construction phase.

Olympic Family Hotel, attended the daily venue management meetings to which all ACOG functional areas reported and assisted in the exchange of information to ensure the smooth processing of any specific requests or problems raised by the IOC.

CONSULAR AND DIPLOMATIC CORPS

In 1994, the Olympic Family Department began to manage an active liaison program with the consular and diplomatic corps. The program with the diplomatic corps in Washington, DC, was very successful, with 127 of the 162 embassies naming diplomats to facilitate Olympic-related issues directly. Direct contact with the consular corps was maintained through meetings between Olympic Family staff and a consular corps working group and meetings between the managing director of International Relations and the dean and vice dean of the consular corps. With the assistance of the State

Department, a briefing was also held for the ambassadors of the diplomatic corps in February 1996 in Washington, DC.

In order to facilitate communication with foreign diplomatic missions, Olympic Family requested that each mission name an Olympic contact. These Olympic contacts proved helpful when Olympic Family needed to contact an embassy directly regarding an Olympic Games issue. Additionally, Olympic Family hosted a large number of diplomatic visitors, including heads of state, ministers, first ladies, ambassadors, consuls general, and consuls for briefings and tours of Olympic venues. The tours were arranged by Guest Services, using volunteer tour guides. The office also assisted the State Department in establishing a liaison program between US diplomatic Olympic coordinators in each US embassy or consulate overseas and senior representatives of the NOCs and IFs.

INTERNATIONAL DIGNITARY RELATIONS

Olympic Family was responsible for coordinating visits during the Games from high-level government dignitaries and members of royal families. While such dignitaries were considered guests of their respective NOCs, International Dignitary Relations coordinated all NOC requests for dignitary accreditation, accommodations, and other arrangements, serving as the liaison with advance NOC, government, and/or ministry representatives of the visiting dignitary. The dignitary program worked internally with Accommodations, Accreditation, Airport Operations, Guest Services, Security, and Transportation to provide an appropriate level of service to each individual.

International Dignitary Relations functioned from the Olympic Family Hotel during the Games. Each visiting delegation was assigned a protocol liaison officer to coordinate details of the visit. All details were also coordinated with the Secret Service and Diplomatic Security detail leaders responsible for dignitary protection. Logistics coordination, particularly for Opening and Closing Ceremonies, was facilitated by protocol officers from the State Department Office of Protocol.

All arrangements for government dignitaries were made through the NOCs. ACOG did not hold hotel accommodations for this group, but urged governments to work independently or through their NOCs to secure rooms. For convenience and security purposes, efforts were made to house the highest ranking dignitaries at the Olympic Family Hotel.

Staffing for International Dignitary Relations included a director, a protocol liaison coordinator, a ceremonies logistics manager and assistant, a protocol liaison coordinator, and nine protocol liaison officers, each responsible for a group of countries and staffing the hotline/information desk.

Discussions were held with visiting NOCs as well as consular and diplomatic contacts concerning dignitary attendance, but very little information concerning visiting dignitaries was available prior to early 1996. Actual international dignitary attendance was 12 heads of state, 10 heads of government, 104 ministers of sport, and 57 ambassadors. There were 19 world leaders present at the Opening Ceremony and 3 at the Closing Ceremony.

INTERNATIONAL ENTRY ISSUES

Olympic Family included within its management an officer on loan to ACOG from the US Department of State for two years, commencing August 1994. Obtaining visas became this officer's main responsibility, principally for international athletes and officials needing regular visitor's visas to come to Atlanta during the two years before the Games for Olympic-related activities or events. Many visitors coming for meetings in Atlanta, pre-Olympic test events, and other reasons requested assistance in obtaining visas from US embassies and consulates overseas.

Olympic Family and International Relations worked with three main offices at the State Department: the Visa Office, the Office of Protocol, and the Office of International Relations. In addition, the managing director of International Relations consulted regularly with senior government officials such as the undersecretary of state for Political Affairs, the deputy director of

Immigration and Naturalization Services, and the assistant secretary of state for the Bureau of Consular Affairs concerning entry issues. Certain political issues and situations were monitored closely and information was forwarded regularly to ACOG senior management.

OBSERVER PROGRAM

The Observer Program was developed under the direction of Olympic Family to manage relations with future Olympic organizing committees

and facilitate requests of observer organizations. The Observer Program was coordinated by one manager, two coordinators, and ten volunteer assistants. The primary responsibilities of the Observer Program were to:

■ establish and maintain a positive relationship with the organizing committees, Olympic bid cities, and international multisport organizations;

■ provide hospitality services to visiting observers, including organizing and coordinating accommodations, transportation, and venue tours; communicating with ACOG representatives; and providing informational documents for use;

Representatives of organizing committees for future Games participated in the Observer Program.

■ serve as a liaison with the IOC Candidate Cities Department;

■ develop and manage the observer accreditation policy in conjunction with the Accreditation Department;

■ develop an Observer Exchange/Loaned Employee Program that allowed future Games organizers to send employees to Atlanta to work with ACOG prior to and during the 1996 Games;

■ develop and conduct the Observer Seminar held in May 1996;

■ develop an observational tour schedule for all venues during the Games in conjunction with the Venue Management and Sports Departments; and

■ maintain an office for the Observer Program located in the Olympic Family Hotel during the Games period.

Observer Delegations

The Sydney Organizing Committee for the Olympic Games in 2000 (SOCOG), the Organizing Committee for the XVIII Olympic Winter Games in Nagano, Japan, in 1998 (NAOC), the Salt Lake City Organizing Committee for the 2002 Winter Games, and 11 candidate cities sent delegations to Atlanta for the Games.

SOCOG sent a delegation of approximately 150 people. In the years leading up to the Games, ACOG hosted approximately 40 SOCOG officials, including the premier of New South Wales. Prior to and during the 1996 Games, approximately 20 people from SOCOG participated in the Observer Program. In addition, approximately 40 security personnel from Australia participated in the Security Task Force Volunteer Program and were assigned to security duties at the venues.

NAOC sent a delegation of approximately 65 people. Prior to and during the Games, approximately 10 NAOC representatives participated in the Observer Program. An NAOC staff member served as one of the Observer Program's coordinators.

The Salt Lake City Organizing Committee sent a delegation of approximately 25 people to the 1996 Olympic Games.

Eleven candidate cities for the 2004 Olympic Games—Athens, Greece; Buenos Aires, Argentina; Cape Town, South Africa; Istanbul, Turkey; Lille, France; Rio de Janeiro, Brazil; Rome, Italy; San Juan, Puerto Rico; Seville, Spain; Stockholm, Sweden; and St. Petersburg, Russia—sent delegations to the 1996 Olympic Games.

Other multisport observer delegations that attended the 1996 Games included: APOC and the committees organizing the XVI Commonwealth Games in Kuala Lumpur, Malaysia; International World Games Federation; the Goodwill Games; organizers of the 1998 Hockey World Cup, Netherlands; 1998 World Cup, France; and the Asian Games in Seoul, Korea.

ACCREDITATION POLICY

Olympic Family worked with the Accreditation Department to define the accreditation policy for Olympic Family members. This policy determined the levels of service for the various constituents, including seating, transportation, and access to zones at venues. Olympic Family also worked with Accreditation and Government Relations to develop procedures for the Olympic identity card and entry into the US for the Games through negotiations with the US government.

PUBLICATIONS

Olympic Family provided information for various ACOG publications and was responsible for working with Creative Services to publish an Olympic Family guide, which included information about accommodations, accreditation, arrivals and departures, the Cultural Olympiad, entertainment, Olympic Villages, and transportation. A total of 16,000 copies were produced in

French and English for distribution to IOC members, IF and NOC presidents and secretaries-general, organizing committees, and various guests.

CONCLUSIONS AND RECOMMENDATIONS

Olympic Family existed to facilitate and nurture relationships between Olympic Family constituents and ACOG functional areas in order to promote and uphold the IOC standards of the Olympic Movement. The following recommendations are offered to future organizing committees.

■ Appoint specific liaisons between ACOG and the respective organizations to ensure successful interchange.

■ Coordinating all aspects of diplomatic relations, from entry visas to dignitary visits, is of central importance.

LANGUAGE SERVICES

Because the Olympic Movement has two official languages and involves people who speak many different languages, a competent Language Services staff was essential in planning and conducting the Centennial Olympic Games. Accurate oral and written messages were critical to all types of communication, from high-level meetings of the IOC Medical Commission and IOC Session to press conferences at the Main Press Center (MPC) and the competition venues. Additionally, the Language Services Department worked with all ACOG functional areas to assess translation and interpretation needs.

Language Services was comprised of Translation, Interpreting, and Operations divisions. The Translation division translated all documents and official publications from English into French, and both the Operations and Interpreting divisions facilitated spoken communication. During the Olympic Games, a Language Services communication center (LCC) was established to provide central coordination for all language-related issues, thereby integrating the three different divisions into one operation.

TRANSLATION SERVICES

The *Olympic Charter* mandates that French and English are the official languages of the Olympic Games. ACOG created all written materials in English, and the Translation division provided written translation from English into French. Certain critical documents were also translated into Spanish. To ensure accuracy, all official publications were translated by professional translators who followed a strict quality-control process. Language-skilled volunteers assisted translating into English all documents written in other languages. French translation was also provided for Info'96, signage, Opening and Closing Ceremonies speeches, and selected phrases displayed on scoreboards.

Translation management personnel were responsible for the initial receipt of documents and assigning and scheduling the appropriate technical staff to perform the translation quality-control process within a certain time frame. A database was used to track all pertinent information regarding each translation.

The first step in the process was the initial translation. Once this was completed, the original document and the corresponding translation were sent to an editor, who ensured that all sentences were translated properly using established ACOG terminology and style guidelines and adhering to grammatical rules. The final step was proofreading. The proofreader examined the translated document for basic grammar errors, ambiguity, and other visible mistakes. The original document was referenced for clarification only.

To ensure consistency between documents, the Translation division created style guidelines and sport-specific and Olympic-based glossaries. Glossaries were initially created by volunteers who compiled and researched terminology in publications from previous Olympic Games. Once a basic glossary of terms was established, French glossaries were sent to INSEP (l'Institut National du Sport et de l'Education Physique / National Institute for Sports and Physical Education) for review by French technical delegates and/or athletes. Upon return of the information, ACOG translators with sport-specific expertise reviewed the documents for accuracy and clarified any questions with IFs or other authorities. For Spanish glossaries, ACOG consulted TERMCAT, an organization that provided electronic copies of its glossaries for the Translation terminology database. The glossaries were extremely valuable to the Translation staff, professional interpreters, and volunteers.

Staffing

The core of the Translation division staff was a team of personnel fluent in French and/or Spanish with experience in the language services industry. The program director, hired in May 1993, supervised all translation projects. Joining the staff in June 1994, the translation manager assisted with the day-to-day organization and management of all translations. Two translation coordinators were hired in October 1994.

Prior to September 1994, when a senior translator was hired, a team of freelance translators and editors translated most ACOG documents. All ACOG translators were fluent in French and English. Some freelancers were chosen to work on specific projects that required their area of expertise. A native French-speaking translation technology specialist was added to the staff translation team in October 1995, as the extensive use of computers and computer tools warranted adding a technology expert.

In June 1995, a request for proposal was sent to more than 35 translation service companies throughout the US to secure a competent company to provide auxiliary translation services. Inlingua, a company with an Atlanta presence and the ability to provide translations in more than 60 languages, was selected.

The Games-time translation team consisted of a manager, an administrator, a technology specialist, 5 coordinators, 4 staff translators, 2 French translation students, 35 freelance translators, 9 volunteer Games-time translation assistants, and 47 Games-time translators.

Pre-Games Translation

Translation services were necessary for a variety of documents, ranging from general correspondence to highly technical documents.

French and Spanish translation services were provided daily for the International Relations Department, to aid correspondence with the Olympic Family. In addition to these documents and letters, French translation services were required for formal presentations and reports to the IOC and various IOC commissions.

Some of the more challenging translation projects originated in Sports Logistics, including translations of explanatory books and team leader guides for each sport, as well as numerous sport-specific forms and reports. A substantial amount of translation work was associated with Info'96 and the commentator information system (CIS). ACOG signs were translated into French, with the signs at the MPC, Olympic Villages, and AWC also translated into Spanish. Numerous translations were also required for Opening and Closing Ceremonies, including but not limited to programs, scripts, storyboards, speeches, pre-show videos, and press guides.

Technology

Translation services made use of state-of-the-art translation management tools. A database was established in October 1994 to monitor and track all pre-Games translation activities. Simultaneously, Translation explored the capabilities of an IBM product called Translation Manager. This computer-assisted program recognized previously translated text and sections of text that matched sections of a new document. For sections that matched exactly, it allowed for incorporation of the previously translated text. When the new text was similar, but not identical to previously translated text, the system displayed the similar translation, allowing the translator to modify accordingly. This system guaranteed consistent terminology and phraseology in translated documents. Translation Manager also contained a glossary tool that further ensured proper term usage when more than one translation option existed. Another IBM product, FlowMark, was used for Games-time translation. This program automatically routed and tracked documents through the translation process.

Translation Center

The translation center, located at the Inforum adjacent to the MPC, was operational from 17 June through 7 August 1996. From 17 June until 14 July, the center operated Monday through Saturday from 0700 until 2300. From 15 July until 4 August, it operated 24 hours a day, seven days a week. The main purpose of this center was to translate the contents of the Info'96 system, including biographies, news, historical results, schedules, and other general information about the Games. The minutes of the daily chefs' meetings were translated into French and Spanish each afternoon for same-day delivery to the chefs. Translation of weather reports was performed by the National Weather Service.

The translation center also handled miscellaneous requests for translation services, regardless of language, for documents including speeches, venue announcements, and signs.

Requests for translation services from the venues, Villages, and NOCs were also handled through the center.

Translation center staff was also responsible for translating 32 issues of the Olympic Village newspaper, the *Daily Olympian,* into French. The majority of the material for translation arrived at various times during the day, and because of publication deadlines, involved four to six translators per issue.

INTERPRETING SERVICES

Interpreting services were provided for designated meetings, such as IOC meetings, press conferences at the MPC and certain venues, selected IF congresses, and at other pre-Games and Games-time events. In addition to actual interpreting services, Language Services was responsible for renting all simultaneous interpreting equipment and the required technical support.

The chief interpreter, named in April 1994, was responsible for selecting and supervising the simultaneous interpreters as well as other associated details. The chief interpreter worked directly with the IOC to schedule services for its meetings. In those instances, Language Services served as a liaison between the chief interpreter and the responsible organizations.

In the fourth quarter of 1995, I.S.T.S. was selected to provide the rental, transportation, installation, and operation of all simultaneous interpreting equipment. In January and April 1996, site visits to all the facilities ensured adequate space and defined specific equipment needs. Technicians arrived during the first week of July to survey all requirements and begin installation according to the established schedule.

Pre-Games Activities

Simultaneous interpreting services and the associated equipment rental and technical support were required for the following meetings held prior to the 1996 Olympic Games:

- ASOIF and IOC Executive Board meeting—French, Spanish (March 1993)
- ANOC General Assembly—Arabic, English, French, German, Russian, Spanish, (December 1994)
- Chefs de Mission Seminar—English, French, Spanish (May 1995)
- Third IOC World Congress on Sports Science—English, French (September 1995)
- Other IOC and commission meetings held in Atlanta—English, French (periodically, 1992–95)

Games-Time Activities

During the Centennial Olympic Games, simultaneous interpreting services were provided in many meeting places and locations on a regular basis.

Simultaneous interpreting services and technical support for IF congresses and other Olympic-related meetings were coordinated through Language Services on a reimbursement basis. Consecutive interpreting services were provided at venues for the following sports:

- boxing—Russian, Spanish
- fencing—French, Italian, Spanish
- handball—French, Korean, Spanish
- shooting—French, German, Korean, Russian
- wrestling—Korean, Russian

Every effort was made to have either a professional interpreter and/or language agent available at all venues for press conferences and interviews upon request. Depending on the venue, the interpretation services provided were exclusively simultaneous, exclusively consecutive, or a combination of both.

Staff Housing and Transportation

Securing accommodations for interpreters and technicians was challenging, as interpreters and technicians were obliged to reside within approximately 20 mi (32 km) of the Olympic Ring. As a result, daily planning of work schedules for the interpreters was critical, and last-minute requests for services were not easily accommodated.

Ten rooms were reserved at the Olympic Family Hotel where interpreting staff members could coordinate all IOC meetings that were difficult to schedule in advance. Additionally, ACOG's chief interpreter and deputy chief interpreter resided at the Olympic Family Hotel to coordinate these activities.

Because of the location of interpreting staff housing, transportation was critical to ACOG's ability to utilize its interpreters. In addition to the staff and spectator transportation systems, the interpreting staff was allowed to utilize the media transportation system.

OPERATIONS

The primary focus of the Operations division was to facilitate conversation between ACOG representatives and Olympic Family members, including media, who did not speak a common language. These services were provided by volunteers called language agents. At all competition venues and selected noncompetition venues, such as the Atlanta Olympic Village, the MPC, and the Olympic Family Hotel, Language Services maintained a response team of language agents with expert skills in principal languages.

Primary clients consisted of Doping Control, Medical Services, Olympic Family, Olympic Villages, Opening and Closing Ceremonies, Press Operations, Protocol, Security, and Sports. Language agents also assisted in press

FLAG OF THE
INTERNATIONAL
OLYMPIC COMMITTEE

conferences, medical emergencies, and security problems by serving as communication facilitators, rather than information providers. Due to the high level of language proficiency required in these situations, the majority of language agents spoke English and one additional language only.

Recruitment

Recruiting efforts targeting international organizations and other groups began in June 1993 in conjunction with the Envoy Program

were abundant; however, during the first quarter of 1996, it was necessary to recruit volunteers fluent in other languages. These efforts were extremely successful with languages such as Korean and German; however, languages such as Arabic, Russian, Polish, and many other Eastern European languages required greater efforts. In some cases, Language Services was required to find volunteers outside the Atlanta region. In these instances, specific languages were targeted, and only candidates with substantial prior interpreting experience

FLAGS OF THE
PARTICIPATING
DELEGATIONS
JULY 1996

AFG / Afghanistan

ALG / Algeria

ANT / Antigua and Barbuda

ARU / Aruba

AUT / Austria

BAN / Bangladesh

BEL / Belgium

AHO / Netherlands Antilles

AND / Andorra

ARG / Argentina

ASA / American Samoa

AZE / Azerbaijan

BAR / Barbados

BEN / Benin

ALB / Albania

ANG / Angola

ARM / Armenia

AUS / Australia

BAH / Bahamas

BDI / Burundi

BER / Bermuda

created by Olympic Villages. Language Services representatives made presentations to organizations throughout the Atlanta area to encourage people to volunteer, and in September 1995, Language Services established a telephone number to inform callers about the requirements necessary to become a language agent.

Prospective volunteers were interviewed by Language Services from September 1995 through May 1996. More than 3,000 candidates were interviewed for language agent positions.

Because of extensive time commitment associated with being a language agent, including the 10-day minimum volunteering requirement established by ACOG, every effort was made to recruit volunteers from Atlanta and the surrounding regions of Georgia and the South. Qualified French and Spanish speakers

or those enrolled in a university program for professional interpreters were accepted.

Language Proficiency Evaluation

A placement device was used by Language Services to evaluate candidates. In addition to evaluating all candidates for language agent positions, Language Services also conducted evaluations for other ACOG department positions for which language skills were critical, such as Olympic Villages.

The language evaluation consisted of three increasingly difficult sections of recorded oral exercises, including an evaluation of speaking skills and memory recollection. Evaluations were conducted in the language laboratories at Kennesaw State University and Georgia State University, where 20–30 people could be evaluated simultaneously. In total, 3,787 evaluations were administered—75 percent for Language Services purposes and the remaining 25 percent for other ACOG functional areas.

Training

A comprehensive training program was developed for language agents by a Language Services training coordinator in conjunction

intent of this program was to provide language agents with interpretation tools and techniques, as well as an opportunity to practice, thus ensuring they were well-trained and capable of handling situations that might arise during the Games.

Training sessions for language agents were conducted prior to large events, including, but not limited to, Atlanta Sports '95 and the ANOC General Assembly meeting in December 1994. Language Services also provided basic training for other functional areas with lan-

BHU / Bhutan

BLR / Belarus

BRA / Brazil

BUL / Bulgaria

CAM / Cambodia

CGO / Congo

CHN / People's Republic of China

BIH / Bosnia and Herzegovina

BOL / Bolivia

BRN / Bahrain

BUR / Burkina Faso

CAN / Canada

CHA / Chad

CIV / Ivory Coast

BIZ / Belize

BOT / Botswana

BRU / Brunei Darussalam

CAF / Central African Republic

CAY / Cayman Islands

CHI / Chile

CMR / Cameroon

with an outside consultant. This program assumed an advanced or expert level of language ability in English and at least one other language and focused on the appropriate usage of these language skills in a variety of situations, such as press conferences and medical emergencies.

Training included a mandatory six-hour primary training session, with at least two additional three-hour workshops. During primary training, basic job responsibilities were described, interaction with other departments was explained, and techniques and ethics of consecutive interpretation were presented. The workshops were smaller sessions during which volunteers participated in role-playing, memory retention, and note-taking exercises. The

guage-skilled staff, such as Security and Olympic Villages.

In addition to training the language agents, three mandatory training sessions were held for all Language Services management and coordination personnel. Managers were also required to attend supplemental training sessions that focused on managing all venues and emphasized differences and unique requirements of their respective assignments. Additionally, managers were encouraged to participate in international sports events prior to the Games to ensure adequate understanding of the event environment.

Staffing

The Operations division consisted of an operations manager, a recruitment coordinator, a training coordinator, a venue operations coordinator, 4 regional coordinators, a training consultant, a database project coordinator, and 15 office volunteers. Volunteers played a significant role in the daily operations of Language Services.

Venue Operations

Language Services was part of the management team at each venue, attending meetings and participating in all planning sessions prior to the Games. During the Games, each coordinator became a venue language services manager (VLSM), resulting in a Games-time staff

language agents wore a badge at all times indicating the language(s) they could speak. The VLSMs were given temporary passes that they managed and distributed as needed when language agents were called upon to provide assistance in areas where they were not accredited.

Requests for language assistance were communicated to Language Services either through the venue communications center or directly, and the language agent was temporarily dispatched to the appropriate functional area. A pager was provided to facilitate communication.

COK / Cook Islands

CPV / Cape Verde

CUB / Cuba

DEN / Denmark

DOM / Dominican Republic

ESA / El Salvador

ETH / Ethiopia

COL / Colombia

CRC / Costa Rica

CYP / Cyprus

DJI / Djibouti

ECU / Ecuador

ESP / Spain

FIJ / Fiji

COM / Comoros

CRO / Croatia

CZE / Czech Republic

DMA / Dominica

EGY / Egypt

EST / Estonia

FIN / Finland

of 39 VLSMs, 56 volunteer assistant VLSMs, 9 volunteer Language Services coordinators, and approximately 1,400 language agents. In total, 42 Language Services offices were maintained in all competition and selected non-competition venues. Each Language Services office was staffed with a VLSM and 1–3 assistant VLSMs, supported by a team of 15–20 language agents per shift.

Efforts were made to provide services to as many people as possible with as few languages as possible. Based on sport-specific available information such as qualifying countries, historical results, and world championship data, Language Services established a list of languages to be covered at each venue. Input from Sports and Communications was critical to these decisions.

In general, Language Services followed standard operating procedures at all venues. During an event, language coverage was provided at each Language Services venue office during predetermined hours. To ensure easy identification,

Because Language Services operated as a response team in the venues, the daily activities varied. Assignments ranged from the scheduled press conferences and tours to assisting with doping control, ceremonies, sports technical meetings and weigh-ins, security incidents, and severe medical problems.

Communications Center

A central control center, the LCC, was established to provide overall support of Games-time Language Services operations. Direct and immediate access to senior Language Services management staff, as well as to the translation center, was also available through the LCC. Every day, reports were faxed to the LCC for compilation into a single daily activity report used to monitor all venue operations on a regular basis.

The services provided by this operation varied substantially, from routine procedural questions and venue-specific concerns requiring immediate resolution, to personnel problems and cultural questions and challenges. Therefore, if there was an unexpected shortage of speakers of a particular language in one venue, the LCC could reappoint underutilized speakers from another venue. The LCC had the authority to

agents 18 hours a day. AT&T's Language Line Services provided supplemental assistance to the language agents from 2400 to 0600. All calls were answered within 45 seconds, and complete language coverage was always maintained. The language switchboard had transfer and conference capabilities, enabling the language agent to remain on the line in order to facilitate conversation between parties not able to communicate with each other directly.

Languages covered by the language switchboard included Amharic, Arabic, Bulgarian,

FRA / France

GBR / Great Britain

GEQ / Equatorial Guinea

GRE / Greece

GUI / Guinea

HAI / Haiti

HUN / Hungary

GAB / Gabon

GBS / Guinea-Bissau

GER / Germany

GRN / Grenada

GUM / Guam

HKG / Hong Kong

INA / Indonesia

GAM / Gambia

GEO / Georgia

GHA / Ghana

GUA / Guatemala

GUY / Guyana

HON / Honduras

IND / India

move volunteers from one venue to another as needed. The LCC also handled requests for written translation services in the venues and provided professional interpreters for sensitive situations. This operation proved to be the cornerstone of Language Services during the 1996 Olympic Games.

Language Switchboard

In addition to the LCC, Language Services also established a telephone switchboard service to provide general support to all functional areas and support spectators in medical and security emergency situations. The 24-hour language switchboard, covering 31 languages, was situated in the Atlanta Olympic Village to ensure its easy and direct access to all Village departments and NOCs. It was staffed by language

Czech, Dutch, Farsi, Finnish, French, German, Greek, Hausa, Hebrew, Hindi, Hungarian, Igbo, Italian, Japanese, Korean, Mandarin, Norwegian, Polish, Portuguese, Romanian, Russian, Slovak, Spanish, Swahili, Thai, Turkish, Vietnamese, and Yoruba. From 7 July to 8 August 1996, the language switchboard received approximately 2,600 calls, 20 percent of which were directed to AT&T's Language Line Services.

LIAISON WITH THE FRENCH GOVERNMENT

The French government provided substantial support to Language Services through various governmental and private associations, including the Office of the Consul General of France in Atlanta, the Alliance Française of Atlanta, the French Ministry of Foreign Affairs, and the French Ministry of Youth and Sport.

A translator training program, financed by the French Ministry of Youth and Sport, was active from 1 June 1995 to 10 August 1996. Every two months, two students from l'Institut Supérieur d'Interprétation et de Traduction (ISIT) or l'Ecole Supérieure d'Interprétation et de Traduction (ESIT) were sent to Atlanta to assist ACOG's translation efforts. The students, enrolled in translation programs at these schools, were carefully selected by the schools' administrations and were provided round-trip airfares, accommodations, and per diem expenses. ACOG reimbursed students for their insurance.

Observatory of the French Language, awarded a "Gold Medal in the French Language" to ACOG in his critique of its performance.

CONCLUSIONS AND RECOMMENDATIONS

The importance of providing translation and interpretation services in a wide range of languages is central to planning and providing for an international environment in which to stage the Games. In addition, measures taken to maintain high standards for French transla-

IRI / Islamic Republic of Iran

ISL / Iceland

ITA / Italy

JOR / Jordan

KEN / Kenya

KSA / Saudi Arabia

LAT / Latvia

IRL / Ireland

ISR / Israel

IVB / British Virgin Islands

JPN / Japan

KGZ / Kyrgyzstan

KUW / Kuwait

LBA / Libyan Arab Jamahiriya

IRQ / Iraq

ISV / Virgin Islands

JAM / Jamaica

KAZ / Kazakhstan

KOR / Korea

LAO / Lao People's Democratic Republic

LBR / Liberia

Terminology assistance was also provided. INSEP reviewed glossaries and also produced its own French/English sport-specific lexicon. Eight hundred copies of this publication were provided free of charge to Language Services to distribute to its French-speaking staff and volunteers.

The Ministry of Foreign Affairs, with assistance from the Ministry of Youth and Sport, financed a program called FOCUS (Français Olympique Communicatif à l'Usages Spécifiques/French Olympic Terminology). This program, conducted entirely in French, provided native and non-native French speakers the opportunity to study issues and terminology unique to the Olympic Movement and Atlanta.

The French government maintained a strong interest in all ACOG activities that involved usage of the French language and was pleased with both the quantity and the quality of the written and oral French language services provided. M. Yves Berger, president of the National

tion are rewarded by consequent international credibility and the ability to fulfill the mandate to provide all documents and announcements in both French and English. The following recommendations are offered to help future language services departments in these endeavors.

■ A senior translator should be appointed three years prior to the Games to establish procedural guidelines. The services of an auxiliary language services company can also be very beneficial and should be contracted early.

■ Material used in connection with information systems, commentator information, and other technical systems should be translated as soon as possible. Efforts should be made to standardize all terminology usage and test and refine the translation process many months prior to the beginning of the Games.

■ Some centralized management of all signage should be done from both a planning and implementation perspective. Develop a way to produce signs without rekeying all the translation work to ensure accuracy.

■ The accommodations and transportation needs of professional interpreters and technicians should be considered early in the planning process. Because the technical demands of their work require long and erratic hours, it would be helpful to locate them close to their assignments.

■ Venue Management should provide sufficient availability of day passes for language agents, as there are many instances in which they are required to provide language assistance in a zone for which they are not accredited.

■ A central Language Services communications center should be incorporated into the early planning stages so all facets of Language Services can function together as one central unit.

LCA / Saint Lucia

LIE / Liechtenstein

MAD / Madagascar

MAW / Malawi

MEX / Mexico

MLI / Mali

MOZ / Mozambique

LES / Lesotho

LTU / Lithuania

MAR / Morocco

MDA / Republic of Moldova

MGL / Mongolia

MLT / Malta

MRI / Mauritius

LIB / Lebanon

LUX / Luxembourg

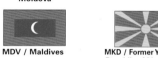
MAS / Malaysia

MDV / Maldives

MKD / Former Yugoslav Republic of Macedonia

MON / Monaco

MTN / Mauritania

PROTOCOL

The Protocol Department was responsible for protocol services in the Olympic Village, competition venues, and the Olympic Family Hotel; general protocol and seating at special events, such as the opening ceremony of the 105th IOC Session and the Opening and Closing Ceremonies of the Games; and victory ceremonies.

OLYMPIC VILLAGE SERVICES

Protocol services in the Olympic Village included the organization of team welcome ceremonies, tours for Olympic Family members and distinguished guests, and distribution of

Olympic diplomas for the first- through eighth-placed athletes and commemorative medals and certificates for accredited athletes and officials.

Staffing and Training

The program manager for protocol services in the Olympic Village joined ACOG in June 1995 and was assisted by a protocol coordinator beginning January 1996. A team welcome ceremonies coordinator joined the staff in February of the same year. During the operation of the Village, a tour coordinator was redeployed from NOC Relations. In addition, a multilingual staff of 82 members, many selected from among international students at Georgia Tech (site of the Atlanta Olympic Village), were available at Games-time, as were 25 flag raisers/bearers and escorts. The Village protocol program manager reported directly to the Protocol division but interacted extensively with Olympic Village management.

Both staff and volunteers were trained in overall Olympic matters, basic protocol, and cross-cultural sensitivity. Training on country specifics and details of the Olympic Village was given to those volunteers handling the tours.

Facilities

The Olympic Village protocol office was housed in a 2,400 sq ft (216 sq m) tent located at the guest entrance. The tent housed the Olympic Family lounge, the venue protocol program manager's office, the Olympic Village

mony was held. Teams with between 100 and 300 members were welcomed separately or with one other NOC. For teams of 50–100 members, ceremonies were held in conjunction with three or four other NOCs. Six NOCs were welcomed simultaneously if each had fewer than 50 team members.

Upon an NOC's arrival to the Olympic Village, its chef de mission was contacted and schedules were established. The Protocol office tried to group together teams with similar languages or geographical locations.

 MYA / Myanmar
 NED / Netherlands
 NIG / Niger
 NZL / New Zealand
 PAN / Panama
PHI / Philippines
POL / Poland

 NAM / Namibia
 NEP / Nepal
 NOR / Norway
 OMA / Oman
 PAR / Paraguay
PLE / Palestine
POR / Portugal

 NCA / Nicaragua
 NGR / Nigeria
 NRU / Nauru
 PAK / Pakistan
 PER / Peru
PNG / Papua New Guinea
 PRK / Democratic People's Republic of Korea

mayor's office, a kitchen/pantry, a waiting room for dedicated hosts and hostesses, and an enclosed terrace. Several Info'96 terminals were available.

Team Welcome Ceremonies

Team welcome ceremonies for the 197 NOCs were held between 6 July 1996, the opening of the Olympic Village, and 20 July 1996, the day after Opening Ceremony. The venue protocol program manager organized and conducted these ceremonies.

Ceremonies were held in a covered amphitheater in the international zone of the Village, a facility that held 300 people in standing room. A platform at the rear of the amphitheater was provided for the press.

The number of NOC teams welcomed at one time depended on their size. If teams had more than 300 members, an individual cere-

Envoys assisted in confirming dates and times with the various chefs de mission. Each welcome ceremony began with the team or teams being ushered into the amphitheater. The Village protocol program manager acted as the master of ceremonies, announcing the name of the team being welcomed and introducing the mayor or one of his five deputies. ACOG's executive management also conducted ceremonies. The speaker welcomed teams in English, while translations of the welcome speech in French, Spanish, German, Russian, and Arabic were displayed on television screens. The country's national anthem was played as its national flag was raised.

The Village mayor then gave the chef de mission a quilt. The Quiltmakers of Georgia had prepared approximately 400 quilts for presentation to the chef de mission and the flag bearer of each NOC. Each quilt was different and represented the history and culture of the South.

Following the ceremony, each NOC was escorted by a protocol representative to the chefs' meeting hall for a reception, where the official flag bearer of each NOC was recognized and presented with the second quilt.

Team welcome ceremonies were also organized for yachting teams at the Savannah Village by the venue protocol manager.

Tours

Many Olympic Family members and guests from the various countries, including heads of

the Olympic Family lounges and seating and for locating the Olympic Family members who were to present medals and flowers at the victory ceremonies.

During the Games, each protocol team in the competition venues consisted of a venue protocol manager, 2 venue protocol coordinators, and 10–72 protocol officers, depending on the capacity of the venue. Selection of managers and coordinators began in 1995, enabling ACOG to start training at pre-Olympic test events. In January 1996, sessions began on

 PUR / Puerto Rico
 RSA / South Africa
 SAM / Western Samoa
 SIN / Singapore
 SLO / Slovenia
 SOM / Somalia
 SUD / Sudan

 QAT / Qatar
 RUS / Russian Federation
 SEN / Senegal
 SKN / Saint Kitts and Nevis
 SMR / San Marino
 SRI / Sri Lanka
 SUI / Switzerland

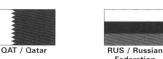 ROM / Romania
RWA / Rwanda
 SEY / Seychelles
 SLE / Sierra Leone
 SOL / Solomon Islands
STP / Sao Tome and Principe
SUR / Suriname

state, members of royal families, and other high-ranking government officials, also visited the Village. Protocol worked with the Olympic Family services desk at the Olympic Family Hotel as well as with Security to coordinate visits. Protocol used its own guest passes for access to the residential zone when needed.

No more than six tours were conducted at any one time. Tours were given in eight different languages: French, English, Spanish, German, Russian, Arabic, Japanese, and Mandarin.

VENUE OPERATIONS

As part of each competition venue planning team, Protocol was responsible for managing

venue-specific matters, Olympic protocol, and cross-cultural sensitivity.

Olympic Family Lounges

Olympic Family lounges were located near seating areas reserved for Olympic Family and the Olympic Family entrances to each venue. In preexisting facilities, the spaces used for lounges had to be selected from available locations. At the outdoor venues and those that were newly constructed, large tents were used with an average space of 8 sq ft (.7 sq m) allowed per person. Adjacent to each lounge was a small office for Protocol venue management.

In each lounge, which was decorated with plants, artwork, and Look of the Games items, the Food and Beverage Department provided refreshments. Beer and wine were provided in most lounges beginning at 1700 on each competition day. Closed-circuit televisions, Info'96 terminals, and telephones were also provided. Lounges opened generally one hour before competitions and closed approximately 30 minutes after the end of the day's events.

Olympic Family Reserved Seating

In accordance with IOC guidelines and Rule 58 of the *Olympic Charter*, designated areas or stands were reserved for accredited Olympic Family members at each venue. The size of these areas related to the overall seating capacity of the venue. Several high-demand events were designated as prime events. For these prime events, complimentary tickets were required for

people from the IF regulating the sport being staged at that venue. Access required accreditation in the IF, Gt, B, B guest, or J categories.

For the Opening and Closing Ceremonies, the following stands were reserved for the relevant accreditation categories: IOC, IF, NOC, G, Gt, Ac, Aa, B, and J in addition to the media and broadcast seating areas. Complimentary tickets for Olympic Family members could be obtained in the Olympic Family Hotel beginning 48 hours before the Opening and Closing Ceremonies.

 SVK / Slovakia

 SYR / Syrian Arab Republic

 THA / Thailand

 TOG / Togo

 TUN / Tunisia

 UGA / Uganda

USA / United States of America

 SWE / Sweden

 TAN / United Republic of Tanzania

 TJK / Tajikistan

 TPE / Chinese Taipei

 TUR / Turkey

 UKR / Ukraine

UZB / Uzbekistan

 SWZ / Swaziland

 TGA / Tonga

 TKM / Turkmenistan

 TRI / Trinidad and Tobago

 UAE / United Arab Emirates

 URU / Uruguay

  VAN / Vanuatu

certain categories (G, Gt, some B), which were distributed one day before the session from the Ticket Sales office in the Olympic Family Hotel. Removable stickers showed the accreditation category of members with access to each stand. Access was checked by Security and Protocol officers. GI-accredited individuals had free access to the stand of honor for all events, except prime events and ceremonies, when purchased tickets in spectator areas were required.

During the Games, the venue protocol officers managed the seating access. On certain occasions when the stands were overcrowded, individuals with a certain category of accreditation were asked to relinquish their seats and watch the event from the Olympic Family lounge. Generally, however, sufficient seats were set aside in each venue.

Venue day passes and Olympic Family lounge passes were issued to allow guests of accredited individuals access to the Olympic Family lounge.

The federation stand, implemented for the first time in Olympic history, was reserved for

A presidential box was used for distinguished guests for the Opening and Closing Ceremonies. For other competitions, the following stands were reserved for persons with certain categories of accreditation.

■ official stand: IOC, IF, NOC, G, ACOG

■ stand of honor: B, GT, Ac, GI (except for prime events and ceremonies)

■ federation stand: IF, GT, B, B guest, J

■ A stand: athletes and officials, excluding extra officials, attachés, chefs de mission

■ J stand: jury members, judges, referees, and other such constituents

Olympic Family Hotel Services Desk

The Olympic Family services desk at the Olympic Family Hotel was open from 0700 to 2200 daily from 9 July through 7 August 1996.

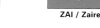

VEN / Venezuela

YUG / Yugoslavia

VIE / Vietnam

ZAI / Zaire

**VIN / Saint Vincent
and The Grenadines**

ZAM / Zambia

YEM / Yemen

ZIM / Zimbabwe

The desk provided a variety of services to residents at the Olympic Family Hotel, including information about restaurants, shopping, the competition schedule, and Cultural Olympiad events. Together with Protocol, Ticket Sales also coordinated the distribution of complimentary tickets for Opening and Closing Ceremonies and prime events.

The Olympic Family services desk was staffed by a protocol manager, six protocol coordinators, and volunteer protocol officers. The IOC also provided staff for the desk from prior to the IOC session until the end of the Games.

VICTORY CEREMONIES

The victory ceremonies were conducted following the procedures outlined in the *Olympic Charter* and in accordance with the protocol determined and approved by the IOC. Victory ceremonies staff was responsible for conducting all 271 medal award ceremonies, obtaining all national flags and anthems from the 197 NOCs, and supervising the installation of all protocol and country flags at the Olympic Village and the competition venues.

Organization

Research for victory ceremonies began in October 1993, when a project coordinator joined ACOG to verify the national anthems and the correct display of the national flags of the 197 countries participating in the Olympic Games. Planning for the victory ceremonies began in October 1994. A second project coordinator responsible for staffing the victory ceremonies themselves joined ACOG in October 1995. A deputy victory ceremonies program manager was appointed in April 1996. Shortly before the Games, a volunteer deputy victory ceremonies program manager was appointed.

Eleven venue victory ceremony managers and 11 assistant venue victory ceremony man-

agers were recruited. These paid staff members were all theater stage managers recruited to manage the ceremonies in the venues. A total of 308 volunteers were used during Games-time and were divided into 11 teams, each assigned to a specific group of venues.

Four additional teams were used for victory ceremonies in the venues outside Atlanta. These volunteers were recruited from the venues' surrounding areas and worked under the guidance of existing venue victory ceremonies managers and their assistants.

Teams consisted of a venue victory ceremonies manager, an assistant venue victory ceremonies manager, two runners, three flag bearers, three flag raisers, one flag timer, three flower/medal bearers, one presenter escort, one athlete escort, one escort coordinator, one flower/medal coordinator, and one flag coordinator.

Volunteers were recruited nine months before the Games, primarily from the 300 Dream Team members. *(For more information, see the Youth and Education chapter)*. The remaining volunteers came from high schools and colleges in the Atlanta area. All escorts, flower/medal bearers, and runner positions were filled by women aged 18–25. The flag bearers and flag raisers were men aged 18–25. Coordinators were usually teachers.

Volunteers were trained in groups at the Wolf Creek shooting venue to allow practice with both indoor and outdoor ceremonies. They were trained in marching drills, posture, flag usage, and the operating plans. Rehearsals at each venue followed, with the volunteers practicing as a team. Second and third full dress rehearsals were held with Atlanta Olympic Broadcasting (AOB) and competition management. Training was principally conducted by a venue victory ceremony manager.

During the Games, the teams arrived at their venue three hours before the first ceremony. Additionally, several volunteers were available for three- to four-hour shifts each day for substitution purposes.

Costumes and Uniforms

Victory ceremony managers and assistant managers wore the standard ACOG staff casual uniform at the victory ceremonies, as did all regular departmental staff. The escorts, runners, flag bearers, flag raisers, and flag timers wore ACOG full business dress with a gold-colored tie or scarf. The flower/medal bearers wore cream-colored southern-style dresses with large straw hats and cream shoes. A total of 125 dresses and hats were ordered.

Podiums

Designed to accommodate individual as well as team event winners, the podiums were modular so that components could be lifted on and off the field of play. With compatible fasteners, they were expandable to hold up to 60 athletes.

The podiums were built by an ACOG fabrication shop and differed in length according to the number of athletes per sport. A width of 2 ft (.6 m) per person was allowed. Fourteen 12 ft (3.6 m) podiums, seven 24 ft (7 m) podiums, and two 72 ft (21.6 m) podiums were made. One podium each was made in sizes of 36 ft (10.8 m), 48 ft (14.4 m), 96 ft (28.8 m), and 108 ft (32.4 m).

Underlays or carpets were used to provide a flat surface and protect existing flooring. At certain indoor venues, special mats were used underneath podiums to protect the flooring. Six large pots of flowers surrounded the podiums on the field of play at the outdoor venues to enhance the ceremonial environment. For the two wheelchair events in athletics, a ramp was added.

Medals

Each evening during the Games, a member of the Victory Ceremonies division retrieved medals from storage in a bank vault for the fol-

lowing day. These were then stored in a secure place before being transported to the various venues the next morning.

At the venues, following the awarding of the medals, the medalists were given presentation boxes to hold their medals. *(For more information on Olympic medals, see the Creative Services chapter.)*

Victory Bouquets

A bouquet was presented to each medalist consisting of flowers and leaves representing

various qualities that symbolized the meaning of Olympic victory. The flowers in the bouquet were sunflowers for loyalty, cockscomb for immortality, larkspur for swiftness, tuberose for hospitality, and tiger lily for pride. The greenery was an olive branch for peace, laurel for glory, palm fronds for victory, magnolia for perseverance, and leucothoe for friendship. This bouquet reflected the Games' ancient roots, traditional southern hospitality, Georgia's

left: Many victory ceremonies volunteers were recruited from the Dream Team Program.

right: The costume for victory ceremonies flower/medal bearers was a traditional southern dress.

• SIMONE COPELAND • SUE J COPELAND • TASHAWN J COPELAND • TIFFANY COPELAND • VALARIA Y COPELAND • WILLIAM E COPELAND • TAMMY S COPEMAN • GEORGE W COPENHAVER • KELLIE F COPENHAVER • ROBBIE H COPENHAVER • DAVID M COPHER • SUE A COPLEY • SHIRLEY A COPPEDGE • CELISSE F COPPEL • BARBARA COPPOLA • TISH A COPPOLINO • ANDRIA COPRICH • DAVID CORADINI • CHRISTINA I CORAZALLA • JOANN M CORBAN • GERALDINE M CORBETT • HELEN A CORBETT • HELEN E CORBETT • SALLY A CORBETT • SHIRLEY R CORBETT • TEANER M CORBETT

315

botanical interest, and the qualities that make an Olympian.

Two thousand bouquets were used. They were made in a local warehouse every night by volunteers under the guidance of a local florist and delivered each morning to the appropriate venue.

Medal/Flower Trays

The trays, designed to carry up to four medals and four bouquets each, were approximately 24 x 15 in (61 x 38 cm). They were

top: **Podiums designed for victory ceremonies were modular and expandable to accommodate both individuals and teams.**

bottom: **Victory bouquets were composed of a variety of flowers and leaves symbolizing the meaning of Olympic victory.**

made of a light wood painted ACOG green, with gold leaves decorating the inside and the handles. A total of 85 trays were used.

Anthems

In mid-1994, ACOG requested that each NOC submit a certified audiotape and a printed copy of its country's national anthem. The NOCs could send these or bring them to Atlanta during the ANOC General Assembly. The anthems were recorded by the US Army Band. At the ANOC General Assembly in December 1994 and the Chefs de Mission Seminar in May 1995, a representative from each NOC was asked to listen to the recording and sign a form certifying that the version was correct.

Under the supervision of the victory ceremonies program manager, anthems were edited at a sound studio to not exceed 75 seconds in length. They were produced as CDs containing all the national anthems, together with processional and recessional music to be used at each venue by the competition producer, who was responsible for coordinating the music.

Victory Diplomas

In accordance with the *Olympic Charter*, diplomas were awarded to athletes who placed first to eighth. Designed by the Creative Services Department, they bore the sport's pictogram, the name of the event, the position placed by the athlete, and the citation "For Outstanding Achievement." Each diploma was signed by the IOC and ACOG presidents. The names of the diploma winners were displayed on the scoreboard during the victory ceremonies. Diplomas preprinted without names to cover all eventualities totaled 10,646.

Flags

The Victory Ceremonies division was responsible for ceremonies and the placement of permanent flags at all venues. After a competitive bid process, ACOG contracted with a manufacturer to supply all requisite flags. NOC representatives were asked to approve color illustrations of their flag, shown in both the horizontal and vertical positions. Where required, adjustments were made, and revised illustrations were sent to the NOC for approval.

A book displaying all 197 flags vertically and horizontally was available at each venue during the Games as a reference for installation purposes.

Each victory ceremony location was examined to ascertain whether flags would be flown horizontally, as on flagpoles, or vertically, as on battens from the ceiling.

After determining which NOCs had entered athletes in which events, victory ceremonies planned on the most extreme scenario: the possibility of one country winning the gold, silver, and bronze medal in an individual event. Through careful monitoring of the results of the preliminaries and qualifying rounds, the actual number of flags needed was found to be less than had been originally anticipated.

Operations

The victory ceremonies office at ACOG headquarters served as a communications center during the Games. The central office monitored results in order to assist with flag selection and dispatch from the warehouse. It also maintained the victory ceremonies master schedule and rehearsal times.

The office also received lists from the IOC of the IOC members awarding the medals and of the IF representatives presenting the bouquets. These names and any changes were entered regularly into Info'96 and communicated to the venue victory ceremonies managers and ACOG's protocol office. The latter was responsible for transmitting the information to the venue protocol managers, who would locate the presenters in the stands or Olympic Family lounge one hour prior to the victory ceremonies. If the presenters were not present, the IOC member responsible for that sport would either award the

medal or choose another IOC member to present the award. The office also supervised the calligraphy of the victory certificates.

An off-site warehouse was used to store the flags, which had been sorted by size and labeled by country. Each flag was also labeled to show which way it was designed to be flown.

The warehouse manager distributed on a daily basis those flags needed for the following day's ceremonies. At the end of each day, the flags, trays, and podiums were returned to the warehouse and inventoried. Medals not used

The Austrian delegation studies a model of Olympic Stadium.

were stored in the bank. The warehouse was staffed by six paid managers/drivers.

The flags and trays needed were loaded at the warehouse onto trucks that were dispatched to the various venues before dawn. The podium pieces also were dispatched on the trucks except when it was more efficient to leave them at the venues. Those were then transported between venues once one sport had been completed. The truck drivers also received the relevant number of bouquets, plus a few extra in the case of ties, from the flower assembly warehouse and stored them in cool chests. The medals and presentation boxes were similarly loaded onto the trucks.

Once at the venue, the logistics manager would accept delivery of the materials, which would then be stored in the victory ceremonies staging area. Logistics was responsible for moving the podium, carpet, and ornamental flowers. At a few venues, such as the Olympic Stadium, the podium remained on the field of play at all times.

The venue victory ceremonies manager attended the morning venue meeting each day. The other members of the team arrived three hours before the ceremony to be briefed, rehearse, and change into their uniforms or costumes. Competition results were closely monitored in order to prepare flags and medals.

Shortly before each ceremony, the escort runners would meet the IOC member and IF presenter in either the Olympic Family lounge or seating area and escort them to the staging area. The presenters were briefed with the aid of a simple diagram showing the route of the processional and recessional. In the meantime, the athlete liaisons, provided by competition management, escorted the athletes from the field of play to the staging area. The competition producer signaled the start of the proceedings.

Advertising on Uniforms

To enforce Rule 51 of the *Olympic Charter* restricting advertising on athlete uniforms, ACOG had extra-large white T-shirts distributed throughout all venues to cover any advertising, but none of these were needed.

Venue Protocol Flags

Flags representing the country of each NOC with participating athletes at a venue were flown at that venue. Some of these were hung from the ceiling of the venue, as at the indoor venues, others on flagpoles, as at outdoor venues. In cluster venues, such as the Georgia World Congress Center, the flags of all NOCs participating in all sports taking place there were displayed in one central location—usually the main entrance.

A full set of all 197 flags was hung vertically from the rim of the Olympic Stadium, and another full set flew on flagpoles in the Main Transportation Mall at the Olympic Village. A third full set was displayed on stands at the Olympic Family Hotel.

A protocol set of flags consisting of the Olympic flag, the US flag, the ACOG flag, and any relevant IF flags was also flown at each venue. ACOG either obtained the IF flag designs from the IFs themselves or copied the artwork of IF logos.

The flags carried in at the Opening and Closing Ceremonies by each NOC flag bearer were also ordered by the Victory Ceremonies division, and managed by the Ceremonies Department.

For those flags displayed in the venues, victory ceremonies worked with Construction and Venue Management with regard to flag placement and the installation and removal of poles and other apparatus. AOB and the press department were also involved in these decisions to ensure good camera shots of the winning athletes on the podium with the medalists' flags also in view.

Flags flown from flag-raising devices in indoor venues hung vertically. Two pipes of equal length and size accommodated any configuration of ties. Devices were raised either manually or electronically, depending on the venue.

CONCLUSIONS AND RECOMMENDATIONS

The Protocol Department existed to promote and uphold the IOC standards for the Olympic Movement. The accurate rendition of guiding protocol is essential to preserving the traditional significance and symbolism upon which the Games are based. The following suggestions are offered to help future protocol departments in this effort.

■ Planning for the team welcome ceremonies at the Olympic Village should include consideration of the needs of the media, especially photographers.

■ All components of the victory ceremonies should be approved and finalized no later than six months in advance to allow sufficient time for orientation and training.

■ Processional and recessional music for victory ceremonies should be composed to accommodate various lengths of processionals and recessionals due to different venue sizes and configurations.

■ Flag design and correct horizontal and vertical orientation as well as national anthems should be approved not only by the NOC, but also by the embassy of the country, if possible.

■ It is preferable to provide one size flag for each venue.

■ Rehearsals for victory ceremonies should be conducted in at least three different venue environments and should begin at least three months prior to the Games.

■ Medals should be stored with an armored car service or bank with 24-hour access, and vehicles and drivers with flags, medals, and flowers should be given priority access to all venues.

■ The location and installation of the venue protocol flags should be determined very early in the venue planning process to save time and expense.

NOC Relations

The NOC Relations Department was formed in November 1992 to facilitate all contacts between the NOCs and the various departments within ACOG. Important areas of contact included most sport- and competition-related affairs, marketing, licensing, press- and other media-related issues, accommodations, and transportation.

Besides fulfilling these responsibilities, the department coordinated the visits of NOC delegations to Atlanta, managed the Attaché Program, and produced a quarterly newsletter to send to each NOC and IOC member and IOC staff. The department also coordinated the Adopt-a-Family Program and the pre-Olympic training program, working in conjunction for the latter with the Georgia Olympic Training Alliance (GOTA). The NOC Relations Department coordinated Games-time hotel accommodations for all NOCs.

NOC Relations was headed by a program director and supported by four coordinators. NOCs were divided into four groups, each with its own coordinator. Coordinators were matched with NOC groupings based on their nationality or heritage, language skills, travel experience, and personal interests. In several cases, the NOC groupings themselves were based on factors other than geography, such as shared linguistic, cultural, or historic ties. Dividing the NOCs into established groups at an early stage helped the development of relationships with the NOCs, as this allowed them to become accustomed to contacting their particular coordinator on a regular basis.

Coordination with the NOCs was also enhanced by reports to each of the five continental associations of NOCs at their regular meetings. These reports were given by the managing director of International Relations.

NOC Visits

In preparing for the Olympic Games, ACOG received regular visits of delegations from the participating NOCs. The NOC Relations staff coordinated the various elements of these visits. Not only did an NOC delegation's visit offer ACOG an opportunity to learn about the visitors and their concerns, but it also gave the visiting delegates an opportunity to see how ACOG operated.

When an NOC notified the NOC Relations Department of its plans to send a delegation to Atlanta, the NOC Relations coordinator communicated these plans to Airport Operations and Guest Services, which were responsible for various aspects of delegation visits.

KIMBERLY R CORSINO • ARTURO CORSO • JOE M CORSO • STEPHEN G CORTELYOU • CLAIRE B CORTER • BECKY J CORTEZ • CLAUDIA CORTEZ • CYNTHIA C CORUM • CHARLES CORVI • CINDY CORVI • KEITH J CORY • KELLIE R COSBY • KATHERINE COSENTINO • KRISTA L COSGROVE • MICHAEL E COSGROVE • PETER C COSMIANO • MANUEL A COSTA • TANJA COSTA • JEAN J COSTANTINO • WILLIAM E COSTANTINO • JUANITA S COSTELLO • JUDITH B COSTELLO • KATHERINE T COSTELLO • MICHAEL S COSTELLO • PATRICK E COSTELLO • RICHARD P COSTELLO • WARREN K. COSTIKYAN

319

The coordinator's next responsibility was to establish a schedule to meet the delegation's needs. To this end, information was received including the days of the guests' stay in Atlanta, which ACOG personnel the visitors wished to meet, and specific issues, problems, and details that the NOC wished to address during their visit. A complete itinerary was thereby constructed and delivered to all personnel involved in the visit, as well as the NOC.

With responsibility of handling all arrangements for each country's official delegation

left: **The Irish NOC delegation met with Billy Payne to discuss ACOG's plans for the Centennial Olympic Games.**

right: **The Greek delegation tours Olympic Stadium.**

within the Olympic Village, the Olympic Village NOC Services division was closely involved in almost every NOC delegation visit. Integrating the NOC Relations Department's activities with those of the NOC Services division demanded close cooperation prior to and during every visit. Delegations met with Village personnel and received a tour of the Olympic Village. Tours were also given of Olympic competition venues that were either completed or under construction.

Before an NOC delegation arrived, the coordinator ensured that the country's national flag was displayed in the International Relations reception area. This practice was very successful, as the delegation frequently wished to take pictures in this area.

A typical visit from an NOC lasted two or three days. During this time, the coordinator

was occupied with the visitors for approximately one full day while they attended meetings in the ACOG offices. The coordinator normally did not accompany the guests on venue tours or visits to the Olympic Village. After the delegation had departed, the coordinator prepared a written report of the visit.

THE ATTACHÉ PROGRAM

The Olympic Charter allows for the appointment of an attaché for each NOC to facilitate contacts between the NOC and the Organizing Committee. ACOG provided assistance to ensure communications.

When requested, the NOC Relations Department identified potential attaché candidates and submitted their résumés to the NOC. The department requested that the NOCs send an official letter notifying ACOG when a new attaché had been appointed.

The first forum was held on 8 June 1994 at ACOG headquarters. In all, five such gatherings were held. Their purpose was to give the attachés the opportunity to meet each other and discuss the tasks that their respective NOCs had asked them to perform. During these gatherings, the attachés also met with ACOG staff members and received informative presentations from various departments on such issues as accommodations, accreditation, security, transportation, protocol/State Department concerns, sports, and ticketing.

During the ANOC General Assembly and the Chefs de Mission Seminar, the attachés met in person, often for the first time, with delegates from their NOCs.

Some of the attachés collaborated on projects such as pre-Olympic training sites, media relations, and plans for NOC hospitality centers. During the Games, the attachés were fully accredited as members of their NOC's official delegation. In general, their role was to accompany and assist their delegations. Outside the Olympic Villages, their responsibilities varied. A total of 175 attachés were appointed.

NOC NEWSLETTER

In November 1994, the NOC Relations Department began production of a quarterly newsletter to provide NOCs with regular information on ACOG preparations. Some of the issues covered were: pre-Olympic training; venue construction; the Envoy Program; attaché appointment procedures; the ANOC General Assembly; the Chefs de Mission Seminar; ticket ordering procedures; customs and freight-forwarding information; Olympic Family accommodation request procedures; announcements of various mailings and deadlines; and general information regarding transportation, logistics, medical services, and pre-Olympic events. The articles were either written directly by representatives of the departments concerned or by an NOC Relations coordinator.

Published in-house in cooperation with Creative Services and Sports, the newsletter was originally produced in one trilingual version with English, French, and Spanish text. As content increased, NOC Relations and Language Services began to produce separate versions. Approximately 300 English, 100 French, and 100 Spanish copies of each issue were produced. One copy in the appropriate language was sent to each NOC, each NOC's attaché, and the IOC.

OUTSIDE PROGRAMS

NOC Relations took part in two programs involving partners outside ACOG: the GOTA Program and the AT&T Adopt-a-Family Program. The department served as the liaison between these programs and the NOCs.

Georgia Olympic Training Alliance

ACOG created GOTA to help NOCs find suitable training sites for their athletes prior to the 1996 Games. Atlanta was the first host city to offer this type of program for training and acclimation. The effort provided athletes with an opportunity to acclimate themselves to the area and also enabled communities throughout the southeastern US to be involved in the Olympic experience.

Initially, ACOG gathered information from potential sites concerning available training and lodging facilities, compiled this information into a binder, and sent it to all 197 NOCs. The intention was to facilitate negotiations between NOCs and their respective communities, and this facilitation was coordinated through the NOC Relations Department.

As a result of this program, the state of Georgia hosted delegations from 105 countries in 65 communities. Throughout the Southeast, cities hosted 6,900 athletes and officials from 112 countries. Many participating communities financially supported athlete housing, food, training facilities, equipment, local transportation, and insurance needs.

Adopt-a-Family

The Adopt-a-Family Program was an extension of AT&T's past involvement in helping families of US athletes attend previous Olympic Games. For the 1996 Games, AT&T expanded the program to enable the families of athletes from other countries to participate. Under the company's direction, a coalition of community organizations identified families in the Atlanta and satellite venue areas who were interested in hosting families of visiting Olympic athletes. With the assistance of NOC Relations, AT&T contacted the NOCs to identify athletes' families to participate.

Upon arrival in Atlanta, athletes' families were met by AT&T representatives and introduced to their host families. During a typical five- to eight-day stay, the host family provided accommodations, at least one informal meal per day, and access to the Spectator Transportation System. Some host families grouped together to sponsor receptions or other events for their guests.

As part of the Adopt-a-Family Program, AT&T created a hospitality center in Centennial Olympic Park called the AT&T Global Olympic Village. In this center, families were provided with hospitality televisions and meeting space. A crisis management team was established to deal with medical, liability, and security issues 24 hours a day.

The program proved to be a significant success, with 2,500 participants from 75 countries being hosted by 850 families. The largest number of families came from the US, Canada, and Australia. Furthermore, 17,000 credentials were issued to athletes and family members for the AT&T Global Olympic Village.

ACCOMMODATIONS

In late 1995, NOC Relations assumed responsibility from Accommodations for coordinating Games-time hotel accommodations for the NOCs. Bookings were divided into two main categories: the Olympic Family Hotel and extra accommodations.

Each NOC was allocated a maximum of four rooms in the official Olympic Family Hotel. This was the largest number of rooms ever available to an NOC. Most chose to reserve all four rooms offered, although some reserved fewer and many desired more.

NOC Relations provided NOCs with a list of the number of rooms available in other hotels along with a list of the possible room-class categories and prices from which to make extra room requests. The department then coordinated the distribution of rooms, a task complicated by the number of hotels involved, each with a different price list, location, and room availability.

GAMES-TIME OPERATIONS

During the Games, the NOC Relations Department was located at the Olympic Family Hotel and was staffed by seven people. The department worked very closely with other functional areas, especially Guest Services and Olympic Villages, to provide many services to the NOCs during Games-time.

Once NOC delegations arrived for the Games, NOC Relations confirmed reservations at the Atlanta Marriott Marquis. Challenges included delegations not reserving the anticipated number of rooms for their guests and difficulties with paying for the total number of rooms in advance for the entire period of stay.

NOC Relations coordinated problem solving with the NOCs upon request.

CONCLUSIONS AND RECOMMENDATIONS

NOC Relations is the interface between the NOCs and the functional areas. To allow the department to fulfill its role, it is important that other functional areas understand this. Most recommendations for the department involve facilitating communication with NOCs and functional areas.

■ Procedures and regulations for NOC visits should be communicated to each of the NOCs prior to their visit. Request NOCs to communicate questions and issues for discussion to NOC Relations prior to their visit so that meetings can be arranged in advance.

■ A general guide should be prepared for attachés informing them of their responsibilities and duties.

■ A centralized communication system must be established no later than one year prior to the Games to handle the huge volume of inquiries from the NOCs.

■ All accommodation requirements should be coordinated with one department, with especially close attention paid to problems involved in collecting payments from NOCs.

■ Create one department to handle NOC relations, and then subdivide this department into smaller divisions, including one for Olympic Villages.

CHAPTER EIGHTEEN
OLYMPIC VILLAGES

OVERVIEW—The concept of the Olympic Village was first applied at the 1932 Los Angeles Games, when two separate Villages housed 1,400 male participants and 100 female participants. The concept was so successful that it became part of the protocol for all subsequent organizing committees. In this tradition, the Centennial Olympic Games featured Villages that were conceived and designed for the ultimate convenience and enjoyment of 16,500 athletes and officials.

The largest site, the Atlanta Olympic Village, was located on the campus of the Georgia Institute of Technology. Located just inside the northern circumference of the Olympic Ring, this facility was less than 3 km from competition venues for 16 of the 26 sports presented in the Centennial Olympic Games.

The Atlanta Olympic Village was a special place to live and visit. A completely secured and self-contained community, the Village offered a full range of amenities and free services for living, training, and sports administration. Newly constructed facilities accommodated two people per room, and for the first time, all Olympic Village accommodations were air-conditioned.

Transportation services and five dining locations were available 24 hours daily, providing a high level of convenience and accommodation to the culturally diverse tastes of the Village population. The international festival zone, located in the center of the Georgia Tech campus, offered entertainment, recreation, and other amenities in an atmosphere that encouraged the friendship the Games were conceived to inspire.

Making a home for 197 delegations with different expectations for comfort and convenience was a unique challenge. Whether an athlete desired the solitude of the religious center and music listening rooms or the revelry of the dance club, the options were numerous and convenient. Virtually every service found in a city was provided within the perimeter of the Atlanta Olympic Village.

In addition to the main Olympic Village in Atlanta, ACOG established and operated eight satellite Villages for athletes and officials participating in yachting, football, softball, canoe/kayak–slalom, and rhythmic gymnastics competitions. Each satellite location was selected for its proximity to competition and training venues and the convenience of its facilities. These Villages offered residents a level of comfort and service similar to that found in the Atlanta Olympic Village, yet each one had its own character.

VILLAGE PREPARATIONS

Members of the ACOG Olympic Villages Department visited the Olympic Games in 1992 to observe the Barcelona Village and its satellite Villages. This experience helped management define the physical and operational preparations that would be necessary to develop athlete Villages for the Centennial Olympic Games.

While in Barcelona, ACOG observers paid special attention to the needs and expectations of the NOCs. Most apparent was the need for convenient access to allotted office, storage, and medical spaces, assigned or motor pool vehicles, and Village information. ACOG determined it important to provide 24-hour assistance desks in the residential areas and well-trained, mature personnel to assist each NOC delegation. The experience also confirmed the need for air-conditioned accommodations and an internal Village transportation system.

The observations in Barcelona altered some of the Village management's operations and resulted in definitive changes in ACOG's original plan for the Atlanta Olympic Village. Perhaps the most significant change in plans was the decision to locate NOC office spaces in residential areas instead of at centrally located facilities in the Village. This decision immediately won the praise and approval of the IOC Coordination Commission and NOCs. Another change was that ACOG decided to develop a comprehensive Envoy Program through which specially trained volunteers would be assigned to assist each NOC.

Village Site Selection

Several factors motivated the selection of Georgia Tech as the home of the Atlanta Olympic Village. The university campus provided numerous suitable facilities, especially in the areas of housing, dining, recreation, and training. As one of the premier technical institutions in the US, Georgia Tech offered a wide array of existing technology and technological expertise that would be useful to Olympic Village planning as well as other areas of ACOG. When it became apparent that the Village would require an augmented technological infrastructure, the campus was found suitable for

the installation of permanent and temporary technology. Additionally, Georgia Tech had its own trained support organization of more than 400 people available to meet the majority of the Village's custodial, physical, and mechanical maintenance needs.

Approximately 270 acres (109 ha) of Georgia Tech's 325 acres (132 ha) were within the secured Village perimeter, and some 200 permanent facilities on the campus were utilized. The majority of these facilities were residence halls and apartments used for housing and NOC offices. Other places utilized included academic, student services, entertainment, retail, sports and recreation, parking, and operational support facilities.

ACOG and the Board of Regents, the state agency that administers and controls the facilities of state universities, negotiated seven separate agreements to govern the use of those Georgia Tech facilities required for the operation of the Atlanta Village.

Campus Adaptation

In order to develop the permanent facility infrastructure required by the Olympic Village and to make long-term improvements to the Georgia Tech campus, the Board of Regents undertook construction of new housing projects, numerous housing renovation projects, and the Georgia Tech plaza, an attractive, new, open area that was the main gathering place in the international zone.

New Housing. One 8-story building and one 13-story building were constructed in the southeast corner of the campus. After the Games, these facilities would be used and managed by Georgia State University, another public institution located nearby. They would provide the first university-owned, dormitory-style housing available for Georgia State students. The Board of Regents also constructed six other midrise buildings on the east and west sides of the campus.

The new construction program required the collaboration of many entities, including

ACOG, the Board of Regents, Georgia Tech, Georgia State University, the Atlanta Housing Authority, the National Historic Register, and the Georgia State Financing and Investment Commission, which managed the project contractors. The projects were funded by ACOG contributions and state of Georgia revenue bonds, to be amortized over 20 years through student rent revenues.

The new housing facilities provided space to house 9,384 Olympic athletes and officials. All new housing projects were designed with

This artistic rendering of the Georgia Tech plaza shows how the central area of the international zoneof the Atlanta Olympic Village would look during the Games.

apartment-style accommodations, typically with four single- or double-occupancy bedrooms, two bathrooms, a kitchen, and a living room. Olympic athletes and officials resided in double-occupancy rooms, with private rooms for NOC chefs de mission.

Existing Housing Renovation Program. The Board of Regents also completed renovations of several existing residence halls. These projects not only enabled Georgia Tech to accelerate its long-range plan for housing renovation, but also raised the aesthetic and functional standards of existing facilities to meet ACOG guidelines and contractual specifications. Renovations were completed in June 1996.

Georgia Tech Plaza. The Georgia Tech plaza project, which became the centerpiece of the international zone, included a permanent central fountain, a bell tower gathering area, and

an amphitheater used for NOC team welcome ceremonies. ACOG provided a significant portion of the funds required for this project.

Temporary Construction. Probably the most demanding challenge facing ACOG in connection with the Atlanta Olympic Village involved building approximately $17 million worth of temporary and portable structures in 16 days to transform the Georgia Tech campus into a completely secure and functional Olympic Village. Agreements with the institution prevented this construction from beginning before 15 June 1996. In the time available, construction efforts had to be coordinated with other equally time-sensitive activities, such as perimeter security fence installation and the movement of massive amounts of furniture and equipment. This project required very detailed planning and close coordination. During this construction period, crews worked 24 hours a day.

ACOG's Role

Throughout all Olympic-related construction on the Georgia Tech campus, ACOG performed various significant functions. ACOG reviewed new facilities at various stages, providing Olympic criteria and verifying specifications, and participated in final reviews and the preparation of showrooms for NOC viewing of housing options. ACOG's financial contributions and the promotional value of the Olympic Games played critical roles in accomplishing the projects and preparing them for marketing and occupancy.

Liaison with Georgia Tech

During its years of involvement, ACOG developed a close working relationship with Georgia Tech. During ACOG's lease period of the campus, 15 June to 15 August 1996, daily scenarios required constant communication and coordination in many functional areas including staffing, access, deliveries, maintenance, and security. Most problems were resolved expeditiously. ACOG temporary structures and adaptations were offered to Georgia Tech for purchase as part of the agreements. As ACOG vacated the Village site after the Games, Georgia Tech and Georgia State assisted with inventory, direction, coordination, and restoration processes. Contracts were given final review by all parties before the facilities were returned to Georgia Tech and Georgia State.

ORGANIZATION

Reporting to the ACOG managing director of International Relations, the executive director of Olympic Villages was responsible for the detailed planning, management, and operations of all Villages. The Atlanta Village mayor, a volunteer position, oversaw protocol, ceremonies, and relations with the Board of Regents. Village directors, which were staff positions, reported to the executive director and were assigned distinct functional duties. Each director recruited an assistant director or manager, who was an important factor in ensuring a sustained high level of performance from all management staff throughout the Village operating period.

The director of Village administration oversaw administration, human resources, day pass distribution, lost and found, finance, training, communications, and media relations. The marketplace, recreation, entertainment, religious services, and medical services were supervised by a director of athlete services, who also coordinated sports and ticketing. A director of logistics was responsible for material logistics, purchasing and procurement, Village technology systems, and the material and waste transfer areas. Village construction, design, maintenance, and grounds keeping were managed by the director of facilities. The director of NOC Services coordinated chef relations, the NOC

Services center, Language Services, and reception. Food services, housing, housing allotment, and Village internal transportation were handled by a director of operations. A protocol director organized visits and tours, team welcome ceremonies, participation medals and diplomas, and the daily honorary mayors program. Satellite Villages operations were managed by the director of satellite Villages. The director of special projects facilitated the production and distribution of Village information, publications, and videos, and implemented sig-

nage and Look of the Games decorative elements for all Villages. Program planning, coordination with Georgia Tech and its surrounding community, and coordination with the Atlanta Paralympic Organizing Committee (APOC) was the responsibility of the program manager of planning and development.

The personnel operation of Olympic Villages began in May 1993 with the hiring of the director of Village administration. The first major effort to staff the Village operation was the recruitment of volunteers for the Envoy Program. Members of this core volunteer unit were identified during 1993 and 1994 and began an intensive two-year training program in June 1994. Mandatory attendance at weekly envoy meetings served to train not only the envoys, but also Village staff.

The newly constructed athlete housing was provided to Georgia State University for use as student housing after the Games.

The greatest period of staff hiring was during the last quarter of 1995 and the first quarter of 1996. Guided by the experience of past Games, Village administrators recruited 80 percent of all required staff by March 1996, adding the remaining 20 percent in the following two months. At Games-time, Village staff included 1,923 volunteers, 335 paid ACOG staff, and 3,981 contract staff. These numbers do not include people who were assigned to the Village representing other functional areas such as Accreditation, Atlanta Olympic Broad-

The Atlanta Olympic Village residential zone provided both housing and relaxation space.

casting (AOB), Financial Services, Language Services, Medical Services, Security, Press Operations, Protocol, Sports, Technology, and Transportation.

This strategy enabled ACOG to control costs effectively and engage staff in training programs. In April and May 1996, general orientation sessions and supervisor training were conducted for all Village staff, including those from other ACOG departments.

Village Mayor's Office

The Village mayor's office was located at the main guest entrance to the Atlanta Olympic Village. Working with the mayor were four vol-

unteer deputy mayors, a director of protocol, and a team welcome ceremonies coordinator. Also assisting were hosts and hostesses, guest escorts, protocol assistants, and photographers. This staff, which formed the mayor's operations team, was responsible for planning and coordinating welcome ceremonies for the delegations housed at each Village, officially welcoming special guests, and receiving high-level NOC officials. As part of their welcoming function, these staff members conducted tours of the Village for IOC members and their guests, royal families, heads of state and other high-level government officials, bid-city delegations, corporate sponsors, and team officials. The mayor's staff was also responsible for issuing Village day passes to these special guests and for working closely with AOB throughout the Village operating period.

DESIGN AND FEATURES

The architectural style of the Georgia Tech campus, which combines traditional red brick with modern design, was adapted to serve as the style for the Olympic Village. New housing was built to complement the existing Georgia Tech buildings and facilities.

During the Games, the Atlanta Village became a multifaceted home and activity center for 16,500 athletes and officials. To accomplish this while adhering to IOC guidelines, the Village operated with two distinct areas—an international zone and a residential zone. Each zone provided comfort, service, and the appropriate security to ensure the privacy and enjoyment of all Village residents.

The Village residential zone was divided into five different color zones: red, blue, green, gold, and purple. All residential buildings were identified by a number and the respective zone color. Street-level banners in zone colors were used to mark pathways. Removable street paint provided additional directions for pedestrians. All signage incorporated the Look of the Games graphics and colors. This wayfinding system effectively transcended language and cultural barriers.

The facilities and services provided in the international zone, the Olympic Village equivalent of a town center, are described in detail later in the chapter.

Food Services

Olympic Village food services was responsible for serving nutritious and appetizing meals to Village residents, guests, and staff. The department organized and directed the operations of ARAMARK Food Services, McDonald's, The Coca-Cola Company, and Crystal Springs Water Company. These Games sponsors and suppliers supported the food and beverage operations in providing a high level of quality food service 24 hours a day.

The goal was to provide a harmonious and flexible food service operation that would not impede or distract athletes during training or competition. To accommodate different tastes and meet the basic dietary needs and diverse nutritional requirements of persons from all participating countries, daily menu selections featured international cuisine. Pasta, rice, soup, and fish were served every day. Three to five entrees, 20 or more salad items, sliced cold meats, and assorted cheeses were provided at every meal. Food selections were identified in English, French, and Spanish, and with pictograms. Strict access-control measures were employed at dining halls.

The greatest number of meals served in one day was 63,000 on 19 July. The average number of meals served daily between 15 July and 4 August was 58,000.

Food Service Sites. Located in the residential zone, the 3,500-seat main dining hall was a tent with hard walls and a raised floor, constructed on an 85,000 sq ft (7,905 sq m) parking lot. The structure was built in 21 days and disassembled in 7 days. A preexisting parking garage was remodeled as a supporting facility. It housed food service offices, a 7,000 sq ft

(651 sq m) walk-in freezer/refrigerator, shelving for dry food storage, a newly constructed dock receiving area of approximately 105,000 sq ft (9,765 sq m), and the 26 newly installed, interconnected tractor trailers (28,000 sq ft/2,604 sq m) that comprised the main kitchen.

McDonald's operated three supplemental full-service dining halls strategically located in or adjacent to residential buildings on the north, east, and west sides of the Village. These allowed athletes to eat quickly without traveling to the main dining hall. Operations in the north and the east each provided seating of 200 in air-conditioned tents. Supplemental dining on the west side of the Village was an 8,550 sq ft (795 sq m) existing food service facility with a seating capacity of 350. Supplemental dining locations operated from 6 July to 5 August 1996.

Guest dining services were provided in a preexisting facility in the international zone. This 36,000 sq ft (3,348 sq m) location could seat 500 people. It was operated by ARAMARK from 6 July to 7 August, and was open from 0730 to 2400 for athletes and from 0900 to 1900 for guests. McDonald's also operated two kiosks, located in the main dining hall and the guest dining hall. Each offered a limited menu of McDonald's products.

Food Procurement and Delivery. ARAMARK and McDonald's procured food and related nonfood merchandise daily. Quantities were based on Village occupancy projections, anticipated team arrival and departure dates, projected menus, food perishability, and available storage capacity. Suppliers loaded vehicles at their respective operation sites, and delivery operations were conducted between 2400 and 0600 hours.

Special Food Services. Boxed lunches were available for athletes and team officials whose training or competition required their absence

STEPHEN M CRABTREE • JON P CRACIUN • CHRISTINA A CRADDOCK • MICHAEL D CRADDOCK • DEBORAH J CRAFT • DONNA CRAFT • GARY O CRAFT • JOEL P CRAFT • MICHAEL B CRAFT • RYLAND G CRAFT • BRYAN C CRAFTS • MELBOURNE E CRAGWELL • ANDREW CRAIG • CONNIE A CRAIG • DANIEL G CRAIG • DANIEL G CRAIG • DINA L CRAIG • DONALD L CRAIG • ERIC E CRAIG • HEATHER K CRAIG • JAMES S CRAIG • JAMES W CRAIG • JASON A CRAIG • JEFFREY W CRAIG • JOEL W CRAIG • LYNN M CRAIG • MELANIE J CRAIG • MELINDA J CRAIG • MONICA A CRAIG • RHONDA C CRAIG •

329

from the Village for four hours or longer. The program served all competition sites except those for boxing and aquatics, which were located immediately adjacent to the Village. Boxed lunch service was not available to noncompeting or spectating athletes and team officials.

Using Info'96, the electronic information system that served the Games, team leaders placed orders no later than 1900 on the date prior to delivery. Boxed lunches were produced in an assembly line in the main kitchen between 1600 and 0100 hours. Checkers inspected and verified the contents of each box, affixed a security seal, and stamped the box with the production date. The meals were refrigerated until distribution to the various venues via refrigerated vehicles. In total, 57,915 boxed lunches were produced.

Food services planned and directed catered receptions and meetings at various locations throughout the Village. Chefs de mission or their designees could place catering orders at the NOC Services center, where menus and price lists were available. Orders had to be placed no later than 1900 two days before the order had to be filled. Three facilities were available for catered events. Each accommodated up to 350 people for seated or standing service.

Beverage Sponsors. The Coca-Cola Company was the official soft drink supplier of the Games and was responsible for providing all carbonated soft drinks and juice products in the Village. It also supplied any equipment required for dispensing, including 350 beverage vending machines. Restocking supplies were stored in refrigerated trailers near housing areas.

Crystal Springs, as the official water supplier of the Games, placed 400 water-dispensing machines throughout the Village. Its 5 gal (19 l) bottles were stored away from the sun in a multilevel parking structure, and distributed

continuously to machines throughout the Village. Beverages were free to Village residents.

Village Transportation

Accredited athletes and team officials could use the internal Village shuttle system and the external athlete transportation system. *(For information about the external system, see the Transportation chapter.)* An electric golf cart was provided to each chef de mission for personal transportation within the residential zones. ACOG also provided each NOC with two bicycles. NOCs could bring additional bicycles, but no cycling training was permitted inside the Village.

Shuttle System. The Village shuttle system (VSS) was designed to transport athletes to and from practice sessions at training venues located in the Village, as well as to and from other sites in the Village, such as entertainment facilities and the cafeteria. Additionally, VSS provided transportation to and from all scheduled practice and competition sessions located at the Georgia Tech Aquatic Center and Alexander Memorial Coliseum, which were adjacent to the Village. Shuttles ran continuously during the Games. Athletes could depend on VSS service arriving within five minutes at any of the system's 14 stops. Staff access to the system during peak hours was restricted to those staff members who worked in Village zones located a considerable distance from the staff entrance and to physically challenged staff.

The VSS used both electric trams and electric buses, which were efficient, environmentally friendly vehicles that were unobtrusive to activities of the Village population. Trams consisted of three 12-passenger carts pulled by an electric tow vehicle. Passengers could board and disembark from either side. Seventy trams were available for use, with 60 being the most used during peak periods. Eight 30-passenger electric buses complemented the trams and provided transportation to housing areas at the northern-most section of the Village. Another bus transported staff between the staff entrance on the east side and various locations on the west side of the Village.

The VSS operated both clockwise and counterclockwise routes. Each VSS stop was identified by number and the color of the zone in which it was located. Signage at each stop included directional information and pictograms of the facilities located in the zone, as well as facilities located at the next VSS stop. Staff was present to supervise loading and unloading at high-volume VSS stops and during critical time periods. One third of the vehicles were equipped with a wheelchair ramp, and all were equipped with two-way radios.

Parking. All motor vehicle parking in and around the Village required an ACOG parking pass. NOC parking at the Village was located near the Village's innermost security fence.

Technology

Planning for the technological infrastructure of the Olympic Village began in early 1994. At that time, the wiring needed to support telephones, computer networks, televisions, and other technology was determined for each functional location. A collaborative effort with AT&T, BellSouth Corporation, and Georgia Tech was established to upgrade the existing fiber infrastructure to meet ACOG's needs during the Games. Through this project, named Futurenet, more than 1,700 mi (2,736 km) of new data, voice, and video fiber-optic cabling was installed to connect more than 125 buildings, tents, and trailers in the Village. After the Games, this infrastructure was left as a legacy for Georgia Tech.

Detailed drawings were created that showed the exact placement of each technology item in each building. These drawings were used to develop a temporary cabling plan to serve each location. Beginning four months prior to the Games, this internal cabling was installed and tested. Prior to the Village opening, the end devices were attached to the new and existing cabling, and all systems were activated. The tedious project of activating all the token ring networks was made easier by the prior placement of hubs and routers. Without advance installation of these elements and temporary cabling, moving into the Village would have been much more difficult.

All technology equipment installed by ACOG had 24-hour service available, and 24-hour assis-

The Village shuttle system, comprised of electric trams and buses, was used to transport athletes within the Village.

tance was available by telephone or in person for all users. The Village help desk responded to 8,443 requests for service and assistance.

Each NOC office in the Village was equipped with one Info'96 terminal, provided free of charge. Every housing facility's front desk had an Info'96 terminal that could be used by any Village resident. Additional Info'96 terminals were located at the NOC Services center and at all information stations in the international zone. NOCs could obtain additional terminals through the Olympic Village rate card.

Village residents used the E-mail system available on these terminals to send and receive messages, read bulletin boards, and request services using E-forms. E-forms were used to request NOC guest day passes and boxed lunches, update arrivals and departures, schedule team welcome ceremonies, reserve meeting rooms, and request maintenance or repairs.

Venue Logistics

ACOG's Venue Logistics division was responsible for preparing and dismantling the Village's residences, offices, and operational and recreational areas, and keeping them supplied with furniture, fixtures, equipment, and other needed items during the operating period. Preparation took place between 15 June 1996, when ACOG assumed control of the Georgia Tech site, and 1 July, when access was restricted to accredited individuals. This staff worked 24 hours a day to resupply facilities during the 1 July–10 August lockdown period and to restore the campus to its original state after the Village closed on 7 August 1996. Retrofitting was a monumental challenge, as the Paralympics followed immediately after the Olympic Games, and Georgia Tech scheduled a summer class session as well.

Residents and staff used a Village logistics hot line during the Village operating period to request assistance for a variety of activities, including relocation of tables, beds, and chairs. This hot line also offered assistance with placement of additional office equipment and supplies or housing furniture. Coordination with the main distribution center helped to locate assets within the ACOG materials management system. Approximately 65 structures, including existing Georgia Tech facilities and temporary structures (tents) built specifically for the Games, needed to be adapted to the Olympic configuration and then restored or removed in a short time period. Approximately 15,000 beds and 4,000 desks in 94 buildings needed to be arranged or moved during the preparation and restoration periods.

(For information on the materials transfer area [MTA] and other security measures taken for all shipments to the Village, see the Security chapter.)

Equipment Maintenance. All major systems were tested and inspected prior to the commencement of Village operations. Additionally, spare parts were stocked for components with a known history of failure in order to minimize repair time. Because of the short duration of Village operations, maintenance was generally restricted to breakdown repairs with only minimal preventative maintenance performed. During the Games period, Village maintenance received about 6,000 work orders through a centralized job order desk and about 12,000 requests via telephone and facsimile transmission.

Major heating, ventilating/air conditioning, electrical, natural gas, water, and sewer systems exhibited few problems and were not overburdened, as the size of the Village population was very similar to Georgia Tech's student population. Newly constructed residential buildings required little maintenance, except for routine warranty maintenance and repair of some vandalism. Assistance from the city of Atlanta and the municipal utility systems was minimal. Installers continued elevator maintenance during the Games period as part of their existing contracts. Two companies provided service 24 hours daily.

The maintenance work force combined the existing maintenance divisions of Georgia Tech and Georgia State. Subcontractors provided additional staff for a total work force of 480. Planning and scheduling the work force was slowed due to the late accreditation of university employees. Some Georgia Tech employees chose to avoid Olympic Village operations completely, because of work schedules and site access restrictions. These individuals were reassigned to other positions outside the Village.

The Village Maintenance division took operational control of all Georgia Tech and Georgia State maintenance operations during ACOG's campus lease period of 15 June to 15 August 1996. Existing Georgia Tech procedures were used, with some modifications made to meet the special needs, time restrictions, and security requirements of the Village.

Waste Management. Development and implementation of an effective waste removal concept was critical because of the high population density of the Village. Self-contained high-capacity compactors were utilized to meet the Village's strict sanitation standards. These compactors were strategically placed, primarily at high-volume food preparation and paper waste-generation sites and remote areas of the Village. Individual waste receptacles were used mainly in housing areas to promote custodial efficiency.

The contents of full units were transported to a waste transfer area (WTA). At this secured, fenced service area, units were unloaded from internal transport vehicles and retrieved by vehicles outside the Village security fence for transport to the contractor's waste disposal site. Empty replacement receptacles were returned to the Village, inspected by security personnel, and returned to service through the WTA port. In total, 870 tons (789 t) of waste were removed from the Village during the operating period.

Hazardous substances and chemicals were brought into the Village only with special approval by the maintenance manager. Medical wastes and sharps were properly handled and marked for disposal. Approximately 2,500 lb (1,134 kg) of medical waste was removed from the Village during the operating period.

Recycling. All vendors, residents, and guests participated in the recycling program. A major donor of recycling services implemented an extensive program of educating residents on recycling issues, composting wastes, and avoiding use of landfills. Supplying products in bulk avoided individual packaging, excessive crating, and overestimation of perishable goods. Nearly 150 tons (135 t) of recyclable material was collected from the Village during the operating period.

Cleaning Service. Housekeeping was a major challenge. The housekeeping contractor was selected in late 1995 and had some difficulty hiring sufficient staff to do the job satisfactorily. Cleaning rooms for the athletes and officials was complicated by communication problems, inability or lack of permission to gain entry to rooms, and the challenge of cleaning rooms with many personal items of the occupants filling the space. This area should be addressed very early in the planning process and requires a dedicated and well-trained staff in order to work efficiently.

Access Control

ACOG obtained exclusive access to the Georgia Tech campus on 15 June 1996 in order to commence the adaptation of facilities for Olympic use and the construction and installation of temporary and portable structures. During the period from 15 June to 1 July, limited access control procedures were enforced, with access limited to accredited persons and those given temporary passes by Village management to enable them to perform their functions during the final preparation of the Village. Village ports of entry included the main/guest entry, media entry, staff entry, and athletes' and officials' access points.

Security Sweep. The Village security sweep was conducted from 1 to 5 July 1996, requiring the commencement of strict access control procedures and the implementation of a day pass system for all unaccredited persons and those whose accreditation did not permit Village access.

A more restrictive system was used to control access to the residential zone of the Village. Biometric identification was used for the first time in Olympic history. This system relied on the unique structural characteristics of the individual's hand to grant or deny access.

FIGURE 1: DAILY ATLANTA OLYMPIC VILLAGE DAY PASS ALLOCATION TO NOCS

NOC delegation size (Village residents)	Passes per day
1–24	3
25–50	5
51–100	6
101–200	8
201–300	10
301–400	12
401–500	14
+500	16

Day Passes. The NOC day pass center monitored all guest pass requests from NOC delegations, sponsors, vendors, observers, and ACOG management. All requests for day passes had to be submitted by 1900 the previous day, by E-form in Info'96, by manual form at the day pass center, or by facsimile machine. Many NOCs, however, submitted requests or changed guest lists at the last minute. Each guest surrendered photo identification, such as a passport or Games accreditation badge, for the guest pass. Passes were issued between 0900 and 2030. Guests were required to exit the Village and return their passes to the day pass center by 2100 each day. Photo identification, held as collateral, was returned to the guest upon surrender of the day pass.

NOC day passes were rotational, allowing a new guest to use a pass previously issued to and returned by another guest. The larger NOCs would often rotate guests in and out of the Village in two-hour shifts, allowing an extremely high volume of individuals to be processed each day. No NOC day passes were available for 19 July (Opening Ceremony day) or 4 August (Closing Ceremony day). A total of 39,864 guest passes were issued during the Village's operational period. *(For the daily day pass allocation to NOCs, see Figure 1.)*

The Village was closed to noncredentialed vehicles, making it difficult for invited guests to visit without walking a considerable distance. To assist guests, ACOG's Transportation Department provided round-trip shuttle service from the Village guest center, located adjacent to a nearby MARTA rail station outside the Village. The operating dates mirrored the schedule of the day pass center, and an average of 800 guests per day utilized the shuttle service to access the Village.

Nonaccredited staff needing temporary Village access, as well as accredited staff who arrived at work without their credentials, obtained day passes at the staff pass center.

Housed in a tent immediately adjacent to the staff entry, this center operated 24 hours daily to support all shifts. Village managers submitted requests for day passes for nonaccredited staff by 1900 the previous day, using E-mail, manual form, or facsimile transmission. Staff day passes were issued only with the authorization of the functional area manager for whom the pass bearer worked. To obtain a day pass, staff were required to submit photo identification, which was held at the staff pass center until the day pass was returned. A total of 24,152 staff passes were issued during the Village's operation, primarily for late accreditation issuance and entertainment and recreational service people.

The MTA pass center was open 24 hours daily to issue staff day passes to nonaccredited persons accompanying deliveries. The MTA pass center also accommodated other service personnel, such as maintenance, construction, and material logistics staff. Procedures for requesting and obtaining day passes were identical to those employed at the staff pass center.

In keeping with *IOC Media Guide* requirements, ACOG issued no more than 400 media (200 press, 200 broadcast) day passes to the Village at any one time. These were issued on a first-come, first-served basis, and were not transferable. A valid Centennial Olympic Games accreditation badge was submitted in exchange for the pass and held until the pass was returned. Media day passes allowed access only to the international zone. Access to Village residential areas was obtained only via an ACOG tour (10–14 July), or at the express written invitation of an NOC, signed by the chef de mission. Chefs were required to provide journalists with their NOC's designated guest pass and an escort to accompany the guest within the residential zone.

The media pass center operated on the same schedule as the NOC guest pass center. A total of 4,556 media day passes were issued.

Media Subcenter

The Village media subcenter was located in the Georgia Tech research zone, near the media entry to the international zone. This facility served as a small operating base, similar to the Main Press Center (MPC) and International Broadcast Center, for media personnel covering the Village and its activities. All accredited press and broadcast personnel had access to the media subcenter.

The Village media subcenter housed AOB and ACOG Press Operations on the first level and the ACOG host broadcasting operation on the second. A reception desk and lounge area were shared by both operations. Interview rooms, workstations, telephones, facsimile machines, copiers, competition results, information, and televisions showing competitions were also available. Press Operations occupied the facility from 6 July to 7 August, operating daily between 0700 and 2200, and AOB operated between 0800 and 2100, from 15 July to 5 August.

Four interview rooms within the international zone of the Village operated between 0900 and 2100 and were available for the convenience of athletes and team officials wishing to be interviewed in the Village. Scheduled at the subcenter reception desk, interviews in these rooms occurred 105 times during the operating period.

The media subcenter was also available for chefs de mission to schedule meetings, hold briefings, post notices, and use for other related activities.

Lost and Found

A lost and found center was established in the main recreation center, a central location that would be easy to access. All lost or found items could be claimed at or returned to this site. Village supervisors were responsible for transporting found items to the information stations, where they were recorded in a log book. Items were then taken to the lost and found center, where they were received and entered into another log.

Many items were submitted to the center, but only a small percentage were of significant monetary value. Most were never retrieved by their owners.

Residential Zone

The residential zones provided housing for athletes, officials, and chefs de mission, NOC offices and storage space for NOCs, and training sites for athletes.

Athlete and Official Housing. NOC athletes and officials were housed in a combination of apartments, residential halls, and smaller new and existing residential houses. There were 15,078 beds in the Atlanta Village: 9,384 in newly constructed apartments, 4,509 in existing apartments and residence halls, and 1,185 in smaller residential houses.

Each apartment accommodated 4–14 residents, although most units accommodated 8 residents. Most apartments consisted of bedrooms, one bathroom for every four residents, a living room, and a kitchen. Except for the refrigerator, kitchen appliances were inoperable during the Games. Each apartment bedroom contained two beds, one wardrobe, and one three-drawer chest. Each living room contained a sofa, two end tables, one coffee table, two armchairs, a dining table, four chairs, and a wastebasket.

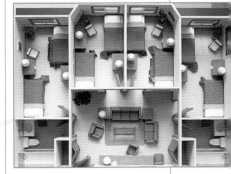

Some athletes and officials were housed in apartments consisting of four bedrooms, two bathrooms, and a living room.

Residence hall accommodations consisted of double-occupancy rooms with a central bathroom and lounge. Sleeping rooms did not have carpets, but hallways were carpeted. Residence hall rooms contained two beds, wardrobes or closets, three-drawer chests, desks, and chairs. Each floor was designated male or female, and more than one NOC could share a floor.

Some smaller NOC delegations were assigned to residential houses normally used by campus social organizations. Thirty-five such houses were used, holding 8–80 beds. Each house accommodated one to three delegations. Living rooms in these houses were each furnished with one sofa, one coffee table, two end tables, and two armchairs. Kitchens were closed to the delegations, but a dining area in each house was furnished with tables and one chair per resident. Each house also provided space for residing NOC offices as well as medical and storage areas.

All sleeping rooms were air-conditioned and equipped with screened windows. Two towels, two sheets, one pillow, one pillowcase, one mattress pad, and one blanket accompanied each bed. Extra-long beds (7.25 ft/2.2 m) could be ordered in advance by the NOCs at no extra charge. All 3,000 available extra-long beds were used. Each room in the Village was decorated to reflect the Olympic Spirit, the spirit of the South, and Atlanta.

Nineteen front desks operated 24 hours daily; seven operated 16 hours daily. At any front desk, residents could use Info'96, get general information, obtain complimentary laundry detergent, exchange linen, request housekeeping services, file complaints or problems, and receive assistance.

Chef de Mission Housing. Chefs de mission were housed in single-occupancy rooms within their respective NOC housing areas. In addition to regular furnishings, each chef's room was equipped with a desk, telephone, typewriter, refrigerator, safe, bulletin board, and coffee maker. Complimentary technology items furnished included a color television with both the international broadcast and general cable channels, a telephone providing access to the Olympic five-digit dialing network, and an alphanumeric pager.

NOC Offices and Storage. Every NOC delegation with 25 or more members residing in the Atlanta Olympic Village received its own office space equipped with one Olympic cable-equipped color television, one Olympic network telephone, an Info'96 terminal, and an alphanumeric pager. If an NOC delegation had fewer than 25 members, the chef's residential space was used as its office space. Six shared medical spaces were also available to accommodate smaller NOCs. All delegations could order additional technology items using the NOC rate card.

Each NOC delegation was also assigned a separate, enclosed storage space for nonperishable supplies and equipment. Located throughout the residential areas, these storage spaces varied in size from 300 sq ft (28 sq m) to 3,000 sq ft (279 sq m) according to the number of members in the NOC delegation.

Sports Training Sites. In accordance with the *Olympic Charter*, ACOG provided facilities for athlete training in the Olympic Village. Four training sites and one warm-up site were available in the residential zone to accommodate athletics, baseball, tennis, and strength training. ACOG's Sports Department coordinated site operations from its Village information center.

International Zone

The idea behind the international zone was to create a town center for Village residents and guests that would be festive, memorable, and conducive to international friendships. The Georgia Tech plaza area became the international festival zone.

Temporary features included two tower pavilions, 100 ft (30 m) and 86 ft (26 m), decorated with banner and shade fabric. The size and color of these elements transformed the open plaza into a festive backdrop for Games activities, complete with evening theatrical lighting. Within one pavilion, a tent covered the team welcome ceremony amphitheater.

The fountain area was decorated with flags from previous Olympic Games host cities. Numerous information, refreshment, and other miscellaneous tents dotted the plaza adjacent to the pavilions, the largest being a covered entertainment stage for cultural events. Large graphics, banners, and towers accented the gateway entrance to the main recreation center and the Village marketplace, both housed in existing buildings adjacent to the open plaza. A covered walkway connecting these external elements added to the festive atmosphere and provided protection from sun and rain.

Design and construction also included a temporary queuing plaza for athlete transportation to training and competition sites, 20 tram stop tents, material and waste transfer areas, a temporary in-ground swimming pool, a temporary coffee house and dance club, and an integrated temporary dining facility with kitchen. Other projects included the installation of general outdoor lighting and more than 40,000 sq ft (3,720 m) of trailer space used for offices and storage. Many existing spaces required remodeling, including offices, the main recreation center, and the Village marketplace, and many required the installation of temporary power, sewer, natural gas, and water systems.

Adjacent Venues

The Georgia Tech campus was also the site of two competition venues: the Aquatic Center, bordering the Village on the west side, which was the location for diving, swimming, synchronized swimming, and water polo competitions, and the Alexander Memorial Coliseum

on the northeast side, at which boxing competitions were held. While this was convenient for participating athletes and officials, who could enter these venues from within the Village, both venues posed operational challenges. While each venue's management, staffing, security, and operations were conducted separately from Village operations, the venues did share a perimeter fence, which made advance loading and staging at the sites necessary in order to meet Village security requirements.

SERVICES TO NOCS

Because NOCs were most directly responsible for the success of each athlete's experience at the Games, it was imperative that ACOG cultivate a good relationship with them. While the NOC Relations Department of Olympic Family and Protocol primarily coordinated relations between ACOG and all NOC delegations, Olympic Villages' NOC Services division focused on serving the primary Village clients, the chefs de mission.

NOC Services was the single most important point of communication with the chefs, keeping them informed concerning all aspects of preparation required for bringing their delegations to the Centennial Olympic Games. To facilitate this role, NOC Services was staffed with multilingual, multicultural personnel divided into teams, with each team serving an assigned region of the world. Beginning in 1994, the staff created databases to track critical information, were actively involved in hosting NOC visits to Atlanta, and assisted with recruiting and training envoy teams. NOC Services participated in the December 1994 ANOC General Assembly in Atlanta, managed the logistics of the Chef de Mission Seminar, and planned the

The fountain area of the Georgia Tech plaza was decorated with flags from previous Olympic host cities.

operations of both Village reception and the Village NOC Services centers.

Pre-Games Communication

A three-tier approach was developed for pre-Games communication with NOCs. The comprehensive publication, the *Chef de Mission Manual*, was assembled and mailed to the 197 NOCs in April 1995. It contained all pertinent policies and described services affecting team preparation and Village and other venue facilities in detail. The release of this document preceded the Chef de Mission Seminar.

The Chef de Mission Seminar, held in Atlanta 17–21 May 1995, was attended by more than 300 delegates. Information was provided in accordance with chef responsibilities rather than depicting ACOG's activities on a departmental basis. Two days of presentations discussed what chefs should know and do before and upon arrival at the Games, including policies and preparations as they applied to each sport, each venue, and the Villages. Numerous workshops were held to elaborate on the issues presented and to encourage participant response. The seminar also included a comprehensive tour of Village and competition sites.

Attendees received an assortment of printed materials, including a calendar of important deadlines before the Games. In addition, participants had the opportunity to meet individually with Olympic Villages and ACOG managers. Participants praised the seminar and the invaluable information exchanged.

As a next step, Olympic Village management prepared the *Chef Manual I*, mailed in October 1995. Printed in English, French, and Spanish, this publication contained all ACOG policies, regulations, and guidelines, with heavy concentration on chef responsibilities before and upon arrival in Atlanta. Major issues such as reception, accreditation, extra officials, transportation, and finances were described in great detail. Satellite Villages were also highlighted.

The *Chef Manual II* was distributed in June 1996, providing practical information to guide chefs through the logistics of their stays in Atlanta.

Chefs with prior Games experience indicated that these communications efforts for the chefs de mission created a new, higher level of cooperation between organizers and NOC delegations.

Envoy Program

Providing each NOC with a well-trained and language-proficient envoy team to assist the chef was one of ACOG's most important and ambitious projects. Envoy teams comprising an envoy, associate envoys, and drivers were trained for two years, and each participant made a tremendous commitment to preparing to serve his or her assigned NOC. The size of NOC delegations determined the size of the teams, which ranged from 4 to 27 people.

Volunteers were chosen through a competitive process that included interviews, language evaluation, and security background screening. Envoys began training in July 1994 by attending mandatory weekly two-hour sessions, supplemented by occasional weekend meetings and activities such as venue tours. Training also included individual study projects and periodic examinations. Envoys were first introduced to NOC presidents and secretaries-general at the ANOC General Assembly and to the chefs de mission at their seminar.

During the Games, each envoy served as the chef's primary point of contact with ACOG and was given authority to make certain decisions and solve problems. Envoys were considered members of Village management. NOC Services managers and coordinators were also available to the chefs 24 hours a day to address issues at a higher level.

Envoy teams offered assistance with routine procedures, including scheduling the team welcome ceremony, informing ACOG of the NOC's arrival and departure plans, and notifying ACOG of any special visitors anticipated by the NOC.

Housing was provided in the Village for one member of each envoy team, enabling an envoy or associate to be available to the chef 24 hours a day. Envoys were housed separately from the NOCs.

NOC Housing Allocation

The Village Housing Allotment division determined placement of all delegations in Village housing during the Games. This staff gathered as much detailed information as possible before NOC arrival, including estimated team size, expected number of men and women, expected event participation, and arrival and departure dates. The monitoring of the IOC qualification systems throughout the pre-Games period led to development of a team profile, which was critical to the housing allocation process. NOCs were also asked to indicate any preferences in housing type or location within the Village. The allocation process took several factors into consideration, including political sensitivities and cultural diversity.

Preparations for the allocation process began in May 1995 at the Chef de Mission Seminar. NOC Services staff met individually with each chef of the larger delegations to obtain the anticipated number of Village residents. Each chef was required to complete an estimated team size form, itemizing athletes and officials by sport and gender. Afterward, these estimates were verified and adjusted based upon qualification information from the Sports Department as well as historical data. Using the data collected, rooms for 11,200 residents from 51 NOCs were allocated in August 1995. Representing 83 percent of the total NOC population, these were the larger NOCs,

which planned to bring more than 100 residents each. Security-sensitive NOCs were also allocated in August 1995, to ensure accommodation within predetermined areas. Other NOCs received their housing assignments in June 1996.

Team size estimates were continually reviewed, updated, and changed. A database tracked sports qualification information, expected occupancy for all Villages, including room and bed allocations, and calculation of eligible officials for the individual NOCs by *Olympic Charter* Rule 42.

ACOG's Village housing allocation system performed a wide range of functions, including recording manually entered allocations, providing for Games-time manipulation of allocations, displaying room status in graph form, producing floor plans of room allocations for the NOCs, and producing reports for the Village housing offices and building staffs. The system used Access application and user interfaces developed for AutoCAD.

Reception Process

The Chef Relations subdivision coordinated the NOC reception process at the Airport Welcome Center (AWC). Operations began 25 June and concluded when the last of the 197 delegations was processed on 19 July.

At the beginning of the process, the chef, an NOC Services representative, and the envoy met with a Sports Inscriptions representative and an Accreditation representative to verify applications, verify all qualification data, and make a preliminary Rule 42 calculation to determine the total delegation size. The Accreditation staff member reviewed these lists to determine access privileges for each delegate.

Financial Services then computed the amount of funds owed to ACOG for residents of the Village during the paid period, 6–14 July, and collected any other funds due for rate card services or extra officials' housing. The official or officials normally arrived prior to the team to complete the processing, which took an average of four hours.

The Village Housing Allotment division finalized building and room assignments for the Atlanta Olympic Village and notified each satellite Village of the number eligible to be

housed there. Each chef received a housing packet to review. Arrival and departure information was collected, and Transportation was notified of expected arrival dates, times, and numbers of delegates. Welcome ceremonies were also scheduled at this time. Upon completion of these functions, the chef and delegation proceeded to accreditation badging and prepared for transport to the Village.

NOC Services Center

The NOC Services center in the Village consisted of chef relations offices, an NOC Services center desk, finance office, envoy work room, and general lounge areas for the chefs. This facility, for use by the chef or a designee, was located in the international zone near the chefs' meeting hall and operated from 0600 to 2400. These hours were varied to accommodate peak periods including additional hours during the competition period. Multilingual staff provided general Village information and many other services at no charge, including the distribution of NOC mail and incoming facsimile transmissions or telexes, scheduling of meeting rooms, assistance with transportation information and arrangements, updating of arrival and departure plans, and service of NOC accounts.

Services available for various fees included photocopying, word processing, and translation of documents into English, French, or Spanish. Circle International, ACOG's official freight forwarder and customs broker, processed materials and answered questions on shipping and customs. Office supplies were sold, and available rate card items were offered for rent. (For rate card items ordered, see Figure 2.) Staff at the center also provided menus and helped to arrange catering for special NOC events.

The NOC Services center desk proved to be a very valuable information source, and customers quickly came to depend upon staff for assistance with nearly every subject imaginable. Staff researched issues until a satisfactory solution was found. The staff also assisted with

FIGURE 2: NOC RATE CARD ORDERS

Item	Total	Item	Total
Refrigerator	85	Desktop computer	12
Ice machine	31	Desktop printer	12
Lockable cabinet	29	Printer toner cartridge	34
Stretcher bed	11	Info'96 workstation	25
Heating unit	10	Info'96 printer	30
Massage therapy table	67	20 in television	183
Ultrasound unit	21	51 in television	16
Electrical stimulation unit	16	27 in television	41
Chilling unit	9	Television stand	40
Inferential stimulation unit	16	Cable TV connection	369
Typewriter (English keys)	3	Combination TV / VCR	59
Typewriter (French keys)	3	VCR	36
Typewriter (Spanish keys)	1	VHS tape	65
Loveseat	4	Compact VHS cassette tape	10
Coffee table	2	Small copier	17
Executive desk	52	Midsize copier	27
Desk	32	Large copier	1
Swivel chair	111	Facsimile machine	67
Safe	25	Toner cartridge for facsimile machine	59
File cabinet	37	Headset	10
Coat tree	149	Analog two-way radio	43
Coffee maker	63	Spare battery	23
Folding chair	206	Power surge protector	46
Marker board	43	Power cord	89
Folding tables	26	Power bar with surge protection	44
Desk lamp	77	Telephone line surge suppressor	12
Telephone line set	420	Power bar (no surge protection)	15
Speakerphone line	6	Village parking passes	259
Facsimile phone line	116	Minivan 30-day rental	20
Cellular phone service	432	Minivan weekly rental	60
Cellular phone air time	425	Sedan rental	55
Pager	376		

chef room and pager check-in and check-out and had the daily responsibility of ensuring that the chefs' meeting hall and lounge were ready for all meetings.

Chef Meetings

Chef meetings were held in the chefs' meeting hall at 0730. Twelve meetings were conducted during the operation of the Village. In general, meetings were held every other day beginning 8 July. These meetings were conducted in English, with simultaneous interpretation available in French and Spanish. The Language Services Department coordinated all aspects of the required equipment and technical support for the interpreting function.

Village management used these meetings as opportunities to update the chefs, listen to their concerns, and address any issues raised. A team of three or four people translated the minutes of the meeting into French and Spanish. Chefs were able to obtain minutes of the meeting at their mail slots in the NOC Services center before the next meeting.

Language Services

The Language Services Department provided linguistic assistance to athletes, Olympic Family members (including media), and other ACOG departments during the Games. These services included conversation facilitation, written translation, and simultaneous interpretation. The Language Services' operations headquarters was located in the Atlanta Olympic Village. *(For more information, see the Olympic Family and Protocol chapter.)*

Team Welcome Ceremonies

Team welcome ceremonies, coordinated by the Protocol Department, were held between 6 July 1996, the opening day of the Olympic Village, through 20 July 1996, the day after the Opening Ceremonies. *(For information concerning these official ceremonies, see the Olympic Family and Protocol chapter.)*

IOC Representation

Two IOC functions were located in the international zone for the convenience of Village residents. The NOC Relations office provided support to NOC officials and access to the IOC for NOCs to make suggestions. Furnished and staffed by IOC personnel, the office was open from 1100 to 2200 from 17 July to 4 August.

The IOC Athletes Commission occupied a two-room office suite, furnished and staffed by commission members. The primary mission of this office was to broaden communication between currently active athletes, as well as advise the IOC Executive Board in matters of current or contemplated policies and programs. This office was open daily from 1100 to 2200 during the competition period, 20 July to 4 August.

IOC Athletes Commission Election

Rule 24 of the 1994 *Olympic Charter* states that, "An Athletes Commission shall be constituted, the majority of whose members shall be athletes elected by athletes participating in the Olympic Games." As a result, these elections

Quilts were presented to the NOCs upon arrival at the Village as part of the team welcome ceremonies.

were held for the first time in the history of the modern Olympic Games. Athletes in all nine Olympic Villages were able to vote.

Prior to the Centennial Olympic Games, there were 13 athlete members of the IOC Athletes Commission. The new commission will consist of 19 athletes. Seven athletes, representing summer sports, were elected during the Atlanta Olympic Games. Three additional athletes, representing winter sports, will be elected to the commission during the 1998 Winter Games in Nagano, Japan. Nine athletes will be appointed by the IOC president to ensure a geographical distribution and a gender balance to obtain the best possible representation of all athletes.

In April 1995, each NOC was asked to nominate one male representative and one female representative from its athletes. These candidates were required to have French or English language skills. The IOC Athletes Commission electoral college narrowed the number of nominees to 35 athletes who were featured in an IOC-produced manual published in six languages (Arabic, English, French, German, Russian, and Spanish), which was distributed at the AWC.

Voting began 20 July and continued through 31 July at the main Olympic Village. Each satellite Village scheduled specific days for voting. Athletes cast their votes confidentially at polling stations adjacent to each Village's main dining facility. Twenty full-time volunteers assisted with the voting process, supervised by IOC representatives. At 2200 each day, all unused ballots and ballot boxes were secured by IOC representatives to prevent tampering.

At the conclusion of voting, members of the IOC electoral college and its designees counted the votes. Votes were counted twice by the IOC, and results verified by the electoral college, which had full authority to resolve any issues relating to the voting procedure, were considered final. President Samaranch announced the election results on 2 August at the MPC. *(For a list of the athletes elected, see Figure 3.)*

A total of 5,734 athletes (54 percent of eligible voters) participated. The IOC considered the election, which offered competing athletes a voice in the Olympic Movement, a success.

Sports Information Services

Located near the main dining hall, the sports information center was the headquarters for all sports-related issues. Team leaders and officials were permitted access to the sports information center to access inscriptions, sports desks, training sites, and results distribution. Team officials could also order boxed lunches, obtain directions to venues and training sites, address sports equipment issues, leave or retrieve messages, and coordinate athlete transportation.

■ Inscriptions—Coaches/team leaders addressed issues concerning the registration of athletes, replacement of injured athletes, activation of alternate athletes, and athlete name corrections or changes.

■ Sports Desks—Sport-specific information was available on each sport at dedicated sports desks. Personnel at these desks could also verify entries, schedule training sites, distribute sport-specific notices, verify start lists, distribute results, and accept orders for boxed lunches.

■ Training Sites—Use of all training sites was scheduled in the sports information center. Issues concerning site preparation, shutdown, and recovery were handled by the training site staff.

■ Results Distribution—Results and competition updates were available at the sports desks. Results books were compiled and copied for each sport.

■ Boxed Lunch Coordination—Orders for boxed lunches were placed manually at the sports desks and then entered on Info'96.

■ Sports Equipment Coordination—A sports equipment desk was available to address problems concerning sports equipment provided to the competition or training site.

**FIGURE 3:
ATHLETES ELECTED
TO THE IOC ATHLETES
COMMISSION**

Roland Baar
Germany

Hassiba Boulmerka
Algeria

Sergey Bubka
Ukraine

Charmaine Crook
Canada

Robert Ctvrtlik
United States of America

Alexander Popov
Russian Federation

Jan Zelezny
Czech Republic

■ Transportation Coordination—The transportation desk, operated by ACOG's Transportation Department, facilitated transport of athletes to and from training sites and competition venues.

■ Message Center—Messages for team leaders and officials were given and received via facsimile transmission or telephone.

■ Language Services—A Language Services representative was available for language translation and interpretation.

RESIDENT SERVICES AND AMENITIES

To provide residents of the Village with relaxing and enjoyable ways to spend time when they were not training or competing, a variety of entertainment and recreation activities were developed that appealed to an audience of diverse nationalities, cultural backgrounds, and ages.

Entertainment

Village entertainment programs operated from 6 July through 5 August 1996. Most activities were located in the international zone. The support of various suppliers and promotional partners was central to the success of the Village entertainment program. The logistical challenges of moving large numbers of performers and their equipment in and out of the Village on a daily basis required planning and daily communication with Village logistics. Performers entered the Village by using the day pass system.

Olympic Theater for the Arts. This second largest venue in the Village seated 1,200 people. It showcased culturally diverse national and international performances, featuring local and international dance troupes and well-known entertainers.

Cultural Pavilion. This open-air stage with benches and grass seating areas offered local, regional, and ethnic entertainment such as jazz ensembles, gospel choirs, and bluegrass, rhythm and blues, and country western music.

Dance Club. A highlight of the entertainment program, this 25,000 sq ft (2,325 sq m) facility was one of the liveliest and most frequented places in the Village, featuring state-of-the-art audio technology, special effects, disc jockeys playing popular music, and occasional live performances.

Coffee House. Adjacent to the dance club, the coffee house provided a relaxed social environment in which Village residents could gather and enjoy complimentary gourmet coffee drinks, teas, and cold beverages. During the day, entertainment included solo performers, classical guitarists, acoustic musicians, and string quartets. In the evenings, patrons could watch and enjoy dance club activity.

Bobby Dodd Stadium. This 45,000-seat outdoor arena was the venue for the Village All-Star Farewell Evening, featuring the international premiere of the movie *Eraser.* An opening concert was given by the Goo Goo Dolls, and appearances were made by the movie's stars, Arnold Schwarzenegger and Vanessa Williams, as well as Olympians Bruce Jenner and Evander Holyfield. The purpose of the event was to honor the athletes for their courage, dedication, and hard work and express appreciation to Village staff and volunteers.

Centennial Olympic Festival Area. This area, the focal point of the Olympic Village, was brightly decorated with flags and Olympic banners and filled daily with performers, magicians, jugglers, clowns, mimes, and other live entertainment. The fountain in the center of the area, designed to commemorate the Games, served as a backdrop for television feeds. Volunteers served as hosts and hostesses, answering questions and directing Village residents to various entertainment and recreation activities.

Cinemas. Five Village cinemas featured a variety of international, classic, popular, and first-run films, providing residents with another place to relax and escape the pressures of training and competing.

Olympic Memorabilia. On display in the main recreation center, this exhibition of a private collection included material from various

Games ranging from Olympic pins to the very first Olympic torch.

IOC Museum Collection. This outdoor exhibition was filled with memorabilia from the Olympic Movement and past Olympic Games.

Recreation

Recreational programs were divided into vendor-run programs, constructed and operated at the sole expense of the promotional partner, and programs funded, constructed, staffed, and operated solely by ACOG. Promotional partner programs included the day spa, the laser tag arena, the health club, and the world information center and World Wide Web pavilion. ACOG-operated programs included the sports video viewing and taping center, external excursions, a recreational pool, television lounges, and athlete gift bags.

Olympic Village Day Spa. Residents could escape from the pressures of competition and training in the day spa, with services including aromatherapy, massage therapy, European hydrotherapy, audio therapy, a sauna, spa, a variety of facials, and body wraps. All athlete relaxation massage services were provided by certified massage therapists. Those needing massage for physical therapy purposes were referred to the sports medicine center. Approximately 4,900 people used the day spa during the Games.

Olympic Village Health Club. The first full-service, technologically advanced health club to be available in an Olympic Village, this facility featured the cardio theater, where participants could view or listen to any of 32 radio or video channels built into the wall while using various types of personal exercise equipment. Additionally, the 7,000 sq ft (651 sq m) facility was equipped with 50 pieces of cardiovascular equipment and two lines of strength-training equipment. There was also a full-stage

area for aerobics classes led by certified and nationally known aerobics instructors. A unique aerial walkway above the exercise areas allowed media to report on activities without intruding. The club operated 0600–2200 from 15 July to 4 August and 0900–2000 from 6 to 14 July and 5 to 6 August. It was used by more than 6,300 athletes.

Olympic Sensory Performance Center. Open daily from 1000 to 2100, this state-of-the-art testing facility was developed to heighten awareness of the important relationship between sports performance and the visual, auditory, and dental characteristics of the athlete. Trained staff conducted tests for visual acuity, as well as the speed with which an athlete responded to visual stimuli. Hearing tests were conducted, and the center provided education on hearing loss for athletes, coaches, and trainers. Dental and medical referrals were made as needed. However, to avoid having a negative influence on training or competition performance, results were sent to the NOCs for distribution to individual athletes after the Closing Ceremony. More than 1,450 athletes participated in these tests.

Sports Video Viewing and Taping Center. This center allowed athletes to view their own performances and performances of others in their competitions. There were 20 individual viewing stations and 6 team viewing rooms. Each area was equipped with a television, video cassette recorder, and comfortable seating. A taping schedule was developed based on AOB's live transmission schedule. All broadcast events were recorded and available to residents in the Village soon after the actual event occurred. Once events were taped, labeled, and catalogued, athletes could submit their credentials to check out tapes from 0900 to 2300 from 19 July through Village closing. More than 1,300 athletes used this service.

Recreational Pool. A 75 x 45 ft (23 x 14 m) in-ground recreational pool was a popular site for relaxation, attracting more than 4,000 athletes. Adjacent to the pool were saunas and a spa, and water games were available to be checked out. The pool operated from 0900 to 2100.

Music Listening Center. The Georgia Tech music listening center gave patrons the choice of 120 cable music channels which provided a variety of music from all over the world as well as a regular inventory of compact discs. The facility could accommodate 36 people at one time. More than 1,250 athletes visited the center, which was open daily from 0900 to 2300.

Television Lounges. One hundred and fifty television lounges were located throughout the various types of Village housing for communal use. Seven other such lounges were available in other areas of the international and residential zones. Lounges were open 24 hours a day.

Video Games Arcade and Laser Tag Arena. This facility featured 300 state-of-the-art video games and two laser tag arenas. Laser tag, a very physical activity, provided much-needed stress reduction and release of energy. Open from 0900 to 2300 daily, the facility received more than 54,370 visitors during the Games.

Bowling, Billiards and Other Recreational Activities. An existing bowling and billiards facility in the main recreation center was renovated by a supplier that also hosted instructional clinics and a three-day bowling tournament during the Village operating period. Extremely popular among the athletes, more than 30,000 games were played in the facility during Village operation.Other recreation equipment was also available, and outdoor areas were allocated for its use.

Residents could also register to participate in Atlanta excursions in the Village marketplace travel agency. Excursions ran from 1000 to 2200. Each attraction allowed free entry for Village residents with proper accreditation, and some sites also distributed souvenirs to the athletes. A total of 566 people participated in eight different excursions between 6 July and 4 August.

Information Resources. Established as an example of a library of the future, the world information center and World Wide Web pavilion was a 3,000 sq ft (279 sq m) facility that housed 25 computers linked to the World Wide Web. Residents could browse the Web, participate in Internet and on-line service chat rooms, read newspaper articles from their native countries, and view any of more than 150 CD-ROM titles. In the information center, open 0800–2300, IBM provided newspapers from around the world and a video wall, upon which messages sent to athletes were displayed for public view.

The *Daily Olympian,* the Olympic Village newspaper, spotlighted the athlete community through feature stories and photographs depicting Village life and athlete activities. It was produced daily during Games-time and distributed to all Village residents. *(For more information about the* Daily Olympian, *see the Creative Services chapter.)*

Athlete Gift Bags. Each resident of the Village received a coupon for a complimentary gift bag containing a Village pin and an assortment of gifts, ranging from souvenirs to toiletries. Bags were assembled and stored until distribution. Notices were posted in residential buildings to remind participants to claim their bags. More than 12,800 gift bags were distributed, and all unclaimed bags were donated to local charities.

Tickets to Events

ACOG Ticket Sales operated a counter, operational from 0800 to 2200 between 7 July and 4 August, in the Village shopping area. Tickets for many competitions and Olympic Arts Festival events could be purchased at this location. A limited number of complimentary tickets to

MARY A CUMMINGS • SONYA Y CUMMINGS • STEVEN A CUMMINGS • TIMOTHY L CUMMINGS • JOANN C CUMMINGS-ARNOLD • DONDII J CUMMINGS ATC • NANCY H CUMMINGS CATC • DAVID J CUMMINS • LISA-ANNE CUMMINS • TODD T CUMMINS • EDWARD CUMMISKEY • ELIZABETH A CUNARD • TIFFANY R CUNDITH • CHRISTINE M CUNDY • ROSE K CUNDY • LOUIS E CUNEO • ANNE M CUNIC • JILL J CUNICO • RANDALL W CUNICO • BARBARA A CUNNINGHAM • BARRETT C CUNNINGHAM • BRETT M CUNNINGHAM • CHAD F CUNNINGHAM • CLARISSA B CUNNINGHAM • CYNTHIA L CUNNINGHAM •

345

competition events were also distributed to NOCs and athletes. *(For more information on this subject, see the Ticket Sales chapter.)*

The Marketplace

The Village marketplace offered a wide variety of goods and services in a protected and festive environment. Marketplace vendors operated daily from 0800 until 2300 during the Games, and were carefully selected to provide the highest quality at an affordable cost. The building, which normally housed a student bookstore and other small retail operations, lent itself well to the shopping center atmosphere.

A 12,000 sq ft (1,116 sq m) department store sold Centennial Olympic Games souvenir merchandise, as well as health and beauty aids, sundries, and electronics. The department store housed an international newsstand, where residents could find daily and weekly newspapers and magazines from around the world and books in many languages. Dry cleaning, laundry, clothing alterations, and shoe repair were available in various sections of the department store.

A preexisting hair salon provided free haircuts to Village residents. Services also included manicures, pedicures, hair coloring, and permanent waves and relaxers.

Eastman Kodak Company provided a full-service photo shop that sold film, cameras, camera equipment, and supplies, and offered one-hour film processing.

A travel agency provided ticketing services and booked travel excursions. It also sold tickets to local attractions and entertainment events.

AT&T provided a 24-hour communications center, which offered assisted international long-distance telephone service, prepaid calling cards, facsimile service, data terminals, and electronic messaging. The area featured several calling stations and some private booths.

A courier service provided hand-carried local delivery of documents and small parcels. The couriers used golf carts in the Village and bicycles outside the Village.

United Parcel Service (UPS) supplied a full range of packaging and shipping services. Incoming parcels were held for residents. UPS also sold postage stamps and sorted incoming mail for the NOC Services center.

NationsBank opened a banking branch in the marketplace, which provided currency exchange, safe-deposit boxes, checking accounts, vendor accounts, and all other regular banking functions. It also sold Olympic commemorative coins. The branch operated from 0900 until 2100 every day. After hours, customers could use an automated teller machine and a night depository.

Religious Centers

Meeting the religious needs of athletes and the Olympic Family is an important aspect of the Olympic Games. In 1991, ACOG formed the Interfaith Advisory Group (IAG), which consisted of local leaders of various religions. The IAG held discussions with representatives of each faith group to determine requirements for scheduling, special fixtures, furniture, and equipment. Two existing student religious centers on the Georgia Tech campus were used. *(For more information on the IAG, see the External Relations chapter.)*

The primary center provided space for Hindu and Buddhist meditation and a multi-purpose space for Protestant Christians, Eastern Orthodox Christians, Jews, and other faith groups as requested. This center also provided a lounge for watching television, conversing, and relaxing. Compact discs and players were available, and a variety of reading material was provided. A second religious center provided space for Muslim and Roman Catholic prayer and worship services. These religious centers required little modification other than a divider in the Muslim prayer area to separate men and women as required by Islamic law.

The non-Muslim religious centers were open daily from 0800 to 2300 from 6 July through 6 August except for special services as noted. The Muslim prayer center was open during daily prayer sessions held at 0500, 1200, 1600, 1800, and 2000. On Fridays, the Muslim prayer center opened for a two-hour period for the special prayers of this Muslim holy day. A local leader was selected by the Atlanta Muslim community to lead the Friday prayers and meditation.

The Roman Catholic worship center was open from 0800 to 2300 to allow access to the Blessed Sacrament Chapel. A resident Roman Catholic priest provided primary supervision of the chapel. Mass was said each day at 0730 and 1730, as well as at 1100 on Sundays, led by either the resident priest or a priest serving as a volunteer chaplain. A priest was available for confession before Mass on Saturday evenings, before all three Sunday Masses, and at other times, as needed.

No special services were scheduled for the Buddhist and Hindu meditation rooms, which remained open from 0800 to 2300. Jewish Shabbat services were held on three Fridays at 1830. A Protestant Bible study was held each night at 2130, and services were held each Sunday at 0830. Eastern Orthodox Christians scheduled their worship service at 0700 on Sunday mornings. All guests presiding over prayer and worship services were escorted by Village staff.

Volunteer chaplains, representing Protestant, Catholic, Jewish, Islamic, Buddhist, Eastern Orthodox, and Hindu faiths, committed to eight-hour shifts between 6 July and 6 August. Chaplains were given specific assignments in the religious centers or elsewhere in the Village. Assignments were rotated, and volunteers selected as chaplains of the day ensured all areas were adequately staffed. During Village operation, 3,775 visitors came to the religious centers.

Medical Services

Village medical facilities consisted of a polyclinic, sports medicine center, and a first-aid station. The polyclinic handled all emergency care procedures. All individuals with serious medical conditions occurring in the Village were stabilized at the polyclinic, then transported to Crawford W. Long Hospital, located approximately 1.5 mi (2.4 km) away. The polyclinic also conducted gender verification as required by the IOC. (For more information, see the Medical Services chapter.)

The sports medicine center provided physical therapy and athletic training facilities. This facility was consistently utilized by athletes during their stay in the Village.

Because visitors, guests, media, and staff had limited access to the polyclinic, a separate first-aid facility was provided in the international zone. Additionally, American Red Cross first-responder teams covered the international zone, providing people with medical assistance as needed.

Information Stations

The Olympic Village provided five information stations designed to answer questions and distribute information, including competition and shuttle schedules, daily results publications, flyers about Village events and entertainment, and the Daily Olympian newspaper. Atlanta maps and guides were also available, and all stations were equipped with at least one Info'96 terminal. These kiosks were used extensively by Village residents, guests, and even staff. Although most questions asked concerned the Villages, information clerks often found themselves called upon to solve minor problems as well.

SATELLITE OLYMPIC VILLAGES

Planning for the Villages outside Atlanta began three years prior to the Games with the selection of other host cities. Local organizing committees (LOCs) in each of the eight satellite cities supported and organized the Games at the local level.

Management Structure

Satellite Villages had organizational structures similar to that of the Atlanta Village, but on a much smaller scale. Directors of satellite Villages joined the ACOG team one year before the Games to organize, plan, and work with the LOCs. All operational control was under the supervision of these directors. They served as the primary contacts with all other ACOG functional areas, including Financial Services, Logistics, Sports, Transportation, and Venue Management.

The directors reported to ACOG's director of satellite Villages, who was responsible for planning, contracting, developing, and coordinating the satellite Villages, as well as training their directors. In each of the Villages, the key staff members reporting to the satellite Village director included managers for NOC and athlete services, operations, logistics, administration, and security.

Operations

All athlete housing in the satellite Villages was air-conditioned. Food service was consistent with Olympic standards at all Villages, offering 24-hour dining adjacent to housing areas and providing boxed lunch service. Like the Atlanta Olympic Village, recreation services for satellite Village residents included a coffee house and dance club, television and game rooms, a hair salon, cinema, telephone calling card center, postal center, and shop for souvenirs and sundries. Religious services were also available, as was a variety of types of live entertainment.

Arrival and accreditation procedures differed slightly for each satellite Village. Yachting athletes and team officials flew directly into the Savannah International Airport, were

transported to the Savannah accreditation center, and from there, shuttled to the Savannah Village. Athletes and officials residing at the Ocoee, Columbus, and Athens Villages arrived at Hartsfield Atlanta International Airport and were accredited at the AWC. Ocoee and Columbus residents were transported by bus to their respective Villages. Athens participants resided in the Atlanta Olympic Village until 29 July, when they were transported by bus to the Athens Village. Football athletes and officials in the Washington, Orlando, Miami, and Birmingham Villages flew directly to airports in those cities and were accredited at the competition venues. They were transported by bus from these venues to their respective Villages.

An ACOG bus system ran daily between the Atlanta Village and the Ocoee, Columbus, and Athens Villages for athletes and officials. Residents of Villages in Savannah, Columbus, Athens, and Cleveland were transported to and from Atlanta to participate in the Opening Ceremony on 19 July. Residents of the football Villages participated in opening ceremonies held in their respective cities. (For operating dates of satellite Villages, see Figure 4.)

Savannah, Georgia, Yachting Village. Located at the Savannah Marriott Hotel on the banks of the Savannah River in the city's historic district, the yachting Village housed 682 athletes and officials representing 76 NOCs. All accommodations were hotel rooms furnished with two beds, a bathroom, television, and telephone. Savannah Village residents also had use of a fitness training facility and an outdoor pool.

The Olympic Marina, located at Turner's Creek on Wilmington Island, was approximately 12 mi (19 km) from the Savannah Village. An ACOG shuttle system of buses and other vehicles transported athletes and officials between the marina site and the Savannah Village. From the marina, athletes and officials traveled 8 nautical mi (15 km) on water taxis to the competition site, located on the Atlantic Ocean in Wassaw Sound.

FIGURE 4:
OPERATING DATES OF SATELLITE VILLAGES

Savannah Village
6 July–4 August

Ocoee (Cleveland) Village
6 July–31 July

Columbus Village
11 July–2 August

Athens Village
29 July–4 August

Washington, DC, Village
13 July–28 July

Orlando Village
10 July–28 July

South Florida (Miami) Village
6 July–31 July

Birmingham Village
13 July–31 July

Ocoee (Cleveland, Tennessee) Canoe/Kayak–Slalom Village. Lee College provided the satellite Village location for the 201 athletes and officials participating in the canoe/kayak–slalom competition. Participants represented 29 NOCs. The competition venue, located on the Ocoee River, was 25 mi (40 km) from the Cleveland Village. A shuttle bus system transported athletes and officials to the competition site.

The Village at Lee College consisted of six buildings, including four residential buildings of both apartments and residence hall accommodations. Food service was available in the college dining facility adjacent to the athlete housing. The international zone included a modern recreation building that housed a small gymnasium, indoor practice courts, exercise/fitness rooms, television and game rooms, and lounges.

Columbus, Georgia, Softball Village. Fort Benning, a US military installation located near Columbus, provided the satellite Village for 170 softball athletes and officials from eight NOCs. Competition was held at Golden Park, located 6 mi (10 km) from the Village, with a shuttle system of team buses providing transportation.

The Columbus Village consisted of one three-story residential building. All rooms were single-occupancy, furnished with a double bed and bathroom with shower. Athlete and NOC services were located on the building's ground floor, and lounges were available on the upper floors.

Athens, Georgia, Rhythmic Gymnastics Village. The University of Georgia (UGA) served as the satellite Village for athletes and officials participating in rhythmic gymnastics in Athens. Competition was held at the UGA Coliseum, .2 mi (.3 km) from the satellite Village. An ACOG shuttle bus transported athletes and officials to and from this site.

The Athens Village consisted of one college residence building with connecting sections and exterior walkways. All accommodations were air-conditioned, dormitory-style, double-occupancy rooms with shared bathrooms. The Village housed 160 athletes and officials from 23 competing NOCs.

Athlete and NOC services were located on the ground floor of the residence hall, with additional lounges and facilities on the upper floors. A dining facility in the same building provided food service to residents.

The UGA campus also hosted indoor volleyball preliminaries and football medal-round competitions. The Athens Village served as a dining, resting, and relaxing site, or day village, for these two sports.

Washington, DC, Football Village. The Washington Olympic Village was located at Mount Vernon College, 20 mi (32 km) from the competition venue, Robert F. Kennedy Memorial Stadium. Athletes and officials traveled to and from the stadium on team buses. The Washington Village consisted of 10 buildings, 5 of which contained apartment and residence hall–style accommodations, while the other 5 provided space for athlete and NOC services, lounges, and entertainment and recreational activities. Food service was provided in the college's dining facility.

Orlando, Florida, Football Village. The University of Central Florida in Orlando hosted a Village for football athletes and officials that was 20 mi (32 km) from the competition venue, the Florida Citrus Bowl.

The Orlando Village consisted of eight buildings, which included five resident housing units with 12 apartments each. Other buildings housed athlete and NOC services, lounges, and entertainment and recreational activities. Residents could dine in an air-conditioned tented facility adjacent to athlete housing.

South Florida (Miami) Football Village.
NOVA Southeastern University, located in Fort Lauderdale, Florida, provided the South Florida satellite Village location for athletes and officials participating in the preliminary and quarterfinal rounds of football competition. The campus is located 29 mi (47 km) from the competition venue, the Orange Bowl.

The South Florida Village was housed in one four-story residential building. Athlete and NOC services were located on the first floor, with additional lounges and facilities on the upper floors. An adjacent air-conditioned tented dining facility housed the food service operation.

Birmingham, Alabama, Football Village.
Birmingham Southern College hosted a satellite Village for football athletes and officials located .6 mi (1 km) from the competition venue, Legion Field.

The Birmingham Village consisted of five buildings on the southern area of the campus. Three residential buildings contained double-occupancy and air-conditioned apartments and residence hall accommodations. All rooms were double occupancy and air-conditioned. Other buildings housed athlete and NOC services, lounges, entertainment, and recreational activities. An adjacent tent provided dining services to residents.

CONCLUSIONS AND RECOMMENDATIONS

The Olympic Villages were conceived and designed to provide all necessary services athletes might need during their stay and enhance their performance at the Games. The department was committed to supplying a secure, relaxed, and comfortable environment with air-conditioned accommodations, training sites, cafeterias, and multiple entertainment facilities in order to promote international friendships and a feeling of camaraderie.

In addition to planning the Villages, extensive communication took place with the NOCs prior to and during the Games. Extensive communication with all NOCs prior to the Games is essential to the success of an Olympic Village program.

The recommendations that follow will help future organizing committees plan an Olympic Village.

Village Facilities and Layout

■ Use facilities over which the organizing committee has exclusive control for all Villages.

■ Use multilevel parking structures as on-site warehouses.

■ Divide the Village residential areas into zones which are clearly demarcated using a directional system of a universal language such as colors, numbers, and pictograms.

■ Place all entertainment and recreation activities in one zone of the Village.

Village Operations

■ Alert all functional areas to the fact that the starting date of operations for the Villages is earlier than that of other venues.

■ Maintain good communication with all law enforcement and security organizations and Village departments.

■ Install a lockable storage space, such as a wardrobe or safe, in each residential room to decrease opportunity for theft.

■ Install multiline telephones with voice mail capabilities.

■ Link all computers via a local area network between the Village and any remote venues with Village functions.

■ For housing allotment, complete information should be obtained from NOC Services concerning each NOC, including type of government, political issues, religion, culture, and current affairs. Design a housing allotment tracking system that can identify whether or not an NOC has arrived. A building occupancy report that shows which rooms are occupied and who is occupying them is also helpful.

■ Hire a reception manager at least one year prior to the Games to begin the coordination of NOC Services, Sports Inscriptions, Accreditation, and Transportation. Having a sufficient number of trained staff for reception is also imperative. Operate all reception functions with the same service hours.

■ Rotate menus frequently in the athlete dining facilities.

OPENING AND CLOSING CEREMONIES

CHAPTER NINETEEN
OPENING AND CLOSING CEREMONIES

OPENING AND
CLOSING
CEREMONIES
EMPLOYEES

Date	Staff Number
May 1994	1
January 1996	3
July 1996	3

Note: These staff numbers do not include DMP contract, VIK, and volunteer personnel.

OVERVIEW—There were no scripts, no famous actors, no familiar story lines upon which to base the productions. There was only the certainty that the Opening and Closing Ceremonies of the Centennial Olympic Games would have to communicate with and inspire the 85,000 attendees, as well as an international broadcast audience of 3.5 billion. A production that would fill an expanse equivalent to four football fields had to be created that would be simultaneously spectacular and dynamic, yet intimate and meaningful.

Presenting a program for a worldwide audience is a challenge every organizing committee faces. Atlanta had the added responsibility of celebrating the Games' centennial without sacrificing the city's and country's expectations of offering the world a new perspective on the American South. ACOG readily defined three themes that would provide a basis for all the creative development and production planning that would follow:

■ representing the American South, especially Georgia;

■ celebrating the centennial of the modern Olympic Games; and

■ celebrating youth.

Fulfilling the mission to portray these themes required a massive creative and logistical endeavor. ACOG gathered the world's most talented artists in many disparate fields, and together they created a spectacular, unforgettable tribute to the Centennial Olympic Games, the American South, international youth, and the 10,500 athletes who gathered in Atlanta to represent their countries.

Historical Background

From the first modern Olympic Games in Athens, official Opening and Closing Ceremonies have been a critical part of the Olympic Games, and today they are considered among the Games' most significant events. The ceremonies draw an enormous television audience—especially the Opening Ceremony, which attracts billions of viewers and has become the single greatest concentration of global attention for peacetime events in human history.

Opening Ceremony. All Games, except those of the II and III Olympiads in 1900 and 1904—held in conjunction with the Universal Parks Exposition in Paris and the Louisiana Purchase Exposition in St. Louis—have staged formal Opening Ceremonies.

Each Opening Ceremony is comprised of official protocol segments, which are closely supervised by the IOC, and artistic or cultural performance segments, which are largely a product of the creativity and initiative of each organizing committee.

In 1896, the protocol segments included the formal welcome of the head of state into the stadium, the host country anthem and flag raising, a parade of national athletic delegations, a speech by the organizing committee president, the formal declaration of the opening of the Games by the host country's head of state, performance of the Olympic hymn, and release of doves of peace. Subsequent Games saw the addition of the IOC president's speech, the Olympic flag arrival, the athletes' and judges' oaths, the Olympic flame lighting, and the Torch Relay to the stadium. The symbols of the Olympic Games thus attained the prestige and prominence to begin the days of the world's finest sports competitions properly.

While expressions of local culture were present in the earliest modern Olympic ceremonies, the Games of 1932 and 1936 introduced more elaborate music, dance, and pageantry. Such cultural elements have become increasingly prominent, as has the significance of the ceremony itself.

Closing Ceremony. From the 1896 Games in Athens to the 1928 Games in Amsterdam, the Olympic Games Closing Ceremony focused on the distribution of prizes—medals, diplomas, and special trophies—to victorious athletes. During this period, individual victory ceremonies were not conducted after each competition.

During the Olympic Games held in the 1930s, Closing Ceremony activities and traditions assumed the format familiar today. Victory ceremonies held to award medals after each competition, in the same place and before the same audience that had witnessed their athletic performances, began during this epoch.

As a result, the Closing Ceremony was at liberty to express the equality and solidarity of the Olympic Family. The Closing Ceremony is now a time for the warmest social interaction, as it celebrates the capacity for human friendship across cultural and political boundaries, which has been tested and proven throughout the Games. The artistic segments became magical and evocative, but also lighthearted, humorous, and even carnivalesque.

In recent decades, the most important innovations to the ceremony's protocol segments have contributed to the themes of international solidarity and joyous festivity. Beginning with the 1956 Melbourne Games, athletes have

entered the Closing Ceremony en masse, without formal distinction of national identity or degree of athletic success. The athletes have authenticated this symbolism by claiming the Closing Ceremony stage for a truly international party.

ORGANIZATION

While ACOG mandated that the ceremonies must use as much local talent as possible, it was felt that creative direction could come

David Goldberg, Don Mischer, Billy Payne, and former Atlanta mayor Maynard Jackson commemorate the announcement of the company selected to produce Opening and Closing Ceremonies.

from anywhere. In spring 1993, ACOG began a worldwide search for a production company to develop and stage the ceremonies. A 14-member ACOG selection committee conducted a -2

In October 1993, ACOG selected Emmy award–winning Don Mischer Productions (DMP), a Los Angeles creative firm, and a contract was executed in May 1994. DMP formed a Georgia-based subsidiary, Centennial Events, Inc. (CEI), to stage the production. The company's president, Don Mischer, a 12-time Emmy award–winning creative producer/director, served as executive producer and director of the Opening and Closing Ceremonies. The company's vice president of production, David Goldberg, a 14-year veteran of the ABC television network and three-time Emmy award winner, served as the producer.

In early 1994, DMP assembled a team of professionals with backgrounds in theater, music videos, performance art, motion pictures, concert tours, and large-scale stadium events to direct the various aspects of production. The team included Peter Minshall, an acclaimed artist famous for his dancing mobiles, as artistic director of costume design; Kenny Ortega, director and choreographer of feature-length films, theater, television, music videos, and concert tours, as artistic director for special staging and choreography; Judy Chabola, with her background in staging, directing, and choreographing international special events, as the staging director and choreographer; Mark Watters, an award-winning composer, conductor, and arranger of both popular and classical music, as the music director; Bob Keene, with his extensive experience in set design, as the production designer; and Bob Dickinson, lighting designer and a nine-time Emmy and three-time Ace Award winner. Many of these key members of the creative team had worked on the Opening and Closing Ceremonies of previous Games. Selected as creative consultants were Cirque de Soleil's founding president, Guy Laliberte, and vice president of creation, Gilles Ste-Croix. The DMP ceremonies creative staff eventually grew to 175. *(For a list of the creative and production team, see Figure 1.)*

CREATIVE DEVELOPMENT

From the outset, ACOG and DMP agreed on three important policies that drove the creative process and shaped the ceremonies' development.

■ Creative development would be a collaborative process between DMP and ACOG.

■ The directors of the production team would report directly to ACOG senior management to ensure that communications between the two parties would be clear and timely.

■ All creative elements would be kept extremely secret to maximize public anticipation and response to the ceremonies.

During the first year of researching and assembling the key members of the production staff, the creative team held a series of meetings with ACOG senior staff in Savannah, New Orleans, and Los Angeles. After the themes and elements were finalized, the creative team began to engage the production staff and to hold biweekly internal staff meetings in Los Angeles as well as week-long creative sessions with the entire staff in Los Angeles, Atlanta, and Montreal. At the first of these meetings, held in Los Angeles in June 1994, they discussed the protocol elements, the three themes, and how the various people involved would work as a team. At this meeting, ideas were conceived and discussed without regard to budget or logistics. Another significant meeting occurred the following September at the Amateur Athletic Association in Los Angeles, where the team surrounded itself with Olympic memorabilia to inspire the creative process. Many meetings were held with ACOG senior management to discuss creative direction. During these sessions, the concepts introduced were rejected, accepted, enhanced, or further refined.

Throughout this process, the team sought ways to portray the three themes of the ceremonies both individually and in such a way that they would culminate in a powerful global statement—that Atlanta was calling all the nations of the world to gather for the Centennial Olympic Games.

Cultural Diversity of the South

ACOG, like every host committee, was sensitive to regional anxieties concerning the manner in which the Opening and Closing Ceremonies would reflect the local community. To overcome perceived and real difficulties that the producer would face in creating the ceremonies, ACOG and DMP devoted the first six months of their contract to local research. Mischer and key members of his team made more than a dozen trips to Atlanta to familiarize themselves with the landscape and to interview local historians, area residents, and leaders of the civic, civil rights, arts, and business communities. These interviews proved invaluable. Mischer gained important insight into the spirit of Atlanta and the South and into Atlantans' hopes and fears concerning the ceremonies. Atlantans had the genuine opportunity to contribute and respond to ideas for the ceremonies before any were formally developed.

It was especially important to ACOG that the South be portrayed appropriately in the Opening Ceremony, since it would introduce the region's people, history, culture, and traditions to many people around the world. The challenge was to portray the culture and diversity of the South in a manner that would accurately reflect its history and truly display its beauty.

It was ultimately decided to create a very youthful, high-energy segment welcoming the world to Atlanta, contrasted with a peaceful, lush, pastoral evening in the South. As on many such evenings, and as an important element of the history of the South, a storm comes but is followed by a wonderful rebirth at dawn. The costumes and music were perhaps the most important elements in depicting this southern theme, enhanced by a traditional southern sunflower distributed to each member of the audience.

Centennial of the Modern Games

Many possible concepts and elements were considered for honoring the centennial of the Games and their ancient heritage. It was decided to include centennial tributes throughout the program, highlighted by a dramatic portrayal of the ancient Games. To ensure accuracy in the interpretation, DMP researched the traditions of the ancient Games and in October 1995 traveled to Olympia and other parts of Greece to verify and further develop these concepts.

Other accolades to the centennial of the Olympic Games included a tribute to the founder of the modern Olympic Games, Pierre de Coubertin; a tribute to previous host cities of the Olympic Games; and a tribute to athletes who had achieved great success during the one hundred years of the modern Olympiad.

Celebration of Youth

From its inception, ACOG intended to celebrate young people for their contributions to the Olympic Movement and because the legacy of the Olympic Spirit truly belongs to the future they represent. DMP developed many creative concepts that included youth participation and that depicted the enthusiasm of youth.

Two of the most important of these segments were the youthful, energetic Welcoming of the World to Atlanta segment in the Opening Ceremony, and the Sport as Art segment designed to entertain the athletes in the Closing Ceremony. Sport as Art featured a demonstration of the skill and beauty of extreme sports—skateboarding, in-line skating, and mountain biking—combined with daring stunts. In addition, trained and uniformed youths were stationed in every section to encourage audience participation during both ceremonies.

Protocol

The DMP creative team placed great emphasis on producing a magnificent, dramatic, and entertaining program that also honored the traditional protocol elements of the *Olympic Charter* and the US. These included the

top: Constructing the Greek temple made of fabric and columns for the Opening Ceremony Tradition of the Games segment required extensive rehearsal.

bottom: Rehearsal time in Olympic Stadium for the Closing Ceremony was limited to one short session.

Olympic flag and anthem, the US national anthem, the entrance of the president of the US, and the lighting of the Olympic flame. To continue and yet add great emphasis to two other traditional protocol segments, DMP enhanced the release of the doves of peace and the parade of participants. The release of doves was creatively depicted by having youths fly dove kites over the heads of the athletes gathered on the field.

Parade of Participants. The parade of participants has become one of the most important aspects of the ceremonies. In the Opening Ceremony, the athletes traditionally parade into the stadium in formal dress, following their national banners, demonstrating for the world the magnitude and scope of the Olympic Games. During this assembly the field resembled a giant patchwork quilt, each nation distinct but joined together during those few magnificent moments. DMP created an entrance ramp into the stadium to allow all participants a view of the entire stadium and to emphasize the entrance of each nation.

As an amendment to the host city contract for the 1996 Games, DMP's plan first required the approval of the Athletes Commission and the IOC Executive Board. Implementing the parade required detailed plans for transportation to and seating in the adjacent Atlanta–Fulton County Stadium, where the athletes would wait before entering Olympic Stadium. Tickets were produced and distributed to each NOC based on *Olympic Charter* rules for numbers of athletes from each country allowed to march.

The participants began to arrive at the stadium at 1900, and were given time to refresh and enjoy watching the artistic segments of the ceremony on large video monitors. At approximately 2100, the Greek delegation was asked to begin the move to Olympic Stadium. One by one, the other countries were called in alphabetical order. When their turn came, the athletes of each nation crossed between the stadia following their national flag and a placard bearing their country's name. Television monitors were positioned along the route so the athletes could continue to watch the ceremony as they proceeded. Volunteers assisted the athletes and officials in positioning themselves in lines eight abreast in preparation for their entrance.

There were challenges in trying to maintain an orderly procession between stadia. The athletes were justifiably excited and enjoying the moment, and stern demands for their attention and proper behavior would have lessened this important experience for them. The physical structure of the Atlanta–Fulton County Stadium, with its narrow aisles and stairs, sometimes resulted in an irregular flow of athletes, causing larger gaps than anticipated between countries. Language differences also accounted for some lack of response to requests for athletes to proceed more quickly.

The Greek delegation made its entrance over the ramp into Olympic Stadium at approximately 2140 as the orchestra played "Bugler's Dream" by Leo Arnaud. An international collection of march music was played for the other countries. Delegations proceeded down the ramp and circled the track in formation, saluting US President Bill Clinton and IOC President Juan Antonio Samaranch at the appropriate moments. As prescribed by the *Olympic Charter*, the delegation from the host country, the United States of America, was last to enter. As the US team entered over the ramp, the orchestra played "Olympic Fanfare and Theme" by John Williams, the theme of the 1984 Olympic Games in Los Angeles.

After the athletes of each country had completed their walk around the track, they were positioned on the field by 650 field marshals. The marshals then stood hand-in-hand around the perimeter of the infield to ensure that the athletes would not overflow onto the track area. For the first time, the protocol stage was positioned in the center of the field surrounded by the athletes. In the past, this stage was placed just inside the track closest to the presidential box.

During the Closing Ceremony, the placard carrier and flag bearer entered the stadium as part of a formal parade, and all the athletes were invited to enter en masse, as friends rather than competitors or representatives of their nations, to celebrate the closing of the Games together.

IOC Approval

The first presentation of creative elements to the IOC Executive Board in Paris in August 1994 was very well received. Board members emphasized that the representation of the ancient Greek Games should be historically accurate.

The final creative plan for the Opening Ceremony was presented at the December 1995 IOC Executive Board meeting in Nagano, Japan, and was approved by a positive response.

In March 1996, the final Closing Ceremony plan was presented at the IOC Executive Board meeting in Lausanne, Switzerland. Artists' renderings and original music were presented to the Executive Board, which again provided enthusiastic approval.

TECHNICAL DEVELOPMENT

Technical development began in 1993, when DMP reviewed the design of Olympic Stadium, and continued throughout the creative planning phase. By summer 1995, most key creative elements had been established, and research and development of the ceremonies' technical aspects intensified. Costume and prop design began at this time, and audition schedules for recruitment of cast and volunteers were confirmed.

One important technical aspect was establishing the start and end times for each ceremony, which were determined in consultation with ACOG, the IOC, Atlanta Olympic Broadcasting (AOB), and NBC. With an on-air time of 2000 eastern standard time for both the Opening and Closing Ceremonies, the lack of daylight quickly became an important issue. Theatrical lighting would be required for virtually the entirety of each ceremony. Though costly, this allowed ACOG and DMP to make creative use of available daylight while maximizing the dramatic effects of theatrical lighting.

The magnitude and importance of the ceremonies required full coordination and support from most ACOG functional areas, especially Accommodations, Marketing/ACOP, Technology, Ticket Sales, and Transportation. To facilitate this coordination, ACOG provided an internal ceremonies director and two additional staff members to ensure that DMP's support requirements were communicated to and supplied by the ACOG functional areas. To facilitate contracting, ACOG's ceremonies staff also assumed responsibility for leasing space requirements outside the stadium venue, including the costume facility and audition and rehearsal halls.

In addition to these services, DMP coordinated directly with AOB, Communications, Construction, and Creative Services, and Venue Management.

Budgeting

One of the most difficult aspects of planning the ceremonies was to develop a realistic budget. Although ACOG had set a budget, it was virtually impossible to finalize cost requirements until the plans for the ceremonies were established and confirmed.

ACOG initially determined its ceremonies budget based upon prior Games. Later, DMP

• CAROL G DANA • JOSEPH W DANAHEY • MISSY DANAS • LINDA M DANAVALL • MICHAEL DANBOM • VICKIE S DANCE • REGINALD C DANCIL • MICHAEL J DANCKERT • W ANTHONY H DANDA • GEORGE C DANDELAKIS • CARMELITTA D D'ANDRADE • MARTEN H DANE • SUSAN DANESHGARI • JANICE K DANFORD • MARK W DANFORD • TOM DANFORTH • NGOC-ANH N DANG • ANN D DANGAR • REBECCA A DANGAR • PAUL M DANGEL • LIHONG L D'ANGELO • VICTORIA S D'ANGELO • DALE A DANGLER • KARRIE L DANHOF • WAYNE P DANIEL • ALEX DANIEL • CAROLENE D DANIEL • CHARLES M DANIEL

357

submitted a budget according to the creative plan that had been developed, which was significantly higher than ACOG's predetermined budget. Through negotiation and compromise between ACOG and DMP, certain budget increases were approved, especially for dramatic lighting and enhanced sound systems.

Construction Coordination

Ceremonies planners were fortunate that Olympic Stadium was still under construction during the creative planning phase and could

Don Mischer and David Goldberg incorporated Olympic Stadium design into the plan and design of the ceremonies.

be modified in certain ways to accommodate the ceremonies. ACOG senior management asked DMP to review the design of Olympic Stadium and recommend any changes that might be required. After evaluation of the venue, DMP produced a report outlining several requirements to ACOG Construction, including specifications for lighting, sound, electrical power sources, and access.

Certain requirements would change as the creative process continued. Construction did not initially alter its stadium plan, but when DMP was officially selected, its scenic, lighting,

and sound design teams became involved in the construction of Olympic Stadium. They were able to incorporate key features, such as additional street access for loading props, scenery, and performers and an underground tunnel in the center of the field to enhance dramatic entrances for performers.

Designers also modified the seating plans. The northeast corner of Olympic Stadium was constructed so that it could be removed just prior to the ceremony to construct the temporary ramp used for the parade of participants. The seating section was replaced in time for the start of the athletic competitions. The southwest corner was modified to construct a temporary ramp for the Centennial Chorus and the Atlanta Symphony Orchestra. A portion of this ramp stayed in place throughout the Games, while another portion was removed to provide space for photographers. Also, lighting facilities were modified to accommodate theatrical lighting fixtures, sound equipment, and other special effects apparatus.

Some of the modifications adopted were difficult to keep secret, such as the athlete's entry ramp and the tunnel to the center of the field. The digging of the tunnel also revealed drainage problems that required attention.

Because Olympic Stadium interior space was still in a formative stage while the ceremonies were being planned, DMP was able to establish on-site office space and shops to support show production and operations. Two additional facilities, within the perimeter of the security fencing surrounding the stadium, housed the entire wardrobe and costume shops along with ACOG's ceremonies management offices. This convenient location provided cast members with easy access to fitting and final dressing areas while at the stadium for rehearsals. It also afforded DMP an excellent staging area during rehearsals and the show. A parking lot adjacent to the stadium was equipped with large tents to provide additional work space.

Venue Management

The DMP team began planning its space requirements and facilities services with ACOG's Venue Management Department in fall 1995. As the team would require space for 200 individuals, DMP mostly used large rooms with rows of desks. Extra lighting, air-conditioning, technology cabling, food and beverage service, and security had to be provided. Maintenance and installation of equipment and access for rehearsal groups were coordinated daily with the venue team.

The space utilization of Olympic Stadium and Atlanta–Fulton County Stadium proved too restrictive for cast assembly, so DMP coordinated with Transportation to marshall the cast at a location more than a mile away and bus them to Olympic Stadium immediately before their entrance at the Opening Ceremony.

Television Production

For the first time in Olympic history, the executive producer of the ceremonies, Don Mischer, was also asked to direct the television coverage for the world broadcast. Because of his vast experience in television direction and his familiarity with every aspect of the show, it was appropriate for him to determine the best camera angles for conveying the ceremonies to television viewers around the world.

Mischer and his directorial team worked closely with the AOB production team. The television crew—140 technicians, camera operators, and support personnel—was provided by

AOB, with the exception of two associate directors, the head audio engineer, and two camera operators who maneuvered specialized long-arm cranes.

The ceremonies were broadcast from an AOB control room. The directorial team, audio engineer, lighting director, commentator, and stadium video screens operated from this control center. Twenty-six cameras were used—8 on the field, 17 positioned around the stadium, and 1 in a blimp airship shared with NBC.

DMP coordinated equipment, schedules, and logistics with the AOB venue broadcast manager. There were two days of rehearsals with the full television crew on 13 and 14 July 1996.

Media Relations

Though ACOG and DMP aimed to keep the content of the Opening and Closing Ceremonies secret, both realized that local media in particular would be aggressive in their attempts to uncover the story, and also recognized the benefit of seeking publicity in the entertainment trade media for appointments made to the ceremonies team. Working with ACOG Communications, the media was invited to cover selected auditions, recording sessions, and elements of early rehearsals in Olympic Stadium. With only one exception, local, national, and international media cooperated fully with ACOG's ceremony press guidelines and appreciated the opportunity to document ceremony preparations.

In addition, both broadcast and, for the first time ever, print reporters were given thorough briefings prior to each ceremony. After consulting with historians, sociologists, and others in academia who study the worldwide interpretations of Olympic ceremonies, ACOG and DMP concluded that international media should be assisted in interpreting the artistic portions of the ceremonies. In the past, the host broadcasters would receive a broad briefing from the

During auditions, choreographers tested the strength and balance of prospective cast members and their ability to manage the large puppets used in the Opening Ceremony.

NELDIA M DANIEL • PETER K DANIEL • PETER K DANIEL • REBON L DANIEL • ROBERT O DANIEL • RUTH DANIEL • SAM T DANIEL • TOMMY J DANIEL • TONYA DANIEL • WILLIAM G DANIEL • SHARON D DANIEL-BROADNAX • DEBBY A DANIEL BRYANT • BOBBY H DANIEL II • JAMES R DANIEL JR • LYDIA DANIELI • BETH M DANIELL • JAMES B DANIELL • KENNETH F DANIELL • ANTHONY DANIELLY • ANTHONY L DANIELLY • BRENDA J DANIELS • ELEASE D DANIELS • ELSIE T DANIELS • J DANIELS • JAMES M DANIELS • JOYCE A DANIELS • JUDITH C DANIELS • KATHRYN L DANIELS • KENNETH E DANIELS

359

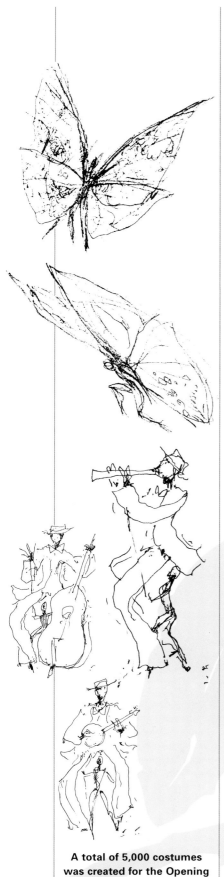

ceremonies producer. For the Centennial Games, broadcasters received an in-depth briefing book, complete with storyboards and useful narratives they could incorporate into their broadcasts. This briefing was held in the International Broadcast Center two days prior to each ceremony.

Print journalists were briefed at the Main Press Center one day prior to each ceremony and received materials similar to those given to broadcasters, but without the storyboards. Unlike the broadcasters, who always cooperated fully with the host broadcaster, ACOG and DMP realized that print journalists would report on these briefings. For this reason, ACOG and DMP allowed selected elements—such as facts about the cast and costumes and a general outline of the ceremony—to be published before the ceremony. These items were clearly noted in the front of the *Press Guide* that was distributed to print reporters. The remaining information was embargoed until the ceremony began. Without exception, print journalists worldwide honored the embargo.

PRODUCTION ELEMENTS

Preparations for the staging of the Opening and Closing Ceremonies focused on selecting performers, choosing and composing musical selections, constructing necessary props and costumes, and finalizing all other details to make the ceremonies memorable and enjoyable.

Cast Formation

The first auditions for the thousands of cast members who would perform during the Opening and Closing Ceremonies were held in November 1995 in a high school gymnasium in Atlanta. These auditions were open only to qualified groups in order to facilitate communications and training. DMP, which conducted the auditions, particularly sought talented

cheerleading squads, dance troupes, gymnastic teams, and flag corps. A total of 3,216 people were auditioned at this time. DMP also auditioned several Atlanta high school bands for the high-stepping band segment. During this time, the National Cheerleaders Association formally agreed to recruit, select, and train cheerleaders for the ceremony. These cheerleaders were selected from throughout the US and were housed outside Atlanta.

The second series of auditions, open to individuals, was held in February and March 1996. These auditions focused on recruiting musicians, dancers, audience leaders, and placard bearers. Also, the production staff contacted local elementary schools and auditioned groups of children who wished to participate. During auditions, choreographers tested the strength and balance of prospective cast members using large puppets similar to those introduced at the Barcelona Opening Ceremony.

Music

In creating music for the show, the producers chose composers that would represent a wide range of American musical talent, from the traditional and highly acclaimed John Williams and major film composers, such as Basil Poledouris and Michael Kamen, to successful popular music writers. Mark Watters was selected as music director for the Opening Ceremony, and was joined by Harold Wheeler as co–music director of the Closing Ceremony. Other members of the team were Mickey Hart, Stephen Taylor, Dr. David Morrow (director, Morehouse College Glee Club), and Dr. Norma Raybon (director, Spelman College Glee Club).

The composition of new music for the Centennial Olympic Games required much creative collaboration between DMP and individual composers. Each piece was developed around a central theme appropriate to a particular element of the show. Five pieces were composed especially for the ceremonies: "Summon the Heroes", an Olympic fanfare with full symphonic orchestra composed by John Williams; "Welcome to the World", a contemporary hip-hop song with strains of bluegrass

A total of 5,000 costumes was created for the Opening and Closing Ceremonies.

and country composed by Jimmy Jam and Terry Lewis; "Power of the Dream", the popular theme song of the Games composed by David Foster and Kenneth "Babyface" Edmonds with lyrics by Linda Thompson; "Faster, Higher, Stronger", an anthem of encouragement and inspiration for Olympic athletes composed by Mark Watters with lyrics by Lorraine Feather; and "The Flame", a poignant choral ballad reflecting on the departure of the athletes and the extinguishing of the Olympic flame composed by John Jarvis with lyrics by Joe Henry.

Creation of the musical scores began eighteen months before the Opening Ceremony. Demo tracks, or scratch tracks, were made to provide directors and choreographers with timing, tempos, and melodies. In most cases, several scratch tracks were made before a musical composition was accepted.

Preliminary recording sessions were held in San Francisco, Los Angeles, and New York in spring 1996. The final and principal recording sessions were held in June 1996 with the Atlanta Symphony Orchestra.

Props and Costumes

Each member of the creative team had a role in developing the 87 different kinds of costumes and over 5,000 props that were used.

DMP's design team submitted numerous costume designs for each segment of the show. The proposed costumes were coordinated within and between segments to create an effect of colorful, dramatic emphasis and subtle beauty. Eighty-seven different costume designs were selected and more than 5,000 costumes created. To facilitate costume production and fitting, a wardrobe shop with a team of tailors was assembled in the area adjacent to the stadium. At the close of each ceremony, volunteer cast members were allowed to keep their own costumes as a keepsake of their particiaption in the event.

Two companies were engaged to create and maintain the major props—the stage, ramps, Greek columns, the Old Man River boat, the

thundercloud, puppets, and others. This was a large operation that required work space in addition to the shops within the stadium, including tents, parking lots, and nearby buildings. A large labor force from the Atlanta area was needed to develop and maintain the props. Volunteers assisted with the final decorations to such items as butterfly wings and puppets.

One of the most difficult props to develop was the field cover. It was constructed of durable, heavy canvas to ensure it would re-

Costume production, fitting, and repair took place in a wardrobe shop adjacent to Olympic Stadium.

main intact, since it was used during all rehearsals. It was also easily removable to accommodate other activities and regular maintenance of the athletic fields. It was painted just prior to the Opening Ceremony for dramatic effect.

Despite efforts to maintain the grass, the field cover and large cast rehearsals damaged

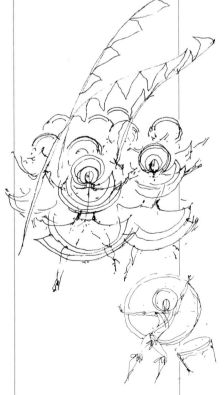

the turf, which was completely replaced during the six days between the Opening Ceremony and the first athletics competition.

Star Performers

From the beginning of the creative process, ACOG and DMP chose to develop the dramatic elements of the ceremonies as an all-inclusive production and to rely on individual performers to enhance the show as a whole. In the Opening Ceremony, individual performances by musical entertainers were interwoven among the artistic segments. In the Closing

Volunteers placed an Opening Ceremony gift kit on every seat in Olympic Stadium.

Ceremony, the individual talent first performed alone and then in concert as a celebratory tribute to the athletes. DMP recommended the performers and negotiated all contracts. The production team worked with ACOG Accommodations and Guest Services to provide the support required for the perform-

ers' stay in Atlanta. In all, 20 star performers enhanced the Opening and Closing Ceremonies of the Atlanta Games.

Final Torchbearers and Cauldron Lighting

In early 1996, ACOG and DMP began selecting final torchbearers to carry the torch in Olympic Stadium. It is a Games tradition that all such runners are from the host country, but in celebration of the Olympic Centennial, ACOG decided to include a Greek athlete to honor the origins of the modern Olympic Games. As a result, Evander Holyfield, renowned Olympian from Atlanta, shared the torch with Greek athlete Voula Patoulidou during one segment. Olympic swimmer Janet Evans, who represents US athleticism, was also selected to run a segment. Muhammad Ali, the 1960 Olympic gold medalist in heavyweight boxing, was chosen to be the final torchbearer and to light the Olympic Cauldron.

In February 1996, as the cauldron designed by Siah Armajani was being finished in Hugo, Minnesota, DMP and ACOG senior management and the artist met there to conduct a test event. *(For more information about the design of the cauldron, see the Cultural Olympiad chapter.)* Four runners from the University of Minnesota women's track team tested and timed the running of the torch across the bridge and up the stairs of the cauldron. The run was made both in daylight and at night. After the cauldron was installed in Atlanta, tests from the camera positions in the stadium confirmed that in following this path, the flame would disappear three times from the view of most spectators in Olympic Stadium. It was then that alternate methods for lighting the cauldron were explored. With Muhammad Ali as the final torchbearer, the need for a new approach was manifest, as Ali's physical condition would prevent him from running across the bridge and ascending the stairs.

Kits and Programs

In collaboration with Creative Services and a graphics design firm, DMP created an Opening Ceremony gift box for each member of the audience. The ceremonies kit, as it is traditionally called, contained a colorful 48-page program describing the show in English and French and illustrating many of the show's elements with newly created graphic art. The kit also contained a special ceremonies pin, audience participation props including scarves and flashlights, and a specially designed Nations-Bank debit card. At the Closing Ceremony, audience members were each supplied with a Closing Ceremony program book and a disposable Kodak camera. Production of the kit and program books for the Opening and Closing Ceremonies was managed by Creative Services in consultation with DMP, and was not included in the ceremonies budget. Each kit and closing book was covered in plastic and placed on every seat in Olympic Stadium by volunteers the day before each ceremony.

TESTING AND REHEARSALS

In early 1995, an exact replica of the ramp that would be used for the parade of participants was secretly constructed in Duarte, California. Students from an area school were recruited to test safety and timing issues. In March 1995, selected ACOG staff members gathered in Duarte to walk the ramp and test its surface under varying conditions. Another major test, involving Greek silhouette figures, Olympic spirits, and various fabric effects, was conducted in October 1995 in the Los Angeles Coliseum.

In fall 1995, technical team members began to make periodic trips to Atlanta to conduct surveys at Olympic Stadium, with thorough site tests beginning as the entire production team moved to Atlanta in April 1996. For several weeks, intense tests of the shows' mechanics, such as mounting the Greek columns used in the Tradition of the Games segment and flying the US Army Rangers into the stadium, were conducted.

Rehearsals incorporating the main body of the cast began on 10 May 1996. Rehearsals were scheduled from early morning until midnight and were held four or more days a week. Strict rules of attendance and conduct were established from the beginning. Rehearsals were held at two alternate locations, South Atlanta High School and Fort Gillem Army Post, during periods when Olympic Stadium was not available. These facilities provided easy access and excellent security.

The first rehearsals were held in the school gymnasium, where choreographers taught the cast dance steps and movements. After several practices, the rehearsal group was transferred to a field similar in size to the one in Olympic Stadium, and each cast member was assigned their position on the field. The basic steps, positioning, and movement were built upon at each rehearsal, until each cast member knew the entire routine. Fortunately, Atlanta enjoyed good weather in the months leading to the Games, so the rain dates built into the schedule were seldom needed.

On 15 July 1996, the first full dress rehearsal occurred at Olympic Stadium. Featured star performers participated, and final costumes were selected. This was the first full run of the show in its performing venue, and because of excellent preparation, there were few

top: Learning to use many of the props, such as this four-drum unit used in the welcoming segment of the Opening Ceremony, required extensive practice.

bottom: Stars performing at the ceremonies, like Stevie Wonder, rehearsed with the volunteer cast members.

FRANK DASPIT • TAMARA E DASSO • GUILLAUME D'ASSY • AIZAD DASTI • SALMAN DASTI • KATHERINE S DATER • NILANJAN DATTA • MARY T DAUBE RN • THOMAS E DAUCH • DESHA DAUCHAN • ANN M DAUFFENBACH • AVIS G DAUGHARTY • HARRY DAUGHARTY • EDWARD D DAUGHERTY • EDWARD L DAUGHERTY • JEFFREY A DAUGHERTY • KEVIN DAUGHERTY • MARLENE M DAUGHERTY • MARLYS B DAUGHERTY • CLAYTON L DAUGHTREY • BOBBIE R DAUGHTRY • TODD DAUGHTRY • FREDDIE M DAUM • LAWRENCE F DAUM • MARIE DAUM • NANCY L DAUM • HAROLD C DAUME III pauses in the show's progress. The second and final full dress rehearsal was on 17 July 1996. ACOG staff and volunteers were invited to this rehearsal in appreciation of their work. ACOG President and CEO Billy Payne thanked all the people in the audience for their hard work and dedication.

Rehearsals for the Closing Ceremony were more difficult. Many of the individual elements had to hold rehearsals in separate facilities. Several complete technical rehearsals took place, but because access to the stadium was limited during the Games, a full dress rehearsal was not possible until the day of the show.

CONCLUSIONS AND RECOMMENDATIONS

Because of their magnitude, visibility, and importance to the Olympic Games, Opening and Closing Ceremonies require substantial attention from the organizing committee. It is important that an organizing committee assess and express the themes and concepts for the ceremonies carefully, and then develop a creative plan capable of communicating these themes and concepts to both a stadium audience and a worldwide television audience. Also, the large number of participants and limited access to the performing venue requires a massive scheduling and coordination effort to ensure that the ceremonies will proceed smoothly.

In Atlanta, 20 stars performed, 5 new songs were written, and 8 musical scores were composed. A volunteer cast of some 5,500, mostly from Atlanta and other parts of Georgia, performed in the Opening and Closing Ceremonies. An additional backstage crew of 2,100 volunteers and 650 field marshals helped make both shows possible.

Many challenges of a show of this importance require special attention:

■ Design the ceremonies venue in collaboration with the ceremonies production team. Many of the ceremonies' creative elements would not have been possible without this collaboration. It is also helpful to have a model of the site available at all creative meetings to help design and structure the ceremonies' individual elements.

■ Atlanta's contract with the IOC to host the Centennial Olympic Games contained elements that limited the ceremonies' creative development. Contractual issues involving the ownership of residual rights of individual star performers and musicians arose. All of the performance artists considered for the program would not agree to release their rights. It took more than a year of contract negotiations to satisfy all parties involved.

■ Finalize the creative elements of the ceremonies at least one year in advance to allow ample time for refining technical operations.

■ Although Atlanta's rehearsal schedule was sufficient, it was interrupted by sporting test events held in the stadium prior to the Games. Future organizing committees should schedule test events earlier to avoid similar problems.

Security

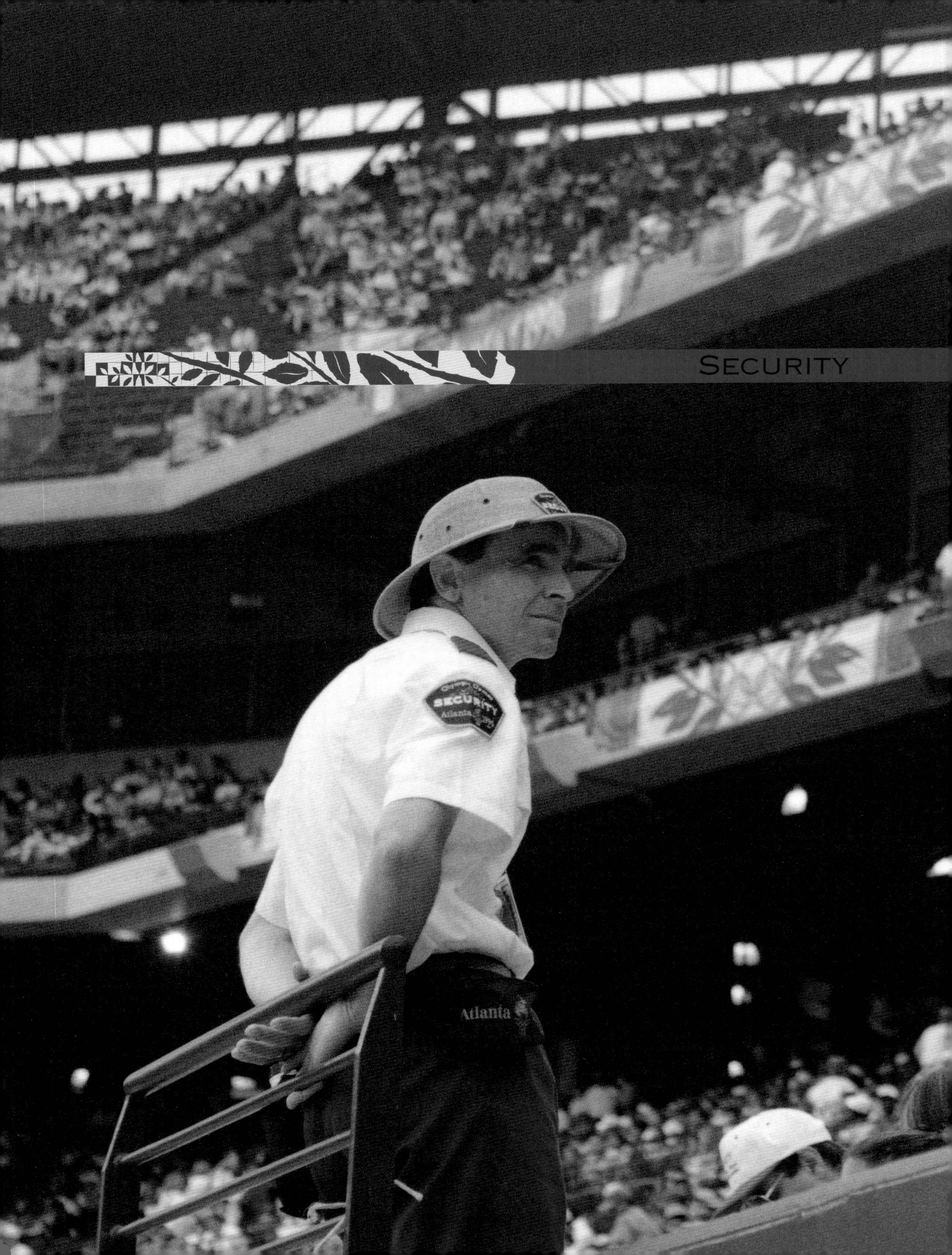

Chapter Twenty
Security

OVERVIEW—The mission of ACOG's Security Department was to coordinate the various police and security forces necessary to provide a protected environment in which all Olympic constituents could prepare for and enjoy the 1996 Games. Unlike other countries, the US does not have a single national police force, therefore, authority to enforce laws is granted to individual geographical and specialized jurisdictions.

ACOG was required to facilitate the coordination of the security function among more than 40 local, state, and federal law enforcement and public safety agencies, including police and military personnel; contracted security firms; and ACOG Security personnel.

ACOG Security had responsibility for communicating and facilitating the planning efforts of all law enforcement agencies that provided security for the Centennial Olympic Games. The complexities of such a task were recognized in the goals which guided the planning process:

■ to accomplish security in a manner that allows athletes to fulfill their Olympic dreams and spectators to enjoy the competitions;

■ to assemble a large professional force of Games-time security personnel that is well-trained, proactive, and highly visible, yet unobtrusive; and

■ to use technology to the greatest extent possible to facilitate rapid communications and consistency of methods and procedures.

The ACOG Security Department did not control the law enforcement agencies. Security roles and responsibilities were determined by law, tradition, and agreement. ACOG Security did control efforts to secure areas within ACOG-controlled venues, enforce ACOG policies and procedures within those facilities, and protect all ACOG assets.

The challenge of providing consistent security procedures for use by more than 40 different agencies at widely dispersed and very concentrated venues required a significant degree of planning and cooperation. Due to the number of venues and their locations, experienced professionals coordinated security operations at each venue and were primarily responsible for problem resolution at remote venues. Alternatively, the high concentration of venues in the Olympic Ring increased the requirement for local coordination and communication.

At each venue, one law enforcement agency had designated jurisdiction. Law enforcement, which encompasses all agencies authorized to enforce current statutory obligations at local, state, and federal levels, was responsible for duties such as making arrests, conducting criminal investigations, showing a uniformed presence, and providing dignitary protection and emergency response capability.

ACOG's Security Department also managed access control, which ensured that individuals had the proper accreditation or ticket and/or that their names appeared on an authorizing list before admittance, and asset protection, which involved grounds surveillance and control of materials moving into and out of designated areas.

ORGANIZATION

Recognizing the magnitude of the preparations necessary to secure the Games, ACOG organized a task force—the Olympic Security Support Group (OSSG)—in 1991 to develop the plan for a coordinated security effort among all law enforcement agencies and jurisdictions. The IOC delegate for security assisted in the planning process, providing the unique insight and experience gained from security planning for numerous other Olympic Games. In March 1993, an individual with extensive prior Olympic and special event security experience was appointed director of ACOG Security, and Security moved from Operations to its own independent department.

The Security Department was organized along functional and geographic lines. Responsibility for managing security operations extended from the director, through the responsible deputy director, to the appropriate venue security manager (VSM). Nine deputy directors and executive managers reported to the director. Three of them supervised competition venues based on location—urban, suburban, and remote; the other six divided responsibility for noncompetition venues, sites, and facilities, the management of administrative support and liaison personnel.

A VSM at each venue or other major site was responsible for managing Security operations. Groups of two or more contiguous venues, which shared common challenges due to their close proximity, were known as clusters, and security was managed by a single VSM designated as the cluster manager. If problems involving personnel or other resources arose at one of the venues, the cluster manager attempted to solve the problem with cluster resources prior to seeking additional resources.

While Security had a wide range of tasks and responsibilities, the following were the most critical.

- protecting athletes at the venues, villages, and training sites and while they were in transit between those locations
- protecting all Olympic venues, sites, and facilities, and all ACOG property and assets
- protecting designated ACOG and IOC officials
- coordinating all planning and security operations with law enforcement and other public safety agencies
- carefully considering and developing a plan for staffing, recruiting, selecting, training, scheduling, uniforming, and managing a security force of nearly 17,000 persons
- coordinating the integration and utilization of military personnel provided by the US Department of Defense
- using the most sophisticated technology available to establish consistency in access control and to provide other critical support
- securing sponsorships and suppliers of personnel, equipment, and technology to support the mission
- performing background screening of persons prior to their accreditation
- coordinating and supervising security planning for the four cities hosting preliminary football competitions: Miami and Orlando, Florida; Birmingham, Alabama; and Washington, DC
- providing air transport for ACOG and IOC officials and official Olympic broadcasters

Security Personnel

The importance of having a well-trained, professional force was paramount to the success of ACOG Security's mission. Having experienced, professional security managers was also critical to successfully integrating ACOG's plans with those of law enforcement agencies, and to decentralizing venue operations. The limited number of local law enforcement officers available for Olympic Games assignments required ACOG to recruit a large security force. To achieve the desired degree of professionalism in the security force, recruiting efforts extended nationally and internationally.

Five different types of security personnel—ACOG, military, Security Team Program (STP), access control (volunteers), and private (contract) security—comprised the Games security force.

ACOG Personnel. ACOG staff members included the executive management staff, VSMs and assistant VSMs, and the administrative support and liaison personnel. While this group numbered 275 during Games-time, two-thirds were hired during the three months preceding the Games. The enormous growth during this short period challenged staff administration and training.

People who comprised the core of the Security Department were experienced professionals, the majority of whom came to ACOG from successful careers in law enforcement, the military, or private security.

Military Personnel. ACOG Security also benefited from the assignment of military personnel to assist the Olympic organizing and security effort. Military personnel staffed a total of 3,525 positions; however, because most were National Guard or Reserve personnel fulfilling their yearly two-week training requirement, approximately 10,000 people actually participated in staffing the positions. A military venue officer (MVO) was assigned to each venue or other facility where military personnel were deployed to serve as the liaison between the military and ACOG Security.

Unarmed personnel performed venue interior and perimeter security, asset protection, and sanitization and command center duties under the direction of ACOG Security personnel. While they were not permitted to perform tasks requiring them to deny, limit, control, search, or direct nonmilitary personnel, they worked within their guidelines and often assumed additional responsibilities when needed.

Their military discipline and dependability were a significant factor in the overall success of Security operations.

Security Team Program Personnel. The STP was presented for the first time at the 1996 Games. This volunteer program, open to active and retired law enforcement officers from around the world, provided ACOG with a core group of experienced security professionals.

The participants, who were responsible for their own transportation to Atlanta, provided services at Olympic venues on a private security basis. These officers were not certified to enforce laws in the state of Georgia and therefore did not have peace officer status. Their security function was to enforce the ACOG policies and procedures of sanitization, asset protection, and internal venue security. ACOG provided these volunteers with training, uniforms, and room and board.

Access Control Personnel. Over 8,700 security positions were filled by professionals recruited as volunteers; people filling these positions were assigned almost exclusively to access control duties, excluding the late-night shift of 2400–0800.

Finding the needed number of volunteers within the metropolitan-Atlanta area was a tremendous challenge. Several thousand people who applied for nonspecific volunteer opportunities were assigned to security positions. Substantial recruiting efforts resulted in the enlistment of volunteers from sponsor companies, businesses, schools, religious groups, existing volunteer groups, associations for retired people, fraternal and civic organizations, as well as hundreds of other individuals.

Private Security Personnel. As the official Olympic sponsor for protective services, Borg-Warner Protective Services was responsible for supplying over 2,000 unarmed private security officers on peak days. These officers were primarily assigned to access control duties, often during the critical 2400–0800 shift.

To meet this demand, Borg-Warner conducted an extensive recruiting effort in the

Security Team Program personnel were given gold security badges in addition to security uniforms.

Atlanta area. In addition, they deployed 1,000 college students from outside the Atlanta area, whom they housed in a local school dormitory.

Law Enforcement Personnel. Law enforcement agents from designated jurisdictions maintained a uniformed presence at each venue to provide an immediate response capability when police intervention was necessary and to supplement and support ACOG Security. The price for these services was negotiated with each agency and reimbursed by ACOG for services provided within ACOG facilities or in direct support of ACOG operations.

Training and Uniforming

Critical to accomplishing Security's mission was the recognition that many members of the security force would require extensive training. To handle this requirement, Security developed 12 separate classes, presenting a total of more than 163,000 hours of training.

All members of the security force received training appropriate to their positions and responsibilities. The initial basic course, designed for home study, enabled prospective security personnel to learn the basics of Olympic security at their own pace. Students studied a workbook supplemented by a one-hour videotape depicting both typical and potential situations. The course took an average of four hours to complete, and required that the student perform a self-test at the end of each chapter. New security personnel then received an intermediate training class. Security supervisors received an extra three-hour supervisor class that emphasized management skills.

Security personnel were given site-specific training prior to operations at their assigned site. This on-the-job training included classes on x-ray access control technology and communications, magnetometer programming and operation, and in-transit security. At least one trainer was available at each venue to conduct these classes.

Security designed and procured its own uniforms in collaboration with the sponsor uniform provider. Designing and producing the security uniform separately from other uniforms increased the visibility of security personnel.

The security uniform was distinctive and authoritative in appearance. It included dark green pants, a traditional white uniform shirt with epaulettes, a tan pith helmet, and black Reebok shoes. Patches on the shirt and hat identified the wearer as a member of the security force. STP members and the ACOG security managers also wore gold badges. The uniform was worn by all security personnel except military personnel, who wore their service uniforms.

OPERATIONS PLANNING

ACOG Security was responsible for providing 24-hour security at all ACOG venues, sites, and facilities. ACOG assumed responsibility for security when it received exclusive use of a facility, and maintained an appropriate level of security through the assembly, competition, and recovery periods. The primary focus during assembly and recovery was the protection of ACOG assets. During the competition period, focus shifted to access control and communication with law enforcement for safety, although asset protection remained a priority.

Operational Cornerstones

The gathering and dissemination of intelligence information, the prevention of disruptive activities, and the ability to respond to contingencies were the cornerstones of the ACOG Security operational philosophy and were encapsulated in the intelligence/prevention/emergency response model described below.

Intelligence. Under the direction of the Federal Bureau of Investigation (FBI), the Olympic intelligence center was responsible for the collection, analysis, and dissemination of all intelligence data related to the Olympic Games. The center served as a formal interface for the intelligence functions of the local, state, and federal agencies involved in Olympic security, and prepared daily threat assessments for dissemination to all agencies involved in Olympic security.

Prevention. The prevention strategy involved three elements. First, physical, electronic, and human countermeasures were designed and installed to protect Olympic facilities and personnel. Second, security personnel were made highly visible through distinctive uniforms and conspicuous deployment. Last, the media was used to publicize the far-ranging measures being taken to secure the Games. This public information campaign was patterned after a successful program used for the 1984 Olympic Games in Los Angeles.

Emergency Response. Planning and preparation were identified as essential prerequisites for an effective response capability. Standardized policy and procedure statements were developed to guide actions to be taken when certain predictable situations arose. Specific operations plans for each ACOG facility were developed to ensure that the unique challenges of each location were considered and addressed. Law enforcement, with other agencies sharing responsibility, participated in this planning process, so agreement regarding individual roles, responsibilities, and responses was reached long before Games-time.

After the plans, policies, and procedures were developed, ACOG Security personnel were trained not only to perform their daily responsibilities, but also to respond to a wide variety of emergencies and contingencies. Security and other involved law enforcement agencies participated in a number of mock exercises sponsored by the FBI. The exercises were conducted to test and improve operational responses and emergency capabilities.

At athlete Villages and other high-security areas, counterassault teams (SWAT teams specifically trained for repelling any criminal or terrorist assault) were present at all times as an emergency response force.

Detailed Planning

A comprehensive security plan covering the precompetition, training, competition, and postcompetition phases was developed for each venue. Each plan included a CAD drawing and detailed description of the site, sport and venue schedules, command and control procedures, staffing needs, job descriptions, equipment needs, training information, ACOG policies and procedures, post orders, and policies and procedures for access control, accreditation, sanitization, and other Security functions.

The tasks to be performed were defined, as well as when and where they needed to be performed and the number of personnel required to perform them. The plan also indicated which security force constituent group(s) should perform each task (i.e., regular staff, military, volunteers, STP, or private security officers) and where law enforcement personnel would be deployed.

A contingency plan was developed in case of a staffing shortage. Each position was prioritized, so the most critical could be filled first.

ACOG Security developed standardized policies and procedures to guide what action should be taken in certain situations. These policies and procedures were integrated with those of law enforcement to ensure consistency. Olympic test events, held at every venue, provided an opportunity to test each security plan so refinements could be made where necessary before Games-time.

Games-Time Command and Control

ACOG Security was organized as a Games-time command and control center to facilitate a smooth transition from the planning stage to the operational phase. Prior to Games-time, the VSMs worked closely with their immediate supervisors to develop their venue security plans and resolve any problems and issues that arose. However, at Games-time, VSMs had much greater authority under the management by exception principle, which required that issues be resolved at the lowest level possible.

All VSMs were expected to resolve situations and problems at their venues by utilizing resources available either at that venue, or, if the venue was part of a cluster, within the cluster. Requests for intervention or resources were referred to the command center when a situation was beyond the capability of the VSM or the venue team. This concept was adopted for two reasons. First, the sheer number of incidents that could occur simultaneously during the Games would make a centralized command structure inefficient. Second, the amount of people and traffic involved in Olympic activities would make it extremely difficult to move additional resources to venues in time to affect problematic situations.

As part of the Games-time management strategy, the Security executive managers responsible for supervising the urban, suburban, and remote venues were deployed in the field. Their duties were to conduct on-site inspections, participate in high-level issue resolution, and respond to requests from VSMs. The domain of their duties allowed them to be available when needed and to identify problems.

To address exigent circumstances, a small cadre of personnel with expertise in access control, crowd management, and communications formed a response team to be dispatched to venues or other facilities if immediate assistance was required.

Approximately 150 members of the ACOG Security force were assigned as a reserve force contingency response to staffing shortages. This group, composed primarily of volunteer federal employees recruited through a program created by US Vice President Al Gore, assembled at ACOG headquarters and were deployed to locations with critical staffing needs.

Venue Command and Control. Each VSM was responsible for communicating venue security operations in collaboration with the law enforcement agency assigned to the venue. The VSM had authority only over ACOG Security staff, STP members, and private security guards. The VSMs coordinated activities with the military venue officer (MVO) and law enforcement commanders who oversaw venue law enforcement personnel.

Security operated a security command center (SCC) at each of the competition and noncom-

petition venues, athlete Villages, and functional sites. These SCCs were the nerve centers for all security operations and provided continuous security supervision and administration. Each SCC was designed and staffed in accordance with a standard plan scaled to the size of the venue. The SCCs were equipped with a variety of communications equipment and facilities to monitor intrusion alarms as well as the venue closed-circuit television (CCTV) cameras and commercial television feeds.

Security command centers at each venue provided continuous security surveillance, supervision, and administration.

ACOG Security and venue law enforcement personnel, stationed together in each SCC, maintained a clear delineation of authority and responsibility, which allowed for instantaneous communication and quick decision making.

Each venue also had a venue command center (VCC) operated by the Venue Management Department and staffed by representatives from all ACOG functional areas assigned to the venue. This concept allowed expedient communication and coordination between members of the venue team. The SCC coordinated with the VCC.

ACOG Security Command and Control Network. The SCCs were linked together through a central ACOG Security operations center (ASOC) located at ACOG headquarters. The ASOC operated continuously from two weeks before Games-time to when the Atlanta Olympic Village closed, three days after competition ended.

The ASOC's primary purpose was to serve as a coordination center for all ACOG Security activities with a deputy director of Security always on duty and ready to assume command if an emergency situation arose. A number of military personnel and ACOG Security personnel were assigned to the center during the Games. The ASOC monitored all activities occurring at each venue and facility, communicated pertinent situation reports to senior management, and responded to requests for assistance when problems could not be resolved at the venue level.

The ASOC and the SCCs were linked together by radio, facsimile, telephone, and the incident tracking and reporting system (ITS), developed by IBM and Lotus Notes, and installed at the ASOC and at the SCCs in all 31 competition venues. The system allowed each SCC to enter, prioritize, and monitor to completion all incidents that occurred at the venue.

Any occurrence, decision, or observation that directly related to the security of the venue could be entered into the ITS. A "quick step" feature allowed access to the policy and procedure that applied to a particular situation, thus providing guidance on handling an incident.

Because the ASOC monitored the ITS for all venues, it was able to stay abreast of the status of each venue on a real-time basis. In addition, the ITS provided a permanent and readily accessible means to store venue information and produce management reports. A separate but identical system was also used by law enforcement to track law enforcement incidents, and to monitor the ACOG ITS.

The ASOC also served as Security's contact with the ACOG main operations center (MOC) and the law enforcement joint coordination center, which was staffed with representatives from the primary law enforcement agencies involved in Olympic security and served as a conduit for information sharing. ACOG Security staff were assigned to both centers.

These three centers united the components of ACOG, ACOG Security, and the law enforcement community, and provided a mechanism for processing information and handling requests for service not handled at the venue level. These interfaces allowed pertinent information to flow throughout ACOG and to and from the law enforcement community.

Also, because all ACOG functional areas were represented in the MOC, problems that involved several areas could be resolved quickly.

AREAS OF OPERATIONS

Security operated in four general areas: Villages, competition venues, noncompetition venues, and special programs. Factors such as apparent risk, venue configuration, size, location, and other considerations were taken into account to develop specific categories with specific minimum standards of security for each. For example, at some venues, standards required that everyone entering be screened through magnetometers. At others, hand-held magnetometers were used to detect metal objects. These systems managed resources while providing security.

Olympic Villages

Security in athlete Villages was a primary concern. Village security entailed the following components: double perimeter fencing, electronic intrusion detection systems, internal and external access control, high grounds surveillance, enhanced security for high-risk delegations, counterassault teams, bus and vehicle screening, and vehicle barriers. ACOG Security and law enforcement agencies coordinated response procedures for a spectrum of incidents ranging from criminal activity to emergency contingencies.

Risk assessments were carefully evaluated in order to plan athlete Village housing assignments. Security and Olympic Village staff minimized potential danger to certain high-risk delegations by placing them in strategically advantageous locations.

Atlanta Olympic Village. Securing the largest Olympic Village in history was an enormous task. The effort was supported by the most technologically advanced tools and a large contingent of security personnel. A director of Village security implemented access control, threat assessment and deployment, command post coordination, and security coordination.

Security in the Village was provided by an integrated force consisting of members from all constituents of ACOG Security and members of the State Olympic Law Enforcement Command (SOLEC), a management unit established by the governor of Georgia to incorporate and operate all state law enforcement personnel and resources deployed for the Games. Each group had specific roles, but all were managed from a common command center. This team was able to achieve the highest level of security without major incident or interference in the athletes' experience.

Security was responsible for operating all access control points, with assistance from the US Border Patrol. Members of SOLEC, assisted by military personnel, controlled the double perimeter fence. Military personnel also staffed posts in the command center, and secured and monitored the vast tunnel system traversing the campus.

Security operations at the Village required extensive planning. Due to the configuration and topography of the Village site, a large number of CCTV cameras and security officers were required to secure the area.

The Village security sweep was conducted from 1–5 July, requiring commencement of access control procedures, the locking of perimeter fence gates, and the implementation of the day pass system for all unaccredited persons.

The Village had two distinct parts: the international zone and five residential zones, each supplied with an appropriate level of external and internal security. These zones were delineated by security fences. Security staff at all internal access points checked accreditation badges as people moved from one zone to another. Biometric identification was also utilized, for the first time in Olympic history, to control access to the residential zones. The system relied on reading the unique structural characteristics of an individual's hand to grant or deny access. The hand geometry system was used in addition to a radio frequency badge that enabled quick and accurate retrieval of the individual's coded hand geometry description. This system allowed properly accredited people to enter such areas without having to manually enter a personal identification number each time they required access. Further, by automating access control verification, reliance on the discretion of access control personnel was minimized, thereby greatly improving security.

A large scientific research facility containing some toxic chemicals and a nuclear reactor on the Georgia Institute of Technology campus

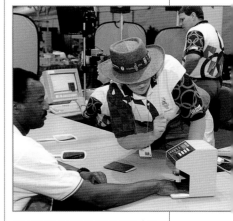

Hand geometry was used to regulate access into the residential zone of the Olympic Village.

had to be secured to an extremely high degree. The entire area was separated from the main Village by an enclosed fence and those requiring access were provided supplemental credentials that authorized entrance.

All materials entering the Village were required to be screened. The material transfer area (MTA) in the Village was the entry and exit point for all materials, packages, equipment, and other freight. The MTA received deliveries 24 hours daily, where they were sorted and inspected visually and electronically. Once

ACOG Security staff were required to search for prohibited items before permitting a spectator to enter a venue.

Prohibited Items
Alcohol, Coolers, Chests
Food & Beverages
Glass Bottles
Banners, Signs, Ball
Frisbees, Fireworks
Noise Makers
Pets, Strollers
Weapons
Illegal

cleared, the materials were taken through the security fence.

For special delivery of large-volume items such as food, delivery trucks were loaded and sealed in secure, off-site locations. These trucks could enter directly into the Village through a vehicle screening entry point called the salle port, adjacent to the MTA. Military security

personnel ensured the safety and security of all inbound Village supplies by visually inspecting and scanning delivery vehicles with a magnetometer. Only such sanitized vehicles could enter the Village.

No private vehicles were permitted within the perimeter of the Village unless they had a vehicle permit and entered through the salle port for inspection.

Outlying Olympic Villages. Some remote competition venues included an athlete Village. Because they were smaller than the main Village, they required less personnel and equipment to produce the same level of security. They did require extra fencing, lighting, and barricades, and adjustment for the difference in the physical layout of each site and area terrain.

Security at remote sites involved ACOG and a more extensive role of local law enforcement agencies. A deputy director for remote Villages provided coordination and direction and established standards for these Villages. Reporting directly to this director were venue managers stationed at each outlying site, who had been selected and trained by ACOG. Security personnel were provided by the law enforcement agencies that had jurisdiction over the venue site.

Venues

All competition venues received security personnel and resources most suitable to their location, configuration, traffic flow, and security risk potential. As with Village operations, venue security teams were comprised of law enforcement, military, ACOG Security, and private security personnel. All competition venues and venue clusters were surrounded with a single perimeter fence.

All urban competition venues were located within the 1.5 mi (2.4 km) radius of the Olympic Ring. Because of the need to coordinate resources in the area, Security operations for all competition and most noncompetition venues were coordinated from the shared security command centers at each of the three venue clusters in the Olympic Ring—the Olympic Center cluster, the Olympic Stadium cluster, and the Atlanta University cluster. The Olympic Center cluster included the downtown area, making traffic and crowd control an essential part of its security operations. The cluster command centers could relocate personnel and resources quickly in response to changing operational requirements.

The suburban competition venues were located within a 60 mi (96.6 km) radius outside the Olympic Ring, and offered a challenge because they tended to be isolated from other ACOG facilities. This required that they be self-sufficient in terms of security personnel, equipment, and problem-resolution capabilities.

All noncompetition venues had unique security requirements. Because of their critical Games support roles, some noncompetition venues were among the highest priority sites from a security perspective. Among these were the International Broadcast Center (IBC), the Main Press Center (MPC), the athlete bus system, and the Olympic Family Hotel.

International Broadcast Center. The IBC, located on three levels of the Georgia World Congress Center, was within the security perimeter established for the Olympic Center cluster. As it was utilized by 9,000 accredited members of world broadcast organizations, accreditation and access points specific to the IBC were established to ensure that only authorized persons entered the facility. Because of the amount of time needed to install and remove the associated technology, ACOG's exclusive use period encompassed 170 days. Daily security staffing levels ranged from 68 during the initial period to 384 during Games-time.

Main Press Center. The MPC, the primary base of operations for the accredited journalists and photographers of the international press

corps covering the Games, was located in non-contiguous space in the Inforum and Atlanta Apparel Mart buildings. Open 24 hours daily for a 31-day period, the MPC required the daily deployment of 600 security personnel. Both buildings that housed the center had large underground parking structures and businesses that were open to the public during the Olympic period; therefore, an extremely secure environment had to be maintained.

Athlete Bus System. The safe and expeditious movement of Olympic athletes and team

officials between Villages, venues, and practice sites was paramount, as Security regarded the time athletes were in transit as their greatest security risk. ACOG Security and law enforcement shared responsibility for this task.

Three hundred twenty buses transported athletes and team officials, including 37 teams designated as high-risk by the FBI, between their housing locations and competition and practice sites.

Each bus was completely sanitized and then retained in a secure holding area until dispatched on a transportation assignment. All

Spectators were required to pass through a security checkpoint before they were allowed to enter a venue.

buses transporting athletes were driven by military personnel to ensure an appropriate reaction in a crisis situation. After athletes and team officials entered the bus, it traveled on a predetermined secured route to its destination. The Georgia State Patrol (GSP) maintained security on these routes, using roving patrol units. The US Marshals Service provided over 50 armed marshals to serve as protective details on the buses for the high-risk teams. Security for these teams was supplemented by law enforcement vehicles that escorted the buses.

Olympic Family Hotel. The Olympic Family Hotel, which provided lodging for approximately 4,000 Olympic Family members during the Games and was also the site of numerous meetings, receptions, and other special events, required the deployment of 360 security personnel each day during the Games. Because it shared an underground parking lot with two adjoining business towers, all vehicles entering the parking facility were sanitized. Strict access control methodology was implemented via a holographic sticker attached to the accreditation badge and rigid guest registration procedures.

Special Programs

Security supported a number of ancillary programs, special events, and support functions. Most significant among these were the Centennial Olympic Park, the Cultural Olympiad, the Olympic Torch Relay, background screening, and aviation.

Centennial Olympic Park. From its inception, the Centennial Olympic Park was intended to be a public gathering spot where all people could enjoy the Olympic experience and festivities without needing to purchase a ticket. More than 5.5 million people visited the park during the competition period. Because it was open to the public, accreditation badges were not required for admittance, and park

visitors were not screened for prohibited items prior to entry. Security was coordinated by ACOG Security, with law enforcement services provided by SOLEC.

Shortly after midnight on the morning of 27 July, a security guard spotted an unattended bag at the base of a sound and light tower and summoned police to evaluate it. Bomb squad officers who examined the bag saw what appeared to be three pipe bombs inside and began to move people away from the area. The device exploded at approximately 0125, before the site could fully be evacuated. Emergency personnel and police responded to the explosion by providing medical care and closing the park.

After the bombing, the FBI assumed control of the investigation and coordination efforts with other law enforcement agencies. Additional SOLEC personnel and members of the US Border Patrol were assigned to access control duties. After the park was reopened to the public, they searched all bags brought into Centennial Olympic Park, and conducted a visual inspection of people for prohibited items as they passed through entry points.

The Cultural Olympiad. The Cultural Olympiad's four-year, multidisciplinary arts program consisted of four separate arts festivals from 1993–1995 and culminated with the summer-long 1996 Olympic Arts Festival (OAF). The OAF, with its multiple locations, diverse environments, large numbers of participating organizations, and many unexpected receptions and events, was challenging to secure. With the limitation on available resources, all personnel and technology available at each site had to be utilized. This often required supplementing existing security with off-duty law enforcement personnel. During the operating period of 24 May to 9 August, approximately 98 security personnel provided security for these events.

Olympic Torch Relay. Security for the Olympic Torch Relay was provided by the GSP and supported by the FBI, the US Secret Service, and ACOG Security. Safety personnel from the state of Georgia escorted the torch along its entire route across the US.

Background Screening. It is standard practice to require background security checks for everyone associated with staging Olympic events. This is considered essential to providing a secure environment for the Games.

The FBI and the Georgia Bureau of Investigation (GBI) created a special system for processing Games-related background checks that queried the following state and federal databases:

- Georgia Crime Information Center criminal history information files;
- GBI intelligence files;
- GSP driver history records;
- FBI National Crime Information Center criminal history information files;
- FBI intelligence files and case files;
- US Secret Service;
- US Department of State; and
- US Immigration and Naturalization Service.

All ACOG and ACOP employees, loaned and VIK employees, subcontract employees, volunteers, vendors and subcontractors requiring access to ACOG facilities, and construction employees with access to sensitive information were subjected to the screening process. Others were exempted from the process, such as certain Olympic Family groups, law enforcement personnel, and all military personnel except the National Guard and Reserves. Individuals subjected to the process were required to execute a waiver of confidentiality, or not be considered for employment and other Games affiliation. Throughout the life of the program, 191,975 individuals and some 313,000 background checks by name were processed through this system. If name checks revealed inconclusive information, a fingerprint background check was conducted.

Aviation. ACOG Security managed ACOG's aviation operation. Security coordinated logistical support in planning efforts for missions

such as landing zones at remote venues, and it coordinated all efforts with the Federal Aviation Administration (FAA), including designations on restricted air space. It provided services to Atlanta Olympic Broadcasting (AOB) and NBC broadcast operations, executive and VIP transport, and emergency movement of equipment and key staff members.

Security was selected to manage the aviation operation because of its responsibility for coordinating with the FAA. The function of Security and aviation operations also overlapped because helicopters were used for surveillance and transportation of certain officials. In accordance with the sponsorship agreement, Textron, Inc., supplied ACOG with four fixed-wing airplanes and 17 helicopters on a VIK basis. This included eight helicopters for AOB, five helicopters for NBC, three VIP and executive helicopters, and two reserve helicopters. Furthermore, two blimps were provided by the Goodyear Tire and Rubber Company as camera/broadcast platforms.

Aviation operations were administered by ACOG's flight operations center at DeKalb Peachtree Airport. The flight operations center was staffed by an operations manager and two assistant operations managers, all volunteers.

CONCLUSIONS AND RECOMMENDATIONS

ACOG was required to facilitate the coordination of the security function among more than 40 local, state, and federal law enforcement and public safety agencies, including police and military personnel, contracted security firms, and ACOG Security personnel. Training qualified personnel, utilizing innovative technology, and establishing effective communication among functional areas were essential to

arrange and ensure adequate security for the largest peacetime gathering in history.

The following four factors are central to planning a successful security operation for a large event: intelligence gathering; prevention; contingency planning; and management by exception.

The following elements should be incorporated as fundamental components of any event security plan:

■ Integrate committed multi-agency plans early and provide clear delineation and documentation of jurisdiction, roles, and responsibilities of the organizing committee's security department versus law enforcement and public safety agencies.

■ Define technological requirements carefully and coordinate with technological experts early in the planning process.

■ Train security members to work in a Games environment by cultivating sensitivity to cultural differences.

■ Develop a standard personnel plan for each site based upon venue design and crowd management procedures. All venues should be kept at the same level of protection.

■ Train all security personnel extensively concerning the accreditation system and its various subsystems.

■ Perform careful evaluations of job requirements before assigning Games staff to perform asset or entry control functions, and provide supervisory personnel for conflict resolution.

Chapter Twenty-One
Sports

OVERVIEW—The responsibilities of Olympic organizing committees are extensive, but the ultimate goal is staging the sports competitions. Five years before the Games began, ACOG established the Sports Department to plan, organize, and manage the best sports competitions in Olympic history. ACOG also wanted to leave a legacy for amateur sports, especially those included in the programme of the Olympic Games.

To ensure that the Olympic Games fostered a truly world-class level of competition and provided playing conditions that were fair and free of distractions, the Sports Department served as an advocate for the interests of athletes, IFs, and officials. The mission of the Sports Department included the following objectives:

■ meet or exceed the sports requirements of the IOC, the USOC, and the IFs;

■ schedule competition and create an environment that would optimize the athletes' performances and the spectators' experiences, in keeping with ACOG's resources and logistical plans;

■ stage Olympic sports events in a way that would promote the growth and development of the sports programs after the Games;

■ identify and arrange for pre-Olympic training and acclimation facilities that showcased Atlanta, the state of Georgia, and the Southeast as locales for world-class sports competitions;

■ provide training facilities that would meet the requirements of the athletes, IFs, and technical delegates; and

■ assist in the preparation of nationally designated technical officials (judges, referees, and umpires).

In addition, the Sports Department was responsible for providing guidance to all other ACOG departments and programs on sports requirements and matters affecting the athletes, IFs, and officials. The department's duties also included selecting and coordinating the Athletes Advisory Committee and procuring and disposing of the sports equipment required for the competitions.

The Programme of the Olympic Games

The programme for the 1996 Olympic Games consisted of 26 sports, 37 disciplines, and 271 events in which more than 1,860 medals were awarded. For this Olympiad, the IOC decided not to include exhibition or demonstration sports.

Approximately 3,700 women participated in the Centennial Olympic Games, representing the largest number of women ever to compete in Olympic medal competition.

For the first time, women's softball and men's and women's mountain bike racing and beach volleyball were added to the sports programme. In addition, ACOG included the slalom discipline as part of the sport of canoe/kayak. This was the third appearance of this discipline in an Olympic Games, but the first time it was held at a natural site.

Some competitions were restructured after 1992, and certain events were added in 16 sports and disciplines. Among the events that were added were the women's triple jump in athletics, badminton mixed doubles, women's football, and the women's 4 x 200 m freestyle relay in swimming.

ORGANIZATION

At its creation in early 1991, the Sports Department consisted of a senior vice president, a vice president, an assistant, and two full-time volunteers. Initially, the Sports Department focused on developing relationships with the IFs and obtaining information about the technical requirements of the competitions. This information aided the Sports Department in developing the specifications for both adapting existing venues and constructing new venues. In 1991, it became apparent that several venues proposed in the Bid would have to be changed. Specifically, this involved moving the tennis venue because of neighborhood concerns, moving the canoe/kayak and rowing course due to environmental and construction concerns, and establishing permanent equestrian and shooting venues as opposed to the temporary facilities originally proposed.

The Sports Department led the effort to locate new venues for these sports and obtain the approval of the respective IFs for the venue changes. As a result of these efforts, it was agreed that a new tennis facility would be constructed at Stone Mountain Park; a canoe/kayak and rowing course and facilities would be constructed on Lake Lanier, near Gainesville, Georgia; a major equestrian complex would be constructed in Conyers, Georgia, and a world-class shooting facility would be constructed at Wolf Creek in Fulton County. These changes resulted in the establishment of better venues than had been originally proposed and also ensured that a physical legacy would remain for each sport following the Olympic Games.

In early 1992, three planning managers and two volunteers were added to the Sports Department, making a total of 10 staff members as the Barcelona Games approached. In order to gain as much information and experience as possible concerning the sports competitions, ACOG engaged several sports experts to attend the Barcelona Games to observe the competition venues and consult with the competition and venue management staffs. Each observer then submitted a written report on his or her sport and participated in debriefings with appropriate members of the ACOG staff.

Following the Barcelona Games, the senior vice president of Sports was elected president of the USOC and left ACOG. The Sports Department then became part of the International Relations Department, reporting directly to the managing director of International Relations, and a director of Sports was hired in 1993.

In addition to observation of the Barcelona Games, a primary focus of the Sports Department in 1992 was the completion of venue agreements, relocation of venues where necessary, and the approval of additions to the sports programme that required the verification and selection of additional venues. This process continued throughout 1993–1994.

The most difficult negotiations involved Olympic Stadium. Because Atlanta had no identifiable need for a new stadium of this size, it was determined during the Bid process to construct a stadium that could be converted after the Games into a new stadium for the Atlanta Braves major league baseball team. It was anticipated that this stadium would be located adjacent to the existing Atlanta–Fulton County Stadium. This plan required the review and approval of the city of Atlanta, Fulton County, the Atlanta–Fulton County Recreation Authority, the Atlanta Braves, and the local neighborhoods, which insisted that the construction of

SR • CYRIL DE LOPEZ • GREGORY J DE LUCCA • ANTHONY L DE MAIO • KATHLEEN DE MARCO • MICHAEL DE MAURO • BENJAMIN DE MAYO • CLAUDIA P DE MAYO • ANA M DE MELLO • NATIVIDAD A DE MESA • VALERIE DE NAEYER • AMY L DE NARDO • ANN M DE NARDO • FLORENCE DE NAVACELLE • DUSTIN JAMES DE NUNZIO • DAVID DE PALMA • SUSAN DE PALMA • MARIA F DE POORTER • CLARICE DE PROSPERO • EDITH M DE REYS • DANIEL L DE RIEMER • CRISTIANNE F DE ROSE • EDUARDO R DE ROSE • MICHAEL D DE ROSE • INGRID DE SAINT-GEORGES • JOSEPH G DE SANTIS •

381

a new stadium would lead to the ultimate demolition of the existing stadium. Further approval was also required from the International Amateur Athletic Federation (IAAF). All negotiations were completed, and the groundbreaking was held in June 1993.

As planning progressed, Sports became a separate department, and its director assumed the function of managing director of Sports. Initially, the department was divided into two distinct areas, the Sports Competition Planning division, which coordinated information and developed specific operating plans for the competitions, and the Sports Logistics division, which managed the competition logistics needed to support each sport. Later, a Sports Operations division was added that supported the entire Sports Department in administrative, budget, and staff needs and developed the Games-time program for results criteria and competition production. While each division within Sports had distinct functional responsibilities, each had the ultimate goal of supporting the sports competition programme. The coordination and interaction among these divisions ensured the acclaimed success of the competitions and individual athletes in the 1996 Olympic Games.

SPORTS COMPETITION PLANNING

A director of Sports Competition Planning was named and five sports planning managers (SPMs) were hired, each responsible for several sports. The assignments given to the SPMs were based on the locations of the sports and their proximity to each other.

To assist the SPMs, each sport's national governing body (NGB) in the US was requested to submit a recommendation for an expert at the Olympic level to advise the SPMs. By May 1993, there was one advisor for each sport. The goal was to secure the best experts in each sport as volunteer advisors until competition managers for each sport could be hired. The sports advisors met quarterly with the corresponding SPMs. In the early stages of planning, these advisors played a significant role in the development of construction plans for each venue, a master schedule of projects, and a critical generic competition management plan for all competitions. The advisor program continued throughout 1993 and part of 1994.

Approximately six months were required to develop and verify the Competition Management Plan, incorporating the sports event management concept of having one competition manager per sport. If the sport competition required a second venue, a deputy competition manager would assume responsibility of the second venue and report to the competition manager.

Assistant competition managers were named for each sport for the areas of administration, implementation, results, and training sites. The assistant competition manager in charge of administration managed administrative support, athlete services, and competition secretariat. The assistant competition manager in charge of implementation organized the sport's competition officials, competition production, field of play, results/timing/scoring, and sports equipment.

To identify potential competition managers for each sport, recommendations were requested from the IFs and NGBs. Qualified candidates included Olympians and former athletes with known sports administration experience. The competition managers eventually selected included Olympians and former athletes as well as other professionals renowned in their respective sports.

Depending on the demands of the sport, managers started either full-time or part-time beginning in January 1994. Those managers hired part-time were present in Atlanta for a minimum of two days a month. SPMs continued to work with both full-time and part-time competition managers throughout 1994. In January 1995, competition managers for all sports became full-time and included all former SPMs. These competition managers began to develop the competition management manuals. The format for the manuals was developed by Sports in September 1994, with completion scheduled for July 1995.

Each competition manual included the detailed competition activity schedule (DCAS), which outlined by hour and by minute the activities of competition management in each venue. This DCAS was provided to Venue Management to create the venue preparation schedule for Games operations.

Other areas addressed in the manuals included job descriptions, staff numbers and schedule, history of the sport, list of sports equipment, and lists of furniture, fixtures, and other equipment needed for that competition.

Technical Delegates

As outlined in the *Olympic Charter*, each IF appointed technical delegates (TDs) to coordinate competition planning operations with each respective Sports competition management team. TDs also scheduled all equipment requirements with Sports Logistics. A total of 58 TDs worked in the 26 sports areas.

The number of TDs varied according to the sport. For example, badminton had one TD, while aquatics had four. Football did not designate any TDs prior to the Atlanta Games, as the International Association Football Federation (FIFA) preferred to have its secretary-general coordinate all competition-related activities before the Games.

ACOG was financially responsible for two official visits by these TDs prior to the Games for coordination of venue construction plans and for consultations with competition managers and other functional areas on the technical

aspects of the competitions and fields of play. Additional visits by the TDs were scheduled as requested.

After the competition sites were approved, the TDs began focusing on aspects of the fields of play. These aspects included competition schedules, layout of the field of play, approval of training sites, selection of equipment, approval of the sports explanatory books, construction of IF offices at the venues, approval of technical installations for establishing results, and the selection of international officials, judges, and referees.

ACOG was also responsible for transporting TDs to Atlanta at least five days prior to the start of the first event in their sport to enable them to assist with any arrangements regarding athlete entries. All reasonable expenses incurred by the TDs during their stay, including board and lodging, were ACOG's responsibility. The TDs were housed in designated IF hotels. In the cases of those sports in which the TDs were also presidents or secretaries-general, they stayed in the Olympic Family Hotel.

Competition Officials

The number of international competition officials for each federation was determined by the IF with the assistance of the IOC's director of sports, who acted as a coordinator and liaison between the IFs and ACOG. The list of competition officials was given to ACOG as a basic form from which to plan operational requirements. *(For numbers of international and national officials, refer to individual sports in Volume 2.)*

For the first time in the history of the Olympic Games, the organizing committee provided housing and meals for the more than 1,000 international competition officials. The Host City Contract, signed at the time the Games were awarded to Atlanta, stipulated this new obligation for the organizing committee.

There were many challenges connected with housing the international competition officials because of the contract's nonspecific language regarding the type of housing ACOG was expected to provide.

In agreements with the IFs, ACOG provided plans of appropriate housing for these officials similar to the officials' village in Barcelona. The plan called for all officials to be housed in double-occupancy, air-conditioned rooms in college residence halls on Atlanta campuses. However, many IFs and NOCs requested that competition officials be housed in hotels. As a compromise, accommodations in single or suite-style rooms were offered. In an attempt to provide enough of these single rooms for all competition officials, Sports contracted the campuses of Emory University and the Georgia Baptist College of Nursing as housing centers for officials of the Atlanta-based sports.

In order for future organizing committees to avoid similar problems regarding officials' housing, specific standards and guidelines should be provided by the IOC. The lack of guidance and support in this area was a distinct disadvantage to ACOG in preparing for the Games.

ACOG was responsible for all Games-time local transportation for international and national competition officials, including transportation from the Airport Welcome Center (AWC) to ACOG-sanctioned housing sites; transportation to clinics, training sessions, training sites, and competition venues; and transportation to the airport for departure.

Meal service for international and national competition officials included breakfast at a dining hall for those in residence halls and a daily food allowance of $30. For those B- or J-accredited competition officials residing in hotels, a daily food allowance of $38 was provided, although breakfast was not included.

Upon arrival at the AWC, ACOG provided each official with the following uniform package: one dress jacket, two golf shirts, one hat, two pairs of khaki pants (men) or two khaki skirts (women); two dress shirts (men) or two dress blouses (women); one tie (men) or one scarf (women); one belt; one pair of shoes; and three pairs of socks. Officials requiring sport-specific, field-of-play uniforms received them at that time as well.

International competition officials were eligible to receive one ticket to the Opening Ceremony and one ticket to the Closing Ceremony of the 1996 Olympic Games. Transportation was provided to and from these events from the officials' housing.

A sports information desk was located at each housing center to serve as a link between the officials and the competition managers. Messages and information were received and relayed to the appropriate persons by desk personnel. Dedicated telephone and telefax lines were available at each sports information desk. A message board was available for officials and their coordinators to post and receive messages. The sports information desks operated from 0500 to 0100 daily.

SPORTS LOGISTICS

The Sports Logistics division defined and delivered the necessary support required to execute the sports competition programme. The director of Sports Logistics was hired in December 1993. Areas managed by this division were IF Relations, the sports competition schedule, sports equipment, training sites, publications, inscriptions, and volunteers.

IF Relations

The supervision of each of the 26 sports of the 1996 Olympic Games was the responsibility of its corresponding IF. According to the *Olympic Charter*, each IF's role is to "assume responsibility for the technical control and direction of their sport at the Olympic Games" and to "establish and reinforce the rules concerning the practice of their respective sport and to ensure their application." Each federation's president, secretary general, or technical delegate was involved in the planning stages of their sport. *(For listings of the sports and their IFs, refer to Volume 3.)*

As suggested by the IOC, ACOG drafted memoranda of understanding (MOUs) to establish the essential parameters between the IFs and ACOG functional areas. The IOC felt that if the MOUs covered most functional areas early, the understanding of the respective roles would be enhanced, and fewer problems would arise during the planning process.

The following areas were among those outlined in each MOU: the number of athletes participating in each sport, coordination of entries, venue location, field of play, competition management, venue management technology requirements, competition officials, technical delegates, financial responsibilities, accommodations, transportation, accreditation, medical services, press and photographers, television, radio, and congresses.

The MOUs were designed to generate coordination between the IFs and the functional areas. They were useful references during subsequent sports competition planning; however, they attempted to address too many details too early in the planning process. It was projected that each would have addenda at various stages, but the amount of planning time required for documentation was prohibitive. The first MOU was signed in September 1993 and the last in January 1995. The IAAF did not sign an MOU.

For the IF offices at the venues, ACOG provided standard provisions including fixtures, furniture, and technology. The precedence for these standard provisions was derived from documents obtained from Barcelona's organizing committee. The IF rate card directory was created to offer additional furniture and technology items that the IFs requested.

The Sports Logistics manager (SLM) for IF Relations developed the rate card and the corresponding order process with the departments of Logistics, Accounting, Planning and Budget, Purchasing, and all other departments that published rate cards for their constituents. The SLM was responsible for the order process and the fulfillment, delivery, installation, and recovery of all items ordered from the rate card directory.

The rate card directory for the IFs was mailed in August 1995, with an order deadline of mid-October 1995. Ten of the 26 federations placed orders from the rate card directory by the order deadline. In addition, many IFs placed Games-time orders (after 1 March 1996), which were filled subject to availability.

Six IFs held congresses in Atlanta prior to the Games. During the congresses, the IFs typically conducted federation business, which, in some cases, included the election of officers and the passage of rules and regulations governing their sports. ACOG assisted in securing hotel accommodations, meeting spaces, and language services for these congresses.

Competition Schedule

The sports competition schedule was originally developed in late 1992, taking into account the following areas:

■ *rest*—sufficient time in the schedule to allow athletes to rest between sessions and recover from the effects of competition and heat;

■ *overall coordination of the 1996 Games*—balancing the level of activity throughout the Games to sustain the energy of spectators and television viewers;

■ *popularity of a sport*—planning the schedule so as to avoid an overlap of the more popular sport competitions and control the capacity of the venues;

■ *venue preparation*—sufficient time to empty, clean, and restock venues with food, merchandise, and general necessities for the spectators between sessions; and

The basketball draw was conducted to establish the match pairings for men's and women's competition.

■ AIMEE A DEBOYACE ■ RON F DEBRANSKI ■ ANITA L DEBRO ■ CAROLINE A DECAMINADA ■ FRANK B DECAMINADA ■ CAROLYN E DECAPRIO ■ JOAN B DECARIE ■ LEE A DECARLO ■ TERRI H DECARLO ■ JASON DECESARE ■ KIRTLAND A DECHERD ■ DEANA M DECK ■ JULIE J DECK ■ HOLLY A DECKEBACH ■ CASSANDRA T DECKER ■ DAVID M DECKER ■ DAVID R DECKER ■ DEEANNE R DECKER ■ ERILYNNE DECKER ■ SHANE DECKER ■ JILL S DECKMAN ■ SANDRA A DECKMAN ■ KRISTEL DECKX ■ FRANKLIN DECONINCK ■ VIDA R DEDINAS ■ KAREN L DEDO ■ KEVIN T DEE ■ HISHAM H DEEB ■ DONNA L DEEGAN

385

FIGURE 1:
SPORTS EQUIPMENT SUPPLIERS AND NUMBER OF TECHNICIANS PER SPORT

AB Finessa 10
yachting

Accusplit 4
athletics, wrestling

Adidas, Inc. 2
football, handball

**Adolph Keifer
& Associates** 18
swimming, water polo,
synchronized swimming,
diving

American Athletics, Inc. 33
artistic gymnastics,
rhythmic gymnastics

Astroturf 6
hockey

Atlanta Soft Spa 8
diving

B & K Rental 6
judo, weightlifting,
wrestling, synchronized
swimming, fencing

Beiter 1
archery

Brunswick 40
yachting, rowing,
canoe / kayak–sprint,
canoe / kayak–slalom

Cloudburst 4
athletics, hockey, football

Composite Engineering 2
canoe / kayak–sprint

Cool Concepts 7
equestrian

Easton 2
baseball

**Federal Sports
Technologies, Inc.** 10
judo

FITA 2
archery

Hydra Rib 10
basketball

JOOLA 2
table tennis

K1 Ergo 2
canoe / kayak–sprint

Kajakbyggeriet 2
canoe / kayak–sprint

Kookaburra 2
hockey

Leisure Health and Fitness 4
wrestling, boxing

Lower Brothers 5
tennis

Maple Leaf Press 1
archery

Mavic, Inc. 28
cycling

McKenzie Sports Products 5
archery

Mercury Marine Corp. 20
rowing,
canoe / kayak–sprint,
yachting

Mettler-Toledo, Inc. 30
diving, synchronized
swimming, water polo,
athletics, boxing,
canoe / kayak–sprint,
canoe / kayak–slalom,
rowing, equestrian,
artistic gymnastics,
rhythmic gymnastics, judo,
shooting, volleyball,
weightlifting, swimming,
yachting, wrestling

Mikasa, Inc. 6
volleyball, water polo

Mistral Sports Group 10
yachting

Mizuno, USA 16
baseball, rowing,
canoe / kayak–slalom,
diving, yachting, softball

Molten, Inc. 6
basketball

MONDO, S.p.A. 18
athletics, diving,
synchronized swimming,
water polo, swimming

Nagase Kenko 2
table tennis

Nittaku 2
table tennis

O'Jump 3
wrestling

Penn Racquet Sports, Inc. 2
tennis

Perry Sports 4
boxing

Pocock Manufacturing 7
rowing,
canoe / kayak–sprint

Robbins Sport Surfaces 12
basketball, handball,
volleyball, table tennis,
badminton,
rhythmic gymnastics

Senoh 12
indoor and beach volleyball

Sietech 2
yachting

Speedo 8
swimming, water polo,
diving, synchronized
swimming

Sport Supply Group, Inc. 30
athletics,
canoe / kayak–sprint,
canoe / kayak–slalom,
rowing, tennis, baseball,
softball, handball, hockey,
football, archery, boxing,
weightlifting, basketball,
indoor and beach
volleyball, cycling

Sunfish Laser 4
yachting

Taraflex 5
volleyball, handball

Top Ten 4
boxing

**Tuf-Wear
Manufacturing, Inc.** 6
boxing

Uesaka Iron Works 4
rowing,
canoe / kayak–slalom,
weightlifting

Victor Boats 2
yachting

Yakima 4
cycling

Yonex 12
badminton

■ *medal ceremonies*—sufficient time to present medal ceremonies.

The competition schedule was revised at least once per quarter and no more than once per month. The published revisions of the schedule were as follows: three times in 1993; eight times in 1994; three times in 1995; and twice in 1996. A total of 16 editions of the sports competition schedule were published between February 1993 and July 1996 for the appropriate constituencies to review.

Constituencies that should review the competition schedule are the host broadcaster (Atlanta Olympic Broadcasting (AOB)) and rights-holding broadcasters. Initial requests from rights-holding broadcasters regarding the schedule were for competitions to be held on particular days with general time guidelines (focusing primarily on the end times of competition) for selected events. As work on the sports competition schedule progressed, requests from broadcasters became more Games-specific. The time requests placed on previous Olympic schedules by the US rights holders (NBC) were not as strict for the 1996 Summer Games as for previous Games because of Atlanta's location in the eastern time zone, which is convenient with respect to other time zones around the world. NBC televised Olympic events Monday through Friday with morning, prime time, and late night broadcasts. Weekends featured live events on Saturday afternoon and evening and all day on Sunday.

The competition schedule was approved by the IOC Executive Board in September 1994 with open issues remaining in only a few sports.

The schedule was presented at the First World Broadcasters Meeting in May 1994, with explanations of the changes made since the previous Olympiad in Barcelona. A presentation of the revised schedule was given at the May 1995 meeting along with information on the proposed road cycling and marathon courses and two new venues, Atlanta Beach

(beach volleyball) and the University of Georgia Coliseum (rhythmic gymnastics and volleyball).

Sports Equipment

The Sports Equipment program was responsible for the identification, procurement, and disposal of all field-of-play equipment required for competition and at training sites. Approximately 200,000 necessary pieces of equipment were identified in a comprehensive database. Lists of each sport's IF's exclusive suppliers or approved vendors were also obtained. Written proposals were solicited worldwide from all potential suppliers.

ACOG selected more than 50 sports equipment manufacturers, including 23 that were granted supplierships and received limited marketing rights and benefits packages. In addition to equipment, suppliers also provided 300 technicians to install and service the equipment. *(For sports equipment technicians per sport, see Figure 1. For a list of sports equipment suppliers, see the Marketing/ACOP chapter.)*

One year before the Games, Sports Equipment staff established offices in the main warehouse to direct all operations related to field-of-play equipment, including receipt, storage, inventory control, deployment to and recovery from venues, and post-Games disposal. Staff ensured quality control and verification of receiving information and shipping activities. Large items received in the warehouse were stored in venue pods. Smaller items were stored in secured sport-specific areas. Sports Equipment staff assembled all the items for a venue, completed the necessary documentation, and loaded all trailers for venue delivery.

During the Games, Sports Equipment staff served as a support unit to resupply equipment as needed and ensure that an adequate reserve was available at each venue.

After the competitions, recovery plans were implemented immediately. The Sports Equipment office coordinated with the freight forwarder for direct shipment of items being returned to foreign suppliers. The disposal plan of all other equipment began by inventorying and then returning goods to the main warehouse, from which they were sold to local high schools and colleges or at auctions.

Training Sites

Athlete preparation for the Games took place at official warm-up venues, competition venues, and exclusive training sites. A total of 39 individual sites for 21 sports were used for training. Seven sports conducted training at a warm-up area at the competition venue in ad-

dition to exclusive training sites. For 10 sports, training was conducted at the competition venue only. Exclusive training sites were selected based on technical requirements of the sport, proximity to the Olympic Village, and the current condition of the site. *(For a list of training sites for each sport, see Figure 2.)*

The necessary equipment was provided for each sport according to the International Federation requirements.

FIGURE 2:
CENTENNIAL OLYMPIC GAMES TRAINING SITES

Aquatics—diving
Georgia Institute of Technology
   competition venue

Aquatics—swimming
Emory University
Willis Park

Aquatics—synchronized swimming
Emory University

Aquatics—water polo
Dynamo Swim Center

Archery
Stone Mountain Park
   competition practice field

Athletics
Olympic Village: George C. Griffin Track
Emory University
Grady Stadium
Morehouse College: Edwin C. Moses Track
Lakewood Stadium
Panthersville Stadium and auxiliary field

Badminton
Georgia International Convention Center

Baseball
Emory University: Chappell Park,
   Candler Field
Lovett School
Olympic Village: Russ Chandler Stadium

Basketball
Columbia High School
Henderson High School
McNair High School
Southwest DeKalb High School
Towers High School

Boxing
Georgia Tech: O'Keefe Gymnasium and
   freshman gymnasium

Canoe / kayak—slalom
Ocoee River competition venue

Canoe / kayak—sprint
Lake Lanier competition venue

Cycling—mountain bike
Georgia International Horse Park:
   equestrian endurance course

Cycling—road
City of Atlanta competition course

Cycling—track
Stone Mountain Park competition course

Equestrian
Georgia International Horse Park

Fencing (semifinals and finals)
Georgia International Convention Center:
   international ballroom

Football
Agnes Scott College
Marist School: Gellerstedt Field

Gymnastics—artistic
Georgia International Convention Center:
   six training gymnasiums

Gymnastics—rhythmic
Emory University: Woodruff Center
University of Georgia Coliseum

Handball
Georgia International Convention Center
Mays High School
Redan High School
Stone Mountain High School

Hockey
Lakewood Stadium

Judo
Grady High School: two gymnasiums

Modern pentathlon (individual sports)
Competition training sites

Rowing
Lake Lanier competition site

Shooting
Wolf Creek competition site

Softball
Columbus, Georgia:
   South Commons Softball Complex

Table tennis
Druid Hills High School

Tennis
Olympic Village: Bill Moore Tennis Center

Volleyball
Avondale High School
Agnes Scott College: Woodruff Gymnasium
Holy Innocents Episcopal School
Mercer University: Sheffield Gymnasium
Jean Child Young Middle School
Southwest Middle School

Weightlifting
Georgia World Congress Center: Hall A

Wrestling
North Atlanta High School

Yachting
Savannah, Georgia competition venue

After sport-specific sites were selected, Sports, along with ACOG Venue Management, contacted individual owners to begin the contractual process. Once it had contracted a facility, ACOG Sports began site-specific operational planning. All exclusive training sites were fully operational on 6 July 1996.

The assistant competition manager for training sites was responsible for the implementation of the sport-specific operational plan and facilitation of communication to the teams. The managers' offices were located in

Volunteers were recruited for pre-Games test events, including the Atlanta Sports '95 rowing competition.

the sports information center at the Olympic Village. Each site was managed by a supervisor who was responsible for daily operations. This involved coordination with site owners and all

ACOG functional areas. At the completion of training, Sports implemented its retrofit plan for each site.

Publications

The Sports Publications subdivision was responsible for producing all necessary sports documents related to the staging of the Games. Approximately 25 percent of all publications generated by ACOG were produced by the Sports Department.

Foremost among these publications were the 26 sports explanatory books—one for each sport—that were sent to IFs in September 1995.

The explanatory books included qualification information, competition schedules, and information about Atlanta and the Olympic Village. All explanatory books were approved by the IFs and the IOC before publication.

Team leader guides with the most current information were produced for each sport in the months prior to the Games. These guides contained information that athletes, coaches, and teams needed for their preparations, including a list of event personnel; arrival, transportation, Olympic Village, and accreditation information; competition-specific information; and detailed venue maps.

Coordination with the competition managers was imperative for Sports Publications, as information changed constantly until the Games. The Sports Publications staff was also responsible for the production of the Games-time competition forms, inscription forms, manuals, IF newsletters, and results books.

Original plans for publications called for the production of a daily spectator program for each sport. The project was later limited to start lists and results for 13 individual sports.

Before the Games, Sports Publications provided spectator information for ACOG's official World Wide Web site, including overviews, a guide to watching and understanding each sport, a competition preview, and historical information. During the 16 days of the Games, the Sports Publications staff of 6 paid employees and 25 volunteers produced more than 1,400 action reports and feature stories for the Internet.

Inscriptions

The process by which every competitor in the Olympic Games is verified as qualified and registered for competition is called Inscriptions. Because all invited NOCs accepted their invitations, the Centennial Olympic Games registered 197 countries, including 10,705 athletes and 4,155 team officials.

During a two-year process, more than 52 Inscriptions forms were created. These forms included numerous sport-specific registration (entry by name) forms, summary of participation forms (which captured estimated sports participation and numbers of team officials and horses), request for invitation forms (used by the NOCs to request wildcards), official alternate forms, and eligibility code forms.

Final approval of the forms by the IFs and the IOC was not given until late fall 1995. This timing presented several logistical challenges, because forms needed to be printed in three-part sets and ready for distribution in January 1996.

The Centennial Olympic Games also marked the introduction of the Olympic qualification system. In March 1995, the IOC sent to all 197 NOCs the Qualification and Participation Criteria document, which consisted of the qualification rules for all sports represented at the Olympic Games. This initial mailing was followed by an update a few months later.

All IFs were informed that information concerning the qualification status for their sports

The explanatory books for all Olympic sports were developed by ACOG in conjunction with the IOC and the IFs and mailed to all National Olympic Committees in 1995.

D. BRAD DELAY MD • VALERIE L DELBY • ROSEMARY A DELCORIO • CHRISTOPHER E DELEE • ANTHONY G DELEEDE • MEGHAN B DELEHANTY • RICK R DELEO • CRISTINA DELEON • RICARDO DELEON • RUBEN P DELEON • MATTEA DELEONNI STANONIK • KIT DELEOT • MADELINE E DELESKI • ANGELIQUE DELEVA • TAMMY L DELEVER • COLOMBE DELFERIERE • FERNANDO I DELGADO • ISIDRO R DELGADO • LORETTA DELGADO • MARIA DELGADO • MARISOL DELGADO • MERCEDES LUISA DELGADO • STEVEN V DELGROSSO • MICHAEL B D'ELIA • SUSAN WOODHOUSE DELIE • SALLY B DELISLE

389

(qualification dates, teams and individuals qualified, quota places filled, and quota places remaining) were to be reported to ACOG on three dates during 1996: 20 April, 20 May, and 23 June. The last date was also the deadline for the completion of qualification selections; however, several IFs continued to determine qualifiers well after this deadline.

Completed entry forms were submitted to ACOG on 5 July 1996, the day before the opening of the Olympic Village. This deadline was established by the IOC. Several of the larger NOCs—including Australia, Canada, France, Great Britain, Russia, and the US—submitted their forms early to avoid the large number of submissions expected 5 July. The first completed entry by name forms arrived 25 June.

While many countries mailed completed forms, the vast majority were hand delivered to Inscriptions at the AWC. Entry forms had to be verified before teams could move into the Olympic Village. If there was a disagreement regarding qualification status between the chef de mission and Inscriptions, the matter was referred to the competition manager, the IF, or the IOC, as needed.

Before the delegation arrived, changes by the chef de mission were managed at the AWC. After the arrival of the delegation, changes were made in the Olympic Village. When an NOC arrived at the Village, all of its forms were coded by sport and distributed to the data entry staff for input. Once completed, forms were returned to supervisors to be proofread and filed. Reports were then generated daily for competition staff and to NOCs as needed.

Volunteers

The Sports Logistics manager for volunteers began working full-time in January 1994. This individual worked with competition managers to develop sport-specific volunteer questionnaires, which were sent to various national and international sports organizations and federations for distribution to qualified individuals. The information received was used to develop a database of experienced and knowledgeable people who could be considered for positions as volunteers within the Sports Department.

Each competition manager assigned a staff member to coordinate volunteer recruitment. These coordinators were responsible for selecting volunteers to work on the field of play, accrediting their volunteers, assigning uniforms, and providing sport-specific training.

ACOG's Volunteer Services Department coordinated the mailings of official Games packets to potential volunteers. This packet included the official volunteer application, liability release, uniform sizing form, and security waiver form. Completed, returned information was entered into the ACOG Games staffing technology system. Once selected, volunteers received the ACOG Games staffing training materials and uniforms.

Throughout the five-year sports program, internship positions were available to students at the graduate or undergraduate level. Internships were required to be part of an academic, credit-bearing program, and all expenses were paid by the applicant.

SPORTS OPERATIONS

A third division of the Sports Department, Sports Operations, was defined in 1993 to be responsible for budget management, human resources, competition production, and sports results operations.

Budget Management and Human Resources

In coordination with Financial Services and the Procurement and Contract Administration division of ACOG, Sports budget management responsibilities included asset planning and assignment and financial reporting. A primary responsibility was the direct financial management of the budget for test events, which required additional corporate sponsorships and ticket revenues.

The human resources processes included recruitment, selection, and assignment of a staff that evolved from 5 people to 8,133 at Games-time.

Competition Production

The objective of the Competition Production subdivision was to present during Games-time all elements of Olympic competition to the audience in a knowledgeable, appreciative, and responsive manner, respecting the dignity and grandeur of the Olympic Games.

The Competition Production team reported directly to the competition manager, and at Games-time consisted of production consultants as well as scoreboard, video board, victory ceremony, announcer, staffing, and audio coordinators. The Competition Production team also coordinated the evaluation and hiring of all competition producers and announcers.

Announcers were ACOG's voice to the world. At each venue, there was at least one French-language and one English-language announcer. Dignified, neutral tones of voice were expected, without bias shown toward any team, individual, or nationality. Scripted announcements were developed for the official welcome and departure messages and for introductions.

Music played an important and varied role in ACOG's production plan. Because the Olympic Games are an international event, producers were required to have diverse selections of music for programming. In addition to the five CDs developed by ACOG, a 32-hour competition enhancement music library was created, including classical, pop/rock, jazz, rhythm and blues, country, contemporary instrumental, soundtracks, and international genres.

Musical chimes were used to call spectators' attention to videos, official results, and the start of a competition, heat, match, or event.

The instant replay equipment system, also referred to as "Music on Demand," was the key to audio programming success. This system used digital audio storage, which allowed quick recall of 16 hours of music. The instant replay equipment is recommended as the primary audio source machine for production musical programming in future competitions. Digital audio tape (DAT) recorder-players were used to preprogram music for use during long breaks in action, and during the periods between individual competitors.

The scoreboard served as the primary source of results information, and also functioned as an enhancement medium, providing educational information and entertainment. Standard scoreboard displays were developed for use at each venue. Sport-specific displays were developed by the competition managers and the producers.

Video provided spectators with historical, educational, and entertaining information about the sports and the Olympic Games. Video boards were also used to give spectators a unique view of the competition through pre-produced video features and a live broadcast feed provided by AOB. Generic video programming consisted of features on Atlanta and the Olympic Games developed by ACOG. Sport-specific video features were developed in conjunction with the individual competition managers and sports producers.

Producers were responsible for cuing victory ceremonies to the prerecorded music of John Williams's *Summon the Heroes*. The programming of specific athlete/technical official parade music was a key to providing uniformity across venues and using music to preserve the prestige and dignity of the Olympic Games.

The interaction between Competition Production and the host broadcaster was critical to the success of the broadcast media. Competition producers synchronized their clocks daily with AOB producers and made every effort to keep all competition to the prescribed time limits. The number of late or early starts was minimal.

Atlanta Sports '95 concentrated a large number of sports competitions in Georgia, and specifically in Atlanta, in July–August 1995.

Results Operations

The Results Operations subdivision was created to coordinate the development of the results system by detailing the sports criteria and providing event experience to the Technology Department. The results system was designed based on the requirements imposed by the individual sports, the press, and television; therefore, it was very important for these three areas to work together in identifying their needs.

The effectiveness of the results system depended directly on the accreditation and

sports inscription systems capturing the necessary information on athletes and officials. The data ownership process among Accreditation, Inscriptions, and Results Operations was cumbersome with the large amount of data to be entered in a short period of time. The problem of entering large amounts of data, as well as the difficulties in acquiring complete data from each of the NOCs, make ownership of information critical to the process. Deadlines for receiving data prior to competition were very difficult to enforce, which created challenges in preparing for draws and technical meetings.

During competition, the system was managed and operated by the assistant competition manager for results (ACMR). When the results system was ready for testing and approval, involving the ACMR in defining the results process and its requirements proved to be essential.

The ACMR was also responsible for the development and printing of start lists and results. The necessary equipment was well supported by Xerox technicians, with support staff requiring proper training to produce each sport's results in a timely manner. The degree of advance testing on the fully operational system directly corresponded to its success. The infrastructure to operate these systems needed to be in place at least one month before competition began.

The distribution of print reports in the quantity needed for each constituent was a large task: 1.3 million sheets of results were produced during the Games. A report distribution table was developed in advance detailing the results report requirements of all constituents so as to be prepared for Games-time and not overburden the system.

As competitions ended, bound results books were assembled for each sport. These books were provided for every NOC participating in a sport, and were distributed through the sports desks at the Villages.

Test Events

The Sports Department was responsible for the implementation and coordination of all operations of sports competition test events held before the Olympic Games. ACOG departments took advantage of the 27 advance competitions to test, refine, and reevaluate their systems and competition plans. There were single-sport as well as multisport events, ranging from events that included small numbers of athletes (as in weightlifting) to events that were larger than the actual Olympic competition (as in yachting and shooting). ACOG created Atlanta Sports '95 to bring a concentrated number of events to Georgia, and specifically to Atlanta, during a two-week time period to prepare selected communities, staff, and volunteers for the Games. The organization and administration of the sports competition events played a major role in assuring the IFs that Olympic-quality events would be hosted in 1996.

Letters of agreement were developed by the Sports Department for any event that was cohosted with an NGB, sponsor, or IF. These letters outlined the responsibilities, both financially and operationally, of ACOG and the other parties involved. The budget for each event ranged from $150,000 to $500,000, depending on the agreement.

ACOG planned these events to test the venues, people, and departments for the baseline requirements absolutely necessary to stage the event without compromising the quality of competition. The test event budget was $10 million, including $1 million of income from incremental sponsorships, donations of value-in-kind goods and services, and ticket sales.

When planning their Olympic marketing budgets, most sponsors did not provide for the use of resources to support test events and therefore participated primarily with incremental products and services.

As ACOG ticket sales were focused on Games-time tickets, Sports relied heavily on direct mail to targeted audiences to promote the competitions and advance ticket sales.

Most broadcast rights for the events were either very limited or totally owned by the sport involved, and therefore AOB production was limited to documentation of the event.

During the test events, the overlap of functional systems was brief and not of the same level as planned for 1996, so testing of all systems was not provided. For example, a transportation system was customized for each event; thus, no overall transportation system was built to service several events at once.

The main accreditation center did service many sports at once during the test events and received pre-Games testing. Due to the nature of some of the test events, registration information was not obtained in advance, which resulted in delays when the athletes and officials arrived. Other accreditation difficulties resulted in a reevaluation and modification of the accreditation system for the Games.

These competition test events provided ACOG the opportunity to build the organization's policies and procedures in various areas. The experiences helped to define departmental roles and responsibilities, as well as to identify staffing and operational needs. For example, because so many staff members were hired immediately prior to the test events, only minimal training sessions were provided for understanding of the event.

Test events such as the Pan American Race Walk gave ACOG staff and volunteers the opportunity to prepare for their Games–time activities.

ALLISON L DENMARK • HERBERT W DENMARK • JACKIE M DENNARD • PATTY W DENNARD • SHAWN K DENNARD • JENNIFER N DENNEE • DANIEL D DENNETT ATC • CHRISTY G. DENNEY • ERIN L DENNEY-JONES • ANYETTA R DENNIS • CHARLOTTE C DENNIS • DARRYL B DENNIS • JANET A DENNIS • JAYE DENNIS • JEREMY A DENNIS • KEITH A DENNIS • LOU E DENNIS • MARIE DENNIS • RENATA L DENNIS • THOMAS W DENNIS • TRINA L DENNIS • VERNA C DENNIS • VICKI L DENNIS • JUDITH J DENNIS MD • ANTHONY DENNIS SR • CAROLYN M DENNISON • FLORENCE A DENNISON •

393

The test events were a key step in preparing for the 1996 Games, providing the basis for developing venue-based teams and giving them a sense of participation, and affording the ACOG family its first feeling of accomplishment from jointly planning sporting events. IFs gave high approval of these competition events.

GAMES-TIME OPERATIONS

The Sports Department's Games-time operations were aimed at effective management of all aspects of the sports programme. To accomplish this, Sports focused on competition management, the establishment of a sports coordination center and a sports information center, and a presidential representatives program.

Competition Management

The organizational structure of competition management at Games-time followed the same format as that developed in the 1995 competition management manuals. Each competition manager was responsible for a team consisting of assistant managers for administration, athlete services, competition production, field-of-play equipment, and results/timing/scoring.

Each team met two hours prior to the opening and immediately following the conclusion of every competition to coordinate all activities. During the competition, communications were facilitated by cellular telephone service, dedicated radios, and intervenue telephone lines.

ACOG's structure, which made both sports competition managers and venue managers equally responsible for the overall success of the venues, required constant communication and coordination of their respective functional responsibilities. As the number of spectators, broadcasters, and press attending, as well as the scope of services provided to athletes and officials, were defined for each venue, the structure was confirmed as being appropriate. *(For more information, see the Venue Management chapter.)*

Sports Coordination Center

As part of the competition management plan, the sports coordination center (SCC) provided competition managers a center where they could share information and resolve issues that could not be solved at the venues. Located adjacent to the main operations center (MOC), the SCC served as the conduit of competition information to the MOC.

The SCC began limited operations on 6 July 1996 from 0900 to 2200. On 19 July, it began 24-hour operation, divided into 12-hour shifts with a director, supervisor, and sports desk attendants present.

The Competition Secretariat at each venue reported the start and completion of each competition session to the SCC. Furthermore, the training site representatives in the sports information center (SIC) at the Olympic Village were required to report the number of training sites being used each day and their schedules. All of this information, as well as the competition managers' daily report, was recorded in the SCC and forwarded to the MOC.

Sports Information Center

The SIC opened on 6 July 1996 to inform team officials in the Olympic Villages of developments or changes at each venue and to distribute data about athlete registration, boxed lunch coordination, competition results, Inscriptions, training site scheduling, and transportation. It also supported and assisted the sports desks located both at the SIC and at the competition venues.

The SIC general information counter provided assistance with language services and transportation, and distributed the athlete transportation guide, calendars of events, and the training site confirmation form, which was readily available before the Village opened. Five sets of boards providing information and results were placed adjacent to dining areas. These boards were updated by SIC staff two to four times a day. *(For additional information, see the Olympic Villages chapter.)*

Presidential Representatives

In the first quarter of 1996, ACOG President and CEO William Porter "Billy" Payne selected outstanding community leaders and business people to serve as presidential representatives at the sports venues during the Games. These representatives were ambassadors to the Olympic Family, providing the same warmth and hospitality for which Atlanta's Bid effort was known.

Their responsibilities included both hosting the Olympic Family and communicating with venue managers and competition managers on specific plans.

CONCLUSIONS AND RECOMMENDATIONS

As judged by athletes, officials, and IFs, the sports competitions of the Centennial Olympic Games were an outstanding success. Fairness and equity on the fields of play and at training facilities assured the athletes that the years they spent training for their sports competitions were respected. Achievements of more athletes from more countries than ever before attest to this accomplishment.

■ Though an often-criticized and challenging process, changes of venues, both competition and training, can be accomplished with a positive impact on the sport.

■ The MOU process helps define the expectations of IFs, the IOC, and the OCOG, but must take into account any changes needed as detailed planning progresses.

■ Early clarity of the numbers of competition officials and the responsibilities of the OCOG is necessary for proper planning.

■ Continued development of the criteria, testing, and implementation of the results systems is necessary.

■ In staff planning, it is of paramount importance that staff have extensive experience in event administration.

■ Detailed planning for the recovery of assets needs to be completed three months prior to the Games and enforced strictly after the Games.

■ In order to receive the full value of holding test events, the events should be staged within a short time period and requirements of all functional area support should be mandated.

PAULYNE F DEPP * LAURA H DEPREE * ANTHONY R DEPROSPERO * JOSEPH DERBES * MARY H DERBES * JENNIFER S DERBY * ROBERT R DERCK * FRANCIS P DEREIMER * MCKAY L DEREK * ANN W DERGARA * JACK S DERHAM * MARIJKE E DERICKS * PETER W DERICKS * ART J DERICO * ANTHONY J DERIGGI * CHRISTINE M DERISO * BARBARA A DERKETSCH * ROBERT D DERKSEN * DANIEL J DEROSA * THEODORE J DEROUSSE * LUBA L DERR * ROSEMARIE DERR * GEORGANN E DERRICK * MICHAEL A DERRICK * TRACY K DERRICK * DAVID DERU * OLUSESAN B DERU * BRIAN P DERWIN *

395

SPORT BY SPORT PLANNING DETAIL

AQUATICS

For the first time in Olympic history, all four of the aquatics disciplines—diving, swimming, synchronized swimming, and water polo—were held at the same venue, the Georgia Tech Aquatic Center, located on the campus of the Georgia Institute of Technology, adjacent to the Atlanta Olympic Village. In addition, the swimming portion of the modern pentathlon was held at the main pool. With the downtown Atlanta skyline in the background, this open-air venue was one of the most spectacular settings of the Centennial Olympic Games.

Designed and built in a cooperative effort between ACOG and Georgia Tech, this state-of-the-art facility included three permanent pools (50 m main swimming pool, diving well, and 50 m warm-up pool) and an adjacent 33 m temporary pool. Seating for the main pools accommodated 15,000. The water polo pool had approximately 4,000 temporary seats.

Ten meters of the floor of the main pool could be raised or lowered between 0–3 m depending on the demands of the competition. This unique feature and the pool's wide lanes and gutters were designed specifically to create opportunities for faster times.

The facility was covered with a permanent roof 110 ft (33.5 m) above the pool deck. A sun shade was built over the spectator stands on the north side.

The diving well, 24 x 22.75 m, had a minimum depth of 4.5 m and included two springboards (1 and 3 m) and several platforms (1, 3, 5, 7.5, and 10 m).

The swimming pool was 50 x 25 m with a minimum depth of 3 m. Starting platforms were between .5 and .75 m above the surface of the water. Synchronized swimming used a 30 x 25 m area

within the main swimming pool. The water polo pool was 33 x 22 m with a depth of 2.2 m. The final day of competition for water polo was held in the swimming competition pool.

Two sets of locker rooms served athletes of all disciplines and officials.

Training Sites. The main pool was used as a warm-up area for lap swimming only, until after the swimming competition was completed.

Competitors in synchronized swimming, after warming up by swimming laps, could practice in the main pool between the 30 m mark and the 40 m mark. The swimmers then rotated to the competitive area, one country at a time, for practice with music.

In addition to the four pools at the venue, there were three training sites (see Figure 2). Two of these locations contained eight-lane, 50 m pools, and one site also included a dance room with mirrors for land drills and a complete selection of strength equipment and aerobic machines.

Test Events. The Aquatic Center was completed in June 1995, and six test events were held there during August and September: Synchronized Swimming World Cup, Pan Pacific Swimming Championships, Diving World Cup, Water Polo World Cup, International Paralympic Swim Trials, and the Modern Pentathlon World Cup Final. A new world record was set in the men's 4 x 100 m freestyle relay during the Pan Pacific Championships, as well as 17 national records.

Competition. The competition format and other various requirements for the aquatics disciplines were established in an agreement signed in October 1994

between ACOG and the International Amateur Swimming Federation (FINA).

DIVING

The diving competition was to include the 3 m springboard and 10 m platform events for both men and women. The schedule was held over eight days (26 July–2 August), with a total of 122 divers (66 men and 56 women).

SWIMMING

The agreement for the swimming competition set forth a number of firsts. For the first time in Olympic history, the swimming events were scheduled over seven consecutive days (20–26 July), with no rest day. The Games also introduced the women's 4 x 200 m freestyle relay into Olympic competition, bringing the total number of medal events to 32. In another Olympic first, countries entered swimmers based on two levels (A and B) of qualifying standards. In order for a country to enter two swimmers in an event, both swimmers had to meet the faster A standard. Otherwise, a country could enter just one athlete per event. There was a total number of 985 athletes competing in swimming events.

SYNCHRONIZED SWIMMING

Synchronized swimming became a team sport for the first time in Olympic history in 1996. The traditional figures competition was replaced with a technical routine in which required elements were to be executed in a prescribed order and, with the exception of one required cadence action,

synchronized. In Atlanta, 80 women (eight teams of 10) competed on 30 July (technical routine) and 2 August (free routine).

WATER POLO

Scheduled 20–28 July 1996, a total of 156 men (12 teams of 13) competed in water polo in a round-robin format with single-elimination finals.

Equipment and Staff. All equipment provided by ACOG complied with FINA rules. Diving boards were Maxiflex Model B on Durafirm stands. The platform surfaces were supplied by Mondo S.p.A., while B & K Rental supplied the podia.

For swimming, Swatch Timing/Omega supplied the starting blocks.

For synchronized swimming, Speedo provided apparel. Sound equipment included the following: Panasonic 3800 DAT recorder, Ramsa Mixer-3 channels, SPL M-3 mike input, Ramsa Air speakers, Ocean Engineering underwater speakers, and a Clark synthesizer to monitor underwater sound from a sound booth. All equipment had emergency backup systems.

Water polo competition balls were supplied by Mikasa, Inc. All other required equipment was supplied by Adolph Keifer & Associates.

The aquatics competition manager began in April 1993 as the sports planning manager for aquatics, boxing, and cycling. In January 1995, she was designated competition manager for the four disciplines of aquatics. In addition, a competition manager for each discipline was added in May 1994, ultimately reporting to the aquatics manager.

The diving staff included 14 paid staff and 65 volunteers. The swimming staff included 8 paid staff and 114 volunteers. For synchronized swimming, there were 17 paid staff and 58 volunteers. Water polo, which had the largest staff of the aquatics disciplines, had 69 paid staff and 86 volunteers.

ARCHERY

The archery competition was held at the Archery Center in Stone Mountain Park, a magnificent 3,200 acre (1,295 ha) facility in the Atlanta suburb of Stone Mountain, approximately 16.6 km from the Atlanta Olympic Village. The 5,200-seat Archery Center rested in a pastoral valley at the base of the mountain's south side. The park also served as the venue for the tennis and track cycling competitions.

Training Sites. Adjacent to the competition range, a 22-lane practice range was available to athletes during non-competition times. This field served as the site for the ranking round, where the 22 targets were placed in a single row with their centers 3 m apart from each other.

Test Event. ACOG's archery test event, the Atlanta Grand Prix Archery Tournament, was held in April 1996 at the practice range. More than 120 athletes from 30 countries attended.

Competition. The MOU signed in February 1994 between ACOG and the International Archery Federation (FITA) outlined the competition format for the Games, which included a variety of alterations in the way the contest was played. Under the MOU, the tournament was divided into four events: men's and women's individual and team competitions. In an Olympic first, countries could qualify up to three archers for individual competition. In addition, a single-elimination match format was introduced, in which archers shot from a

single distance of 70 m at a 122 cm target face divided into 10 scoring rings.

As a result of various enhancements, including the change of format and the use of cameras placed in targets and video boards, spectators were more involved than in any previous Olympic archery competition.

The competition was scheduled for six days, 28 July–2 August 1996, with 128 athletes (64 men and 64 women) competing.

Equipment and Staff. All equipment provided by ACOG complied with FITA regulations and was used at the test event in April 1996. McKenzie Sports Products provided 90 (including 50 replacement) 50 x 50 in (127 x 127 cm) target mats, along with 40 metal stands, which replaced conventional wood stands. Maple Leaf Press supplied the plastic-backed 122 cm target faces.

The competition manager for archery began in June 1994, and the assistant competition manager in July 1995. Additional staff members began work in April 1996 for the test event and returned for the Games in June 1996. The competition was conducted with 10 paid staff and 51 volunteers.

ATHLETICS

Two key components intensified the planning for the athletics competition—the stadium and the schedule. Constructed as the centerpiece of the Centennial Olympic Games, the 85,000-seat Olympic Stadium located 2.7 mi (4.3 km) from the Atlanta Olympic Village served as the site of the athletics competition and the Opening and Closing Ceremonies. It was planned to be converted into a baseball stadium after the Games, requiring a very specialized design to accommodate both the Games-time and the permanent use, as well as an extraordinary amount of construction approvals.

A hard-surface Mondo track was installed for both track and field events, providing one of the fastest tracks in the world for the sprint races. The 400 m oval contained eight lanes, with a ninth lane on the sprint straightaway. The stadium also contained two long jump/triple jump runways, two high jump areas, three pole vault runways, two javelin runways, one hammer circle, two discus circles, and four shot put circles. A complete array of athlete facilities and services was available within the stadium venue.

Training Sites. Training facilities met IAAF surface requirements and were equipped with athlete and management support facilities such as locker rooms, showers, and offices. All sites (see Figure 2) were within a 20-minute drive from the Olympic Village. The warm-up site was Cheney Stadium, .5 km from Olympic Stadium. A call track was provided in the stadium for final athlete preparation.

Test Event. Held 3–4 May 1996, the Atlanta Grand Prix served as the test event for athletics and was the first competition held inside Olympic Stadium. Nearly 440 athletes from 30 countries competed. Other test events included the Pan American Race Walk Championship in September 1994 and the US Olympic Trials in June 1996.

Competition. An MOU was proposed to the IAAF that confirmed the schedule of events for the Games but remained in constant flux until June 1996, primarily regarding the time of the men's marathon, which was changed to an early morning event, and the scheduling of the men's 200 m and 400 m events.

Olympic Stadium was the venue for all track and field events, including the race walk and marathon events, which started and ended inside the stadium.

The competition extended over nine days, 26 July–4 August, with a single rest day (30 July). A total of 2,259 athletes (1,407 men and 852 women) competed in 44 medal events.

Equipment and Staff. All equipment provided by ACOG complied with IAAF rules. Sport Supply Group, Inc., furnished throwing implements, throwing cages, landing pits, hurdles and jumps, and starting blocks. Vaulting poles, supplied by the athletes, were inspected at the venue prior to both individual and decathlon competition to ensure compliance with regulations.

The work of the professional staff began in January 1993. The competition manager began working full time on 1 January 1994. The assistant competition manager began in early 1995. Games-time competitions were directed by 26 paid staff and 284 volunteers.

BADMINTON

The badminton competition was held in the 3,500-seat Georgia State University gymnasium 3.3 km from the Olympic Village. The venue featured three competition courts measuring 6.1 x 13.4 m with a 2 m clearance on all sides. The ceiling height was 12 m.

Training Sites. In addition to the three competition courts, a pair of warm-up courts were available for athletes at the venue. (For the additional training site, see Figure 2.)

Test Event. Held at the Georgia State University gymnasium in August 1995, the Yonex US Open Badminton Championships served as the sport's test event. The competition program contained a full slate of events with 200 competitors from 15 countries.

During the test event, athletes and IF representatives noted that the ventilation system in the venue was affecting the flight of the shuttlecocks during

competition. Under the guidance of the federation, this problem was corrected before the Games.

Competition. Signed in October 1993, the MOU between ACOG and the International Badminton Federation (IBF) established the competition format and set forth various competition requirements.

The agreement introduced the mixed doubles event into the Olympic Programme. The other four events in the nine-day competition schedule (24 July–1 August) included men's and women's doubles and singles. A day was added in respect to the Barcelona schedule to accommodate the mixed doubles competition.

The athletes competed in five medal events, each a single-elimination tournament consisting of the best-of-three-set matches. In another Olympic first, bronze-medal playoffs determined third place.

In the badminton tournament, 96 men and 96 women competed.

Equipment and Staff. All equipment complied with IBF statutes. As the official badminton equipment supplier of ACOG, Yonex furnished the majority of badminton materials, including 16 courts and 8,400 shuttlecocks.

The competition manager and assistant competition manager started work in March and May 1994, respectively. The competition was conducted with 12 paid staff and 114 volunteers.

BASEBALL

Atlanta–Fulton County Stadium, home of the Atlanta Braves major league baseball team and site of four of the last five World Series, was the venue for the Centennial Olympic Games baseball competition. Located adjacent to Olympic Stadium, this 54,000-seat venue was 2.7 mi (4.3 km) from the Atlanta Olympic Village.

The dimensions of the field were the same as for major league baseball: the outfield fence measured 330 ft (100.6 m) to left and right fields, 385 ft (117.4 m) to the power alleys, and 402 ft (122.5 m) to center field.

Four locker rooms were provided. Locker rooms and their respective dugouts were connected by tunnels.

Atlanta–Fulton County Stadium is scheduled to be razed when Olympic Stadium becomes the new home of the Atlanta Braves in 1997.

Training Sites. Training sessions for Olympic baseball took place at Russ Chandler Baseball Stadium within the Olympic Village as well as the sites listed in Figure 2. Meeting IF specifications for training, these sites also were fully equipped with the necessary athlete and management support facilities such as locker rooms and administrative offices and were used for the umpires' clinic.

Competition. Signed in July 1994, the agreement between ACOG and the International Baseball Association (IBA) established the competition format and set forth various requirements for the competition.

The tournament extended from 20 July to 2 August. The tournament span of 14 days contained 12 scheduled competition days and two rest days available as game make-up days. A total of 160 athletes (20 per team) were slated to compete in the eight-team, 28-game, round-robin tournament. To accommodate Olympic competition, the Braves' 1996 schedule included an extended series of games away from Atlanta.

Equipment and Staff. All equipment provided for the teams by ACOG for training and competition complied with IBA rules. Mizuno, USA, along with Easton, supplied team equipment such as balls, bats, and gloves, while Sport Supply Group, Inc., furnished miscellaneous equipment such as batting cages and bases.

The competition manager began working full-time in July 1992. The assistant competition manager began work in April 1994. The competition was conducted with 22 paid staff and 147 volunteers.

BASKETBALL

With the addition of more teams, two venues were needed to host the men's and women's basketball competitions at the Centennial Olympic Games: the Morehouse College Gymnasium and the Georgia Dome.

The main site was the 69,000-seat Georgia Dome, the largest cable-supported stadium in the world. This was one of three facilities—along with the Georgia World Congress Center (GWCC) and the Omni—that comprised the Olympic Center cluster, the most concentrated cluster of venues in the Olympic Ring. In addition to basketball, the Georgia Dome hosted artistic gymnastics and the men's handball finals. The Georgia Dome, divided in half by a soundproof curtain with 34,500 seats on each side, hosted 66 preliminary and final rounds of basketball (20 July–4 August).

The 6,000-seat Morehouse College Gymnasium hosted 26 of the preliminary-round games (20–30 July) prior to becoming the new home of the college's men's and women's basketball teams.

Numerous locker room facilities were available and were assigned randomly.

Training Sites. At Morehouse College, a full-sized gymnasium next to the competition court was available for practice. At the Georgia Dome, a temporary half-court was created for teams to practice shooting.

Training sessions also took place at various high schools *(see Figure 2)*. These sites met IF specifications for training and were fully equipped with the necessary athlete and management support facilities. All sites were within a 25-minute drive from the Olympic Village.

Competition. The agreement between ACOG and the International Basketball Federation (FIBA) established the competition format and set forth various requirements for the competition.

For the first time in Olympic history, with the addition of four teams to the women's tournament, the basketball competition included an equal number (12) of men's and women's teams, with 144 men and 144 women competing in identical competition formats. The increased number of teams required the use of a second venue. The preliminary round consisted of two pools of six teams that played in a round-robin tournament, with the top four teams in each group advancing to the quarterfinals, semifinals, and the medal-round games. There were also classification games that determined places 5–12.

Equipment and Staff. All equipment complied with FIBA rules. Molten, Inc., supplied the basketballs, and Hydra Rib supplied the fixed and portable goals, nets, and backboards. Robbins Sport Surfaces supplied the floors, while Daktronics furnished the scoreboard and shot clocks.

The competition manager began working part-time with ACOG in 1995. The deputy competition manager was hired in July 1995. The competition was conducted with a paid staff of 28 and 166 volunteers at the Georgia Dome, 3 paid staff and 111 volunteers at Morehouse College, and 90 additional volunteers at training sites.

BOXING

The boxing competition took place at the 10,000-seat Alexander Memorial Coliseum, home to Georgia Tech's basketball team and adjacent to the Atlanta Olympic Village.

The boxing field of play, constructed on the basketball court, was 6.1 x 6.1 m, rising no less than 91 cm or more than 1.22 m above the floor. Four ropes were drawn tightly from the corner posts.

The facility's locker rooms, coaches' offices, and storage rooms were converted to accommodate the needs of both athletes and competition management.

Training Sites. The primary training venue for boxing was Georgia Tech's O'Keefe Gymnasium, located less than 200 m from Alexander Memorial Coliseum. O'Keefe contained 10 practice spaces complete with a ring and workout station. Equipment was available for teams to use for practice. Saunas and trial scales were also available.

Plans required the gymnasium to be operational each day commencing 6 July 1996 from 0900 to 1900. Countries were assigned a rotating time each day through 24 July.

The secondary training venue for boxing was Georgia Tech's freshman gymnasium, also adjacent to the competition venue.

Test Events. In March 1995, IF technical delegates were invited to observe testing of the electronic scoring, results, and scoreboard technology at the US

National Championships in Colorado Springs, Colorado. In October 1995, competition production was tested at the World Championship Challenge in Macon, Georgia. Final preparations were tested in May 1996 at the Atlanta Boxing Classic in the newly renovated Alexander Memorial Coliseum.

Competition. Signed in October 1993, the MOU between ACOG and the International Amateur Boxing Association (AIBA) established the competition format and set forth various competition requirements, including age limits of 17–34 years.

In accordance with the ACOG and AIBA agreement, the boxing competition was a single-elimination tournament with a separate draw for each weight class held just before Games competition. Each bout consisted of three rounds of three minutes each with a one-minute interval between rounds. An electronic scoring machine only recorded a scoring blow if three of the five judges pushed their buttons within one second of the punch being landed. The jury verified the judges' scores when the bout was completed.

The boxing competition extended over the entire Games, 20 July–4 August, with a single rest day (29 July). Competing in 12 different weight classes were 355 male competitors.

Equipment and Staff. All equipment met AIBA rules. The competition ring and 12 training cubicles were supplied by Perry Sports. Top Ten supplied all training and competition gloves in blue and red. Much of the remaining support equipment was supplied by Tuf-Wear Manufacturing, Inc., and Everlast, Inc.

A competition manager was selected in April 1994. Early in 1995, the assistant competition manager was hired. The competition was conducted with a paid staff of 17 and 162 volunteers.

CANOE / KAYAK

CANOE / KAYAK–SLALOM

The sport of canoe/kayak consisted of two separate disciplines: slalom and sprint. The slalom competition was held on the Ocoee River at the Ocoee Whitewater Center in Cleveland, Tennessee, 26–28 July 1996, while the sprint took place on Lake Lanier in Gainesville, Georgia, 30 July–4 August.

Several entities formed a partnership with ACOG to create the stunning venue for the slalom events, as well as to stage the competition. The state of Tennessee created the Tennessee Ocoee Development Agency (TODA) to coordinate the partnership. The US Department of Agriculture Forest Service led the construction effort at the venue, much of which involved reshaping the river channel to enhance the rapids. The Tennessee Valley Authority (TVA), one of the nation's largest electric-power producers, provided water-management expertise for the competition.

Slalom athletes competed on a natural river for the first time in Olympic history. Deemed the most challenging course in the world, the waters carried the athletes through a beautiful rocky gorge in the Appalachian Mountains in the Cherokee National Forest near Cleveland, Tennessee, 130 mi (209 km) from the Olympic Village in Atlanta. The course ran approximately 415 m, with a gradient of 9 m and a water flow of

1,200 cu ft (34 cu m) per second. Bleachers along the narrow riverbank provided seating for up to 14,400 spectators.

Training Sites. All training was held on the Ocoee River upstream from the competition course. Several short stretches of whitewater were available for warm-up.

Test Event. The 1995 Ocoee Slalom Challenge served as the test event. Held 3–6 August 1995, more than 125 athletes competed in four events: canoe and kayak singles and doubles.

Competition. The agreement between ACOG and the International Canoeing Federation (FIC) was signed in December 1994 and established the competition format and requirements. Four medal events were established: men's canoe single, men's canoe double, men's kayak single, and women's kayak single. In all, 135 athletes (105 men and 30 women) in 120 boats participated.

Equipment and Staff. All equipment and material provided by ACOG complied with FIC regulations. ACOG had boats available for hire by the competing teams.

The deputy competition manager began full-time in May 1994, with the assistant competition manager starting part-time in April 1995. The competition was conducted with 15 paid staff and 223 volunteers.

CANOE / KAYAK–SPRINT

The canoe/kayak–sprint competition course was located on scenic Lake Lanier, a beautiful Georgia resort area near the city of Gainesville, 55 mi (88 km) northeast of the Atlanta Olympic Village. The venue was also the location of the rowing competition.

There were 17,300 seats available for general spectators, located across the

lake from the event management and athlete areas. Spectator seating was composed of temporary grandstands resting on a floating platform on the lake surface. To aid spectators, a video board was placed near the finish line.

Air-conditioned day village facilities were shared by the almost 1,000 canoe/kayak–sprint and rowing athletes. Two tents were equipped with workout facilities and recreational areas. Team tents were assigned by sport and by country based on team size. These tents were equipped with stretching mats and team lockers.

The venue also included two boathouses with a capacity of 250 boats, and two separate locker rooms.

The field of play was defined as the practice course, the competition course, finish-line tower, and two boat-control areas. The practice and competition courses were water based with no direct land access. All servicing was done by boat, requiring a fleet of 50 motor vessels for safety officials and traffic marshals as well as for coaches' viewing, course umpires and officials, and broadcasters.

Security of the field of play was also water based and included three traffic-restricting barriers and a 24-hour patrol.

The race course consisted of nine lanes, each 100 m long and 9 m wide. At each start (1,000 m and 500 m from the finish) there was a starter/aligned platform, a 25 m judges platform, a boat-holder's platform for each lane, and a mechanical starting mechanism, which was connected to the timing/scoring system. At the 750 and 250 m points, platforms existed for recording intermediate times.

Training Sites. Training began when the venue opened on 6 July 1996. Plans called for the practice course to be used extensively during the week prior to canoe/kayak–sprint competition, while the rowing competition was being held. The practice course consisted of six lanes, each 1,000 m long.

Ample area beyond the start line was utilized as the warm-up area.

Test Event. Held 22–24 September 1995, the Lake Lanier Sprint Challenge drew 350 athletes to the Olympic venue. Spectators were seated on the north side of the lake because the large area of temporary seating had not yet been constructed.

Competition. The agreement signed in December 1994 between ACOG and the FIC set forth various requirements for the competition, which involved a total of 350 athletes and 192 boats, competing in 12 medal events between 30 July and 4 August. The three women's events were 500 m races in kayak single, kayak double, and kayak fours. The nine men's events were 500 m and 1,000 m races in canoe single, canoe double, kayak single, and kayak double, as well as a 1,000 m kayak fours race.

Equipment and Staff. Motor boats required to support the canoe/kayak– sprint event were provided and maintained by Pocock Manufacturing and Mercury Marine Corp. At the request of the IF, competition canoes and kayaks were purchased and rented to countries that requested them, and after the Games were sold to various local canoe/kayak clubs. The manufacturers agreed to perform the necessary boat maintenance prior to and during the competition.

The competition manager was hired in October 1994, with the deputy competition manager starting full-time in

May 1994. There was a total of 22 paid staff and 183 volunteer staff.

CYCLING

Each of the three cycling disciplines utilized different venues. The mountain bike course was constructed in the woods of the Georgia International Horse Park in Conyers, Georgia. The road cycling events took place on the streets of Atlanta. The track cycling velodrome shared a complex with archery at Stone Mountain Park.

While road and track cycling had already been part of the Olympic Programme, the mountain bike discipline made its first appearance in the Olympic arena at the 1996 Games. Its entry into the Games was made official when ACOG and the International Cycling Union (UCI) signed an MOU in April 1994 outlining the competition format for all three disciplines.

CYCLING—MOUNTAIN BIKE

The venue for the inaugural event of mountain bike racing was the Georgia International Horse Park, a 1,139 acre (461 ha) site in Rockdale County near Conyers, Georgia, approximately 35 minutes (33 mi/53 km) east of the Atlanta Olympic Village. Racing took place on the park's equestrian endurance course. (In addition to mountain bike racing, the Georgia International Horse Park also hosted the Olympic equestrian competition and both the riding and running events of the modern pentathlon.)

Each lap for the mountain bike athletes measured approximately 6.6 mi (10 km), with the men's race consisting of four and one-half laps and the women's race consisting of three laps.

Athlete compounds were created that included tent cabins for athletes' use while they were on-site to compete or train. An athlete lounge, medical facilities, Mavic neutral service, and toilet and shower facilities were located in the athlete compound areas.

Training Sites. Mountain bike racing training was held on the course from 27 to 29 July, the three days prior to competition.

Test Event. On 20 August 1995, mountain bike racing held its test event. For the one-day event, more than 250 athletes competed on the mountain bike course at the Georgia International Horse Park.

Competition. In accordance with the agreement, the mountain bike competition consisted of two events: men's and women's cross country. A total of 44 men and 29 women competed, and both the men's and women's races were held on 30 July.

Equipment and Staff. All equipment complied with UCI rules. Mavic, Inc., supplied the neutral services. In mountain bike racing, the rider cannot receive any external technical assistance or spare parts during the race. A violation would result in disqualification.

The mountain bike competition was conducted with three paid staff and eight volunteers. More than 500 volunteers from the marathon provided marshaling support for both mountain bike racing and road cycling.

CYCLING—ROAD

After frequent reviews of a variety of potential road courses, the IF and ACOG agreed on a course through Atlanta's historic Buckhead community, located less than 10 mi (16 km) from the Olympic Village. The start/finish area

was located near three 100-year-old churches. From there, the course of approximately 8.1 mi (13 km) proceeded through a shopping district, before winding through a residential neighborhood that included stately mansions and the home of Georgia's governor.

The road cycling competition was open to the public. In addition to temporary seating at the start/finish area, spectators gathered along the course route.

Athlete compounds at the road racing course included tent cabins, an athlete lounge, and neutral services.

Training Sites. Training on the Olympic road course was provided prior to each day of competition. In addition, athletes trained on other city streets.

Competition. The MOU signed with the UCI in 1994 provided for two Olympic firsts in the road cycling competition at the Centennial Olympic Games: professional riders were allowed to compete for the first time, and racers competed in individual time trials. Another change in the programme concerned the elimination of the men's team time trial event.

A total of 189 men and 60 women competed in the four medal events of road cycling. Competition began with the women's race on 21 July, followed by the men's race on 31 July, and both the men's and women's individual time trials on 3 August. In the mass-start road race, the cyclists raced over a distance of 17 laps (137.85 mi/221.85 km) for men and 8 laps (64.87 mi/104.4 km) for women. In the time trials, cyclists started individually from a starting ramp at 90-second intervals, with the men racing four laps (32.4 mi/52.2 km) and the women racing two (16.2 mi/26.1 km).

Equipment and Staff. All equipment complied with the UCI rules. Mavic, Inc., supplied the neutral services.

ACOG provided 32 spare bicycles for competitors. The spare bicycles and other equipment were carried by the neutral support vehicles, which followed the riders in case of mechanical difficulty.

In addition, road cycling utilized approximately 100 cars for the road race and general purposes. BMW and GM vehicles supported the road cycling events.

The competition was conducted with nine paid staff and 180 volunteers. In addition, more than 500 volunteers from the marathon provided marshaling support.

CYCLING—TRACK

The track cycling competition at the Centennial Olympic Games was held in picturesque Stone Mountain Park *(see also the archery section)* and utilized a temporary 5,200-seat velodrome with a revolutionary new wood surface. The 250 m oblong track, featuring 42-degree banking in the turns and 13-degree banking along the straightaways, had a surface of plywood panels covered by a textured surface called Teak Skidguard— a smooth, slip-resistant resin that also reduced track moisture.

Each team was provided with a secure outer cabin where the competitors could store equipment, repair bikes, and rest. Shower trailers and an athlete lounge were located in the athlete compound. Team cabins on the infield were equipped with tables and chairs and provided shade for the riders during competition.

Training Sites. All training was done at the competition site. Training on the velodrome began when the Village opened on 6 July. During competition, a warm-up area was provided on the infield for the riders.

Test Event. The Atlanta Cycling Invitational, held 13–15 October 1995, was the test event for track cycling. Approximately 260 riders from 32 countries competed in five men's and three women's events.

Competition. Among the programme modifications for the Atlanta Games established by the 1994 MOU with the UCI was the addition of the women's point race, bringing the number of medal events in track cycling to eight: men's and women's sprint, individual pursuit, and point race; and men's time trial and team pursuit. A total of 152 men and 54 women competed (24–28 July).

Equipment and Staff. All equipment complied with UCI rules. Mavic, Inc., supplied the neutral services. ACOG supplied teams with spare parts and technical assistance as well as training facilities at the Stone Mountain Park Velodrome.

The track cycling competition was conducted with 9 paid staff and 37 volunteers.

EQUESTRIAN

All three disciplines—three-day event, dressage, and jumping— of the equestrian competition were held at the Georgia International Horse Park. This world-class equestrian facility was constructed especially for the Centennial Olympic Games through a joint venture between ACOG and the city of Conyers.

The Olympic equestrian competition spanned a 15-day period (21 July– 4 August, including two rest days). Individual and team medals were awarded in all three disciplines.

Shaped and constructed from a natural bowl-shaped area, the park's magnificent 32,000-seat (8,000 permanent) main arena featured a 60 x 20 m rectangular sand dressage piste and a 100 x 145 m sand jumping area. The surrounding countryside contained a 25-obstacle, 700 acre (283 ha) endurance course.

The facilities also included stables (five barns with 92 stalls each), a covered arena, a hacking field with grass dressage and jumping areas, a track course, trails, a steeplechase oval, 11 sand training areas, a complete veterinary clinic, grooms' housing complex (with accommodations for 300 people), athlete lounge and locker room, and administrative offices.

Training Sites. Training facilities included five dressage arenas, five jumping arenas, one modern pentathlon arena, and one arena isolated and dedicated for piroplasmosis-positive restricted horses. In addition, the hacking field, a galloping area, and the covered arena were available.

The footing in the dressage, jumping, and covered arena was the same and was maintained in the same manner as the competition arena. Dressage arenas were standard 20 x 60 m areas enclosed by boards, and jumps were single standards and rails.

Test Event. The facility hosted approximately 60 riders for the Atlanta Cup Three-Day Event, 17–20 August 1995.

Competition. The agreement between ACOG and the International Equestrian Federation (FEI) signed in March 1994 established the competition format for all three disciplines.

The staging of the equestrian competition occurred only after long negotiations involving a variety of constituencies. The discussions involved not only the FEI at all levels, but also the state of Georgia and the US Department of Agriculture. These discussions were held due to the fact that Georgia has strict rules prohibiting animals with a communicable disease to enter the state. The issue in regard to the horses was the disease piroplasmosis, which has been eliminated in Georgia.

The competitions proceeded, however, after ACOG and the state agreed to special handling procedures, including building quarantine facilities and providing special attention for horses carrying the potential for piroplasmosis. Horses testing positive for piroplasmosis were not allowed to compete in the three-day event.

In addition to the piroplasmosis issue, animal rights advocates in the US were very vocal about the potential dangers to horses, especially during the three-day event, which might be affected by Georgia's summer heat and humidity. In response to these concerns, ACOG in cooperation with the FEI made minor adjustments to the three-day event program and added cooling stations to the course. These cooling stations were giant fans which sprayed a fine, cool mist on the competing animals.

■ *Three-Day Event.* For the first time in Olympic history, the three-day event (21–26 July) was held as two separate competitions: a team event followed by an individual competition. Eighty-nine athletes participated in the three-day event competition.

■ *Dressage.* A total of 50 athletes (required to be at least 16 years old) competed in the dressage events (team and individual) in the Centennial Olympic Games. Team competition took place on 27 and 28 July, and the individual competition took place on 3 August.

■ *Jumping.* The jumping competition (25, 29 July and 1, 4 August) was held in the jumping ring in the main arena. A total of 83 athletes (required to be at least 18 years old) qualified for the competition (each country could enter a maximum of four competitors and six horses).

The only format modification involved qualification for the individual competition. Results from the qualifying competition were combined with the scores from the first two rounds of the team event to determine the competitors eligible to compete in the individual jumping event, held on the last day of the Games. Only the 45 riders with the best scores qualified for the semifinals of the individual event, from which only the top 20 advanced to the finals.

Equipment and Staff. All equipment provided by ACOG complied with FEI regulations. ACOG contracted with Linda Allen for the design construction of the show jumps and with Roger Haller for the obstacles on the cross-country course of the three-day event. The competition dressage arenas and letters were provided by Jump PVC. Floral decoration was by Richard Jeffery. Additional dressage training arenas and letters were loaned by Bloks, USA.

The footing for all the training areas and competition arena was prepared and maintained by Hermann Duckek, Denmark.

The competition manager was hired in December 1993. The competition was conducted with 23 paid staff and 478 volunteers.

FENCING

The modern Olympic Games began in 1896 with fencing as one of the nine original sports; moreover, fencing is one of only four of the original sports to have been conducted at every modern Olympic Games. While the 1896 competition in Athens, Greece, consisted solely of the individual foil and sabre, the Centennial Olympic Games hosted both individual and team events in men's and women's foil and épée and men's sabre.

The competition was held in the GWCC, Hall F, one of the many venues located in the Olympic Center 3 km from the Olympic Village. Spectators had 2,200 general admission seats for the preliminaries and 3,900 assigned seats for the finals.

The field of play for the preliminaries was surrounded by two rows of parallel barriers to which the noncompeting athletes, national coaches (no personal coaches), nonworking referees, athletes' and officials' escorts, and scorers had access.

The locker rooms and athlete lounge were located in the warm-up area and were temporary structures. The warm-up area contained eight strips for warm-up, practice, and lessons, and a staging area for athletes, officials, and escorts during competition.

Training Sites. Fencing had one dedicated training site with 15 training strips (see Figure 2).

Competition. The entire Olympic fencing competition format was altered by the agreement between ACOG and the International Fencing Federation (FIE), signed in April 1994. From the 1992 Games, the competition was condensed from nine days to six days, adding women's épée for the first time. For these Games, the competition was scheduled for 20–25 July 1996. The number of athletes was set at 42–46 per weapon, with 233 athletes competing (140 men and 93 women).

The competition format was altered to facilitate the smoothest and most efficient flow of events possible. The athletes competed on five strips (for the individual events) in a direct-elimination format with no repechage. Each strip produced one finalist, creating a high level of competition in each bout as well as a format that was more easily followed by the audience. The format of the best two out of three bouts formerly used to determine the winner was changed to one bout of 15 touches. The team event was also altered. The scoring system was changed to a relay format, with the winning team scoring 45 touches.

The field of play for the preliminaries consisted of six Leon Paul elevated strips, SC31 scoring machines, and Kabcom scoreboards. The finals used one Leon Paul elevated strip with the SC31 scoring equipment and the Kabcom scoreboard incorporated into its front panel, all mounted on a 4 ft (1.2 m) high stage. Two Lorrymage video walls were used for both the preliminaries and the finals.

To allow the audience to see their faces, fencers wore translucent masks. Also, ACOG improved the posting of scores to keep spectators closer to the progress of competition.

Equipment and Staff. All equipment provided for the fencers by ACOG for training and competition complied with FIE rules. Swatch Timing provided all timing-related devices including the scoreboards and the timing/scoring machines that registered a scoring hit by an athlete. Other equipment providers included Grainger, Leon Paul, and Lectrotech Company.

The competition manager was hired in mid-1994 and the assistant competition manager in January 1996. A total of 16 paid staff and 121 volunteers managed the fencing competition.

FOOTBALL

Football was the most geographically diverse sport, as five cities in four southeastern states served as venue sites. The competition manager coordinated all transitional elements of the tournament including coordination with FIFA. The competition spanned 15 days, from 20 July through 3 August 1996.

Satellite Venues

■ *Sanford Stadium.* Sanford Stadium, located on the campus of the University of Georgia in Athens, was the venue for the semifinals and finals of both the men's and women's football tournaments. Located 65 mi (105 km) northeast of the Atlanta Olympic Village, this venue is the fourth largest university stadium in the country with a seating capacity of 86,100. Converting the field of play from American football to international football standards required removal of the renowned hedges that surrounded the field.

The field provided an excellent grass surface for the competition. Athletes competing at this venue were housed in the main Olympic Village at Georgia Tech in Atlanta.

■ *Legion Field.* Used primarily for American collegiate football, Legion Field is an 81,700-seat stadium located in Birmingham, Alabama, 148 mi (238 km) from Atlanta. Athletes were housed in dormitories at Birmingham Southern College.

■ *Orange Bowl.* A 1994 World Cup venue and host to numerous other international football matches, the Orange Bowl in Miami, Florida, has a seating capacity of 72,700 and is located 668 mi (1,075 km) from Atlanta on the southeastern coast of Florida. Athletes were housed at Nova Southeastern University.

■ *Florida Citrus Bowl.* Also a 1994 World Cup venue, the Florida Citrus Bowl in Orlando, Florida, accommodates 65,000 spectators and is located 321 mi (517 km) from Atlanta in central Florida. Athletes stayed in the dormitories at the University of Central Florida.

■ *RFK Stadium.* Also a 1994 World Cup venue, Robert F. Kennedy (RFK) Memorial Stadium in Washington, DC, has a capacity of 56,500 and is located 640 mi (1,030 km) from Atlanta. Housing for athletes was at Mount Vernon College.

Training Sites. All training site fields had the same dimensions as the competition fields. Warm-up space was located adjacent to all five venues.

In Atlanta and Athens, training sessions for the semifinals and finals of the Olympic football competitions took place at Agnes Scott College and the Marist School, both within a 15-minute drive of the Atlanta Olympic Village.

In Birmingham, all training sites were located within a 20-minute drive of the Village. This included a lighted on-site facility at Birmingham Southern College and fields at the University of Alabama Birmingham and Hoover Park and Recreation Complex.

Training in Miami took place at the four fields on the campuses of Nova University and Nova High School, both within walking distance of the Village.

Training in Orlando took place on two fields on the campus of the University of Central Florida, within walking distance of the Village.

Training sites in Washington, DC, were Reeves Field at American University and

Harbin Field at Georgetown University. Both were less than 10 mi (16 km) from the Washington Olympic Village.

Competition. A total of 416 athletes (288 men and 128 women) participated in the football competition. The men's tournament featured 16 teams split into four groups. The teams played a round-robin format in the preliminary round with the top two from each group advancing into the quarterfinals. The women's tournament featured eight teams separated into two groups with the top two teams from each group advancing into the semifinals.

The draw, held 5 May 1996 in Atlanta, determined the four groups of four men's teams and two groups of four women's teams, as well as the locations of the matches.

In the first round of competition, groups competed in Orlando and Miami or in Birmingham and Washington, DC, with the men's quarterfinals scheduled for Birmingham and Miami. The semifinals and finals for both men and women took place in Athens.

Equipment and Staff. All equipment provided by ACOG complied with FIFA rules. Sports Supply Group, Inc., supplied goals, nets, corner flags, etc., while Adidas, Inc., supplied the competition balls.

In early 1995, the SPM for football became the competition manager. The deputy competition managers were hired in fall 1994. At Athens, the competition was conducted with a paid staff of 14 and 75 volunteers.

ACOG provided the deputy competition manager and the competition production management team for the preliminary-round football cities. Each of the four competition staffs was designed differently, in cooperation with the LOC.

GYMNASTICS

GYMNASTICS—ARTISTIC

The Georgia Dome, the largest indoor arena for gymnastics in Olympic history, provided the setting for the artistic discipline during the Centennial Olympic Games. Also the site for the basketball competition, the Georgia Dome was located in the middle of the Olympic Center, 3 km from the Olympic Village.

The Georgia Dome was divided into two sections to accommodate both the gymnastics and basketball competitions. In order to properly separate the two competitions, a soundproof curtain was suspended from the Dome's ceiling to the floor with the gymnastics and basketball events placed on either side.

The competition field of play included the gymnastics podia and production table located within a corral (fence) measuring 202 x 136 ft (62 x 41 m). The five podia (95 cm high) each staged an apparatus for both the men's and women's events. Competition officials and television personnel were positioned on the floor of the arena inside the corral.

Training Sites. At the training site (see Figure 2), six sets of equipment were available in the three training gyms for men and three training gyms for women. The equipment in the training gyms was identical to the equipment at the competition venue. The six training gyms were located within 20 minutes of the Olympic Village. The training schedule permitted training for all athletes from 6 through 29 July. Delegations were assigned a minimum of 4.5 hours training for each day, comprising 2.5–3 hours for the first session and 1.5– 2 hours for the second session.

The warm-up gymnasium was constructed adjacent to the competition floor, permitting excellent access for the athletes and coaches.

Test Event. Held 16–17 November 1995, the Atlanta Gymnastics Invitational served as one of the final test events prior to the Games. The individual event competition welcomed 18 men and18 women to the Georgia Dome.

Competition. Signed in September 1994, the agreement between ACOG and the International Gymnastics Federation (FIG) established the competition format and set forth various requirements for the competition.

The IOC approved invitations for five additional men and three additional women athletes. The Centennial Olympic Games artistic gymnastics competitions included 218 athletes (113 men and 105 women) competing in the team competition. The top 36 gymnasts from the team competition qualified for the all-around finals, with the top eight in each event qualifying for the individual apparatus finals. Competition was scheduled for 20–25 and 28–29 July 1996.

In addition, the MOU added the Gala event to the Olympic artistic gymnastics competition for the first time. A non-medal event, the Gala closed the competition and allowed the gymnasts to perform a routine especially for the spectators.

Equipment and Staff. All equipment provide by ACOG complied with FIG regulations. American Athletic, Inc., was the exclusive supplier for the gymnastics equipment.

The competition manager was hired in March 1994. The assistant competition manager was hired in June 1995. The competition was conducted with a paid staff of 57 and 219 volunteers.

GYMNASTICS—RHYTHMIC

The rhythmic gymnastics competition was held at the 10,000-seat University of Georgia Coliseum in Athens 1–4 August 1996. The competition included the individual all-around event as well as the team competition, a new event for the 1996 Olympic Games.

The field of play featured two individual and team competition carpeted areas, each 13 x 13 m. The field of play was surrounded by a corral enclosing the two competition carpets and the seating for the competition officials. The production table accommodated seating for the results team, IF committee members, delegation leaders, and the production staff. The ceiling height for the rhythmic gymnastics competition was 12 m.

The athlete locker rooms and the warm-up gymnasium were located in the same area and were adjacent to the competition venue.

Training Sites. The athletes trained from 6 to 29 July in Atlanta, at a site 15 minutes from the Olympic Village (see Figure 2). The training site was equipped with eight Mitufa floor systems identical to the competition floor.

The music for the athlete performances was recorded onto DAT audio system tapes to ensure consistency in training and performance. The recording process was accomplished at the training site gymnasium.

Athletes from countries participating in one event could train 3 hours, twice a day, while athletes from countries participating in both the individual and team competitions could train 4.5 hours, twice a day.

Training during the competition was limited to 2 hours per day at the University of Georgia Coliseum in Athens. The training at the Coliseum was organized as podium training for individuals and groups.

The warm-up gymnasium was constructed adjacent to the Coliseum and equipped with three Mitufa floor systems and carpets identical to the competition area. The warm-up gymnasium served as the staging area for the athletes during each competition session. The warm-up gymnasium and competition hall were scheduled for two days of formal training and a session following each competition.

Competition. Signed in September 1994, the agreement between ACOG and FIG established the competition format and set forth various requirements for the competition.

Thirty-seven individuals qualified for the all-around competition, and 53 athletes qualified for the team competition. The team competition was based on the performance of two exercises, one with five hoops and the other with three balls and two ribbons. Individual competition involved four exercises, each with a rope, ball, club, or ribbon.

Equipment and Staff. Each athlete was responsible for providing her own equipment, which had to comply with FIG regulations and be measured before each competition. Failure to comply with these regulations resulted in a one-point deduction.

The competition manager for rhythmic gymnastics was hired in March 1994. The deputy competition manager was hired in June 1996. Many Games-time positions were shared between

artistic and rhythmic gymnastics. The competition was conducted with a paid staff of 9 and 80 volunteers.

HANDBALL

All women's competition, men's preliminaries, semifinals, and placement finals were held in Hall G of the GWCC, a facility that also hosted six other Olympic sports and the International Broadcast Center. The playing site for handball allowed for 7,300 spectator seats. The men's medal matches were held in the Georgia Dome, where approximately 34,500 seats were available. The competition was held 24 July–4 August 1996.

The condition of the competition halls was nearly ideal, with handball-specific lighting, precise temperature controls, a specially designed handball subfloor, and 12-camera television production.

The fields of play at both the GWCC and the Georgia Dome were 40 x 20 m.

Training Sites. Training sites for the Olympic handball competition (see Figure 2) met IF specifications and were fully equipped with support facilities such as locker rooms, showers, and administrative offices. The four handball training sites were available from 6 July to 4 August. Each training site and the warm-up court in the GWCC were equipped with Taraflex sport flooring, the same surface used on both competition courts.

Test Event. Although not held at the GWCC, the Handball USA Cup served as the test event for the handball competition. Held at the Georgia International Convention Center, the event extended from 6 to 13 August 1995 and welcomed six men's and six women's teams for the tournament.

Competition. Signed in January 1995, the agreement between ACOG and the International Handball Federation (IHF) established the competition format and set forth various requirements for the competition.

The draw for the handball competition was held in January 1996 on the occasion of the World Cup in Stockholm, Sweden. It was organized by the Swedish Handball Federation and was cohosted by ACOG and the IHF.

The Olympic handball competition consisted of 12 men's and 8 women's teams, totaling 191 male and 128 female athletes. The teams were placed in two groups (A or B) of four teams each for the women's matches and six teams each for the men's matches. In the preliminary rounds, teams competed within their own pools, with the top two teams in each pool advancing to the semifinals. Teams not advancing to the finals played the teams with the same rank in the other pool to determine final placement.

Equipment and Staff. The IHF approved the equipment and suppliers. Adidas, Inc., supplied balls for the competition and training, and Robbins Sport Surfaces supplied the suspended wood floors for the competition and training areas, while Taraflex supplied the seven synthetic playing surfaces. Goals and backdrop netting were provided by Sport Supply Group, Inc.

The competition manager was hired in May 1993, with the assistant competition manager starting full-time in July 1995. The competition was conducted with 17 paid staff and 133 volunteers.

HOCKEY

The hockey competition took place between 20 July and 2 August in two adjacent stadia at the Atlanta University Center, 3.5 km from the Olympic Village. The new competition pitch at Morris Brown College Stadium was the primary venue and site of the finals. It was supported by a competition pitch, warm-up pitch, and new stadium at Clark Atlanta University. The stadium at Morris Brown College seated 15,000, and the Clark Atlanta University Stadium seated 5,000.

Each stadium had four oversized locker rooms with commercial fans.

Training Sites. In addition to a specific training site (see Figure 2), the competition pitches and the warm-up pitch also were used for training. All were equipped with synthetic turf.

A separate warm-up pitch was provided at Clark Atlanta University. Teams scheduled to play at Morris Brown College warmed up on the competition pitch.

Test Event. Clark Atlanta University hosted the Atlanta Hockey Challenge Cup '95, which served as the sport and the venue's test event. The tournament was held 6–11 August 1995, and four men's and four women's teams competed.

Competition. Immediately following the signing of ACOG's agreement with the International Hockey Federation (FIH) in December 1993, the city of Atlanta began working to increase the sport's exposure in the southeastern US. Local communities and schools were introduced to the sport, and the effort was aided by the relocation of the US women's team to Atlanta in July 1995, giving Atlantans an opportunity to watch Olympic-level hockey as the team prepared for the Games.

For the Games, the MOU stipulated that the tournament would consist of 12 men's and 8 women's teams. In the men's preliminary rounds, the teams were divided into two pools. The preliminaries were followed by classification matches to determine places 5–12 and semifinals and finals to determine the medal winners.

For the women's teams, pool matches consisted of an eight-team round-robin format. The gold medal match was contested between the first- and second-place teams, while the third- and fourth-place teams played for the bronze. The remaining four teams were ranked according to the number of points each accumulated during the pool matches.

A record number of 318 athletes (190 men and 128 women) participated in Olympic hockey competition.

Equipment and Staff. All equipment provided by ACOG complied with FIH specifications. Presidential Sports, Inc., supplied the synthetic turf for all fields. Sport Supply Group, Inc., supplied the goals, netting, and team shelters.

The competition manager was hired in May 1994. The assistant competition manager was hired in May 1995. Fourteen paid staff members and 115 volunteers were at Morris Brown College, and another 8 paid staff members and 115 volunteers worked at the Clark Atlanta University complex.

JUDO

The venue for the judo competition was Hall H of the GWCC, which provided a total of 151,000 sq ft (14,043 sq m). The final configuration provided 7,300 seats. The GWCC was an exceptionally adaptable venue for all functions required to support both the competition and all preparatory activities.

The field of play consisted of two judo mats (tatamis, which are covered mats of pressed foam) laid over a podium. Each competition area provided a 10 m, U-shaped space, bordered on each of three freestanding sides by an additional 3 m of safety zone. The shared side provided 4 m of safety zone between the two competition areas.

An additional layer of .75 in (1.9 cm) plywood was added to level the top of the podium, which measured .5 x 18 x 32 m. A 1 m border covered in teal carpet surrounded the tatami.

The field of play was surrounded on three sides by a corral. Sports marshals were available at each opening as well as at the corners of the closed sides.

Locker rooms and shower rooms were provided for both male and female athletes and officials. Footlockers were provided in all locker rooms.

An athlete lounge was located adjacent to the warm-up area and in close proximity to the athlete locker room.

A 20 x 20 m warm-up area covered with tatamis was provided, which was installed atop a wooden subfloor. The warm-up area was enclosed and had two video monitors, permitting the athletes to follow their competition categories.

Training Sites. Judo had one exclusive training site (see Figure 2). Seventeen cubes, each providing 64 sq m separated areas as well as locker rooms, medical stations, and six saunas, were provided in the air-conditioned facilities. The site provided a very effective training environment, as well as a sewing area for affixing the country-code back placards.

Each delegation was scheduled for one hour of training time daily, according to a predetermined rotating matrix, between morning, mid-afternoon, and late afternoon. Delegations could request alternative training times.

Competition. In accordance with the MOU signed with the International Judo Federation (IJF) in September 1993, judo had a limit of 400 athletes. A total of 392 athletes (241 men and 151 women) competed from 20 to 26 July.

Each weight category on a single day competed in a direct-elimination draw format. A double repechage system allowed athletes who lost a match to reenter the competition for a chance to reach the final medal rounds.

Equipment and Staff. All Agglorex judo mats and other required equipment were supplied by Federal Sports Technologies, Inc. Each mat had two electronic sport-specific scoreboards provided by Swatch Timing. B & K Rental supplied the podia used during the Games.

The competition manager was hired full-time in January 1995, and the assistant competition manager in May 1995. For the judo competition, 34 paid staff and 122 volunteers worked at the venue.

MODERN PENTATHLON

The modern pentathlon competition took center stage at three Olympic venues: the GWCC, the Georgia Tech Aquatic Center, and the Georgia International Horse Park.

The shooting and fencing events were held in two separate sections of Hall F of the GWCC, both of which seated approximately 2,000 spectators.

Following the shooting and fencing competitions, pentathletes and staff were transported to the Georgia Tech Aquatic Center for the swimming events. The covered natatorium featured a 50 m pool with eight lanes and electronic timing.

The final two phases of the modern pentathlon—riding and running—were held at the Georgia International Horse Park. The pentathletes were transported from the Aquatic Center in specially designed buses that also served as locker rooms. Inside these buses, athletes had the opportunity to change clothes, relax, and have refreshments.

The riding competition took place in the main arena, which featured a beautifully decorated course. The running course began in the center of the main stadium arena. Each of the four 1,000 m loops of the course passed through the specially prepared track inside the arena for approximately 400 m and then left the arena to continue on an adjacent, level grass field.

Athletes had access to locker rooms at each of the three venues.

For the fencing, running, shooting, and swimming phases of the modern pentathlon, the warm-up area was the same as the field of play. For the riding phase, a warm-up area containing one vertical jump and one oxer was adjacent to the main competition arena.

Training Sites. Training took place at particular sites in Atlanta for each specific phase: shooting training took place at the competition site; fencing training was at the Georgia International Convention Center; swimming training took place at either the Georgia Tech Aquatic Center or the student athletic complex at Georgia Tech; and running training was at Grady High School, which is 4.8 km from the Atlanta Olympic Village.

Test Event. Held 10–11 August, the 1995 Modern Pentathlon World Cup Final served as the test event for the competition. Unlike the Games, the test event included a women's event. The Georgia International Convention Center served as the site for shooting and fencing, while the other sites were the same as during the Games. The Games-time enhancements of the format were tested at this time.

Competition. ACOG and the International Modern Pentathlon and Biathlon Union (UIPMB) established that the modern pentathlon competition would be held in one day for the first time in Olympic history. Traditionally spread over five days, this demanding Olympic event was held on 30 July 1996. A total of 32 athletes were required to shoot, fence, swim, ride, and run in a 12-hour test of skill and endurance.

The shooting area included a 10 m shooting range with electronic standing targets and scoreboards that featured the athletes' names. The fencing area featured eight electronic competition pistes, with two alternate pistes, set in an H-shaped configuration. Scoreboards on each strip showed the names of the fencing pentathletes, with the winner of each bout clearly indicated, and a video wall gave spectators current rankings.

Several days prior to the riding competition, a jury ride allowed officials to select 16 horses, plus 4 alternates, from a pool of 25 horses. On the day of competition, the computer draw provided a fair method of distributing the horses to the pentathletes. The draw was simulcast to the spectators.

Several enhancements were proposed to the running portion of the modern pentathlon. In addition, a staggered start for the running competition provided a dramatic close to the event. With points tallied after each of the five modern pentathlon events, the pentathletes started the race at intervals that corresponded to the total number of points separating them from the leader. Therefore, the first three competitors to cross the finish line—the three highest

scorers—would be the medal winners. And finally, a newly developed audio computer start system allowed the competitors to use only two lanes instead of the traditional three.

Equipment and Staff. All equipment provided by ACOG complied with the UIPMB Modern Pentathlon Competition Rules. The shooting equipment was supplied by Suis-Ascor, including targets, competitor monitors, and individual target printers. The fencing equipment included 10 Leon Paul fencing pistes and equipment supplied by Swatch Timing. The swimming phase used existing equipment supplied by the swimming venue, including equipment by Adolph Keifer & Associates, Mikasa, Inc., and B & K Rental and touch pads provided by Swatch Timing. The exact course for the riding phase's 12-jump course was created by Linda Allen, and electronic eye start/finish technology was provided by Swatch Timing. Running utilized equipment by Sport Supply Group, Inc., and Mondo S.p.A. Two clocks and photo timing systems were provided by Swatch Timing.

There were 11 paid staff for the modern pentathlon, excluding the competition manager, who also served as equestrian competition manager. The administrative support of the modern pentathlon was managed by the equestrian administrative staff. Aquatics, fencing, and shooting also contributed volunteers to the staffing of the modern pentathlon competitions. Of the 250 volunteers needed to staff modern pentathlon only 30 were exclusive to modern pentathlon.

ROWING

The sport of rowing has been on the Olympic Programme since the beginning of the modern Games. For these Games, the rowing competition schedule was 21–28 July 1996.

The clear waters of Lake Lanier served as the venue for the competition. The venue, constructed on a calm stretch of water with forested banks, provided excellent racing conditions, sheltering crews from the wind. It included spectator seating, a permanent cabling system, a finish tower, two permanent boathouses, and a six-lane 2,000 m race course. A 1,000 m training course adjacent to the course was also provided. The venue was also used for the canoe/kayak–sprint events.

One of the best courses in the world due to its flat water, the rowing venue provided seating for 17,300 spectators. Docks constructed directly along the southeastern side of the course provided spectators the most complete view of the races ever offered in an Olympic rowing event. Also unique to the event, a newly developed start system for the competitors was the first mechanical start system to be used in rowing for an Olympic Games.

The separation between the boating area and the spectator areas helped divide the different activities, providing the athletes with a screened environment during the competition.

A day village at the Lake Lanier venue provided the athletes with a lounge, refreshments, exercise facilities, and a recreational area.

Training Sites. Lake Lanier was a training site as well as a competition venue, serving exclusively as a training site until 20 July 1996. Once the rowing competition began, the venue was both the competition venue for the rowing athletes and a training site for noncompeting rowing athletes and the canoe/kayak–sprint athletes.

Test Event. Held 22–24 September 1995, the Lake Lanier Challenge served as the rowing test event. Spectators were seated on the northeastern side of the lake.

Competition. Signed in November 1994, the agreement between ACOG and the International Rowing Federation (FISA) established the competition format and set forth various requirements.

The competition was divided into separate weight classes for women and men and a variety of single, double, and eight-person racing shells. All together, 597 athletes (392 men and 205 women) participated in the rowing competition. During the Games, athletes competed in a total of 14 medal events, making rowing one of the largest sports represented in the Centennial Olympic Games. Rowers competed in eight events for men and six events for women. The newest addition to the rowing program was the inclusion of lightweight divisions in three medal events.

Depending on the number of entries, rowing events included preliminaries, repechages, semifinals, and finals. A draw held just prior to the first day of competition determined the starting order in the heats, in accordance with FISA international competition rules.

Equipment and Staff. All equipment provided by ACOG complied with FISA rules. A manufacturer's marking could not appear more than once on an item of equipment. Equipment suppliers included Brunswick, which supplied boats and various boating equipment, and Fast Signs, which supplied the distance markers.

The competition manager was hired in May 1994. The assistant competition manager was hired in April 1995. The competition was conducted with 16 paid staff and 245 volunteers.

SHOOTING

The Centennial Olympic Games welcomed 423 athletes (295 men and 128 women) to the Wolf Creek Shooting Complex, which was 21 mi (33.7 km) from the Olympic Village.

In order to accommodate this large contingent of athletes and nations, ACOG constructed the Wolf Creek Shooting Complex especially for the Games. The venue was acclaimed by the International Shooting Union (UIT) and national shooting federation leaders as one of the finest and most modern shooting venues in the world. The new venue had three separate rifle and pistol buildings and three combined skeet and trap fields, all located around a common spectator plaza. The venue featured finals seating for 5,000 for the clay target events and 2,500 for the rifle and pistol finals.

In order to encourage spectator interest, Wolf Creek offered six different opportunities for viewing the competition. To facilitate the flow of spectators, the 10 m range served as overflow seating for the rifle and pistol finals. The venue included a manufacturer exhibition area, an Olympic memorabilia exhibit, and numerous spectator information and educational sites.

Temporary facilities also were constructed at the venue for arms and equipment storage, team rooms, competitor rest areas, and additional offices. Four trailers were provided for arms storage that were kept under 24-hour security during the period of 5 July–7 August.

Four large air-conditioned tents were constructed as locker rooms. To provide secure storage, a basement storage facility in the 50 m range was allocated for athlete equipment. Another large air-conditioned tent was used as the athlete lounge.

Wolf Creek featured the most modern target and results system ever installed in a shooting range. All rifle and pistol events utilized Suis-Ascor electronic targets provided through ACOG's Swatch Timing sponsorship. For the first time in Olympic history, no paper targets were used. The results of every shot fired were initially scored; displayed on electronic monitors and scoreboards for shooters, media, and spectators to see; and recorded in the computerized results system.

Training Sites. All training for shooting took place at Wolf Creek on the competition fields of play. The venue opened for training on 6 July 1996. Training times and shooting positions were scheduled by the classification office according to the number of NOC entries in each event. Official training for each event was provided the day before each competition event.

Test Event. One of the final test events prior to the Games, the Atlanta UIT Shooting Cup was held from 22–29 April 1996. The 15-event competition was held at Wolf Creek, and approximately 450–500 athletes attended.

Competition. An MOU between ACOG and the UIT was signed in November 1993 establishing the format and other requirements for the competition.

With the test events completed, the shooting competition was set to start on 20 July and continue through 27 July 1996. Two new Olympic clay target events—men's and women's double trap—were on the Olympic Programme for the first time at the 1996 Games, bringing the total number of events to

15—10 men's and 5 women's. Each competition began with a preliminary round followed by a shoot-out final. Scores in the final were added to each shooter's preliminary total; the winner was the shooter with the most points (or clay targets hit). In the case of ties, there were shot-by-shot tiebreakers.

Equipment and Staff. All shooting equipment provided for the competition by ACOG complied with UIT regulations and was inspected by UIT technical delegates. Suis-Ascor electronic targets provided by ACOG sponsor Swatch Timing were used for all 10, 25, and 50 m pistol, rifle, and running target events. Clay target traps were provided by Matarelli through Swatch Timing.

Technical services were provided at Wolf Creek by each selected equipment manufacturer.

For the shooting competition at Wolf Creek, ACOG employed 7 paid staff and 98 volunteers.

SOFTBALL

To further the opportunities for women in the Olympic Games, the IOC added softball to the Olympic programme.

The competition was held at Golden Park Stadium in Columbus, Georgia, approximately 105 mi (169 km) southwest of the Atlanta Olympic Village. Located along the Georgia and Alabama border on the banks of the scenic Chattahoochee River, Golden Park is currently the home of minor league baseball's Columbus Red Stixx.

Golden Park was an extensively remodeled baseball stadium. The complex had an 8,800-seat capacity and consisted of a standard fast pitch softball field with a skinned infield and an outfield fence at 200 ft (61 m).

Two large locker rooms were located inside the stadium with two reserve

locker rooms at the adjacent Civic Center. The athlete lounge was located near the left field foul line.

Teams warmed up at the training site, with final loosening up on the playing field. Each team had designated bull pens where pitchers could warm up.

A satellite Village for athletes and officials participating in the Olympic softball competition was located in Columbus, with housing, meals and recreational amenities on-site. The Village was located at Henry Hall on the US military installation at Fort Benning, Georgia.

Training Sites. Training sessions for the competitions were located at the South Commons Softball Complex, an eight-field facility adjacent to Golden Park. Each country was assigned a field on the first day. Field assignments were rotated daily.

Competition. Signed in 1993, the agreement between ACOG and the International Softball Federation (ISF) established the competition format and set forth various requirements for the competition.

The Olympic competition consisted of a pool of eight fast pitch teams competing in a single round-robin tournament, with the top four teams progressing to the semifinals and medal-round games. The nine-day tournament was held from 21 to 30 July (with a rest day on 28 July). A total of 120 women (eight teams of 15) competed in the first-ever Olympic softball tournament.

Equipment and Staff.

All equipment provided by ACOG complied with ISF rules. Sport Supply Group, Inc., supplied the backstops, pitching machines, pitcher's rubbers, pitching screens, and other equipment. Mizuno, USA, supplied the softballs, and Rogers Break Away Base System

supplied the bases and home plate. All suppliers complied with ISF rules.

The competition manager was hired in March 1994 on a full-time basis. The assistant competition manager was hired in June 1995. There were 17 paid staff and 127 volunteers at the venue.

TABLE TENNIS

Held from 23 July through 1 August 1996, the table tennis competition was one of seven different competitions housed in the halls of the GWCC.

The seating capacity of Hall D was 4,100. The spacious 89,000 sq ft (8,277 sq m) competition area contained eight playing tables lined in a row. The dimensions per playing area were 16 x 8 m. A suspended wood floor 3 in (7.6 cm) high, covered by approved playing mats, served as the playing surface.

The playing conditions for the athletes met all standards of the International Table Tennis Federation (ITTF) and were of the highest quality. Through the use of specially designed air-locks on all outside doors, air movement over the field of play was limited to a level of 10 cm per second. At the same time, temperatures were kept at a comfortable level for both athletes and spectators. Every table featured a computerized statistics system that was located courtside. This system provided the most detailed point-by-point breakdown ever provided at a table tennis event. Furthermore, scoring information was immediately available to the press, broadcasters, athletes, and coaches.

Training Sites. In addition to the eight competition tables, the hall contained 16 practice tables for training and warm-up. The secondary practice site (see Figure 2) provided 14 practice tables. Each team was guaranteed training time and table space twice daily.

Test Event. One year prior to the Games, the venue site hosted its first competition—the Table Tennis World

Team Cup. As the sport's test event, the three-day competition differed from the Olympic format by focusing solely on team competition, with 16 men's and 12 women's teams in attendance.

Competition. In November 1993, ACOG and ITTF signed an MOU that established the format and other requirements for the competition.

During the Centennial Olympic Games, 64 men and 63 women competed in the men's and women's singles tournaments, while the men's and women's doubles tournaments each had 31 pairs competing.

Initially, athletes competed in 16 groups of four (eight groups of four for doubles) in a round-robin format against competitors within their own group. In this preliminary stage, the matches were best-of-three games. The winners in each group then advanced to the next single-elimination stage of play, which consisted of best-of-five matches.

Equipment and Staff. Joola supplied the tables, surrounds, nets, umpire tables, manual scoring devices, and athlete towel boxes. The colors and design of the equipment were coordinated with the ACOG Look of the Games. The tables were purple and blue, with blue surrounds and matching umpire equipment. Nagase Kenko provided the wine-colored court mats. Nittaku provided orange balls.

The competition manager was hired in May 1994. The assistant competition manager began in May 1995. The competition was conducted with 12 paid staff and 114 volunteers.

TENNIS

One of three venues at Stone Mountain Park, the newly constructed Stone Mountain Park Tennis Center hosted competition between 23 July and 3 August 1996.

This permanent state-of-the-art facility was built for the 1996 Olympic Games in Stone Mountain Park, one of the most popular tourist attractions in Atlanta and the state of Georgia.

Comprised of 16 hard courts, the Stone Mountain Park Tennis Center featured seating for 10,400 spectators at the main stadium center court, 4,900 spectators at court 1, and 500 spectators at court 2. The additional surrounding 13 courts each had a seating capacity of 500. The area containing the outdoor court bleachers was also designed to be transformed into more tennis courts if needed. All 16 court surfaces were made of Plexipave, an acrylic cushioned hard surface.

The facility also included adequate locker rooms, an athlete lounge, and additional support areas for the judges, referees, and technical officials.

Training Sites. The training sites at Stone Mountain Park and elsewhere *(see Figure 2)* for the tennis competition featured the same court surfaces as the match courts at the Stone Mountain Park Tennis Center. Both training sites were equipped with the necessary athlete and management support facilities.

Competition. The agreement between ACOG and the International Tennis Federation (ITF) signed in March 1994 instituted certain modifications to the tennis program.

Instead of geographical qualification tournaments, athletes qualified based on computer ranking or wildcard selection. In addition, bronze-medal playoff matches in all four medal events were added to the Olympic programme.

The single-elimination tournament format was changed from best of five sets to best of three sets, with the exception of the men's singles and doubles finals, which remained best-of-five sets. The tiebreaker was used in all sets except the third set and in the men's singles and doubles finals, where advantage scoring applied in the fifth set.

The final modification involved changing the tournament draw to ensure that players from the same country would not meet before the quarterfinals.

For the competition, a total of 185 athletes (96 men and 89 women) competed in four medal events: men's and women's singles, and men's and women's doubles.

Equipment and Staff. Umpire's chairs, squeegees, roll dries, singles sticks, and nets were provided by Sport Supply Group, Inc. Penn balls and Babolot stringers were provided by Penn Racquet Sports, Inc.

The competition manager was hired in September 1994. The assistant competition manager was hired in August 1995. The tennis competition staff consisted of 14 paid staff and 283 volunteers.

VOLLEYBALL

VOLLEYBALL—BEACH

Added to the Olympic Programme in 1993, beach volleyball made its inaugural appearance in the Games as a full medal competition from 23–28 July 1996.

The Atlanta Beach venue, located in Jonesboro, 20 mi (32 km) south of the Atlanta Olympic Village, was a unique sports and entertainment park, featuring three constructed lakes, large sandy beaches, and permanent office facilities. The competition took place in two stadia: center court, with a seating capacity of 9,600, and the second court with seating for 3,000. The field of play for each court was 28 x 19 m.

Training Sites. Six courts at the venue were available for training. Two warm-up courts and two practice courts separated from the spectators were provided for the athletes.

Competition. The MOU between ACOG and the International Volleyball Federation (FIVB) signed in June 1994 established Tybee Island near Savannah,

Georgia, as the competition site. However, because of access and transportation challenges, the venue was moved to Atlanta Beach.

Beach volleyball is played with four players, two per side, on an 18 x 9 m court.

The Olympic competition consisted of 24 men's teams and 18 women's teams. All teams competed in a double-elimination format. All preliminary sets were scored one game to 15 points. Medal matches were the best two out of three sets to 12 points; the third set was played as a tiebreaker to 12 points with a 2-point lead.

Equipment and Staff. Only FIVB-approved equipment was used. Mikasa, Inc., provided the balls, while the field-of-play equipment was made by Senoh, including lines and nets.

The competition manager was hired in May 1994. The assistant competition manager was hired in March 1995. There were 23 paid staff members and 141 volunteers working at the Atlanta Beach complex.

VOLLEYBALL—INDOOR

The XXVI Olympiad was particularly significant for indoor volleyball, as the 1996 Games represented the centennial anniversary of competition. Fans could enjoy watching indoor volleyball throughout the entire period of the Games, from 20 July to 4 August.

The main venue for the indoor volleyball competition was the Omni Coliseum. A multipurpose arena, the Omni hosted part of the preliminary competition and the finals with seating for 16,500 spectators. With the addition of more teams, a second venue was required. Originally, it was proposed to be at Cobb County's Galleria Centre. The site was changed, however, in 1994 to the University of Georgia Coliseum, which hosted six preliminary matches in a 10,000-seat facility. A day village located near the venue in Athens was provided for the athletes and officials from Atlanta.

The fields of play (36 x 21 m) at each of the arenas were identical. The court dimensions at both sites were 18 x 9 m. The ceiling height exceeded 12.5 m.

Training Sites. *(For volleyball training sites, see Figure 2.)* Each team received two two-hour training sessions prior to 15 July as well as one two-hour training session from 15 July through the end of the Games or until elimination from competition. All courts at these sites met IF training specifications. In addition, all sites were equipped with the necessary athlete and management support facilities such as locker rooms and administrative offices.

Test Event. The USA Volleyball Centennial Cup held 15–19 August 1995 included four teams and served as the test event for the sport and the venue.

Competition. In June 1994, ACOG and the FIVB signed an MOU setting the basic requirements for the sport, the accommodation of more teams than in previous years, and the requirement of two competition sites.

The competition format was expanded for the 1996 Games to include 12 women's teams for the first time. The tournament consisted of 288 athletes playing in 24 teams (12 men's and 12 women's). The tournament format, identical for men and women, involved preliminary competition with two six-team pools playing a complete round-robin. The top four teams in each pool advanced to the quarterfinals, semifinals, and finals.

Equipment and Staff. FIVB-approved equipment was used for indoor volleyball. Senoh was the supplier of nets and posts, while Mikasa, Inc., supplied the volleyballs. Taraflex provided the green and orange flooring that covered the plywood floor. Mizuno, USA, supplied uniforms for referees and other officials.

The deputy competition manager joined ACOG in April 1994 and became the competition manager in January 1995. The competition staff at the Omni was composed of 17 paid staff and 178 volunteers, and the Georgia Coliseum operated with 16 paid staff and 88 volunteers.

WEIGHTLIFTING

Hall E of the GWCC was the site for the weightlifting competition. Events took place on a 12 sq m stage raised 1 m. On top of the stage rested a 4 x 4 m solid wood competition platform. In the two front corners and in the front center of the stage, sections were created for the referees. In order to withstand the demands of weightlifting, the center section of the podium was reinforced with an extensive support structure built with 6 x 6 in (15 x 15 cm) boards. The podium was carpeted and skirted.

For the first time in the Olympic Games, a television camera was placed beneath the competition platform to provide a unique angle for filming. This camera was placed beneath a piece of frosted Lexan that was strong enough not to break and textured to provide good footing for the athletes.

The athletes were flanked on either side by a pair of stadium-sized video screens designed to show replays. The 10 x 25 ft (3 x 7.5 m) scoreboard showed results for up to 16 competitors and was one of the largest in the Olympic Games.

The venue supplied spectator seating for 5,000. Seats that were unusable due to a large support pillar that blocked the view of competition were covered with Look of the Games fabric in order to avoid distraction.

Weightlifters were provided 18 private cubicles, each including a massage table. Nearby was a separate room with portable showers, sauna, and scales for weight checks.

The warm-up area was located immediately behind the competition podium, and separated from it by a floor-to-ceiling drape and a sound-dampening wall. The warm-up room contained 10 platforms, four closed-circuit monitors showing the competition platform, and four results system monitors showing current standings and scheduled attempts for each lifter. In addition, a more traditional marker board system showing future attempts was provided.

Training Site. One training site, Hall A in the GWCC, was available to weightlifters. The site contained all necessary training equipment, 35 platforms, saunas, showers, and spas. Five two-hour sessions were provided each day, with countries scheduled on a rotating basis. Schedule alterations were allowed subject to availability of equipment.

Test Event. Held 13 August 1995, the Super Heavyweight Weightlifting Championships served as the test event for the competition. The event was held at the Georgia International Convention Center.

Competition. By agreement between ACOG and the International Weightlifting Federation (IWF) signed in November 1994, the sport format was altered from that of the 1992 Games. The 10 weight classes were changed and organized into the following categories: 54 kg, 59 kg, 64 kg, 70 kg, 76 kg, 83 kg, 91 kg, 99 kg, 108 kg, and +108 kg. The weightlifting tournament consisted of 253 men, all given three attempts each in the snatch and the clean and jerk. The gold medal was awarded to the athlete with the greatest successful lift in his weight category. Competition was held 20–24 and 26–30 July.

Equipment and Staff. All equipment complied with IWF rules. Uesaka Iron Works supplied barbells and other necessary equipment, as well as the competition platform. The competition podium was rented from B & K Rental in Maryland.

The competition manager was hired in June 1994. The assistant competition manager was hired in April 1995. In total, 16 paid staff and 86 volunteers worked at the weightlifting competition.

WRESTLING

The GWCC hosted both wrestling disciplines, Greco-Roman and freestyle, in Halls G and H, respectively. Each hall seated 7,300 people.

According to the IF, the field-of-play and athlete preparation areas were the best ever assembled for the Olympic Games. The field of play was a fully carpeted podium 132 ft x 52 ft x 32 in (40 m x 16 m x 81 cm), containing three O'Jump octagonal wrestling mats placed side by side. It was bordered on four sides by corrals.

Seven temporary locker rooms and four portable showers were available to the athletes. The locker rooms were divided among the participating teams. In addition, an athlete lounge was provided within the complex.

The warm-up area contained six warm-up mats for Greco-Roman and four for freestyle. Also located in the warm-up area were a bank of televisions, exercise bicycles, and saunas. All weigh-ins were held in an area constructed within the warm-up area.

Training Sites. Two training sites were used by wrestling. The GWCC was used on weigh-in days. The other site *(see Figure 2)*, about a 10-minute ride from the Village, featured 14 mats, exercise bicycles, saunas, dummies, and scales. Separate workout spaces for teams allowed privacy while training.

Test Event. Approximately 300 athletes participated in the sport's test event. The World Freestyle Wrestling Championship was held at the Omni Coliseum 10–13 August 1995.

Competition. The agreement between ACOG and the International Federation of Associated Wrestling Styles (FILA), signed in December 1993, established 20 medal events (10 freestyle and 10 Greco-Roman weight classes). A total of 406 men competed. The Greco-Roman competition was held 20–23 July, and the freestyle competition was staged 30 July–2 August.

Equipment and Staff. All materials provided for training and competition complied with FILA rules.

The competition manager was hired in April 1994, and the assistant competition manager in May 1995. The staff for wrestling consisted of 20 paid staff and 114 volunteers.

YACHTING

The yachting competition was held in an area of Wassaw Sound and the Atlantic Ocean off the coast near Savannah, Georgia, from 22 July to 2 August 1996.

The venue consisted of three main parts: a satellite Olympic Village located in downtown Savannah, the Olympic marina located on Wilmington Island, and the day marina, a 150,000 sq ft (14,000 sq m) temporary barge system located on the north side of Wassaw Sound at the mouth of the Wilmington River. The day marina served as a forward launch area for all competing boats except the Stars and Solings, which were towed between the Olympic marina and their race areas on alternate days, generally spending one night in the water at the day marina.

The day marina concept was the first of its kind and enabled competitors to store their boats safely and securely in close proximity to their racing areas. A long sail or tow was eliminated for all events except the keelboats. During the Bid process and original planning phase, the Olympic marina was to be located at Priest Landing. This site is located on Skidaway Island on the Wilmington River and was 2–3 mi (3–5 km) closer to the racing areas than the actual Olympic marina. However, environmental concerns about endangered wildlife made this venue unusable, so an alternate site was chosen, necessitating the creation of a day marina in close proximity to the competition.

The final site of the Olympic marina, a former resort hotel property, was originally planned to be the satellite Olympic Village. After the hotel closed, the Village location was moved to the Riverfront Marriott in downtown Savannah. A portion of the hotel property and contiguous properties were used as the Olympic marina facility.

The yachting field of play consisted of an area of the Atlantic Ocean and Wassaw Sound encompassing approximately 22 sq mi (57 sq km). Athletes prepared their boats at the day marina and either sailed or were towed to their assigned racing area for the day. An athlete lounge was provided at the Olympic marina. This facility also housed the sports information desk for the Olympic marina. At the day marina, teams were assigned tents, in which they stored their equipment. Access to the day marina was strictly controlled, and members of the press were not permitted until the competing athletes had left the field of play.

Spectator and Olympic Family seating was provided on seven spectator boats that could accommodate approximately 1,000 people per day.

Training Site. The Olympic marina was available as a training site from 1 April 1995 through 31 May 1996. The facility was not used extensively until May 1996. A practice area was defined within the field of play. Additionally, noncompeting boats were allowed to practice during Games-time in any of the four race areas not in use.

Test Event. More than 600 athletes participated in the 1995 Savannah Olympic Classic Regatta, which served as the test event.

Competition. The yachting competition consisted of 10 medal events, involving 459 athletes (359 men and 100 women). It was the largest regatta in Olympic history, and for the first time, the IF set the maximum number of athletes for the yachting events. A total of 145 athletes participated in the three men's events and 96 in the three women's events: board (Mistral), single-handed dinghy (Finn for men, Europe for women), and double-handed dinghy (470). In the four open events, 202 men and women competed: centerboard dinghy (Laser), two-person multihull (Tornado), two-person keelboat (Star), and three-person keelboat (Soling).

Event modifications for the 1996 Games were: Laser replaced Flying Dutchman in the centerboard dinghy classification; Mistral supplanted the Division 2 sailboard; and the IMCO one-design board made its Olympic debut, replacing the Lechner sailboard. Event pairings were: Laser and Europe; Star and Finn; Soling and Tornado; 470 (men and women); and IMCO one-design (men and women).

The racing format established by ACOG and the International Yacht Racing Union (IYRU) called for two races a day rather than one. The races were managed

to target times rather than distances. To accommodate racers who had their boats damaged in the first race and could not return in time for the second race, the scoring was modified to include one "throw out" race if four to eight races were sailed. If more than eight races were sailed, two throw outs were allowed.

The racing took place in Wassaw Sound for the IMCO one-design events, and in three race areas in the Atlantic Ocean just outside Wassaw Sound for all other events. A new trapezoidal course configuration was used for the 470s, Europes, Lasers, and Solings.

Equipment and Staff. ACOG provided all of the single-handed boats. All materials for these craft were secured at one time to ensure uniformity, and boats were inspected throughout the building process.

Boats and equipment were measured before and during the regatta and were selected at random for daily post-race measurement. Boats provided by athletes (470, Soling, Star, and Tornado classes) were fully measured prior to competition. The spars and sails of the Finns and Europes also were measured. All measurement was supervised by the class measurers under the direction of the IYRU. ACOG was responsible for supplying all measurement equipment and staff.

ACOG provided teams with furniture, a nautical spare parts store, sunshades, and workshops for conducting repairs.

The competition manager was hired in January 1994, with other members of the staff hired subsequently through July 1996. The staff was composed of 21 paid staff and 810 volunteers.

Chapter Twenty-Two
Staffing of the Games

OVERVIEW—Among ACOG's greatest assets in organizing and staging the largest Olympic Games in history were the people who staffed the effort—talented, diligent, enthusiastic, hospitable individuals dedicated to contributing to the success of the 1996 Centennial Olympic Games.

From the beginning, the organizing committee recognized staff as a critical resource that would greatly affect the quality of the Games, and thus endeavored to create a comprehensive staffing plan that would identify and meet ACOG's needs, as well as those of its constituents, while providing a rewarding experience for each individual. Equally significant, plans had to reflect ACOG's belief that each job was crucial to the success of the Games.

A challenge for ACOG was creating a procedure to identify, process, and assign the staff—comprised of volunteers, contractors, loaned employees as part of sponsorship agreements, and salaried and hourly employees—into a cohesive team known collectively as the Olympic Games Staff (OGS). Also challenging was planning and implementing programs that addressed the diversity of the OGS and technology systems to support processing and assignment within an extremely compressed time frame.

Throughout all functional areas of the organization, the development of staffing plans was a time-consuming process. Management from each department and venue first identified the needed staff functions and positions and provided brief job descriptions, summaries of the qualifications needed, and the hours of operation for each position. From this information, functional areas estimated the number of individuals needed to staff each area of their operations. This was a complicated process that was constantly reviewed as department and venue staffing plans evolved until Games-time.

In January 1995, before the final staffing demand was identified or technology systems fully developed, ACOG began its recruiting process and the development of one of the most comprehensive staff and volunteer training programs in Olympic history.

Once recruited, staff were assigned to Games-time functions and notified by mail. Upon acceptance of a position, OGS received background materials regarding their position and were then trained at the venue to which they were assigned. Venue training was beneficial to the OGS, as it offered staff an opportunity to gain experience, meet colleagues, and ask questions.

The creation of the staffing process, although challenging, was successfully achieved by intensive planning and teamwork among all ACOG departments. At Games-time, 131,788 individuals comprised the OGS, each contributing immeasurably to the success of the Games.

This chapter describes how the thousands of staff members required at Games-time were assembled. ACOG's staffing process is described on the following pages in its logical sequence, beginning with the development of the consolidated staffing plan and concluding with recognition programs.

ORGANIZATION

The staffing process began in 1991 as the AOC progressed from a bid committee managed by volunteers to an Olympic organizing committee directed by paid employees who would establish policies for recruiting, assigning, training, and managing all who would provide services on behalf of the 1996 Centennial Olympic Games.

In order to assemble the required number of individuals to staff the Games, staffing responsibilities were ultimately divided among three departments: Human Resources (HR), Volunteer Services, and Total Games Staffing (TGS).

During the period of 1991–1994, HR, a part of Administration, was responsible for determining the number of paid employees that would be required up to and through the Games and for processing these paid employees. HR also helped create ACOG's organizational structure prior to the Games. *(For information regarding the organizational structure of ACOG, see the Management chapter.)*

Volunteer Services, a part of Olympic Programs, focused on compiling information regarding functional area and venue volunteers for the Games, processing all volunteers, and managing the Internal Volunteer Program. *(See the Management chapter.)*

TGS, a part of Planning and Integration, was created in 1994 to manage the development of an overall staffing plan for the Games.

These departments assisted ACOG functional areas in defining their staffing needs, and then recruited, assigned, and trained staff on their behalf; however, the functional areas were responsible for managing their respective staff.

Demand Assessment

In October 1993, Volunteer Services began to survey ACOG departments to identify the positions needed and determine the number of volunteers required to staff the Games. Concurrently, HR was assessing the number of necessary paid employees and ACOG Financial Services' Procurement and Contract Administration

(P&CA) division was addressing requirements for contract staff. The desired result of these early independent efforts was not to identify the exact number of people required to fulfill Games-time demand, but to emphasize the need for a consolidated staff plan to ACOG management.

In summer 1994, Planning and Integration helped consolidate the data that had been continually updated and modified by Volunteer Services, HR, and P&CA into the first overall staffing plan for the 1996 Games. Between August and October 1994, two databases were developed to capture a wide variety of staffing-related information for both paid staff and volunteers. These were called the TGS FoxPro volunteer database and the TGS FoxPro employee database. At that time, these departments also assigned members of their staff to the new department, TGS. TGS's primary mission was to assess, integrate, standardize, and streamline staffing requirements in order to construct an optimal consolidated staffing plan. The Volunteer Services staffing manager supervised the TGS team, reporting to the directors of both Planning and Integration and Volunteer Services.

As the TGS team proceeded in developing a consolidated staff plan, it became apparent that more specific development was needed to standardize staff planning parametrics and methodologies, eliminate duplication and overlap between job positions, and ensure that operational plans matched staffing projections. It also became evident that the development of this consolidated staff plan would be more efficient if the management of the staffing plan was confined to a single department, TGS, under the direction of Planning and Integration. In January 1995, a new TGS program director was appointed to manage this effort.

Operational Reviews

In early 1995, TGS began intensive operational reviews and financial analyses that provided a new foundation for staffing, and from

• NEAL H DOROW • LAUREL J DORR • JOHN R DORRIS • ROBERT A DORRIS • KEINYA M DORSETT • A ELAINE DORSEY • BELINDA T DORSEY • CAROL E DORSEY • CECIL D DORSEY • CURTIS DORSEY • DEBBIE K DORSEY • FARRAH M DORSEY • GLORIA H DORSEY • HENRY C DORSEY • JAMES JR E DORSEY • JENNIFER L DORSEY • JOSEPH C DORSEY • JOY E DORSEY • MICHELLE S. DORSEY • RONALD A DORSEY • SARAH DORSEY • SHIRLEY A DORSEY-DAVIS • ALFRED S DORSEY JR • LEO E DORSON • CAROLE A DORTCH • CHRISTINE L DORY • FRANCHESCA D DOS REMEDIOS • DEREK J DOSS •

419

which all departmental staffing plans were reconstructed. This assessment, which focused on organizational charts and job descriptions, resulted in the creation of an ACOG master staffing plan that remained the standard structure, with modifications, through the Games.

Important steps in the development of the master staffing plan were standardizing titles and creating methodologies for calculating the exact number of staff needed at each venue for each functional area.

When TGS began conducting review sessions with each department, some 2,500 unique staff titles already had been created for venue-based personnel. Standardizing the titles significantly reduced this number and revealed areas where different departments were planning to assign staff to the same responsibilities.

ACOG departments were also using a variety of planning assumptions to estimate the number of staff needed for similar work, ensure coverage for several shifts per day, and account for attrition. By using consistent methodologies to develop this data, the estimated total number of people required to staff the Games was significantly reduced.

Organizational Charts. Though functional area plans continued to change until and in some cases through the Games, organizational charts were developed that provided the necessary framework for staff planning.

In early 1995, based on principles from Venue Management, a master venue organizational chart was developed that graphically depicted the overall organizational concept for the management of competition venues. This chart served as the model for the charts to be developed by each functional area operating within a venue, and created a consistent organizational approach that was used throughout ACOG.

The master organizational chart was included in the Venue Operations Manual, a document that established the primary policies, procedures, and guidelines for competition venue operations.

Job Descriptions. Organizational charts had to be accompanied by job descriptions for each position identified in the management structure for use in the ACOG Venue Job Description Manual. The preparation of these descriptions assisted departments in developing more detail for their operating plans and provided direction for those who would recruit and fill the positions.

TGS assisted in standardizing and editing the descriptions and managed the schedule for their development. In April 1995, the first edition of the Venue Job Description Manual was compiled and distributed to all functional areas. An update was prepared the following month, and a final edition was distributed in November 1995.

THE CONSOLIDATED STAFF PLAN

By May 1995, TGS was producing weekly reports pertaining to the consolidated staff plan that provided the first comprehensive view of the number of part-time, temporary, and full-time staff members by department; the volunteers required to stage the Games by quantity, job description, location, and department; and the full cost of paid employees and volunteers by department.

Initial estimates for necessary paid employees were more than 9,000, and volunteer estimates were almost 74,000. TGS was able to reduce the number to 7,900 and 61,000, respectively. From the viewpoint of experience with previous events, operational efficiency, and cost management, these estimates were still too high; however, more analysis was required before further reductions could be made.

Estimates for contractor positions for cleaning, food, and other services were 46,000, but because the data was largely incomplete, indications were that this number was too low.

Some departments required help planning staff quantities, as staff was estimated for various functions which were already estimated by another department, and planners could not always deduce how many volunteers or what type of staff would be needed at specific venues. Moreover, some departments planned to schedule volunteers to work three or four days per week, while others planned six or seven; some departments planned for 50 percent attrition, and others estimated none. To help resolve these issues, TGS developed and implemented specific staffing policies, such as a standard number of shifts and days a volunteer was expected to work.

Total Games Staffing Task Force

The TGS task force was formed in May 1995 to establish ACOG's staffing priorities and resolve staffing issues that were raised as staff plans were being consolidated. This group was comprised of senior management representatives from Financial Services, HR, Planning and Integration, Venue Management, Volunteer Services, and the office of the COO.

Numerous meetings were held between early June and late July. TGS used the results of these meetings to formulate recommendations regarding staffing quantities and costs. The TGS task force required all departments to submit written responses to issues and questions regarding the quantity and cost of their staffing plans.

Following these meetings, it was recommended that volunteer positions be reduced to 43,500, and paid employees to 6,400. Allocations for each functional area were delivered to the managing directors in mid-September. By 6 October, 85 percent of these departments had refined their plans to match the allocations.

Reports by Total Games Staffing. Changes to each department's staffing plan were continuous; therefore, accurate and detailed record maintenance by TGS analysts was critical to sustain these changes, which were reported to Financial Services, HR, Volunteer Services, and other departments.

An extensive data report was developed using the TGS FoxPro database. This report, called a change management report, was delivered to Volunteer Services each week from 20 October 1995 through 8 July 1996. It noted all additions, deletions, and changes to existing positions and included a complete, updated list of all volunteer quantities, titles, and venues. A summary report was also produced for and delivered to Financial Services every four weeks to track staffing costs. Changes were less frequent for paid employees; therefore, reports of changes were provided to HR on a daily basis via E-mail and voice mail, with master reports produced every 4–5 weeks.

The entire organization relied heavily on both the standard and customized reports for volunteer, paid, and contractor staff generated by TGS. TGS analysts provided approximately 1,000 different types of reports from the data maintained in the TGS database.

By April 1996, the number of volunteers requested increased to 54,511 based on the additional requirement of 1,800 ticket-takers and ushers, 2,800 security personnel, and 2,000 drivers for the ACOG Transportation Department. The final number approved by July 1996 to staff the Games was 51,881 volunteers, 6,560 paid employees, and 78,240 individuals accredited as contractors.

IMPLEMENTATION OF THE STAFFING PLAN

To coordinate the efforts of the various departments involved in the staffing process, a staffing integration group (SIG) was formed just prior to the test events in 1995 (Atlanta Sports '95). SIG consisted of a core planning group and an extended group.

The core group, managed by TGS, included representatives from Accreditation, HR, Planning and Integration, Security, Technology, and Volunteer Services. This group met weekly

• BRANDON R DOTY • CHANDA KAY DOTY • CLAUD R DOTY • NINA N DOTY • PETER G DOUBLEDAY • VANESSA P DOUCET • JENNIFER J DOUCETTE • BRIAN DOUD • EDWARD I DOUDA • STEPHAN I DOUE • STACEY DOUGAN • CHRISTINE A DOUGHERTY • KIMBERLY C DOUGHERTY • LINDA M DOUGHERTY • ROBERT B DOUGHERTY • HEIDI LYNN DOUGHERTY ATC • BERNADETTE G DOUGLAS • BIRGITTA M DOUGLAS • CARLA L DOUGLAS • CAROL A DOUGLAS • CERELLE F DOUGLAS • CHAKA DOUGLAS • CHARLES D DOUGLAS • JANE L DOUGLAS • JOHN DOUGLAS • MCLEAN R DOUGLAS • MICHAEL DOUGLAS

421

and Volunteer Services. This group met weekly to plan and manage an integrated time line and answer staffing questions raised by functional areas.

The extended group, consisting of approximately 100 staffing representatives from the functional areas, participated in 12 SIG forums from September 1995 to June 1996. The forums included presentations from the core group on a variety of staff-related topics, such as job descriptions, shift dates and times, and services provided, as well as a question and answer ses-

FIGURE 1:
GAMES STAFFING TECHNOLOGY SYSTEM (GSTS)

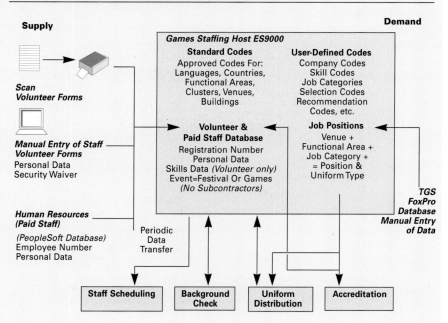

sion. These forums were crucial to the implementation of ACOG's staffing plan, as they identified critical issues, served as a communication link to all departments, and provided a progress report on the consolidated time line.

Games Staffing Technology System

The Games staffing technology system (GSTS), one of the operations management systems (OMSs) developed for the Games, was created as a centralized database of volunteer and paid employee information. The software

application had the capacity to qualify, confirm, assign, train, uniform, and accredit electronically. Once the initial database of personal data —or supply data—was created, the number of job positions—or demand quantities, determined by the approved staffing budget from the TGS FoxPro database—were entered manually.

Qualification criteria such as the skill, geographical location, and availability of applicants were utilized in selecting, and ultimately assigning, a person to a position. Various queries and reports were available, including confirmation and summons letters for training, staff lists, venue assignment rosters, and management status reports.

GSTS shared data with other OMSs, such as the accreditation, background check, staff scheduling, and uniform distribution systems. The system's most significant interface, with the accreditation application, was designed not merely to transfer personal data from one system to the other but also to help streamline the process to match access privileges (accreditation) with job assignments (GSTS).

Data for ACOG paid employees was primarily managed by HR through PeopleSoft, a personnel application. However, since a large percentage of paid employees would also perform a Games-time function requiring accreditation, data was transmitted from PeopleSoft into GSTS and eventually, the accreditation system.

The background check application retrieved information from GSTS to support the security clearance process. GSTS transferred information to the uniform distribution application to ensure accredited persons were issued the correct uniform for their Games assignment. From April 1996 through the end of the Games, GSTS provided a daily extract of names, addresses, and assignments to the staff scheduling application.

GSTS was available to users working within Volunteer Services on the ES9000 host via their desktop personal computer (PC). The core user group consisted of a systems operations manager and four assistants, in addition to users from HR and Security. During the nine months prior to the Games, the venue staffing managers (VSTMs) in Volunteer Services and their assistants were also given on-line access to the system. Other functional areas received periodic printouts of their respective staffing groups from Volunteer Services.

TGS initiated the development of FM3, a centralized scheduling system, to provide a tool that would allow each department to specifically enter titles, staff numbers, shift start and end times, and venues, in order to create a staff schedule. This system provided summary information to departments to allow them to validate their planning assumptions and make any necessary adjustments. Individuals from Technology, TGS, and Volunteer Services cooperated to define the scheduling process and system requirements so Technology could begin designing the system. FM3 was released in phases from mid-November 1995 to mid-April 1996.

Several key reports generated by FM3 assisted users in tracking staff scheduling information, determining scheduling gaps, and identifying individuals who had not been scheduled. The Personal Schedule Report reflected all shift times, dates, positions, and venues to which an individual had been scheduled in FM3. In addition, FM3 was used to generate the daily duty rosters, which sorted the staff reporting information by functional area and were vital to the smooth and efficient operation of the check-in process. A wide variety of management reports were also produced using data from FM3.

This system was linked to a network prior to the Games so that functional areas could enter their own schedules. In early July, the system became independent at each venue. With the exception of Security and Transportation, the VSTM entered all staffing changes in the system. *(For the operations flow of the GSTS and FM3 systems, see Figures 1 and 2, respectively.)*

RECRUITING AND PROCESSING

Recruiting and processing the more than 100,000 people required to staff the Games

was the primary responsibility of HR and Volunteer Services, with assistance from all ACOG functional areas.

ACOG Paid Employees

In order to recruit and hire the required number of people to fill Games-time positions, the HR Department established in September 1995 its objectives to:

■ process paid employees, including ACOG, Randstad, loaned, value-in-kind (VIK), and some individual contract staff;

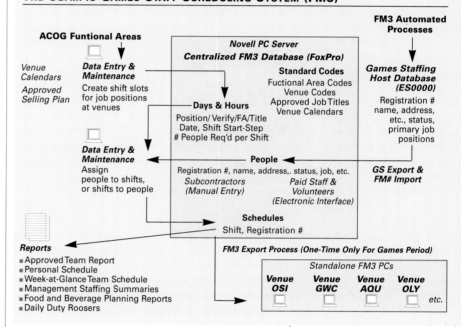

FIGURE 2:
THE OLYMPIC GAMES STAFF SCHEDULING SYSTEM (FM3)

■ implement and manage a mass hiring process beginning 1 November 1995; and

■ cooperate with each functional area to implement all internal redeployment.

Employee Processing. It was critical that paid employees be identified and processed by

HR as early as possible, in order to meet other staffing deadlines. This process was complicated by the lack of a common staffing database at ACOG.

Although detailed records for paid employees were maintained in the HR database, PeopleSoft, data for all paid employees performing Games-time duties had to be entered in GSTS. HR matched the supply data—or staff member—from the HR database to the demand data—or position—from the TGS database, then entered the combination of supply and demand in GSTS. These systems were not linked, so managing and processing paid-employee assignments through GSTS was extremely challenging.

Technology developed a partially automated interface to transfer supply data from PeopleSoft to GSTS, but this process was terminated in March 1996, as it was easier to enter and assign paid employees manually than to match the supply data from PeopleSoft to the correct position in GSTS.

HR worked with Accreditation, Uniform Distribution, and Volunteer Services to develop time lines for paid employee processing. Most employment information was delivered to current staff through publications or voice mail. Paid employees with start dates after May 1996 received information in their letters offering employment.

Mass Hiring. Recognizing the need to fill Games-time positions rapidly, HR implemented an accelerated recruiting process, known as the mass hiring process, in November 1995. Paid employee information from the TGS database was used to create mass hiring requisitions for functional areas, which included the total positions available and the titles, duration, staff type, and budgeted salary amount for each po-

sition. The HR coordinator contacted the functional area manager to verify the mass hiring requisitions data and determine the staffing and sourcing requirements.

Positions were filled by candidates identified by the hiring manager, HR, or Randstad, or by redeployed ACOG staff. Functional area managers identified numerous employment candidates for their departments due to the specialized nature of many Games positions, and HR mailed employment information to more than 1,000 of these candidates. Once the package was returned and the candidate had completed the employment process successfully, including a background check and drug screen, HR verbally offered employment and issued a confirmation letter, which included start-date instructions.

HR continued to seek candidates for open positions from the résumé database and conducted jobs fairs in February and April 1996.

Randstad Staffing Services. In September 1994, under terms of its sponsorship agreement, Randstad became the sole provider of hourly paid personnel for ACOG. In February 1996, ACOG and Randstad adjusted procedures to expedite the mass hiring process for the many Randstad employees that would be needed for Games-time.

Under the new process, two additional Randstad staffing managers were assigned to ACOG headquarters full-time to assist in recruiting, interviewing, and hiring 1,000 hourly paid employees. Randstad staffing managers used the staffing projections provided by GSTS to determine which positions needed to be filled and then identified and hired candidates with the appropriate skills to fill the positions. After an employment offer was accepted, the appropriate ACOG functional area manager was given the new employee's name and start date.

Randstad also opened an office in an ACOG warehouse in March 1996, where two staffing managers screened and hired logistics crew candidates.

Randstad's support was instrumental in the success of mass hiring for the Games, since it allowed ACOG managers and HR to focus on hiring the additional 2,500 managerial staff members needed. By July 1996, 1,400 Randstad employees were recruited for the Games.

Contractors. ACOG departments contracted with specific companies to provide the services and staff they required for the Games. These contracted companies were responsible for recruiting and hiring the required number of employees or subcontractors. The process of selecting contractor companies was not standardized across ACOG departments. By Games-time, the number of companies ACOG contracted with to provide services was approximately 3,597.

Redeployment. HR was responsible for the internal redeployment of ACOG paid employees between functional areas. All ACOG paid employees received staffing assignments for the Games. When an employee's position was not required for Games-time responsibilities, their manager contacted HR, which then placed the individual in an appropriate Games-time position. Only 25 employees were redeployed from one functional area to another for the Games, as most were redeployed within their original functional area.

Volunteers

Volunteer recruiting was largely a function of Volunteer Services, but other departments also recruited people to fill volunteer positions. Volunteer Services recruited for positions requiring minimal training and a maximum availability of four weeks. Generally, ACOG departments were responsible for recruiting volunteers for positions requiring specialized skills (e.g., medical, technology, sports) or long-term availability (hosts and hostesses).

Because the Atlanta community has a strong history of volunteerism and had demonstrated great enthusiasm for participating in ACOG activities, attracting enough volunteers to stage

the Games was achieved successfully, but required standardization and communication of the responsibilities for Games-time assignments.

The Olympic Force. ACOG began building the base of potential volunteers through a program called the Olympic Force. The Olympic Force was comprised of volunteers from ACOG's internal volunteer program; groups from the community such as sports clubs, schools, religious groups, and professional organizations; and the Corporate Council.

The Corporate Council, established on 11

August 1991, was comprised of representatives from 15 of the largest corporations in Georgia. Each company agreed to provide an allocated number of volunteers for the Games as well as an experienced human resources professional to assist with staffing and support the training program and other pre–Games-time volunteer activities. Each corporation loaned an experienced professional to serve as the VSTM for their assigned venue from 1 January 1995 through the Games.

As a part of the recruiting strategy, Volunteer Services also worked closely with ACOG Community Relations to engage community groups and residents of venue host neighborhoods. *(For more information, see the Management chapter.)*

top: **Pre-Games volunteers were at the very heart of ACOG's efforts, as their tireless work and dedication helped ensure the success of the Games.**

bottom: **Volunteer recognition pins were given to all pre-Games volunteers in recognition of their tenure of service.**

Application Process. In March 1994, the volunteer application was developed. It provided as much information as possible to applicants about volunteering for the Games. It also requested comprehensive information from the applicants, gathering enough data for Volunteer Services to recommend volunteers to ACOG functional areas for further evaluation. A list of desired skills based on early staff descriptions, focus groups, market research firms, and ACOG functional areas was identified and compiled by Volunteer Services.

Because of required training, uniforming, transportation, and support costs, it was decided that volunteers must be willing to work at least 14 days. This 14-day minimum requirement resulted in fewer applications than expected. As the Games approached, the minimum requirement was reduced to 12 shifts and, for some positions, 8 shifts.

Volunteers were also required to be 18 years of age by 1 July 1996, pass a security background check, and provide their own housing. For some sports volunteer positions, such as ball kids and gymnastic runners, this age requirement did not apply; applications were approved case by case based on the tradition of the sport. If a specific skill was required and a volunteer was recruited from outside metropolitan Atlanta, ACOG provided dormitory-style housing.

The original application consisted of the application booklet, answer sheet, and security waiver form. So that volunteers could be matched to appropriate positions, applicants were asked about their general background, availability, preferred geographic location, proficiency in languages other than English, professional and volunteer skills, licenses and certifications, sports background and experience, and prior volunteer service history.

More than 75,000 volunteer applications were completed as a result of ACOG's recruiting efforts.

Application Distribution. Applications were distributed in January 1995, and recruiting continued as planned through June 1996. The process was enhanced by a comprehensive media plan executed by the Communications Department that included press releases, targeted mailings, public service announcements, radio and television interviews, and on-site media coverage of recruiting events. The distribution strategy was designed to provide easy access to the application for potential volunteers statewide.

On 17 January 1995, more than 70,000 applications were distributed to members of the Olympic Force at its annual group coordinators meeting. Corporate Council members received approximately 25,000 applications for their employees during the following week.

In an effort to reach the general public, a one-day event, known as Super Saturday, was held on 21 January in five metro-Atlanta locations. After an extensive publicity campaign and broadcasting by local television and radio stations, thousands of potential volunteers visited the centers and completed applications. After Super Saturday, distribution continued at various metro-Atlanta locations and 11 other Georgia cities throughout January and February. A total of 23 distribution locations were used.

The first phase of recruitment focused on encouraging as many people as possible to complete and return the application. Only Corporate Council applications and those for ACOG departments that had specific skill requirements, such as sports, were precoded for assignment.

To ensure the availability of the application, distribution points were established at ACOG and various other locations, such as United Way and libraries throughout the state. An application could be requested and received by mail if a self-addressed, stamped envelope was included.

Approximately 250,000 applications were distributed from January 1995 through March 1996.

Recruiting Process. Original estimates projected that 90–95 percent of the required volunteers would be identified by February 1996, allowing volunteers to be assigned, confirmed, and trained during the remaining months.

The processes and technology systems which supported volunteer recruiting were capable of accommodating the several hundred thousand volunteer applications within a short time frame. However, application submission was staggered over a longer period of time than expected. Approximately 20 percent of the applications had been manually entered into the database two months prior to the Games.

Although ACOG had more than enough volunteers to staff the Games, the recruiting process lasted longer than anticipated and required several changes in strategy and extensions to the time frame to complete.

As Atlanta Sports '95 approached, recruiting for the approximately 9,000 volunteers required to staff the test events was combined with recruiting for the Games. During this phase, functional areas, as well as Volunteer Services, intensified their efforts by addressing specific groups. This effort was also enhanced by a media campaign.

Because volunteers could work in an event related to the Games and choose a particular venue, test events were successfully staffed, and there was an increase in the number of applicants for the Games. As a result of the test events, several changes were made to simplify the recruiting process.

The volunteer application form was simplified to require only basic personal information, geographic location, availability, and preferred venue. Volunteers who worked at the test events were given preference for Games-time assignments.

The final phase of recruiting, based on the staffing plan and the staffing of the test events, occurred after the October 1995 staff plan was completed. These recruiting efforts focused on filling specific positions. Flyers listing positions were widely distributed, and a media campaign highlighting the available positions was begun.

By late spring, the competition venues were approximately 80 percent staffed, but many noncompetition venues and some functional areas had attained less than 50 percent of their recruitment goals.

The successful recruitment of the last ten thousand volunteers can be attributed to functional area staffing coordinators, VSTMs, and the small Volunteer Services recruitment team.

These recruiting efforts generated over 75,000 completed applications, providing ample applicants from which Games volunteers were selected. On 25 June 1996, volunteer demand was 55,261, and the number of valid applications, 58,028. The final number of valid applications was 60,422.

VOLUNTEER ASSIGNMENT

The core requirements for volunteers—flexibility and willingness to fill an identified need—was based on ACOG's belief that the fulfillment of all levels of responsibility was necessary to the success of the Games. Based on this plan, mass assignment, a core function of GSTS, was designed to match thousands of potential volunteers with available positions. Except for venues and functions preassigned to members of the Corporate Council, the two most important criteria for mass volunteer assignment were availability and skill.

A volunteer who filled a position requiring specific skills or long-term availability was called a designated, or direct, volunteer. A volunteer assigned to a position requiring minimal

KATHY S. DRESSEL • NANCY E DRESSEL • JAY DRESSER • DANIEL DRESSLER • BETH R DREW • BUDDIE W DREW • CAY DREW • ELAINE M DREW • FRANCES K DREW • GERTRUDE S DREW • JAMES JESSE DREW • JOHN B DREW • JOHN J DREW • MARY E DREW • MICHELLE T DREW • ANGELA DREW-MORRIS • JOE S DREWRY • VIRGINIA P DREWRY • NORMAN A DREWS • CLINTON HOWARD DREXEL • ADAM J DREYER • DIRK DREYER • FRANCES M DREYER • LARRY W DREYER • LORIN M DREZIN • GARY A DRIBNAK • CHARLES J DRIEBE • THOMAS DRIGGERS • LISA A DRIGGS • VIRGINIA DRIGGS •

427

training and average-length availability was called a mass volunteer. Originally, the terms referred to the method of volunteer assignment: mass volunteers could be assigned positions by the computer, while designated volunteers had to be assigned manually. Gradually, designated volunteer came to mean a volunteer recruited for and assigned to a specific position by an ACOG functional area, regardless of the level of skill or length of availability required. As the Games period approached and recruiting efforts intensified, the distinction between designated and mass volunteers became less significant.

Following the test events, some volunteers expressed their desire to volunteer for specific assignments or venues; thus, ACOG changed its method of mass assignment to honor their requests, encouraging volunteers to indicate their assignment preferences. This change resulted in keeping departments from using the GSTS matching function for assignment; therefore, all volunteers' names were manually assigned to positions.

Prior to assigning individuals to positions in GSTS, Volunteer Services prioritized the groups from which volunteers could be selected. Generally, based on a group affiliation, volunteers were assigned in the following order: ACOG internal program volunteers, Corporate Council members, test event volunteers, and all remaining volunteers. Venues were assigned volunteers for up to 115 percent of available positions. Corporate Council volunteers were assigned to up to 50 percent of available positions in their venue, with the remaining positions being assigned to community volunteers. If a requested venue was fully staffed, volunteers were assigned to their second or third choice.

ACOG determined that competition venues be assigned first, followed by select noncompetition venues, such as the accreditation centers, Main Press Center (MPC), Olympic Family Hotel, Olympic Village, and ACOG functional areas such as Opening and Closing Ceremonies and Guest Services. Within venues, positions in Protocol, Sports, and Venue Management received priority. Generally, positions in food production and cleaning services, in remote parking lots, on rail platforms, or late at night were eliminated, and filled by paid contractors.

All processes involving the use of GSTS were directed by the systems operations manager, supported by two analysts and data entry personnel. The analysts examined the data, produced the status reports, and managed volunteer record changes.

Since all 50,000 volunteers needed to be manually assigned—one volunteer to one position—it was apparent that the systems operations group could not handle the volume of data entry. Following ACOG's progression to venue teams in 1995, Volunteer Services assigned a staff member, including the 15 Corporate Council representatives, to each of the competition venues and many of the noncompetition venues.

Thirty VSTMs were responsible for entering all assignments in the system for their venue as well as the thousands of record changes.

This decision distributed the workload and enhanced the VSTM role as the sole contact for staffing of their venues. With one person reviewing the staffing for one venue, rather than a team reviewing the volunteers assigned to 4,805 positions across 65 venues, the staffing plan became more manageable and deficiencies and overabundances of staff became more apparent.

VSTMs worked directly with venue managers (VMs) and functional area staffing coordinators to complete the recruiting and assigning process. This included providing weekly and sometimes daily status reports, actively recruiting to fill any remaining unstaffed positions, and assisting functional area staffing coordinators in resolving staffing issues, such as duplicate assignments.

The Olympic volunteer center was established as a place for prospective volunteers to learn about the Games and complete the entire application process.

An early assumption was that by 15 December 1995, functional areas would complete the paperwork, including the proposed assignment, for volunteers they recruited. This would allow Volunteer Services to complete the assignment in GSTS of designated volunteers prior to assigning volunteers to all other positions. This proved to be an unrealistic expectation, and the deadline was extended first to 15 March and then to 4 May. As a method of tracking the program of making assignments, detailed reports were distributed to managing directors in the weekly COO meetings.

With only 57 percent of the designated volunteers assigned by March, it was evident that without additional staffing efforts, the organization would be unable to successfully accredit, uniform, and train all the volunteers. At this time, staffing became a priority for the entire organization. Once volunteers were assigned in GSTS by Volunteer Services, it was the responsibility of the appropriate functional area to call the volunteers and confirm their schedules. By 5 June, 41,522 of the 55,720 volunteers in the database had been assigned.

In order to assist the functional areas with confirming the assignment of and scheduling volunteers, Volunteer Services provided candidate lists of all volunteers assigned to positions in their area. The first of these lists was provided to the functional areas in January 1996, allowing them to begin verifying volunteer acceptance of the assignment and commitment to the time requirements. This process was far more time-consuming than originally anticipated.

Functional areas then began scheduling their volunteers. Each department devised its own methods of tracking volunteer schedules, using spreadsheets and written formats. The introduction of the FM3 scheduling system helped standardize the procedure.

Change Management Form

After all volunteers on the candidate lists were contacted, the lists were returned to Volunteer Services along with a change management form if a change in status was required. Volunteers unable to meet the job requirements were deleted from the assignable pool by Volunteer Services. Those who did not accept the assignment offered but still wished to volunteer were contacted by Volunteer Services, which tried to reassign them to another area. Volunteer Services entered the changes of those reassigned to other positions in GSTS.

Many functional areas were also changing their staffing plans through the TGS process. Staffing reductions or increases were requested, but most requests were to change quantities in functional areas among venues.

During a particular two-week period, more than 10,000 volunteer records were changed. In an attempt to stabilize the data, ACOG implemented a policy where no additional staff plan changes could be made after 15 March unless they were operationally critical to functional areas. As a result, only 10–15 changes to staff plans were made each week between 15 April and early July.

The candidate lists were revised to include the names of only confirmed volunteers and were then transferred to the Accreditation Department, which assigned access privileges for the volunteers.

The Olympic Volunteer Center

The method used to process volunteers from receipt of their application through deployment to their Games-time assignment changed from the plan adopted in February 1995 to a simplified process in January 1996. Many operational principles were modified, especially those relating to the use of an Olympic volunteer center (OVC). The OVC, designed as a complete center for volunteer processing, opened in May 1995, and was staffed primarily with volunteers who were

A call center was established within the Olympic volunteer center to provide important information to volunteers.

FIGURE 3: TOTAL GAMES STAFFING BY VENUE

Venue	Paid staff	Volunteers	Total staff
Accommodations sites	12	66	78
Agnes Scott College	8	33	41
Airport Welcome Center	94	573	667
Alexander Memorial Coliseum	81	903	984
Aquatic Center	226	1,538	1,764
Athens—coliseum	75	705	780
Athens—housing	0	1	1
Athens—Sanford Stadium	90	1,126	1,216
Athens—Village	7	57	64
Atlanta Beach	77	773	850
Atlanta–Fulton County Stadium	254	1,266	1,520
Centennial Olympic Park	124	660	784
Clark Atlanta University	65	569	634
Columbus—airport	0	2	2
Columbus—Golden Park	58	555	613
Columbus—Village	7	151	158
Cultural sites	82	522	604
Emory University	24	221	245
Fleet headquarters	80	3,647	3,727
Florida Citrus Bowl	1	0	1
Georgia Dome	396	2,608	3,004
Georgia International Horse Park	122	1,653	1,775
Georgia State University	68	579	647
Georgia World Congress Center	261	2,437	2,698
Hartsfield Atlanta International Airport	18	465	483
Inforum	1,134	163	1,296
International Broadcast Center	13	332	345
Lake Lanier	103	1,259	1,362
Main accreditation center	54	242	298
Main Press Center	107	1,223	1,330
Main ticket center	45	14	59
Mall locations	143	6	149
MARTA stations	19	0	19
Martin Luther King Jr Center	2	0	2
Morehouse College	68	628	696
Morris Brown College	71	882	953
Ocoee—venue	54	737	791
Ocoee—Village	10	166	176
Olympic Family bus operations	29	563	592
Olympic Family Hotel	125	1,723	1,848
Olympic Village	565	4,096	4,661
Olympic spectator bus system	26	0	26
Olympic Stadium—ceremonies*	8	2,643	2,651
Olympic Stadium—competition events	185	3,964	4,149
Olympic Youth Camp	68	59	127
Omni Coliseum	84	1,001	1,085
Parking lots	43	1	44
Road courses	57	730	787
Savannah—airport	30	138	168
Savannah—venue	88	1,177	1,265
Savannah—Village	27	289	316
Sponsor hospitality villages	49	117	166
Staffing sites	82	136	218
Stone Mountain Park Archery Center and Cycling Velodrome	68	787	855
Stone Mountain Park Tennis Center	84	1,603	1,687
Training sites	47	651	698
Uniform distribution center	107	252	359
Warehouse—general	179	37	216
Warehouse—merchandising	8	0	8
Wolf Creek Shooting Complex	71	737	808
Total	**6,074**	**47,466**	**53,540**

Does not include CEI staff

knowledgeable about the process and trained to answer general questions.

Initially, upon ACOG's receipt of completed applications, applicants were sent a letter of invitation and a request to appear at the OVC on a specific date and time to complete required paperwork and be interviewed. Assigned times were based on the assumption that the OVC could accommodate up to 50 people per half hour. Upon their arrival, candidates reviewed their applications for any needed corrections and completed and signed a security waiver and a release of liability form. Candidates then watched an eight-minute video that introduced the volunteer program and outlined ACOG's expectations for volunteer participation. After watching the film, volunteers were interviewed in groups of five. The purpose of the interview was to verify candidates' availability, skills or licenses, and willingness to accept any position and to identify those suited for leadership positions. Once all requirements were discussed, volunteers had their forms notarized and driver's licenses photocopied. They were then measured for uniforms and photographed for accreditation purposes.

Three months after opening the OVC, ACOG changed the processing plan to adjust to the continual rescheduling of appointments. All volunteers were sent a postcard inviting them to the OVC at any time during extended operating hours six days per week. The film, the interview, and uniform sizing were eliminated. ACOG also established a call center to handle the volume of calls associated with rescheduling, which ultimately evolved into a general information center for volunteers.

Once assignments were made and functional areas began the confirmation process, a second telephone call center was established to assist with reassigning volunteers who were not contacted or did not wish to accept the position offered. Since all paperwork had already been completed, volunteers could be reassigned to another open position immediately.

In January 1996, the Accreditation Department acquired the space occupied by the OVC to expand its operations for the Games. Volunteers were then requested to go to the main accreditation center (MAC) for photo capture only and to mail all other information. Beginning in June and continuing through the Games, space in the MAC was allocated to Volunteer Services for a small staffing center.

THE OLYMPIC GAMES STAFF

ACOG's objectives and guiding principles for staffing the Games were based on the philosophy that the successful staging of the Games required the dedication and hard work of every individual, both volunteer and paid. Together, these groups comprised one team, which became known collectively as the Olympic Games Staff (OGS).

Once the assignment process was complete, with support from ACOG, the additional functional steps of accreditation, training, and uniforming OGS were necessary to prepare them for their Games-time roles.

Accreditation

The accreditation badge served as a work permit for the OGS. All access rights were assigned in accordance with the requirements of each position. The Accreditation Department, in consultation with Venue Management and the functional areas, assigned access rights to the venues and the zones within them for all positions identified in GSTS.

On 15 April 1996, the first rosters listing volunteer names, assignments, and venue access privileges were distributed to the functional area managing directors for review. After the lists were reviewed, Accreditation met with each area to confirm the data. Once validated by the functional area, OGS members were ready to be accredited. This process occurred until 15 May.

When the MAC began operating on 15 April 1995, Volunteer Services assisted in expediting the photo capture process. Volunteer Services staff working in all the accreditation centers had access to both GSTS and the accreditation database, so volunteers could be assigned a position and access privileges at the same time. The access privileges for all OGS were finalized from 15 May to 15 June. *(See the Accreditation chapter.)*

One of the most challenging issues regarding OGS accreditation was assigning privileges to OGS who required access to more than one venue. The design of GSTS was based on the premise that each person would be assigned to one position in one venue. When the data was reviewed with the functional areas, it was determined that 9,400 OGS members required multivenue access.

A multivenue access committee comprised of representatives from Accreditation, TGS, Venue Management, and Volunteer Services was formed to assess the operational necessity of positions requiring access to more than one venue. It was determined that all OGS members be assigned to a primary venue in GSTS by Volunteer Services or HR and that all additional access privileges be manually assigned in the accreditation system by Accreditation staff. A multivenue access matrix was developed to assist Accreditation with this task.

All OGS members who were assigned, confirmed, and photographed by 4 May were included in Accreditation's bulk badging process. The 22,000 bulk-produced accreditation badges were printed in mid-May and delivered to the MAC for paid employees or the Uniform Distribution Center (UDC) for volunteers. Volunteers could receive both their badge and uniform at the UDC beginning 1 June.

OGS processed after 4 May were individually badged at the MAC beginning in early June.

Approximately 5,000 volunteers—most from outside the metro-Atlanta area—were individually badged at the Airport Welcome Center (AWC).

In mid-June, paid employees were invited to the MAC to retrieve their badges and then asked to report to the UDC to receive their uniforms. Staff in the MAC help office had access to the HR database to facilitate any problems.

The final number of ACOG paid, Randstad, loaned, and VIK individuals accredited was 6,082. *(See Figure 3.)*

Contractors. Contractors were responsible for ensuring that all their employees or subcontractors completed data forms and sent them directly to Accreditation for data entry into the accreditation database. Background checks were then conducted and used as a basis for approving and assigning accreditation. The majority of these subcontractors were not given an assignment in the GSTS system. Venue access privileges were determined by Accreditation based on the functions that subcontractors needed to perform at Games-time.

Training

In 1993, a subcommittee of the Corporate Council, comprised of training professionals, began researching the requirements critical for a successful training program.

Georgia Power, an Olympic sponsor, and its parent company, the Southern Company, agreed to provide training support for OGS, which included a loaned executive to coordinate training, printing and publishing services, and design assistance. The training manager joined Volunteer Services in April 1994. The training subcommittee developed as the guidelines and objectives for the training program to:

■ develop a knowledgeable, motivated, friendly, and guest-oriented OGS;

■ convey and instill the knowledge of the Olympic Games and the Olympic Movement worldwide to the OGS;

■ provide OGS the tools needed to perform their assignments to the highest level; and

■ provide encouragement to the OGS that will assist them in fulfilling their responsibilities.

One of the guiding principles of the program was that training was viewed as an integral part of the staffing process.

The staff resource kit consisted of a staff handbook, training video, planning calendar, bumper sticker, and Opening Ceremony dress rehearsal invitation.

In early 1995, ACOG contracted with a local firm, Deeley Rechtman Communications, to help develop training materials. Given the goal of making every moment count, the program consisted of general and venue orientation and leadership and job-specific training.

General Orientation. General orientation material included a resource kit consisting of a 50-page staff handbook, 20-minute training video, planning calendar, bumper sticker, and an invitation to the Opening Ceremony dress rehearsal. Also included in the kit was confirmation of the volunteer's assignment as well as notification of the venue orientation date and location.

This kit, designed for self study, was distributed to all staff via UPS beginning 29 April 1996. After 24 May, volunteers could receive their kits at the MAC.

Leadership Training. Leadership training included both printed material and classroom-style instruction. Leadership/management training packets contained a print-based self-study manual which focused on communications, performance management, practical operational procedures, and common-sense approaches to problem solving. Managers, supervisors, and team leaders were encouraged to attend at least one session at their venue one week prior to venue orientation. During these sessions, special considerations regarding personnel issues and conflict resolution were discussed. In total, 5,000 leadership training manuals were produced and distributed.

Venue Orientation. All OGS members were invited to attend one of 42 four-hour orientation sessions held to increase their knowledge of their venue and its operations. This innovative program was one of the most important components of training. Although many staff members had worked at the test events, numerous venues had been reconfigured for the Games. Held on 22 and 29 June, the venue orientations, known as Super Saturdays, were very successful, with more than 20,000 OGS members attending. Between 4 May and 4 July, additional orientation sessions were held for the OGS.

VSTMs were responsible for organizing the orientation for their respective venues. A session began with an overview of the venue operations, including the introduction of the VM, the sports competition manager, and the functional area managers. OGS members were then separated into their functional area for a venue tour. Attention was given to areas that would be of particular interest to spectators, such as concessions, exits, first-aid stations, restrooms, and ticket sales booths. Details of emergency procedures and staff transportation plans were emphasized. At the conclusion of the session, job training was conducted for those OGS members with jobs requiring specific instruction.

A venue pocket guide was distributed to each OGS member to reinforce the information provided at the orientation. The pocket guide included space for volunteers to record additional information and information applicable to their job or venue.

Each functional area conducted additional training sessions and venue tours for OGS members unable to attend the orientation sessions. The majority of these individuals were staff from outside the metro-Atlanta area who were assigned to positions requiring specific skills.

Job-Specific Training. For certain ACOG-developed support programs requiring substantial knowledge, training began well in advance of distribution of the resource kit. For example, the training for the Envoy Program began two years prior to the Games. Training for the Dedicated Host and Hostess Program and positions in the Protocol Department began in January 1996.

Volunteers from the Corporate Council received additional training at their corporation, and many assisted the VSTMs by serving as trainers for the venue orientations. Their resource kits and leadership materials were distributed in February 1996.

Uniforming

The development and implementation of the uniforming function required the coordination of several departments. Volunteer Services directed the uniform program, serving as ACOG's liaison to the uniform sponsor—the Hanes division of the Sara Lee Corporation—and managing the VIK budget. The Creative Services Department was responsible for coordinating the design of the uniforms. Planning and Integration was responsible for uniform distribution and established the Uniform Distribution division for this function.

The Sara Lee Corporation sponsorship agreement established that the company would manufacture, ship, and tailor the garments, while ACOG would be responsible for warehousing and distribution. Sara Lee provided outfits for all volunteers, ACOG paid employees, and contractors in positions where their appearance should reflect the Look of the Games.

The design team, directed by Creative Services and including representatives from Hanes and Volunteer Services, developed three basic types of uniforms with several color variations to denote certain positions—dress, business, and casual. After the initial concepts were accepted, the team refined the designs and produced prototypes. The designs incorporated the Look of the Games Quilt of Leaves pattern as well as the torch mark logo and the Olympic Rings. The shoe designs were coordinated with the uniforms.

Torch Relay uniforms were an addition to the Sara Lee contract. Security staff uniforms were provided by Borg-Warner Security Corporation. *(See the Torch Relay and Security chapters.)*

The design of the uniforms, examples of which are shown in the preliminary sketch above, was coordinated by Creative Services.

A fashion show was held to showcase the different types of staff uniforms that were selected for the Games. From top to bottom, they were: competition officials, casual, business, and dress *(see Figure 4)*.

Uniform shoes were provided by Reebok. In addition, staff received a watch from Swatch and a water bottle provided by Crystal Springs.

Allocations and Distribution. The total number of OGS members to be uniformed was derived from GSTS data. Uniforms were ordered for 60,119 individuals. Volunteer Services designated one uniform type for each OGS position created in GSTS.

A general purchase order for uniforms was issued in September 1995, listing the components to be ordered and an estimate of the total quantity needed. The specific quantities and sizes were determined through a staff sizing database. The purchase order was finalized and reissued on 15 February 1996.

All uniforms were shipped directly from the manufacturers to the UDC between 27 February and 18 July 1996. Approximately 600,000 labels with bar codes containing the component description, size, and item number were provided to the uniform manufacturers, which affixed them to the lower portion of each package.

The Uniform Distribution division was responsible for efficiently distributing uniforms to a very large number of people over 74 days; ensuring each OGS member was provided a uniform appropriate to his or her position; and processing OGS members in a maximum of 20 minutes for casual and security uniforms and one hour for competition official, business, dress, and field marshal uniforms.

In early 1996, ACOG determined that uniforms and accreditation badges be distributed at the same location. A large warehouse in the Decatur distribution center was selected as the UDC, and was the central warehouse staging area and distribution facility for uniforms.

Uniforms could be acquired at the UDC only by the recipient, and a valid accreditation badge or UDC uniform voucher was required. For staff in remote cities, the VSTM provided the necessary authorization for uniform distribution.

Each individual received only one type of uniform which had multiple components, such as three shirts and two pairs of pants. All uniform types were predetermined by ACOG management and no changes were made unless authorized by Volunteer Services. *(For a description of the types of uniforms and their components, see Figure 4.)*

Uniform distribution was complicated by the number of people who changed positions, thus requiring different types of uniforms.

The UDC was equipped for uniform distribution with 12 check-in stations, multiple stations for distribution of uniform components, a tailoring area, and 14 check-out stations. Volunteers were directed on a one-way path designed to minimize congestion and queuing.

The check-in and check-out process at the UDC was automated using PCs and scanners. At the check-in station, the accreditation badge was scanned to retrieve the individual's information from GSTS. A data sheet was printed and the appropriate uniform checklist attached. OGS members were then directed to the measurement and dressing room area. A customer service desk was available if any OGS members required assistance.

Once the required size was determined, OGS members proceeded to a distribution station to receive their components. Individuals could try on sample garments in group dressing rooms. Tailoring was provided at the UDC for dress and business uniforms.

After receiving all uniform components, OGS members proceeded to the check-out area, where the uniform checklist and the bar code of each component were scanned. OGS members then signed the checklist form to acknowledge receipt of their items.

At the exit of the UDC, OGS members received a poncho, map, uniform appearance standards, and laundering instructions. Check-out processing averaged 12 people in three minutes.

An inventory reconciliation was produced approximately every 30 minutes. The accurate inventorying of certain components was difficult to manage, due to incorrect bar codes, returns, bulk orders, and continuous updates.

Extra uniform components were given to the VSTMs to distribute as needed at the venues. Following the Games, remaining uniform pieces were sold to the OGS at the post-Games recognition party, and subsequently to the general public.

Other Distribution Sites. The initial inventory was received in the UDC and then shipped to the remote cities (Athens, Columbus, Ocoee, and Savannah) and the AWC from 15 June through 3 July based on their predetermined inventory requirements. Most sites' distribution systems were similar to the UDC, but used manual check-in and check-out systems. AWC distribution was augmented to service the 2,500 officials who received uniforms between 6–29 July.

Shoe Distribution. Shoes were provided by Reebok to accompany all ACOG uniforms. Due to the complexity of stocking and distributing shoes in such large quantities, staff picking up uniforms at the UDC location received shoe vouchers which were redeemable at any of five retail locations in metro Atlanta. Reebok representatives were available at the other uniform distribution locations to dispense shoes.

GAMES-TIME OPERATIONS

During the Games, Volunteer Services had both a centralized headquarters operation and decentralized venue-based operations. The headquarters operation supported staff activities across all venues and served as the liaison and support for VSTMs. In the decentralized operations located at the venues, VSTMs were

FIGURE 4: TYPES OF UNIFORMS AND THEIR COMPONENTS

Uniform type	Men	Women	Position

Dress	Hat
	Blue blazer
	Tie
	Dress pants
	Socks and shoes
	Men provided own
	    white dress shirt
		Hat
		Blue jacket
		Blouse
		Scarf
		Skirt
		Dress shoes
			CEO; COO
			Managing directors
			Venue managers
			Competition managers
			Venue press chiefs
			Venue protocol
			    managers
			Dedicated host/hostess
			Designated ACOG
			    spokespersons

Business	Hat
	Pinstripe button-
	    down shirt
	Belt
	Casual pants
	Socks and shoes
		Version I
		Hat
		White dress blouse
		Scarf
		Skirt
		Hose
		Dress shoes
		Leather pouch
		
		Version II
		Hat
		Pinstripe button-
		    down shirt
		Belt
		Skort
		Socks and dress
		    shoes
			Olympic Family Hotel
			    staff
			Venue protocol officers
			
			Envoys
			Associate envoys
			Dedicated drivers

Casual	Hat
	Golf shirt
	Belt
	Belt bag
	Casual pants
	Socks and shoes
		Hat
		Golf shirt
		Belt
		Belt bag
		Skort
		Socks and shoes
			Majority of Olympic
			    Games staff; color
			    of rings dependent
			    on functional area:
			Red rings—medical
			Gold rings—ushers/
			    ticket-takers
			Blue rings/teal ground—
			    sector coordinators
			Blue rings—all others

Competition Officials	Hat Dress shirt Teal blazer Tie Casual shirt Belt Casual pants Socks and shoes	Hat Dress blouse Teal jacket Scarf Casual shirt Belt Skirt/skort Socks and shoes	All competition officials Ceremonies Marshalls

Note: All Olympic Games staff also received Swatch watches

• DAWN L DUNCAN • DELORIS D DUNCAN • DONALD E DUNCAN • ELEANOR A DUNCAN • FRANCES M DUNCAN • HOWARD A DUNCAN • IMOGENE J DUNCAN • JAMI T DUNCAN • JEFFREY DUNCAN • KATHERINE DUNCAN • KELLY J DUNCAN • KENNETH E DUNCAN • KIM D DUNCAN • KIMBERLY W DUNCAN • LEE C DUNCAN • MICHAEL S DUNCAN • PATRICK A DUNCAN • ROBERT G DUNCAN • ROBERT K DUNCAN • STEPHEN J DUNCAN • SUZANNE M DUNCAN • TIFFANY DUNCAN • WIEDA M DUNCAN • WILLIAM K DUNCAN • WILLIAM P DUNCAN • ANNETTE P DUNCAN MALLORY • STEPHEN F DUNCAN

435

the chief advocates for staff and the single point of contact for any personnel-related issues at their venue. VSTMs reported to the VM regarding all venue operational matters and to either Volunteer Services or HR about personnel matters.

Headquarters Operations

The Olympic staff center (OSC) served as the centralized headquarters and coordination center for all OGS members and provided support for the AWC, MAC, main operations center

All visitors were required to register at the reception desk at ACOG headquarters before proceeding inside.

(MOC), and UDC. Personnel assigned to the headquarters were the managing director of Olympic Programs, the director of Volunteer Services, and four Volunteer Services managers. The director and the managers worked in both the OSC and the MOC.

Olympic Staff Center. The OSC was designed to provide the MOC and ACOG executive management with a centralized information and communications system to support the VSTMs. Information conveyed from the VSTMs to the OSC included a predefined daily written report covering key data such as attrition, morale, and other staffing issues, as well as periodic updates by telephone.

Responsibilities of the OSC included:

■ daily contact with the VSTMs to assist with problem resolution;

■ reassigning staff who had finished their assignments and wished to continue working;

■ personnel issue consultation and resolution, including medical issues, ACOG policy issues, and separation confirmation;

■ processing new volunteers; and

■ OGS ticket distribution.

At least one management staff member was present in the OSC from 0700 until 1800. Remaining hours of operation were staffed by MOC personnel. At 0700, the staff member on duty reviewed the previous evening's daily staffing reports and voice mail messages.

Management staff met daily to review the status of the staff at the venues and discuss any concerns. Following the meeting, management staff met with VSTMs at the venues to resolve any outstanding issues.

Typically, issues handled by the OSC involved improvements to operating procedures, such as producing materials to assist volunteers or recruiting additional volunteers to assist with crowd control.

OSC staff delivered mail and other necessary items, such as snacks, to the VSTMs for distribution. In order to accomplish this task, Volunteer Services was allocated two ACOG fleet vans with parking permits.

Main Operations Center. In addition to their responsibilities in the OSC, the director of Volunteer Services and the managers worked at the staffing desk in the MOC from 0600 to 2400 daily.

Throughout early planning, Volunteer Services assumed that the communication link between the VSTMs and Volunteer Services and other ACOG department headquarters would be through the OSC. However, once the Games began, the MOC emerged as the best communication link, because functional area representative desks were in close proximity to each other. The OSC thus became a conference and work center.

In addition to the MOC, Volunteer Services established a presence in three accreditation centers—the AWC, MAC, and UDC—to assist with volunteer staffing and assignment issues. Twelve individuals staffed the help desks seven days a week, 20 hours a day. Technology provided PCs, printers, and phone lines to support these operations.

Because the VSTMs served as the single point of contact for personnel issues at their venues, HR employees were not assigned to venues, with the exception of two members assigned full-time to the Olympic Village to facilitate communications. The majority of HR employees were assigned to ACOG headquarters, and through rotating shifts, staffed a 24-hour HR hot line to handle any personnel-related issues or emergency situations involving ACOG paid employees or contractors, and communicated to the VSTMs or the MOC. Other HR staff continued to process new employees while also preparing for post-Games termination procedures.

Venue Operations

The VSTMs served as the single point of contact for staff at all competition venues as well as the MPC and Olympic Family Hotel. The other noncompetition venues were managed by the functional areas with primary responsibility for their operation.

All major personnel issues were managed by the VSTM except for those regarding wages and hourly reporting and issues involving ACOG-paid employees, vendors, or contractors. The size of the VSTM's team was proportionate to the staff assigned to the venue.

The daily management of all OGS was the responsibility of the functional area manager or supervisory personnel in that area. To assist the functional areas in effectively managing their staff and informing them of ACOG's expectations for performance and standards of conduct, specific policies and procedures were outlined in staff and leadership handbooks and emphasized in the training program. *(For the typical venue chain of command, see Figure 5.)*

Each morning, all VSTMs were contacted by Volunteer Services headquarters staff members to discuss the general status of staff at the venues and any issues that had been raised by the venues' morning team meetings. This discussion allowed the VSTMs and the management staff to discuss immediate and potential problems and assess the overall morale of the OGS at each venue.

All VSTMs were issued a pager and a radio. At the venues, a PC and special printer were configured to run the check-in system. Phones were located in each check-in area and some break areas.

In order to maintain a high level of morale at the venues, the VSTMs used creative approaches to motivate staff and thank them for their work. These approaches included special daily recognition for outstanding service, photographs taken and posted in the check-in area, and impromptu celebrations. During competition, the VSTMs and their staff continually monitored the venues to ensure the OGS were provided enough break time and water.

Comment cards were available in the break areas at each venue, which allowed OGS members to comment on their experience and suggest any changes. The VSTM reviewed the cards and forwarded any significant information to the OSC for action.

Check-In. Each competition venue had a centralized check-in system for OGS at the beginning of every shift. This allowed the VM, competition manager, and VSTM to ensure all staff assignments were filled each day.

At the beginning of each shift, staff checked in—usually at a tent outside the staff entrance to the venue—and received food coupons and any last minute instructions. All staff scheduled to work were listed on a duty roster. Individuals then reported for a pre-shift briefing prior to beginning their assignment.

If an individual's name did not appear on the duty roster, the individual was sent to the

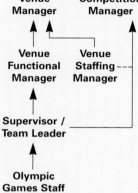

FIGURE 5: TYPICAL VENUE CHAIN OF COMMAND

Venue Manager / Competition Manager

Venue Functional Manager / Venue Staffing Manager

Supervisor / Team Leader

Olympic Games Staff Member

staff service desk, where his or her supervisor or functional area manager was contacted. If the supervisor or manager verified that the individual was scheduled to work that day, the individual continued the normal check-in procedure. If, however, the individual was not scheduled to work that day, entrance to the venue was denied. This procedure was designed to discourage unassigned staff from entering the venue.

Management staff which had access to all venues were not listed on a duty roster and therefore checked in at the staff service desk, indicating who they were visiting at the venue and the reason for their visit.

The Security and Transportation Departments established their own check-in procedures at each venue. In many cases, OGS members who worked the perimeter of venues were checked-in at another location; food coupons were distributed by a supervisor and the staff received meals at an off-site location.

Contracted staff members were handled separately by Venue Management with a sign-in procedure.

Staffing Contingency Plan. The size and diversity of the OGS and the number of systems needed to support venue operations required that the venue staffing plan be as precise as possible. However, each venue team was asked to develop a plan to handle absences, tardiness, and attrition, as deviations from the staffing plan during operations can always occur. The purpose of the staffing contingency plan was to establish the absolute minimum number of staff required to effectively operate the venue and define procedures for redeploying staff within the venue and requesting outside staff if necessary.

The VSTM was responsible for implementing the staffing contingency plan at the venue and assisting functional area managers with temporary and permanent reassignments to fulfill the needs of the venue team. Each functional area manager was asked to develop a description of duties, or job aid card, which could be given to temporarily redeployed OGS members.

Functional area managers were asked to inform the VSTM of their staffing status after all OGS member checked in. This status report indicated whether the functional areas were adequately staffed and provided the VSTM with information needed if staff redeployment was necessary.

With the exception of Security and Transportation, which scheduled their personnel centrally rather than at the venue level, significant redeployment across venues was not required during the Games.

The attrition rate for volunteers was minimal. Prior to the start of the Games, 51,881 volunteers were accredited; 47,466 completed their assignments.

RECOGNITION AND POST-GAMES ACTIVITIES

To thank the OGS members for their commitment to the success of the Centennial Olympic Games, Volunteer Services implemented several ways of recognizing OGS efforts before, during, and after the Games.

Opening Ceremony Dress Rehearsal

All OGS approved in the GSTS database were invited to attend the Opening Ceremony dress rehearsal on 17 July 1996. Invitations received in the orientation kits were exchanged for one dress rehearsal ticket.

Tickets to Events

In June 1996, Jet Set Sports—a sports marketing firm—donated more than 20,000 tickets for a variety of events to ACOG for distribution to the OGS. These tickets were given to all VSTMs to distribute to their staff. Some VSTMs awarded tickets to individuals for their dedication or excellent performance, while others awarded them through contests and games.

Certificates of Recognition and Thank-You Pins

ACOG presented all OGS with a commemorative certificate of recognition for their participation in the Games. Volunteers also received a thank-you pin from the IOC.

One volunteer was selected by each management team to represent their venues or functional areas at a farewell breakfast held by the IOC on 5 August 1996. At this event, IOC President Juan Antonio Samaranch personally presented these volunteers with their recognition certificates and pins.

Each VSTM was required to provide a final staffing roster at the conclusion of the Games, allowing Volunteer Services to eliminate the names of OGS members who did not complete their assignments before certificates or pins were distributed. One month following the Games, a mailing service was contracted for the calligraphy on all certificates and for mailing the individual recognition items.

Olympic Games Staff Recognition Party

A party was held on 10 August 1996 in Centennial Olympic Park to recognize all OGS members. The park was closed to the general public and Games credentials were required to enter. OGS were invited to the party through flyers available at each venue.

Various refreshments were served. The Superstore offered a 20 percent discount, Olympic items were raffled, and other items were sold throughout the park. ACOG CEO Billy Payne addressed the staff for the final time. As people left, they received a commemorative poster created specifically for OGS. More than 20,000 people attended this function.

In addition to this party, most venues also held their own farewell/recognition functions.

Employee Retention

In early 1995, preliminary meetings were held regarding the implementation of a retention program which encouraged paid employees to remain with ACOG through completion of their assignment. Details regarding a salary transition plan and an outplacement program were released in October 1995.

All full-time employees hired by 31 December 1995 were eligible for the Employee Transition Payment Program, whereby employees received two weeks salary for each full year of employment, with a maximum of eight weeks pay. Employees were required to remain with ACOG through their established end date to receive transition pay.

Employee Termination

The post-Games procedure for out-processing ACOG staff was developed by HR. During May and June 1996, HR conducted 24 post-Games termination process seminars for ACOG paid employees and loaned staff to explain and distribute packages containing termination guidelines and documents. All paid employees were asked to complete the appropriate documents and bring them to the out-processing center upon completion of their assignments. The out-processing center, located at ACOG headquarters, operated daily from 5 August through 15 September 1996, and twice monthly through 31 December 1996.

All ACOG paid employees were eligible to participate in the outplacement services program, provided through Drake Beam Morin, Inc. Outplacement services were conducted at ACOG headquarters in an outplacement center which was operational from 15 April until 25 October 1996. Consultants helped employees with résumé writing skills, interviewing techniques, and following job leads. They also conducted counseling sessions and presented a series of programs on career placement. More

• DEBORAH E DURAND • LARRY K DURAND • EDWARD W DURANT • LEAVEAN B DURANT • LILLIAN D DURANT-DAVIS • CHARLOTTE G DURANTE • KENNETH DURANTE • LORI J DURANTE • BIRGITTE T DURBAN • CAROLINE M DURDEN • CHRISTOPHER T DURDEN • JENNY L DURDEN • JERRY L DURDEN • KYLA A DURDEN • VERONA C DURDEN • WANDA S DURDEN • BARBARA G DUREN • KAREN BELL DURFEE • AMY L DURHAM • AMY P DURHAM • BRYCE V DURHAM • CARLA Y DURHAM • CYNTHIA A DURHAM • DANIEL A DURHAM • JAMES D DURHAM • JAY CLIFFORD DURHAM • JOANN A DURHAM •

439

than 2,300 employees utilized the services offered by DBM, which also conducted a job fair for ACOG-paid employees on 17 August 1996, in which 175 companies and almost 3,000 employees participated.

Upon termination, all ACOG paid staff were required to return any applicable assets to Administration, Technology, and Transportation and settle any outstanding financial obligations.

Volunteer Services Dissolution

ACOG-paid VSTMs remained after the Games to assist in compiling data from the venues and archiving materials such as duty rosters and waivers of liability forms.

CONCLUSIONS AND RECOMMENDATIONS

It is important that organizing committees recognize the complexity and length of time involved in staffing an Olympic Games. Staffing efforts require a flexible staffing plan and experienced management through the conclusion of the Games. People are a valued resource to the success of the Games and must be carefully selected, trained, managed, and recognized for their contributions. The following points are critical to implementing a successful consolidated staffing plan.

■ House all staffing responsibility—from the development of the staff plan through recognition activities for paid employees, contractors, and volunteers—in one department.

■ Develop an integrated staffing system and a centralized database to ensure all staffing data, terms, procedures, and forms are standardized.

■ Develop a consolidated staff plan, including job descriptions, start and end dates, and approximate numbers, before beginning the recruiting process.

■ Use the 80 percent rule when planning for required resources to support staff: plan to need only 80 percent of meals, space, and other support resources, as estimated staff numbers will always be higher than the actual number of staff required.

■ Encourage functional areas to recruit both paid employees and volunteers, but ensure that the process is centrally managed.

■ Simplify the application, recruitment, and assignment process as much as possible, and caution against relying too heavily on technological systems.

■ Operate a staffing center at least one year prior to the Games, and keep it operational through the Games.

■ Establish only one uniform distribution site if possible. It is important to locate staff processing, accreditation, and uniform distribution at the same facility.

■ Minimize the number of uniform types and limit the distribution period to a maximum 6–7 weeks.

■ Recognize that the staffing process is extremely labor-intensive. It will require at least two and a half years of concentrated effort and will probably not be completed until the beginning of the Games.

CHAPTER TWENTY-THREE
TECHNOLOGY

TECHNOLOGY EMPLOYEES

Date	Staff Number
December 1993	26
January 1996	63
July 1996	112

Note: These staff numbers do not include contract, VIK, and volunteer personnel.

OVERVIEW—The mission of the Technology Department was to provide integrated, state-of-the-art applications for the 1996 Games throughout all venues and around the world (through the Internet and television broadcast signals), as well as support pre-Olympic special events and the administrative needs of the organizing committee before, during, and after the Games.

Technology provided the foundation for many Olympic Games functions, making it possible for ACOG to reserve more than 800,000 nights of accommodations, market 10.5 million tickets, manage approximately 6,000 vehicles, deliver scoring and timing results at 31 competition venues, and broadcast more than 3,000 hours of television to a cumulative worldwide audience of 19.6 billion.

The scope of Technology operations was enormous, as was the amount of equipment necessary to support the Games: 7,000 desktop and laptop computers, 3 mainframe computers, more than 1,000 laser printers, more than 250 local area networks (LANs), 7,700 pagers, 12,000 mobile and hand-held radios, 700 copiers, 700 facsimile machines, 10,000 televisions, and 20,000 telephones. The budget for Technology was the second largest of all ACOG functional areas.

During initial planning, ACOG recognized the importance of delivering technological solutions with computer systems that users with minimal training could easily operate. Such solutions reflected a high degree of technological integration and were designed to be as available and flexible as possible.

Existing commercial software packages met many of ACOG's requirements, thus minimizing the necessity to develop new applications. The applications enabling methodology (AEM), used before the Games for applications development, consisted of several phases, including requirements definition, design, systems development, and systems testing. Each phase of development required an exit review before the next phase could begin. A post-Games evaluation phase was also conducted.

Multiple backup copies were provided for all applications, and numerous redundancies were built into each system. As a result, virtually any problem that occurred could be resolved on-line without affecting spectators and the worldwide television audience.

Olympic sponsors and suppliers AT&T, Bell-South Corporation, Eastman Kodak Company, IBM, Motorola, Inc., Panasonic, Scientific Atlanta, Sensormatic, Swatch, and Xerox provided the wide range of equipment, services, and resources that allowed ACOG to plan and implement Games technology. The technology sponsors, many of whom retained ownership of their equipment, were involved during the design, implementation, operation, and asset recovery. *(For services provided by technology sponsors, see Figure 1.)*

Many products and services of the technology sponsors were offered for rent or sale during the Games to the print media, broadcasters, NOCs, IFs, and other sponsors and vendors through a rate card process.

ORGANIZATION

Technology staff had to plan for both the technological needs of the sporting events and all administrative needs for every ACOG functional area. As ACOG staff quickly grew, associated technology needs grew along with it. The dramatic growth of Technology operations required a corresponding growth in its staff to ensure the development of technological solutions to enable ACOG staff to work effectively.

The Technology Department began in September 1990 with one manager who focused on the daily operations of the organizing committee. By summer 1991, the department had separated into two divisions—Information System Services and Technical Services—each headed by a director reporting to the ACOG COO. Information Systems Services developed all the computer-related applications, such as results, Info'96, and accreditation, and designed the internal computer network. Technical Services was responsible for noncomputer equipment and applications, such as telephone systems, cable access television (CATV) systems, radio systems, security and access control systems, and timing and scoring systems.

In late 1991, AT&T, BellSouth, IBM, and Motorola loaned executives to ACOG to help document technical requirements and potential applications for use during the Games. Additionally, a visit to the 1992 Games in Barcelona provided a view of the technical operations needed to support an Olympic Games.

By late 1993, additional loaned executives and new employees were added. Project managers coordinated the development of Info'96, operations management systems, Games applications, computer network delivery systems, telecommunications and document services,

cabling and radio frequency (RF) systems, timing and scoring applications, imaging and security systems, and the Games staffing technology system.

Throughout 1994 and 1995, administrative staff, analysts, programmers, contractors, consultants, facility engineers, and venue technology managers (VXMs) were also added.

The Technology Department continued to grow and began the transition to a Games-time organizational structure in 1995. The managing director of Technology assumed responsibility for both Information Systems Services and Technical Services. In addition, a director for both divisions and additional program directors for consulting and budget supervision reported to this managing director.

During the Games, volunteers staffed such positions as technical services specialists (TSSs), information systems specialists (ISSs), rate card specialists, and results distribution runners. TSSs monitored the operation of copiers and facsimile machines. ISSs assisted in computer systems operation. Rate card specialists ensured that all technology provided was installed and operating properly. Results distribution runners delivered printed results to the press, broadcasters, and Olympic Family locations at the venues. At Games-time, Technology staff totaled approximately 5,500.

During the test events in summer and fall 1995, the technology implementation center (TIC) and the technology operations center (TOC) began operations. Both centers provided a base for managing tasks performed at the venues and provided support for issue resolution. The TIC scheduled and managed technology implementation at the venues, and the TOC provided support to management regarding technical problems that arose or escalated and could not be resolved at the venue level.

When the test events in spring 1996 began, both the TIC and TOC were fully operational

---

FIGURE 1: SERVICES PROVIDED BY TECHNOLOGY SPONSORS

AT&T
Venue telephone or PBX systems and associated equipment, cabling, and long-distance services

BellSouth
Local voice and data network and cellular and paging services

IBM
Computer support, technical support, and information systems applications, including results and Info'96

Kodak
Worked with the IBM accreditation application to develop the accreditation badging system

Motorola
Radios, cellular telephones, and pagers

Panasonic
Televisions, videocassette recorders, and cameras

Scientific Atlanta, BellSouth, and Panasonic
Collaborated on the ACOG CATV system

Sensormatic
Equipment to control venue access and monitor security

Swatch
Timing and scoring—integrated its systems with both the IBM results application and the Xerox results printing solution

Xerox
Engineering printing and plotting, copiers, facsimile machines, and DocuTech 135 Publishing Systems for the ACOG publishing center

KATHLEEN A DYAR • SARA J DYCK • SUSAN F DYCK • DANIEL B DYCUS • COBOLEA DYE • ERIC M DYE • STEVEN S DYE • TREVIN GERARD DYE • GEORGE D DYER • JOHN O DYER • MIKE DYER • NATHANIEL O DYER • PATRICIA A DYER • PHILIP M DYER • PHILLIP A DYER • ROHAN D DYER • ROLSTON A DYER • WILLIAM R DYER • JAMES K DYER II • DRURY N DYER JR • GLENN W DYKE • BETTY W DYKES • JEFFREY T DYKES • MARIAN A DYKES • KAREN C DYKSTRA • TAD DYNAKOWSKI JR • AMANDA A DYSART • SCOTT L DYSART • JEANNIE N DYSON • NELSIE B DYSON • TANIA L DYSON • BOZO DZAKULA

443

and would remain so throughout the installation, operation, and dismantling of technology at Olympic venues. The TIC, staffed by ACOG Technology prior to and during the Games, primarily supported venue installation and recovery, while the TOC staff, which included technology sponsor representatives, provided technical and computer network support during testing and venue operations. The TOC operated continuously from 1 July to 7 August.

INFORMATION SYSTEMS SERVICES

The Information Systems Services division developed all computer-related applications and designed the ACOG administrative and Games computer networks. These applications were sourced to the presenting sponsor, IBM, and other specialized service suppliers. IBM was the systems integrator for all applications and for systems dependent on other sponsors' services.

Competition Results System

Competition results for the 1996 Olympic Games were produced by an integrated system of Swatch Timing, IBM, Xerox, and Scientific Atlanta. All competition results were delivered to broadcasters, press, and sports managers using a client-server application with an IBM ES9000 host, a network of IBM AS/400s, and venue-based IBM personal computers (PCs) attached through LANs. All these components were interconnected via high-speed wide area networks (WANs). During the 16 days of competition, the results system was used for more than 7,500 events held in 31 venues—the largest coverage ever in an Olympic Games.

The system produced:

■ venue-based timing, scoring, and results for all Olympic events;

■ printed information for distribution to media at the venues and other locations, competition management, and the Olympic Family;

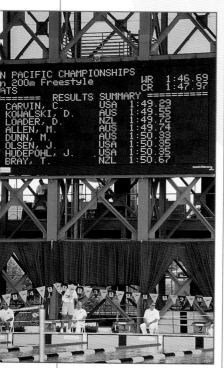

Technology provided boards for the display of venue-based timing, scoring, and official results for all Olympic events.

■ 15,000 results reports containing more than 40 million pages;

■ real-time data for TV graphic overlays, start lists, rankings, statistics, points needed to medal, and overall results;

■ real-time, interactive commentator information system (CIS) for nine sports;

■ near real-time results and flash quotes to the press and broadcasters through the press data system (PDS) for eight sports;

■ start lists, results, and statistics to 1,800 Info'96 touch-screen terminals; and

■ similar results information via the World News Press Agency (WNPA) feed contained in more than 300,000 reports sent to news agencies and the Internet.

The competition results system was newly developed by IBM based on requirements from ACOG sports competition managers, the IFs, ACOG Press Operations, Atlanta Olympic Broadcasting (AOB), and from analysis of prior Games results systems. The system was tested in a laboratory and at test events.

Data for the competition results system were compiled from athlete and sports-specific information received from Accreditation and Sports; athlete biographies, records, and rankings in Info'96; and time, score, and race-in-progress results entered through Swatch Timing. The information produced by this system included start lists, results, and statistics, which were sent to television graphics, CIS, PDS, the scoreboard, Xerox DocuPrint 390 HC systems, Info'96, the WNPA feed, and the Internet.

Results were released only after being declared official. Print reports were usually available for distribution less than 10 minutes after release of official results. The CIS usually received results within three seconds from the time data were available. The PDS was typically updated within five or six seconds.

Two significant problems were identified during the first days of the Games. The WNPA feed, which sent data directly from the results system to specified world press agencies, was not providing all information correctly. This was primarily caused by coding errors not identified during testing due to the difficulty of simulating a Games-time environment. An interim solution was created while these errors were being corrected. Planned operations resumed, but the system never met expectations.

An additional problem was related to the flow of information from where it was entered or recorded to other locations on the system. The function that allowed production of print reports from the results system was most affected. Results information reports were quickly

available for a venue's competition; however, other locations also able to receive the reports—the International Broadcast Center (IBC), Main Press Center (MPC), and the Olympic Village—often encountered considerable delays in receiving data from venues. The difficulty related to errors in the distribution parameters for report types and quantities at various locations. Corrections were made rapidly, but isolated reoccurrences were noted.

Current technologies, such as client-server, relational databases and object-oriented development, were selected by IBM as key building blocks of the system. Reusing this system in future Games while focusing development activity on evolutionary, incremental enhancements would decrease the possibility that

future Games will experience the difficulties encountered in Atlanta.

A detailed assessment of both the successes and difficulties encountered with the results project has been conducted and will be shared with future organizing committees through the IOC-sponsored InfoTech Guidelines project.

Info'96

Info'96, a touch-screen information system containing Olympic Games information and E-mail capabilities, was one of the most impor-

tant tools available to the media, athletes, officials, staff, and other members of the Olympic Family. In total, 1,800 Info'96 terminals were located at competition venues, the IBC, MPC, Olympic Village, Olympic Family Hotel, and accreditation centers. Two hundred terminals were housed in specially created kiosks that incorporated the ACOG Look of the Games visual profile and were wheelchair accessible. The Info'96 system was developed by IBM based on requirements defined by ACOG. The data resided on a centrally located master IBM

left: A total of 1,800 Info'96 terminals provided information and E-mail capabilities for media, athletes, staff, and other Olympic Family members.

right: Results were compiled and released after being declared official.

DARLENE A EARL • JENNIFER A EARL • JENNIFER A EARL • FRANKIE L EARLE • JIMMIE L EARLE • MAYRENE T EARLE • MERRICK K EARLE • MITCH EARLE • CHARLES L EARLEY • BRIAN D EARLS • LISA A EARLS • BILL A EARLY • KATHLEEN M EARLY • MICHAEL W EARLY • JACK G EARLY JR • CECELIA ANN EARNEST • LISA M EARNEST • BRUCE EARP • DENA EARP • DOROTHY A EARP • WILLIAM EASLEY ESSIE J EASON • JUDITH H EASON • KEENAN T EASON • LATRICIA L EASON • ANNA V EASON-HORTON • MICHELE EASTALL • CHERYL F EASTBURN • KAREN K EASTBURN • AARON M EASTERLEY

445

AS/400 database as well as local AS/400 databases at Olympic venues. The IBM data network managed the data flow to all Info'96 terminals and the Games World Wide Web site. *(For Info'96 main menu touch options, see Figure 2.)*

Info'96 E-mail, which could be accessed by all accredited persons, was based on a similar application implemented at the Albertville, Barcelona, and Lillehammer Games. E-mail included interfaces to electronic paging, X.400 external E-mail, telex, and facsimile. E-mail notice boards were created automatically according to

country, organization, and accreditation category. Individuals were assigned to a general notice board for all users and selected notice boards based on their category of accreditation.

Other user-friendly Info'96 features included main menu touch screens, the option to view text in either French or English, help information on the contents, and print capabilities for E-mail.

Info'96 experienced some difficulties related to results, similar to those encountered by the WNPA feed; however, the problems were of far less magnitude and were resolved quickly. Response time for the system—the time it takes to move from one screen to another—was slower than had been anticipated, but overall Info'96 was a valuable tool that worked well.

Olympic Games Promotion

One of ACOG's goals was to use computer-based technology to promote the Centennial Olympic Games by providing a variety of information to the broadest possible audience.

An Internet-based strategy for Olympic Games promotion was developed by Technology and subsequently approved by ACOG senior management.

The 1996 Centennial Olympic Games web site, at http://www.atlanta.olympic.org, was launched on 11 April 1995 as a joint project of ACOG and IBM. This was the first Olympic web site and Internet-based information system established by an organizing committee.

The site included: official results of competition events, news, athlete biographies, radio broadcasts, photographic images, electronic purchasing of tickets and merchandise, competition schedules, and information on travel, sponsors, the Cultural Olympiad, the Olympic Arts Festival (OAF), and the Torch Relay. New technologies in video streaming, massive video image and still photo capture, and live results feeds allowed people worldwide to use this site as an immediate source of Games information.

FIGURE 2: INFO'96 MAIN MENU TOUCH OPTIONS

- Biographies of athletes, coaches, Olympians, dignitaries, and artists

- Sports competition schedules, entry lists, start lists, results, statistics, summaries, medals, and sports facts

- News stories from competition venues, ACOG, the IOC, NOCs, and IFs

- Results from past Olympic Games and World Championships

- Venue weather conditions, forecasts, and bulletins, as well as international weather from the National Weather Service

- Current and historical Olympic, world, area, national, and all comers records, including the day's sport and country records

- Schedules of sports competitions, press conferences, OAF and Olympic Village events, and ceremonies

- Current and historical medal counts from all Olympic Games, as well as the day's medalists by sport and country

- Shuttle schedules for media as well as transportation services and bulletins

- Profiles of all Olympic competition venues and cities

- Information on the IOC, NOCs, IFs, and Olympic Games

- Olympic Village information on athlete and NOC services, event schedules, and the Olympic Village map

- OAF event schedules, artist and performer biographies, and information on the Cultural Olympiad

- Information on ACOG departments and programs

- The capability to send and receive E-mail messages, create and view notice boards, and send E-mail via interfaces to electronic paging, X.400 external E-mail, telex, and facsimile

Information from the web site was duplicated on several computer databases, or servers, located across three continents. During the Games, about 200 million inquiries were made to the Olympic web site worldwide. *(For more information, see the Communications chapter.)*

In addition to the official Centennial Olympic Games web site, ACOG worked with IBM to develop public information kiosks, several of which were deployed throughout Atlanta to showcase the Games. The kiosks used touch screens, photographic images, video, audio, and text to deliver information about the Games. IBM maintained the kiosks and updated the information in each until the start of the Games.

Operations Management Systems

Technology also assisted in developing and implementing various computer-based operations management systems (OMSs) for functional areas.

Accommodations. Accommodations developed an application to allocate university housing for press and sports officials. The system worked with the facilities' own inventory systems for room assignment and arrival. The Corporate Services Department created a system for room allocations during the years prior to the Games. The Olympic Family Hotel had its own PC-based system for room assignment and check-in during the Games. Security used a PC-based system to allocate rooms to its volunteers.

Olympic Village Room Allocations. The largest computer application for accommodations assigned housing to athletes, coaches, and numerous officials. The system, which operated at the Olympic Village and the Airport Welcome Center (AWC), was PC-based using Microsoft Access and a room inventory with a link to Microsoft Windows 3.1 computer-aided design (CAD) drawings.

Its four subsystems included: room inventory accounting by building, floor, sector, room, and NOC; room allocations accounting by NOC; reports production; and response to CAD-based queries.

During the pre-Games period, the system was used to track manual allocations and provide NOCs with graphic displays of room and building allocations. During the Games, updates were made to the inventory based on the athlete reception process, which determined how many athletes were qualified to compete, and *Olympic Charter* Rule 42, which provided guidelines on the number of team officials eligible for a Village room. Reports were produced for housing offices, building staffs, and cleaning organizations; CAD-based reports were also produced for NOCs, using information contained in the inventory database.

Accreditation. The accreditation system was purchased from the Barcelona Olympic Organizing Committee and modified by the SEMA Group, a software development firm, to support ACOG requirements. The registration database drew from two sources: electronic interface with the Games staffing technology system (GSTS) for volunteers and staff, and manual data collection using forms from Olympic Family, vendors, and Security. The final registration database included 265,811 entries. After cancellations and elimination of duplicate records, accreditation badges were issued to 228,563 individuals.

As the primary source of information about people, the accreditation database served several other systems, including results (inscriptions and athlete registration), Info'96 (E-mail and athlete biographies), access control (access privileges and badge cancellations), background

BRYAN C EAVES • FRANKLIN C EAVES • LAURA K EAVES • PHILIP S EAVES • ROBERTA R EAVES • CARMEN B EBBING • WAYNE W EBENROTH • MARK W EBERHARD • RHONDA R EBERHARD • KRISTIN EBERHART • SANDRA S EBERLEIN • PETER M EBERSBACH • BRENDA P EBERSOLE • WILLIAM J EBERSOLE • CHRIS J EBERT • BASHIE L EBRON • STEVEN C ECHARD • TIMOTHY A ECHEMANN • ANA ECHEVERRY • LAWRENCE K ECHIKSON • ANTHONY J ECHOLS • ARRITA V ECHOLS • BENJAMIN D ECHOLS • CHRISTOPHER J ECHOLS • JACQUELINE M ECHOLS • LASHUNDRA P ECHOLS •

447

check (new registrations), and Medical Services (accreditation number, status, and athlete gender).

ACOG developed an interface between the host S/390 and the Kodak badging system with the assistance of Kodak, Sensormatic, and IBM. The result was one-step badging with image and text printed directly onto plastic.

Arrivals and Departures. The arrival and departure system was also a Barcelona system enhanced by the SEMA Group. Information was stored on the host S/390 system either by individual members of the Olympic Family or as group information by organization. Once an Olympic Family member was registered, information could be added to the system, which was designed to track any registered person and record expected arrival times and locations, accommodations, and departure details. This information allowed Olympic Family members, either individuals or groups, to be met upon arrival and escorted to the appropriate accreditation center or accommodation.

Transportation, Accreditation, and Uniform Distribution also relied on this information, which was available by individual, by group, by organization, and by hour.

Used at the AWC, the Olympic Family Hotel, Olympic Village, and ACOG's main offices, the system had more than 9,000 individual arrival and departure records and more than 4,800 group records that accounted for more than 27,000 people.

Games Staffing. The GSTS was developed to support Volunteer Services in creating and managing a centralized database for more than 131,000 volunteers and staff. The processes supported by the application were qualifying, confirming, assigning, training, uniforming, and accreditation for staff.

Information was entered into the database either manually or through an automated process. The quantities for job positions were entered manually, based on the approved staffing budget. Games Staffing could then help users match volunteers with positions based on qualification criteria such as skills, availability, and location.

Queries and reports available included confirmation and summons letters for training, staff listings, venue assignment rosters, and status reports for management. The application also worked with the background check application to track security clearances in preparation for accreditation.

The GSTS was available to personnel working in the Volunteer Services Department, who could use the application from their desktop PCs.

During the Games, the focus of staffing database activity was to query assignments and aid in the redeployment and proper accreditation of volunteers. Changes in volunteer status and personal data were also tracked and updated.

FM3—Staff Scheduling System. The FM3 staff scheduling system was a PC-based system using the FoxPro database. This centralized scheduling tool was developed to assist ACOG functional areas in planning, documenting, and communicating the venue work schedules of more than 60,000 paid, volunteer, and contractor Games staff covering more than 200 venue and building locations.

Prior to Games-time, the system was networked so functional areas could enter their own schedules. The application was available to ACOG internal users, usually via desktop PC. A staff scheduling center with five shared-use PCs was also established. Support and updates to the FM3 system were provided by the Total Games Staffing Department.

Functional area staff manually entered shift times and quantities for job positions into the central database, eventually creating more than one million work shifts. The records of paid employees and volunteers approved to fill venue positions were electronically transferred from GSTS to FM3. Contractor staff records were manually entered into FM3 by functional areas. Individuals were scheduled for specific days and shifts, with the functional areas taking responsibility for printing and delivering the information to their staff.

In early July, a version of the scheduling system was created that was not connected to the central Games network. All competition venues and several noncompetition venues received a PC and a printer containing the respective venue's unique data regarding personnel and shifts. These PCs were used to refine schedules and print daily duty rosters to support staff check-in, functional area roll calls, and distribution of meal coupons. The centralized database remained available, largely for inquiry purposes, at ACOG headquarters.

Incident Tracking. A tracking system—the Olympic incident tracking and reporting system (ITS)—was developed using Lotus Notes, and allowed ACOG to record incidents and then access the data through reports or electronic searches. Because the data was shared centrally, communications and reporting between the venues and operations centers for both ACOG and law enforcement were greatly enhanced.

Materials Management and Planning. The materials management and planning system supported ordering, receiving, inventorying, and asset tracking for Logistics, Procurement and Contract Administration, and Technology. More than 30,000 purchase orders were entered into this system. The assets tracked included technology, sports equipment, and furniture, totaling 200,000 individual items. Identification of assets by bar coding was done at the warehouse. Bar code recognition systems were used at the warehouse and at ACOG headquarters.

The system was a customized version of an inventory software program, running on an AS/400. The modules used were purchasing, receiving, inventorying, and order processing. Finance used the general ledger, accounts payable, accounts receivable, and contract administration modules.

Extensive modifications were made to the system to support serial number tracking of items such as pagers, computers, radios, and cellular phones. Serial numbers could be issued individually to a person or in bulk to a venue, where each recipient signed for the rented device.

Intermec 1545 scanners and wedges were used to scan the serial numbers into and out of the warehouses. Intermec Janus 2020 portable scanners were used to move assets at the operation locations and perform cycle counting. The portable scanners ran dcLink software for inventory transfers and cycle counting. Docking stations were used to transfer the data into the system.

The system was also used to book, fulfill, and collect payment for technology products and services provided by AGOG to constituencies through rate cards. *(Discussed later in this chapter.)*

Medical Services. A medical encounter tracking and reporting system (METARS) was developed to meet the information needs of the IOC, NOCs, ACOG Medical Services, and local, state, and federal health surveillance agencies. METARS was a hybrid system with host and PC components. The host component, developed by ACOG OMS/Technology, concentrated on data collection, validation, extraction, and daily NOC reporting. The PC component, developed by the US Centers for Disease Control and Prevention (CDC), concentrated on data analysis and IOC daily summary reporting, with data provided through the host data extraction process.

More than 10,000 physician-assisted medical encounters and more than 3,000 first-aid encounters were recorded in the host system between 4 July and 9 August 1996. The host application was developed for an IBM MVS/CICS environment using CSP and COBOL II. The

CDC's EPI INFO PC application is a public domain software package for a PC MS-DOS environment.

The medical reporting application, based on MVS and CICS, supported the IOC Medical Commission and the ACOG Medical Services Department, which used it to compile and report on basic medical assistance at all venues, specialized assistance at the Olympic polyclinics and hospitals, hospitalization and home emergencies, and tracking of patients.

Technology Materials Planning and Management. The technology materials management database (TMMD) was used to plan technology materials requirements at the venues.

The system was developed using Microsoft FoxPro for Windows 2.6. Standard ACOG codes for venue, function, and building were loaded onto the database to ensure data integrity. The item master was transferred from the inventory system, and each entry was validated against the codes.

The two primary sections in the database were allocations and requirements. Allocations, entered by the manager of technology materials management, represented the equipment designated for each venue and functional area after a review of requirements and budget limitations.

The facilities engineer for each venue then added the delivery dates and other information for each piece of equipment. Reports were printed from the database to plan and coordinate delivery schedules with Logistics. As each shipment was delivered, the technology materials management group noted delivery in the TMMD and entered the transfer on the inventory master.

TMMD contained records for approximately 200,000 individual pieces of equipment distributed to approximately 150 locations.

Ticketing. ProTix and Integrated Systems Solutions Corporation (ISSC), a wholly owned subsidiary of IBM, partnered to provide technology solutions for ACOG's spectator ticketing process. ISSC provided project management and IBM RISC/6000 computer servers, and ProTix supplied software solutions.

ISSC used Gage Marketing to scan and validate domestic mail orders and Voice Integrators, Inc., to provide an interactive voice response (IVR) information system.

ProTix management and programmers customized their software, Prologue, for the Olympic ticket system. The system integrated numerous functions into Prologue's basic ticketing programming. *(For more information, see the Ticket Sales chapter.)*

Uniform Distribution System. The uniform distribution system supported the supply of uniforms to the more than 60,000 Olympic Games staff requiring uniforms for the 1996 Games. The system was an integration of both host-based and AS/400 technology, coupled with a process developed by the Volunteer Services Department. The system could process up to 300 people per hour.

The uniform distribution system had modules for uniform check-in and check-out. Uniform check-in was a set of custom screens added to GSTS on the ES/9000. The check-in station scanned the customer's accreditation badge using Intermec 1464A02 2D scanners (PDF417 bar code type) to validate the badge and verify that a uniform had not been already issued.

The uniform check-out system was added to the existing inventory module. This system used Intermec 1545 scanners to scan the uniform type from the customer's uniform checklist and concurrently update the existing inventory database.

Security Systems. Technology was also instrumental in supporting the various security systems used during the Games.

■ *Closed-Circuit Television Systems.* Closed-circuit television (CCTV) systems consisted of

SpeedDomes, remotely controlled movable cameras, and fixed, or stationary, cameras feeding to a security command center (SCC) at each venue. Each SCC was an independent system with controls for the cameras, monitors, multiplexers, and videocassette recorders. Two transmitters at each venue returned video feeds to the central security operations center at ACOG headquarters.

The system included 186 SpeedDomes, 275 monitors, 56 fixed cameras, and 23 SCC consoles.

■ *Access Control System.* The access control system consisted of on-line PCs, using the ACOG WAN to link with the main ACOG computer. Information on any accreditation badge reported lost or stolen was downloaded to a PC via the ACOG network. The PC at each venue, running Sensormatic interface software, admitted only certain badges at particular entrances. The privilege level, along with the lost or stolen lists, was downloaded to the hand-held reader through a cradle attached to the PC. The readers, which totaled 450 at 23 venues, were updated at four-hour intervals.

Approximately 4,700 badges were lost or stolen during the Games. An estimated 3 million badge scans were conducted.

■ *RFID Access Control System.* Security at the Atlanta Olympic Village was greatly enhanced by the use of the RFID system, which was based on an on-line RISC/6000 PC, using the ACOG WAN to link with the main ACOG computer. Accreditation records were copied into a DB2 table at the host and then downloaded to the PC. The Sensormatic software on the RISC/6000 translated the information (privileges and accreditation number) into access groups and issue levels. The information was then transferred by a fiber backbone at the venue to the wiring closets.

The system read the accreditation number and hand geometry information of the badge wearer who passed through, and then the system communicated information to the portal.

The hand geometry was checked for a match, and the accreditation number was checked for access privileges and against the database of lost or stolen badges.

Equipment included 62 portals and 28 wiring closets installed at 16 entry-control points. Four reenrollment stations, 36 SpeedDomes, and 128 fiber modules were also installed.

CAD Systems/Physical Planning

The CAD function at ACOG was based in Technology, although different departments used the centralized technical and operational resources in different ways. Most ACOG departments relied primarily on printed information from the CAD systems, but some departments acquired technical tools from the CAD systems and generated derivative works for their own purposes. Still other functions (e.g., Look of the Games) used similar technology but were not connected directly to ACOG's CAD efforts.

Olympic sponsors IBM and Xerox provided the base infrastructure of computing hardware and large format output for the CAD systems function and worked with Auto Desk, Inc., supplier of AutoCAD software, to support ACOG's needs.

ACOG created a hybrid of both centralized and decentralized CAD operation options. The CAD systems function provided service to as many internal clients as possible and helped users within ACOG learn to use AutoCAD. These users were then provided licenses to perform their own work.

CAD Technologies. PC-based AutoCAD was chosen to run on standard PCs used throughout ACOG. An IBM RISC/6000 server was installed to support the needs of clients by running IBM's Netware for AIX protocol. Additional RISC/6000 graphical workstations provided more capability to key CAD personnel by allowing larger dataset manipulation, including three-dimensional review of Olympic venues.

ACOG Technology used an IBM RISC/6000 model 970B as the central CAD server, with six model 41Ts for AutoCAD and ArcView use. Two IBM RISC/6000 model 41Ts with GXT1000-2 graphics accelerators were used for real-time interactive three-dimensional review of major Olympic venues, using IBM's 3-D Interaction Accelerator software. To meet document management needs required for vaulting auditable CAD drawings, the IBM ProductManager document control module was implemented on the primary server. The document management system utilized the RISC/6000 version of the DB2 database system.

Physical Planning Efforts. CAD systems' primary service was delivered through its facilities planning group. These eight professional CAD planners delivered venue master plans developed in conjunction with Venue Management. The plans described venue operational issues in an easily understood graphic form.

Drawings of venue master plans were issued monthly during the final year, with content that covered: a cluster area map, site plans and site plan enlargements, floor plans and floor plan enlargements, field of play layout elements, building sections, accreditation zone plans, broadcast plans, and disability circulation routes.

In addition to the centralized CAD function, AOB and Olympic Villages developed CAD plans that focused on their specific functions and areas.

Technology also used AutoCAD software to record technology operational and construction issues. The department contracted with an outside source for services related to cable placement and design documentation.

While CAD systems were used throughout ACOG, three-dimensional modeling was done for selected projects, such as seating configurations and victory ceremonies requirements for the placement of 197 flags on the roof of Olympic Stadium.

Network Delivery Systems

All computing equipment used during the Games was connected through a large number of both WANs and LANs. The size of a particular venue and the applications supported at each determined how the networks were implemented.

Most venues had one LAN with application-specific LANs attached to it by local LAN bridges. Each main LAN was connected by remote LAN bridges to both the primary and backup LANs at the primary data center (PDC). Telecommunications circuits with transmission speeds ranging from 128 kbps (ISDN) to 1.544 Mbps (T-1) were used for these remote bridge connections.

In addition, communications controllers (3745s) were located at the PDC and a majority of venues. Telecommunications circuits ranging from 64 kbps (DS-0) to T-1 were used to connect the 3745s at the venues to 3745s at one of four concentration sites. The majority of those circuits used the public frame relay network, which minimized the number of communications ports required at the concentration sites. The 3745s at the four concentration sites in turn formed a private frame relay network using point-to-point T-1 or T-3 (45 Mbps) circuits.

The Info'96 application used the AS/400 platform as its application server. Venues that required large numbers of Info'96 terminals had one or two AS/400 computers which connected to multiple token-ring networks via multiple token-ring cards. A master Info'96 server located at the PDC distributed all necessary data to each venue-based Info'96 server.

Office systems were Microsoft applications, except for Auto Desk for CAD and Schedule Publisher for project management. EMC2 was the E-mail system used at ACOG headquarters.

Systems Integration

The systems integration and quality-assurance function tracked and reported the schedule progress and delivery performance of the application development groups (Games management systems, results, Info'96). The reporting standards followed the AEM development manual provided by IBM and adapted by the systems integration group for ACOG's needs.

Systems integration managed the testing required to prepare for an integrated application platform for the Games. During the year prior to the Games, the independent test team coordinated development of this testing program and assumed responsibility for the function and integration testing of Games applications. The transition to function and integration testing was coupled with a quality-assurance function to ensure a clear management view of the product.

Systems integration also prepared and maintained the enterprise data model of the primary Games applications and the delivery of the enterprise codesets. These data tables contained common data on venues, athletes, and events shared by all Games management applications.

In addition, problem- and change-management processes for Technology during pre-Games phases and Games-time were the responsibility of systems integration.

TECHNICAL SERVICES

Technical Services negotiated and managed sponsorships with noncomputer technology providers and developed associated solutions with multiple technologies. Technical Services was responsible for a range of operations from telecommunications, pagers, and radios to document processing and the CATV network.

Telecommunications

Prior to the Games, office PBX systems, and later ESSX (Centrex), supported the growing telephone requirements for the primary office buildings as well as for several remote locations, such as the warehouse and fleet management centers. A Meridian SL1 PBX system was donated when ACOG headquarters offices opened in the Inforum in May 1991. In 1994, Lucent Technologies (then AT&T) added a Definity G3r PBX to fulfill AT&T sponsorship requirements. The two switches were linked with tie lines, and the five-digit dialing scheme was introduced. A Definity G3i was installed at ACOG headquarters at 270 Peachtree Street to handle the 15 floors of additional administrative space and, specifically, to accommodate the heavy call volume for Ticket Sales. The central office-based ESSX system was used at remote administrative sites, such as warehouses and transportation centers. As PBX and ESSX systems were added, they were incorporated into the five-digit dialing plan. The administrative station-to-trunk ratio was 9:1. At peak periods, call volumes indicated blockages (60 percent usage), and additional trunks were installed.

ACOG's IVR system offered a menu for information that allowed callers with touch-tone telephones to press selected numbers for explanations about volunteering, conducting business with ACOG, and purchasing tickets. A caller could press zero to reach a live operator. Typically, a team of three to five operators answered the main ACOG telephone number. Their responsibilities included providing and recording information and transferring calls. Recorded general information for frequently

asked questions was integrated with the consoles for directory assistance and call transfer. A second database developed with Microsoft Access software was used to collect name, address, and area of interest information used by Games Services to forecast ticket sales and interest in merchandising.

During the Games, the five-digit dialing network of more than 15,000 lines linked all venues except the Washington, DC, football stadium and its Village. Ten-digit dialing was required to communicate with the systems there as the city was beyond BellSouth's communications area. Primary service was provided by AT&T Definity PBXs, with BellSouth ESSX serving as a backup service at venues in case of power interruption. The station-to-trunk ratio for Games operation was 3:1 with virtually no blockage during the Games period.

Calls to the primary ACOG telephone number averaged 7,000 per day during the Games. Pre-Games volumes averaged 2,500–3,000 calls per day.

Wireless PBX (AT&T Transtalk) offered solutions to mobile users within a venue. This phone could send and receive calls like any other PBX telephone but did not work outside the venue. Transtalk coverage ranged from 400 to 1,000 ft (122 to 305 m) from base stations, and was more effective in open areas without concrete barriers.

More than 1,200 ACOG-provided cellular telephones were also used within and between venues. The need for cellular telephones arose before the venue telephone systems were installed. BellSouth Mobility implemented a digital cellular network that separated ACOG and rate card users from users on the existing analog network. Motorola provided the dual-mode cellular telephones for the digital network. For ACOG cellular telephones, the average per station usage was 1,000 minutes a month, peaking at over 4,000 minutes for one month.

Long-distance calling was implemented in a variety of ways. ACOG staff used authorization codes for long-distance calling. These calls traveled the software-defined network (SDN), a discounted long-distance network for the Olympic Family. For the ACOG voice and data networks, AT&T extended dedicated circuits to the remote venues and provided an ISDN for all switched long-distance service. AT&T sold prepaid calling cards to the press, broadcasters, and athletes at AT&T calling centers.

AT&T provided Public Phone 1,000 Plus, commonly known as charge-a-call, telephones for work areas at the MPC and press subcenters. The phones used only AT&T cards, so AT&T offered instant credit to the press to obtain a card. Prepaid calling cards, however, could not be used on telephones for long-distance use with laptop computers because the prompting on the prepaid calls required more time than the computers' systems had programmed. Again, the AT&T calling card was the solution. Another issue with Public Phone 1,000 Plus was that the press used a variety of communications packages with their laptop computers that often caused system interruptions.

BellSouth public telephones augmented telephone services at the venues for staff, volunteers, and spectators. Telephones with telecommunications devices for the deaf were available at every venue.

The data network was primarily DS-1, Frame Relay, and ISDN, using Motorola data communications equipment (CSUs, DSUs, terminal adapters, modems). The BellSouth SONET ring architecture supported the intra-LATA (local long distance) voice, data, and video services for the Games.

Paging

MobileComm, then a subsidiary of BellSouth and later a division of MobileMedia, Inc., provided 1,100 alphanumeric pagers and associated service prior to the Games, including a paging connection to ACOG's E-mail system so users could send text messages. For the Games, the MobileComm pagers were returned, and

Motorola provided 7,700 alphanumeric pagers for local, regional, and nationwide use, using the MobileComm paging network. Pagers were allocated to functional areas, which assigned individual pagers within a department.

The link to the Info'96 E-mail system allowed text messaging over the MobileComm paging network. As pagers were assigned, the paging and associated accreditation numbers were entered into the Info'96 system to activate this feature for an individual pager.

Recovery efforts were successful, though lengthy. The loss rate was only 5 percent.

Radios

Reliable radio communications were essential to Games operations. Radio systems were designed to provide redundancy and backup and were hardened to ensure reliable operation. Two simulcast trunked radio systems were interconnected with redundant microwave radio systems. Uninterrupted power supply and standby power generators ensured that the system could operate in the event of power interruption.

Multiple radio systems were used during the Games to meet most requirements for coverage, reliability, interoperability, and acceptable time delays.

The talk group was introduced as a concept that eliminated the need for users to understand the complexities of radio technology. It required determining who needed to talk together and could share radio channels.

Detailed reviews determined which groups would be better served with wired solutions such as headsets, phones, and intercoms, or with wireless solutions such as cordless phones or cell phone technology. A balance of the number and types of users on a talk group was then implemented. Too few users limited the number of frequencies that could be utilized to communicate with other groups; too many users or excessive traffic on a talk group rendered it unusable.

The strategy was to secure a contiguous radio spectrum that provided an integrated solution for interoperation and modification as requirements changed. Radio sponsorship depended on radio equipment that could be resold after the Games. The only available radio frequency spectrum that met these criteria was the public safety band in the 821 Mhz range, where 92 duplex frequency assignments were secured. The challenge was to design a radio system that included management of the 92 radio channels. Within the Olympic Ring, the use of these radio channels had to be maximized to handle the traffic.

Simplex Radio Systems. Simplex radio systems were used where radio-to-radio direct communications were adequate. This worked well at most venues outside the Olympic Ring. Frequencies could be reused between these locations.

Simplex systems were also used when time was critical and range could be easily defined; the primary areas of use were short-range communications within venues for AOB, Opening and Closing Ceremonies, and critical event operations for Sports.

Trunked Radio Systems. Trunked radio systems allowed frequencies to be reused and were more efficient than radio channels dedicated to each user. The radio system automatically assigns an available frequency, or channel, to users for their conversation talk group. Additional advantages include improved radio coverage over simplex operation and the ability to reconfigure the systems. Radio channel loading was balanced to optimize priorities. However, the system was more complex and required user training. In total, five trunked radio systems were used for the Games, with 256 different talk groups on the system.

Other Radio Systems. A number of additional radio systems were utilized during the Games that were not initially contemplated because of geographic and operational considerations. The integrated digital enhanced network (iDEN) radios provided two-way radio communications suited to small talk groups with the capability for private conversations. The system could also be used for cellular telephone conversations. The system was used by the Olympic Family host/hostess program, primarily for driver to host/hostess communications and emergencies, and by the ACOG executive management team. Also, a number of commercial radios, both simplex and trunked, were rented to meet extra requests.

Operations. Radios were a scheduled and managed resource moved between venues to meet requirements. They were assigned to individuals at venues and required a signature for accountability. This approach resulted in a minimal loss of equipment. A single location was established at each venue for the distribution and recovery of radios.

In total, Motorola provided 12,000 mobile and hand-held radios. ACOG's radio group, with the Federal Communications Commission, established the Olympic Frequency Coordination Committee to accommodate all requirements for radio frequencies operating during the Games. User requests were for frequencies around 20 MHz. Peak traffic averaged 300,000 calls per day with more than 1.4 million seconds of air time used. Importantly, there were virtually no busy system issues.

Documents

The paper flow from Xerox copiers, facsimile machines, and printers was enormous before and during the Games. Before the Games, the ACOG publishing center produced more than 2,000 professional quality documents using a variety of layouts and paper stock comprising 110 million images. The center used the Xerox DocuTech 135 Publishing System and a 5775 color printer to provide an electronic interface to the user.

An analysis of the potential documents to be printed was conducted, with an assessment of ACOG-produced versus contracted printing costs. Implementation of the ACOG publishing center to replace the outsourcing of publications to local printers saved ACOG more than $2 million over a four-year period.

A print server directly linking Xerox DocuPrint systems to competition results printing was used for the first time in an ACOG-sponsored sports event prior to the Games. At nine pre-Olympic events and at the road cycling event during the Games, the DocuPrint systems shared a trailer with the AT&T Definity PBX. The mobile trailer was dubbed OTTO for Olympic technology trailer operations.

The unique link of 128 DocuPrint systems to the results system produced more than 40 million results for the 26 sports. The publishing center remained in operation during the Games and produced the results books, which compiled official results for every sport. The total Games volume was more than 140 million images.

Cable Access Television Network

The ACOG CATV network was comprised of two parts: venue video feeds from the local AOB feed distributed on an ACOG CATV system, and return video providing all AOB feeds from all Atlanta venues to selected venues. The number of local feeds per venue varied according to the number of local feeds provided by AOB, typically from one to seven, providing coverage to broadcasters, the press, the Olympic Family, volunteers, and competition participants. The return video network was capable of transporting up to 48 channels from the IBC to predetermined locations such as the MPC, the Olympic Family Hotel, the Olympic Village, major press subcenters, and selected sponsor locations. In addition, local nonoperating channels for weather information and news feeds were included in the network. The Olympic Village had 12 channels of international programming plus entertainment channels.

The CATV network supported the implementation of CIS for broadcasters and PDS for the print media. A collaboration between Scientific Atlanta, BellSouth, and Panasonic, the system used digital MPEG2 video and audio compression over a digital SONET OC3 network to more than 10,000 television sets (13-, 20-, 27-, and 51-in) with 6,000 addressable television set–top decoders and combination television/videocassette recorders located in accredited areas for the Olympic Family. The network offered a view of the events with no commentary, only ambient sound.

Video Boards

At some venues, the video feed was projected onto large-screen video boards to enhance the spectator experience. In addition to providing replays, the feed also served as an entertainment feature. The primary sources of video material were the AOB host broadcaster world feeds and the ACOG CATV system.

At Olympic Stadium, the main video board was a high-resolution model, the largest of its kind in the world, approximately 30 x 40 ft (9 x 12 m). There was also a temporary auxiliary board in the stadium. An additional temporary board was installed to provide the AOB host broadcaster feed of the Opening Ceremony to the athletes during their procession from Atlanta–Fulton County Stadium. During the marathon, video boards were used in the stadium to provide spectators with the host broadcast feed covering the competitors along the course.

Temporary video boards were installed for aquatics at the Georgia Tech Aquatic Center and archery at Stone Mountain Park, as well as in Centennial Olympic Park. Existing video boards were used at Atlanta–Fulton County Stadium and the Georgia Dome.

To ensure that the operation of the boards and their location did not affect competition, personnel were required to operate the value-added video replay systems and the sports-specific video content portions of the program. Large video boards proved even more valuable because they provided information for safe entrance and exit of venues.

Headsets and Intercom Systems

Technical Services coordinated implementation of headsets, intercom systems, public address systems, and other sound systems that allowed instantaneous communication within the venues.

Cabling

LAN and telecommunications were connected by 40,000 AT&T Systmax cabling drops. ACOG used 2 million ft (610 km) of fiber cable and 5 million ft (1,524 km) of copper cable to satisfy Games-time requirements.

Support of Special Events

From fall 1992 until the Games, ACOG hosted a series of events and meetings that required technological support. The smaller events, typically workshops, required telephones, radgers, facios, cellular phones, pasimile machines, small copiers, and workstations with printers. The larger meetings, typically in support of the IOC, NOCs, IFs, and AOB, required substantial technology for meeting rooms and offices.

Technology also supported 25 sporting events from spring 1995 through spring 1996. The results system (the Swatch timing/scoring system, IBM results application, Xerox DocuPrint results print solution, and the BellSouth/AT&T Datacom networks) was tested for the sports represented at the events, as were other technologies. An early release of the Games accreditation system was used, as well as the bar code and RF identification features of the access control system.

Video boards were used to display graphic images as well as text results.

BRUCE L EKIN • DON G EKLUND • ERIK A EKLUND • JENNIFER D EKLUND • KARL M EKLUND MT • RICHARD A EKMAN • SCOTT E EKMAN • SUZANNE E EKMAN • ELIZABETH C EKMEKJIAN • CHRISTOPHER N EKSTRAND • MATS N EKTVEDT • FAREED A EL-AMIN • RANDA A EL-HAJJE • JEAN EL GUINDI • ALADEEN M EL KORDY • LYNDA ELAM • WHIT ELAM • RICHARD H ELAN • HESHAAM A ELBATOUTI • CARLA J ELDER • CHARLES E ELDER • DIANE H ELDER • DOUG ELDER • GREGORY E ELDER • JAMES R ELDER • JEFFREY S ELDER • JIMMY W ELDER • LUTHER F ELDER • PEGGY ELDER • ROGER ELDER •

On average, events required 10 cellular phones, 3 copiers, 30 radios, 30 pagers, 5 facsimile machines, 45 telephones, workstations, and intercom and public address systems. Rate card telephone lines were installed for the press and concessionaires. Broadcasters, when in attendance, ordered telephone and program audio and video lines. Info'96 was tested at the gymnastics event in November 1995.

Technology Rate Card

Technology products and services were available on rate cards that were provided to different ACOG functional areas that offered services to external clients, including AOB, the Olympic Family Hotel, Olympic Villages (for NOCs), patron suites (for the patron suite ticket holders), Press Operations, Sports (for IFs), and Venue Management (for all other services to be installed at a venue).

The technology rate card offered 367 different items. Technology negotiated with sponsors and suppliers for services and equipment such as CATV feed, cellular telephones, the CIS, computers, copiers, facsimile machines, Info'96, pagers, radios, telephones, and televisions. The department then processed orders with the appropriate providers. A rate card manager in the department oversaw the implementation, customer satisfaction, and recovery of the technology. During the Games, more than 30 rate card specialists assisted in this process.

Cumulatively, 400 customers ordered a total of 10,850 items. *(For the scope of rate card technology, see Figure 3.)*

CONCLUSIONS AND RECOMMENDATIONS

The extraordinary amount of technology necessary to support both the infrastructure of the Olympic Games and worldwide broadcasting to a cumulative audience of more than 19.6 billion people required intense planning and collaboration with ACOG functional areas, sponsors, and technical experts. State-of-the-art broadcasting applications, coupled with the first Olympic Internet web site, ensured real-time worldwide communications.

The overall success of technology support is largely dependent upon two critical factors: early and continual support of the technology sponsors that offer solutions and staff, and the experience of staff and sponsor personnel who managed technology at previous Olympic Games. The following recommendations are offered for future organizing committees.

■ It is essential to have experienced and knowledgeable sponsor personnel manage the technology projects. The commitment to supplies and delivery dates must be met, and penalties considered if they are not.

■ Comprehensive planning and design of staff technology needs, along with a conservative staff allocations plan, will help stabilize the budget without hampering Games operations. The budget must include a contingency (financial and resources) to support administrative and special events leading up to the Games.

■ Adhere to a set date for the introduction of new technology.

■ Although it is difficult to simulate an actual Games-time environment, testing the results systems and a deadline for early completion of the application is essential. Have sponsors and the organizing committee agree to a testing schedule that can accomplish systems testing at least one year before the Games.

■ A central clearinghouse concept such as the TIC/TOC process can ensure and provide for continuous communication and coordination among all participating entities.

■ The rate card implementation process requires a dedicated resource person to coordinate, verify, and ensure timely implementation of all rate card services.

■ A centralized CAD function model is recommended, making an early analysis of technology and choosing flexible systems that work within the existing and planned technology infrastructure.

FIGURE 3: SCOPE OF RATE CARD TECHNOLOGY

Item	Orders
Cellular telephones	825
CIS terminals	130
Copiers	169
Data jack conversion kits	360
Desktop computers	70
Facsimile machines	351
Info'96 terminals	220
Laser printers	50
Pagers	525
Radios	300
Telephone lines	6,600
Television cable	735
Televisions	500
X.400 external E-mail	15
Total	**10,850**

Atlanta 1996®

TICKET SALES

CHAPTER TWENTY-FOUR
TICKET SALES

OVERVIEW—The mission of ACOG's Ticket Sales Department was to optimize ticket revenue, maximize attendance, provide an efficient and clearly communicated ticket distribution system, and give customers fair access to tickets at reasonable prices. The large available ticket inventory coupled with ACOG's philosophy of making the Centennial Olympic Games the most accessible ever, required that Ticket Sales develop and implement both innovative selling techniques and a fair distribution process.

The Ticket Sales Department operated as a self-contained business unit responsible for pricing, promoting, packaging, selling, accounting, delivering, and servicing its ticket products for all sporting and Olympic Arts Festival (OAF) events. The amount of ticket inventory and changes in inventory standards necessitated the development and implementation of an on-line, computerized ticket system.

When estimated ticket revenue grew from 15 percent of all Olympic revenue to 25 percent in September 1995, it was mandated that the department focus primarily on selling tickets, especially for the two sports with the most available tickets: football and baseball.

Ticket Sales accomplished its mission, selling a record 8.6 million Olympic tickets, surpassing the Los Angeles record by 2.9 million and generating $468.2 million in total sales.

ORGANIZATION

The Ticket Sales Department was established in May 1993 as part of Games Services. Managers and staff were recruited from the ticketing operations of other major sporting and cultural events. By January 1996, the Ticket Sales Department totaled 80 staff members, with specific skills in computerized tickets, languages, contract negotiation, box office management, manifest development, sales, and accounting.

The management team began in July 1993 and was divided into six areas of responsibility: Operations, Distribution, Vendor Contract Management, Special Sales, Ticket Marketing, and Venue Operations.

ACOG also employed consultants with expertise in specific phases of planning. The Los Angeles Games ticket director was consulted early to validate ticket distribution procedures and offer other guidance. A technology expert from the Barcelona Games helped plan and execute the quota system and later served as a liaison between Ticket Sales and ProTix, the third-party vendor whose software, Prologue, was used to develop the computerized ticket system. Services from ticket promotions consultants were utilized to assist in the sales of football and baseball tickets.

The department also relied on legal counsel to review issues relating to public sales, ticket brokers, and scalping. The law firm engaged by ACOG reviewed all vendors and contracts, drafted the terms and conditions printed on the back of the tickets, and reviewed all Ticket Sales policies and procedures.

OLYMPIC TICKET SYSTEM

The large inventory of available tickets along with changes in industry standards since the 1984 Olympic Games necessitated an on-line, computerized ticket system. To shift ticket sales successfully from a hard ticket environment to an on-line environment, it was critical to select the proper vendor.

ACOG sought a company with a sophisticated understanding of the business, including direct experience with phone centers, box office operations, and outlet networking, and an existing presence in the domestic market. It was also important that the company have the appropriate staff and resources to support customized programming. The company selected had to maintain its commitment over the several phases of the project, as well as be compatible with ACOG corporate structure.

A request for information was sent to 20 ticket agencies. Upon review, only six were invited to bid on the project. The requirements, combining current ticket industry standards as well as high-tech enhancements, were translated into a request for a proposal.

ProTix and Integrated Systems Solutions Corporation (ISSC), a wholly owned IBM subsidiary, presented a partnership arrangement to ACOG. ISSC's financial and computer hardware strength, coupled with ProTix's ticket software and service capabilities, made an appealing combination, and they began work in September 1994.

ISSC used additional subcontractors to meet ACOG's needs: Gage Marketing, to scan and validate domestic mail orders; IBM, to provide scanning technology; and Voice Integrators, Inc., to provide an interactive voice response (IVR) information system.

ISSC and ProTix operated on site at ACOG, occupying a secured floor near the Ticket Sales Department. ISSC provided project management and IBM RISC System/6000 computer servers. ProTix supplied software solutions and an in-house phone room with 50 sales stations, which eventually expanded to 100 stations. The other two contractors operated from their own corporate headquarters.

Consultants from the Sema Group, whose ticket system was used in the 1992 Olympic Games, helped develop enhancements to the ProTix system, providing continuity and quality assurance for the Games.

ProTix management and programmers customized and enhanced the ProTix software, Prologue, into what became known as the Olympic ticket system. Mail order requests were processed using FairTix, a specifically designed software program developed to randomly award space for oversubscribed sessions. An automated program assigned space in blocks of seats. Domestic customers awarded space were assigned seats on a first-come, first-served basis. Nondomestic customers were one of several separate market segments, discussed later in this chapter, for which tickets were allocated against a quota. The redistribution of sponsor tickets was automated through bar code scanning.

To offset the cost of the customized ticket system, service fees for ticket accounts and individual tickets were necessary.

BETTY L ELLIOTT • BOBBY ELLIOTT • BOBBY J ELLIOTT • BRANDON F ELLIOTT • CHRISTI E ELLIOTT • DANIEL C ELLIOTT • DANIEL G ELLIOTT • DEXTER L ELLIOTT • EUNICE S ELLIOTT • JAMES M EL-LIOTT • JAMES S ELLIOTT • JAN E ELLIOTT • JESSE R ELLIOTT • JOHN W ELLIOTT • KARL E ELLIOTT • KATHRYN D ELLIOTT • KELLIE L ELLIOTT • KRISTEN M ELLIOTT • LARRY P ELLIOTT • LEAH M EL-LIOTT • LESTER F ELLIOTT • MARY ELLIOTT • MARY E ELLIOTT • MATTHEW B ELLIOTT • MICHELLE D ELLIOTT • PAMELA R ELLIOTT • ROBERT S ELLIOTT • RONALD E ELLIOTT • RYAN M ELLIOTT •

461

Contrary to the ticket industry standard of charging an order fee for every unique order, a one-time account fee was created, which helped develop true customer relationships. Based on the theory that existing customers represent future customers, the fee structure rewarded repeat business.

TICKET OPERATIONS

Operations was responsible for creating Ticket Sales' business plan, establishing accounting controls and procedures for ticket transactions, advising pricing strategies, managing seat assignments, and overseeing ticket printing and delivery.

Business Plan

The department began to develop its business plan and corresponding budget in September 1993, incorporating sales and distribution strategies to help maximize revenues. There were small modifications to the original plan due to fluctuations in sports schedules, construction, seating capacities, and venue sites. Yet the plan developed in 1993 was essentially followed. The initial budget and revenues forecasts were submitted to senior management in October 1993. The budget was approved without changes. Three years before the Games, the goal was to achieve revenue projections by the time the Opening Ceremony began. Because of aggressive ticket pricing, direct marketing, innovative distribution, and premium packaging, revenue projections more than doubled by September 1995.

Expenses. The expense budget was derived from costs associated with selling and distributing a projected 7.5 million tickets out of a projected salable inventory of 10.5 million. Costs were calculated only for projected sales, not total inventory. The most significant cost items were payroll, ticket printing, and ticket delivery. Costs were also calculated for creating, supplying, and managing box offices at each venue.

Revenues. Ticket Sales worked closely with Financial Services and Technology to forecast revenue potential, ensuring a comprehensive approach. The complexity of variables and scope of the project challenged forecasters until a database was created using a customized version of Microsoft's FoxPro software.

The database incorporated and could calculate changes in the variables that would affect revenue: venue size, price scaling, scheduling, percent of tickets sold, amount of stand seating for the Olympic Family and broadcast media, and allocations to customer groups within 15 ACOG-defined market segments. Calculations were made at all levels (session, price, venue, sport, or grand total), and the ability to compare different scenarios quickly became invaluable in the decision-making process. The program also enabled Ticket Sales to determine initial quotas for customers and market segments and to track the number of unsold tickets by price category for each session.

Pricing. Ticket Sales began establishing ticket prices in January 1994 by reviewing current rates for individual sports and for world-class competitions and national and international championships. Sport advisors and focus groups of potential customers across the country were consulted. Ticket prices at the Los Angeles Games, adjusted for inflation, were considered. A transportation fee was also incorporated into prices, reflecting that tickets served as free passes to the spectator transportation system.

Using baseline numbers established from the above research, final ticket prices were derived using supply and demand theory. The sessions anticipated to be highest in demand, because of popularity or limited seating, were priced accordingly. Ticket prices for the best seats at Opening and Closing Ceremonies were $636, whereas some baseball tickets were priced as low as $7 because of Atlanta–Fulton County Stadium's large capacity and the frequency of baseball sessions.

To provide the general public with fair access to tickets, not every seat was priced at its going market value. A percentage of tickets was priced no higher than $27 for every sport. The pricing plan was presented to the IOC in June 1994 and approved with no changes.

Quotas. A quota system was required to manage ticket availability. In late 1994, preliminary quotas were set according to past Olympic allocations, the size of each venue, contractual obligations, and anticipated demand for each of the 540 sports sessions.

The quota system grouped ticket sales into 15 categories: The Olympic Programme (TOP) sponsors; Centennial Olympic Partner (COP) sponsors; broadcast rights holders; other sponsors and suppliers; contingencies; citizens with disabilities; other individuals needing modified aisle seating; NOCs; IOC; IFs; special accommodations packages; other ACOG contractual commitments; direct marketing programs; Georgia lottery winners; and *Olympic Charter* Rule 58 accredited individuals. All market segments were included in the system except for the domestic public, which was given the freedom to choose preferred sessions.

The quotas were managed with a customized version of Microsoft Excel spreadsheet software, which allowed Ticket Sales to limit the number of tickets for each of the categories. This function was particularly important in high-demand sessions because it saved a percentage of tickets for the domestic public and prevented sessions and price categories from being oversubscribed. The system also provided for daily quota adjustments, which permitted Ticket Sales to redefine a market segment's limit as necessary. Final quotas were confirmed in December 1995, when ticket demand for most contractual customers (e.g., Olympic Family) was known. The system was used until January 1996, when seat assignments were completed and inventory control was accomplished.

Seat Assignments

Ticket Sales began converting space allocations at venues into seat assignments in December 1995. Until then, customers had been sold space but had not been guaranteed specific seats because some venues were still under construction, and in other instances, obstructions and unusable seats, known as seat kills, had not yet been determined.

Almost all seats were assigned using the Prologue system based on rules created by Ticket Sales. It was important to finalize all existing customer assignments as soon as possible so account information could be formatted for printing.

As a starting point, Ticket Sales obtained current manifests for existing venues. For newly constructed venues, manifests were created using blueprints and CAD drawings. Of the 31 sports manifests created, 16 were built for reserved seating and 15 for general admission. All four OAF manifests were built with reserved seating. Some general admission capacities were restricted by the number of people Security, Transportation, and Venue Management could control, given the logistics of the venue and the session's time frame.

Seating information was assembled using an Excel spreadsheet and then entered into a Prologue test database. The test database was scaled for pricing, ranked for viewing preference, and assigned hold codes. The quantity of tickets within each hold code corresponded to

FIGURE 1: COMPREHENSIVE STATEMENT ON REVERSE SIDE OF TICKET

ACOG 1996 Olympic Games Spectator Rules

(1) Spectators assume all risks and danger incidental to the event, whether occurring prior to, during, or after the event, including, among other things, injuries caused by other spectators. Spectators assume all risks of property loss.

(2) This ticket is a personal license and may not be resold or transferred. Persons selling or reselling tickets in violation of law are subject to arrest and prosecution. Ticket prices include all applicable taxes and are subject to a $15 nonrefundable order processing fee. The license granted by this ticket may be terminated, without cause, by refunding the face value of the ticket.

(3) Tickets obtained from unofficial sources may be lost, stolen, or counterfeit and may not be honored for admission. All spectators, regardless of age, must have a ticket. ACOG is not responsible for lost, stolen, forgotten, defaced, or destroyed tickets. No replacement tickets will be issued.

(4) Spectators grant the IOC, ACOG, and third parties authorized by them permission to use photographs, film, tape, or other images or likenesses of spectators without compensation. Images of the Olympic Games obtained by spectators with cameras, video and/or audio devices, or other means cannot be used for broadcast, publication, or any commercial purposes under any circumstances.

(5) This ticket may not be used for political, advertising, or other promotional purposes (including prizes, contests, or sweepstakes not licensed by ACOG). Spectators may not solicit contributions or distribute literature on the premises or wear or bring political, advertising, or other promotional items into the venue.

(6) The following is a partial list of prohibited items and activities: smoking, broadcast through the use of cellular phones or other transmitting devices, use of flash photography or other lighting devices, strollers, bottles, cans, coolers, ice chests, food and beverages brought into the venue, weapons, fireworks, illegal drugs, horns, poles, banners, large flags, flags

other than those of participating countries, animals of any kind (except service animals), signage of any nature, balls, and Frisbees. All spectators consent to inspection of prohibited items. Persons refusing inspection may be denied entry and ticket prices will not be refunded. No storage is available at venues.

(7) ACOG reserves the right to refuse admission or eject any spectator who fails to comply with these rules or is disruptive to the session or the enjoyment, comfort, or safety of other spectators; ticket prices will not be refunded. No readmission or pass-outs will be allowed.

Postponement, Cancellation, and Exchange Policy

All session dates, times, and descriptions are subject to change. If, prior to commencement, a session is canceled or postponed to a later date, spectators may exchange tickets in person for tickets to any subsequent sport or Olympic Arts Festival session, for equal or lesser face value, subject to availability. No refunds are allowed. There will be no refunds or exchanges if a session is canceled or postponed after it has commenced or if a session description or participants change.

Transportation Information

A portion of the purchase price of this ticket is for transportation on MARTA and the Olympic Transportation System, for the 17-day period from 19 July 1996 through 4 August 1996, on the day of the session, to venues in the Atlanta area. There will be no ACOG-provided spectator transportation furnished between Atlanta and within the following cities and areas: Lake Lanier (rowing, canoe/kayak), Columbus (softball), Ocoee (canoe/kayak), Athens (football, gymnastics, volleyball), Savannah (yachting), or the satellite football cities. No smoking, eating, or drinking will be permitted on any transportation vehicle.

Spectators agree to abide by all other rules and safety regulations which may be posted at the venue or on the Olympic Transportation System.

the limits established by the quota system. Ticket Sales used 14 hold codes, including disability seating, modified aisle seating, wheelchair companion seating, permanent seat kills, temporary seat kills, Rule 58–accredited individuals, camera positions, press tables, international sales, special sales, Georgia lottery commitments, sponsor sales, session-day contingencies, and reserved interim sales.

The test database was examined several times for accuracy and completeness and then became the actual database. Within each sport, a completed manifest was copied across all pertinent sessions of that sport, making it possible to assign seats. Automated seat assignment began in January 1996 and took six weeks to complete. Assignments were performed venue by venue, sport by sport, session by session, and price by price. Before starting the process, sponsors were polled about features desired in seat assignment. The most consistent request was that ACOG provide seats in blocks of 40. The Olympic ticket system was customized to accommodate this request.

Immediately following automated assignments, Ticket Sales used the corresponding hold code ticket inventory to complete manual assignments. The patron category ticket packages had to be manually assigned to accommodate requests for seating next to other patrons. ADA category accounts were also assigned manually to provide the mix of wheelchair, companion, or modified aisle seating needed for each order. Manual seat assignment was completed by March.

Ticket Content and Design

Ticket Sales was responsible for the production and distribution of tickets, but decisions on the printed content and security of tickets were made with the assistance of Protocol, Security, Transportation, and Venue Management.

ACOG's Creative Services Department designed all aesthetic elements of the tickets.

Because printing on the tickets had to be large enough to be legible to customers, bus and train attendants, and ticket takers, they were printed only in English, the common language of the majority of spectators. Specific security measures involving paper, ink, and the printing process were also incorporated into the design. Three holograms commemorating the Centennial Olympic Games fulfilled both artistic and security requirements.

Each ticket was imprinted with the session's venue name, geographic location of the venue, sport name, a pictogram of the sport, the date and time the session would take place, a unique session code, and seating information. One challenge was to create a common way of describing gates or portals, aisles or sections, rows, and seats at the various venues. Tickets for the arts events included additional descriptions for balcony and orchestra sections.

The final format allowed for four character fields with alterable title fields. For venues with fewer than four categories of seat specifications, the excess fields were suppressed during imprinting. Most tickets read "Gate, Section, Row, Seat."

Other details imprinted on each ticket included the price in US dollars and the price level (A, B, C, or D), the session code, a bar code used for redistribution purposes, and the customer account number. Tickets complied with Rule 51 of the *Olympic Charter* prohibiting advertising. *(The disclaimer on the reverse, which included all spectator rules, is shown in Figure 1.)*

Ticket Sales produced distinctive, commemorative tickets for both Opening and Closing Ceremonies and souvenir tickets for all other sessions. For box office sales, thermal ticket stock incorporated design features similar to the souvenir stock. Ticket dimensions for the Opening and Closing Ceremonies were 3.75 x 8.5 in (9.53 x 21.6 cm), and souvenir ticket dimensions were 2.5 x 7.5 in (6.35 x 19.05 cm). The thermal stock dimensions were 2 x 7 in (5.08 x 17.78 cm). Ceremonies tickets were designed differently than other stock because they commanded higher prices and were therefore more vulnerable to counterfeiting efforts. All four ticket designs corresponded with the Look of the Games motif. Creative Services worked closely with the ticket printer, Weldon, Williams & Lick, to ensure that design ideas were feasible from a printing standpoint. For additional security, the agency was

left: Opening and Closing Ceremonies tickets were designed differently from other stock.

right: Souvenir tickets were especially designed to prevent counterfeiting.

FIGURE 2: OLYMPIC GAMES TICKET SALES PERFORMANCE

Code	Discipline	Tickets sold
AR	Archery	42,114
AT	Athletics	1,134,558
BB	Baseball	1,134,203
BD	Badminton	56,314
BK	Basketball	1,068,032
BV	Beach Volleyball	108,909
BX	Boxing	162,742
CS	Canoe/Kayak—Slalom	41,846
CA	Canoe/Kayak—Sprint	103,137
CM	Cycling—Mountain Bike	27,789
CT	Cycling—Track	29,961
DV	Diving	128,360
ED	Equestrian—Dressage	110,544
EJ	Equestrian—Jumping	81,740
ET	Equestrian—Three Day	164,715
FN	Fencing	24,308
FB	Football	1,255,173
GA	Gymnastics—Artistic	474,209
GP	Gymnastics—Artistic Podium Training	72,695
GR	Gymnastics—Rhythmic	46,490
HB	Handball	186,901
HO	Hockey	282,135
JD	Judo	76,298
MP	Modern Pentathlon	10,648
RO	Rowing	129,048
SB	Softball	120,132
SH	Shooting	37,050
SW	Swimming	151,476
SY	Synchronized Swimming	22,051
TE	Tennis	162,389
TT	Table Tennis	53,393
VY	Volleyball	508,279
WF	Wrestling—Freestyle	45,374
WG	Wrestling—Greco-Roman	45,781
WL	Weightlifting	64,855
WP	Water Polo	88,712
YA	Yachting	8,086
ZC	Closing Ceremony	55,796
ZO	Opening Ceremony	68,047
Total		**8,384,290**

referred to generically as the ticket printer, rather than by its company name.

Ticket Printing

The ticket printer produced 12.2 million tickets in a short time. The process involved printing the base design and then imprinting specific seating information. ACOG ordered quantities of 200,000 ceremonies, 8 million souvenir, and 4 million thermal tickets.

On 15 November 1995, after final ticket designs were approved, the printing of the base design on stock was begun and completed in January 1996. In February, seat assignments had been completed and tickets began to be imprinted with seating information.

The key to success during this phase of production was maintaining a well-organized printing and shipping schedule. ACOG forwarded electronic data files from the Olympic ticket system to the ticket printer at regular intervals. Each file consisted of multiple customer accounts within their customer group, allowing Ticket Sales to manage one group at a time. The customer account number was used as the main control device, preventing the imprinting of duplicate seat locations. There were 220 individual electronic files sent to the printer between February and July 1996.

Because of required delivery schedules, tickets were first printed for TOP and COP sponsors, then for other sponsors and NOCs, and finally for the general public. Many customer accounts required both ceremonies and souvenir tickets. Because the imprinting process was organized by individual customer accounts, two printing production lines operated simultaneously. Once an entire account was imprinted, tickets were assembled into boxes and pouches for shipping.

For aesthetic and security purposes, the department fulfilled as many ticket orders as possible on souvenir stock, including all phone orders through June. All ceremonies ticket requests were imprinted on ceremonies stock. Therefore, ceremonies tickets were not available for sale at all box office locations. Use of thermal ticket stock was limited to venue box office transactions, which did not commence until June 1996. Each venue box office was equipped with on-line computer terminals and a BOCA printer that used heat instead of ink to imprint, therefore requiring thermal or heat-sensitive paper.

Ticket Delivery

TOP and COP sponsors were required to pick their tickets up in person at the ticket printer. Sponsor accounts totaled more than 40,000 tickets. Before accepting their tickets, sponsor representatives, assisted by Ticket Sales staff, verified both the content and quantity of their tickets against an itemized manifest list. Once verified, sponsors signed for their tickets and received ownership of them. Tickets were then shipped to their corporate headquarters by a secure means of delivery.

NOCs and other sponsors collected tickets in person at the main ticket center located in downtown Atlanta in the same building as ACOG headquarters. The balance of tickets, mostly for the general public, was delivered via UPS.

UPS shipped 426,000 general public ticket packages directly from the ticket printer. Accomplished in 14 days, this delivery was the largest by any express carrier in history. UPS only delivered packages to the address that appeared on the shipping label, and all deliveries required a receiver signature. Using an on-line tracking system called Parcelink, UPS was 99 percent effective in delivering packages. Only 48 packages were lost or destroyed.

After three delivery attempts had been made, the package was forwarded to the main ticket center in Atlanta, where UPS and ACOG staff attempted to locate the owner. Some ticket packages were still unclaimed just prior to the Games. The tickets in these packages were then destroyed, and the customer's account information was updated. The tickets could then be printed again at the venue; however, very few of these tickets were claimed by customers.

SALES

The sale of tickets to the domestic public occurred in three phases. The mail-order phase took place from May through December 1995 and resulted in the sale of 3,275,327 tickets. The telephone phase lasted from February to August 1996 and generated the sale of 952,253 tickets, including Internet and IVR system sales. Venue box office sales from June to August 1996 totaled 510,327 tickets. Sales volumes generated for a given phase dictated the strategy used for the next phase. *(For summaries of ticket sales by sport sessions and OAF events, see Figures 2 and 3, respectively.)*

ACOG assisted Ticket Sales with research, direct marketing, and mass advertising, as well as editing the mail-order brochure and planning the media campaign. An ACOG Communications Department staff member planned press conferences to launch and promote each sales phase, handled numerous requests for interviews, and provided advice on all policy issues.

Ticket Sales introduced several technological innovations during domestic public sales, including ticket sales via the Internet and IVR information system, and on-line ticket access, which allowed customers to purchase tickets

FIGURE 3: OLYMPIC GAMES OAF TICKET SALES PERFORMANCE

Code	Discipline	Tickets sold
DA	Dance	27,458
DF	Dance	,428
DM	Dance	11,575
EA	Exhibition	12,242
EE	Exhibition	3,496
EG	Exhibition	18,554
EH	Exhibition	81,136
EM	Exhibition	7,318
MC	Classical music	29,459
TA	Theater	12,111
TC	Theater	,624
TF	Theater	6,346
TG	Theater	3,333
TP	Theater	10,824
TS	Theater	3,587
Total		**228,491**

for any venue at any venue or mobile Olympic ticket outlet (MOTO) van.

Media Campaign

Tickets were the topic of extended media coverage long before they went on sale. ACOG Communications used the news value of tickets to strengthen publicity by announcing ticket prices a year before sales began, establishing the day tickets would be available for sale six months in advance, and explaining the procedure for

obtaining and completing the order form. Sponsor promotions accompanied the launch of ticket sales.

The launch of each ticket sales phase was previewed during a news conference and accompanied by a photo opportunity. In addition, ACOG released frequent updates on the number of orders received.

Mail-Order Sales

Central to the general public mail-order campaign was Ticket Sales' 48-page, four-color brochure featuring a description of each sport

and its corresponding sessions, highlights from past Olympic Games, and the US athletes' medal chances. The brochure included a one-page, two-sided ticket request form, which could be scanned into a computer, and a self-addressed envelope.

Ticket Sales policies were explained and the guidelines for FairTix eligibility, ACOG's random selection system for ensuring equitable access to tickets, were repeated several times within the brochure to reinforce the processing rules. The deadline for participating in FairTix was 30 June 1995, instead of the regular mail-order deadline of 1 December 1995, to encourage early response. The brochure also included information about accommodations and transportation in Atlanta.

ACOG allowed interested corporate sponsors to promote their products in conjunction with the ticket sales campaign in return for advertising and brochure distribution.

Corporate sponsor–affiliated retail outlets were the sole distribution points for the 36.5 million brochures. In May and June 1995, 15,000 grocery stores carrying Coca-Cola products and all Home Depot stores had brochures available. VISA was the only credit card payment method accepted for tickets, and all payments were processed through NationsBank.

ACOG publicized the campaign through press releases and paid advertising in national magazines and newspapers. Advertising coverage was emphasized in Georgia and the four satellite cities hosting preliminary football sessions. VISA and NationsBank sent promotional announcements to 20 million cardholders. ACOG's information phone line was staffed with 24 agents daily from 0800 to 2100. Agents directed callers to retail outlets that carried brochures and helped callers complete their ticket request forms.

Season Tickets. Season ticket packages were also featured in the brochure and sold only during the mail-order phase. Season tickets guaranteed spectators with a particular interest in a sport a seat for every session of that sport in a particular venue. Season tickets were available for all sport disciplines, but were not

Ticket Sales' 48-page, four-color brochure featured a description of each sport and its sessions, highlights from past Games, and other pertinent information. A total of 36.5 million brochures was printed and distributed throughout the US.

available for ceremonies or OAF sessions. As with individual session tickets, season tickets were subject to the FairTix computerized random selection process used for oversubscribed sports. A limit of four season tickets was placed on athletics, basketball, diving, gymnastics, swimming, and volleyball. Although spectators were guaranteed a seat in the same price category for every session, they were not guaranteed the same seat.

Processing FairTix Requests. To handle the anticipated volume of mail-order ticket requests, ACOG and ISSC hired a fulfillment specialist company to review each request form for accuracy and completeness and convert each form into an electronic account. High-speed electronic scanning technology could read up to 3,000 forms an hour.

Only valid accounts were electronically forwarded to ACOG and loaded into the Olympic ticket system. Of the 326,000 orders received, 286,122 were considered valid. The most common reasons for disqualification were lack of a customer signature and improper payment.

Before FairTix processing, ACOG conducted its own audit of accounts to confirm compliance with set ticket limits and to enforce its rule of allowing only one order per customer. Accounts failing to comply were not eligible for FairTix processing.

The purpose of FairTix was to award each customer venue space at random in anticipation of future seat assignments. Although modeled after the systems used in Los Angeles and Barcelona, FairTix eliminated the postselection customer waiting list because ACOG could sell tickets on-line and by phone. FairTix was applied only to domestic mail-order requests received between 1 May and 30 June 1995.

Order processing began in July 1995. The first step was to determine which sessions were oversubscribed. Of the 540 sports sessions available, 397 sessions had at least one oversubscribed price category, and the following 14 sports were oversubscribed in every

category: badminton, cycling, diving, equestrian jumping, fencing, rhythmic and artistic gymnastics, judo, modern pentathlon, swimming, synchronized swimming, table tennis, tennis, and freestyle wrestling. In addition, both Opening and Closing Ceremonies were oversubscribed.

Customers requesting undersubscribed sessions were automatically allocated space. For oversubscribed sessions, the FairTix random selection process was utilized. Using a cascading model, the system allowed customers who did

not receive space for a session's higher price to be eligible for the session's lower priced spaces. The FairTix system was considered equitable because customers received additional chances to be awarded space at their most desired sessions. For customers who were not awarded space at any price level for their preferred choice, the system attempted to fill the customer's first alternate choice, then second alternate choice.

Ticket Sales staff reviewed each FairTix ticket request for accuracy and completeness before converting it to an electronic account for high-speed scanning into the Olympic ticket system.

To ensure that ticket requests were being handled fairly, a separate certified public accounting firm reviewed the FairTix process. Their review confirmed that the procedures were executed as described in the mail-order brochure.

The total number of tickets awarded through FairTix processing was 2,895,747. Nearly 87 percent of accounts were awarded at least one session. The average number of tickets requested per customer was 17, and the average number awarded per customer was nine. A credit balance account was established for customers with at least one unfulfilled order.

Sessions were awarded as follows: 85 percent, the customer's preferred choice; 10 percent, the first alternate choice; and 5 percent, the second alternate. Accounts that received no awards were usually ones that requested only oversubscribed sessions or did not offer any alternates. Many requested one to three sessions only, predominately ceremonies, diving, or swimming.

Additional Sales. Customers were notified in September 1995 of the tickets they would receive as a result of the FairTix system. These ticket confirmations itemized awarded sessions and notified customers of their account balance. Ticket Sales mailed a list of available sports sessions and an OAF brochure to customers with a credit balance before sending a refund check.

To assist FairTix customers with add-on ticket requests, confirmation packets included a list of available sports sessions and additional order forms. Customers had the option of using their credit balance as payment, or if they did not wish to purchase additional tickets, could donate their credit balance to the USOC or receive

Olympic tickets could be purchased by telephone when the telephone sales to the domestic public phase began in February 1996.

a refund check or VISA credit. If no correspondence was received, a refund check was automatically issued in December 1995.

Additional ticket requests were filled on a first-come, first-served basis as available after FairTix processing. During this process, 74,732 customers purchased 255,191 additional tickets.

During this same time, new customers, referred to as post-FairTix customers, also submitted mail-order ticket requests. Post-FairTix orders were filled on a first-come, first-served basis subject to availability after FairTix processing. There were 23,296 post-FairTix customers who purchased 124,389 tickets.

Telephone Sales

The telephone sales phase to the domestic public began with the sale of remaining tickets from the mail-order phase and most OAF sessions. Customers in cities hosting preliminary football matches had the option to call their local sales offices to purchase tickets to those matches.

The ACOG phone center operated from 10 February through 4 August 1996. The phone center drew the most calls during its first weekend of operations, with 5.3 million call attempts. During the entire phase of telephone sales, there were 11.3 million call attempts. Ticket Sales' goal to sell one ticket per agent call minute was achieved; telephone agents sold nearly 800,000 tickets.

The phone center sold tickets through telephone agents, the IVR system, and ACOG's World Wide Web home page. A one-time processing fee was charged to all new ticket customers but was waived for those who participated in the mail-order phase. All sales were subject to a minimal per ticket fulfillment fee.

ISSC and ProTix provided all phone and computer equipment to support the operation and hired, trained, and supervised all phone center agents, whose hours were 0900 to 2100, six days per week except on the opening weekend and other high-volume days. ACOG's original contract with ISSC required a phone room staff of 50 agents; yet ACOG and ISSC management remained flexible, allowing for staff increases to accommodate the sustained demand over the phone room's six-month operation.

Having periodic ticket releases helped maintain interest and demand for Olympic tickets. During March, April, and May 1996, the phone center also handled sales for tickets released after the completion of final venue seating configurations (e.g., for the press) and other contingencies. As tickets to formerly oversubscribed sessions became available, press releases and advertising announcements were made. Customers were encouraged to check the availability of each session regularly.

Interactive Voice Response System. ACOG was the first in Olympic history to use an IVR telephone system to service and sell tickets to customers. Millions of spectators used this enhancement to the Olympic ticket system from 1 May 1995 through the Games period. Provided by Voice Integrators, Inc., the IVR system managed 150 phone lines using IBM Direct Talk/6000 computer hardware.

Customers telephoned to request ticket information or purchase tickets, depending on the selling phase (mail-order or telephone sales). Recorded messages provided information about available sessions, individual accounts, special ticket packages, accommodations, and transportation and procedures for purchasing tickets. Customers had the option of speaking to an operator during regular business hours. Existing customers with an Olympic account number and a VISA payment card could purchase tickets without having to speak to an operator.

Regularly updated, recorded messages were carefully scripted to be complete, yet concise. Much effort was applied to organizing information logically to enable callers to reach their desired options quickly.

Approximately 300 hours of script was recorded for changing circumstances, such as the availability of new seating. Incoming calls were tracked and recorded daily.

During the mail-order phase, from 1 May until 1 December 1995, recorded messages explained each sport and its related sessions, ticket policies and procedures, and step-by-step instructions for completing ticket request forms. The system also promoted test events, season tickets, group packages, patron packages, and suite sales. During this period, customers could receive information but not purchase tickets because the FairTix system was still in place. The IVR handled 344,948 information-only calls during this phase, and the average duration of each call was 182 seconds.

During the interim period between the mail-order and telephone phases, from 1 December 1995 to 9 February 1996, IVR messages explained the mail-order ticket confirmation process, announced the dates of the upcoming telephone sales phase, and offered individual customer account details. The IVR handled 46,998 interim calls, and the average duration of each call was 120 seconds.

From 10 February to 4 August 1996, the IVR was the direct ticket order mechanism as well as an information service. In March 1996, customers could purchase tickets with or without the assistance of an operator. Existing Olympic customers, using their Olympic account numbers and VISA payment cards, could order tickets using touch-tone telephones. IVR sales totaled 31,148 tickets.

Internet Orders. On 5 March 1996, ACOG's World Wide Web site became another way for customers to check availability and purchase tickets. Once a selection was made, users accessed an electronic order form and entered their personal information. The information was sent securely via the Internet to the phone center for fulfillment. The customer was sent an electronic mail confirmation of the purchase within 24 hours. During the first week in March, the ACOG web site received more than 98,000 "hits" daily from around the world, reflecting an increase from February's average of 62,000. This is partly attributed to the start of on-line ticket sales. Internet sales totaled 130,662 tickets.

The web site was updated hourly and allowed customers to search remaining sports and OAF sessions at any time. To ensure that purchasing was secure, IBM used secure sockets layer (SSL) technology and new IBM electronic commerce technology. SSL, an industrywide communications protocol, encrypts data as it is entered by the web browser so it can be sent securely without allowing other Internet users to view it. The data was received by an IBM Internet secure computer server and entered into the Olympic ticket system. In order to purchase tickets on-line, users required an SSL-enabled web browser, a US shipping address, and a valid VISA account.

Policies and Procedures

Ticket policies and procedures for the sale, delivery, and use of tickets were drafted by Ticket Sales and reviewed by a law firm in Atlanta. Terms and conditions of ticket sales were explained either verbally or in writing to every customer prior to every sale. Terms and conditions were also included in the Games spectator rules printed on the back of each individual ticket.

Customers requesting a refund or other exceptions to the terms and conditions of sales were asked to submit their request in writing.

Spectators purchasing modified aisle or wheelchair tickets were provided with a clear line of sight to the field of play.

Written correspondence was reviewed and responded to by Ticket Sales staff. Fewer than 5,000 written complaints were received, representing 1 percent of domestic customers.

Americans with Disabilities Act

In 1992, the US federal government passed the Americans with Disabilities Act (ADA), instituting broad fair access regulations for public facilities. Measures were taken at all stages of the sales process to ensure fair access. Sales communication materials were available in multiple mediums, which made information accessible to hearing- and visually-impaired spectators. Large inventories of tickets were reserved for ADA seating with the same range of ticket prices offered for conventional seating.

Ticket Sales attempted to match ADA spectator requirements with available seating throughout the sales process. Spectators purchasing wheelchair spaces or modified aisle seats were guaranteed the opportunity to purchase at least one adjacent companion seat. There were no limits on the total number of companion seats that could be purchased except for sessions with established ticket limits.

Ticket Sales also reserved a percentage of wheelchair, modified aisle, and companion tickets until the start of each session. Some spectators were not aware of the opportunity to reserve ADA seating in advance and waited until they arrived at the venue to make their request. Also, in some instances, spectators were involved in disabling accidents between the time of the ticket purchase and the ticketed session. These spectators were also relocated at the venues by the venue ticket manager.

The Olympic Arts Festival

The OAF exhibitions, concerts, and dance, theater, and other performances represented 1.2 million in ticket inventory. Initially, the sale of OAF tickets was to be handled by ACOG's Cultural Olympiad Department. In December 1994, however, it was decided that Ticket Sales would sell all OAF tickets, so that OAF promotional material could reach a broader audience.

Integrating OAF sales and operations into Ticket Sales presented significant challenges due to the substantial increase in ticket inventory, the three-month extended schedule for box office operations, and the different revenue-sharing agreements for each attraction. It was therefore necessary to reallocate existing Ticket Sales resources and staff to support ticket sales, fulfillment, and box office management for OAF sessions.

In September 1995, an OAF ticket mail-order brochure was created and mailed to existing Olympic sports session customers. OAF sessions were also integrated into the Olympic ticket system. By combining OAF sessions with sports sessions, Ticket Sales increased its ability to offer customers OAF alternatives on days with oversubscribed sports sessions. The final number of OAF tickets sold was 228,491.

Ticket Sales provided four on-line venue box offices to support OAF sessions: Atlanta Civic Center, 14th Street Playhouse, High Museum of Art, and Woodruff Arts Center. Because OAF sessions began as early as June 1996, the Woodruff Arts Center and the High Museum of Art were among the earliest box offices to open.

SPECIAL SALES

A Special Sales division within Ticket Sales managed ticket allocations for ACOG's diverse group of contractual customers, including the IOC, NOCs, other Olympic Family members, broadcast rights holders, sponsors, suppliers, and hotels. The Olympic Family and NOC obligations were established by the *Olympic Charter*, whereas other contractual obligations were established primarily by ACOP. The total number of tickets sold to this diverse group was 2,452,704.

Special Sales implemented consistent communication, record-keeping, and distribution strategies. Each contractual customer was required to designate one authorized ticket buyer. Likewise, only one Special Sales representative was authorized to fulfill a customer's request. Once assigned, the same Special Sales representative managed the account throughout its cycle. The representative maintained comprehensive account records, including copies of the contract or obligation, all communications, ticket requests, ticket allocations, adjustments, payments, and deliveries. This approach enhanced accuracy as well as customer service.

ACOP Contracts

To fulfill sponsor contractual obligations, Ticket Sales categorized Olympic tickets into two groups: type 1, or high-demand tickets, and type 2, or low-demand tickets. Almost all contracts provided for the opportunity to purchase type 1 tickets. Depending on the contract, customers were allowed to purchase maximum limits of type 1, or an incorporated ticket ratio of at least an equal number of type 2 tickets for every type 1 ticket purchased. Some contracts required the purchase of four type 2 tickets for every type 1 ticket purchased. More than 2 million tickets were sold through ACOG contractual agreements.

As contracts were signed and ratios and terms became known, Special Sales solicited ticket requests from the designated buyer. Most of the sponsor, hotel, and broadcast contracts were signed by early 1995. Buyers were asked

to submit their ticket requests as soon as possible to allow time to adjust quotas accordingly. With few exceptions, demand for tickets matched the allotted market segment supply. The final deadline for requests was 1 December 1995, after which time customers could not return any tickets, but could add tickets to their accounts, subject to availability. As new contracts were signed, customers had a shorter time frame to select their tickets and were afforded less flexibility.

The Special Sales division was also responsible for confirming receipt of payment before accounts were sent to the ticket printer, and reserved the right to retract tickets from partially paid accounts. Tickets were not delivered to accounts with outstanding balances.

Olympic Family Tickets

As a part of the IOC agreements for hosting the Olympic Games, Olympic sports competition tickets are provided for sale to the IOC and NOCs or designated agents for international sale. In addition, for the 1996 Games, OAF tickets were also offered for sale. The allocation of tickets for international customers initially was based on quotas derived from prior Olympic trends. Ticket information packets were distributed to the NOCs and designated agents as early as August 1994. Each NOC submitted an initial request for tickets, due by 1 December 1994. Requests were matched with the initial allocation and the market segment quota was adjusted accordingly. Adjustments to NOC requests were accepted through 1 December 1995. With the extensive ticket needs of the host country, the USOC had a separate allocation process.

More Olympic Family tickets were purchased than for any other Olympic Games: 130 NOCs purchased 622,519 tickets, the USOC purchased nearly 200,000 tickets, and IFs purchased 77,277.

In accordance with Rule 58 of the *Olympic Charter*, ACOG also provided an allocation of venue seats to the Olympic Family. These seats were complimentary and required appropriate accreditation for access to venues and seating areas. *(For a full description of this subject, see the Olympic Family and Protocol chapter.)*

Staff Tickets

In September 1995, the ACOG Family Ticket Program was finalized, whereby ACOG staff could purchase tickets directly from Ticket Sales and retrieve them in person at ACOG headquarters. ACOG's Human Resources Department defined eligibility and managed the program by obtaining payments and answering questions. Ticket Sales was responsible for fulfilling employee ticket requests. This popular program resulted in the sale of 29,800 tickets.

Participating staff followed the same rules and submitted the same forms as the general public during the mail-order campaign. All requests were subject to availability, and no discounts were offered.

Games-Time Sales

During Games-time, ticket outlets with online selling capabilities operated at the sponsor village adjacent to Olympic Stadium, the Olympic Family Hotel, and the Olympic Village. Special Sales representatives were also available at these locations to provide customer service and fulfill ticket requests for Olympic Family members and other customers.

The Olympic Village outlet managed distribution of athlete tickets. Athletes held accreditation for the venue(s) where their sport was contested and therefore were allowed to sit in designated stand seating at their competition venues.

The IFs and NOCs requested that ACOG allocate a quantity of tickets to all sessions for use by athletes competing in other sports, coaches, and team officials; therefore, 60,000 tickets were allocated for this purpose. During Games-time, that number increased slightly, when ACOG redistributed unsold tickets.

Tickets for athletes attending other sports competitions were clearly marked, requiring appropriate accreditation for venue access. Seating was available in the athlete stand area. Only the chef de mission of each NOC was authorized to request and retrieve complimentary tickets. Requests had to be submitted one day in advance of the desired session. Due to the limited number of tickets, demand for tickets almost always exceeded supply. In order to distribute tickets fairly, a computerized quota system, based on delegation size, determined how many tickets were allocated to each delegation. Management prerogative was used to ensure that the large delegations did not receive an unfair advantage.

Redistribution

In their mission to maximize attendance, Ticket Sales designed the first automated ticket redistribution program. Ticket redistribution offered TOP/COP sponsors, the USOC, and NBC the option to return tickets for resale and the first opportunity to purchase returned tickets. Suppliers, sponsors, NOCs, and the IOC could also return tickets for resale, but did not share the same priority access to purchase tickets as the first group.

The program was popular with sponsors, as it provided a means to avoid unused ticket inventory. It was also popular with spectators, as it increased their chances of purchasing tickets to formerly oversubscribed sessions.

Automated redistribution was made possible by enhancing the Olympic ticket system software. Each ticket's unique imprinted bar code was read by a hand scanner, which identified tickets being returned and validated that tickets had been originally issued to the sponsor. Scanned data was then transmitted to the Olympic ticket system for processing. ISSC sponsored the development of the software and provided staff; therefore, ACOG incurred no costs in developing this service.

Tickets ordered by the original customer were eligible for return, but tickets that had been traded or exchanged were not. Tickets returned by TOP/COP sponsors, the USOC, and NBC at least 48 hours in advance of the session were placed in a hold code category for 24 hours. Tickets in this hold category could be purchased by other program participants. Hold code sales were credited with full face value for each ticket. After 24 hours, and for returns within 48 hours of the session, returned tickets still unsold became available on-line to the general public. If they sold, the returning account was credited 50 percent of face value. Unsold returned tickets earned no credit.

Ticket Sales provided participants with on-line Olympic ticket equipment configured to purchase tickets from the special redistribution hold code, purchase any available tickets on the Olympic ticket system, and review the status of returned tickets. Ticket Sales trained users in Prologue software and also provided them with BOCA ticket printers. Tickets could then be purchased and printed on site, eliminating the need for will-call ticket pick up or a courier service.

No payment was required at the time of purchase. After Games-time, a statement was prepared indicating the value of tickets purchased and returned. The net amount was then paid to or collected from the participant.

Instead of dedicated on-line access, sponsors, suppliers, NOCs, and the IOC were provided an exclusive phone line for ordering tickets. Extended operations hours at the redistribution center, part of the main ticket center, allowed them to return and purchase tickets before the main ticket center opened. Returned tickets were not placed in a hold code; instead, they were immediately available for sale to all customers. Accounts with returns that sold were credited with 50 percent of the face value; unsold returned tickets earned no credit. All sales were settled immediately. The statistics demonstrate the success of ticket redistribution.

TICKET MARKETING

In addition to the strategies that supported mail-order and phone sales to the domestic public, the Ticket Marketing division implemented direct response strategies for Olympic baseball, football, yachting, and high-end ticket products. Football and baseball ranked first and second in terms of the total volume of ticket inventory. To avoid substantial numbers of unsold tickets, marketing efforts began early to develop awareness of ticket availability and to solicit support from existing fans of each sport. Yachting had its own marketing, management, and administration functions in Savannah, Georgia, due to its venue configuration and coastal location.

Patron packages and suites, considered more costly ticket products, required their own sales strategies for their narrow identified audiences.

Baseball

The Centennial Olympic Games not only had the largest Olympic baseball ticket inventory ever, but also sold the largest quantity of baseball tickets in Olympic history—1,134,203 tickets. Record sales were reported in both domestic and nondomestic markets—760,000 tickets and 460,000 tickets, respectively. Sales were enhanced by marketing strategies based on the availability and affordability of tickets, and other promotions. To support this theme, some baseball tickets were priced as low as $7, the least expensive of any Olympic sport.

Ticket Sales solicited support from US Baseball and Atlanta's major league baseball team, the Braves. Innovative marketing programs were developed for each group's constituency. In February 1995, a sales promotion was extended to Braves season ticket holders. The Olympic package included access to four sets of tickets to all 32 sessions of baseball, four sets of tickets to the six sessions of football in Athens, and four sets of tickets to the first four morning sessions of athletics. Customers had the option of buying just baseball tickets from the package, but were required to purchase both baseball and football tickets before they could purchase athletics tickets. More than 95 percent of all buyers purchased the entire package. A cover letter, Olympic baseball information, and an order form were mailed to the Braves season ticket accounts. The offering generated the sale of 1,350 packages, totaling 180,000 baseball tickets.

Baseball group packages were defined at 40 tickets per session. Baseball tickets became the only option for many group customers, as other sports did not have enough ticket inventory to provide 40 contiguous seats.

In February 1996, in conjunction with the launch of the phone phase for domestic sales, ProTix phone agents began promoting baseball tickets. Agents were trained to promote the affordability and availability benefits of baseball as well as the sessions featuring the US team. This effort contributed to early sellouts of US baseball sessions.

Football

Sales of football tickets offered the greatest challenge. Football ticket inventory far surpassed the inventory of any other sport, with 2,411,210 available tickets. In addition, football matches were held at five separate venues in five cities: Legion Field in Birmingham, Alabama; Florida Citrus Bowl in Orlando, Florida; Orange Bowl Stadium in Miami, Florida; RFK Memorial Stadium in Washington, DC; and Sanford Stadium in Athens, Georgia.

To help overcome these challenges, Ticket Sales hired a dedicated football sales manager in January 1994 as well as a football consultant. To avoid any possible confusion among US ticket buyers, ACOG always promoted football as soccer. Football ticket sales results placed the sport first with the most tickets sold, 1,255,173.

Although ACOG retained control of the 2.4 million ticket inventory, it shared ticket revenues with each local organizing committee (LOC). Given the number of participating cities and overall scope of the project, ACOG centralized marketing and management in Atlanta. LOCs received support and direction from ACOG. Traditional sports marketing strategies were used, including sponsor promotions; print, broadcast, and outdoor advertising; a direct-mail campaign; a football community campaign; and phone sales.

Yachting

Managed separately from the sale of other Olympic sports tickets, yachting ticket sales were facilitated by a full-time ACOG Ticket Sales representative located in Savannah, Georgia, who worked closely with the Atlanta

Ticket Sales office. Tickets became available in February 1996 and were sold only through mail orders. Final sales totaled 8,086 tickets, over 80 percent of the venue's total capacity.

Ticket Sales created the viewing area for the venue in cooperation with two charter boat services—one departing from Savannah and the other from Hilton Head, South Carolina—which provided cruises around the venue. The charter companies became contractors for ACOG and shared the financial risk of the venture. The charter services were responsible for all operational aspects of each session's cruise, including food and beverage services, while ACOG performed all ticket functions, including marketing, administration, security, and payment collection. ACOG and the charter companies shared ticket revenues.

Seating capacities for each session were limited by both the available dock space at the two ports and the eight-spectator-boat limit set by the yachting competition managers. Individual boat capacities ranged from 50 to 250 persons. A 50-person capacity boat was reserved as a suite.

Yachting sessions lasted seven and one-half hours and included food and beverage services, commentary on the competition, and views of historical sights along the coasts of South Carolina and Georgia. On their ticket request form, spectators were required to sign a yachting-specific terms and conditions policy, detailing yachting's unique session cancellation rules. Just prior to boarding the boats, they were required to sign a waiver of liability for potential injury or sea sickness.

Yachting tickets were only sold via mail order due to the special terms and conditions signature requirement. The order form with yachting venue rules was sent to target audiences, including yachting clubs on the east coast of the US and local Savannah businesses.

Patron Program

ACOG created a package similar to the successful patron program ticket package offered

---

FIGURE 4: COMPONENTS OF PATRON PACKAGES

- Two tickets to both Opening and Closing Ceremonies
- Four tickets per day (two each to the top two sessions)
- Preferred access to luxury rental accommodations
- Two invitations to pre-Olympic receptions
- Olympic gifts and patron ID badge
- Access to transportation system and parking as available

at the 1984 Los Angeles Games. The elements and pricing of ACOG's package were determined in May 1994, and offered exclusive amenities, along with premium tickets to high-demand sports sessions. *(For components of patron packages, see Figure 4.)*

One thousand packages were reserved for sale, and a two package per customer purchase limit was established to prevent patron packages from competing with sponsor benefits. The final number of packages sold was 692.

Ticket Sales launched its sales and marketing plan for patron packages in November 1994. Each potential sale was reviewed and approved by ACOP to prevent ambush marketing. For example, a competitor of an existing sponsor was not eligible to purchase a patron package or a suite.

During November and December 1994, patron packages were offered exclusively to sponsors and broadcast rights holders, allowing them the first right of refusal. In February 1995, Ticket Sales began a direct-mail campaign to non–ACOG-affiliated potential buyers. The identified audience was established through research conducted by an Atlanta market research company. Their list of 100,000 prospective customers included smaller businesses, corporations, and individuals. Ten staff members handled all facets of sales to this group.

The final sales campaign for suites and patron packages was in March 1996. Ticket Sales created spirit packages, or a one-half patron package, to accommodate customers who wanted to attend only one week of sessions. These packages could be purchased only by customers who had already purchased a complete patron package. Print advertising was used in local and national newspapers announcing their availability. The smaller patron packages sold quickly, but not all suites sold as a result of this final campaign.

Suites

The Centennial Games were the first in Olympic history to have suites, also referred to as skyboxes, available for spectator viewing. Six venues had a total of 316 suites, of which 120 were leased for the duration of the Games period. *(For a list of venues with suites and their respective sessions, see Figure 5.)*

Suite leases included tickets to every session of a sport that could be viewed from the suite. They were fully furnished, featuring climate-controlled environments, private restrooms, and concierge service. Parking and food and beverage services were offered at an incremental cost. In addition, in January 1996, suite holders could rent technology items, including telephones, facsimile machines, two-way radios, cellular phones, cable television, and audiovisual equipment.

Suites ranged in size from 10 to 54 seats, depending on the venue. Price range depended on the number of seats in the suite, number of sports sessions held in the venue, number of suites available in the venue, popularity of the sport, and location of the suite in the venue.

Advertising and marketing for suites were combined with that for patron packages, as their potential customers were the same. During November and December 1994, sponsors, broadcast rights holders, licensees, and suppliers were offered the option to purchase suites before the program became available to non-ACOG affiliates in February 1995. Each sale was then preapproved by ACOG senior management and ACOP to ensure the protection of sponsor agreements. In March 1996, Ticket

FIGURE 5: VENUES WITH SUITES AND THEIR RESPECTIVE SESSIONS

Alexander Memorial Coliseum
Boxing
12 suites

Atlanta–Fulton County Stadium
Baseball
32 suites

Georgia Dome
Basketball, Artistic Gymnastics
199 suites

Olympic Stadium
Athletics, Ceremonies
55 suites

Omni Coliseum
Volleyball
7 suites

Sanford Stadium
Football
11 suites

Sales created combo suites, tickets for a combination of sports in venues where suites were still available. Customers could purchase half the sessions in one suite and, if desired, half the sessions in a different venue's suite.

Beginning in June 1995 and continuing through the duration of the Games, Ticket Sales provided daily customer service to its suite holders. Representatives of the Suite Services group acted as liaisons between the suite holder and ACOG departments such as Food and Beverage, Technology, and Venue Management. Suite Services also approved all caterers' menus and distributed menus to suite holders.

During Games-time at each of the six venues, a suite services center (SSC) operated to provide on-site assistance and support to suite holders. Located on the suite level, this concierge-type station was facilitated by ACOG staff and volunteers recruited from the Association of Luxury Suite Directors and the Atlanta Sports Council.

VENUE OPERATIONS

The Centennial Games were the first to offer customers the opportunity to purchase tickets for any available sports competition, at any venue. Ticket Sales had operations at every venue with the ability to sell tickets, print tickets, and provide customer service. Ticket Sales also introduced its MOTO vans during this sales phase. Total venue box office sales were remarkable at 510,327 tickets. In order to create this presence, Ticket Sales needed to establish locations for 33 venue box offices; create box office policies and procedures; equip each location with on-line computer equipment and fixtures; and recruit, hire, and train staff to manage each box office location.

Planning for venue box office operations began in January 1994. Ticket Sales integrated box office operations into each venue's site plan, using existing box office facilities where available. At venues where the secured perimeter did not allow the use of the existing facilities, temporary trailers were used.

By January 1996, all box office and temporary trailer locations had been confirmed. At this time, Ticket Sales assigned staff members to specific venues to represent the department as venue ticket managers (VTIMs).

From January through July 1996, VTIMs attended weekly venue meetings. Subsequent to these meetings, VTIMs met to establish venue box office procedures. A unified approach was defined for handling issues such as obstructed view complaints, duplicate tickets, ADA complaints, and session cancellation and postponement. Weekly meetings ensured consistent implementation of Ticket Sales policies and procedures from venue to venue.

Along with a VTIM, venue box offices were staffed with an assistant manager, a seller supervisor, ticket sellers, and volunteers. Managers and supervisors were recruited, hired, trained, and assigned by the Ticket Sales Department. Recruiting was performed in conjunction with the trade organization Box Office Managers International (BOMI). There were more than 550 total ticket staff during Games period.

Box office operations began officially on 8 June 1996 when Ticket Sales opened the first of its 33 box offices—the main ticket center—which was the hub of all box office operations. It provided training for other venues' staff, who could observe or work at the main ticket center prior to the opening of their box office. Other box offices opened in conjunction with the first session of the venue or the anticipated level of traffic near their venue.

The main ticket center's layout was designed to accelerate retail sales by providing customers the ability to wait in a lobby after taking a number. By offering information both outside and inside the building, customers could find out the availability of tickets before they were called to the counter. This approach decreased customers' waiting time.

Ticket Sales operated a central communications center during Games-time. Each VTIM was equipped with an electronic pager and a two-way radio, allowing instant communication between the central communications center and the venue. When an issue arose, center staff devised an action plan and resources to

Mobile ticket outlet vans (MOTOs) were very popular, as they enabled customers to purchase tickets quickly and conveniently.

address it. The center was staffed 24 hours per day during Games-time.

Mobile Ticket Outlet Vans

Also on 8 June, in conjunction with the opening of the main ticket center, Ticket Sales launched the first MOTOs, consisting of four vans capable of selling on-line tickets. The vans became very popular with customers, as they offered the convenience of buying tickets quickly rather than at crowded box office sites.

Each 15 ft (4.6 m) white van was decorated with sports pictograms, the Olympic logo, and the BellSouth Corporation's logo. BellSouth Mobility technologically equipped the vans. MOTO ticket sales totaled 43,588 tickets.

MOTOs were able to dial directly into the Prologue system using a combination of cellular or land line communications and an internal generator or shoreline power. Each van had three selling terminals.

Prior to Games-time, vans were deployed to sell tickets in nearby cities in the Southeast while one van followed the Torch Relay, selling tickets en route from New York to St. Augustine, Florida. During Games-time, vans supported venue box office operations as needed.

CONCLUSIONS AND RECOMMENDATIONS

The Ticket Sales Department was notably successful in its efforts to promote, sell, and deliver tickets. The software system used to allot tickets to the public was designed to offer all ticket buyers fair chance to receive their desired sessions. Utilizing innovative sales techniques, such as promotions for low-demand sports, and technology, such as the Olympic web site, ACOG sold more Olympic tickets than any other organizing committee in Olympic history. The greatest challenge faced by Ticket Sales concerned the volume of tickets, transactions, and accounts involved.

The following recommendations are offered to future organizing committees.

■ It is necessary to conduct substantial research to predict customer trends in purchasing tickets. Once ticket sales begin, focus the department's attention on recognizing buying trends and promoting availability.

■ To optimize revenue, utilize new technology and adjust to trends in consumer demand.

■ Recruit a professional staff with event ticketing experience, particularly in the area of launching new ticket sales campaigns.

CHAPTER TWENTY-FIVE
TORCH RELAY

ꞏꞏꞏ The 1996 Olympic Torch Relay ꞏꞏꞏ

The 1996 Olympic Torch Relay logo was inspired by pictures on ancient Greek vases.

OVERVIEW—The mission of the 1996 Olympic Torch Relay was to bring the Olympic flame and its celebration of the human spirit, diversity, friendship, and peace to as many people as possible in a fitting preface to the Centennial Olympic Games. ACOG and the Hellenic Olympic Committee (HOC) conceived and developed the event to include Greece, the former Olympic host cities, and the US. The HOC staged the portion in Greece and the former host cities, and ACOG managed the event in the US.

The Flame Relay, as it is called in Greece, began when the Olympic flame was ignited by the sun in Olympia on 30 March. Over the next eight days, more than 800 torchbearers carried the flame 2,141 km throughout Greece. The flame arrived in Athens on 6 April. In honor of the Centennial Olympic Games, the HOC held a celebration as the flame was brought into the Panathenean Stadium.

This celebration of Greek traditions and the reenactment of the first modern Olympic Games in 1896 concluded as representatives from 17 cities that had previously hosted the Olympic Games each received a safety lantern, lit from the sacred Olympic flame. During the next 21 days, these flames were celebrated in each former host city while the original flame burned in Athens.

The flames were extinguished as the original flame left Athens for Los Angeles aboard a Delta chartered flight accompanied by ACOG CEO Billy Payne, other ACOG officials, and senior members of the HOC. Upon arrival, the flame was received with a welcoming celebration.

Olympian Rafer Johnson began the Torch Relay in the US on 27 April at the Los Angeles Coliseum, the site where he ignited the last Olympic flame to burn in the US at the 1984 Games. On the journey to Atlanta, which would last 84 days, 12,467 torchbearers carried the flame along a 16,700 mi (26,875 km) route that passed within a two-hour drive of 90 percent of the US population. On 19 July, it arrived at Atlanta's Olympic Stadium, where the final torchbearer, two-time Olympic heavyweight boxing champion Muhammad Ali, lit the cauldron to begin the Centennial Olympic Games.

The 84 days of the Torch Relay, together with the 16 days of the Games, reflected the centennial of the Olympic Games, as the flame burned in the US for a symbolic 100 days.

THE FLAME RELAY IN GREECE

Traditionally, the relay and flame lighting ceremony in Greece are organized by the HOC in collaboration with the organizing committee. In this partnership, ACOG wanted to show its respect for Greece's role in the Olympic Movement and the history of the flame. In 1994, a delegation of HOC representatives arrived in Atlanta to discuss the goals of the Torch Relay and the flame lighting. Extensive meetings resulted in a strong friendship based on the mutual desire to stage the most memorable flame lighting and Torch Relay in Olympic history.

In the final agreement, ACOG agreed to abide by several core principles to ensure the sanctity of the Olympic flame. ACOG committed to refrain from selling the honor of carrying the Olympic flame, to control and minimize commercialization of the flame or relay imagery, to prohibit any sponsor identification from appearing on the torch or torchbearer uniform, and to protect and acknowledge only one Olympic flame.

ACOG also agreed to subsidize Greek relay expenses and, in the spirit of one flame and

one relay, create and provide the HOC with torches, uniforms, posters, US and ACOG flags, and diplomas for torchbearers; to host a reception the night before the flame-lighting ceremony; and to invite the HOC president, high priestess, and two Greek Flame Relay managers to the Games in Atlanta, providing all-access credentials.

The HOC agreed to organize all elements of the ceremonies and relay in Greece, host a reception after the flame-lighting ceremony,

and provide accommodations for the six members of the ACOG delegation. ACOG received the right to film and photograph the lighting ceremony and obtain proper credentials for media upon request. ACOG also received Greek flags to be used in the relay in the US.

The Lighting of the Flame

For each Olympiad, a flame is ignited from the sun's rays in a historic ceremony dating back to 700 BC. The ceremony marks the beginning of the Flame Relay, and presents an op-

portunity for each organizing committee to pay homage to the legacy Greece has bequeathed to the modern Games. In April 1995, ACOG and the HOC began their important collaboration by unveiling the torch to the press and public simultaneously in Athens and Atlanta.

Following tradition, the majestic ceremony took place in the ancient stadium in the city of Olympia. It was attended by thousands of Greek citizens in a public celebration of Olympic ideals. After presentations by the Greek government, HOC, ACOG officials, and the first lady of the US, the high priestess and accompanying priestesses performed an ancient and private ritual in the Sacred Grove of Altis, invoking the Greek gods to bless the Games and light the flame.

The flame was then presented for view to the public by the high priestess, and the first Greek torchbearer began the Flame Relay through Greece. This beautifully executed

left: The Greek high priestess ignites the flame from the reflected rays of the sun.

right: In Athens, Billy Payne prepares the flame for its journey to Los Angeles.

ceremony was a truly emotional experience for all who attended. The ACOG representatives returned to Atlanta energized for the final months before the Games.

The portion of the relay that took place in Greece was the most extensive in history. At each relay stop, officials conducted a 15–20 minute public ceremony that included lighting a cauldron, raising the US and Greek flags, playing the national anthems, remarks by Greek and ACOG representatives, traditional Greek dances, and gift exchanges between ACOG officials and the local government representative.

The Flame Relay in Greece united ACOG and the HOC in respect and sentiment for the flame, epitomizing the true spirit of the Olympic Games.

ORGANIZATION OF RELAY IN THE US

ACOG managed and organized all logistical operations and strategic decisions of the 1996 Olympic Torch Relay in the US. Torch Relay staff were responsible for developing and communicating the route, selecting and placing torchbearers, securing cooperation from law enforcement entities, seeking funds and other support from Games sponsors, recruiting and training volunteers, managing media relations, and managing the event.

A Torch Relay director was hired in May 1993 to begin research for the event. The senior manager for advance operations, charged with the initial route development, was hired in February 1994. Torch Relay operated within the Special Events Department until January 1995, when it became independent, reporting to the managing director of Corporate Services.

The preliminary route was divided into seven regions, each staffed with two regional advance managers. The advance team was responsible for refining the route; working with

communities to implement the torchbearer selection process and create community celebrations; and working with local, regional, and state law enforcement entities to ensure the safe, timely passage of the Torch Relay caravan. A media relations manager finalized preparations for the route announcement scheduled for 23 July 1995, and an accommodations manager booked hotel rooms, planned meals, and surveyed sites.

The transition from office staff to an on-the-road crew was planned by project area. Approximately 10 staff members were assigned to Atlanta. On the road, Torch Relay staff numbered 230.

Volunteer support was vital to Torch Relay operations. Volunteers were confirmed in March 1996 after the caravan evaluation tested applicants' performance with various responsibilities. Most were assigned to the torchbearer shuttle bus area.

Successful implementation of the 1996 Torch Relay required a collaborative effort among ACOG departments. Senior management offered support and guidance during the planning phase. Creative Services managed the production and design of all relay materials. Special Events assisted with large celebrations throughout the country. Volunteer Services assisted with intern and volunteer recruitment. Accounting and Financial Services processed last-minute requests and budget plans.

The event also required outside support and expertise in specific operational areas. A company specializing in competition services provided basic logistical support for the caravan including hiring and supervising approximately 70 professional drivers and building and retrofitting all caravan vehicles. State of Georgia public safety personnel helped establish law enforcement cooperation along the route and coordinated information from federal agencies. An Atlanta public relations firm supported media relations by providing crisis management training, media operations personnel, and other communications operations.

The US Route

The US route, designed to reflect the geographic and social diversity of the country as well as its history, crossed deserts and prairies, wine country and farmland, rivers and lakes, and big cities and small towns. In addition to being carried by torchbearers, the flame traveled by train, steamboat, canoe, horseback, sailboat, and other modes of transportation that reflected the character and history of surrounding communities. The route included three US Olympic host cities: St. Louis (1904), Los Angeles (1932 and 1984), and Atlanta.

Development. Prior to its announcement on 23 July 1995, the route was a closely guarded secret to prevent political lobbying from dictating route decisions. However, officials along the route were contacted and their support garnered before a public announcement was made. This announcement marked the culmination of months of committee planning, cross-country test drives, and community celebration planning that had begun in February 1994. Communities announced as being part of the 1996 Olympic Torch Relay celebrated with local flag-raising ceremonies.

The most heavily populated cities across the US were used as the framework for the initial plans in keeping with the goal to have the flame reach as many people as possible. ACOG expanded the skeletal route, incorporating alternative transportation modes such as rail travel through part of the western states, the Pony Express from Colorado to Missouri, the *American Queen* steamboat up the Mississippi River, a laker across Lake Erie, and a sailboat into the port of Savannah, Georgia. The torch was carried by bicycle through sparsely populated areas; while in rural areas, it was carried by motorcycle to ensure punctual arrival at each city celebration.

Torch Relay staff researched historical sites and key moments in US Olympic history to create a route that would showcase the US. In summer 1994, the senior manager of operations secretly journeyed cross-country to determine the initial proposed route and undertake an initial mileage measurement. He also drove the secondary roads to ensure the route was passable, tracked mileage for a preliminary distance estimate, and researched local folklore and landmarks to choose celebration sites that ensured the route would pass by places important to the

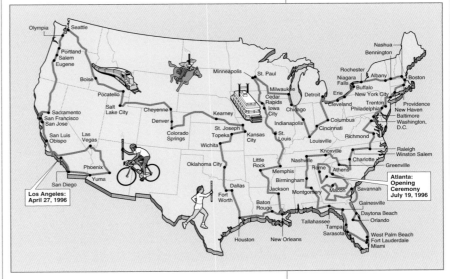

local population. Many ideas generated on that drive were adopted in the final route.

Mapping of City Celebrations. As the route was developed, lunch and overnight locations showcasing the diversity and history of US cities were chosen to hold daily midday and evening celebrations. ACOG envisioned events displaying local flavor, honoring local community hero torchbearers, and culminating with the lighting of the ceremonial Olympic cauldron. Each community was given the opportunity to develop its own program within certain guidelines, with ACOG staging the final 15 minutes prior to the flame's arrival.

Map showing the route of the US Torch Relay.

FIELD • MITCH FAIRFIELD • KENIN L FAIRLEY • SHEVA G FAIRLEY • WILLARD L FAIRLEY • MARK S FAITH • NIKI S FAITH • ROY L FAITH • GUS FAKHARIAN • ZAHRA S FAKHRABADI • HARTLEY L FALBAUM • JOAN FALCONE • SANDRA K FALCONER • RUTH E FALEIDE • LAURIE FALESTO • JUDY M FALETTI • DENISE B FALK • MIKKEL C FALKENLOVE • JANNA L FALLE • ANGELA M FALLEN • EMMA FALLINS • DANIEL J FALLON • GLORIA S FALLON • MICHAEL P FALLON • NANCY R FALLON • ROBERT D FALLON • STACEY E FALLON • MARTHA A FALLWELL • PAULA FALOCCO • DOROTHY FAMBLE • JOYCE H FAMBLE   485

City planning guides were issued to all communities, containing sponsor guidelines, a sample show time line, dimensions for the stage truck, volunteer plans, street banner order information, security requests such as road blocks and traffic control, and other event planning suggestions.

Other significant US Olympic sites were added, such as Olympic training centers in San Diego, California, and Colorado Springs, Colorado; Salt Lake City, Utah, host of the 2002 Winter Games; Indianapolis, Indiana, home of

Torch Relay staff tested the timing of the cycling segments in early 1996.

seven national governing bodies for Olympic sports; and communities that were homes to many famous US Olympic athletes. The additions to the route also had to be driven and modified.

The initial route traveled through 42 states. Because of the size of vehicles within the caravan, a route was mapped along US highways allowing time for celebrations and for the flame to spend the night in designated cities. Special attention was paid to historical landmarks, open places such as town squares or university campuses for public celebrations, and roads where large crowds could view and

experience the flame. *(For the seven regions created using the proposed route, see Figure 1.)*

The Georgia route was announced in September 1995. Ten days were allocated for the flame's travel, with the route reaching within 40 mi (64 km) of all Georgians. The daily schedule was lengthened, with activities during most days in Georgia lasting for nearly 20 hours.

The metropolitan-Atlanta route was the final Torch Relay element unveiled. An announcement in early July 1996 revealed a route leaving Stone Mountain Park, the site of Olympic archery, track cycling, and tennis, in early morning 18 July. The route was scheduled to travel almost continuously to virtually every area of Atlanta until 1400 on 19 July, when the flame would rest at Atlanta City Hall. The final portion of the route would travel from City Hall, past the Martin Luther King Jr. Memorial, ending at Olympic Stadium at the conclusion of the Opening Ceremony for the Games.

Timing Calculations and Final Route. The regional advance staff charted the route, documenting landmarks and mile-markers. Timing estimates for the different segments—geographical spaces referred to as slots—were made and revised during planning. The estimates for running required the most consideration because running slots had to accommodate each torchbearer's level of ability, without affecting arrivals to celebration sites. Eventually, the average running speed chosen was 8.5 km/hr for all slots. The cycling estimates used were: 31 km/hr for fast, 29 km/hr for average, and 18 km/hr for slow. Motorcycling slots were added to help maintain the 84-day schedule: 45 km/hr (slow segments) and 75 km/hr (fast segments).

As a result of these adjustments, the caravan rarely ran behind schedule, and such occasions were due to inclement weather and other uncontrollable circumstances. Adjusted timing estimates did result in changes to the operational plan of the Torch Relay the month before it began. The average length of 13.5 hours per day grew to approximately 15 hours per day, causing shifts in hotel planning, staffing, and other important support details.

A televised Olympic special on 23 July 1995 revealed that a Torch Relay destination, Yale, Oklahoma, had been erroneously identified as the birthplace of Olympic gold medalist Jim Thorpe. Prague, Oklahoma, was his actual birthplace, and a campaign was launched to have the relay rerouted. Prague was added to the route in December 1995 without excluding any originally scheduled cities.

A second route change added Kittery, Maine to honor and celebrate the accomplishments of native Travis Roy, an athlete paralyzed in his first collegiate hockey game. The final route traveled through 43 states and the District of Columbia.

Torchbearer Program

The Torchbearer Program for the 1996 Olympic Torch Relay was designed as the most inclusive and diverse in the history of the Games, and an estimated 12,000 torchbearers would be needed.

Torchbearers had to be 12 or older on 27 April 1996 to be eligible to carry the Olympic torch. There was no fee or purchase requirement for any part of the torchbearer selection processes or participation in the actual relay. ACOG supplied and mailed to all torchbearers, through a fulfillment firm and UPS, a uniform complete with shorts, a T-shirt, and socks along with an exchange-point flag. Once chosen, all torchbearers were treated the same, regardless of the method by which they were chosen. There was no separation in services provided or in the actual participation, and each signed

a waiver of participation. Each torchbearer carried the Olympic flame for up to 1 km, and the average slot length was 500 m.

Community Heroes. The Torch Relay was an ideal opportunity to honor outstanding citizens; thus, the concept of community heroes was born. The great honor of carrying the Olympic flame is most deserved by people who have donated their services to the community. Through the Community Heroes Program, communities celebrated these heroes. Applicants nominated themselves as community heroes or were nominated by others through an entry process that included an essay of 100 words or less describing the qualities of the nominated person. ACOG's core criteria for a community hero included: outstanding volunteer work; service as a community leader, role model, or mentor; acts of generosity or kindness; and extraordinary feats or accomplishments. The nationwide search was conducted from 1 November to 15 December 1995. Well-orchestrated local publicity programs, such as applications published in newspaper ads and public service announcements, promoted the program.

Torchbearer entries totaled nearly 40,000. Judging panels comprised of respected leaders and outstanding citizens in local communities chose 5,500 community hero torchbearers. The judging process was deemed extremely fair. By using 147 judging locations, the majority of communities along the route were ensured torchbearer representation. United Way of America facilitated the application process, and the judging panels worked with more than 1,300 local United Way organizations.

On 23 February 1996, the names of the community hero torchbearers were announced to the public. Communities nationwide honored their hometown torchbearers with ceremonies

FIGURE 1: US REGIONS CREATED USING THE PROPOSED TORCH RELAY ROUTE

Region 1
Los Angeles, California, to Ogden, Utah

Region 2
Salt Lake City, Utah, to Memphis, Tennessee

Region 3
Cape Girardeau, Missouri, to Cincinnati, Ohio

Region 4
Columbus, Ohio, to Philadelphia, Pennsylvania

Region 5
Wilmington, Delaware, to Nashville, Tennessee

Region 6
Brentwood, Tennessee, to Jacksonville, Florida

Region 7
Georgia

LETIZIA FARISATO • JERRY H FARKAS • COLLEEN M FARLEY • KERI E FARLEY • LAURIE B FARLEY • LINDY C FARLEY • RANDY H FARLEY • RAPONZEL E FARLEY • SANDRA S FARLEY • ADOLF M FARLEY-THOMPSON • MARILYN M FARLEY-THOMPSON • SAMANTHA S FARLEY-THOMPSON • ANN L FARMER • ANNETTE R FARMER • ANTHONY E FARMER • ASHLEY M FARMER • DONALD C FARMER • EARNEST T FARMER • EDWARD B FARMER • FREDERICK K FARMER • JAMES C FARMER • JAMES H FARMER • JAMES N FARMER • JAMES V FARMER • JASON C FARMER • JEFFREY H FARMER • JINNY T FARMER

487

and press conferences. Each torchbearer received an Atlanta logo T-shirt from ACOG, and newspapers everywhere printed group photographs of local torchbearers wearing their T-shirts. The media extensively publicized the Torchbearer Program by profiling these exemplary citizens.

Share the Spirit. The Coca-Cola Company, the official presenter of the Torch Relay, was invited to offer 2,500 people the chance to "Share the Spirit" by choosing torchbearers they thought deserved the honor. Nomination forms were distributed in stores throughout the US in January 1996 and processed locally in the Torch Relay regions. There were no costs associated with the program's nomination process.

Five hundred people from other countries participating in the Olympic Games were also selected for the Share the Spirit Program. The program continued The Coca-Cola Company's tradition, initiated in Barcelona's 1992 Torch Relay, of including torchbearers from other countries to carry the flame.

Olympians and Other Torchbearers. More than 700 Olympian torchbearers carried the flame, honoring 100 years of Olympic athletic competition. The USOC selected these athletes from the family of Olympians who participated in previous Olympic Games.

The opportunity to become a torchbearer was also offered throughout the US to media members, those chosen by the corporate providers of the 1996 Olympic Torch Relay, guests of the USOC, and other Olympic Family members.

Approximately 400 amateur athletes from the US Cycling Federation transported the Olympic flame between towns on specially equipped bicycles. These cyclists, some Olympic hopefuls, pedaled outside major metropolitan areas traversing long distances in sparsely populated areas quickly. Cyclists were ranked through the US Cycling Federation and assigned to relay slots suited to their skill level.

Escort Runners. A group of 2,500 high school students was selected by The Coca-Cola Company to escort torchbearers. They ran alongside the torchbearers, ready to assist if required. They were awarded the honor for their athleticism, character, and leadership qualities.

Slotting Process

For each day of the Torch Relay, a specific number of torchbearer positions (slots) was determined by the distance to be covered and hours of operations. The number of slots each day averaged 145, but the process was completed on a daily basis. Community heroes were assigned to the day the Olympic torch was closest to their hometown. Exceptions to this rule were community heroes selected from states not included in the Torch Relay route. These torchbearers were slotted for the state closest to their own, and were responsible for their own travel arrangements and accommodations. United Way held fund-raisers to help finance trips. Share the Spirit winners selected the location where they wanted to run. If the winner was slotted more than 150 mi (241 km) from home, The Coca-Cola Company assisted with a travel stipend.

Olympians were asked to choose three cities where they would like to run, and every effort was made to accommodate these requests. Providers, that is, companies that provided support for the Torch Relay operation (*see Figure 2*), were given a predetermined number of slots at the time of their commitment. Relay slots were then allotted by city to each provider.

Special needs torchbearers were given primary consideration in the slotting process. It was very important that all special needs be accurately recorded. All road notes needed to be carefully considered when slotting, as route segments uphill, downhill, or through a high-traffic area made mobility difficult.

Local task forces submitted slotting requests in writing to the Atlanta command center or to their regional advance manager. All requests were considered and allowances made when possible. Once torchbearers were placed into a relay slot, the placement was entered into the torchbearer transportation manifest database.

The original intent was to notify the torchbearers of their slots approximately 2–3 weeks before their relay day and deliver their uniforms a week or more prior to their slot. This was very difficult to coordinate due to the limitations of the Torch Relay database system and incomplete torchbearer information. Although most torchbearers received notification 3–5 days before their relay day, some did not receive notification until the night before their slot.

Some slots needed to be filled during the course of the Torch Relay for torchbearers who did not arrive. A rewarding time-sensitive option was to obtain a recommendation from local high school counselors or principals. Torchbearers chosen in this manner required a parent or guardian to sign a consent for participation. The torch support team filled any remaining empty slots with Torch Relay and The Coca-Cola Company support staff when possible.

Torch Production

The torch was designed by Malcolm Grear Designers and engineered under the direction of the Georgia Institute of Technology School of Engineering, with further input from the Atlanta Gas Light Company. The pecan wood for the center handle was collected and donated by the Georgia Forestry Commission. Receiving parts from 15 different suppliers, American Meter Company assembled and tested the torches to ensure quality control. *(For a detailed description of the torch, see the Creative Services chapter.)*

After the Flame Relay in Greece, minor modifications were made to enhance flame visibility. The fuel was changed from propane to propylene, a fuel containing more carbon, so it burned more brilliantly. Approximately 5,000

torches already manufactured were disassembled to change the fuel. In some instances during the relay in Greece, the reeds on the torch melted. A crown to protect the reeds was added to the first 1,000 torches used in the relay in the US, but it affected torch performance by causing the flame to occasionally extinguish. Georgia Tech and American Meter then developed a screen that protected the reeds without affecting torch performance, and torch performance was outstanding for the duration of the Torch Relay.

Sponsorship/Marketing

The Torch Relay was designated as an ACOG signature event, with a separate budget from other ACOG properties. All funds had to be secured outside Olympic Games marketing efforts.

left: Olympic torches were 30 in (76 cm) in length and weighed 3.5 lbs (1.6 kg). They were lit by pushing in and rotating the brass plate at their base to activate fuel release, and then touching the top of the torch to a flame. Torches could burn for 20 minutes, and were extinguished by turning off the gas.

right: Torch Relay banners decorated the US route.

FIGURE 2:
**VIK PRODUCTS AND
SERVICES SUPPLIED BY
THE OFFICIAL PROVIDERS**

BellSouth Corporation
Communications services
along the route

BMW
Use of automobiles,
motorcycles, and bicycles
for the caravan and the
construction and decoration
of all support vehicles,
such as stage trucks

Delta Air Lines
A charter flight to transport
the Olympic flame from
Greece to the US and
nationwide air transportation
for the Torch Relay crew

Holiday Inn Worldwide
Hotel accommodations,
meeting rooms, and
office space

IBM
Computer technology

Motorola, Inc.
Cellular phones, pagers,
radios, and accessories and
technical support for the
wireless communications link

Sara Lee / Champion
Torchbearer and escort
runner uniforms

Sara Lee / Hanes
Crew and community
volunteer uniforms

Texaco USA
Gasoline and motor oil

United Way of America
Community support and
volunteer services, assistance
in planning the torchbearer
selection process, and
recruitment of volunteers for
community celebrations

Union Pacific Railroad
Use of a 19-car
passenger train

On 16 February 1995, The Coca-Cola Company contracted with ACOG to expand its Olympic sponsorship and become the presenter of the 1996 Olympic Torch Relay. After much negotiation, the presenter was given specific marketing rights and allowed to select 2,500 torchbearers and 2,500 escort runners. Additionally, The Coca-Cola Company was the only entity allowed to create Torch Relay–related advertising. The agreement provided that ACOG would manage all logistical planning, operations, and media efforts, and The Coca-Cola Company would enhance community awareness, develop product promotions, and manage the licensing program.

The Coca-Cola Company maintained a presence on every level, from the executive ranks to local task force meetings across the nation. One of the most beneficial aspects of participation was the activation of its extensive bottler network along the route. Bottler representatives were present in most communities to assist with planning celebrations and encourage interest in the project.

In addition to the presenter, nine official providers supplied the Torch Relay with VIK products in exchange for certain privileges. *(For a list of these providers, see Figure 2.)*

To build interest in the Torch Relay, several marketing initiatives were developed. A line of commemorative Torch Relay merchandise including pins, T-shirts, hats, and pennants were jointly merchandised by ACOG and The Coca-Cola Company. The Coca-Cola Company made Torch Relay items available nationwide by moving several tractor-trailer trucks containing merchandise from celebration to celebration. To build awareness of the route, sets of street banners were sold to communities. One of the three banners in the set displayed the name of the city where the celebration would occur and the arrival date of the Olympic flame. Community promotions were held two days before the arrival of the Olympic flame in local retail outlets along the route.

TORCH RELAY OPERATIONS

From coast to coast, Torch Relay operations produced the mobile and touching celebration of the Olympic Spirit throughout the US. Careful planning of complex logistics and attention to thousands of details were always behind each smile, each touch of hands, as the flame passed from torchbearer to torchbearer.

Modes of Transporting the Flame

To accommodate route expansions and enrich the symbolism of the Torch Relay, modes of transportation other than runners, bicycles, and motorcycles were used. Modes were chosen that reflected American history and the character of the surrounding community, including a rowing shell, train, ferry, cable car, horseback, canoe, biplane, street car, steamboat, Great Lakes laker, packet boat, sailboat, seaplane, and tall-masted sailing vessel. The flame was always transported either by a torchbearer or in a cauldron. The cauldron was used on trains, ferries, and some boats to allow the flame to be more visible.

Union Pacific Railroad's passenger train carried the Olympic flame and about 200 staff members and special guests for more than 3,500 mi (5,633 km) in the western US. A steel, flatbed special edition car was designed to act as both a caboose and a stage for the flame. At the rear, a retractable cauldron matching the design used on Torch Relay stage trucks during community celebrations was mounted to carry the flame. This car had a sound system and a torchbearer pictogram decorating the backdrop for the flame. Before each Torch Relay train departure, a torchbearer would board the train and light the cauldron. During the course of a train slot, a series of whistle-stop celebrations enabled communities along the way to host the flame. Usually 5–10 minutes in length, these celebrations included brief remarks about the Olympic message by an ACOG representative and a short welcome from the mayor or other local official.

Passenger ferries transported the flame across Puget Sound in Washington state and across the Hudson River in New York City. A visible cauldron mounted on the deck of each ferry held the flame for these voyages.

More than 300 members of the National Pony Express Association recreated 544 mi (875 km) of the old Pony Express route between Julesburg, Colorado, and St. Joseph, Missouri, traveling exclusively on horseback for 58 continuous hours. Much like the original Pony Express, the riders carried mail—over 1,000 formal letters from ACOG spreading the message of the Olympic Games—in a mochilla, or mail bag, placed over the saddle. Each rider wore a traditional Pony Express uniform and carried a hand-held torch.

A 128 mi (206 km), 34-hour journey up the Mississippi River on the *American Queen*, the largest steamboat ever built, was designed to recognize and thank providers and other special guests for their contributions to the Torch Relay. The trip unfortunately was abbreviated due to inclement weather and flooded riverbanks, but all aboard enjoyed the luxurious, traditional decor and endless buffets of the *American Queen*.

Flame Carriers

Twelve inch (30.5 cm) safety lanterns with the capacity to hold 20 hours of liquid paraffin were designed to hold backup flames. One version could be lit by inserting a wick into a side opening, and the other by unscrewing the lantern and inserting a wick through the top. The lanterns were housed at remain-overnight (RON) Holiday Inn Worldwide hotels, the command car, emergency medical services and other motorhomes, and a security location in

Atlanta. Twenty-four inch (61 cm) decorative lanterns were used to transport the flame on bicycles, motorcycles, and during ceremonial occasions. Decorative lanterns were lit by placing a safety lantern into the decorative encasing, but because they were more time-consuming to light and access, they were used for display purposes only.

A torch mount for torchbearers in wheelchairs was designed to employ brackets adaptable to all wheelchairs. The bottom half of the torch slipped into a clear plastic cylinder, held

by brackets on the side of the wheelchair. Although the mounts were time-consuming to affix and remove, they worked well.

At the start of every day, a flame tender—a staff member who traveled with the flame to attend to it—lit a transfer wick from a safety lantern, then lit a transfer torch from the wick. The transfer torch lit the torch of the first torchbearer.

left: A bicycle torch mount is tested at the Georgia Institute of Technology.

right: Safety lanterns that could hold 20 hours of liquid paraffin were designed to hold backup flames.

During the first few days of the Torch Relay, torchbearers were charged with engaging the gas flow of the torch. However, after many ignitors were damaged by excited torchbearers, a staff person was assigned to turn the torches on and off.

Transfer of the Flame

When transferring a flame from runner to runner, the torchbearer would light the next runner's torch directly with his/her flame, assuring the torch was lit before extinguishing the flame. When transferring a flame from runner to cyclist, a flame tender used a transfer wick to light a safety lantern from the runner's torch, carried the flame into the service vehicle, reemerged with a lit decorative lantern, and mounted it to the front of the torchbearer's bicycle. When transferring a flame from cyclist to runner, the process was reversed. A flame tender transferred the flame from cyclist to cyclist by using a transfer wick to light one lantern from another.

A runner transferred the flame directly to the cauldron by lighting it from the flame of his/her torch, and a runner meeting a train or boat lit his/her torch directly from the cauldron. When transferring the flame from cyclist to cauldron, a flame tender detached the lantern from the bicycle and carried it into the service vehicle, where he/she ignited a transfer torch by a transfer wick. The flame tender then left the service vehicle with the transfer torch to light the cauldron. Transferring the flame from cauldron to cyclist was the reversal of this process. At the end of the day, the last torchbearer would light the cauldron with the flame from his/her torch. A flame tender then ignited a safety lantern from the cauldron using a transfer wick. Most individuals assigned to tend the flame were Georgia State Patrol (GSP) personnel.

Advance Operations

The advance teams working to ensure a safe route and helping communities plan local

Media-1, a customized 31 ft (9m) motorhome, was the caravan's primary media vehicle.

events thought it necessary to have ACOG stage managers and representatives assist in the local planning efforts to ensure each event would proceed in a manner consistent with ACOG's plan for the celebration of the Olympic flame. While the advance team managers for each region remained with the caravan, advance staff on loan from other regions arrived two days prior to the Torch Relay to help communities prepare for the arrival of the flame. Days were divided into manageable slots based on the complexity of the events and distance between communities. In general, advance staff organized an evening celebration, morning celebration, and a break, or a lunch celebration and two or three breaks. Advance managers held conferences with the local security team, event organizers, and any other involved association.

Ensuring that the 15-vehicle Torch Relay caravan moved unimpeded through urban streets required planning and information exchange continuously, until the last minute. One day before the Torch Relay arrived, an advance staff member attended prearranged security briefings where local police departments were presented the final daybook and last-minute route issues were addressed. Any necessary information concerning the presence of local police and emergency vehicles was relayed to the caravan manager.

Also, a pilot car drove the entire next day's route, marking torchbearer exchange points with slot numbers by placing fluorescent stickers along the route and confirming daybook directions. When last-minute rerouting was necessary, the pilot was responsible for planning alternate routes, and the change was communicated in the following day's daybook. The pilot team then led the caravan through the areas marked the day before.

The Daybook. The daybook, produced in the RON center two days before the day it outlined, was a working log for staff use during the Torch Relay. Single update sheets were used to add any recently gathered information before distribution. The daybook was the most important information tool, used by all Torch Relay staff and volunteers. The first page contained a day sheet with an overview of the day, including start time and location; all cities on the route; time, location, and duration of all breaks; distance accrued; modes of transporting the flame; and the address and telephone number of the night's RON.

Crew shift information such as wake-up calls, departure times, and locations were listed after the day sheet. Next, route sheets documented every turn the route would take that day and each significant landmark it would pass. They also included detailed directions for caravan movement, reflecting exchange and collection points. Every torchbearer slot was marked clearly on the document. Included on the written route were insertion points marking where torchbearer shuttle buses would enter the caravan; the day's total travel distance and time, based on timing estimates; and the length and projected time for each slot.

A map tracing the day's route was produced along with detailed maps of celebration sites, break sites, caravan staging vehicle placement during breaks, and torchbearer paths to the staging area. Enlarged maps of the region and directions were also included for the benefit of advance teams needing alternate routes that would allow them to reach a point early enough to prepare for the arrival of the flame.

The daybook also supplied torchbearer names, escort runner names, slot numbers, and the collection points and host teams that would be assigned. A table including shuttle bus insertion point times, first and last runner estimated drop times, and collection point arrival times outlined the day's schedule for the shuttle system. Phone numbers of the primary law enforcement contact for each jurisdiction the route would travel through during the day, primary contact names and phone numbers

for collection points, and break and celebration sites were also included. Daybooks were distributed during hotel registration.

Staging Community Celebrations. To ensure that lunch and evening celebrations ran smoothly, ACOG stage crews traveled in advance to the celebration sites. The A-stage crew traveled with the largest mobile stage for public events reaching 20,000 people in attendance. The B-stage crew traveled with the smaller stage truck and was primarily used at lunch sites for crowds of 5,000 or more. The C-stage crew traveled with an Olympic backdrop and props for use on existing stages for large-scale celebrations.

Because the route scheduled approximately two or three 5- to 15-minute breaks a day, a break team was created several weeks into the Torch Relay. This team preceded the caravan to prepare for its arrival at the break site. Although these breaks were originally planned to give the staff a reprieve, this advance team proved necessary, as the breaks often attracted as many spectators as the celebrations.

Caravan Configuration

The caravan configuration accomplished the essential need for safety, while allowing the greatest exposure for the torch. The vehicles in the caravan also provided facilities for most operations that supported the Torch Relay while on route.

A group of vehicles preceded the core caravan by about five minutes. First, the pilot vehicle advanced the Relay route. This automobile, fitted with flashing yellow lights and an external public address (PA) system, announced the approach of the Olympic torch. The pilot's primary functions were to check and establish predetermined torchbearer exchange points and to alert the torchbearer shuttle driver to the drop points. Next came the 18-passenger shuttle bus to drop torchbearers and escort runners several minutes in front of the core

The Torch Relay daybook was the indispensible working log for staff use which contained essential information relating to the route, location, schedule, and torchbearers.

caravan. A host or hostess on the shuttle timed the runners' exits to reduce torchbearers' waiting time. Three of the six vehicles used were fitted with wheelchair lifts. Where available, a local law enforcement vehicle helped protect torchbearers exiting the shuttle. The last part of this caravan segment was Pace, a vehicle used to set the speed of the caravan under the direction of the caravan command manager.

Home-1, a state or local law enforcement automobile or motorcycle(s), escorted the core caravan. In smaller jurisdictions, local law enforcement agencies sometimes deferred to state or county coverage for this position.

A sedan followed with two GSP officers assigned as internal torchbearer security providers. Media-1, a customized 31 ft (9 m) motorhome, was the caravan's primary media vehicle. The rear of this vehicle was modified to allow electronic and print media representatives an unobstructed view of the torchbearer, and the front compartment provided a media workspace.

The torchbearer and escort runner followed, accompanied by a security unit that shielded the torchbearer from the crowd while enabling spectators and supporters to see the Olympic flame. The security unit was composed of six specially equipped motorcycles, and was augmented by as many as four GSP security runners deployed to keep the street free of obstacles.

Command, the caravan command vehicle, was positioned directly behind the torchbearer. This sedan was equipped with a variety of communications systems and specialty equipment including an external PA system and a flashing, yellow light bar on its roof to alert crowds of the torch's arrival. All caravan management and movement decisions—including liaison with local law enforcement and government agencies—were made from this vehicle by the Torch Relay director, caravan manager, and security team leader. G-2, a second identical sedan (used occasionally), followed, transporting staff and guests into and out of the caravan as needed.

The caravan services center followed: a retrofitted, 31 ft (9 m) motorhome with seating and workstations for staff and guests. It served as a deployment platform for GSP security runners and carried the reserve flame, used to relight the torch when necessary, in four safety lanterns ignited by the original flame in Greece.

Emergency medical services were housed in the 31 ft (9 m) motorhome that followed, providing primary medical care for ACOG staff and torchbearers. This vehicle was also the backup to the command vehicle and served the additional role of carrying all specialized radio and com-net systems, including the radio repeater system.

Cycle-1, a station wagon equipped with bicycle racks, support materials, and a mechanic to service bicycle torchbearers completing their slots ensured the operational consistency of the bicyclists. During bicycling slots of the Torch Relay, the torchbearer shuttle was replaced by Cycle-1 and Cycle-2 support vehicles.

Near the end of the caravan, a second torchbearer shuttle provided transportation for torchbearers as they completed their slots. A GSP vehicle was also at the rear to address any security issues. The broom wagon, equipped with a light bar and external PA system to attenuate traffic, marked the end of the core caravan. A state or local law enforcement vehicle followed. During passage through larger crowd venues, this vehicle helped prevent incursion into the core caravan from behind.

Ahead of and behind the core caravan was a small group of vehicles used to support the drivers and equipment in the core. They included mechanical support trucks, motorhomes, and sedans. These vehicles traveled on their own, usually on side or alternate-route highways and roads.

Caravan Operations

RON Operations. While the caravan was traveling during the day, the team of approximately 10 RON staff members formed constructed offices in hotel conference rooms for the entire staff. The RON operation was managed by the caravan services manager and the command center manager. The RON operations center handled luggage delivery, daybook production, volunteer reception, room list/key packet assembly, mail and message distribution, shipping and receiving, and other tasks. Complete with computers, printers, a facsimile machine, a copier, and snacks, the RON offices were the traveling headquarters for the Torch Relay.

RON staff were also responsible for confirming and handling last-minute arrangements for accommodations and meals. They also coordinated with a local affiliate to provide laundry services.

Each morning, a RON staff member arose before the caravan was scheduled to depart, sometimes as early as 0300, to ensure breakfast arrangements and provide snacks for the caravan staff to carry for the day. After the caravan departed, the RON operations center closed and relocated to the next RON. Three trucks, loaded with luggage and equipment, drove the most direct route to the next RON. Staff members followed shortly thereafter in sedans after finalizing all hotel business. When the trucks arrived at the next RON, a staff member coordinated office space. The trucks were taken to the secured parking area at the hotel. Once the remaining RON staff arrived, preparation of the daily operation commenced.

Holiday Inn Worldwide provided accommodations and primary meals for Torch Relay personnel. When possible, all staff stayed in the same hotel.

Communications. The ability to communicate with other staff members was critical. Relay operations functioned through the use of radios and cellular phones, MobilComm pagers, a QualComm system, and a traveling 800 number at the RON. The QualComm system was a communications system, similar to E-mail, that worked through a modem and could function when other communications systems were inoperative or out of range.

In February 1996, the Federal Communications Commission granted the Olympic Torch Relay the authority to use 15 frequencies including five 12.5 kHz offset repeater pairs and ten 12.5 kHz offset simplex frequencies selected by the Personal Communications Industry Association. As requested, they provided 50 w output power and 20k0F3E emission on a noninterference basis.

All vehicles were equipped with mounted radios, and approximately 50 percent of the staff were given hand-held radios. This permitted communication between the caravan and the celebration site staff.

The QualComm system was mounted in the emergency medical services motorhome, allowing the Atlanta command center the opportunity to send text messages directly to the caravan when it was outside cellular coverage areas. QualComm was also installed on the Union Pacific train.

Vehicle Fueling and Maintenance. Caravan vehicles were fueled and serviced at designated Texaco stations. Motorcycles, requiring frequent fuel replenishment, were fueled as necessary during midday celebrations or breaks also at designated Texaco gasoline stations. Roadside assistance for repair or removal of all caravan vehicles was provided by BMW service technicians. Vehicles were washed every night in the RON parking lot by a professional crew that traveled with the Torch Relay. They were also secured overnight in RON parking lots by a combination of private and local security groups.

ID System. In order to facilitate handling staff room and board essentials, an ID system was developed whereby each staff member was assigned an exclusive three-digit number marked on all luggage, laundry bags, picture

IDs, credentials, and key packets. Staff members were required to mark each item of clothing, personal or uniform, with the ID number.

Media Relations. The media relations team, comprised of approximately 30 Torch Relay staff members, accommodated the requests and needs of print and broadcast representatives and escorted them at all times. The team's objective was to present the story of the Torch Relay to the public as it unfolded. Focusing on three elements—torchbearers, city celebrations, and the Look of the Relay—media relations reported positive accounts of the relay that would convey the uplifting experience for all who witnessed the flame pass through their communities.

Torch Relay press kits, containing background with historical information and relay operations materials, were available to all media representatives.

Stories were identified and offered to the media each day. Some focused on community torchbearers and city celebrations, while others were of national and international interest, reporting more general aspects of the relay.

ACOG contracted with NBC to air a 30- to 60-second Torch Relay update during prime-time each night. The segments focused on a key torchbearer or other visual opportunity and helped build enthusiasm and awareness of the Torch Relay by reaching large portions of the population. Each segment was produced by the Torch Relay video crew and sent by satellite from a local affiliate to NBC's Burbank, California, studio.

A local briefing took place in each community one or two days before the Torch Relay caravan arrived. A media guide, produced daily, was distributed to the press at the morning briefing. This guide provided information on the caravan schedule and route, torchbearers, and media access to secured caravan areas and celebration sites.

To access secure areas of the Torch Relay, reporters were required to possess a credential issued by ACOG, which they could obtain by contacting the Torch Relay media hot line in the Atlanta command center.

A specially designed media motorhome located in the core caravan seated several members of the press, with space allocation determined and assigned by the press chief. Positions became available in every section on a rotating basis—usually every hour during the day. Additional media positions were available at the discretion of the press chief in media cars, on media motorcycles, in the torchbearer shuttle, at celebration site platforms, hotel sites, and other select caravan vehicles. Priority was given to local media.

Only specified ACOG Torch Relay media relations staff made statements or conducted interviews with the media, and responses to the media in a crisis situation were made only by designated media relations or management personnel. Appropriate responses and a chain of command were developed for such situations. Staff was instructed to direct reporters to media relations for interviews and press information.

Torchbearer Shuttle System

The purpose of the torchbearer shuttle system was to give each torchbearer and escort runner a memorable three-hour Olympic group experience in addition to their flame-carrying slot. On a typical day, a host/hostess and driver team was scheduled for 2–3 collection points. Most Torch Relay host and hostess positions were filled by volunteers and interns. Staff rotated, bringing new people to the project every few weeks. Ten hosts and hostesses were present in the caravan at all times. While their jobs were demanding, the responsibilities of torchbearer hosts and hostesses were among the most rewarding of the Torch Relay.

Torchbearers were instructed to arrive at the collection point in uniform with an exchange-point flag at least one hour prior to the first torchbearer in the group's slot. Torchbearers, always eager to begin their Olympic experience, would almost always arrive 30 minutes to one hour earlier than necessary. For this reason, all hosts/hostesses and drivers were instructed to arrive at least 30 minutes prior to the time listed in the daybook. The high percentage of torchbearers that gathered at the collection point was impressive—and the diversity rewarding.

The shuttle host/hostess began by registering each torchbearer. The registration process involved ensuring each torchbearer and escort had the proper uniform. At this time, torchbearers also confirmed whether or not they would purchase their torch. Torchbearers completed forms and were questioned to determine if any had special needs to be met. Next, the host/hostess and driver ensured the torchbearer's family and friends knew the correct location to cheer for their torchbearer. A presentation followed, wherein an official greeting issued by the ACOG CEO was extended on video, and The Coca-Cola Company and other providers of the Torch Relay were acknowledged. Video highlights of previous days and of the flame lighting ceremony in Greece were also shown. Torchbearers were given the opportunity to introduce themselves to the group and share why they were chosen to carry the flame. Torches were distributed and all mechanisms and significance were explained in detail. The host/hostess and driver then escorted their guests on the shuttle and proceeded to the insertion point.

The shuttle bus dropped torchbearers at the insertion points, indicated with a sticker and a volunteer holding an exchange-point flag. For identification purposes in photos and documentaries, torchbearers and escort runners were given stickers to wear that corresponded to their slot number. The same number was marked on the bottom of the torches to ensure that the torchbearers received the correct torch.

An escort runner was assigned to accompany each torchbearer on his/her slot for companionship and in case of terrain needs. Exchange-point flags in four different colors were held by a family member or friend of the torchbearer to mark the end of his/her slot.

Most torchbearers took advantage of the shuttle back to the collection point, sharing stories on the return trip. At the return collection point, torches were purged for safety reasons by turning them upside down before the torchbearers took them home. The sanctity of the Olympic flame was explained—that the torch should never again be lit with any other

flame. Used torches were moved to the RON truck for shipment to Atlanta.

Of the 12,467 torchbearers who carried the flame, only 104 substitutions were required due to failure to appear. These torchbearers were escorted by 2,500 runners. The majority of these runners were met and returned to the

The torchbearer shuttle system offered torchbearers a memorable Olympic experience in a group setting.

1,040 collection points from Los Angeles to Atlanta. Most torchbearers have commented positively about their 1996 Olympic Torch Relay experience.

CONCLUSIONS AND RECOMMENDATIONS

The Olympic Torch Relay celebrated the Centennial of the Games, honored the role Greece played in the modern Olympic Movement, and brought the Olympic flame within reach of hundreds of thousands of Americans. The detailed planning of the relay route and the innovative transportation of the flame showcased the many different cultures within the US to the worldwide viewing audience. In addition, the torchbearer selection process, which acknowledged exemplary US citizens, modeled and promoted the qualities of the Olympic Spirit.

Following are some key points to remember in the planning process:

■ Set clear internal and external guidelines and rules for commercializing the activities surrounding the Torch Relay.

■ Hire key staff members, particularly senior managers and advance teams, at least two years prior to the Torch Relay.

■ Consider staff fatigue when planning the route and program. Plan for days off and alternating teams.

■ Allocate a significant budget contingency (15 percent minimum) for use in the few weeks prior to project launch and during the road trip.

■ Clear goals and objectives need to be established early and communicated to all relay staff and the public. ACOG established early that the top priority was to give torchbearers and the general public a positive experience with the flame.

■ Number and location of running slots should be predetermined by relay staff after final route confirmation and implemented by relay staff only.

■ An accurate, dependable database system that will allow torchbearer searches as well as eliminate duplicate slotting is required. This system should allow all involved staff to obtain needed information, and a limited number of staff to make changes.

■ All torchbearers should be notified of their selection and slotting three months prior to the relay. At least one month prior to the relay, their acceptance should be confirmed. All torchbearers should agree in writing to run in available slots.

■ Torchbearer special needs should be accurately recorded into a reliable database system and integrated into daybooks.

■ Beginning at the time of the route announcement, be prepared for thousands of phone calls. Staff the home office with enough personnel to respond to issues and solve problems after the relay begins.

■ All torchbearer shuttles should be wheelchair-accessible. Restroom facilities are not a requirement for the shuttles. Storage and an efficient refrigeration system need to be provided.

■ A communication system that allows uninterrupted contact between torch support, shuttles, and the caravan is critical. All hosts, drivers, and torch support team members should be equipped with portable cellular phones, radios, and beepers, and all shuttles should have mounted radios and cellular phones.

Atlanta 1996®

No Smoking

Southbound   Northb

Directory

TRANSPORTATION

51

153

AIRPORT

Chapter Twenty-Six
Transportation

Games-Time Transportation Staff

Category	Staff Number
ACOG paid	136
Volunteers	6,279
Contract	9,000*
Total	**15,415***

*estimate

OVERVIEW—The mission of ACOG's Transportation Department was to augment the transportation system in Atlanta so as to meet Games-time requirements safely, conveniently, and efficiently. The population of the metropolitan-Atlanta area was 3.4 million, and an additional 2 million people were expected to arrive in the city for the Games. Every day during the Games period, 100,000 working Atlantans, 200,000 Olympic Family members, and more than 2 million spectators required transportation in and around the Olympic Ring, an imaginary circle in the central business district of Atlanta with a 1.5 mi (2.4 km) radius.

According to the Host City Contract with the IOC, the organizing committee is responsible for providing a specified level of transportation for those constituents that comprise the Olympic Family: athletes and team officials; IOC, NOC, and IF representatives; competition officials; media; organizing committee staff; sponsors; and special guests. Because of the tremendous amount of Olympic activity concentrated within the Olympic Ring and the magnitude of event-specific additions to the roadways, ACOG decided to assume the challenge of providing a transit system for an unprecedented number of Olympic spectators that would also meet the needs of Atlanta residents and workers requiring access to the Olympic Ring. All systems were coordinated through the Olympic Transportation System (OTS).

To determine the circulation and transportation requirements for all constituents' needs and to fulfill the department's mission, ACOG began an extensive planning process in 1991 that involved analysis of the area's existing transportation infrastructure and reports from previous Olympic Games, as well as evaluation of constituency needs, resources, and available coordination with federal, state, and local transportation experts.

A tremendous undertaking, Olympic transportation required a vast amount of resources and personnel. During Games-time, the Transportation staff numbered approximately 15,500 members. Among other resources, ACOG Transportation directly or indirectly acquired, managed, and maintained more than 2,000 buses, more than 200 rail cars, 4,250 other vehicles, and approximately 120,000 parking spaces. In the process of developing and executing the OTS, ACOG created a legacy of transportation infrastructure enhancements and interagency coordination and communication.

Organization

Throughout the years of the planning process, a regional circulation plan was developed, and the ACOG Transportation Department was divided into operating systems to fulfill its mission. These areas were: Olympic Family transportation, spectator transportation, regional

WENDALL R FERGUSON • GERALD M FERLAAK • MARIA J FERLAAK • ALISHA D FERMAN • LINDA G. FERMAN • BENEDICT MONTEGOMERY FERMIN • BEVERLY R FERMON • DENEEN C FERNANDES • GHENN R FERNANDES • OLIVIA F FERNANDES • YANIS D FERNANDES • CLARISSE FERNANDEZ • DICKIE FERNANDEZ • EDWIN V FERNANDEZ • JORGE FERNANDEZ • LOURDES A FERNANDEZ • MARIA T FERNANDEZ • MARICELA CH FERNANDEZ • SONIA FERNANDEZ • ZAIDA M FERNANDEZ • MANUEL FERNANDEZ-GUZMAN • JORGE C FERNANDEZ-TRAVIESCO • LARRY B FEROLIE •

traffic management, and Games-time operations, which included venue transportation, airport operations, and resources.

Early Planning

Early research showed that Atlanta's existing transportation infrastructure would not be sufficient to serve the volume of people who would be visiting Atlanta during the Games. Planners concluded that adapting the Atlanta transportation infrastructure to support the Olympic Family also required transporting all spectators throughout the region and adding to or expediting adaptations already in progress or planned by local, state, and federal government agencies. ACOG therefore established a support and planning advisory group and procured a contractor to develop the transportation plan.

Olympic Transportation Support Group. The Olympic transportation support group (OTSG), formed in February 1992 and comprised of community, local, state, and national transportation agency representatives, advised ACOG on the development and implementation of the 1996 Games transportation plan. The OTSG met on a regular basis to discuss issues, share perspectives, and report on its progress. Twenty of approximately 100 OTSG members represented various ACOG departments such as Government Relations, Logistics, and Transportation.

The following business and government entities were represented in the OTSG: the US Department of Transportation; the US Department of Energy; the Georgia Department of Transportation (DOT); the Georgia Public Service Commission; various local county departments of transportation; the cities of Atlanta, Conyers, and Stone Mountain; Hartsfield Atlanta International Airport; the Metropolitan Atlanta Rapid Transit Authority (MARTA); the Atlanta Regional Commission (ARC); Central Atlanta Progress; the Georgia Institute of Technology; the Atlanta Paralympic Organizing Committee; the Atlanta Police Department (APD); the Georgia State Patrol (GSP); the city

of Atlanta Public Works and Planning Department; and the Atlanta and DeKalb Chambers of Commerce.

The OTSG named teams to research and plan for five areas: an Olympic Ring traffic management plan, which outlined the need for traffic circulation plans in the downtown area; an outlying venue circulation plan, which focused on the need for traffic circulation plans around outlying venues; spectator transportation system transit operations, which focused on maximizing the use of rail transportation and encouraging walking within the Olympic Ring (also included subcommittees for taxi company relations and transportation for people with physical disabilities); transportation demand and incident management, which focused on developing a Transportation Demand Management Program for the Atlanta region; and data/model management and refinement, which focused on implications made by transportation-related data. These five teams, comprised of ACOG Transportation staff, ARC staff and subcontractors, and representatives from OTSG member agencies, provided recommendations and assistance during the planning process.

Regional Plan. While the OTSG studied transportation options and made recommendations, ACOG contracted with the ARC to develop the specific OTS plan. Along with their expertise, ARC also provided numerous contacts that enabled ACOG to obtain funding for a portion of the cost of ARC's services. Additionally, ARC subcontracted with local transportation consultants to assist in the planning effort.

The OTS plan was designed to complement ARC's Regional Transportation Plan, which recommended the addition of high occupancy vehicle (HOV) lanes to freeways and three more MARTA rail stations. It also called for the development and implementation of the advanced transportation management system (ATMS), a multimillion-dollar state project to integrate the management of freeways and surface streets, allow state and local engineers to inter-act and participate in real-time transportation decisions, provide a high-speed/high-capacity communications network, and serve as a clear-inghouse for public information. To prepare for the Games, the implementation of these pro-jects was accelerated.

During its strategic planning process, the ACOG Transportation Department worked with the OTSG and ARC to develop goals and measures of performance, study and assess the available modes of transportation, and esti-mate the demand that would be placed on each mode with regard to venues, events, park-ing facilities, and times of day.

A number of methodologies were used to analyze the demand that would be placed on Atlanta's existing modes of transportation. First, statistics revealed that certain modes might require enhancement. For example, past research done by MARTA provided the mass transit authority with the maximum number of people who could safely be accom-modated at rail stations or fit on rail cars and buses at one time. To determine how many buses would be needed and how often rail cars would have to operate during the Games, MARTA recalculated its standard travel equa-tions using the anticipated number of travel-ers during the Games. The same method was used when the Georgia DOT analyzed the need for improvement on the highways, due to the increase in traffic during the Games.

To help determine what road closures and lane restrictions would be necessary to control downtown and highway traffic during the Games, consultants using computerized traffic flow simulations and local agency personnel for-mulated a Games-time traffic management plan.

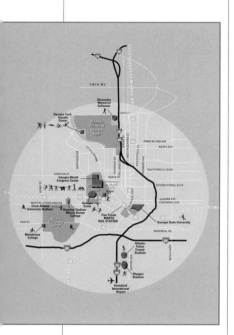

Transportation routes were established throughout the Olympic Ring, a 1.5 mi (2.4 km) imaginary circle.

After analysis, the department developed its transportation service concepts, compared ex-isting capacities to estimated demands, and ad-justed accordingly.

OLYMPIC TRANSPORTATION SYSTEM

The department was structured around the major operating systems of the OTS: the Olympic Family transportation system, which included the Parking Permit Program and a Special Services division; the Olympic specta-tor transportation system (OSTS); and the re-gional traffic management system. Other ACOG Transportation operating components provided support: Staffing, Command Centers, Venue Transportation Management, Airport Opera-tions and Resources. Other groups within the department provided functional support to the operating components: administration and fi-nance, facilities, telecommunications, and planning and technical support.

OLYMPIC FAMILY TRANSPORTATION SYSTEM

The Olympic Family, the group for which ACOG was contractually obliged to provide transportation services, comprised athletes and team officials; competition officials; IOC, NOC, and IF members; media; and special guests. The Olympic Family transportation system also pro-vided services to sponsors and Games staff.

Planning for Olympic Family transportation began with the following standards to move 150,000 Olympic Family members each day.

■ Each Olympic Family member would be provided arrival and departure services.

■ Most service to venues for athletes, offi-cials, and the media would begin two hours prior to an event, while service for staff and volunteers would begin three hours prior to an event. Sponsors would have special service available with equipment assigned on a pre-scheduled basis.

■ Immediate clearance from a venue after an event would be provided for Olympic officials and guests, and within one hour or less for all remaining members of the Olympic Family.

■ Replacement vehicles would always be available in the event of a mechanical breakdown or other service interruption.

■ All vehicles used to transport members of the Olympic Family would operate at or below their normal seating capacity.

The planning group also determined that routing plans for Olympic Family vehicles were to be designed to minimize travel times through the use of the one-way pair systems in downtown Atlanta and the HOV lane system. Routes were selected to avoid, where possible, the streets used for general spectator transportation or pedestrians. Entrances, bus boarding areas, and parking areas were provided at each venue site for members of the Olympic Family.

Transportation systems that met IOC standards were established for constituencies of the Olympic Family, including: 16,500 athletes and team officials; the IOC, NOCs, IFs, and their guests; 2,200 competition officials; 15,000 members of the print and broadcast media; and 53,540 staff members.

As part of Olympic accreditation, each individual was assigned to one of five categories (T1–T5) that would entitle him or her to a designated level of complimentary transportation service. *(For more information, see the Accreditation chapter.)*

Transportation service for members of the Olympic Family included private cars and vans, motor pool service, and bus service. Additionally, the majority of accredited Olympic Family members were provided with a MARTA pass good for use on the OSTS—including the supplemental bus system, MARTA rail, and MARTA regular bus system.

Transportation Operating Components

To meet the needs of the Olympic Family, the Transportation Department operated four distinct programs: the bus system; an assigned vehicle and motor pool program, which provided complimentary vehicles with drivers; a parking permit program; and special guest services, which offered noncomplimentary transportation services.

Bus System. All components of the Olympic Family bus system were planned and operated by a contractor, Event Transportation Associates (ETA). This included all demand modeling, scheduling, routing, and staffing. ETA worked closely with agencies directly involved in regional traffic planning and management.

The bus system was an extensive operation. The system utilized 1,700 vehicles and 2,000 drivers, and managed 74 acres (30 ha) of land in terminals, holding sites, and venue load zones. During Games-time, this system delivered approximately 1.9 million passenger one-way trips.

Assigned Vehicle and Motor Pool Program. According to Accreditation guidelines, members of the Olympic Family were either assigned designated vehicles and drivers or provided access to the Transportation Department motor pools. Assigned vehicles were coordinated by individual departments, such as Guest Services and Olympic Villages. ACOG's Transportation Department created and implemented 14 residential and venue motor pools in the Atlanta metro area to accommodate all T1–T3 levels of accreditation.

Motor pool management supervised facility acquisition, staffing, vehicle inventory, and operations. The largest motor pool was located at the Olympic Family Hotel. Residential motor pools were also available near clusters of ACOG-sanctioned hotels, including Athens, North Perimeter, Olympic Village, South Airport, and Stone Mountain. Residential motor pools were generally larger in terms of personnel, technology, and vehicles than the venue motor pools, which were established to support residential motor pools and the venue staff and functional areas. The venue motor

The Olympic Family bus system was an extensive operation that utilized 1,700 vehicles and 2,000 drivers and managed 74 acres (30 ha) of land.

TERRIE K FICHERA • MARTHA E FICK • RODERICK L FICK • THOMAS M FICK • ELAINA M FIEDLER • MARK A FIEDLER • AMY E FIELD • DONNA S FIELD • ERIC G FIELD • GARY D FIELD • W. MICHAEL FIELD • KARIN K FIELDER • RENEE W FIELDER • VICKI K FIELDER • JONI L FIELDING • ALFREDA S FIELDS • ARTHUR L. FIELDS • BARBARA J FIELDS • BETTY J FIELDS • BEVERLY A FIELDS • BRUCE FIELDS • CAROLYN H FIELDS • CHRIS A FIELDS • DAVID FIELDS • DOLLIS FIELDS • DONNA L FIELDS • JANE A FIELDS • JANET M FIELDS • KITTY FIELDS • LUCINDA E FIELDS • MACK A FIELDS • MARY CATHERINE

503

pools were smaller (5–10 vehicles) and supported the following competition venues: Atlanta Beach, Atlanta–Fulton County Stadium, Georgia International Horse Park, Lake Lanier, Olympic Stadium, and Wolf Creek Shooting Complex.

A reservation system was implemented at each residential motor pool, using telephone or facsimile machine requests submitted at least 12 hours in advance. Venue motor pools operated on an immediate request system.

A total of 712 vehicles were utilized by the 14 motor pools—a sufficient number of vehicles to serve the constituents requiring this type of support.

Parking Permit Program. Parking for Olympic Family and people living in certain restricted areas was managed by the ACOG Parking Permit Program. This program was responsible for securing, providing, and operating approximately 40,000 Games-time parking spaces in more than 100 separate lots, each serving a particular venue. Some venues were served by as many as 10 lots (totalling more than 5,000 parking spaces). The parking team for the Olympic Family consisted of more than 2,500 staff, including management, construction, and maintenance personnel, and venue-specific parking staff. Parking operations at venues were the responsibility of venue transportation management. The Atlanta Olympic Village and Olympic Family Hotel managed parking at their facilities. Most lots were in service and staffed at all times during the Games.

Access to ACOG-operated parking areas was controlled through the ACOG Parking Permit Program with 15 different types of permits, including multivenue permits, venue-specific permits, Opening and Closing Ceremonies permits, and date-specific permits. More than 200,000 permits were printed, about 150,000

of which were actually used. A limited number of permit types were also supplied to local residents or businesses located in restricted areas, to provide access to a home or workplace.

The ACOG Parking Permit Program staff identified potential permit users through a demand survey conducted among staff members, contractors, vendors, and venue owners; special guests, including IOC members, IF members, NOC members, government dignitaries, guests of the organizing committee, patrons, and competition venue suite holders; and ticketed guests with accreditation that allowed them to acquire parking near venues. Permits were allocated on the basis of work-related need or contractual obligation, or purchased from the parking permit office. Separate permit programs were established for charter buses, limousines, hired cars, and private vehicles.

Permits were designed to allow access control personnel to identify and grant vehicular access to restricted roadways or to direct vehicles to the correct parking areas. Each permit had distinctive components that verified validity and identified access privileges: a logo, a venue identifier, a user-group identifier, and a date, when appropriate. Each permit also had three security features: a custom hologram, an imbedded design that could only be detected with special equipment, and a custom print design on the back of the permit. Most permits contained a temporary adhesive that allowed the permit to be transferred between vehicles; some permit types had a permanent adhesive that would cause the permit to be destroyed if removed.

The ACOG Parking Permit Program was managed from an office located in downtown Atlanta. Venue-specific, work-related permits were distributed through venue transportation managers. Daily permits were sold at the permit office and the Main Press Center (MPC).

Access to ACOG-operated parking areas was controlled through the ACOG Parking Permit Program, which used 15 different types of permits.

Special Services. Olympic Family members often had special transportation needs beyond traveling to and from venues and accommodation sites. Although not officially responsible for addressing these needs, the Olympic Family transportation system met such requests through the Special Services division.

Prior to the Games, Special Services created relationships with local and national transportation providers and tour operators and used these relationships to accomplish its Games-time role of acting as a transportation reservation and referral service for members of the Olympic Family. Special Services made reservations for motor coaches, limousines, passenger vans, and hired cars. Referrals were made for tour companies, car and helicopter rental, cargo transport, and any other type of transportation requested.

From 1 January to mid-July 1996, Gray Line of Atlanta supplied needed vehicles; from 13 July to 5 August 1996, Gray Line/Vancom was the primary provider of motor coach, limousine, and hired car service. Special Services also used several other local motor coach suppliers during the Games.

Special Services operated at the Olympic Family Hotel from 6 July through 5 August 1996. Requests for transportation were submitted by telephone or facsimile machine. Special Services had field operating areas, or load zones, south of the Olympic Family Hotel and east of the Olympic Village, with space for 20 buses. The most common requests were for transporting IOC members and spouses, the IOC Executive Board, patrons of the 1996 Olympic Games, and many delegations to events, hospitality functions, local attractions, restaurants, and meetings.

The largest effort coordinated by Special Services was transporting all Cultural Olympiad performers and athlete spectators to the Olympic Stadium and Olympic Center. Special Services also coordinated transportation for larger groups of Cultural Olympiad performers and all Southern Crossroads Festival artists to other venues.

Constituents

Each group served by the Olympic Family transportation system received a level of service that corresponded to its level of accreditation and determined transportation needs. These transportation services were in accordance with the standards established by the IOC and ACOG.

Athletes and Team Officials. The athlete transportation system (ATS) was designed to accommodate accredited athletes and team officials traveling to and from Villages, training and competition sites, and Opening and Closing Ceremonies in accordance with IOC guidelines. All athlete buses operated within Security guidelines and were staffed with Security personnel. Approximately 16,500 passengers used the ATS, including athletes, team officials, and extra team officials residing at the Atlanta University Center. The ATS served individuals with Aa (athletes), Ac (chefs de mission and attachés), Am (team medical officials), Ao (team officials), and As (extra team officials) accreditation.

The ATS operated according to a hub-and-spoke design, providing transportation service from the Village following a preestablished schedule. Village residents accessed the ATS at the Main Transportation Mall, a secured area adjacent to the Village with 20 sport-specific load zones. The athlete bus system maintained three types of sanctioned, complimentary bus services: dedicated team buses, sport-specific shuttles, and special event transportation to Opening and Closing Ceremonies and other sanctioned events. The Olympic Stadium shuttle was added after the Games began and operated at 30-minute intervals each day, beginning at 0800 and concluding at approximately 2300. An additional shuttle to the Olympic Center operated during a limited period of time.

Dedicated team bus transportation was provided for scheduled sessions of baseball, basketball, football, handball, hockey, modern pentathlon, softball, and volleyball. Requests for schedule variations were managed on an individual team basis.

Sport-specific transportation was also provided for scheduled sessions of archery, athletics, beach volleyball, canoe/kayak–sprint, cycling, equestrian, fencing, gymnastics, judo, rowing, shooting, table tennis, tennis, weightlifting, wrestling, and yachting. Buses arrived at the venue approximately 15 minutes prior to the scheduled start time for practice sessions. Services were equivalent to dedicated team transportation, but members of different NOCs shared buses, and athletes determined when they wished to travel based on published bus schedules. Service was provided at frequent intervals throughout each practice and competition session.

Daily transportation to the Village was available for the accredited extra team officials housed at the Atlanta University Center. Limited transportation was also available from the satellite Villages in Athens, Columbus, and Cleveland. Limited bus service was available for athletes visiting a competition as spectators, based on venue seating availability by sport discipline. Athlete spectators from the same sport were allowed to travel with competing athletes, except for team sports and those sports where the venue configurations did not allow athlete spectators easy access to their seating areas from the bus loading area, in which case transportation was not provided. Athlete accreditation badges determined rider eligibility. Athlete spectators with tickets utilized dedicated buses to the Georgia Dome and the Olympic Stadium venues. These operated on a continuous basis, beginning one hour prior to each scheduled competition session and continuing until one hour after each session. Athlete spectators attending other venues were directed to use the OSTS.

Upon returning to the Village after competition, training or spectating athletes and officials were unloaded from the bus at the same location where they had boarded. For Opening and Closing Ceremonies, buses were loaded at the residential zones instead of the Main Transportation Mall. Approximately 300 buses with 45-person seating capacities were utilized to transport participating athletes and officials between the Village and the Olympic Stadium.

Alternate transportation services were available from Special Services and through free access to public transportation services provided by MARTA. Limited motor pool service supported the athlete bus system.

Refer to the Olympic Villages chapter for information about the shuttle system that operated within the Atlanta Olympic Village.

Competition Officials. Approximately 2,200 officials, including judges, desk officials, starters, referees, and umpires, were provided transportation on the competition officials transportation system, which began when the officials' Villages opened. Scheduled service to venues started one day before the first day of a scheduled competition so that officials could orient themselves if they wished. In general, service began one hour before each competition session, and began departing from the venue 15–30 minutes after the completion of each competition session.

The system provided transportation for officials staying in ACOG-sanctioned Villages in Atlanta, Athens, Gainesville, and Savannah. Those staying at nonsanctioned locations drove to the appropriate athlete Village to access the transportation system.

Service was also provided for noncompetition events at which officials' attendance was required. This included transportation between

ACOG-sanctioned accommodations and the Opening Ceremony, mandatory meetings scheduled by IFs, competition venue training that required officials to be in attendance, and uniform distribution.

An additional transportation service, the Emory University tram system, was provided between accommodations, the cafeteria, and sports training sites on the Emory campus for competition officials housed there.

IOC/NOCs/IFs. Olympic Family members residing at the Olympic Family Hotel and Olympic Village—IOC, NOC, and IF members and guests—received transportation support through dedicated cars and resources, access to motor pool vehicles, and a motorcoach and shuttle bus service to the four venues described below.

Guest Services was responsible for organizing and implementing the dedicated driver program for those with T1 and T2 accreditation. Transportation supplied the vehicles and coordinated the routes. *(For more information, see the Event and Guest Services chapter.)* Motor pools provided transportation to all Olympic Family members with T1–T3 accreditation.

Olympic Village cars were assigned to NOC delegations through NOC Services. A certain number of cars in proportion to the size of the delegation was assigned to each NOC, and other requests were accumulated and managed by Fleet Operations.

Dedicated shuttle buses served guests between the Olympic Family Hotel and the Olympic Stadium, Georgia Tech, the Georgia World Congress Center, and the Georgia Dome. This service was available to every guest of the Olympic Family Hotel. Buses began departing from the hotel at 15-minute intervals two hours prior to an event, and the last bus departed from a venue two hours after an event's conclusion. This service was very convenient, as guests could access it at the door of the Olympic Family Hotel and the entrances to the venues.

Olympic Family transportation for the Opening and Closing Ceremonies was a separate effort. Buses were loaded by accreditation category and departed from hotels every few minutes. Approximately 100 motor coaches were used to transport Olympic Family members from the Olympic Family Hotel and four hub locations near other hotels in metro-Atlanta area to within 300 yards (274 m) of the stadium. An additional 10 motor coaches were used to transport IOC members from the Olympic Family Hotel to the Olympic Stadium. These buses made a single trip, escorted by police, and unloaded at the media entrance.

Media. The overall plan for transportation for the press was based on the requirements of the *Olympic Charter* and press colleagues. Dedicated, scheduled transportation was provided for three of the four members of the media population: Atlanta Olympic Broadcasting (AOB), press, and rights-holding broadcasters. Press covering the Cultural Olympiad were not included. Approximately 15,000 members of the media used the media transportation system during the Olympic Games.

Media transportation services—which were complimentary, except for parking—included:

■ arrival and departure services from the point of arrival to an accreditation center and then to ACOG-sanctioned accommodations in Atlanta, Athens, Columbus, Gainesville, and Ocoee, and return from ACOG-sanctioned housing to the point of departure;

■ shuttle service from a central facility—the Media Transportation Mall—to and from accommodations, competition venues except for those in Savannah and the football cities, the International Broadcast Center (IBC), MPC, and Olympic Village;

■ a pass providing free, unlimited travel on MARTA, the mass transit system that serves the Atlanta area;

■ parking at the MPC and the competition venues; and

■ bus service between Olympic Stadium and the Media Transportation Mall for Opening and Closing Ceremonies.

Members of the IOC, NOCs, and IFs with T1 and T2 accreditation received transportation support through Guest Services' Dedicated Driver Program.

The media bus system had a hub-and-spoke design, with the hub at the Media Transportation Mall located in downtown Atlanta, and the spokes including media accommodations, the IBC, MPC, Olympic Village, and competition venues. The Media Transportation Mall, located inside the Olympic Ring, was a well-lit, well-marked parking lot of 4 acres (1.6 ha) that served as a central bus depot.

Two shuttle services from the Media Transportation Mall—one to the IBC and one to the MPC—were designed to provide 24-hour service at five-minute intervals, matching the operating hours of the MPC and IBC. Between 2400 and 0600, less frequent service was planned. Service to the Olympic Village was scheduled at 30-minute intervals between 0900 and 2100 during the period of 6 July–4 August. After the Games began, direct shuttle service from the MPC to Olympic Stadium was added.

Members of the media system were provided regular transportation from the Media Transportation Mall to all competition venues in the Atlanta, Lake Lanier, Athens, Conyers, Wolf Creek, Atlanta Beach, and Stone Mountain areas. Media transportation to and from competition venues in the metro-Atlanta area began three days prior to the start of competition. Service began two hours prior to the first session and continued until two hours after completion of the last session. For Athens, Columbus, and Ocoee, limited service—which included three to four arrivals and departures per day—was provided. No direct transportation between competition venues was available. Transportation was provided to Opening and Closing Ceremonies for members of the media holding complimentary tickets and residing at Atlanta-area ACOG-sanctioned accommodations.

Individual routes serviced clusters of media hotels. Buses ran at least every 30 minutes from each location to the Media Transportation Mall,

with reduced service between 0200 and 0600. Direct service was provided from housing sites to venues where media were housed in remote locations, such as Athens and Gainesville, and shuttles going from the Media Transportation Mall to Athens, Atlanta Beach, Georgia International Horse Park, Lake Lanier, Stone Mountain, and Wolf Creek venues made one stop midroute at a housing cluster on the way to the venue.

Prior to the Games, 116 press agencies ordered 750 parking permits. An additional 70 permits were ordered during the Games. The demand was less than had been anticipated.

The services offered met the requirements established by the *Olympic Charter*; however, implementation was sometimes difficult. A contributing factor was the fairly wide dispersal of media housing—40 sites altogether—which resulted in 31 bus routes for housing. A further challenge was the location of the Media Transportation Mall. This facility was originally planned to be located within a short walk of the MPC, but the hub had to be relocated about .75 mi (1.2 km) away because of plans for the construction of Centennial Olympic Park.

Overall, the planned transportation services for the media met IOC requirements and previous standards. However, the services provided did not meet the proposed operational plans in terms of frequency and efficiency. Considerable improvement in these areas was achieved as the Games continued.

Staff. A basic level of service facilitated ACOG staff's transportation to work assignments. Most ACOG staff were issued a MARTA pass. Because MARTA-designated lots had a limited number of parking spaces, staff members were encouraged to carpool to the rail stations. They were conveyed to their venue destination by MARTA and/or a dedicated shuttle bus service provided by ACOG. While only limited staff parking was available at most competition sites, noncompetition and training sites offered enough on-site or nearby parking to allow staff to rely primarily on private transportation.

Staff with parking permits for lots either within walking distance to a venue or at a staff parking lot with shuttle service were encouraged to carpool to the lot with at least three other people in the car to ensure space availability.

For the Opening Ceremony, approximately 35 buses were used to transport staff and volunteers to the stadium. A parking lot 2 mi (3.2 km) away was also provided for staff and volunteers, along with a shuttle to the stadium.

Sponsors. All three categories of sponsors—The Olympic Programme (TOP), Centennial Olympic Games Partners (COP), and sponsor-level sponsors—were provided support for their self-operated transportation systems.

ACOG arranged for and provided on-site or nearby parking, parking permits, ground staff, limited routing service, and directional signs as assistance for sponsor guests. Ground personnel at boarding areas and shuttle locations coordinated bus activity at sponsor hospitality villages, which were located downtown, east of Atlanta–Fulton County Stadium and Olympic Stadium and west of Centennial Olympic Park, and at Stone Mountain Park, adjacent to the Tennis Center.

To facilitate the operation of sponsor transportation systems within the OTS, ACOG provided sponsors with route narratives from their hotels to all competition venues, as well as assistance in locating housing for drivers and overnight parking for their buses.

ACOG did not provide either buses or financial support for acquiring buses used by sponsors for transportation service. Sponsors controlled their buses with regard to scheduling, ground support, and communications. A few sponsor arrangements included a limited number of assigned fleet sedans.

OLYMPIC SPECTATOR TRANSPORTATION SYSTEM

Although limited spectator transportation support has been provided at past Games, ACOG's decision to take full responsibility for providing Games-time spectator transportation to all venues (except Columbus, Ocoee, and Savannah) was unprecedented. ACOG's aim was to facilitate easy access to venues for all Games participants and spectators. Furthermore, for spectators' convenience, ACOG implemented another unprecedented concept: including the expense of transportation in the price of a ticket.

One of the main considerations in planning the OSTS was spectator points of origin. Planners projected that 74 percent of Olympic spectator travel would originate from within the Atlanta area. Another 22 percent was expected to come from single-day automobile and charter bus trips from outlying hotels or residences, and 4 percent of incoming travel was expected from nearby general aviation facilities. In actuality, almost 35 percent of all spectator travel originated from outside the Atlanta area.

The following strategies were determined for conveying up to one million spectators each day: encourage walking, operate park-and-ride lots outside Atlanta's perimeter highway and shuttles to venues or MARTA rail stations, and use mass transit for spectator movement. OSTS planners therefore focused on encouraging the use of pedestrian corridors, temporary park-and-ride facilities, buses, and trains to accomplish these goals, with an extensive signage system in place to provide the necessary wayfinding.

Tram service for spectators was provided from designated parking lots to certain venues.

A contractual relationship was established with MARTA, Atlanta's publicly funded integrated bus and rail system comprised of approximately 750 buses, 200 rail cars, and 36 rail stations. The resultant agreement made MARTA a full partner in planning and operating the OSTS. The agreement detailed Olympic recognition and funding, outlined the responsibilities of both organizations, and affirmed that taxpayers would not pay for the extra services MARTA would provide during the Games.

MARTA Bus and Rail System

Mass transit plans included three principal elements: the existing MARTA bus system, the existing MARTA rail system, and a supplemental bus system, which operated only during the Games period.

The contract with MARTA stipulated that ACOG would provide resources for the supplemental bus system, would staff and operate parking lots, and would reimburse MARTA for direct incremental costs incurred in operating the expanded OSTS. MARTA's responsibilities included operating the existing MARTA system at an expanded level of service in accordance with Transportation operating plans, planning and supervising the operation of the supplemental bus system, providing transportation on any segment of the system for event ticket holders, and providing 150,000 Olympic Family MARTA passes. A later amendment to the contract stipulated that MARTA would ensure delivery and return, maintain the spectator and Olympic Family supplemental transit bus fleet, and train bus drivers for the spectator and Olympic Family systems.

MARTA's Existing Service. MARTA agreed to enhance its existing service during the Olympic Games period. Rail service was extended to 24 hours daily, three new rail stations and 7 mi (11 km) of additional rail were added, and system capacity was improved by increasing the

frequency of service and removing seats from each rail car to allow more standing area. Bus service was adapted by rerouting 17 existing bus routes around the Olympic Ring area, extending 28 key routes to 24-hour bus service, providing additional buses on 17 high-volume routes, and improving the level of service on all routes by providing a weekday service schedule.

Supplemental Bus System. A supplemental bus system supported the OSTS by providing transportation between Olympic park-and-ride

lots and MARTA rail stations or competition venues and between certain MARTA rail stations and venues. More than 1,400 transit buses were borrowed from more than 65 US transit agencies for use during the Olympic Games. The Federal Transit Administration, in conjunction with the US Department of Transportation, encouraged outside agencies to supply these buses, which were required to be air-conditioned and accessible to the physically disabled.

ACOG contracted with the transit agencies and managed related vehicle insurance issues. MARTA managed all Games maintenance needs, trained the drivers, and handled Games-time operations for the supplemental bus fleet. MARTA and ACOG coordinated the movement of buses into and out of Atlanta before and after the Games. Of the 1,400 buses borrowed from transit agencies, 910 were assigned to the OSTS, and the remainder were used to provide

left: Spectators could board buses to the venues at spectator load zones throughout the city.

right: A total of 1,290 buses supported the Olympic spectator transportation system during Games-time.

Olympic Family bus service. The majority of buses were diesel, although 102 were fueled by compressed natural gas.

Buses for the supplemental fleet were transported to Atlanta by a service contractor and began arriving in March 1996. Buses were initially received and an exterior Olympic bus wrap was applied at one of the temporary operating terminals, where the buses were held until just prior to the Games. Buses were then distributed to one of eight terminals in operation during the Games period. ACOG began re-

FIGURE 1: TOTAL RIDERS PER DAY ON THE OLYMPIC SPECTATOR TRANSPORTATION SYSTEM

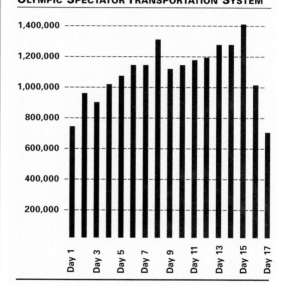

turning buses to transit agencies the week after the Games ended.

The hours of operation for the supplemental bus system were determined by the particular bus service. As a general rule, parking-to-venue and rail-to-venue service began two hours before the start time of the first event at a venue (three hours for venues inside the Olympic Ring) and concluded two hours after the last event of the day, or until all passengers

were cleared from the venue. Parking lots inside the Olympic Ring and at rail stations operated from 0500 to 0200.

Ridership and Usage. The MARTA rail and bus system recorded about 14.4 million one-way rides during the 17-day Games period, while the supplemental bus system reported slightly more than 3.8 million one-way trips during the same time. The peak requirement of loaned transit buses for the OSTS was 910 on 27 July (day 9). Approximately 223 buses from the supplemental bus fleet were used to transport athletes for the Paralympic Games held in Atlanta. (*Figure 1 shows daily ridership on the OSTS, portraying a steady increase that peaked on 2 August, when a total of 1.4 million passengers used the system.*)

In addition to the loaned transit bus fleet, MARTA used buses from its regular fleet to support the OSTS, with three shuttles from rail stations to venues. Depending on the day and competition events, the number of MARTA buses required varied daily, but peaked at 130 buses on day 9. To ensure that enough buses were available in the event of accidents, malfunctions, or unpredicted demand, extra buses from private charter services or school buses were obtained for peak demand days. (*Figure 2 shows the overall bus fleet requirements, which includes approximately 200 school buses used to support spectator transportation to Lake Lanier.*)

Olympic Transportation Accessibility

Transportation provided by the OTS met accessibility requirements under the Americans with Disabilities Act. MARTA rail stations were elevator-equipped, and all buses, including both those in the MARTA system and those brought in from other cities, had wheelchair lifts. At certain venues, however, an additional level of service, called the OTS van service, was provided because ACOG understood that people with disabilities would have difficulty getting from the transport drop zone to the venue entrance. These venues included: Alexander

FIGURE 2: BUS FLEET REQUIREMENTS FOR THE OLYMPIC SPECTATOR TRANSPORTATION SYSTEM

Vehicle source	Total fleet
Loaned transit buses	910
MARTA buses	130
Motorcoaches	50
School buses (including service to Lake Lanier)	200
Total	**1,290**

Memorial Coliseum, Atlanta–Fulton County Stadium, Atlanta University Center, Georgia Tech Aquatic Center, Lake Lanier, Olympic Stadium, Stone Mountain Park Archery Center and Velodrome, Stone Mountain Park Tennis Center, and Wolf Creek Shooting Complex. Service was provided from MARTA rail stations or parking lots near these venues to the competition sites.

A fleet of 35 ramp-equipped vans, each capable of accommodating three wheelchairs and seating three companions, were rented from a local provider for the 17-day Games period and a short pre-Games training and Olympic Family arrival period.

The Transportation Department operated the accessibility van service program throughout the Games. The fleet of vans was stored in a separate motor pool facility and staffed by the federally funded work group AmeriCorps. The staff consisted of 75–80 drivers and dispatchers, who were trained under a program developed by Project ACTION, a federally funded effort of the National Easter Seal Society. The training program included driver training, equipment operation, and sensitivity training.

Based on sales of accessible tickets at venues, a sufficient number of vans were dispatched to select MARTA rail stations, venues, and venue park-and-ride lots to provide continual shuttle service for two hours before and after each event.

Spectator Parking

For spectator parking, ACOG procured and operated approximately 80,000 parking spaces in 43 metro-Atlanta parking lots. Facilities were clustered where possible to make operation more efficient. The park-and-ride lots for spectators fell into one of three categories.

Suburban parking lots were established outside of the perimeter highway along the major roadways to the north, northeast, and northwest, and within the perimeter south of downtown Atlanta. Spectators parked at these lots and boarded shuttle buses for transport to either of the two major Olympic Ring venue clusters—the Olympic Center cluster (the Omni/Georgia Dome/GWCC) and the Olympic Stadium cluster (Olympic Stadium and Atlanta–Fulton County Stadium)—or to a MARTA rail station.

Parking lots established near MARTA rail stations where the anticipated parking volumes were larger than the station's parking lot capacity were called rail overflow lots. At these facilities, spectators and commuters parked and walked or boarded shuttle buses for transport to the MARTA rail system.

Parking lots located near non–Olympic Ring venues were called outlying venue lots. Spectators were transported by shuttle from lots near Athens, Atlanta Beach, Georgia International Horse Park, Lake Lanier, Ocoee River, and Stone Mountain Park to the venues. The Wolf Creek Shooting Complex and Stone Mountain Park Tennis Center were the only competition venues at which spectators could park and walk to the competition areas.

Spectators paid a small fee to use these lots. Most lots contained 400 or more spaces. Lots were paved or graveled, lighted, and staffed with law enforcement personnel or ACOG Security officers.

REGIONAL TRAFFIC MANAGEMENT SYSTEM

Traffic management plans were developed for the Olympic Ring, each outlying competition venue, and park-and-ride lot clusters. In developing each plan, ACOG coordinated with local law enforcement and governmental agencies.

The Atlanta Traffic Management Plan, released to the public in December 1995, encompassed areas within the Olympic Ring. The plan was the result of a collaborative effort chaired by the APD and involving ACOG, GSP, ARC, MARTA, and the Atlanta Public Works and Fire Departments. After closely analyzing the operating plans for the Olympic Games and other

An extensive signage system was established to provide necessary wayfinding for spectators.

Olympic-related events, as well as local traffic patterns, the agencies decided to implement a combination of several traffic restrictions. These restrictions included dedicated lanes for the OTS; part-time and full-time street, lane, and interstate ramp closures; and limited access to areas immediately surrounding Olympic venues. In total, more than 250 restrictions were implemented.

The majority of restrictions were put into effect early on 19 July 1996; a number of restrictions were implemented earlier, such as those on streets within the Atlanta Olympic Village, which were enforced as early as 15 June 1996.

Traffic restrictions were stricter and more pervasive the closer they were to a venue. This was especially true near the Olympic Center cluster, the Olympic Stadium cluster, the Atlanta Olympic Village, and the Atlanta University Center. Beginning in early 1996, the APD and ACOG utilized media releases, Neighborhood Planning Unit meetings, and community and business organization briefings to inform residents and businesses in the affected districts about access to those areas.

Similar but smaller traffic management plans were developed and implemented for all outlying competition venues and Olympic park-and-ride lots.

One of the biggest challenges of Olympic transportation planning was optimizing the roadway capacities in the Atlanta region to ensure that the Olympic Family systems, spectator system, and general public would be able to move throughout the area. To meet this need, ACOG created a transportation demand management (TDM) project, a goods movement plan, a public campaign, and a traffic management planning program.

Transportation Demand Management

The TDM project was tremendously successful and achieved its goal of a 20–25 percent reduction in normal traffic in downtown Atlanta during the Games. The program's message was for people who worked in the downtown area to adopt commuting strategies that enabled them to avoid driving to work, at least during the peak hours of 0730–0930 and 1630–1830. Business cooperation was overwhelming. In fact, the amount of work-related traffic in the downtown area was reduced by 50 percent on many days during the Games period.

Companies also cooperated by allowing employees to leave work by 1500 on the three days when Olympic crowds and OTS traffic were expected to be the heaviest. To gain this cooperation and advocate TDM strategies, the Transportation Department contacted more than 4,000 companies. TDM strategies included: encouraging employees to take vacations and participate in the Olympic experience; asking employees to work from home or other remote work locations; suggesting that employees carpool or vanpool and use the HOV lanes; and allowing employees to work flexible hours to avoid peak travel periods.

Information about how to develop a transportation management plan was sent to Atlanta-area employers. In addition, special presentations were made to companies with 1,000 or more employees in the downtown area. Ultimately, ACOG's efforts were integrated into those of the newly created Commute Connections Network, a group of government and private agencies formed to promote long-term TDM strategies.

Goods Movement Plan

The goods movement plan, which was used to advise the Atlanta business community on the most effective ways to ship and receive goods during the Games, provided required access for clients and suppliers to ship and receive goods, supply services, and maintain operations during the 1996 Olympic Games. The primary challenge was to facilitate the shipment and receipt of supplies required to sustain

In order to facilitate the Olympic Transportation System, ACOG devised traffic management plans and presented them to the Atlanta community.

• BETSY W FLEISIG • ALAN FLEMING • ALLISON FLEMING • ANNE F FLEMING • ANNE M FLEMING • BARBARA R FLEMING • BECKY P FLEMING • CAROL F FLEMING • CATHY L FLEMING • DORIS FLEMING • ERIC A FLEMING • INGRID R FLEMING • JOEL FLEMING • JOHN C FLEMING • JOHN C FLEMING • JOHN F FLEMING • JOYCE P FLEMING • KARIN E FLEMING • KATHLEEN S FLEMING • KIM FLEMING • LAMAR L FLEMING • LESLIE M FLEMING • MARY D FLEMING • MICHAEL L FLEMING • PAUL D FLEMING • POLLY V FLEMING • ROBERT J FLEMING • SARAH E FLEMING • SUSAN L FLEMING • SUSAN L FLEMING •

hotels, restaurants, and local businesses within the Olympic Ring. With major roadway restrictions during the day, most deliveries could be made only in the early morning hours. This required coordination and commitments from both shippers and receivers. Strategies such as stockpiling paper products before the Games and accepting deliveries between 2400 and 0600 were implemented in the central business district of Atlanta.

Public Campaign

The Transportation Department created an information dissemination program to ensure that the public understood the OSTS through regularly updated information. The program prepared residents for the Games by encouraging use of the HOV lanes, carpooling, and mass transit before the Games began and emphasized that the OTS would ensure that spectators would be transported to and from competition venues as smoothly as possible while minimizing the impact on daily life.

Various methods were used to communicate these messages: an ACOG Transportation Public Information Line with information regarding spectator transportation, park-and-ride lots, staff transportation, riding bicycles as a means of transport during the Games, and how Atlanta-area businesses could obtain more information on commuting options; major local media sources; a message to the general public on the Internet; and spectator mailings and other marketing efforts.

Publications distributed to spectators and other groups to convey these messages included: a 32-page phone book insert; the *Guide to the 1996 Olympic Games*; internal publications, including employee handbooks and route manuals, a Special Services packet for charter bus operators and taxi and limousine drivers, and transportation guides for athletes, media, and competition officials; an OTS brochure and special editions of *MARTA* magazine; an OTS van service brochure that detailed service for spectators with physical disabilities;

and a TDM poster, brochure, and information packet for employers.

The local print and broadcast media assisted the Transportation Department with communicating the following primary messages to spectators and the general public:

■ the expansion of MARTA's bus and rail system, coupled with the OTS park-and-ride shuttle system, would provide the most efficient way for spectators and the general public to travel during the 1996 Olympic Games;

■ the Olympic Ring and outlying venue traffic circulation plans were designed to provide safe and efficient traffic flow in and around venue areas for the public, spectators, and the Olympic Family with minimal restrictions; and

■ the goods movement plan would provide the necessary access for local businesses to maintain operations during the 1996 Olympic Games.

These messages were communicated by the media through regular releases and traffic circulation plan updates sent to local newspapers and television and radio stations. Articles appeared in MARTA publications and business, community, and government publications, as well as visitors center, chamber of commerce, and convention bureau publications.

During the Games, information about transportation was distributed to the media through interviews granted by the department director or department media relations specialist; through daily transportation updates distributed to WGST-Radio and NBC affiliate WXIA-TV, the local news outlets for the Games, as well as the Internet; and through news stories broadcast through Info'96.

Games-time media relations were coordinated by the liaison between the Transportation and Communications Departments and by the Atlanta Olympic News Agency, operated by ACOG Communications.

Transportation publications and graphics were handled by the Transportation publications and graphics groups, with production support provided by ACOG Creative Services.

The overall communication of the department's messages through Olympic Family and spectator publications and local, regional, and national media was extremely comprehensive and an important factor in the success of the OTS.

The efforts of ACOG's Transportation Department and the government agencies that worked with it created a legacy which will continue to benefit the city and entire region by changing regional travel behavior. For example, more people began utilizing TDM strategies such as carpooling, flextime working hours, telecommuting, and utilizing MARTA rail and bus systems. Existing key roads, intersections, and bridges were improved, and new ones were developed. Scheduled regional infrastructure projects, such as ATMS, were enhanced to coordinate traffic signals and communicate real-time accident information and alternative routes to motorists. HOV lanes were created on the interstate highways approaching the city. Pedestrian corridors were developed, and freeways were attractively landscaped. Better interagency communication and coordination enhanced by technology links were established, enabling the improvements begun in preparation for the Games to continue.

Sign Program

A committee comprised of representatives from MARTA, ACOG, the Georgia DOT, the city of Atlanta, and the Corporation for Olympic Development in Atlanta (CODA) determined the appropriate types and quantities of signage needed to support the OTS. The committee's mission was to design, locate, and install a seamless system of pedestrian and vehicular signs to direct spectators and Olympic Family members to competition and noncompetition venues throughout the region.

Upon completion of the study, a design was selected and used by each agency in producing signs for its particular jurisdiction. This consistency of design enabled all travelers to identify

Olympic travel directions among the other informational signs that existed throughout the region.

Transportation worked with the Look of the Games team and selected a format of blue and white with the Olympic logo in gold and green. This design format was used for signs on freeways, arterial streets, in parking lots, and along the MARTA rail system. Vehicular directional signs were produced exclusively in English, while pedestrian signs were produced in both English and French.

Signs were placed at venues to guide Olympic Family bus and motor pool drivers to their destination. These signs had a design and color coding that was exclusive to the constituency. For example, all signs for the athlete transportation system were colored with the ACOG signature color—Georgia Green. Each constituency color was used consistently in the Transportation Guides—received by athletes, media, and competition officials—and in signs placed in the windows of Olympic Games buses. All ACOG-operated facilities, including the Airport Welcome Center (AWC), noncompetition venues, and parking lots, as well as Hartsfield International Airport received additional signage to direct both vehicular and pedestrian traffic. Some Olympic Family transportation signs, including bus placards for athletes, officials, and the media, were produced in English and French.

Approximately 6,000 signs were created for the OSTS, and 3,000 were created for the Olympic Family transportation system. In some cases, spectator signage was installed by ACOG, and in others, by state or local government.

At the end of the Games, the spectator transportation signs were returned to the Georgia DOT to be auctioned or reused with new sign

top: **Buses were dressed with the Look of the Games.**

bottom: **This design format was used for signs on freeways, arterial streets, in parking lots, and along the MARTA system.**

DIANA J FLICEK • DAVID R FLICK • KEN FLICKINGER • ERIC M FLICKINGER ATC • LORI B FLIEGELMAN • JONATHON FLIGG • MICHAEL G FLIGG • MAXINE D FLINT • TONY C FLIPPO • CALLIE L FLIPSE • MARY P FLISTER • LESLIE FLO • JEFFREY J FLOAT • STEVEN J FLOERSHEIM • LESTER A FLOHR • BETHANY J FLOOD • JUDITH A FLOOD • KATHY M FLOOD • MARGI G FLOOD • MAUREEN A FLOOD • KATHERINE A FLOR • PATRICIA A FLORA • BARBARA B FLORENCE • BARBARA J FLORENCE • DEBORAH FLORENCE • DWAYNE D FLORENCE • JAMES FLORENCE • LACHANDA FLORENCE •

copy. Olympic Family transportation system signs were returned to the ACOG warehouse for storage until they were auctioned to the public.

GAMES-TIME OPERATIONS

Numerous resources contributed to the effective management of Games-time transportation needs, which benefitted the overall Transportation program.

Staffing

The Transportation Department's Games-time staff consisted of approximately 15,500 paid employees, volunteers, and contractors—more than 6,000 of whom were volunteers. Coordination for the processing and assignment of all staff and volunteers was managed by Transportation staffing operations, a group of 10 people.

The ACOG Human Resources Department was initially solely responsible for recruiting all Transportation contract employees, a requirement of almost 10,000. As the recruitment program progressed, ACOG contracted with a temporary staffing company to recruit, process, and pay approximately 9,000 of these contract employees, more than 2,000 of whom were bus drivers.

The challenge of hiring, processing, and fulfilling payroll obligations for so many people, most of whom were hired after 1 January 1996, was immense. Processing the many newly hired personnel was a lengthy and complicated procedure.

Volunteers represented approximately 40 percent of the total labor force to support Transportation operations. Most volunteers were assigned to competition and noncompetition venues, including the Main Transportation Mall, and to Fleet Operations as transportation specialists and drivers.

The majority of the transportation specialists and fleet drivers needed were recruited between 1 January and 1 July 1996. Transportation specialists performed one of several duties in a transportation system, including permit and access control, bus loading, and volunteer coordination. Fleet drivers provided Games-time transportation for Olympic Family members in sedans and minivans.

Two systems were used to schedule staff—one for bus drivers and one for other personnel. Approximately 350,000 meals were prepared for Transportation staff, a number that proved to be excessive. Eleven staff housing sites with 388 beds were established by Transportation staffing. A total of 283 people were housed in these facilities.

About 80 percent of Transportation staff received ACOG accreditation. The remaining staff members worked in areas where accreditation badges were not necessary and were given generic tags that only allowed them access to necessary facilities. Each program manager had the opportunity to review and define access privileges for each position. During the busiest days of accreditation, Transportation established help desks at the main accreditation center. These desks were staffed by as many as 10 people at a time, and proved to be vital in overcoming accreditation challenges resulting from late hires.

It was intended that every Transportation staff member would be trained for his or her Games-time position. Many volunteers had already worked for Transportation at a number of test events and were well trained and comfortable in the field by Games-time.

Bus driver training was conducted through a company with experience training both school and transit bus drivers. All bus drivers were required to complete 40 hours of training—20 in the classroom and 20 in the vehicle. Maps and routes were developed and disseminated

Buses, shuttles, and dedicated cars and drivers provided Olympic Family members with arrival and departure service between Hartsfield Atlanta International Airport and ACOG-sanctioned accommodations.

through the Transportation Department to all drivers as a part of their training. Fleet drivers also had vehicular training to become acquainted with the vehicles and routes for which they were responsible. The challenge was in training staff who arrived at Games-time and did not have sufficient time to become familiar with the changing routes.

Command Centers

While Transportation operations for the 1996 Olympic Games were primarily decentralized, control lay in three command centers: the ACOG operations center, transportation operations 1, and transportation operations 2. Assignment of Transportation staff to three control centers was deemed necessary as ACOG Transportation coordinated the different systems, but the roadways themselves were controlled by the Georgia DOT (interstate and regional roadways) and APD (surface streets). Executive management for overall transportation and venue transportation had a presence in these centers at all times throughout the Games period.

In the ACOG operations center, Transportation executive management and venue management were part of the Games main operations center and were present 24 hours daily.

Transportation operations 1 was located at the Georgia DOT's management center (TMC), a newly constructed facility designed to accommodate the large number of people necessary to manage Georgia's transportation network during almost any type of emergency or special event. The TMC was headquarters for the newly installed ATMS—a state-of-the-art system designed to monitor, analyze, and help manage real-time traffic issues on regional interstate highways and surface streets by the use of surveillance cameras and other technology. Additionally, ATMS transportation control centers in five adjacent counties, the Atlanta Public Works Department, the APD, and MARTA

were electronically linked to the TMC through ATMS workstations and had real-time data sharing.

The TMC facilitated the coordination and cooperation with other agencies necessary for a seamless transportation network across multiple jurisdictions. The TMC was adjacent to the headquarters of the Georgia Emergency Management Agency (GEMA), which was the Games-time home of the State Olympic Law Enforcement Command (SOLEC), a state command center for the GSP, the National Guard, and other state agencies. ACOG's presence in the TMC enabled ACOG Transportation to work directly and continuously throughout the Games with the Georgia DOT and the other agencies housed there.

Transportation operations 2 was located in the City Hall East building that served as the headquarters for the APD's Agency Command Center. Representatives from state and federal enforcement agencies and ACOG Transportation staffed the operations center 20–24 hours daily throughout the Games period. Transportation operations 2 provided continuous and direct contact with enforcement agencies responsible for controlling traffic and pedestrian movement on all city streets.

All three operations centers were linked by the ATMS and telecommunications, enabling the Transportation representatives in these centers to view the same roads, intersections, and venues simultaneously, and to make decisions based on their expertise and direct impression of a situation.

Venue Transportation Management

All Atlanta competition and noncompetition venues required intensive individual planning. In fall 1994, Transportation assembled a group to create a venue transportation management structure. This group also took responsibility for implementation of the structure.

The Venue Transportation Management division was staffed with regional venue transportation managers (RVTMs) as well as venue transportation managers (VTMs). RVTMs coordinated all Transportation services at a region of venues or venue cluster (e.g., the Stadia Region included the competition and noncompetition venues of Olympic Stadium, Atlanta–Fulton County Stadium, Cheney Stadium, and the sponsor hospitality village), while a VTM coordinated with each Venue Management team to facilitate Transportation operations at a specific venue.

The RVTM and VTM were responsible for coordinating transportation at the venue level with regard to the Olympic Family bus system, Fleet Operations, parking, OSTS, and traffic management. They had to create a plan that coordinated pedestrian flow planning, on-site and nearby venue-based vehicle parking, OSTS access and flow, Olympic Family drop-off and pick-up procedures, Olympic Family transportation system operations, charter bus operations, security interface, and access control. Each venue required a carefully crafted plan that would facilitate each of these activities while not impinging on the general venue operations. Plans also had to take into account the activities of other functional areas, such as waste removal and broadcast production.

Due to the close proximity of most venues, which could result in severe traffic congestion, coordination with adjacent or nearby venues was a major challenge. The VTMs addressed these challenges as they compiled the Venue Transportation Management Operations Manual.

The VTMs were also responsible for managing the implementation of any temporary or permanent transportation-related design changes at the venue. In many cases, owners of lots or roadways required that these temporary adjustments be removed after the Games with restoration to the pre-Games configuration.

Transportation staff from the Olympic Family transportation system, bus and motor pool, parking, and the OSTS were given venue-specific training and were managed during Games-time by the VTM. At the venues, the VTMs ensured that all furniture, fixtures, and equipment required for Transportation operations at the venue were ordered and prepared for Games-time and returned following activity at the venue.

The VTMs also educated other functional areas on how Transportation would operate at a specific venue and coordinated with other functional areas to ensure that any plans would not adversely affect transportation activities at the venue level.

Airport Operations

Transportation's Airport Operations provided an arrival and departure bus system and baggage operations for the Olympic Family. Upon arrival, buses transported Olympic Family members from Hartsfield Atlanta International Airport to the AWC, and then to ACOG-sanctioned accommodations, including the Atlanta Olympic Village. Challenges faced in the arrival and baggage operations systems, due largely to unscheduled arrivals from various places, were overcome after two days of operation.

Departure shuttles ran from ACOG-sanctioned accommodations to the airport approximately every three hours starting at 0300, and more frequently during peak departure days. These services were available from 1 July through the Games period. Transportation was also provided for Olympic Family members arriving at the Savannah airport. Coordination with the NOCs regarding planning and details of Olympic Family arrival and departure schedules was facilitated by the Olympic Family and Protocol Department.

Dedicated cars and drivers, as part of Guest Services, also provided arrival and departure services to and from the airport. For sponsor guests, Transportation only provided services from Hartsfield International Airport to the AWC.

Resources

The Resources division of Transportation provided logistics functions specifically for the Transportation Department. As such, this group supported the identification, requisition, acquisition, distribution, arrangement, and recovery of all vehicles, furniture, fixtures, and equipment needed to support ACOG Transportation systems.

Traffic control devices, tents, trailers, support equipment, and many other assets were under this group's control. To track and coordinate the needs of the department, Resources created and maintained databases on resource/catalog items and venue-by-venue addresses, layouts, and building requirements for 150 locations. Also prior to the Games, Resources tracked the ongoing improvements of sites, which ensured that these sites were prepared on all levels.

Resources was responsible for providing all equipment to entire transportation venues, requiring distribution to 150 locations over several weeks. Immediately following the Games, all resources from these locations were required to be recovered within a few days, creating a significant challenge to ensure that the resources were not lost or stolen. Extensive recovery planning with the Logistics Department was required to help reduce the number of resources stolen from venues and parking lots after the Games.

The Games-time logistics plan was such that every Transportation location was directed by a venue logistics manager based at a specific competition venue or cluster. Having identified the resource requirements at all locations, the Resources group would then contract and coordinate the installation of tents, trailers, portable toilets, storage facilities, support lighting, and trash containers. Resources also identified the requirements for traffic control devices and engaged the Georgia DOT to provide those devices (21,000 cones, 690 water barricades, and 400 barrels). Resources contracted for the installation, tracking, and removal of the above, 2,000 additional cones, and 4,000 ft (1,219 m) of concrete barricades. The group obtained 200 water barricades from the city of Atlanta.

Resources' Games-time role was to support the Logistics Department by providing the daily resupply of Transportation-specific property: flags, vests, flashlights, flares, food, and beverages. To fulfill this role, Resources maintained warehouse operations from a designated section of the Logistics warehouse. During the Games period, the Resources group continuously reevaluated resource needs, based on changing demands of the venue and venue users; as a result, the group was continuously redistributing resources to operating components of Transportation. The Resources group monitored the needs of other ACOG functional areas and controlled the distribution of resources.

After the Games, Resources was responsible for facilitating the recovery of ACOG assets that were utilized by Transportation and monitoring the return of these resources to sponsors or to ACOG warehouses. Resources had a post-Games staff of 20 people. Fleet Operations, the Olympic Family bus system, and the Logistics Department also initiated recovery efforts; the coordination of these efforts facilitated the prompt recovery of assets.

Fleet Operations. The department's Fleet Operations division managed all ACOG light vehicles such as automobiles, light trucks, motorcycles, sport utility vehicles, and vans. Responsibilities involved handling manufacturer/dealer relations; vehicle delivery, inventory, distribution, and return; and driver recruitment, training, and supervision. Reception, maintenance, and return of sponsor-provided vehicles was handled by this division. Most vehicle shipments were received first by the respective dealerships and then transported individually by staff and volunteers to Fleet Operations.

This division also developed and managed the motor pools to transport individuals with proper accreditation. All motor pool facilities required office space and parking. Most of the venue motor pools were allocated space at the venues. Facilities to support residential motor pools, however, had to be arranged for and leased separately.

During Games-time, five Olympic sponsors enabled Fleet Operations to acquire, fuel, and provide necessary maintenance for 1,185 assigned-driver vehicles, 1,230 Olympic Family motor pool vehicles, and 1,835 ACOG staff vehicles. General Motors, BMW, and Nissan provided ACOG with these cars for a set number of car months, defined as 30 days of car usage. The 712 BMW, GM, and Nissan vehicles utilized in the 14 motor pools were sufficient to service clientele.

Texaco USA provided both fuel and general maintenance for ACOG vehicles. Fleet Operations designated specific Texaco gasoline and service stations near competition venues and major highways that could be used by any official ACOG vehicle. Texaco issued credit cards for the sponsor-loaned vehicles, which allowed the drivers to refill with gasoline at the designated stations. A total of 2.55 million mi (4.1 million km) were driven by sponsor-loaned cars during Games-time.

The American Gas Association (AGA) provided ACOG with both cars, vans, trucks, and buses powered by natural gas as well as the natural gas required to fuel these vehicles. Additionally, they provided fuel for the transit buses powered by natural gas loaned to ACOG by transit agencies. AGA provided ACOG with credit cards that allowed the drivers of AGA-supplied cars to refill the gas tanks at natural gas facilities.

Beginning in June 1995, Fleet Operations distributed approximately 100 vehicles to ACOG staff members, primarily in Transportation, Logistics, and Security, with approximately 30 vehicles maintained in a motor pool available to visiting media, sponsors, and special guests. From 1 July to 15 July, the fleet had 650 vehicles in operation.

In the case of vehicle damage, an incident report was completed by the driver and forwarded to ACOG's Risk Management division. A copy of the estimate was retained and forwarded to the manufacturer for disclosure purposes. Mechanical difficulties were handled by each manufacturer's specific warranty program. Broken windows and damaged tires were replaced by outside vendors. General maintenance of sponsor vehicles was supplied through certified vendors.

During the vehicle-recovery period after the Games, Fleet Operations received cars at a staging area. Vehicles not returned to the staging area by a requested date were actively sought and repossessed by Fleet Operations staff. Vehicles were grouped by make and model to await disposition to their respective dealerships.

Volunteer recruitment and coordination for Fleet Operations was accomplished by a staff of 10 people. By Games-time, Fleet Operations had a staff of approximately 4,600 people. Most of these individuals were volunteers who served as motor pool drivers, assigned drivers, or volunteer coordination staff; a number of these volunteers were reassigned to other programs. Assigned drivers transported certain Olympic Family members and special guests, including corporate sponsors and technical delegates.

Transit Buses. Five operating facilities were established to maintain and dispatch buses as supplemental buses in the OSTS, and an additional three garages were established for the Olympic Family transportation system. Two of these were existing MARTA facilities, while the others were temporary facilities.

Regular daily maintenance of buses was performed at each of the operating terminals. Maintenance operations were provided by MARTA's maintenance division. Typical daily maintenance operations included refueling and washing buses and checking engine fluids and tire pressure. Repairs could be performed on buses if the necessary parts and tools were available at the operating terminal. An estimate of bus mileage showed that each borrowed bus was driven an average of 4,200 mi (6,760 km) during Games-time.

Texaco provided diesel fuel for buses. OSTS buses were fueled at each terminal from aboveground diesel fueling stations, eliminating the need for mobile fueling trucks except to replenish the supplies in the fueling stations. The compressed natural gas buses were fueled at an existing MARTA facility, where the compressed natural gas fueling station was operated and maintained by the Atlanta Gas Light Company.

Technology. The Transportation technology systems group was responsible for the planning, distribution, control, and recovery of all types of technology used by Transportation staff. From 1994 until June 1996, the group determined the technology needs of the department, including both the types and numbers of technology equipment that would be needed for each functional area to effectively operate during the Games. Types of technology included cellular phones, computer printers, computer workstations, copy machines, facsimile machines, Info'96 terminals, pagers, radios, stationary phones, televisions, and videocassette recorders.

Prior to the actual Games-time use of technology, the Transportation Department performed a systems acceptance test of the Motorola six-site simulcast radio system. By initiating this test, thereby necessitating the early distribution and trial of equipment, the Transportation Department maintained the schedule for the Games-time distribution of 4,300 radios to 237 separate locations and nearly 2,600 vehicles. Other communication devices, such as pagers and cellular telephones, were distributed at the same time. Technology was provided to support the Olympic Family transportation system and OSTS, 31 competition venues, 47 noncompetition venues (including the Olympic Village, accommodations, and training venues), 14 bus terminals and holding lots, 14 motor pools, 54 park-and-ride lots, 110 venue-associated parking lots, and 11 separate Transportation operations and management centers.

Personal computers used during the Games were moved from pre-Games office spaces to operational locations. Television sets and video recorders, generally used in bus terminal and motor pool drivers' lounges, were issued from a central warehouse location. Copiers and facsimile machines were delivered from a central warehouse and installed by Xerox. Telephone sets were delivered and installed by sponsor installation crews, usually the day before a site was scheduled to become operational.

By 19 July, all Transportation technology systems were distributed and functional with the exception of telephones at all eight park-and-ride operations centers. Cellular telephones were used during this period.

Minor radio maintenance was needed during the first week of operations. Common problems were broken cable connectors and careless handling of radios. Motorola corrected the problems on-site within 24 hours.

Radios were redistributed among competition venues during the Games period, as the need for this equipment increased at some venues and decreased at others in accordance with the competition schedule. Each competition venue was initially allocated 6–10 radios for preparation and closure operations.

Recovery of Transportation technology systems occurred between 5 and 31 August. The department experienced some delay in the recovery process because of the need to support airport departures and Paralympic operations. When all operations of the OTS and the Paralympic Games concluded, technology equipment was returned.

Conclusions and Recommendations

For the first time in Olympic history, an organizing committee was responsible for spectator transportation during the Games period. This decision, based on research of demand and the existing infrastructure and resources, proved extremely challenging. A comprehensive system to provide safe, convenient, efficient transportation for the Olympic Family, spectators, and the general public was a critical function and should be recognized as such through the dedication of resources to support it. Because of the nature of transportation, Games-time requirements often cannot be accurately assessed until late in the development of the overall project, and the vast number of staff required may not be available until Games-time, which can lead to challenges in delivering a successful program. The following recommendations are offered to future organizing committees.

■ Establish general service levels early in a well-written mission statement. Set realistic expectations with comprehensive communication to the various constituency groups.

■ The extended operational period must be recognized in the financial and logistical planning of the program, including food services, land management, staffing, accreditation, technology requirements, and general planning.

■ Include transportation planning and management in venue selection and contract negotiation. Though the concentration of venues facilitates pedestrian movement from one venue to another, it may cause significant general transportation congestion. Additionally, fewer, larger parking lots are preferable to many small lots, as this conserves valuable resources such as buses, staff, and equipment.

■ Identify resource requirements early and ensure that there is a software tracking system for resources—such as automobiles, buses, radios, and pagers—so that people using them can be held accountable for damage or loss.

■ Consider land acquisition early. Any early acquisitions that are not needed can be easily disposed of or converted into a revenue-generating opportunity.

■ Use a temporary staffing agency to hire the large number of drivers required for an event of this magnitude and accomplish hiring early enough to provide proper training.

■ Include a comprehensive transportation program for athletes visiting competition venues as spectators.

■ Situate the media transportation hub immediately adjacent to the MPC.

■ Future groups responsible for developing routes are encouraged to conduct extensive communication with the law enforcement agencies that provide access control.

■ Coordinated and committed standards of service by law enforcement must be provided by the local agencies with legal jurisdiction.

■ Create realistic time lines for the recovery of assets and provide the proper resources and controls to ensure success.

Atlanta 1996®

CHAPTER TWENTY-SEVEN
VENUE MANAGEMENT

OVERVIEW—Staging an international event of the magnitude of the 1996 Centennial Olympic Games successfully required very detailed planning and managing of operations from the smallest venue to crowd management services for cluster venues that might contain 500,000 people at one time. To integrate the planning of all functional areas and manage the competition venues, ACOG established the Venue Planning and Management Department (hereafter referred to as Venue Management) in 1992. Venue Management's first objective was to establish the organizational structure of venue-based teams to plan and manage all competition venues following standardized policies and procedures.

The team concept, known as integrated operations, was an essential approach based on the fact that each activity or occurrence at a venue was likely to have an effect on the operations of more than one functional area. Thus, no functional area could create and implement its plans in isolation. Among the most challenging tasks facing Venue Management was the creation of these teams by combining the many ACOG functional areas, each with its own distinct set of requirements and constituencies to serve.

Venue Management's second objective was to design and set management standards so that each competition venue would be as self-sustaining as possible. The team responsible for managing a venue would be vested with the authority to operate its own site, while depending on other resources for equipment, personnel, and in certain situations, decision making.

To allow venue staffs to operate autonomously during the Games, Venue Management had to develop all central policies and necessary procedures as well as ensure that staff members knew and understood the policies and procedures to promote consistency, fiscal responsibility, and adherence to the laws, regulations, and rules to which ACOG was bound.

The mission to present venues that were world-class competition sites in look and layout, functionality and efficiency, and the enthusiasm they helped inspire in athletes, officials, and spectators was fully accomplished. Throughout the 1996 Games, praise for the venues and the Olympic experience—expressed by thousands of athletes, broadcasters, and journalists and millions of spectators—testified to Venue Management's contribution to the advancement of Olympic ideals.

ORGANIZATION

From 1992 to 1994, the Venue Management team was a division of the Operations Department. Its function was primarily to identify pertinent issues of both permanent and temporary venues which required discussions with representatives of all functional areas to review both the construction and operational plans. Benefits of these meetings included the common understanding of issues to be addressed and the development of cross-functional relationships.

ACOG representatives visiting the 1992 Olympic Games in Barcelona collected information concerning competition venue management and operation to provide the framework for ACOG's organization-wide planning meetings. A continual review of the preliminary policies and operating procedures being developed by the functional areas identified many operational requirements still to be addressed to help ensure a consistent approach to issues, to resolve differences, and to eliminate overlapping responsibilities.

In early 1993, the first venue planning managers were hired. They began creating a database to record for each venue all contractual commitments and other requirements of venue owners, the IFs, Olympic Family members, sponsors, broadcasters and press, and other constituent groups. Development of this database included reviewing construction plans for both new facilities and adaptation of existing facilities.

While venue planning managers made constant revisions as the specific needs of each venue became clearer, Construction proceeded to build new facilities to ensure that completion deadlines would be met and budget goals would not be exceeded; the result was, however, that all operational needs were not, from a major special-event perspective, being addressed on as timely a basis as possible.

A further challenge came in designing new facilities primarily for use after the Games, rather than for their Games-time purpose. This approach offered many benefits, especially in terms of the legacy provided for the city of Atlanta, the state of Georgia, and various educational institutions that would assume ownership of facilities, but it would require alterations and adaptations in the months immediately prior to the Games.

Staffing for Venue Management began to expand significantly in 1994—the same year the function was moved from Operations to become a separate department reporting directly to the COO. The shift reflected Venue Management's assumption of the responsibility for coordinating all ACOG functional areas, vendors, contractors, public safety officials, and venue owners to work as a team within the venues. A new director experienced in event management was hired and subsequently named managing director of Venue Management.

During the 18 months prior to the Games, Venue Management met with staff from various functional areas to develop and build support for the documentation that would determine how the venues would operate. Staff was hired and trained for the management teams for each competition venue. Numerous contracts and site plans were analyzed to determine the physical layout and composition of each venue and the final adaptations necessary for the Olympic Games.

The objectives of the department focused on evaluating existing site plans and developing coordinated operational plans, teams, and training for management of the competition venues with a major special-event focus.

To address site planning, Venue Management concentrated on the functional areas that would have the greatest requirements and impact at the venues, such as Sports, Technology, and Logistics, and examined their plans together with those of Construction.

A comprehensive review of all work on operational plans to date was begun, and the completion and refinement of the plans became a priority.

Preparation for test events, which would begin in late spring 1995, served to force greater integration of plans and to focus on

MARK A FORNWALT • ROBIN D FORNWALT • JUDY A FORRER • DAWN D FORREST • MARKY W FORREST • MICHAEL W FORREST • THOMAS FORREST • EDWARD J FORREST JR • AMY V FORRESTAL • J DANIEL FORRESTAL • JON D FORRESTER • PAMELA G FORRESTER • WILLIAM A FORRESTER JR • NATHAN W FORRISTER • ANDREA L FORS • MAUREEN R FORS • ASA M FORSGREN • MARTHA L FORSS • RICHARD ELLIOTT FORSTALL • GREGORY W FORSTER • KAREN L FORSTER • LISA FORSTER • MARGARET M FORSTER • MICHAEL R FORSTER • ROBIN F FORSTON • ALAN R FORSYTH • PATRICIA C FORSYTH

525

identifying and resolving redundancies and gaps that existed among the functional areas.

In addition to site planning and operations coordination, Venue Management also began to develop plans for event services, such as crowd management, constituency needs, and safety issues. The department first worked with Security for ushers and ticket-takers and Food and Beverage for delivery of water during hot weather and later assumed full responsibility for both planning and implementing these activities.

Functional area planning within a venue site was coordinated and communicated by Venue Management staff.

To communicate the confirmation of decisions and policies, Venue Management developed detailed manuals, schedules, and plans. These most critical tools for guiding the preparation and implementation of venue sites and operations are included in the sections that follow.

INTEGRATED SITE PLANNING

A central factor in Atlanta's being awarded the 1996 Olympic Games was the existence of numerous facilities that could be easily adapted to host various competitions. However, Atlanta's Bid also reflected the fact that a comprehensive construction program would be required to ensure the availability of all needed venues.

Construction projects were developed in different ways: some were funded and built solely by ACOG; some were ACOG-funded but built by other groups; others were built by ACOG with some funding and direction from outside sources that occasionally had conflicting interests; other projects were built without any funding from ACOG. Some projects were entirely temporary, while others were semipermanent. Indeed, virtually every venue presented a unique set of variables.

In 1993, the venue planning managers began refining the construction programming and planning documents (greenbooks) and detailing spaces for spectator flow, service corridors, and ingress and egress. *(For details about construction programming and planning see the Construction chapter.)*

As the importance of detailed site planning became prominent in ACOG's preparations, a site management team of architect consultants was contracted to augment Venue Management. The venue site requirements of each functional area were coordinated and confirmed through planning sessions known as interactive planning process sessions (IPP 1 and IPP 2). The results of these sessions were reflected in the documentation of needed resources, such as power, signage, tents, trailers, and water on each individual venue site plan. One result of the IPP sessions was the understanding of the need for accurate computer-assisted design (CAD) drawings of venues. *(For more details, see the Technology chapter.)*

A venue site plan showed how all space would be utilized. It included everything from temporary structures and adaptations to utilities—essential for designers to prepare permit requests—to signage and areas for spectator queuing and flow. More than any other planning document, the venue site plan needed constant revision, with the latest version made available to Construction, Logistics, Technology, and other departments responsible for venue infrastructure. CAD drawings were used for the documents; however, the number of venues and multiplicity of changes made it extremely difficult to keep CAD production completely current. Inconsistencies in the development of the drawings led to the transfer of venue CAD responsibility to Venue Management in January 1996. In late spring 1996, most changes were being implemented manually, emphasizing the importance of maintaining constant communication through meetings and other exchanges.

Developed in the fourth quarter of 1995, venue program checklists displayed every requirement of the two dozen programs and functional areas that would be implemented at a venue in terms of where they would be located; what facilities, furniture, equipment, and technology would be needed to support them; and how the facility would have to be adapted structurally for Olympic use. The checklists identified all requirements as well as operational issues that needed to be addressed and revealed any discrepancies in the needs already submitted by functional areas.

An adaptation schedule for each venue was created to integrate the plans, requirements, and deadlines of the venue owner, the Construction Department, each functional area, sponsors, and vendors. With the help of this time line, the site manager could effectively track temporary construction, the installation of adaptations, and the delivery of equipment.

In early 1996, a comprehensive signage plan was developed to include all forms of wayfinding tools from the exterior fences to spectator seating areas and within all interior spaces for staff. The production of all signage was coordinated with Creative Services for preliminary development and included a sign production facility at Games-time.

The Site and Facility Management Manual developed in spring 1996 was a compilation of the venue program checklist; CAD venue site plans; CAD construction plans; CAD component plans of the layout of the field of play, access points, seating for spectators and Olympic Family constituent groups, accessible seating, and press and broadcast positions; Look of the Games plans and installations; lists of commodities, facilities, furniture, and equipment; technology lists by end device; electrical and power plans; signage lists and plans; and the integrated adaptation schedule and site manager's operation plan.

VENUE OPERATIONS PLANNING

In addition to determining the site requirements for each venue, Venue Management worked with all ACOG functional areas to produce a generic venue operations plan, which was released in early 1994. This document provided basic summary statements of what each functional area perceived as its responsibilities in a competition venue. Time—in terms of a daily schedule that would be followed—equipment, and personnel were included, but the statements were never compiled as a whole. With a lack of definition of overall requirements and how various areas would impact each other, the usefulness of this plan was very limited.

Two years before the Games, Venue Management collected from each functional area additional definitions of what it perceived its role at the venue to be and a description of how it would execute that role. Information from detailed questionnaires submitted by each functional area was evaluated and incorporated as appropriate into a second venue operations plan. This document provided more precise operational direction than the generic venue operations plan.

An extensive signage program was implemented to provide wayfinding for all constituencies.

527

The functional areas also created organizational charts for their personnel who would be assigned to the venues and for ACOG. Job descriptions and responsibilities of the venue staff were also documented.

This information was assembled in a Functional Area Policies and Procedures Manual. A companion list of responsibilities identified what services one functional area needed from or would provide to other functional areas at the venue.

To facilitate these requests and compilations, Venue Management assembled the Venue Operations Group (VOG) to establish parameters and consistency in operating plans for each venue and for each functional area within a venue. The functional area venue operations representatives submitted plans that gave precise detail and direction based on the specific layout and events to be held at each venue. Review by the entire venue team provided comprehensive understanding of all operations at the venue. The compiled venue-specific plans became an instructional tool for staff and volunteers who joined each area as a venue moved to full operation.

These venue operating plans by function provided a detailed description from each functional area of its responsibilities and activities at a venue. The plan followed a standard format to ensure issues were consistently addressed. The contents included:

■ an overview of the functional area's venue operations, describing the basic responsibilities and/or services provided and the mandate for providing these services;

■ organization of the functional area by headquarters group and venue team, including organizational charts, reporting relationships, approximate size of staff for Games-time, and general staff responsibilities;

■ detailed descriptions of the scope of the functional area's venue operations, including guiding and restricting principles, facilities utilized and provided, and functional area responsibilities;

■ standard policies and procedures guiding the functional area's operations;

■ key contacts with other ACOG functional areas, ranging from interaction and cooperative efforts to areas of interdependency for services and materials. Relationships had to be defined with Accreditation, Atlanta Olympic Broadcasting (AOB), Communications, Community Relations, Federal and State Government Relations, Financial Services, Food and Beverage, Language Services, Local Government Relations, Logistics, Marketing/ACOP, Medical Services, Merchandising, Olympic Family and Protocol, Risk Management, Security, Technology, Ticket Sales, Total Games Staffing, Transportation, and Volunteer Services;

■ time lines showing when milestones in preparing for venue operations needed to be reached and presenting a typical event-day schedule of activities and duties that outlined the process for conducting all aspects of the functional area's operation at the venue; and

■ functional area checklists, contracts, forms, a glossary of terms, maps, and space diagrams.

To assist departments further in preparing their venue operating plans, Venue Management conducted an ACOG-wide information session in December 1995 covering venues in the metropolitan-Atlanta area. A similar session in January 1996 covered venues outside this area. Presenters focused on providing comprehensive descriptions of their functional area's basic role at a generic venue, as well as giving an overview of each functional area and its plan for fulfilling its duties at all venues.

The creation of a common knowledge base for all personnel involved with venue operations was extremely critical. This effort was facilitated by the department's development of defined terms, acronyms, and codes. Ranging from access control to zones dedicated to accredited personnel, the terms provided a consistent framework for discussions and documentation.

A four-volume set of operating plans by venue was prepared initially for instructional training and later adapted for use as a reference and guide for Games-time operations.

The reference tool that resulted from the functional operating plans and the VOG meetings was the Venue Reference Manual. The Venue Reference Manual was designed to assist venue staff with their Games-time duties. The manual outlined detailed information and instruction on objectives and policies not only of ACOG, but also of the Olympic Family.

A general information section of the manual contained an overview of the 1996 Olympic Games and organizational charts showing relationships with the IOC, IFs, and venue owners, as well as the management group of the venue team. *(For other important information included in this section of the manual, see Figure 1.)*

A separate section of the manual contained the basic daily operating procedures that had been developed by Venue Management in conjunction with other ACOG functional areas to ensure clarity and consistency. Procedures described such critical issues as accreditation privileges and restrictions; communications systems and protocols; restocking, maintenance, and cleaning of facilities and equipment; sponsor issues; financial and accounting systems; security; medical services and emergencies; and personnel matters.

Important elements of the manual were condensed into smaller notebooks and pocket guides for the venue team to use during Games-time.

A number of other calendars and schedules were developed as Venue Management tools. Countdown calendars tracked preparatory ac-

tivities after the venue teams had moved to the site, and event-day integrated time lines provided a detailed schedule and checklist of activities for each competition day.

At the same time, the Sports Department was developing the competition management manuals to cover all aspects of competition, from the schedule and plans for implementation to the forms required by the governing IF and other entities. *(For more information, see the Sports chapter.)*

EVENT SERVICES

Developing plans both to manage the large number of athletes, officials, staff, media, and spectators at competition venues and to provide necessary amenities—such as beverage service during hot weather and ushers to queue and direct individuals through venues—was originally the responsibility of other specific functional areas within ACOG. As the site plans, operating plans, and test events progressed, it became necessary for these responsibilities to be assumed and implemented by Venue Management through a division called Event Services.

Of particular concern was the efficient flow of people into and out of venues. Multiple daily event sessions in several venues that were clustered together presented enormous challenges. The challenge was most acute in two primary clusters—the Olympic Center cluster and the Olympic Stadium cluster.

In order to provide the planning necessary for these areas, Venue Management engaged the services of an events contractor experienced in crowd management at other large sporting facilities. The result was a well-conceived patron flow and crowd management plan established in early 1996. This plan safely guided up to 500,000 people a day into and out of these clusters while providing directions, queuing, ticket-taking, and emergency procedures.

As part of the crowd management plan, a

FIGURE 1:
INFORMATION INCLUDED IN THE VENUE REFERENCE MANUAL

■ Maps and directions for all venue areas

■ Schedules ranging from the master Olympic schedule to the event-day integrated time line for that venue

■ A glossary with ACOG codes for buildings, cities, clusters, countries, disciplines, and functional areas

■ ACOG terms and pictograms

■ Descriptions of the ACOG-wide communications network and venue communications network

■ Telephone directories for ACOG, venues, the main operations center, emergency contacts, and venue emergency telephone alert systems

■ Staffing schedules

■ Emergency and contingency plans

■ Appendices with the venue budgets and venue contracts, as well as documentation pertinent to the operation of the venues such as the *Olympic Charter*, IF memorandum of understanding, ticket sales terms and conditions, ticket seating manifest, and vendor contracts

■ Copies of the standardized forms developed for the daily venue integrated reports for the main operations center, incident reporting, day pass applications, parking passes, technology change orders, requisitions, venue tour requests, vehicle requests, and public address announcements

RON C FOSTER • ROSALYN FOSTER • RUTH A FOSTER • SARAH L FOSTER • SHANNON FOSTER • STEPHEN A FOSTER • SUSAN B FOSTER • SUSAN B FOSTER • VIRGINIA I FOSTER • WALTER P FOSTER • WHITNEY T FOSTER • YOLANDA M FOSTER • ANDREW N FOSTER JR • JOSEPH FOSTER JR • ANNA MARIE FOSTER RN • GWENDOLYN M FOSTON • BOBBY L FOUCH • ANCA D FOUNTAIN • CURTIS A FOUNTAIN • ELIZABETH A FOUNTAIN • GAIL FOUNTAIN • JAMES A FOUNTAIN • JOHN T FOUNTAIN • KAY C FOUNTAIN • NANCY J FOUNTAIN • STANLEY R FOUNTAIN • CARINE FOUQUET • LAMIA FOURATI   **529**

As part of the crowd management plan, a definitive set of guidelines for the number of staff required and their specific job responsibilities within the venues ensured the ease of movement of the spectators to their designated seats. The plan for each venue defined the ratio of seats to ushers to sector coordinators.

Other necessary plans were the heat management plan, which encompassed a venue response plan based on increases in the heat index, and a volunteer staffing plan for spectator water distribution.

TEST EVENTS

ACOG planned and implemented more than two dozen major sports competitions before the Games, primarily to test venue fields of play. Venue Management also saw test events as an opportunity to move the organization significantly forward in the transition from a centralized functional areas operation to venue-based management.

Overall, the test events were extraordinarily successful, with each field of play providing an outstanding setting for competition. The test events clarified various operational needs, many of which had already been identified in venue operations group meetings and similar sessions but had not yet been resolved.

The test events also provided information on the strategy of management by cocaptains: a competition manager from Sports who had responsibility for the field of play and presentation of the competition, and a manager from Venue Management who directed all other areas and activities in the venue. This division of authority was considered the best option and remained the management approach throughout the Games because of the markedly different experience, expertise, and scope of responsibilities required in the positions.

Lessons learned during the test events led to some reassignment of responsibilities. For example, the task of providing ushers and ticket-takers, which had been placed under Security, was shifted to Venue Management as part of its Event Services division, which encompassed several similar functions.

Test event outcomes led to extensive review of signage, interior design, and layout of venues involving all ACOG functional areas.

Perhaps most importantly, test events inspired ACOG to prepare detailed plans, calendars, and other documents that outlined policies, procedures, and responsibilities as clearly as possible. These would serve as the basis for training programs and day-to-day operations during Games-time.

1996 OPERATIONS

As most test events concluded, preparation for 1996 operations became more focused. Documentation developed to date was subjected to continual review and validation. Simultaneously, ACOG began the process of establishing the actual venue-based teams to implement the venue planning process. Each functional area that would ultimately operate from a venue was requested to designate an individual to join the venue team and begin to work with the other members.

Lack of space in the ACOG offices, as well as the number of staff members yet to be hired, were challenges to the implementation of this process. Measures were taken to provide for functional area staff to attend to more than one venue team until positions were filled and the move to the venues was complete. Once the groups were located at the venues, the original objective of the team concept began to reach its full potential, as the teams worked extremely well together. In some cases, however, due to the venue contracts, the move was not complete until two weeks before the Games.

The test events provided valuable experience for all venue staff.

Venue Management solicited detailed descriptions from each functional area of the support required at the venues from Food and Beverage, Logistics, Technology, Transportation, and Volunteer Services. These requirements were developed in numerous reports and meetings. The largest efforts were in Technology, which procured and installed complex equipment and systems, and Volunteer Services, which assigned thousands of individuals to specific jobs and work schedules.

Requests for support often exceeded the available resources, which usually meant reductions in what the functional areas sought. The resulting negotiations led to the development of organization-wide guidelines, but numerous changes still had to be factored into an already complicated planning process.

Weekly meetings of the VOG began before the test events to plan policies and procedures that served venues as a whole or involved several functions. With each functional area represented at the meetings, it was possible to reach consensus on an issue and translate decisions into written policy or procedure. These meetings generated most of the information incorporated into the venue-specific manuals. Because of the number of issues to be addressed, the group continued to meet and develop policies after the manuals were issued, with new material provided as supplements and weekly updates to the venue-based teams.

Issues were addressed from both a policy standpoint and in detailed procedures. Areas covered were diverse and comprehensive, including such subjects as removing a stalled vehicle from an entry gate, escorting athletes to doping control at the end of a competition, requesting medical assistance for a spectator, and providing venue tours before and during the Games.

Budget Adjustments

Virtually all modifications and clarifications that emerged in the planning process had an impact on budget proposals, which made the task of incorporating changes even more difficult to implement. Because of budget considerations, functional areas intensely debated the priorities and cost-effectiveness of solutions, and Venue Management assumed the role of negotiator and arbitrator.

Many budget issues were resolved by charging them to the venue adaptation allowance, which Venue Management created with Financial Services as part of the overall Games budget. Ultimately, the venue adaptation allowance was used not only for changes implemented to prepare the venue for Olympic use, but also for maintenance and repairs during the Games.

Training

Management training occurred in a series of meetings held in the first quarter of 1996 as key venue team members reviewed specific plans and the status of operations at their venues. These sessions also allowed managers assigned to the venue teams to refine systems and procedures for the adaptation and operation of their sites.

Other members of the venue team already on staff were trained in similar meetings held in April and May 1996. They then received venue-specific briefings from their own team leaders. By June, the majority of personnel at each venue had participated in the sessions. They had also been provided with the resource materials needed not only for their jobs, but also for assisting with training the hundreds and sometimes thousands of additional staff members who would join the venue staff teams just before the Games.

Following overall management and staff training, members of venue teams participated in exercises with facilitators to resolve various

Volunteers were trained within the venues to provide directional information to all spectators.

voted to both typical and extreme problems that demonstrated the necessity of cooperating across functional areas.

During June 1996, drills were staged at each venue to rehearse responses to a variety of emergency situations. Venue team managers, house management personnel, public safety officials, and others reviewed and refined procedures for relatively minor incidents as well as for full evacuation and mass casualty incidents.

In May and June 1996, staff orientation and training took place during full-day sessions held at each venue. Staff members were instructed on entrance and exit points, layout of the field of play and all support areas, food and beverage services, spectator and Olympic Family transportation routes and parking, and other areas. Each session also provided a forum for reviewing information about the event a facility would host and allowed an opportunity for extensive questions and answers.

Also in May and June, venue team members and public safety managers met to discuss jurisdictional issues. Participants included representatives of police, fire, and rescue groups as well as staff from the nearest hospitals and other organizations. The purpose was to provide a final review of operating and contingency plans for the venue, including emergency procedures and communication protocols.

GAMES-TIME OPERATIONS

Although each venue presented a unique set of circumstances, Venue Management defined a sequence of events to be followed from venue opening to closing, standard organizational structures, and basic concepts and systems for use at all sites.

Periods of Operation

Defined specific time periods were established beginning with ACOG's initial move to the venue and continuing through the final removal of all Games assets after competition ended. Whether ACOG was on site six months or six days in advance, all operations were divided into clearly defined periods with predetermined rules and restrictions regarding access control. During the preparation period, ACOG assets were put into place and ACOG Security was present to protect the property and monitor the arrival and departure of all personnel.

The two periods influencing ACOG activities at a venue were the periods of nonexclusive and exclusive use. Nonexclusive use was the period during which ACOG shared use of a venue with the owner and any tenants. The extent of this term was determined by contracts with the site owner. During this period, the activities ACOG could conduct on the site were subject to the needs of the owner and other tenants. Security was generally the responsibility of the owner, although ACOG usually provided enhanced security if significant Games assets were located at the site. Exclusive use defined the period during which ACOG could use all space within a venue.

During both nonexclusive and exclusive use periods, different levels of access control were enforced. Limited access control took effect when parts of the venue were subject to strict security because athlete training had begun, while other parts of the venue could function under less restrictive rules.

Restricted access took effect after sanitization and allowed access only to those with an Olympic Games accreditation badge or a ticket. During the sanitization exercise, only staff members responsible for the inspection were permitted on the site.

Following sanitization, zone access control was instituted, with entry to the various parts of the venue provided on the basis of accreditation privileges as shown on a badge or, in the case of spectators, on the basis of a ticket. All vehicles without appropriate permits for admission to the venue were thoroughly inspected to determine eligibility of entrance.

The recovery period and the period immediately following the last Olympic event at the facility were referred to by employees as venue lock down. Venue Management was responsible for consolidating all assets, ensuring that all staff had departed, and closing and securing the venue. As Olympic accreditation was no longer valid, access was restricted to those with a special recovery badge or whose names appeared on the list of personnel scheduled to be at the site. All assets were inventoried and removed from the facility, and the facility was cleaned and restored to its pre-Games condition.

As venues advanced through the periods of operation, Games-time preparations proceeded on the following schedule: initiation of most adaptation work—March to early June; cabling, wiring, and other infrastructure requirements—mid-May through June; delivery and placement of equipment, furniture, and Look of the Games materials—mid-June to mid-July; and arrival of venue teams at their respective sites—mid-June.

Organizational Structure

The primary organizational element of the venues was the venue team, consisting of ACOG paid staff, volunteers, contractors, vendors, preexisting facility staff, and public safety officials. A venue manager and one or more competition managers led each team. The ACOG component of the team included functional area representatives who had specific responsibilities in support of the venue and the event.

Each manager was responsible for a staff that ranged in size from three to several hundred people per shift. For large staffs, managers

were supported by assistant managers and supervisors so that one individual was responsible for no more than 35 staff members.

Because each venue team was designed to operate autonomously, all functional area managers reported directly to the venue manager or competition manager for the facility. However, functional area managers were still required to maintain communication with their departments at ACOG headquarters. This structure ensured both prompt action and quick decision making at the venue and department accountability and support at headquarters. *(For the structure of the venue teams, see Figure 2.)*

Each venue manager was also a part of the overall organizational structure for the Venue Management Department and reported to a venue cluster manager, who directed operations at several venues. The venue cluster manager reported to one of several senior managers working directly for the managing director of the department. Once the Games began, senior managers worked closely with venue cluster managers and venue managers, through staff meetings and visits to venues, coordinating operations through the Venue Management desk in the MOC. Members of the headquarters management staff were always available in the MOC to discuss with venue managers the resolution of issues and coordination of cross-venue activities.

Operations Group. At a typical venue, staff reporting to the venue manager formed the operations group, providing all services that supported the noncompetition elements of the event. Under the direction of the venue manager and two assistant venue managers, the operations group included a site manager, who managed all ACOG site and facility alteration, maintenance, repair, and recovery activities, and coordinated with local government entities, safety inspectors, and utility crews at the venue; a venue communications center manager; and managers who handled functional-area duties. *(For specific responsibilities of staff members, see appropriate functional area chapters.)*

FIGURE 2: STRUCTURE OF THE VENUE TEAMS

Operations Group

Venue Management

Accreditation

AOB (Broadcasting)

Event Services

Finance

Food and Beverage

Language Services

Logistics

Marketing (ACOP)

Medical

Merchandising

Press Operations

Protocol

Public Information

Risk Management

Security

Site Management

Technology

Ticket Sales

Transportation

Venue Communications

Competition Group

Competition Management

Athlete support services

Competition administration

Competition implementation

Competition officials

Competition secretariat

Field of play

Sports equipment

Sports information desk

Timing, scoring / results

Training sites

Competition Group. The competition group, under the direction of the competition manager, included experts in sports, sports medicine, scoring, timing and results, sports equipment, and victory ceremonies. The competition manager, who coordinated with the IF for the sport at the venue, directed all activities related to the field of play and managed the facilities required by the officials and technical support team. Also reporting to the competition manager was a production team headed by a competition producer and includ-

ing announcers, equipment operators for scoreboards, video boards, audio facilities, lighting, and other effects, and the victory ceremonies manager, who had responsibility for the presentation of medals and all aspects of the awards ceremonies.

Venue Features

The venue boundary encompassed the entire area designated for the purpose of the venue, which included various buildings, parking lots, and other facilities surrounding the venue itself. Generally, a perimeter fence defined the area controlled by ACOG, although some venues had only a partial fence or shared a fence with other venues in the same venue cluster. The boundary enclosed an area which no one could enter without a ticket or appropriate accreditation.

A portal system was used for spectator entrances, designed on the modified funnel principle—wide at the beginning, then narrowing to a single-file line in preparation for security inspection. At some venues, security inspection included the use of magnetometers; at others, inspection was visual and hand-carried items were searched. At all venues, sections of the spectator gates were designed to accommodate persons with disabilities.

Exit gates were generally either adjacent to or the same as the entry gates, depending on the event schedule. At venues with multiple sessions daily, oversized exit gates were installed away from the entrance gates to separate the departing crowd from spectators arriving at the venue.

Additional entrances around the perimeter of the venue facilitated entry of staff, media, and other Olympic Family members. Where possible, there were separate entrances for each group. Different entrances were also available for accredited pedestrians and vehicles. While many vehicles carrying accredited persons to the venues received security checks at a different location, some had to be checked upon arrival.

Venue site management teams were responsible for the maintenance within each venue.

Prohibited items and activities ranged from beverages and banners to illegal drugs and weapons and applied to everyone entering a venue. ACOG Security inspected for these items as people entered the venue. If people carrying prohibited items such as beverages and banners wished to proceed into a venue, they needed to dispose of the items in trash bins available near the entrance gates, as ACOG did not provide space for holding prohibited items.

A public address system using prerecorded announcements was installed around the perimeter fence of venues to welcome spectators, advise them of prohibited items, and provide information about competition schedules, entry and exit procedures, and transportation.

Certain areas of the venues were designated for support functions and restricted to accredited personnel. These included:

- venue communications center;
- accreditation offices, always at the outermost perimeter of the venues and accessible from outside the venue for the issuance of day passes;
- AOB compound, central location for broadcasting operations and television production trailers, mobile communication trucks, and large equipment;
- site management compound, for construction and maintenance activities;
- food and beverage compound, operations site for concessionaires with refrigeration trucks, storage areas, and temporary kitchens;
- loading dock for coordination of shipping and receiving;
- logistics central supply area, providing storage and warehousing for equipment, tools, and supplies;
- venue offices and meeting rooms for venue team management;
- venue press subcenter, with work areas and interview rooms for accredited press;

- security command center for ACOG Security management, law enforcement representatives, and medical dispatcher;
- observation booth, for security personnel to observe the seating area and field of play;
- sports information desk, located near the athlete preparation areas as the point of contact with the sports information center at the Olympic Village;
- event production area, where competition management coordinated the competition activity schedule and managed control rooms for video boards and public address, scoring, and timing systems;
- staff check-in and break areas;
- technology help desk, the central location for tracking and handling problems with technology equipment;
- transportation office, for managing bus schedules, arrival and departure information, and the venue motor pool;
- doping control station, the restricted area for administration of the IOC Doping Control Program;
- athlete medical station, adjacent to the field of play to provide sports medicine care for athletes;
- results distribution room, for production of printed copies of start lists and results for press, broadcasting commentators, sports officials, and Olympic Family members;
- Olympic Family lounge, a hospitality area for Olympic Family members;
- Olympic Family medical station, a first-aid station for Olympic Family members;
- athlete warm-up areas, usually near the field of play; and

■ athlete locker rooms, restricted to athletes.

Areas of the venues with facilities and services intended for spectators included:

■ ticket box office, placed along the perimeter fence to allow patrons to obtain tickets held at the venue and to permit customers from inside and outside the venue to purchase other tickets;

■ public information booths, located inside the venue entry and outside the ticket gates, where Games staff answered questions and helped spectators, and where spectators could

Coordination between venue and competition management ensured each venue was prepared for its events.

turn in any items they had found and seek to retrieve lost items;

■ concession and merchandise stands, located throughout the venue area;

■ public drinking water stations, equipped with water fountains, water jugs, or other temporary facilities to ensure free water was readily available to spectators; and

■ venue medical stations, for providing first-aid and emergency care for spectators and staff.

Venues used both permanent and temporary seating structures. Spectator seating was primarily reserved, although some venues offered general admission. Accessible seating was available for persons with disabilities and their companions. Luxury suites provided seating for groups. Olympic Family members were provided reserved seating in the official stand or stand of honor. Seating for press and broadcasters included tabled positions equipped

with electrical service, telephones, and television monitors.

The field of play encompassed the competition and associated areas, with configuration governed by IF agreements. A limited number of photo positions were located on the field of play. Adjacent to the athletes' exit was the mixed zone, for press and broadcasters to interview athletes after competition.

Operational Systems

Several systems and procedures were identified as fundamental to effective and efficient venue operations. The venue teams were responsible for managing the venues based on these procedures and systems. Training emphasized what should be communicated beyond the venue for information, support, or rulings on policy.

Each venue was designed and provided with sufficient technology to support its operations. Inside cabling was installed to establish telecommunications and computer systems.

The venue communications system, located in the venue communications center, focused on sharing information, providing status reports, and conveying requests to appropriate members of the venue team. All radio transmissions were monitored, with the center manager serving as the radio traffic director by connecting users on different channels and maintaining order on the venue airwaves.

Each venue had a telephone system that was part of the overall five-digit dialing network. Most venues had a PBX installed, ESSX service, and basic telephone service as a reserve network. Public telephones and ACOG-network phones were available in the press subcenters, and public telephones and telecommunications devices for the deaf were at every venue.

Communication at the venues was by simplex and/or trunk radio systems and headset intercom systems, which were primarily for competition officials, results operations, and broadcasting personnel.

Cellular telephones and pagers were assigned to functional areas. They were the primary means of venue communication during the installation phase, and were also used during venue operations.

Info'96 terminals in the accredited areas permitted E-mail communication between venues. Selected venues had access to the press information system and the commentator information system. At competition venues, results were provided by the results system and high-speed printers. Venues had an internal cable television network, general use copiers, and facsimile machines.

Accreditation and access control systems followed Olympic mandates and guidelines. Procedures were developed to control access in pre- and post-operational stages and to facilitate the use of a variety of contractors during the Games.

Emergency plans were determined with the objective of ensuring the safety of all individuals at a venue at all times. Detailed venue emergency plans were developed and tested, with the focus on prioritizing incidents in terms of urgency and magnitude, and then following prescribed procedures to resolve situations.

Typical Day at a Venue

On event days, the course of activities at every venue proceeded according to a standard routine.

First, senior representatives from Venue Management and Sports Competition Planning met for a daily briefing and organizational session. Members of the venue team also participated in various inspections, working with the site manager and assistant venue manager to examine structures, equipment, and surroundings to confirm that the site was prepared and free of hazards. Concurrently, the competition group examined all portions of the field of play, and the production team conducted equipment checks to ensure that each system was operative. Any corrective work or repairs that needed to be done were immediately prioritized and assigned.

These meetings and inspections were completed by the time the remainder of the staff arrived for check-in and deployment to their work areas. Functional area meetings followed to provide staff briefings.

Before spectator arrival, the venue communications center broadcast periodic countdown notifications to the venue team. Thirty minutes before the gates opened, sector coordinators for the venue completed their facility and safety checks; confirmed that security, access control, and all staffed positions were filled; and ascertained that the concessions and merchandise stands were ready.

During competition, competition management notified the venue communications center at 15- and 10-minute intervals prior to halftime or intermission and before the end of competition. The venue communications center in turn alerted Event Services, Security, Food and Beverage, and other operations groups so that they could prepare for spectator movement. As a session neared its close, sector coordinators, Event Services, Medical Services, Security, and concessions and merchandise personnel prepared for spectator exit. Transportation and Olympic Family staff were deployed to serve Olympic Family members, and all other functional areas followed their specific procedures for conclusion of the event.

When one session immediately followed another, Event Services staff—working with security personnel and others as necessary—swept the seating areas and cleaned concourses, and each functional area reset its space and facilities.

Post-event meetings followed a similar pattern. Venue team managers prepared daily reports, and team members reset the space for the following day. Restocking and cleaning activities were performed after hours by ACOG Logistics and assigned vendors.

The crowd management team provided important guidance to people entering and exiting venues.

FRAPWELL • SHARON A FRAPWELL • KAREN L FRASCONA • ALEX FRASER • ALLAN W FRASER • ANDREW R FRASER • BARBARA F FRASER • CHARLIE B FRASER • DAVID S FRASER • HOWARD D FRASER • JAMES H FRASER • JANE E FRASER • LAURA H FRASER • LINCOLN THOMAS FRASER • LISA M FRASER • NORMA P FRASER • WILLIAM T FRASER • PAUL V FRASER JR • JESSE L FRASIER • LA DAWN FRASIER • FLORENCE S FRASURE • MARC A FRATELLO • MARIE E FRATONI • ROSANNE FRATTAROLI • RANDELL FRATTINI • ELLEN S FRAUENTHAL • LYNN S FRAVEL • CANDICE C FRAWLEY • PATRICK M FRAW-

537

CONCLUSIONS AND RECOMMENDATIONS

Venue Management developed all venues to meet world-class standards in look and layout, as well as in functionality and efficiency. Department staff provided an exciting atmosphere for the competitions by serving the public with warm southern hospitality and vivacious spirit. Judging from the reactions of both spectators and athletes, Venue Management was successful in all these endeavors.

It is important to recognize the significance of the venue management function and begin the process on a broad scale very early in the planning phase. To accomplish this, it is critical that personnel experienced with Olympic Games or multisport, international events participate in the planning process to provide guidance for contracts and other agreements critical to the management and presentation of venues.

The following recommendations are offered to future organizing committees.

■ Begin the discussion and education process for all functional areas concerning the need for integrated operations at the venues and the assembly of venue teams as early as possible.

■ Initiate preparation of operating plans for venues at least three years prior to the Games.

■ Incorporate the operational needs of each functional area of the organization—from space for spectator flow to extra electrical power requirements—into the construction plans for the venues. Give the venue management department the authority to require detailed descriptions of infrastructure, space, and equipment needs from every functional area at a venue, and obtain this information at least one year prior to the Games.

■ Put the most critical members of the venue management team in place at least two years before the start of the Games and establish a venue organizational structure that clarifies leadership and responsibility.

■ Emphasize pre-Games planning activities related to crowd management, especially for those venues where multiple sessions are scheduled in a single day.

■ Confirm access control procedures with Accreditation and train and manage the personnel responsible for enforcement.

■ When contracting for use of facilities, extend site security and access control requirements to the maximum possible time frame, allowing generous time for preparation and recovery/restoration of the property, in order to coordinate the work of all contractors and vendors.

■ Venue agreements need to specify in detail the responsibilities of the venue owner and those of ACOG.

■ Holding test events or other events at a venue helps ensure its operational viability during Games-time.

■ A significant concern at venues is preparation for weather-related contingencies, including a special water delivery plan for athletes and spectators.

■ Clarify the duties of the different law enforcement agencies and security personnel responsible for the venue.

VENUE BY VENUE REPORT

ALEXANDER MEMORIAL COLISEUM

Owner: Georgia Institute of Technology / State Board of Regents

Location: Olympic Ring

Events: boxing

Approximate seating:

total–10,000

broadcast commentator–189 (63 positions)

broadcast observer–61

camera seat kills–250

press tabled–274

press nontabled–266

athlete–300

Olympic Family–250

accessible–150

net spectator–8,100

Ticketing:

ticketed sessions–26

days with ticketed sessions–15

average sessions per day–2

highest number of ticketed spectators–8,000

Key operations dates:

move-in began–1 May

venue preparation– 7 to 18 June

exclusive use– 15 June to 14 August

venue sanitization– 5 July (for training), 15 July

first and last ticketed sessions–20 July; 4 August

move-out–4 to 29 August

ATLANTA BEACH

Owner: Clayton County

Location: metro-Atlanta area

Events: beach volleyball

Approximate seating:

total–9,600, court 1; 3,000, court 2

broadcast commentator–75 (25 positions)

broadcast observer–20

camera seat kills–60

press tabled–52

press nontabled–100

athlete–56

Olympic Family–255

accessible–20

net spectator–8,600, court 1; 2,900, court 2

Ticketing:

ticketed sessions–11

days with ticketed sessions–6

average sessions per day–2

highest number of ticketed spectators–11,500

Key operations dates:

move-in began–22 June

venue preparation– 29 June to 16 July

exclusive use–22 June to 4 August

venue sanitization– 21 July

first and last ticketed session–23 July; 28 July

move-out–29 July to 16 August

ATLANTA-FULTON COUNTY STADIUM

Owner: Atlanta–Fulton County Stadium Authority

Location: Olympic Ring

Events: baseball

Approximate seating:

total–54,000

broadcast commentator–33 (11 positions)

broadcast observer–36

camera seat kills–n/a

press tabled–147

press nontabled–94

athlete–200

Olympic Family–300

accessible–74

net spectator–52,000

Ticketing:

ticketed sessions–32

days with ticketed sessions–12

average sessions per day–2 to 3

highest number of ticketed spectators–50,000

Key operations dates:

move-in began–16 July

venue preparation– 1 March to 19 July

exclusive use–16 July to 6 August

venue sanitization– 17 to 19 July

first and last ticketed sessions–20 July; 2 August

move-out–2 to 6 August

CLARK ATLANTA UNIVERSITY STADIUM

Owner: Clark Atlanta University

Location: Olympic Ring

Events: hockey

Approximate seating:

total–5,000

broadcast commentator–54 (18 positions)

broadcast observer–34

camera seat kills–n/a

press tabled–57

press nontabled–96

athlete–161

Olympic Family–200

accessible–100

net spectator–4,100

Ticketing:

ticketed sessions–14

days with ticketed sessions–11

average sessions per day–2

highest number of ticketed spectators–4,102

Key operations dates:

move-in began– 15 June

venue preparation– 1 May to 6 July

exclusive use–15 June to 15 August

venue sanitization– 18 to 19 July

first and last ticketed sessions–20 July; 1 August

move-out–1 August to 1 September

FLORIDA CITRUS BOWL

Owner: city of Orlando

Location: Orlando, Florida

Events: football preliminaries

Approximate seating:

total–65,000

broadcast commentator–60 (20 positions)

broadcast observer–35

camera seat kills–n/a

press tabled–140

press nontabled–n/a

athlete–60

Olympic Family–85

accessible–300

net spectator–64,500

Ticketing:

ticketed sessions–6

days with ticketed sessions–6

average sessions per day–1

highest number of ticketed spectators–26,000

Key operations dates:

move-in began–n/a (local organizing committee had continuous access)

venue preparation– 1 June to 15 July

exclusive use–n/a

venue sanitization– 19 July

first and last ticketed sessions–20 July; 25 July

move-out–26 July to 2 August

GEORGIA DOME
(ONE ARENA SPLIT INTO TWO SIDES)

Owner: Georgia World Congress Center Authority / state of Georgia

Location: Olympic Ring

Events: artistic gymnastics, men's basketball, men's handball finals

Approximate seating:

total–34,500 per side

broadcast commentator–900 (300 positions) per side

broadcast observer–150 per side

camera seat kills–1,500, gymnastics; 200, basketball; 500, handball

press tabled–600 per side

press nontabled–960 per side

athlete–300 per side

Olympic Family–500 per side

accessible–340 per side

net spectator–32,000 per side

Ticketing:

ticketed sessions–64, plus 4 sessions of podium training

days with ticketed sessions–16, plus 4 days of podium training

average sessions per day–4

highest number of ticketed spectators–32,000

Key operations dates:

move-in began–1 June

venue preparation–1 June to 14 July

exclusive use–1 June to 12 August

venue sanitization–13 July

first and last ticketed sessions–15 July; 4 August

move-out–4 to 12 August

GEORGIA INTERNATIONAL HORSE PARK

Owner: city of Conyers / Georgia International Horse Park Foundation

Location: metro-Atlanta

Events: equestrian, mountain bike racing, modern pentathlon

Approximate seating:

total–32,000

broadcast commentator–126 (42 positions), arena; 75 (25 positions), endurance; 60 (20 positions), mountain bike racing; 36 (12 positions), modern pentathlon

broadcast observer–50, arena; 20, endurance; 25, mountain bike racing

camera seat kills–150, arena

press tabled–33, arena; 25, mountain bike racing

press nontabled–130, arena; 62, mountain bike racing

athlete–400

Olympic Family–1,600

accessible–327

net spectator–28,500

Ticketing:

ticketed sessions–15

days with ticketed sessions–14

average sessions per day–1

highest number of ticketed spectators–34,000

Key operations dates:

move-in began–8 June

venue preparation–17 February to 20 July

exclusive use–15 June to 31 October

venue sanitization–17 June

first and last ticketed sessions–21 July; 4 August

move-out–4 August to 31 October

GEORGIA STATE UNIVERSITY GYMNASIUM

Owner: Georgia State University / State Board of Regents

Location: Olympic Ring

Events: badminton

Approximate seating:

total–3,500

broadcast commentator–63 (21 positions)

broadcast observer–26

camera seat kills–26

press tabled–52

press nontabled–117

athlete–231

Olympic Family–94

accessible–14

net spectator–3,000

Ticketing:

ticketed sessions–22

days with ticketed sessions–9

average sessions per day–2 to 3

highest number of ticketed spectators–2,800

Key operations dates:

move-in began–17 June

venue preparation–15 January to 23 July

exclusive use–17 June to 13 September

venue sanitization–14 July

first and last ticketed sessions–24 July; 1 August

move-out–1 to 26 August

GEORGIA TECH AQUATIC CENTER

Owner: Georgia Institute of Technology / State Board of Regents

Location: Olympic Ring

Events: diving, modern pentathlon, swimming, synchronized swimming, water polo

Approximate seating:

total–15,000

broadcast commentator–360 (120 positions)

broadcast observer–72

camera seat kills–n/a

press tabled–271

press nontabled–225

athlete–600

Olympic Family–476

accessible–251

net spectator–11,900

Ticketing:

ticketed sessions–53

days with ticketed sessions–14

average sessions per day–5

highest number of ticketed spectators–14,900

Key operations dates:

move-in began–15 June

venue preparation–15 June to 19 July

exclusive use–15 June to 15 September

venue sanitization–6 July (phase 1); 14 July (phase 2)

first and last ticketed session–20 July; 2 August

move-out–3 to 31 August

GEORGIA WORLD CONGRESS CENTER
(FIVE DIFFERENT HALLS)

Owner: Georgia World Congress Center Authority / state of Georgia

Location: Olympic Ring

Events: fencing, handball, judo, modern pentathlon, table tennis, weightlifting, wrestling

Approximate seating:

Fencing (preliminaries)

total–2,200

broadcast commentator–n/a

broadcast observer–12

camera seat kills–n/a

press tabled–n/a

press nontabled–16

athlete–100

Olympic Family–32

accessible–24

net spectator–2,000

Fencing (finals)

total–3,900

broadcast commentator–306 (102 positions)

broadcast observer–34

camera seat kills–n/a

press tabled–32

press nontabled–12

athlete–63

Olympic Family–231

accessible–40

net spectator–3,200

Handball

total–7,300

broadcast commentator–450 (150 positions)

broadcast observer–33

camera seat kills–46

press tabled–144

press nontabled–12

athlete–266

Olympic Family–193

accessible–72

net spectator–6,400

GEORGIA WORLD CONGRESS CENTER (CONT'D)

Judo

total–7,300

broadcast commentator–468 (156 positions)

broadcast observer–33

camera seat kills–n/a

press tabled–150

press nontabled–12

athlete–436

Olympic Family–268

accessible–72

net spectator–6,200

Table Tennis

total–4,100, preliminaries; 4,700, finals

broadcast commentator–324 (108 positions)

broadcast observer–36

camera seat kills–60

press tabled–28

press nontabled–60

athlete–180

Olympic Family–202

accessible–41

net spectator–3,300

Weightlifting

total–5,000

broadcast commentator–450 (150 positions)

broadcast observer–34

camera seat kills–n/a

press tabled–150

press nontabled–54

athlete–120

Olympic Family–165

accessible–42

net spectator–4,300

Wrestling, Freestyle

total–7,300

broadcast commentator–450 (150 positions)

broadcast observer–33

camera seat kills–32

press tabled–144

press nontabled–24

athlete–384

Olympic Family–268

accessible–72

net spectator–6,400

GEORGIA WORLD CONGRESS CENTER (CONT'D)

Wrestling, Greco Roman

total–7,300

broadcast commentator–450 (150 positions)

broadcast observer–33

camera seat kills–28

press tabled–150

press nontabled–24

athlete–351

Olympic Family–169

accessible–72

net spectator–6,400

Ticketing:

ticketed sessions–111

days with ticketed sessions–15

average sessions per day–7

highest number of ticketed spectators–7,340

Key operations dates:

move-in began–26 June

venue preparation–28 May to 18 July

exclusive use–27 May to 6 August

venue sanitization–9 July

first and last ticketed sessions–20 July; 3 August

move-out–3 to 6 August

GOLDEN PARK

Owner: Columbus Parks and Recreation

Location: Columbus, Georgia

Events: softball

Approximate seating:

total–8,800

broadcast commentator–18 (6 positions)

broadcast observer–10

camera seat kills–115

press tabled–100

press nontabled–25

athlete–120

Olympic Family–125

accessible–89

net spectator–8,300

Ticketing:

ticketed sessions–16

days with ticketed sessions–9

average sessions per day–2

highest number of ticketed spectators–8,255

Key operations dates:

move-in began–1 July

venue preparation–1 to 20 July

exclusive use–1 July to 8 August

venue sanitization–20 July

first and last ticketed sessions–21 July; 30 July

move-out–30 July to 8 August

LAKE LANIER

Owner: city of Gainesville and Hall County

Location: Gainesville, Georgia

Events: canoe / kayak–sprint, rowing

Approximate seating:

total–17,300

broadcast commentator–180 (60 positions)

broadcast observer–30

camera seat kills–20

press tabled–90

press nontabled–72

athlete–600

Olympic Family–320

accessible–210

net spectator–15,700

Ticketing:

ticketed sessions–16

days with ticketed sessions–14

average sessions per day–1

highest number of ticketed spectators–15,451

Key operations dates:

move-in began–1 April

venue preparation–1 June to 1 July

exclusive use–15 June to 31 August

venue sanitization–19 July

first and last ticketed sessions–21 July; 4 August

move-out–4 to 31 August

LEGION FIELD

Owner: city of Birmingham

Location: Birmingham, Alabama

Events: football preliminaries

Approximate seating:

total–81,700

broadcast commentator–60 (20 positions)

broadcast observer–30

camera seat kills–n/a

press tabled–90

press nontabled–40

athlete–100

Olympic Family–56

accessible–150

net spectator–80,500

Ticketing:

ticketed sessions–8

days with ticketed sessions–8

average sessions per day–1

highest number of ticketed spectators–80,500

Key operations dates:

move-in began–1 June

venue preparation–1 June to 19 July

exclusive use–22 June to 5 August

venue sanitization–17 July

first and last ticketed sessions–20 July; 28 July

move-out–29 July to 30 August

ROAD COURSES

Owner: city of Atlanta with support facilities provided by various entities

Location: city of Atlanta

Events: athletics, road cycling

Approximate seating:

total–800

broadcast commentator–300 (100 positions)

broadcast observer–100

camera seat kills–n/a

press tabled–100

press nontabled–150

athlete–100

Olympic Family–300

accessible–25

net spectator–n/a

Ticketing:

n/a (except for finish of men's marathon; see Olympic Stadium)

Key operations dates:

move-in began–1 July

venue preparation–1 to 19 July

exclusive use–1 July to 10 August (for support facilities)

venue sanitization–19 July

first and last ticketed sessions–n/a

move-out–4 to 10 August

MOREHOUSE COLLEGE GYMNASIUM

Owner: Morehouse College

Location: Olympic Ring

Events: basketball

Approximate seating:

total–6,000

broadcast commentator–138 (46 positions)

broadcast observer–44

camera seat kills–80

press tabled–82

press nontabled–80

athlete–153

Olympic Family–225

accessible–104

net spectator–5,000

Ticketing:

ticketed sessions–13

days with ticketed sessions–9

average sessions per day–2 for four days; 1 for five days

highest number of ticketed spectators–5,014

Key operations dates:

move-in began–15 March

venue preparation–15 March to 19 July

exclusive use–15 June to 25 August

venue sanitization–18 July

first and last ticketed sessions–20 July; 30 July

move-out–30 July to 24 August

MORRIS BROWN COLLEGE STADIUM

Owner: Morris Brown College

Location: Olympic Ring

Events: hockey

Approximate seating:

total–15,000

broadcast commentator–60 (20 positions)

broadcast observer–30

camera seat kills–40

press tabled–64

press nontabled–76

athlete–375

Olympic Family–368

accessible–300

net spectator–13,700

Ticketing:

ticketed sessions–28

days with ticketed sessions–14

average sessions per day–2

highest number of ticketed spectators–13,821

Key operations dates:

move-in began–15 June

venue preparation–1 May to 6 July

exclusive use–15 June to 15 August

venue sanitization–18 July

first and last ticketed sessions–20 July; 2 August

move-out–2 to 12 August

OCOEE WHITEWATER CENTER

Owner: Tennessee Valley Authority

Location: Ocoee River, Tennessee

Events: canoe / kayak–slalom

Approximate seating:

total–14,400

broadcast commentator–120 (40 positions)

broadcast observer–15

camera seat kills–20

press tabled–40

press nontabled–62

athlete–175

Olympic Family–100

accessible–100

net spectator–13,900

Ticketing:

ticketed sessions–12

days with ticketed sessions–3

average sessions per day–4

total number of ticketed spectators–41,846

Key operations dates:

move-in began–June

venue preparation–fall 1995 to June 1996

exclusive use–19 to 28 July

venue sanitization–24 July

first and last ticketed sessions–26 July; 28 July

move-out–28 July to 20 August

OLYMPIC STADIUM

Owner: MAOGA / Atlanta–Fulton County Recreation Authority

Location: Olympic Ring

Events: athletics, Opening and Closing Ceremonies

Approximate seating:

total–85,600

broadcast commentator–525 (175 positions)

broadcast observer–180

camera seat kills–2,180

press tabled–1,001

press nontabled–800

athlete–2,200

Olympic Family–1,048

accessible–800

net spectator–77,500

Ticketing:

ticketed sessions–18

days with ticketed sessions–10

average sessions per day–2

highest number of ticketed spectators–76,982

Key operations dates:

move-in began–1 March

venue preparation–1 March

exclusive use–1 March to 1 September

venue sanitization–16 July

first and last ticketed sessions–19 July; 4 August

move-out–5 to 30 August

OMNI COLISEUM

Owner: The Atlanta Coliseum, Incorporated
Location: Olympic Ring
Events: volleyball
Approximate seating:
total–16,500
broadcast commentator–156 (52 positions)
broadcast observer–56
camera seat kills–100
press tabled–150
press nontabled–250
athlete–280
Olympic Family–498
accessible–68
net spectator–14,500
Ticketing:
ticketed sessions–32
days with ticketed sessions–16
average sessions per day–2
highest number of ticketed spectators–14,500
Key operations dates:
move-in began–15 June
venue preparation–1 June to 5 July
exclusive use–15 June to 10 August
venue sanitization–13 July
first and last ticketed sessions–20 July; 4 August
move-out–5 to 30 August

ORANGE BOWL

Owner: city of Miami
Location: Miami, Florida
Events: football preliminaries
Approximate seating:
total–72,700
broadcast commentator–54 (18 positions)
broadcast observer–35
camera seat kills–n/a
press tabled–103
press nontabled–n/a
athlete–100
Olympic Family–202
accessible–800
net spectator–71,600
Ticketing:
ticketed sessions–8
days with ticketed sessions–8
average sessions per day–1
highest number of ticketed spectators–56,500
Key operations dates:
move-in began–17 June
venue preparation–17 June to 12 July
exclusive use–22 June to 4 August
venue sanitization–19 July
first and last ticketed sessions–20 July; 28 July
move-out–29 July to 13 August

RFK MEMORIAL STADIUM

Owner: District of Columbia
Location: Washington, DC
Events: football preliminaries
Approximate seating:
total–56,500
broadcast commentator–60 (20 positions)
broadcast observer–35
camera seat kills–124
press tabled–85
press nontabled–20
athlete–78
Olympic Family–154
accessible–100
net spectator–56,300
Ticketing:
ticketed sessions–6
days with ticketed sessions–6
average sessions per day–1
highest number of ticketed spectators–56,300
Key operations dates:
move-in began–5 June
venue preparation–5 to 18 July
exclusive use–5 July to 1 August
venue sanitization–19 July
first and last ticketed sessions–20 July; 25 July
move-out–26 July to 1 August

SANFORD STADIUM

Owner: University of Georgia / State Board of Regents
Location: Athens, Georgia
Events: football semifinals and finals
Approximate seating:
total–86,100
broadcast commentator–186 (62 positions)
broadcast observer–65
camera seat kills–120
press tabled–204
press nontabled–150
athlete–220
Olympic Family–500
accessible–87
net spectator–82,000
Ticketing:
ticketed sessions–6
days with ticketed sessions–6
average sessions per day–1
highest number of ticketed spectators–82,000
Key operations dates:
move-in began–1 April
venue preparation–15 May to 25 July
exclusive use–16 June to 10 August
venue sanitization–24 July
first and last ticketed sessions–28 July; 3 August
move-out–4 to 24 August

STONE MOUNTAIN PARK ARCHERY CENTER AND VELODROME

Owner: Stone Mountain Memorial Association / state of Georgia
Location: metro-Atlanta area
Events: archery, track cycling
Approximate seating:
Archery
total–5,200
broadcast commentator–60 (20 positions)
broadcast observer–20
camera seat kills–12
press tabled–66
press nontabled–65
athlete–140
Olympic Family–355
accessible–62
net spectator –4,600
Track cycling
total–6,000
broadcast commentator–168 (56 positions)
broadcast observer–49
camera seat kills–n/a
press tabled–105
press nontabled–92
athlete –112
Olympic Family–423
accessible–56
net spectator–5,000
Ticketing:
ticketed sessions–16
days with ticketed sessions–10
average sessions per day–2
highest number of ticketed spectators–5,878
Key operations dates:
move-in began–15 March
venue preparation–15 June to 22 July
exclusive use–15 June to 7 August
venue sanitization–22 July
first and last ticketed sessions–24 July; 2 August
move-out–2 August to 30 September

STONE MOUNTAIN PARK TENNIS CENTER

Owner: Stone Mountain Memorial Association / state of Georgia

Location: metro-Atlanta area

Events: tennis

Approximate seating:

total–27,500

broadcast commentator–150 (50 positions), center court; 42 (14 positions), court 1

broadcast observer–50, center court; 35, court 1

camera seat kills–120, center court; n/a, court 1

press tabled–48, center court; 16, court 1

press nontabled–90, center court; 50, court 1

athlete–200, center court; 100, court 1

Olympic Family–300, center court; 150, court 1

accessible–120, center court; 65, court 1

net spectator–10,400, center court; 4,900, court 1; 500, general admission seats per court, courts 2 to 16

Ticketing:

ticketed sessions–12

days with ticketed sessions–12

average sessions per day–1

highest number of ticketed spectators–17,531

Key operations dates:

move-in began– 15 March

venue preparation– 1 June to 15 July

exclusive use–15 June to 15 August

venue sanitization– 20 July

first and last ticketed sessions–19 July; 3 August

move-out–3 August to 4 September

UNIVERSITY OF GEORGIA COLISEUM

Owner: University of Georgia / State Board of Regents

Location: Athens, Georgia

Events: rhythmic gymnastics, volleyball

Approximate seating:

total–10,000

broadcast commentator– 99 (33 positions)

broadcast observer– 45 to 60

camera seat kills–25

press tabled–109

press nontabled–35

athlete–55

Olympic Family–212

accessible–50

net spectator–9,500

Ticketing:

ticketed sessions–16

days with ticketed sessions–14

average sessions per day–2

highest number of ticketed spectators–9,000

Key operations dates:

move-in began– 15 March

venue preparation– 23 June to 16 July

exclusive use–15 June to 10 August

venue sanitization– 17 July

first and last ticketed sessions–20 July; 4 August

move-out–5 to 15 August

WASSAW SOUND

Owners: Sheraton Properties, Yachtworks, Harvey Properties

Location: Savannah, Georgia

Events: yachting

Approximate seating:

total–1,000

broadcast commentator–on boats

broadcast observer– on boats

camera seat kills–n/a

press tabled–n/a

press nontabled– on boats

athlete–n/a

Olympic Family –110 on boats

accessible –n/a

net spectator –n/a

Ticketing:

ticketed sessions–24

days with ticketed sessions–12

average sessions per day–2

highest number of ticketed spectators–1,020

Key operations dates:

move-in began– 24 June

venue preparation– 15 May to 9 July

exclusive use–15 June to 15 August

venue sanitization– 3 July

first and last ticketed sessions–22 July; 2 August

move-out–3 to 14 August

WOLF CREEK SHOOTING COMPLEX

Owner: Fulton County

Location: metro-Atlanta area

Events: shooting

Approximate seating:

total–7,500

broadcast commentator–108

broadcast observer–40

camera seat kills–130

press tabled–132

press nontabled–80

athlete–200

Olympic Family–120

accessible–60

net spectator–6,600

Ticketing:

ticketed sessions–8

days with ticketed sessions–8

average sessions per day–1

highest number of ticketed spectators–4,400

Key operations dates:

move-in began– 12 March

venue preparation– 25 March to 19 July

exclusive use–5 July to 9 August

venue sanitization– 17 July

first and last ticketed sessions–20 July; 27 July

move-out–27 July to 30 September

Chapter Twenty-Eight
Youth and Education

YOUTH AND EDUCATION EMPLOYEES

Date	Staff Number
June 1993	2
January 1996	2
July 1996	55

Note: These staff numbers do not include contract, VIK, and volunteer personnel.

OVERVIEW—The mission of ACOG's Youth and Education Department was to use the unparalleled opportunity of hosting the Centennial Olympic Games to motivate the youth of Georgia to strive for excellence in all areas of their lives by promoting participation in academic, cultural, and sports development projects.

In its pursuit of the Olympic Games, the AOC determined to involve young people in Atlanta's effort to demonstrate its spirit and enthusiasm. Thus, in late summer 1989, the Olympic Day in the Schools Program was created to provide curriculum guides to help teachers incorporate Olympic values into their classrooms. In June 1990, the first Georgia Olympic Day, involving 400 students, was held at Emory University in conjunction with the US Olympic Academy. In 1990, the Dream Team Program was founded, and the first Dream Team, comprised of 58 youth ambassadors, accompanied the AOC to Tokyo, where the IOC announced its selection of Atlanta as the host city for the 1996 Games.

Through these and other early efforts, the youth of Georgia made a vital contribution to the community spirit that was behind Atlanta's winning of the 1996 Games.

The Youth and Education Department utilized the momentum generated during the Bid process, using the Games as a means to inspire and energize Georgia youth. The department broadened awareness of the Olympic Movement among school-aged youth, while promoting physical and mental fitness. It prepared them to be knowledgeable, enthusiastic hosts for the Games and encouraged their participation in sports, educational, and cultural programs.

Community leaders in the fields of education, child advocacy, and sports were invited to help define, develop, and implement programs to meet the department's goals. The mission was guided by educational objectives defined in 1991 by the Georgia Department of Education (DOE). In addition to the core curriculum, educators are expected to teach loyalty and respect for self and others in the classroom. The organizing committee found these educational objectives to be synonymous with values inherent to the Olympic Movement.

In fall 1991, two groups of community leaders and educators—the Educational Task Force and the Youth Advisory Council—joined existing educational institutions to create youth programs that would remain as a legacy after the Games. With input from these groups, Youth and Education determined it could realize its educational objectives by:

■ involving young people statewide in educational programs about the history of the Olympic Movement while fostering teamwork, sportsmanship, and excellence;

■ increasing awareness of and participation in Olympic sports, with special attention given to the lesser-known sports;

■ encouraging young people to develop life-long values; and

■ promoting cultural awareness and physical fitness.

ORGANIZATION

Using the 1996 Olympic Games as a platform, the staff of Youth and Education developed and managed four major programs: Olympic Day in the Schools (ODIS), the Dream Team Program, the Children's Olympic Ticket Fund (COTF), and the Olympic Youth Camp (OYC). From the beginning, the close correlation of objectives between the Georgia DOE and ACOG's Youth and Education Department was instrumental in the success of these programs. The programs were implemented through the existing Georgia educational system and gained continuous support and direction through its curriculum and educators.

OLYMPIC DAY IN THE SCHOOLS

ODIS was an interdisciplinary program for public and private elementary and middle schools that combined classroom instruction with schoolwide athletic and cultural events. Originally developed by the USOC, expanded by ACOG, and endorsed by the Georgia DOE, the program focused on helping students understand the values inherent to the Olympic Movement and showed how they could apply these values in their lives.

The program provided schools with a variety of resources and opportunities to promote excellence through the Olympic Movement. The Educational Task Force developed the curriculum that formed the structure of this program. ODIS distributed curriculum guides and sports training manuals, hosted teacher seminars and

annual Georgia Olympic Days, developed a Speakers Bureau, and instituted annual poster competitions and the Welcome Book Program.

Curriculum Guides

Metropolitan-Atlanta area teachers wrote and developed annual four-unit curriculum guides covering subjects related to the Olympic Movement. The instruction units were: volume 1, *History of the Games*; volumes 2 and 3, *A Worldwide Connection*, parts 1 and 2; and volume 4, *People, Places, and Events: An Olympic Celebration*. The materials were designed to be integrated into existing academic programs, with learning activities intended to stimulate critical thinking and develop problem-solving and decision-making skills. Approximately 5,000 copies of each volume were disseminated to teachers, administrators, and media specialists at more than 1,800 public and private elementary and middle schools in Georgia. In addition, a substantial number of the curricula were mailed, upon request, to schools throughout the US. A series of videos that corresponded to topics in the curriculum was also produced and distributed.

Teacher Seminars

Teachers were given an opportunity to enhance their teaching strategies through participation in annual teacher seminars focusing on the Olympic Movement and using the ODIS curriculum. Beginning in 1989, two representatives from every Georgia school were invited to attend these seminars. Originally, many seminars were planned in centers across the state; however, experience showed that enthusiasm and participation increased when fewer and larger seminars were held in centrally located cities.

The seminars were entitled "Bringing Olympism into the Classroom," and featured guest speakers such as Bud Greenspan, an authority on the Olympic Games; former UN ambassador Andrew Young, co-chair of the ACOG Board of Directors; Olympian Benita Fitzgerald; and school administrators and educators.

KENNY M FRONTIN • BRADLEY W FROST • CLIFFORD B FROST • JOSEPH T FROST • KATHERINE H FROST • MICHAEL FROST • SHEILA FROST • STANFORD FROST • BARBARA A FRY • MARILYN D FRY • RAMONA J FRY • STEPHEN P FRY • NICOLE S FRYDMAN • JACQUELINE J FRYE • RANDALL FRYE • REA FRYE • SARA A FRYE • ZOE FRYE • CONRAD FRYKMAN • KRISTEN FRYLING • AMANDA FRYMAN • BRIAN B FRYMAN • JOAN C FU • TINA FU • NAOMI FUATAGA • GERALD D FUCHS • IRMA C FUCHS • JASON W FUCHS • TRACEY M FUDGE • BERTHA M FUDGEN • ARTHUR W FUDGER • JOANNE FUDGER •

The seminars also recognized schools that participated in the ODIS Program by presenting them with certificates and inviting them to present student performances during seminar sessions.

Youth Sports Program

The Youth Advisory Council took a leading role in developing the Youth Sports Program, intended to increase awareness of Olympic sports not widely practiced in the US. While a sports program is costly, as it involves purchasing expensive equipment, the Youth Sports Pro-

left: Students were provided the opportunity to participate in Olympic sports, such as judo, through the Youth Sports Program.

right: Posters created by youth for the annual Olympic Day in the Schools poster competition were displayed at sessions of the Georgia General Assembly and at the Olympic Youth Camp during the Games.

gram was able to maximize its impact by concentrating resources on areas in and around Atlanta. The program implemented numerous sports manuals, workshops, demonstrations, and exhibitions. Ultimately, student participation sessions were held that focused on archery, handball, hockey, judo, and race walking, all of which require low capital expenditures for equipment. In cooperation with local sports federations and community-based organizations, ACOG provided experts in these sports to assist students and coaches.

ACOG enjoyed a long, successful relationship with the local judo programs operating in metro-Atlanta Boys and Girls Clubs by offering financial support for the purchase of mats and uniforms and scholarship assistance. Citywide judo programs grew from one program in 1988, when the

AOC was first preparing its Bid for the Centennial Olympic Games, to more than 12 in 1996.

The Racewalking Program, organized in conjunction with a test event held in 1994, was also successful. Schools in the Olympic Stadium venue area were selected for participation; some 400 students were reached through educational resources such as training manuals and actual experience through demonstrations and workshops hosted by renowned athletes in this sport.

By localizing its focus, the Youth Sports Program was able to meet its goal to increase

young people's knowledge of Olympic sports less prominent in the US, while permanently enhancing the sports curriculum in metro-Atlanta area schools.

IZZY Appearances and Speakers Bureau

IZZY appearances, which were managed by the Special Events Department, began in 1993. Visits from the Olympic mascot were offered to elementary schools with students aged 5–11. The IZZY character made 571 appearances in schools in collaboration with the Youth and Education Department. *(For further details, see the Event and Guest Services chapter.)*

Teachers were encouraged to have Olympic athletes and ACOG staff members participate in their classrooms to make informative and motivational presentations. A Youth and Education Speakers Bureau, formed in 1989, focused most efforts on students aged 11–15 in middle schools. During this pre-Games period, approximately 300 schools annually were visited by Olympic representatives. The representatives addressed both individual classrooms and school-wide student assemblies, affording thousands of Georgia students the opportunity to participate in the program.

Poster Competition

Youth and Education collaborated with the Georgia Art Education Association to organize an annual poster competition, which stimulated considerable school involvement. The competitions, held each year from 1991 to 1995, inspired the creation of more than 500 posters, each based on an annual Olympic theme. Poster themes corresponded to topics in the curriculum guides and included "History of the Games," "Atlanta Welcomes the World," and "A Worldwide Connection." Students entered their works for potential selection as the ACOG ODIS Poster of the Year, which was printed and distributed to all Georgia elementary and middle schools. Posters were displayed at sessions of the Georgia General Assembly and during the Games at the OYC.

Welcome Book Program

During the 1995–96 school year, students in Georgia created welcome books to share their prose, poetry, and artwork with Olympic athletes. Each school system was invited to compile a notebook of students' artistic and literary work that related to the Olympic Movement. ACOG, in turn, gave a notebook to each NOC as it was officially welcomed to Atlanta at the Olympic Village.

Georgia Olympic Day

The highlight of the ODIS Program was Georgia Olympic Day, a special annual event for middle school students held at Emory University during the spring of each pre-Olympic year starting in 1990. Students participated in athletic and academic festivities patterned after the Olympic Games, including opening, closing, and victory ceremonies. Students from different

schools were grouped into teams representing a country, and all students received medals for participation.

To ensure the success of the program, a steering committee was formed with representatives from Atlanta-area school districts. School districts took turns coordinating the components, which included art exhibitions and an academic bowl that featured questions from the curriculum guides. BellSouth Corporation supported this event annually by providing finances and volunteers.

Georgia Olympic Day offered middle school students the chance to meet peers from across the state in an environment that fostered cooperation, respect, and friendship. Program participation rose steadily among all public and private elementary and middle schools, nearly doubling from 1989 to 1996, attesting to the program's success.

DREAM TEAM PROGRAM

In 1990, the Dream Team Program was founded to help achieve the AOC's goal of showcasing the spirit and enthusiasm of Atlanta through

Georgia students participated in Olympic-themed festivities at the Georgia Olympic Day held annually during the spring of each pre-Olympic year starting in 1990 at Emory University. All students received medals of participation.

CHRISTY D FULLER • DEBBIE A FULLER • EDWARD L FULLER • FREDDIE C FULLER • GEORGIA FULLER • GEORGIANA D FULLER • JOSEPH B FULLER • KELLY A FULLER • LINDA D FULLER • MILLICENT E FULLER • NAN ELLEN FULLER • PATRICIA A FULLER • RICK L FULLER • TODD B FULLER • TRACI M FULLER • TY S FULLER • VIVIAN L FULLER • JAMES M FULLER II PM • ALBERT L FULLER JR • RICHARD L FULLER JR. • BRUCE WILLIAM FULLERTON • RICHARD N FULLERTON • JEANETTE FULLILOVE • KURT D FULMER • LEIGH A FULMER • PAUL W FULMER • TIMOTHY S FULMER SAT • DAWN K FULTON •

549

youth programs. The name of the program was chosen to convey the ideals of the Olympic Movement and the goals of the program.

In September 1990, 58 youth ambassadors were chosen for the first Dream Team which accompanied the AOC to Tokyo, where Atlanta was awarded the Games by the IOC. From 1992 to 1996, a diverse group of 100 of Georgia's brightest high school students was chosen annually to represent the Centennial Olympic Games as ambassadors of the Olympic Spirit in their communities. Students were selected based on

left: **Dream Team members traveled to Tokyo in September 1990, where Atlanta was awarded the Games.**

right: **The first Atlanta Dream Team marches in a parade in Atlanta.**

their oral communication skills, leadership abilities, and commitment to community service.

Given the task of helping prepare Georgia for the Games, Dream Team members led service projects in their hometowns, mentored younger students, acted as hosts at many ACOG functions, and studied world history using the Games as a base. These students were given the opportunity to meet and learn from international visitors and each other, as well as improve the living conditions of their respective communities.

Some students facilitated improvement of their environment by planting a tree or a garden, while others implemented systems for recycling. The Dream Team Program also organized and participated in food and toy drives and literacy programs. Through these activities, high school students provided valuable services to their communities, while making new friends.

Youth and Education also collaborated with the nationally recognized Congressional Awards Program to offer Dream Team members an opportunity to gain congressional recogni-

tion. The Congressional Awards Program, a voluntary, noncompetitive program, recognized young people aged 14–23 who accomplished high goals in voluntary public service, personal development, physical fitness, and expedition activities. Many Dream Team members were rewarded for their initiative, achievement, and excellence with a bronze, silver, or gold Congressional Award medal presented by a member of Congress. These activities corresponded to the mission of the Dream Team Program as well as to the ideals of the Olympic Movement.

As a result of the Dream Team's efforts, Georgia and the US gained a resource of more than 400 students who embraced the Olympic Spirit. Many volunteered for the Games to work at the OYC, the Olympic Village, and Opening and Closing Ceremonies, among other assignments. These young people are now poised to become Olympic and community leaders in the future.

CHILDREN'S OLYMPIC TICKET FUND

The COTF was initiated in July 1991 by ACOG President and CEO Billy Payne. Inspired by a similar program at the 1988 Calgary Olympic Games, the fund was intended to enable children in Georgia, who for economic reasons could not otherwise attend Olympic events, to receive tickets to the Games.

In January 1996, ACOG began soliciting applications from 501(c)(3) not-for-profit organizations that had the primary mission of serving economically disadvantaged children aged 10–18 and were actively involved in conducting an ongoing sports, recreational, or educational program. These organizations also had to have been operating for at least three years and carry a proven record of success. More than 270 organizations representing all geographical regions of the state were selected.

Tickets for the COTF were purchased with proceeds from the Centennial Olympic Games Hanes T-Shirt Auction as well as from honoraria paid to the ACOG Speakers Bureau. Nearly 17,000 tickets to 153 events—including Opening and Closing Ceremonies, 22 sports, and 10 Olympic Arts Festival programs—were distributed to approved organizations. An additional 4,000 tickets were distributed to youth in cities hosting Olympic football competitions.

While overall management of the COTF was the responsibility of Youth and Education, the program was implemented through a collaborative effort among Youth and Education,

Community Relations, and Special Audiences, Inc., a not-for-profit arts organization specializing in ticket distribution. *(For more information, see the External Relations chapter.)*

OLYMPIC YOUTH CAMP

Olympic youth camps have a proud history in the Olympic Movement, dating back to the 1912 Olympic Games in Stockholm, Sweden. Although not a mandate of the *Olympic Charter*, an international OYC was hosted by Youth and

Education as part of the 1996 Olympic Games. The mission was to promote cultural exchange and teach the values inherent to the Olympic Movement in a setting that would reflect the best qualities of the American South, notably its warmth and generosity.

Using an allocation process based on the number of athletes from each country participating in the Games, each NOC was invited to send a designated number of young people, aged 16–18, to represent their country. National delegations varied in size from 2 to 12 campers. Ultimately, 152 countries sent 458 delegates to the camp.

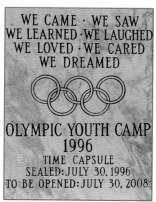

top: **Participants in Olympic Day in the Schools were grouped into teams representing different countries and wore multi-colored shirts to designate their team.**

bottom: **Olympic Youth Camp attendants created a time capsule to be opened 30 July 2008.**

MAUREEN FURLONG · ANTHONY B FURLOW · JOHN D FURMAN · MARGARET E FURNEY · LARRY R FURPHY · ANGELA L FURR · SHERRRY R FURR · CHRISTOPHER A FURR CATC · KRISNA FURROW · SHINKO FURUKAWA · FRANK F FUSARO · LAURIE A FUSARO · ROBERTA J FUSARO · ROBERT J FUSILLO · RAY S FUSS · SANDRA J FUSSEIL · LINDSAY M FUSSELL · MICHAEL T FUSTERO · CRAIG G FUTCH · DELL R FUTCH · MARY E FUTCH · SHELLY R FUTCH · WILTON C FUTCH · LEONARDO J FUTRAL · DAVID M FUTRELL · KIMBERLY N FUTRELL · STEPHEN F FUZIE CATC · AMELIA H FYE · EDWARD M FYE

For the first time in Olympic history, the organizing committee assumed responsibility for all OYC expenses, except the cost of transportation to and from the city of Atlanta. While the NOCs were responsible for meeting these transportation costs, qualifying countries received assistance from Olympic Solidarity, a program of the IOC, and the Freedom Forum.

The OYC was presented by Swatch. Berry College, located in Rome, Georgia, was selected as the OYC site. Situated in the foothills of the Appalachian Mountains 65 mi (105 km) northwest of Atlanta, Berry College has 28,000 acres (11,331 ha) of land and modern sports and living facilities. The city of Rome held an opening day parade for the campers and provided experiences representative of a typical US community.

Organization

The Youth and Education director was responsible for camp management, while the OYC director managed camp operations. The 61 Games-time staff members served as group and team leaders and were directly responsible for the campers. The special presenters—staff and professionals from Berry College—directed arts, sports, and adventure programs and were responsible for implementing class objectives. These presenters were invaluable, as they were familiar with the facilities and equipment at the site.

Games-time staff, professional staff, and volunteers lived at the venue site from 7 July to 2 August 1996. All campers arrived on 15 or 16 July before the OYC officially opened on 17 July, and departed on 31 July, the day the camp closed.

Delegates were organized into teams of approximately 12 delegates each. A team leader (hired and trained counselors) and volunteer were assigned to each team and were available 24 hours daily for the duration of the camp. The team leaders and volunteers lived in the dormitories with the campers, who were housed in separate dormitories based on gender.

To promote cultural exchange, no more than two campers from the same country.were assigned to the same team. However, team assignments were based on language to facilitate communication and interaction among team members from different countries. Team leaders spoke English, French, Spanish, German, Russian, and Arabic.

Programs

There were two types of OYC days: activity days and venue visit days. On activity days, campers were offered classes in adventure, arts, and sports. On venue visit days, campers were escorted on sightseeing trips in Atlanta, to Olympic events, and to the Olympic Village. Each camper was guaranteed five tickets to Olympic sporting and cultural events.

The Adventure Program, one of the most popular OYC programs, allowed students to participate in mountain biking, challenging obstacle courses, and orienteering with a compass. For each activity, campers were asked to act as a team, whether the adventure was climbing a 14 ft (4 m) wall or navigating a journey.

The Arts Program exposed students to a variety of art forms. Standard activities, such as mural painting, dance, and drama, as well as modern communication activities, such as videography and desktop publishing, were offered. Each art class produced a final project for display at the camp, such as a video, slide show, mural, or newspaper based on an Olympic theme. Among other projects, participants produced a video of memorable camp events and created a mural depicting the OYC theme of celebrating the human spirit.

Both individual and team Olympic sports classes were offered. Campers were encouraged to enroll in sports that were unfamiliar to them.

Each day also included free time for trips to the bank, shopping, and watching Olympic events on television. On four evenings, campers were transported to downtown Rome to participate in American leisure activities such as bowling, miniature golf, roller skating, and movies. Some activities were the first such experience for a large percentage of campers. For five evenings, the campers stayed on campus and participated in swimming, arts and crafts, aerobics, and intramural sports competitions, and dances with a disc jockey, which were the favorite on-campus event.

As part of the camp's effort to promote cultural exchange, delegations prepared presentations for their fellow campers on the history, people, customs, and culture of their homelands, as well as camper talent shows. Campers were also involved in an International Café Program, where delegations were given the opportunity to showcase their countries through oral presentations, printed material, pin exchange, and traditional dress, music, and dance. On special evenings, the International Café hosted presentations from the delegations of 20 different countries.

Medical Services

The OYC followed ACOG's Medical Services plan for noncompetition venues, using Berry College medical staff. The staff, consisting of one director, two nurses, and two doctors, managed all campers' medical needs, both on and off campus. The infirmary and the medical director were available to campers and staff, and two local hospitals were readily accessible for medical needs that could not be handled at the infirmary.

Campers had completed health forms before their arrival in Atlanta, and these forms were carefully reviewed to prepare for any medical needs campers might have. Upon arrival, all campers were screened by the medical director. Both the health form and the medical screen-

ing report were filed in the infirmary, and copies were transported with campers during off-campus trips.

Security and Technology

The OYC had a security team of paid and volunteer staff. Campers and staff were required to wear their accreditation badges at all times for identification purposes. Berry College staff and students had access to the campus and were also required to wear a photo ID badge at all times.

Day passes to the camp were issued for Berry College and OYC guests and affiliates. Applications for Berry College guests had to be submitted 24 hours in advance of their visit, but OYC guests were issued passes at the guest registration desk. The only entrance, the front gate of Berry College, had security personnel on duty at all times to ensure that visitors had appropriate ID badges or passes.

Berry College campus police worked with the OYC to staff five campus security posts 24 hours daily during camp operations. Campers

The National Olympic Committees of 152 countries sent 458 delegates to the Olympic Youth Camp at Berry College in Rome, Georgia.

were not allowed to leave the campus unchaperoned at any time.

The OYC was equipped with the latest technology. Three administrative computers were used for producing communication materials with the NOCs and developing the database to register the campers and manage information for program and medical issues. Campers had access to 27 IBM computers connected to the Internet to allow them to communicate with the athletes and receive Olympic events information.

The facility was equipped with a central phone system with 25 primary phones and access to 50 extensions. The system had voice mail and provided access to an emergency mobile phone used by the director. Phones were also available for making and receiving long-distance calls.

Communication at the campus, between buses, and at Atlanta venues was accomplished utilizing 28 high-frequency radios with 20 mi (32 km) range.

Teaching the Value of Fellowship

The OYC was an experience that taught everyone involved to value teamwork, fellowship, and diversity. The camp provided a forum in which young people from all over the world could learn about each other and develop friendships. Programs encouraged campers to work together, and cultural events promoted greater mutual understanding. The success of the camp could be seen on the faces of the campers on the last day as they ended the camp session repeating in one language the theme they had all learned to understand, "We are more alike than we are different."

CONCLUSIONS AND RECOMMENDATIONS

The Youth and Education Department succeeded in educating young people about the Olympic Movement and its values, particularly loyalty and respect for self and others. The implementation of these values through local

school systems, community-based organizations, and the Georgia DOE, all of which lent talent, human resources, expertise, and structure to the programs, accounts for this success. Most programs that were instituted will continue for years to come. This legacy fulfills the mission of inspiring excellence in people's lives and achievements, while giving them hope for the future.

It is strongly recommended that an organizing committee conduct a youth and education program. Implementing programs in collaboration with existing organizations—NOCs, schools, youth organizations, and teacher organizations—provides a framework for programs to continue after the organizing committee completes its work. The following recommendations are also offered to future organizing committees.

■ Develop programs for which the organizing committee can provide materials and guidelines to educational organizations. Involve educators in development and implementation to ensure that the programs will be continued after the Games.

■ An Olympic youth camp is an important component of a youth and education program. In developing this program, early and frequent correspondence with NOCs is of central importance.

■ The venue site for the Olympic youth camp should be selected as early as possible, ideally two or three years in advance. It should be within two hours' travel time to most Olympic competition venues, and the organizing committee should have exclusive use of the facility. An educational facility is ideal because it is equipped with housing and classrooms.

■ Dates of the camp should run concurrently with the Games, making travel easier for campers. Games-time staff should be scheduled to arrive at least two weeks prior to the opening of the camp.

■ The appropriate age range for campers is 16–18 years.

INDEX

ACKNOWLEDGMENTS AND CREDITS

The Atlanta Committee for the Olympic Games (ACOG) acknowledges with warmth and admiration the dedicated efforts of the many ACOG staff members of each department whose insights and experience contributed to the text of this volume. We also acknowledge with equal enthusiasm the talented staff members of Peachtree Publishers, who with the experienced guidance of Margaret Quinlin, assisted in the development of the *Official Report* and creatively enhanced our efforts through their skillful writing, editing, design and typography, and print production.

ACOG STAFF

Editor
Ginger T. Watkins

Managing Editor
Paul F. Acocella

Editorial Assistants
Pamela A. Golden
Stewart Lathan

Design
Andrea Pavone Said
Sheri E. Thomas

Architectural Drawings
John Marshall

Photography
Laine McCall
Leslie E. McCoy

PEACHTREE PUBLISHERS STAFF

Publisher
Margaret M. Quinlin

Senior Editors and Contributing Writers
Melanie M. McMahon
Lucinda G. Tinsman
Sara M. Stefani
Marian K. Gordin
Monica W. Munn

Design and Typography
Loraine M. Balcsik
Nicola Simmonds Carter
Robin Sherman
Dana Celentano

Print Production
Dana L. Laurent
Simone René
  Imago, USA, Inc., NY

Editorial and Administrative
Tiffany Anne Tamaroff
Vicky L. Holifield
Amy R. Sproull
Michael P. Quinlin
Colette Minoque Quinlin
Marsha McSpadden
Lynn Raughley
Alan Neely
Jason Hood

FRENCH EDITION

Editorial
Fabienne Boulongne-Collier
Vicky L. Holifield
Tiffany Anne Tamaroff

Design and Typography
Loraine M. Balcsik
Robin Sherman
Melanie M. McMahon
Sara M. Stefani

PHOTO CREDITS

The Atlanta Committee for the Olympic Games wishes to thank the staff and volunteers who graciously contributed their time and talents to photograph the images found in these pages of Volume I of the *Official Report*.

Roy Ashley—43
Anthony Banks—445L, 515R
P. Cozar—99
Steven Dinberg—328
Wingate Downs—509
Norman Drews—12B, 92, 113T, 113B, 118T, 119B, 124, 148, 170, 190, 320L, 393, 429, 436
Mark Farmer—317, 425B
Lee Heizer—503
Ross Henderson—11L, 12T, 13, 14T, 14B, 25M, 27, 29, 31, 52T, 68, 81, 82B, 83B, 121, 137, 138, 142, 154B, 156, 167, 168, 183, 198, 219, 228, 234, 265, 266, 271, 276, 287, 298L, 298R, 299, 320R, 335, 358, 362, 385, 389, 425T, 432, 434-T1, 434-T2, 470, 472, 483R, 489R, 491L, 491R, 493, 497, 512, 513, 545, 548L, 548R, 550L, 550R, 551B
Billy Howard—152B
Patrick Kelly—165
Stephanie Klein-Davis—52B, 57, 77, 373, 507, 516
Simon M. Kornblit—24B, 85, 374, 377, 445R, 510R
Richard Krauze—232, 252, 315L
Frank Borges Llosa—175, 315R, 316T
Laine McCall—24T, 24M, 25T, 118R, 125, 201, 202, 230T, 259, 327, 341, 387, 428, 480, 504
Theresa Montgomery—375
Jeff Najarian—230B, 457

Rob Nelson—355T, 355B, 359T, 359B, 361, 363T, 363B
Rory O'Connor—120, 286R, 337, 371
Sandy Owens—54T
Michael Pugh—150L, 150R, 158, 235, 236, 353, 481, 483L
John Rossino—73
Bill Rubin—11R
Terry Schmidt—486, 492
Rik Sferra—161B
Sheryl Siegel—60, 177, 510L, 515L, 531, 537
Marilyn Suriani—20, 25B, 119T, 132T, 133L, 133M, 133B, 136, 140, 151, 152T, 161T, 162, 169, 179, 186, 240, 316B, 388, 392, 426, 433, 434-B1, 434-B2, 444, 465L, 465R, 469, 489L, 526, 530, 534, 549
Mandi Wright—331, 536
Jennifer Yard—551T, 553

Artistic renderings on pages 83T and 326 appear courtesy of EDAW.

The graphics utilized in this book are owned by the The Atlanta Committee for the Olympic Games.

Note: Multiple photos on a page are identified with the following abbreviations: T, top; B, bottom; L, left; R, right.

THE ATLANTA COMMITTEE FOR THE OLYMPIC GAMES